Aging,
the Individual
and Society

Readings
in Social Gerontology

Aging, the Individual and Society

Readings in Social Gerontology

JILL S. QUADAGNO

University of Kansas

St. Martin's Press
New York

126380

Library of Congress Catalog Card Number: 80–50014
Copyright © 1980 by St. Martin's Press, Inc.
All Rights Reserved.
Manufactured in the United States of America.
43210
fedcba
For information, write St. Martin's Press, Inc.,
175 Fifth Avenue, New York, N.Y. 10010

typography: Howard S. Leiderman

cloth ISBN: 0–312–01409–0
paper ISBN: 0–312–01410–4

To My Parents

Preface

While searching for a suitable text for my undergraduate course in the sociology of aging, I looked for a book of readings that covered a variety of topics in an integrated manner. In particular, I saw a need for material focused more on the social consequences of growing old and less on the physical and psychological changes that come with age. This collection was prepared to fulfill that need. The basic organization was developed in my own classes over several years. The topics selected provide broad, significant coverage of social gerontology, and they are of both personal and intellectual interest to students.

Throughout, the book explores the changes in the nature of aging that have occurred as a result of modernization. This theme provides a continuity that integrates the diverse topics, but without obscuring other perspectives. Rather it provides a conceptual scheme meant to provoke thoughtful assessment of the position of the aged in modern society.

The introductions to the parts fulfill two purposes. First, they indicate the relationships between the articles and weave them together into a coherent whole. Second, they briefly summarize the literature from the relevant portion of the field, thus extending coverage of the topic. The introductions have proved to be a useful framework around which to organize lecture material.

Valuable suggestions for selecting articles and for improving the organization and clarity of presentation were given by reviewers of the manuscript for this book. I sincerely appreciate the thoughtful contributions of Professor Milton Barron and of the anonymous readers. The articles included here were read and evaluated by students in my undergraduate sociology of aging class. I am grateful to those students for their attentiveness and lively classroom participation.

I would also like to thank Scott McNall for encouraging me to pursue this project, Janet Barber for diligently gathering relevant material, Bob Woodbury of St. Martin's Press for providing ideas and personal concern throughout the writing process, Charles Thurlow of St. Martin's Press for doggedly pursuing permissions, Judy Davis for such fine typing that I hardly needed to proofread, and my husband, David, for many evenings of listening.

Contents

Aging, the Individual and Society

Readings in Social Gerontology

Introduction

Our society has experienced vast technological, cultural, and social changes over the past two centuries. The United States has changed from a rural, agricultural nation to one in which industrial advance influences nearly every aspect of life. Small communities ordered by family ties and personal relationships have given way to a mass society bound by a highly developed economy. This trend has been accompanied by increased reliance on a bureaucratic, administrative network that organizes social action and provides services in a rational, formal setting (Brown, 1976). Our society, once guided by traditional values and beliefs, has been transformed by the social process of modernization.

Traditional society is ideally supposed to be stable and unchanging. Traditional values rest on the repetition of past ways; people seem to accept life as it is. With little variation from one generation to the next, time appears to pass in endless cycles of familiar events. An aged craftsman recalls:

> Our harness lasted for ever, as you might say. It was our downfall, wasn't it! We made these things so well that after a while they did us out of a living. . . . It was all marvellously hand-stitched with ten or twelve stitches to the inch and beautifully set out with a little iron. . . . You don't make much money if you work with your hands. You can't make the turnover. But I have no regrets working so slowly. I began in a world without time (Blythe, 1973, p. 166).

Modern society is idealized as the opposite of the traditional world. Modern life is dynamic rather than stable, ever-changing rather than static. Time is scarce, and life is a race for achievement.

Certainly, these portraits of traditional and modern societies are oversimplified. But startling transformations have occurred all over the world. The questions that provide a theme for this book are: What happens to older people in this transition? How has the situation of the aged changed? How does a modern, industrial, bureaucratic society handle the contemporary concerns of the aged?

The Aging of Societies

Once only a small proportion of the population experienced old age. In 1790, when the first federal census was taken in the United States, less than 20 percent of the people survived from birth to the age of seventy. Now more than 80 percent of the population does so (Fischer, 1978). In other words, the life expectancy of Americans has vastly increased over the past two centuries. A child born in 1900 could expect to live an average of forty-seven years; by 1977 life expectancy was nearly eighty. Women have a survival advantage over men, an advantage which has

1

been increasing. Table 1 illustrates the changes in life expectancy for males and females which occurred in just a seventeen-year period.

With this increase in life expectancy, the proportion of people aged sixty-five and over in the population has increased from only 4.1 percent in 1900 to more than 10.5 percent by 1975. The shift in age composition occurred as a result of both lower birth and lower death rates. A drop in death rates, or mortality, reduces deaths in all age groups, but particularly those of infants and children. Thus the effect of declining mortality alone is likely to be a decrease in the proportion of older people in the population. But when low mortality is accompanied by a decline in the birth rate, the population will begin to "age," as the proportion of older people increases.

The process of moving from a population with high mortality and high fertility to one in which both birth and death rates are low has been termed the "demographic transition." This pattern has been characteristic of most modern industrial societies. Usually it has been assumed that factors associated with modernization, such as improved medical care and a generally higher standard of living, have provided the impetus for the demographic transition to occur. However, non-Western countries have experienced some of the changes associated with early industrialization without having the expected demographic patterns also arise, so the causal relationship between modernization and the demographic transition has come under increasing criticism. Although it may be difficult to identify precisely what factors contributed to the aging of our society, we can and should be attuned to how these demographic changes have affected both the needs of the aged and the treatment of older people.

Changes in the Characteristics of the Aged

As the proportion of older people in American society has changed over the past centuries, so, too, have their characteristics. Cohorts vary in regard to such factors as gender, race, education levels, ethnic origin, and place of residence. Thus when discussing the "aged," it is important to recognize that they are not an unchanging homogeneous group but a diverse population that is constantly altering its characteristics.

TABLE 1   Life Expectancy at Birth, Males and Females, U.S. Population, 1960–1977

Life expectancy at birth	1960	1965	1970	1973	1974	1977
Males	66.6	66.8	67.1	67.6	68.2	72
Females	73.1	73.7	74.8	75.3	75.9	81

SOURCE: *Statistical Abstracts of the United States. 1976.* 97th Annual Edition, Washington, D.C.: U.S. Department of Commerce, Bureau of the Census, July 1976, pp. xiii–xiv, and January 1978.

TABLE 2   Percentage of White Foreign-born Population Aged 60–64
U.S., 1900–1980

Year	% Foreign-born
1900	33.63
1910	30.33
1920	25.83
1930	26.84
1940	24.20
1950	23.26
1960	16.27
1970	9.56
1980°	5.74

SOURCE: U.S. Census of Population: 1950, vol. 11, Table 39; 1960, PC(1)-1D, Table 161; 1970, PC(2)-1A, Table 1; and Current Population Report, series P-23, no. 59 (May 1976).

°Estimates from projections in Current Population Report, series P-23, no. 59 (May 1976).

Ethnic Composition

Over the past century there has been a changing flow of immigrants to the United States, and this has affected the ethnic composition of the older population at different points in time. Most dramatic has been the downward trend in the proportion of foreign-born among the aged (Bureau of the Census, 1976). Until 1950 from one-third to one-fourth of the older population was foreign-born. However, the decline in the rate of immigration between 1920 and 1940 and the additional effects of quotas in restricting immigration after World War II have reduced this figure to less than 10 percent. The decline in foreign-born aged is illustrated in Table 2.

There are several reasons why it is relevant to consider the proportion of the aged who are foreign-born. One is that adjustment to a strange culture is a major difficulty in and of itself, regardless of concerns associated with aging. A second problem concerns relationships with children. The desire of first-generation immigrants to maintain old-world customs often brought them into conflict with children who had begun to adopt American ways. For example, Polish immigrants expressed bitterness about the economic obligations of second-generation adult children to their aged parents. Complaining about their children, the parents stated, "After they finished school, they got married, and they are no help for the parents at all. They leave home and forget their poor old parents" (Wood, 1955, p. 215). The older Poles were not psychologically or financially prepared to maintain themselves independently of their adult children, who would have had clear-cut familial obligations in the old country. The adult children adopted the American perspective which prescribes that one's primary obligation is to one's own children, aged parents being secondary (Lopata, 1976).

Problems associated with acculturation will not continue to affect most older people. For the remainder of this century, over 90 percent of those entering old age will have been born and reared in the United States (Uhlenberg, 1977). Nevertheless, within a complex and diverse society such as ours there will always be subgroups in the population who approach the experience of aging from a unique perspective.

The Urbanization of the Aged

American society has been transformed from a predominantly rural society to one in which most of the population resides in urban areas. This change has, of course, affected all age groups, but it has had a particularly intense impact upon the aged, not only for those who migrated to cities but for those left behind as well. The effects of urbanization are illustrated in Table 3. In 1910 over 50 percent of the older population lived on farms or in small towns. By 1970 more than 71 percent of all aged people lived in urban areas.

In spite of the general trend toward urbanization, the aged still tend to be more heavily concentrated in the countryside than the young, who have migrated toward cities in search of better employment opportunities. This out-migration of young adults has caused problems for the older people left behind, for it jeopardizes the economic stability of the area. In general, the rural aged are among the most impoverished members of society and least likely to have access to needed services. According to one researcher:

> The average older person in a rural area must house himself on an income that is $400 to $700 less than that of the person his age who lives in a metropolitan area, and his housing often lacks things most people take for granted. . . . The rural poor not only are the most impoverished segment of the older population and in the poorest housing, they are also less healthy and have more disabilities, which create problems in dealing with everyday tasks about the home. . . . The rural aged are at a special disadvantage because of the scarcity of younger family members to assist financially and physically (Carp, 1976, p. 57).

The extent of deprivation suffered by many older people in rural areas

TABLE 3   Rural-Urban Distribution of the White Population Aged 60–64, U.S.

Year	Urban	Rural nonfarm	Rural-farm
1910	48.7	25.2	26.1
1920	52.6	20.6	26.7
1930	57.8	19.9	22.3
1940	59.0	19.4	21.5
1950	66.8	18.7	14.4
1960	71.2	20.0	8.9
1970	71.7	22.4	5.9

SOURCE: U.S. Census of Population: 1930, vol. 11, ch. 10, Table 16; 1940, vol. I part 1, Table 6; 1950, PC(1)-1D, Table 158; 1970, PC(1)-1D, Table 189.

cannot be minimized. However, it has also been argued that the quality of life is higher in small towns and the social adjustment to aging less difficult due to a more intimate environment which enhances an individual's ability to maintain control over his or her life situation. For example, farmers have the option of choosing partial rather than full retirement and can move from the farm into town when necessary (Bauder and Doerflinger, 1967). That many have chosen the latter course is evident in Table 3, which shows a decrease in the number of older people on farms but an increase since 1930 in the number in nonfarm areas or small towns.

The urban aged, who comprise over 70 percent of the older population, have advantages denied to older people residing in rural areas but also face problems of a different nature. Services are more readily available, and mass communication makes knowledge about these services easier to obtain (Taietz, 1975). However, the impersonal urban environment makes life lonely and isolated for many older people, and fear of crime further reduces the life space of inner-city residents (Sundeen and Mathieu, 1976).

It would be a difficult task to prove that either urban or rural living provided a life style that was inherently more amenable to the aging process. What is important to recognize is that a major shift in population has occurred, making urban living the mode. While we cannot, as a society, afford to ignore the rural aged, at the same time we must recognize that most older people presently reside in cities and that this pattern is likely to persist for some time.

Increases in Educational Attainments

One of the concomitants of modernization has been mass education, an innovation which initially benefited the young more than the old. Traditionally, the informal knowledge about customs, skills, and community history possessed by older people provided them with authority and prestige. With the onset of mass education, this type of knowledge was quickly outdated as younger people obtained a formal education which they could apply to the new occupations created by modern economic technology (Cowgill, 1974). Now as more highly educated people reach old age, the educational inequities between age groups have begun to disappear. Among those entering old age early in the century, only about 10 percent had completed high school. Nearly 45 percent had less than an eighth-grade education. By the year 2000 it is predicted that over 70 percent of all those over age sixty-five will have attained this level, and over 30 percent will have had some college training as well (Uhlenberg, 1977).

The potential impact of a group of well-educated older citizens cannot be underestimated. They will be more aware of options available to them and better able to function effectively in a complex bureaucratic system. This, in turn, should lead to an improved ability to mobilize resources on their own behalf and to organize to promote their own welfare. Certainly the problems associated with growing old will not disappear, but they will be less fraught with the more basic problems of a permanent underclass of poorly educated individuals.

Aging in Modern Society

Many social institutions have evolved to accommodate the growing proportion of older people in society. The family, the polity, the economy, and the educational system all had to resolve issues concerning the aged. Initially these institutions responded to problems associated with increasingly larger numbers of low-income, often uneducated older people who were inexperienced in handling the demands of a technologically advanced society. Some social scientists believed many of these problems were permanent, necessary accouterments to a modernizing society. However, in retrospect these early dilemmas were merely part of a transitional phase. With the emergence of a more sophisticated cohort of older people, these same institutions have begun a second process of adjustment to deal with a different series of concerns. The effects of these changes can be felt throughout society.

Changes in Family Life

The change in the family life cycle from preindustrial times to the present has altered both the form and style of family relationships. In earlier periods a married couple had many children, who continued to arrive until the parents were well into their late thirties or early forties. When the parents entered old age, it was quite likely that they would have unmarried children still at home. The myth we hold of the three-generation household is a reflection of this childbearing pattern. Evidence shows that children were no more likely to take aged parents into their own household in the past than they are today, but they were often living as dependents with their parents (Laslett, 1972).

As family size decreased, middle age evolved as a distinctly separate phase of the life cycle. People in their forties and fifties found themselves freed from the tasks of child rearing and able to explore other options less tied to familial responsibilities. This phenomenon, coupled with the increase in life expectancy, lengthened the number of years a married couple was likely to spend alone with each other, as well as the number of years an older widowed person might spend alone. However, the evidence shows that even those aged living alone are not isolated from children and other kin but rather form part of an extended network of family members (Shanas, 1973).

Changes in the Economy

The family was not the only institution affected by changes in population structure. The economy also had to undergo revisions to accommodate an increased share of the population no longer in the labor force. The adjustment to an expanded older population was initially made in the 1930s, when social security legislation was passed to provide payments to the retired. The reverberations of that initial legislation are still being felt, as the social security system undergoes renewed scrutiny to balance the amount of incoming funds from contributors with outgoing funds to retirees.

A secondary effect of formalizing a system of retirement benefits has been to encourage more workers to retire. Through the years a wider variety of occupations have been granted social security coverage, so that now nearly all workers are eligible for payments. Although early research seemed to perceive retirement as a negative time of life, there has been an increased awareness of the positive potential that exists for renewed freedom and self-expression. This, of course, is related to the increase in financial benefits, making it less likely that older people will be forced to live out their remaining years in near poverty.

None of these societal changes exists in a vacuum. As each institution responds to an aging population, the adjustments it makes are felt in other social arenas as well. Some scholars were concerned that the increased reliance on impersonal arrangements would erode family ties, as the government took greater responsibility for the social and economic welfare of the aged. The bureaucratization of services to the aged and the formalization of income transfer through a social security system altered but did not destroy family relationships. Rather there are indications that financial independence allows older people to participate in family affairs on a more egalitarian basis and maintain relationships based on mutual interdependence. Further, children often serve as a link between their parents and bureaucracies, providing a buffer against the complexities of large-scale organizations (Shanas and Sussman, 1977).

Conclusion

The theme of the effects of modernization on the position of the aged in society will be explored throughout this book. Part one includes articles which deal specifically with the topic of aging and modernization. Cowgill explains how societies age demographically and explores the meaning this has for the status of the aged. Fischer's excerpt from *Growing Old in America* summarizes the aging and modernization argument and presents historical evidence documenting the turning point in age relations. Palmore provides a cross-cultural example of one culture, Japan, where the status of the aged has remained high in spite of industrialization.

In part two three major theoretical contributions are presented. Rose argues that the aged are in the process of forming a subcultural identity. Riley expands upon the concept of age stratification and speculates on the validity of subculture theory as applied to the aged. Dowd is also concerned with the position of the aged within the social structure and argues that the decline in the position of the aged is due to a decrease in their power resources.

Part three considers the problems associated with age stereotyping. Hess discusses the media as a source which perpetuates age stereotypes by either ignoring the aged or portraying them negatively. This theme is developed in reference to the specific example of television commercials in the article by Francher. Finally, Rubin evaluates one stereotype, that of the sexless older years.

Part four focuses on various aspects of life-cycle research. Neugarten, Moore, and Lowe define the concept of age norms and attempt to determine how age-related expectations for behavior order social interaction. Bengston and Kuypers examine interactions between generations, assessing whether age differences are minor or major sources of conflict. Finally, excerpts from Levinson's *Seasons of a Man's Life* discuss middle age and the mid-life transition.

Part five deals with living environments of the aged. Lopata discusses urban support systems and their use and nonuse by the aged. Youmans describes some of the problems associated with aging in a rural community. Quadagno, Kuhar, and Peterson report on racial tensions in an integrated public housing retirement community.

Part six concerns family relationships. On a general level, Streib discusses the categories of family types in the latter phase of the life cycle and attempts to determine what the family will be like at the end of the twentieth century. One problem which older families face is the death of one of its members. Berardo describes the problems faced by aged widowers. The aged also find themselves in new family roles, and Robertson analyzes one of these, grandmotherhood, and how it is viewed by different women.

In part seven the topics of work, retirement, and leisure are presented. Withers describes some of the irrational assumptions about retirement, such as that sixty-five is the age to retire, that productivity declines with age, and that the aged need less income. Quadagno discusses how a group of professional men and women feel about impending retirement. Finally, Atchley questions the belief that retirement creates an unfillable void, suggesting that leisure activity plays an important role in bridging the pre- and post-retirement gap.

Part eight deals with the plight of minority aged, who have been described as being in "double jeopardy" due to the combined disadvantages of age and minority group membership. Dowd and Bengston confirm that double jeopardy does exist for black and Mexican-American aged in terms of health and income but not in terms of contact with relatives and life satisfaction. Davis describes some of the specific problems faced by aging blacks, such as low incomes and low life expectancy. Maldonado cautions against assuming that the Mexican-

American extended family is strong enough to provide adequate protection for its aged members.

Part nine concentrates on the ways in which the aged influence the political scene. Foner explains why it is unlikely that people will unite on the basis of age to form a cohesive political force. Reimer and Binstock present a case study of Carter's presidential campaign, questioning whether politicians behave as if there were, in fact, an aged vote. Jacobs and Hess look at another source of political power for the aged, the Gray Panthers, who have attracted attention from the media but suffer from organizational problems.

Articles in part ten explore several economic issues. Hollister explains how the social security system works and discusses the myth that it is an insurance program. Kreps asks what effect the change from a personal, informal system of income maintenance for the aged to an impersonal and formal one has had on family relationships. Finally, Burks describes some of the inequities which penalize women, who receive an unfair distribution of retirement income.

Part eleven deals with the health care of the aged, both within and outside of institutions. Coe describes the attitudes of health care professionals toward the aged. Fontana discusses the problem of dehumanization that occurs in a nursing home. Stannard analyzes the conditions which are conducive to patient abuse by aides.

The last part in this book considers death and dying. Pattison discusses four cultural attitudes toward death: death denying, death defying, death desiring, and death accepting; suggesting that our society can be classified as death denying. However, Marshall shows that under certain conditions we can become death accepting. His study of a retirement community demonstrates that people accept and even welcome death when they have adequately prepared for it. In the final article Saunders describes St. Christopher's Hospice, where the acceptance of death becomes translated into superior care for the dying.

The alteration of the demographic structure of society has had a dramatic impact on the ways we age, in regard to both problems associated with aging and to the expansion of the potential for development in later life. As we look at our society now, we can see great improvements in the health care, financial status, and living arrangements for the aged. However, we cannot become complacent, for many problems remain to be solved. Further, we must anticipate change, for there is no reason to assume that the solutions which presently exist will be satisfactory for those who are now young but will one day be old.

REFERENCES

Bauder, Ward W., and Jon A. Doerflinger. 1967. Work roles among the rural aged. In E. Grant Youmans (ed.), *Older rural Americans*. Lexington, Ky.: Univ. of Kentucky Press.

Blythe, Ronald. 1973. *Akenfield: Portrait of an English village*. New York: Dell.

Brown, Richard. 1976. *Modernization, the transformation of American life 1600-1865*. New York: Hill & Wang.

Carp, Francis. 1976. Housing and living environments of older people. In Robert H. Binstock and Ethel Shanas (eds.), *Handbook of aging and the social sciences*. New York: Van Nostrand Reinhold.

Cowgill, Donald. 1974. Aging and modernization: a revision of the theory. In Jaber F. Gubrium (ed.), *Late life, communities and environmental policy*. Springfield, Ill.: Charles C Thomas.

Fischer, David Hackett. 1978. *Growing old in America*. Oxford: Oxford Univ. Press.

Laslett, Peter. 1972. *Household and family in past time*. Cambridge: Cambridge Univ. Press.

Lopata, Helena Z. 1976. The Polish American Family. In Charles H. Mindel and Robert W. Habenstein (eds.), *Ethnic families in America*. New York: Elsevier.

Shanas, Ethel. 1973. Family-kin networks and aging in cross-cultural perspective. *Journal of Marriage and the Family* 35 (August): 505-511.

Shanas, Ethel, and Marvin B. Sussman. 1977. *Family, bureaucracy and the elderly*. Durham, N.C.: Duke Univ. Press.

Sundeen, Richard A., and James T. Mathieu. 1976. The fear of crime and its consequences among elderly in three urban communities. *Gerontologist* 16:211-219.

Taietz, Philip. 1975. Community complexity and knowledge of facilities. *Journal of Gerontology* 30:357-362.

Uhlenberg, Peter. 1977. Changing structure of the older population of the USA during the twentieth century. *Gerontologist* 17:197-202.

Wood, Arthur. 1955. *Hamtramck: Then and now*. New York: Bookman Assoc.

1

Aging and Modernization

Both social scientists and historians have been concerned with the influence of modernization and industrialization on the status of the aged. The pivotal historical dogma is that there has been a *before* and *after* in relations between the generations. In the *before* the aged were venerated, controlling both wealth and power, while in the *after* they were reduced to a secondary role in society.

This theme has been prevalent from the earliest discussions of the position of the aged in the writings of social scientists. In his *Wealth of Nations*, Adam Smith wrote that respect for age was highest in primitive society and tended to fall with the progress of civilization. Emile Durkheim argued in *The Division of Labor in Society* that in primitive societies the aged were the sole intermediaries between the past and present, while in advanced societies all persons of maturity were treated as equals. Similarly, Max Weber viewed "gerontocracy," or rule by elders, as the most primitive type of political authority, whose primary historical effect was to strengthen traditional relations and prevent the development of modern capitalist relations.

Age Relations and Societal Development
In an attempt to examine age relations more systematically, Simmons (1945) compared the position of the aged in over a hundred different societies. His conclusions, published in *The Role of the Aged in Primitive Society*, correlated the treatment of the aged with the mode of economic organization. In nomadic societies where people depended on collecting, hunting, and fishing for survival, the

aged had fewer prerogatives and less access to power than they did in sedentary societies where people engaged in farming and herding. Simmons attributed this pattern to the fact that concepts of property rights were more developed in stable societies and the aged had had more opportunity to accumulate possessions. This ability to accumulate property is an important source of security for the aged in any society.

A second factor affecting the position of the aged in primitive societies, according to Simmons, was their relative scarcity. Few people survived beyond middle age. Because older people were such a small minority and because they were the custodians of tradition and repositories of knowledge, positions of prestige were reserved for them, and they were held in high esteem.

Other scholars have focused their attention on the status of the aged in modern societies. Burgess (1960) was concerned with the effects of the Industrial Revolution on the aged in Western societies. He believed that the trends associated with industrialization contributed to an overall decline in the function, role, and status of the aged in nearly every sphere of life. The most significant effect of industrialization has been the family's loss of its historic functions, a loss which has affected elderly family members most severely. Changes in agriculture destroyed the family as the unit of production and made the large family a burden rather than an asset. This in turn meant the aged were no longer an integral part of a three-generation rural household, a previous source of great personal satisfaction. Unable to count on children for economic support, the aged came increasingly to depend on impersonal bureaucracies which developed with the rise of large organizations. Accompanying industrialization was an increase in life expectancy which expanded the proportion of older people in the population. Since the economy could not accommodate large numbers of older people in the labor force, retirement became a societal institution. Retirement isolated the aged from work companions and forced them to cope with unexpected leisure time. Summing up the series of losses associated with industrialization, Burgess concluded that in contemporary Western society the aged were imprisoned in a "roleless role."

In the reading by Cowgill, the argument presented is similar to Burgess's but further refined. Cowgill views the aging of society as a modern phenomenon which has never occurred in human populations before. Ironically the characteristics of modernization which have increased the proportion of the aged in society have had the simultaneous effect of decreasing their status. Thus modern health technology has created an aging work force and pushed the elderly into retirement. Similarly, the growth of mass education has undercut the role of the aged as transmitters of customs and skills. No longer uncommon, no longer believed to possess special knowledge, the aged in modern society have lost wealth, power, and prestige.

Criticisms of the Modernization Model

Recently social scientists and historians have begun to challenge the prevailing assumptions about aging and modernization. In *Growing Old in America* the historian David Hackett Fischer has demonstrated that many of the changes in the status of the aged, particularly the loss of veneration, occurred prior to industrialization. Using measures such as ownership of property, household and age composition, and age of political figures, Fischer shows that the status of the aged was influenced by the revolutionary ideology of libertarianism and egalitarianism which came to the fore during the French and American revolutions, well before massive industrialization. Summarized excerpts from Fischer's work constitute the second selection in part one.

Other critics have demonstrated that different aspects of the aging and modernization model are invalid. The British sociologist Peter Laslett argues that more continuity exists in age relations than is immediately apparent. He rejects the idea that the emotional, physical, or economic needs of the aged in the past were provided for in a way that is in any sense superior to that found today. According to Laslett,

> the majority of aged persons . . . today are not found in fact to be in the position described . . . as characteristic of the *after*, whatever the stereotypes. Retirement may be widespread and peremptory in high industrial society, but its effect varies with the interest of the job. . . . It is certainly not always felt as a deprivation, or even as a diminution of consequence. Nor are the old so drastically bereft of prestige and respect; they do have recognized functions, especially in respect of their families and their children; they are supported, emotionally and otherwise, by their offspring, sometimes by their siblings, and even by more distant kin (Laslett, 1976, p. 94).

Laslett's view is supported by data from a major cross-cultural study comparing the status of the aged in six countries. In this study Shanas (1973) argues that old people have not become physically and socially isolated from children and other relatives as a result of industrialization. Rather they form part of an extensive kinship network and interact often with children and grandchildren, brothers and sisters. According to Shanas's findings, the isolated nuclear family is merely a myth.

Adding his voice to the argument, Palmore analyzed the effects of rapid industrialization on the status of the aged in Japan. Palmore contends that the Oriental tradition of respect for elders has prevented a decline in the status and integration of the aged in Japanese society, although he does find some erosion of traditional patterns. The last selection in this part summarizes Palmore's study.

Certainly the final answer to the question of the relationship between aging and modernization has not yet been determined. While some indicators point to a deterioration in the position of the aged in Western industrialized societies, others suggest that in some respects the position of the aged may have improved. By idealizing the past, we have obscured continuities in age relations and created several myths. As better-educated, more affluent people grow old, we may find that most of the negative effects associated with industrialization disappear and that it is only those older people who have been socially and economically disadvantaged throughout life who play a secondary role in society.

REFERENCES

Burgess, Ernest W. 1960. *Aging in Western societies*. Chcago: Univ. of Chicago Press.

Laslett, Peter. 1976. Societal development and aging. In Robert H. Binstock and Ethel Shanas (eds.), *Handbook of aging and the social sciences*. New York: Van Nostrand Reinhold, pp. 87–116.

Shanas, Ethel. 1973. Family-kin networks and aging in cross-cultural perspective. *Journal of Marriage and the Family* 35 (August):505–511.

Simmons, Leo. 1945. *The role of the aged in primitive society*. New Haven: Yale Univ. Press.

The Aging of Populations and Societies

DONALD O. COWGILL

As societies modernize, birth and death rates drop, resulting in the aging of the population. Certain forces of modernization have had the dual effect of increasing the proportion of older people in the population and at the same time lowering their position in society. According to Dr. Cowgill, modern health and economic technologies, urbanization, and education have all contributed to a decline in the status of the aged. However, this trend does appear to be leveling off in the most modernized societies, as the aged become increasingly better educated and more affluent and as institutions begin to pay more attention to the needs and interests of this segment of the population.

One of the dilemmas of modern societies is that while sociological processes have fostered a devaluation of old people, demographic processes have led to increasing numbers and proportions of aged in their populations. Thus such societies have larger proportions of older people than ever before, while at the same time older people have less value and utility to those societies. These countertrends give rise to the further anomaly that societies whose relative affluence permits them to provide the greatest comfort and security to their aged members instead deprive them of useful roles and consign high proportions of them to relative poverty.[1]

The purpose of this article is to examine the two horns of this dilemma. First, I shall attempt to explicate the demographic processes which result in the aging of populations; then, I shall seek to unravel the more subtle and complicated sociological processes which currently appear to contribute to the relative degradation of older people.

The Demography of Aging

A population is said to be aging when the elderly segment of that population is increasing faster than the rest of the population. There are several ways in which this change can be measured. However, the most

SOURCE: Reprinted from "The Aging of Populations and Societies" by Donald O. Cowgill in volume no. 415 of *The Annals* of The American Academy of Political and Social Science. © 1974 by The American Academy of Political and Social Science. All rights reserved.

common index—and one of the most useful—is the change in the percent of the total population which is sixty-five years of age and over.

Selected Cases of Aging Populations

Utilizing this index, Table 1 shows that several populations have experienced a remarkable degree of aging in the last 120 years.[2] France had already aged appreciably by 1851, when 6.5 percent of her population was sixty-five and over; the process has continued with only slight variations since then. The latest figures show more than double that percentage—13.4 percent. England is slightly behind France in this aging trend, but the general trend is the same. In 1851 only 4.6 percent of the British population was sixty-five and over. The percentage increased decade by decade with only slight interruptions; the most recent figures indicate that 12.4 percent of the British population is sixty-five and over. Sweden shows the same trend: in 1850 only 4.8 percent of the Swedish population was sixty-five and over; by 1970 the percentage had increased to 12.8. The Netherlands manifests the same pattern, with only a slight interruption at the time of the First World War: from 4.7 percent sixty-five and over in 1849, the aged population has increased to 10.1 percent. A younger population—resulting from the effects of continued immigration—but one which shows the same trend, is that of Australia:

TABLE 1   Percent of Population 65 and Over, Selected Countries, 1850–1970

Date*	France	England	Sweden	Netherlands	Australia	United States
1850	6.5	4.6	4.8	4.7	NA	NA
1860	6.7	4.7	5.2	4.9	NA	NA
1870	7.4	4.8	5.4	5.5	1.7	2.9
1880	8.1	4.6	5.9	5.5	NA	3.4
1890	8.3	4.8	7.7	6.0	NA	3.8
1900	8.2	4.7	8.4	6.0	NA	4.1
1910	8.4	5.2	8.4	6.1	4.3	4.3
1920	9.1	6.0	8.4	5.9	4.4	4.7
1930	9.3	7.4	9.2	6.2	6.5	5.4
1940	NA	9.0	9.4	7.0	7.3	6.8
1950	11.8	10.9	10.3	7.7	8.0	8.1
1960	11.5	11.8	11.2	8.7	8.4	9.2
1970	13.4	12.4	13.7	10.1	8.3	9.9

*Since the date of census-taking varies in different countries, the date used in the table is merely approximate. For actual date in each case, see original sources.

SOURCES: Except for the United States, date for years prior to 1970 are from Edward Rosset, *Aging Process of Population* (New York: Macmillan, 1964), chap. 9, used with permission of Pergamon Press, Ltd. For the United States, data from 1870 to 1960 are from U.S., Department of Health, Education and Welfare, Special Staff on Aging, "Population Trends, National, 1790–1960," *Facts on Aging*, no. 1 (Jan. 1963). Data for 1970 are from United Nations, *Demographic Yearbook 1971* (New York: United Nations, 1973), Table 7.

from 1.7 percent sixty-five and over in 1871, this population has matured to the point that 8.3 percent of the population is now aged by this index. In the United States of America the trend has been from 2.9 percent in 1870 to 4.1 percent in 1900 to 9.9 percent in 1970.

Cross-National Comparisons of the Extent of Aging

It is obvious from the review of these cases (1) that aging is a developmental process and (2) that the process has not proceeded as far in Australia as it has in the other countries used to illustrate the process. We must then infer that at any given time different areas of the world will be in different stages of such a developmental process. Therefore it may be instructive to compare the percentages of population sixty-five and over in various countries at the present time (shown in Table 2).

It will be noted that these percentages range from 1 to more than 22 percent—that is, from only one person who is sixty-five and over out of a hundred persons in the total population to more than one out of five. Of course, Monaco is an abnormal case in which immigration of elderly retired persons has resulted in a high proportion of aged in the population. However, if one disregards such extreme cases, there is probably a fair indication of the normal range of aging in contemporary populations in Table 2—that is, a range from about 1 percent in an extremely young population to about 15 percent in an old, but normally aging, population.

Elsewhere I have proposed a classification of populations according to their degree of agedness, and I continue to use that classification here.[3] Populations with less than 4 percent sixty-five and over are called young; those with 4 to 6.9 percent are described as youthful; those with 7 to 9.9 percent are denominated mature; and those with 10 percent or more sixty-five and over are called aged. Examination of Table 2 indicates that, with the exception of Greenland, all the young populations are in Africa, Asia, Latin America, and Oceania. They range from New Guinea with just over 1 percent to Liberia and Turkey with just under 4 percent. They include Nigeria, Zambia, Korea, Sri Lanka—formerly Ceylon—Colombia, Afghanistan, and Mexico. The youthful populations, while somewhat older, are also found in Africa, Asia, and Latin America. They range from Swaziland to Lesotho and obviously include areas which are in more advanced stages of modernization than those with young populations. The mature populations include the more recently modernized parts of Eastern Europe, Japan and the modernized parts of the New World, which have until recently been kept young by immigration—that is, Iceland, Australia, New Zealand, and Canada. The aged populations are found entirely in Europe, mainly western and northern Europe—that is, those parts first affected by industrialization and modernization.

Aging and the Demographic Transition

It should be evident from the above discussion that the aging of populations is a modern phenomenon, something which has never

TABLE 2 Percent of Population 65 and Over in Various Countries

Country	Percent 65 and Over	Country	Percent 65 and Over
YOUNG POPULATIONS		MATURE POPULATIONS	
New Guinea	1.1	Japan	7.0
Kuwait	1.6	Uruguay	7.5
Nigeria	2.0	Yugoslavia	7.5
Zambia	2.1	Canada	7.9
Greenland	2.3	Australia	8.3
W. Samoa	2.7	New Zealand	8.4
Guatemala	2.7	Poland	8.4
Nicaragua	2.9	Romania	8.5
Colombia	2.9	Finland	8.6
Haiti	3.0	Gibraltar	8.6
Costa Rica	3.1	Iceland	8.8
Ecuador	3.2	Bulgaria	9.5
Korea	3.2	United States	9.9
Bahamas	3.4		
Kenya	3.5	AGED POPULATIONS	
Afghanistan	3.5		
Sri Lanka	3.5	Netherlands	10.1
Tunisia	3.5	Italy	10.4
Mexico	3.7	N. Ireland	10.5
Paraguay	3.8	Czechoslovakia	10.6
Uganda	3.8	Ireland	11.1
Iran	3.8	Switzerland	11.3
Liberia	3.9	Hungary	11.5
Turkey	3.9	Denmark	12.0
		Scotland	12.1
YOUTHFUL POPULATIONS		England & Wales	12.4
		Luxembourg	12.6
Swaziland	4.1	W. Germany	12.6
Algeria	4.4	Norway	12.9
Botswana	4.6	France	13.4
Surinam	4.6	Sweden	13.7
Guadaloupe	4.7	Austria	14.1
Iraq	5.1	E. Germany	15.5
Martinique	5.1	Monaco	22.1
French Guiana	5.3		
Tanzania	5.5		
Lesotho	6.4		

SOURCES: Data computed from *Demographic Yearbook 1971* (New York: United Nations, 1972), Table 7. Effective dates vary from country to country ranging from 1962 to 1971. See original source for actual dates.

occurred to human populations before. It began first in the populations of Western Europe and has progressed to the greatest degree in those same populations. This aging of populations is a by-product of a demographic revolution which is usually called the demographic transition. It has commonly been viewed as a consequence of the Industrial Revolution, but it is much more closely related to changes in public health and education than to changes in modes of production.

In its major outlines the demographic transition is a long-term and presumably permanent change in the level of the vital rates of population change, a drastic and permanent reduction of both death rates and birth rates.[4] The time required to complete the transition may vary from several centuries to only a few decades.

Mortality rates decline first, followed—with a lag of a generation or so—by fertility rates. Since death rates decline first, an early effect of the transition is an increase in the rate of population growth. Since World War II this process has been set in motion with such rapidity and on such a scale in the newly developing areas of the world that it has been dubbed a population explosion.

The scale of the change is dramatic: death rates fall from a range of 25 to 35 deaths per 1,000 persons in the total population per year to a new range of 5 to 15 deaths per 1,000; births drop from a range of 35 to 55 per 1,000 in the population to a low range of 10 to 20 per 1,000. Such major changes in vital rates certainly mark a major transition in human demography; indeed, they probably warrant the application of the more dramatic term, revolution.[5] These revolutionary changes in vital rates result not only in changes in rates of population growth; they also effect drastic changes in the structure of the population in which they are occurring. One of those changes is the age composition.[6]

Declining mortality in the initial stages of the transition permits more babies to stay alive and more children to reach maturity. Thus, since the major reductions in deaths occur with reference to infant and child mortality, the effect of changing mortality alone is more likely to be a younger, rather than an older, population.[7] It is only in the latter part of the transition—when the birth rate begins to decline, reducing the child population—that the population as a whole begins to age. However, the total range of the change which then takes place is highly significant, as we have seen: from as little as 1 percent of the population sixty-five and over to as much as 15 percent.

Aging of the Electorate

It may be assumed that if a population is aging, the segment of it which is of voting age will be aging also. However, this is not a perfect relationship. As we have seen, the proportionate aging of the total population does not begin until the birth rate starts to fall. Similarly, the electorate does not begin to age until about twenty years later, when the constricted cohorts of births begin to come of age. If there are fluctuations in the birth rate, it is possible for the electorate to be aging at the same time that the population as a whole is "younging," as happened in the United States during the baby boom following World War II.

Nevertheless, if we disregard the recent lowering of the voting age, there has been a continuous aging of the electorate of the United States during this century (shown in Table 3). If we take the population twenty years of age and over as representative of the electorate, we can see that while the proportion in the younger ages has steadily declined, the proportion in the upper ages has increased. In fact, more than two-thirds of this adult population were under forty-five in 1900, while in 1970 only slightly more than half were that young. On the other hand, the proportion of this adult population which was sixty-five and over more than doubled during the same period, increasing from 7.9 percent in 1900 to 15.9 percent in 1970. The potential political significance of this shift is emphasized if we remember that larger proportions of older people actually exercise their franchise than people in their early twenties.[8]

Characteristics of the Older Generation

In societies with aged populations the older generation differs from the younger in many ways other than simply age. The older generation has a higher ratio of females and of widows. The elderly have less formal education; they have lower incomes; and they are less mobile.

Older populations usually have higher proportions of females. This is caused by the higher death rate among males, a progressive attrition which occurs throughout the age span. The surplus of males at birth is dissipated by middle age; from that point on, males are a progressively smaller minority in each older age group. Consequently, in the United States in 1970 there were only 72 males per 100 females sixty-five years of age and over.[9] Furthermore, this sex ratio has been declining steadily since 1930, when it was approximately balanced thanks to the carry-over effect of earlier immigration streams, which brought greater numbers of males into the United States population. With the curtailment of immigration in the 1920s, the carry-over effect on the sex ratio of the total

TABLE 3   Composition of Population 20 and Over by Broad Age Groups, United States States 1900–1970

Age Group	1900	1910	1920	1930	1940	1950	1960	1970
20–44	67.6	67.1	64.6	62.4	59.4	56.9	52.4	51.0
45–64	24.5	25.1	27.3	28.5	30.2	30.7	32.7	33.1
65 and over	7.9	7.8	8.1	9.1	10.4	12.4	14.9	15.9

SOURCE: Computed from U.S. Bureau of the Census, *1970 Census of Population: U.S. Summary* (Washington, D.C.: Government Printing Office, 1972), Table 48.

population has been diminishing. Moreover, since most immigrants are young adults at the time of migration, the effects of immigration do not show up in the aged population until several decades later. Thus the impact of immigration upon the aged population of the United States was still quite evident at the time of the 1950 census: 26.2 percent of the white population sixty-five and over was foreign-born.[10] By 1970 this percentage had decreased to 16.3. It will continue to decline for the remainder of this century.

However, this decreasing effect of immigration is less important for the declining sex ratio among the aged than the increasing difference between the mortality rates. During this century female mortality rates have declined much more than male mortality rates. Of course, this results in a much greater increase in female life expectancy and thus in a higher survival rate of females into older ages.

Older populations also differ from younger ones in marital status. Since death inexorably takes its toll and since remarriage of widowed persons is not universal, an older population generally includes a higher proportion of widowed persons. Given the sex ratios and differential mortality rates noted above, one should expect more widows than widowers in the older population. For example, in the United States in 1970, 52 percent of the females sixty-five and over were widows and 17 percent of the males of the same age were widowers.[11]

These sex differentials are widened by two further factors: (1) most husbands are several years older than their wives; (2) widowers have a much greater probability of remarriage than widows. In the United States in 1970, 37 percent of all women sixty-five to sixty-nine years of age were widows, and the percentage increased rapidly with increasing age: more than three-fourths—77 percent—of the women 85 and over were widows. The comparable percentages for males were 9 percent in the sixty-five to sixty-nine age group and 43 percent among those eighty-five and over.

In all modernizing nations the oldest generation has less formal education than younger generations. For example, whereas more than half of all adults in the United States have completed high school, most of the population sixty-five and over have no more than eight years of formal education.[12] It should be noted, however, that this is clearly a generational difference; it is not a function of the process of aging. As will be noted later, this generational gap emerges as an aspect of the modernization process, and it is probable that the difference will diminish in postindustrial society.

In modern societies retirement from the labor force has become increasingly prevalent among older people in the population during the last century. In the United States in 1890 about two-thirds of the males sixty-five and over were still in the labor force.[13] By 1940 the proportion had dropped to 42 percent, and by 1970 it had decreased still further to less than 25 percent.[14] During the same period the proportion of older women who were in the labor force had increased slightly, but still amounted to only 10 percent.[15] There appears to be no doubt that retirement from remunerated employment is becoming the predominant mode for older people in modernized societies.

The societies which have evolved this pattern of retirement are also societies which have become wage economies; hence the livelihood of most people, including the aged, is determined by how much money they receive. For most of those who have retired, this income comes in the form of old-age insurance benefits—administered by the government—and/or private pensions. Unfortunately, such income is only a fraction of the income paid to those who are still active in the labor force. Thus retirement usually entails a considerable curtailment of income. In the United States in 1969 the median income of families headed by persons sixty-five and over was only half the median of that for all families: $4,895 as compared to $9,596.[16] There is therefore a financial penalty attached to aging in modern societies.

Recent news of the growth of retirement communities in Florida and California have fostered the illusion of high mobility of aged people in the United States; yet the fact is that the people who are moving to these communities are the exceptions. In general, older people are much less mobile than those in their younger years. For example, whereas 40 percent of the total population five years of age and over changed residence between 1965 and 1970, only 23 percent of the population sixty-five and over made such a move.[17] The older populations tend to be more stable in residence.

The Limits of Aging

Theoretically, the upper limit to which a population can age in terms of the percent sixty-five and over is 100 percent, but any society which aged to this degree—or even approximated it—would be facing imminent extinction. With no children in the population and all the adult population past the potentially reproductive ages, it would be merely a matter of time until the population would die off. It is also correct to presume that inordinately high proportions of aged persons in a population are a signal of slow growth, stability, or even decline. The question thus becomes: in terms of aging, when do we reach a point of stability?

There is no single answer to this question, but perhaps we may gain perspective on it from noting three types of calculations. In the first place, we may note the degree of aging of those populations which appear to be nearing the end of the transition. Inspection of Table 2 suggests that posttransitional populations may expect to have from 14 to 16 percent of their populations sixty-five and over. This figure varies not only with the current levels of mortality and fertility, but also in relation to their prior histories. A second type of figure is afforded by stable population theory. As an example, Keyfitz and Flieger have calculated the percent of the population which would be sixty-five and over in a stable population characterized by the age-specific birth and death rates extant in England and Wales in 1968; such a population would have 13.3 percent of its population sixty-five and over—only about 1 percent above the actual level in contemporary England.[18] However, this is the level of aging calculated upon actual fertility levels in 1968—fertility levels which were well above mortality levels and still provided a margin of increase in the population. What would the ratio be in a stationary population with the posttransitional mortality rates? One such figure is provided in projections based on the United States. Assuming slightly declining mortality rates to the year 2000, no immigration, and replacement-level fertility— that is, 2.11 births per woman—the population would become stationary in the year 2037, and in that year 16 percent of the population would be sixty-five and over.[19]

Is aging of population, then, a predictable trend? Can we anticipate that those populations which are now young will inevitably age as the populations of western Europe have already done? Of course, the answer to these questions is negative. There is nothing inevitable about the process. There are many developments which could prevent or reverse the process, but most of these are in the nature of disasters—such as nuclear warfare, widespread famine, widespread lethal pollution, or a new virulent epidemic disease—which would reverse the worldwide downward trend in mortality rates.

Indeed, some pessimists believe that such an outcome is more probable than the completion of the transition.[20] Certainly, the assumption that fertility decline is a reflex effect of economic development and will occur automatically in time to avoid such disasters is not warranted.[21] One does not have to be a pessimist to predict that unless fertility rates are drastically reduced in the Third World, some form of lethal disaster is probable. However, if we avoid such disasters and if fertility rates are reduced, this will amount to the completion of the transition, and it will inevitably result in the aging of population.

Societal Aging

The social consequences of demographic aging are exceedingly complex. Since such demographic aging is an entirely new phenomenon—most of it having occurred within the last century—it should not be surprising that traditional cultures provided no ready-made modes of adjustment to the presence of such a high proportion of older people in the population. Nor should it surprise us that there have been some strains and problems involved in the adjustment.

At times the problems loom so large that some people get the impression that demographic aging is undesirable, something to be avoided. This is unfortunate, since it tends to dim the luster of one of man's crowning achievements. Surely, throughout history the prolongation of life has been a perennial preoccupation of individuals and societies.[22] That this objective has been achieved to such a degree in modern societies must rank as one of the greatest boons of modern progress. Indeed, it may be argued that average life expectancy is a more valid and meaningful measure of progress or modernization than the more common indices of gross national product per capita or consumption of electricity per capita.

The demographic transition is a necessary accompaniment of the modernization process. Reduction of mortality is one of the early goals of modernization, and experience has taught that unless fertility is also curtailed, many of the hoped-for economic gains become impossible. However, if fertility is reduced, the population begins to age. We must therefore conclude that the aging of populations is also a necessary accompaniment of modernization. Nevertheless, modernization has thus far tended to devalue old people and to reduce their status.[23]

The Meaning of Modernization

Modernization is such a multifaceted phenomenon that writings about it remind one of the blind men's descriptions of the elephant: such writings usually reflect the disciplinary contexts or the theoretical orientations of the writers. Some see the process primarily in terms of changes in the sources of power—that is, the shift from primary reliance on animate power to extensive use of inanimate sources of power.[24] Closely similar are those who tend to identify modernization with industrialization or with economic development.[25] Without specifying the particular aspects of society which are transformed, some see it as a transformation in imitation of more advanced societies.[26] Social psychologists are likely to stress changes of attitudes and values.[27] Some place the emphasis upon transformation of political institutions, the emergence of nationalism, and the growth of political consciousness, including the demand for citizen participation.[28] The functionalists tend to stress institutional differentiation.[29]

Just as all the blind men were correct, so all of these views of modernization are correct; each writer is merely emphasizing a different aspect of the same process. In an effort to incorporate all of these facets in one statement, I have defined the process as follows:

> Modernization is the transformation of a total society from a relatively rural way of life based on animate power, limited technology, relatively undifferentiated institutions, parochial and traditional outlook and values, toward a predominantly urban way of life based on inanimate sources of power, highly developed scientific technology, highly differentiated institutions matched by segmented individual roles, and a cosmopolitan outlook which emphasizes efficiency and progress.[30]

Comprehensive as it is, even this definition merely samples the range of the societal transformation involved. Its main thesis is contained in the phrase "transformation of a total society"; there is no aspect of the society which is not drastically changed in the process. A second major point to be emphasized about this formulation is that the process is unidirectional; the change is always away from a rural, traditional form of society in the direction of an urbanized, high-energy, highly differentiated type of society. This is not to assert that the process is uniform; it is merely to emphasize that modernization always produces changes in the same direction, regardless of the unique qualities of each traditional society.[31]

Salient Aspects of Modernization

One limitation of the assumption of such a holistic view of the process of modernization is that it is difficult to discuss it without permitting such discussion to develop into a treatise of excessive length and complexity. In order to avoid this pitfall it is necessary to abstract those aspects of the total process which are especially relevant to the problem at hand.

In the present context the problem at hand is the societal response to the aging of population, and this amounts to the analysis of the interaction of modernization and demographic aging. For this type of analysis it appears that the most salient aspects of modernization include (1) the application of modern health technology within a society; (2) the application of scientific technology to economic production and distribution; (3) urbanization; and (4) the extension of literacy and mass education. The question to be examined is How do each of these aspects of modernization contribute to the generally observed downgrading and reduction of status of the aged in modern societies?

Aging and Health Technology

Modern health technology is one of the most obvious exports from modernized societies to contemporary developing—that is, modernizing—societies. Yet there is scant mention of this aspect of modernization in the massive literature about the process.

Since World War II the introduction of modern forms of sanitation and control of communicable disease into erstwhile traditional societies has produced dramatic demographic effects. Initially these are seen in terms of lower mortality rates, especially lower infant and child mortality. Without commensurate reduction in fertility—and, so far, no developing society has reduced fertility as early and rapidly as they have reduced mortality—this touches off a population explosion. Not only is there a rapid increase in the total population; because birth rates remain high while larger proportions of the babies are kept alive, the early effect of these measures upon the age composition of the population is a "young-ing" effect—that is, a disproportionate increase in the number of children in the population. In the long run, however, the application of modern health technology not only prevents death in infancy and childhood but also prolongs life at all stages. Moreover, if this development is coupled with the introduction of contraception—another aspect of such technology—it may produce a reduction of fertility and with it the progressive aging of the population.

As the lives of workers are prolonged, death no longer creates openings in the labor force as rapidly as it once did. Thus competitive pressures are generated between the generations in the labor force. Eventually a social substitute for death as the means of exit from the labor force is instituted in the form of the practice of retirement.

At the same time, at least until the present, modernized societies have been characterized by the work ethic—in its earlier, European form known as the Protestant ethic—which makes the work role the chief role in life and allocates rewards, both material and nonmaterial, accordingly. Consequently, retirement from this most valued and status-giving role is accompanied by a reduction in rewards, including monetary income and psychologically satisfying status.

In sum, then: in the long run the introduction of modern health technology contributes to the aging of population and its work force. This in turn creates pressures toward retirement, forces people out of the most valued and highly rewarded roles, deprives them of utility, curtails their income and lowers their status in the society. This chain of events is depicted in the top line of Figure 1.

Economic Technology and Aging

A second salient aspect of modernization is the introduction of modern economic technology. This creates many new occupations and transforms most of the old ones. It is only natural that the people coming forward to fill these new jobs should be those not yet established in careers—namely, the young. They become the pioneers in a developing society, and they are rewarded both financially and psychologically for filling roles which are highly valued in the society. Older workers carry on in the more traditional work roles, some of which become obsolete and most of which are less highly valued and therefore less well remunerated. Both obsolescence and youthful competition eventually create pressure for retirement and with it the loss of income and status, as previously noted. Thus health technology and economic technology separately and in interaction conduce to the restriction of the roles of the aged in society and toward their relative financial and psychological deprivation. The role of economic technology in this process is depicted on line 2 in Figure 1.

Aging and Urbanization

The third salient factor in modernization is urbanization. The excess rural population created by the population explosion flocks to the cities to take over the new jobs created by economic development. Of course, it is the young who migrate. Their migration produces physical separation from the parental family and tends to foster the establishment of permanently separate residence, thus breaking down the extended family in favor of the nuclear conjugal unit. Neolocal marriage becomes the norm

Figure 1 Aging and Modernization

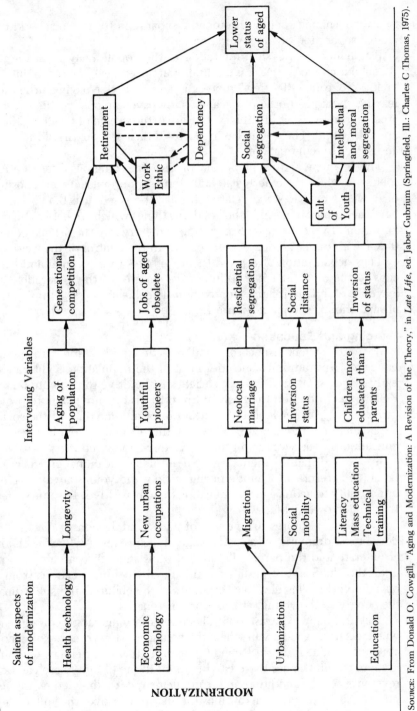

SOURCE: From Donald O. Cowgill, "Aging and Modernization: A Revision of the Theory," in *Late Life*, ed. Jaber Gubrium (Springfield, Ill.: Charles C Thomas, 1975).

in a modernizing society. Residential separation fosters social and intellectual separation of the generations.

Paralleling the physical migration of the young away from the rural parental home to the cities is a subtler, but no less real, social mobility: the young move into the new, more glamorous, better-paying urban jobs, leaving behind—both physically and psychologically—the grubby, archaic, rural way of life. The young are in the stream of progress; the old are left behind. The young have improved their station; the old stand still and suffer by comparison.

This is a new and revolutionary pattern emerging out of a traditional society in which the elderly had high status, important roles, and positions of power. Now the status relationships are reversed; it is the young who have the higher status and who are doing things which are held to be more important. In the process of migration and entry into the urban economy they have, to a large degree, escaped from the control of their elders.

Thus urbanization also provides advantages to the young and handicaps to the aged. It tends to invert the statuses of the generations and leave the elderly in relative deprivation. The dual process stemming from urbanization is shown in Figure 1.

Aging and Education

A fourth salient aspect of modernization with respect to aging is education. In traditional societies most of the population is illiterate. An early effort in all modernizing societies is the drive to promote literacy. Following close upon the heels of this effort is the movement to provide progressively higher levels of education for all the youth of the society. Paralleling this movement, in turn, is the effort to provide vocational education for the workers in the newly developing industries.

Be it noted that the main targets of all such educational efforts are the young. Therefore in a modernizing society the young always have an opportunity to acquire more education than their elders. In some societies this is an avowed objective.

This also constitutes an inversion of status, and the consequences are no doubt most dramatic in the early stage of the process—when the children are literate and the parents illiterate. In this stage the parents must rely upon the children to translate for them many communications from the outside world. This elevates the status of the children and subordinates the elderly to the young, at least for this function.

This dramatic contrast only illustrates the long range consequences which occur in a society in which the young are always more knowledgeable, more skilled, more attuned to the times than their elders. Certainly, in these circumstances there can be no mystique of age; there can be no reverence for the aged deriving from their superior knowledge. In such a society the aged will have lost most of their power over the young within their family and kin group. So, one can see that education, too, contributes to the downgrading of the elderly in modern societies. The process is diagramed on the bottom line of Figure 1.

Aging and the Work Ethic

In this analysis the work ethic is treated as a factor which has thus far conditioned and modified the effects of modernization on the status of the aged, but not as an essential ingredient of the modernization process itself. This is, of course, a moot point. The Weberian point of view would ascribe to it the central role of prime motivator.[32] I do not dispute the key role played by the work ethic, whether derived from Protestantism or from other sources, in the most modernized societies.

However, there appears to be room for reasonable doubt that it is as essential to the process as is generally believed by those whose perspective is derived from Western capitalist countries. Some developing nations, modernizing by selective imitation, may succeed without so great an emphasis upon this cultural value. It also appears that some of the most modernized societies are in the process of softening and modifying the value in the necessity of coming to terms with extensive and increasing amounts of leisure.

Aging and the Cult of Youth

Another persistent, but perhaps extraneous, factor in fostering the devaluation of the aged in the most modernized societies is what is termed here the cult of youth—that is, the prevalent value system which glorifies youth as a symbol of beauty, vigor, and progress and discriminates in favor of youth in employment and in the allocation of community resources. I have already noted that an overwhelming proportion of educational effort and resources is directed to youth. The same point can be made with reference to recreation and, to a lesser degree, to health resources.

In view of the strong tendency toward status inversion during the modernization process—particularly in relation to the creation of new jobs, the migration of the young to the cities, the social mobility of the younger generations, and the superior education of the young—it may appear that the cult of youth is an inevitable accompaniment and conditioner of the modernization process. However, this also is a moot point. It may be that in the later stages of the process—as the center of gravity shifts with the aging of populations—the cult of youth may be partially neutralized, if not by the emergence of a self-conscious subculture of the aging,[33] at least by the sheer weight of the needs and demands of increasing numbers and proportions of the aged.

Aging and the Future

As we have seen, then, modernized societies have large numbers and proportions of the aged. Yet these aged are forced to be nonproductive;

then they are penalized for their nonproductiveness with reduced incomes and relatively low status. Barring catastrophic reversals, populations which have completed the transition will continue to be aged—that is, they will continue to have much higher proportions of older people than any populations in prior history.

Is the temporal correlation between modernization and the reduction in status of the aged a necessary and predictable one? That the correlation is real has been confirmed by Palmore and Whittington.[34] That the relationship is functional—that is, causal—has been one of the main theses of this article. If it has been established that a reduction of the status of the aged has resulted from modernization, it should be possible to predict that the same thing will happen wherever modernization occurs.

Indeed, it is probable that this will happen in other parts of the world as they modernize. However, the relationship does not appear either inevitable or necessarily permanent. Any change in the factors and relationships diagramed in Figure 1 would change the outcome, and, as noted previously, two factors are included which do not appear to be inherent and necessary to the modernization process: the work ethic and the cult of youth. Both of these factors appear to have been present and influential during the development of the presently highly modernized societies, but they do not appear to be essential elements in the process. If either or both of them should be absent or should appear with less strength, the outcome could be significantly modified.

Furthermore, Palmore and Manton find evidence that the relationship is curvilinear, that while the margin of difference between the educational level and occupational pursuits of the aged as compared with the younger adult population is greater in the more modernized societies, there is a point beyond which this is no longer true.[35] In other words, the aged in the most advanced countries suffer from less educational and occupational disadvantage than the aged in countries which are slightly less advanced on the modernization scale. This suggests a possible bottoming-out of the trend and a tendency toward convergence in the most advanced stages of modernization.

This is an encouraging hint, and there are corroborating indicators to give it credence. The late stages of the demographic transition entail convergence of vital rates and a tendency toward stability. As a country becomes highly modernized it is probable that the benefits of medical technology become more widely accessible and, therefore, that the differential effects by social class, area of residence, and age tend to decrease. There certainly is strong indication that the differences between the life styles and standards of living of rural and urban residents diminish in the late stages of the transition. It is also probable that there is an upper limit to the amount of time and resources which a society will devote to mass public education and that as most of the population achieves the general functional level, the differential level of achievement between the generations will begin to decrease. Indeed, this appears to be indicated in the data analyzed by Palmore and Manton.[36] In a more general vein, it is reasonable to suppose that if one out of seven, or even more, persons in a population is sixty-five and over, societies will continue to invent and institutionalize social and cultural means of coping with this condition.

Retirement and social security are two early responses to this phenomenon. However, retirement is largely negative in its impact on the older people themselves in that it deprives them of a key role in life. It is probable that over time new roles for the aged will evolve, roles which have value to the society and provide purpose and status to those performing them. The early forms of social security were intended to provide a minimum income to the retired and some inducement for the elderly to leave the labor market. However, social security benefits have universally been inadequate to provide a satisfying life style. There will be continued efforts to find forms of income maintenance for the elderly which are both socially feasible and individually sufficient. Experimentation will also continue in the effort to provide opportunities for adequate medical care, suitable housing, healthful diet, meaningful leisure and cultural pursuits, appropriate educational experiences, and vital religious life.

Summary

Modern society has made great strides in the application of sophisticated technology to the control of mortality and fertility. Yet, while the application of both forms of technology eventually results in relatively aged populations, these societies have been slow and faltering in adapting their institutions to this new demographic phenomenon. The early, fumbling attempts have been compromises between the interests of youth-oriented society and the needs of the old people themselves. The results have been injurious to the dignity and status of the elderly. Recently, however, there have been some encouraging signs that the more advanced societies may have begun to close the gap, that they are beginning to catch up with their demographic trends, that their institutions and cultures are beginning to reflect more attention to the needs and interests of this increasing segment of their populations. It is predictable that this should happen, particularly in societies in which the political institutions are responsive to an electorate, since the electorate itself is aging. Many of the institutional adaptations which are needed must perforce be proposed, debated, compromised, and adopted within the political arena.

NOTES

1. John Kenneth Galbraith, *The Affluent Society* (Boston, Mass.: Houghton Mifflin, 1958), p. 338.

2. Earlier figures for France, England, Sweden and Australia taken from Edward Rosset, *Aging Process of Population* (New York: Macmillan, 1964), chap. 9; latest figures in each case calculated from *Demographic Yearbook 1971* (New York: United Nations, 1972), Table 7.
3. Donald O. Cowgill, "The Demography of Aging," in *The Daily Needs and Interests of Older People*, ed. Adeline M. Hoffman (Springfield, Ill.: Charles C Thomas, 1970), pp. 35–38.
4. Transition theory was first stated by Warren S. Thompson in "Population," *American Journal of Sociology*, 31 (May 1929), 959–975. It was reformulated by Frank W. Notestein in "Population—the Long View," in *Food for the World*, ed. T. W. Schultz (Chicago, Ill.: University of Chicago Press, 1945). Other statements of it include: Kingsley Davis, "The World Demographic Transition," THE ANNALS, 237 (January 1945), 1–11; Donald O. Cowgill, "Transition Theory as General Population Theory," *Social Forces*, 41, no. 3 (March 1963), 270–274.
5. Ronald Freedman, ed., *Population: The Vital Revolution* (Chicago, Ill.: Aldine, 1964).
6. For a discussion of other changes accompanying the transition, see, Donald O. Cowgill, "Transition Theory as General Population Theory," *Social Forces*, 41, no. 3 (March 1963), 270–274, reprinted in *Social Demography*, ed. Thomas R. Ford and Gordon F. DeJong (Englewood Cliffs, N.J.: Prentice-Hall, 1970), pp. 627–633.
7. For detailed discussions of the relative effects of declining mortality and fertility upon age structure, see Albert I. Hermalin, "The Effects of Changes in Mortality Rates on Population Growth and Age Distribution in the United States," *Milbank Memorial Fund Quarterly*, 44, no. 4, pt. 1 (October 1966), 451–469; and Ansley J. Coale, "The Effects of Changes in Mortality and Fertility on Age Composition," *Milbank Memorial Fund Quarterly*, 34, no. 1 (January 1956), 79–114.
8. U.S. Bureau of the Census, *Current Population Reports*, series P-20, no. 143, p. 9.
9. U.S. Bureau of the Census, "We the American Elderly," Special Report no. 10 on the 1970 Census (Washington, D.C.: Government Printing Office, 1973), p. 6.
10. Henry D. Sheldon, *The Older Population of the United States* (New York: John Wiley and Sons, 1958), p. 13.
11. "We the American Elderly," p. 10.
12. Ibid., p. 11.
13. Margaret S. Gordon, "Work and Patterns of Retirement," in *Aging and Leisure*, ed. Robert W. Kleemeier (New York: Oxford University Press, 1961), p. 18.
14. U.S. Bureau of the Census, *1970 Census of Population: United States Summary* (Washington, D.C.: Government Printing Office, 1972), Table 78.
15. Ibid.
16. "We the American Elderly," p. 12.
17. Calculated from *1970 Census of Population*, Table 196.
18. Nathan Keyfitz and Wilhelm Flieger, *Population* (San Francisco, Cal.: W. H. Freeman, 1971), p. 34.
19. Jacob Siegel and William E. O'Leary, "Some Demographic Aspects of Aging in the United States," *Current Population Reports: Special Reports*, series P-23, no. 43 (February 1973), p. 6.
20. Donella H. Meadows, Dennis L. Meadows, Jørgen Randers and William W. Behrens, III, *The Limits of Growth* (New York; Universe Books, 1972); Paul R. Ehrlich, *The Population Bomb* (New York: Ballantine Books, 1968);

Harrison Brown and Edward Hutchings, Jr., *Are Our Descendants Doomed?* (New York: Viking, 1970).

21. See Donald O. Cowgill, "The Use of the Logistic Curve and the Transition Model in Developing Nations," in *Studies in Demography*, ed. Ashish Bose, P. B. Desai, and S. P. Jain (Chapel Hill, N.C.: University of North Carolina Press, 1970), pp. 157–165.

22. Gerald J. Gruman, *A History of Ideas about the Prolongation of Life* (Philadelphia, Pa.: American Philosophical Society, 1966).

23. Donald O. Cowgill and Lowell D. Holmes, eds., *Aging and Modernization* (New York: Appleton-Century-Crofts, 1972), pp. 322–323; also, Erdman Palmore and F. Whittington, "Trends in the Relative Status of the Aged," *Social Forces*, 50 (1971), 84–91.

24. Marion J. Levy, *Modernization and the Structure of Societies* (Princeton, N.J.: Princeton University Press, 1966); Fred Cottrell, *Energy and Society* (New York: McGraw-Hill, 1955).

25. Walt W. Rostow, *The Economics of Take-Off into Sustained Growth* (New York: St. Martin's Press, 1963).

26. Reinhard Bendix, "Proba Definicji Modernizacji" (Towards a Definition of Modernization), *Studia Socjolgiczno Polityczne*, 25 (1968) 31–43.

27. Alex Inkeles and David H. Smith, "The Fate of Personal Adjustment in the Process of Modernization," *International Journal of Comparative Sociology*, 11 (June 1970), 81–114.

28. Daniel Lerner, *The Passing of Traditional Society: Modernizing the Middle East* (New York: Free Press, 1958).

29. S. N. Eisenstadt, *Modernization: Protest and Change* (Englewood Cliffs, N.J.: Prentice-Hall, 1966).

30. Donald O. Cowgill, "Aging and Modernization: A Revision of the Theory," in *Late Life*, ed. Jaber Gubrium (Springfield, Ill.: Charles C Thomas, 1975).

31. Nettl makes a convincing case that each society is unique in origin, will be uniquely selective as modernization occurs and may be expected to retain its individuality in its modernized form. See J. P. Nettl, *International Systems and the Modernization of Societies* (New York: Basic Books, 1968), pp. 42–57.

32. Max Weber, *The Protestant Ethic and the Spirit of Capitalism* (New York: Charles Scribner's Sons, 1958).

33. Arnold M. Rose, "The Subculture of the Aging: A Framework for Research in Social Gerontology," in *Older People and Their Social World*, ed. Arnold M. Rose and Warren M. Peterson (Philadelphia, Pa.: F. A. Davis, 1965), pp. 3–16.

34. Palmore and Whittington, "Trends in the Relative Status of the Aged"; see also Irwin Press and Mike McKool, Jr., "Social Structure and Status of the Aged: Toward Some Valid Cross-Cultural Generalizations," *Aging and Human Development*, 3 (1972), 297–306.

35. Erdman Palmore and Kenneth Manton, "Modernization and the Status of the Aged: International Comparisons," *Journal of Gerontology*, 29, no. 2 (March 1974), 205–210.

36. Ibid.

Growing Old in America
DAVID HACKETT FISCHER

In these exerpts from *Growing Old in America*, Fischer demonstrates the change that occurred in attitudes toward the aged in the
early nineteenth century in New England. Until around 1790 few
Americans survived until old age, and those who did were held in
veneration. Evidence of veneration for the aged can be found in the
literature and customs of the time. Between 1770 and 1820 a worldwide revolution in social values, as reflected in the French Revolution and the American War of Independence, brought about sweeping changes in relations between generations. Traditional customs
honoring the aged were challenged, as evidenced by the shift from
age to wealth as the principal criterion for assigning seats in
meetinghouses, new clothing styles favoring youthful attributes, the
introduction of pejorative terms for the elderly in the language, and
changes in property inheritance laws and customs.

The Exaltation of Aging in Early America: 1607–1820

We often imagine that our ancestors were older than ourselves, for so they
are whenever we actually meet them. We know the past through its
survivors and easily forget the flight of time. An example of this curious
habit of thought appears in the writings of Oliver Wendell Holmes, Jr.:
"When I went to the [Civil] War," he wrote, "I thought that soldiers were
old men. I remembered a picture of the revolutionary soldier which some
of you may have seen, representing a white-haired man with his flint-lock
slung across his back. I remembered one or two living examples of
revolutionary soldiers whom I had met, and I took no account of the lapse
of time."[1]

That common illusion is, of course, mistaken. Two hundred years ago
the population of America was actually younger than it is today. The
median age of Americans in 1976 was nearly thirty. In 1790 it was barely
sixteen. Sixteen! Half the population was below that age. Few people
were very old; less than 2 percent were sixty-five or older, compared with
10 percent today.[2] That distribution of ages changed scarcely at all during
the first two hundred years of American history. From 1625 to 1810 the
median age was much the same whenever it was measured, and the
relative proportion of the elderly also remained remarkably stable.[3]

The astonishing youthfulness of the American population was caused
more by high fertility than by high mortality. The families of early
America produced great swarms of children; the median age was low

SOURCE: From *Growing Old in America* by David Hackett Fischer. Copyright ©
1977, 1978 by David Hackett Fischer. Reprinted by permission of Oxford
University Press, Inc.

primarily on that account.[4] But high mortality also had an important effect. Two hundred years ago the length of human life in America was only a third of what it is today. In the Chesapeake colonies during the seventeenth century, life expectancy at birth was twenty-five—for both black slaves and their white masters. New England was much healthier. But even in Massachusetts, where life expectancy was highest, it was only thirty-eight. Few seventeenth-century Americans survived to an advanced age. As late as 1726 Cotton Mather guessed that "scarce three in a hundred live to three-score and ten."[5] The evidence of modern historical demography suggests that he was not far off the mark. In Charles County, Maryland, during the seventeenth century only 3.6 percent of white male children survived from birth to the age of seventy.[6] Life chances were much better in New England, where perhaps 20 percent reached Mather's biblical span. But even there mortality was much greater than it is today.[7]

Old age was highly respected in early America, perhaps in part because it was comparatively rare.[8] A large body of literature was devoted to the subject during the seventeenth and eighteenth centuries.[9] It was primarily a literature of prescription, which taught people how they were expected to behave toward their elders. Without exception, it prescribed the ancient ideal of deference and respect for old age. "These two qualities go together, the ancient and the honorable," wrote Cotton Mather. So closely were those ideas linked that they sometimes seemed to be one.[10]

The attitude which the young were expected to assume before their elders was unlike that in any other social relationship. Respect, honor, obligation, and deference were all involved, but there was something deeper than deference, something summarized in a word now largely lost from common usage—"veneration." Old age was to be venerated in early America. The *Oxford English Dictionary* defines veneration as a "feeling of deep respect and reverence." Its Latin root was the verb *veneror*, which meant "to regard with religious awe and reverence." Veneration was more than a form of respect. It was also a form of worship.[11]

. . . .

Early American literature provides copious evidence that veneration of old age was a social idea which was widely preached in that society. But was it also practiced? There are many tests. Most—though not all, as we shall see—suggest a similarity of attitudes and acts. One simple test can be made on the literature itself, where we find, besides the argument that the young should yield to their elders, an assumption that they would naturally tend to do so. The Puritans assumed that respect for age was an ordinary human impulse—even an instinct "written in their hearts by nature." Veneration of the aged was spoken of as natural and normal. Then as now, the strongest social habits were thought to be not cultural, but biological in their basis.

Our memories are so short that we think our social arrangements have always existed, and that they are rooted in some deep, organic structure of our being. Today we tend to assume that youth will *not* venerate age. Modern psychology has taught us to expect trouble between age and youth. Freud believed that fathers would naturally exercise an arbitrary authority over their sons, and that sons would naturally resist. The Freudian model was, perhaps, an accurate description of generational relationships in central Europe at the end of the nineteenth century. But in the seventeenth century the Puritans believed that exactly the opposite behavior was an immutable fact. "The light of nature teacheth men to honour age," one wrote, in a spirit that assumed the proposition to be self-evident. "The law written in their hearts by nature has directed them to give a peculiar respect and deference to aged men. In most civilized nations they have done so."[12] The Puritans assumed that youth *would* inevitably defer to age. Their assumptions, more than their prescriptions, tell us what to expect in their acts.

If we move beyond literature and study the thoughts that the Puritans betrayed in their social arrangements, we find that the ideal of veneration was not merely observed, but also institutionalized in many ways. Old age was ceremoniously honored on public occasions. The most important and solemn public gatherings in a New England town were the moments when the people met to worship together. In their meetinghouses they were carefully assigned seats of different degrees of dignity. The most honorable places did not go to the richest or strongest, but to the oldest. Families and neighborhoods were broken up and the congregation was seated according to sex and seniority. The places of highest honor went to men and women of the greatest age.

Only one seventeenth-century meetinghouse still stands in Massachusetts—Hingham's beautiful Old Ship Meeting, a few miles south of Boston. An historian has tried to establish the exact spot in the meetinghouse where each member of the congregation worshipped on a certain day, January 8, 1682. He has found that Hingham's meetinghouse seats were assigned primarily according to age and sex. Men sat on one side of the aisle, women on the other. The best seat was a single pew beside the pulpit, which was shared by the minister's wife and the aged widow of his predecessor. Next in honor was a bench below the pulpit, which belonged to the Elders. And their title was no euphemism. In 1682 the three Hingham Elders whose ages we know were seventy-three, eighty-six, and ninety-two. They held the bench of highest dignity, though their wealth was much below the average in the town.

The next best seats made a sort of inner circle around the pulpit. They were reserved for the wives and widows of Elders and Deacons on the one side, and on the other the "old guard" that ran the town. Middle-aged men and their wives occupied the front rows in the gallery. Behind them, in an outer ring, were the young bachelors and maids. Young married couples with infants on their laps sat on the first floor and filled the middle of the meetinghouse, and the older children were seated on separate benches around the walls. The worst seats, tucked away in the back corners of the building, were reserved for blacks, Indians, and servants.

Hingham in 1682 was an elaborately stratified society, and its meetinghouse stood as an architectural model of its stratification system. Many different forms of inequality existed together in the Old Ship Meeting: inequalities of wealth, power, order, race, and sex were combined in a pluralistic stratification system of great complexity. It is impossible to say which criterion was most important, for care was taken to be sure that all were respected. The seating committee in Windsor, Connecticut, for example, was instructed that every man was "to be seated according to his age and rates, but no man was to lose his rank." But among all of those many distinctions none was more important than age.[13]

. . . .

The Revolution in Age Relations: 1770–1820

Late in the eighteenth century the Western world experienced a social revolution which was more powerful in its causes and more profound in its effects than any comparable happening in modern history. The American War of Independence and the French Revolution were both parts of that great upheaval; the Russian and Chinese revolutions would be its echoes in the outer world. But the great revolution itself was something larger than those mighty events, and something deeper than the political disturbances which it caused. It was a fundamental change in world culture, which began in the Western nations and spread swiftly to every human society on the face of the earth. In Anglo-America, where its full effects were first felt between 1770 and 1820, radical changes simultaneously appeared in demography and economics, politics and law, stratification and association, ideology and psychology, ethics and aesthetics. Every sort of human relation was transformed by it: relations between nations, classes, races, sexes—and also generations.

The great revolution was, among other things, a revolution in age relations. It was the end of an *ancien régime* which was also a *régime des anciens*, and the beginning of a new order of things built upon a different principle. The revolution created a world without "veneration" on the one hand or "condescension" on the other; a world without eldership or primogeniture. On the surface it introduced a spirit of age equality, which reached its most dramatic expression in the famous public *fêtes* of the French Revolution, where a symbolic harmony of youth and age was celebrated in elaborate rituals. In those public festivals, the old men distributed gifts of figs and raisins to the youths; in turn, the young women presented baskets of bread and fruit to their elders.[14] But beneath that surface a new sort of inequality was being born, a new hierarchy of generations in which youth acquired the moral advantage that age had lost.

In America the first small signs of change began to appear as early as the middle of the eighteenth century. Among the first to be challenged was the custom of "seating the meeting" according to age. In a few New England towns that practice had begun to grow weak early in the century. Northampton, Massachusetts, for example, was still operating according to the old way in 1707, when it instructed its seating committee "first to have regard to a person's age, second to estate, and third to have some regard to men's usefulness." Thirty years later the town decided to reverse the relative importance of age and wealth. In 1737 its seating committee was instructed to "have respect principally to men's estate, to have regard to men's age, [and] voted that there be some regard and respect to men's usefulness but in a less degree."[15]

Northampton was not a typical town. Most others continued to use age as the primary criterion for ranking until the end of the eighteenth century. But then, one by one, they stopped seating their meetinghouses in the traditional way. The transition began slowly in the mid-eighteenth century, reached its peak in the 1790s, and was largely completed by 1830. When the towns stopped "dignifying the seats," they did not abandon the practice of seating altogether. Instead of assigning the seats by age, estate, and place, the committees often sold them at auction, and the best bench in the meetinghouse went to the highest bidder. In that way, the towns shifted from a pluralistic system of stratification to a unitary system based primarily on wealth alone. Rank and status in the meetinghouse thereafter rested upon material possessions, without regard to age.[16]

. . . .

At the same time, a parallel pattern appeared in other evidence—costume. In the sixteenth century there were two styles of men's dress: one for old men and another for young. In the seventeenth century, and still more in the eighteenth, a single style appeared for all age groups, designed to flatter the old. Hair was hidden beneath a wig, or powdered and made white as if by old age. The cut of men's clothing had a similar purpose. During the eighteenth century clothes were cunningly tailored in such a way that the shoulders were made narrow and rounded, the hips and waists were actually broadened, and the backs of the coats were designed to make the spine appear to be bent by the weight of many years. Only one part of the body was revealed—the lower leg, which is, perhaps, an old man's last anatomical advantage. During those two centuries these tendencies became stronger rather than weaker; the pattern of bias toward old age in men's clothing actually grew more intense.

But between 1790 and 1815 men's dress was revolutionized. Artifice remained, but its effect was reversed. The French Revolution introduced fashions that flattered youth. Wigs were replaced by hairpieces and toupees, which were designed to make old men look young again. The white powder that had been used to give men the appearance of age yielded to hair dyes, tints, and preservatives. The cut of a coat was designed to flatter a youthful figure. It was pulled in at the waist and puffed out at the shoulders, and the back was made straight and broad. Knee breeches were replaced by trousers, which was primarily a statement about class relations, but the design of the trousers also made a point about age. The trousers were tightly trimmed, and if they were a bit more trim than the men who wore them, there were corsets for men as well as for women. From about 1790 to our time, fashion has attempted in its endless variety of ways to make old men look young again.

During the transition there was a thirty years' war of the sartorial generations, and a deadly struggle it was, deeply disturbing to those who lived through it. Many old men were left behind by the change—men such as Samuel Curwen (1715–1802), a Salem merchant who had been born in the reign of George I and died in the administration of Thomas Jefferson, By the early nineteenth century he had become a famous sight. "He appeared in our streets, much like a Patriarch," wrote a local clergyman. "The English tye-wig, the long scarlet cloak, the heavy rings, and gold-headed cane attracted notice after the war tho' it was best dress before it, for persons of condition."[17] Samuel Curwen, tottering feebly through the streets of Salem, was an object of respect before the Revolution; afterward, he was a curiosity instead. But the change was most cruel in its effects upon the generation that came after Curwen's— the generation whose unhappy fate it was to be young in an era when age was respected and old in a time when youth took the palm.

The transition occasionally had its amusing moments. In Concord, Massachusetts, an elderly gentleman named Abiel Heywood was, according to his biographer, "the last man in the town, excepting the Reverend Dr. Ripley, who wore the old-fashioned knee-breeches, or small-clothes. When about marrying, he for the first time procured a pair of pantaloons, and informing Mr. Nathan Brooks of the fact, inquired of him how they were to be put on. Mr. Brooks told him he believed that people generally drew them on over their heads, but whether the doctor tried that mode does not appear; if he did, he never made public the result of the experiment, and it is only known that he succeeded in some way or other in getting the strange garment on, became reconciled to the fashion and thereafter followed." It is interesting to observe that Heywood adopted the new fashion on the eve of his marriage at an advanced age.[18]

The history of women's dress is far more complex than that of men's. The primary purpose of feminine fashion was to express a spirit of sexual subordination, and even to promote it. But behind that purpose, attitudes toward age also appeared. We have discovered from some of the earliest feminine costumes which have been found that old women and young women dressed very differently thousands of years ago. Clothing that has survived (by a miracle of preservation) in prehistoric burial mounds shows that young women dressed in a most extraordinary way for that cold climate. The body of a handsome Danish girl of twenty was buried in a brief tunic which barely covered her breasts, and low upon her hips she wore a remarkable short skirt—made not of cloth, but of loose-hanging cords—which revealed more than it concealed. Very different is an old woman's costume which has also survived from the same period. She wore a long skirt, made of closely woven cloth, which rose to meet a bodice and fell nearly to the ground. Thus ancient fashion flattered both youth and age by shrouding an old body in flowing drapery while revealing the grace of a young one.

In the modern era we find a different pattern: feminine costumes were more or less the same for women of all ages. There were many small differences—caps for married women and other symbols of rank, status, and condition, which were codified in what were called "sumptuary laws." But in the seventeenth and mid-eighteenth centuries, every wom-an's body was hidden beneath her dress—all but the shoulders and breasts, which are parts of the body that a mature woman may show to advantage. Torsos distended by twenty years of childbearing were carefully camouflaged, and hips broadened by six or eight deliveries were buried in flowing skirts. Legs were made totally invisible—a service to old age. Women wore wigs and powdered their hair just as men did, and with the same effect. Women's clothing in the early modern era was designed to flatter age rather than youth.

That pattern prevailed until the late eighteenth century. Then the dressmakers of post-Revolutionary Paris began to produce the first feminine fashions in modern history that were designed primarily for youth. The diaphanous gowns of the "Directory" style enormously flattered a youthful body and cruelly mocked an old one. When a Baltimore beauty married the brother of Napoleon, one observer re-marked that her wedding gown was so insubstantial that it could be squeezed into a snuffbox! That style was widely adopted by young women in America during the early nineteenth century despite the stern disapproval of their elders.

But it soon ended. Feminine fashion also had its Thermidor—perhaps because the primary purpose of women's dress was still to show the subordination of women rather than the superiority of youth. The old style returned, and retained its hegemony until the 1920s, when women's clothing suddenly began to be oriented unequivocally toward youth instead of age, with more exposure and less support, higher hemlines and lower necklines. From the 1920s to the 1970s, in summer fashions especially, hemlines moved intermittently higher and necklines progres-sively lower. In the summers of 1973 and 1974, designers added (or subtracted) bare midriffs; in the summers of 1975 and 1976, bare backs. A social historian may await the future with some anticipation.

Still another kind of evidence of the changing attitude toward age is linguistic. As elderly people began to lose their social status, the world developed a more elaborate vocabulary with which to abuse them. The result was the invention of a new language to express contempt for old people. If we consult the *Oxford English Dictionary*, we discover that most of our pejorative terms for old men began to appear first during the late eighteenth and early nineteenth centuries. Some were old words which had earlier carried an honorific meaning—*gaffer*, for example. *Gaffer* had been a title of respect, even a term of endearment, in seventeenth- and eighteenth-century England. It probably arose as a contraction of godfather. But by 1820 *gaffer* (usually *old gaffer*) had been converted from a praise word into a pejorative expressing general contempt for old men. Another such word is *fogy*, which before 1780 meant a wounded military veteran. By 1830 *fogy* had become a "disrespectful appellation for a man advanced in life." The term was put to heavy use in American politics during the 1850s, at the time of the "Young America" movement: the rhetoric of the movement reviled *fogyism* (the characteristic thought of fogies), *fogydom* (the genus of fogies), and *fogyish* behavior in all its forms.

Shakespeare sometimes used the word *greybeard* to describe an honorable old man, and "greybeard counsell" as a synonym for wisdom. But every example from the nineteenth century in the *Oxford English Dictionary* carries a negative connotation. In 1815 *old guard* was a descriptive phrase which was worn like a decoration by Napoleon's soldiers; its first English translations carried the same meaning. By 1880 *old guard* had become an American expression used to describe reactionary, corrupt, and aged politicians.

Superannuated seems also to have shifted its meaning. In the seventeenth and eighteenth centuries, according to the *Oxford English Dictionary*, it referred to people of various ages who were disqualified from some particular service or activity by reason of their age—old maids in their forties, half-pay officers in their thirties, aging courtiers in their twenties, and boys in their teens who had passed the age for school admission were all called *superannuated*. But in the nineteenth and twentieth centuries, *superannuated* increasingly referred to men and women in their sixties and implied a kind of generalized incompetence.

At the same time that old words changed their meanings, new ones were invented, thus enlarging the vocabulary of abuse. They began to appear in the late eighteenth century and multiplied rapidly in the nineteenth. One example is *codger*, a slang word of urban origin, which probably was derived from the verb *to cadge*, or beg. The first clear example given in the *Oxford English Dictionary* dates from 1775. By 1796 *codger* was being used as a specialized pejorative for a "mean stingy miserly old fellow." [19]

In the next century many other terms of specialized abuse were invented. *Old cornstalk* (1824) was an Americanism for "an ineffectual old man." [20] *Old goat* meant a lecherous old man; *fuddy-duddy*, a pompous old man; *granny*, a weak old man; *mummy*, an ugly old man; *geezer*, an eccentric old man; *goose*, a silly old man; *galoot*, an uncouth old man; *bottle-nose*, an alcoholic old man; *back number*, an anachronistic old man. [21] Still another set of words was invented to express an indiscriminate contempt for age—words such as *baldy* (1820), *oldster* (1829), *oldliner* (1855), *old womanish* (1775), and *old womanism* (1828). Those words entered the language at the same time that others, opposite in connotation, were disappearing from use—*progenitor, eldern, beldam,* [22] *grandame, grandsire, forefather, gramfer, granther, grannam.*

The worst pejoratives were rude and vulgar salutations which any arrogant young man might use to greet any old one—words such as *old-timer* (1866) and *pop* (from at least 1889)—which signaled in advance that an elderly man was about to be treated as a member of a generational proletariat. In the eighteenth century, on the other hand, there was a language, now lost, which was the generational equivalent of apple-polishing. Then, *grandfather* was a verb; *to grandfather* meant "to flatter with an excess of veneration." In 1748 Richardson used it that way in his *Clarissa*: "Nor would I advise that you should go to grandfather your cousin." [23]

The semantical pattern we find in the changing language of age relations is similar to all our other evidence. But it is important to observe that words describing old women have a different history. Virtually every term of abuse used for old women appears to be as old as the English language itself. *Hag* was a common term in the fourteenth century; it was used to describe a woman suspected of practicing witchcraft, and also any repulsive and ugly old woman. *Crone* is equally antique. *Old maid* meant nothing good as early as 1530, when she was described as "the most calamitous creature in nature." *Old trot* appears in Shakespeare's *Taming of the Shrew*. [24] The fact that such language existed long before a similar set of words appeared for men strongly suggests that old women were despised not so much for being old as for being women. On the other hand, the language of abuse for old men dates only to about 1800. Before that time there was instead a special vocabulary of abuse for young men—words such as *yongling* and *skipper*—which has become extinct. Dr. Johnson was heard to complain of impudent *puppies* and Mr. Pickwick of *young upstarts*. All of those terms have disappeared from common usage. It is difficult to think of any twentieth-century words that imply contempt explicitly for youth. Some are specially reserved for young people—*young punk*, for instance. But young punks are contemptible because they are punks, not because they are young. Modern words that were originally invented as pejoratives for youth have tended to be transformed by usage into praise words. The word *kid* meant something rude in the early twentieth century, but by the next generation its connotation had been reversed. On the other hand, praise words invented for old people are quickly turned the other way—euphemisms such as *senior citizen* are often laden with a heavy freight of sarcasm. Thus the evidence of language shows, once again, the same pattern and timing of change as the evidence of age bias in census tracts and men's fashions.

Still another sign of change in attitudes toward age appears in a visual form. Group portraits of American families necessarily expressed an ideal of age relationships. The artist, in solving his problem of composition, made each portrait a statement about generations. These statements changed through time, and in an interesting way.[25]

No family portraits are known to have survived from seventeenth-century America. The earliest we have is Feke's *Royall Family*, painted in 1741. Only a few have come down to us from the eighteenth century, but before 1775 all except one portrait had the same composition. The father stood above his family—a stern, unbending, proprietary figure. His wife was seated below him, with other women of the household. And the children were placed below the wife. That vertical composition represented a hierarchical relationship between sexes and generations.

After about 1780 another arrangement began to appear: all the members of the family were placed upon the same horizontal plane. No longer was the father a patriarchal figure, brooding above his wife and children; he and his wife were now on the same level—and so also were the children. That horizontal style remained conventional until the twentieth century; in fact, every family painting we have found from 1820 to 1890 was composed in precisely that way.... Then, in our own time, a pluralistic pattern of composition arose; in some family paintings the children were actually placed above their parents—and a new idea of generational inequality was displayed. Once again, we see the same lines of change—this time reflected in the evidence of American art. The timing of that change was precisely the same as that in our census data, fashion history, and social vocabulary.[26]

Still other evidence appears in the history of inheritance customs. In early America attitudes toward age fixed the flow of power not merely between generations, but also within them. In a world where "older" meant "better," the eldest child received advantages denied to others. The first-born son was better born than any of his brothers. New England, as well as the southern colonies, actually practiced a modified system of primogeniture by which the eldest son commonly inherited the largest share of the property. He rarely received the entire estate, but was favored over his brothers in material possessions, marriage chances, and many other things.

There was no necessary economic reason for favoring the first-born son. The collective interest of the family could have been met by another arrangement, in which the youngest child received the largest share instead. That system was, in fact, actually practiced in some parts of England.[27] In one way it was more workable than primogeniture. When the father died the eldest son had already set up a household for himself, while the youngest was often the child who looked after the parents in their last years and still lived on the homestead. But Americans used a modified form of primogeniture more often than any other method of inheritance. The southern colonists practiced a fullblown form of primogeniture, while in New England the conventional arrangement was for each child to receive an equal share of the property except the eldest son, who was given a double share. That combination of primogeniture and partible inheritance (called "double-partible inheritance") continued to be used from the seventeenth century until the end of the eighteenth. Then it suddenly disappeared—both in law and in custom. Between 1775 and 1800 most states repealed the laws which had given an advantage to the first-born son. At the same time there was also a change in actual wealth holding. Daniel Scott Smith, in studying the town of Hingham, Massachusetts, recently made an ingenious test of that change. He found that eldest sons had a significant material advantage over their brothers in early America and maintained it during the late eighteenth century. If anything, that difference became stronger rather than weaker from 1650 to 1800. But early in the nineteenth century eldest sons suddenly lost their advantage. They have never regained it. After 1810 the wealth of elder and younger sons was virtually the same. The advantage of the elder sons had rested entirely upon age prejudice—upon the premise that older was better. When that premise was destroyed, as it was in so many ways at once, primogeniture and double-partible inheritance vanished overnight.[28]

Patterns of descent changed in names as well as in property. An indication of that trend appears in the frequency with which children were given the same names as their grandparents. The proportion of grandparents honored in that way actually increased from the seventeenth to the late eighteenth century, then fell sharply between 1790 and 1830, and fluctuated at low levels during the nineteenth century. The timing and direction of that change conforms closely to that in other evidence.[29]

All our evidence suggests that a revolution occurred in attitudes toward age between 1770 and 1820. It manifested itself in many ways at once—in

the abolition of "seating the meeting" (*c.* 1770–1820), in the first mandatory old-age retirement laws (1777–1818), in the pattern of age preference
revealed by census data (1787–1850), in the age bias of costume
(1790–1820), in the changing language of age relations (*c.* 1780–1820), in
the inheritance of property (1775–1810), and in the descent of names
(1780–1820). Many other kinds of evidence might be added,[30] but enough
has been introduced to make the point.

NOTES

1. Oliver Wendell Holmes, Jr., *Speeches* (Boston, 1934), p. 61.
2. In New England "old age" was defined in chronological terms, starting at
   about sixty. Cotton Mather wrote of a friend who had crossed the "borders
   . . . of old age" by the "out-living of three-score winters." *The Old Man's
   Honour* (Boston, 1691), p. 2. Compulsory military service ended at sixty;
   many census tracts in early America used that age to subdivide the male
   population. For a more extended discussion see John Demos, "Aging in Pre-
   Modern Society: The Case of Early New England" (unpubl., 1975). In the
   southern colonies, on the other hand, old age may have been understood a
   little differently. Certainly, men and women aged more quickly in the
   Carolinas, where it was said that there "are few old men or women to be
   found in the province . . . we cannot say that there are many in the country
   who arrive at their sixtieth year, and several at thirty bear the wrinkles, bald
   head and grey hairs of old age." Alexander Hewatt, *An Historical Account of
   the Rise and Progress of the Colonies of South Carolina and Georgia* (2 vols.,
   London, 1779), II, p. 294.
3. There were many local variations. The median age was higher in the East than
   the West. Few elderly people were to be found on the frontiers, and were
   explicitly warned away. "I am not sure that English elderly people would do
   right to pass the mountains," one traveler wrote. "For young men, everybody
   agrees that the western territory will be best to settle in. But, alas, it is another
   world." Elias P. Fordham, *Personal Narrative of Travels in Virginia* (Cleveland, 1906), pp. 152–53. A 1773 New Hampshire census shows these percentages of men aged sixty plus:

County	%
Rockingham	5.5
Strafford	4.1
Hillsborough	3.0
Cheshire	2.5
Grafton	2.0

   Rockingham, on the coast, was first to be filled up; Cheshire and Grafton
   were the last. A similar pattern appears in all other colonies for which we have
   evidence. See Robert V. Wells, *The Population of the British Colonies in
   North America before 1776* (Princeton, 1975), p. 72.
4. Ansley J. Coale, "The Effects of Changes in Mortality and Fertility on Age
   Composition," *Milbank Memorial Fund Quarterly*, 34 (1956), 79–114; 35
   (1957), 302–7.

5. Mather, *A Good Old Age* (Boston, 1726), p. 4.
6. This according to recent work by Allan Kulikoff, "Tobacco and Slaves," unpubl. Ph.D. thesis, Brandeis, 1975. Similar findings have appeared in five other unpublished studies of mortality in the Chesapeake colonies.
7. Much of that mortality occurred in childhood—in New England, about 20 percent of it during the first year of life and another 20 percent in the next twenty years. If we take another measure—life expectancy from age twenty to age sixty—the results look a little different, but the major point remains. Only a minority reached old age. Of men aged twenty-one in the Chesapeake colonies during the seventeenth century, less than 30 percent (perhaps closer to 20 percent) survived to age sixty. In Middlesex County, Mass., perhaps 50 percent did so. In the colonies generally, about 40 percent of the males survived from twenty-one to sixty. Mortality among women was greater, particularly in the child-bearing years of young adulthood. Those estimates are consistent with the most recent work on the demography of the Chesapeake colonies, but different from the historiography of New England.
8. In Europe the effect was much the same. Goubert observed that in seventeenth-century France "Only about ten [in 100] ever made their sixties. The triumphant octogenarian, surrounded by an aura of legend that made him seem at least a hundred, was regarded with . . . superstitious awe. . . . His sons and daughters, nephews and nieces long dead, as well as a good half of his grandchildren, the sage lived on to become an oracle for his entire village. His death was a major event for the whole region." Pierre Goubert, *Louis XIV and Twenty Million Frenchmen* (New York, 1970), p. 21.
9. See Job Orton [1717–83], *Discourses to the Aged* (Salem, Mass., 1801), and the works by Cotton Mather cited above. See also William Bridge, *Word to the Aged* (Boston, 1679); Increase Mather, *Two Discourses Shewing, I, That the Lord's Ears Are Open to the Prayers of the Righteous, and II, The Dignity and Duty of Aged Servants of the Lord* (Boston, 1716); Cotton Mather, *Address to Old Men and Young Men and Little Children* (Boston, 1690). There is a vast sermon literature, particularly in the form of anniversary addresses, which often took up the same question.
10. Mather, *A Good Old Age*, p. 4. The evidence of prescriptive literature is reinforced by another sort of literary evidence. For a social historian who wishes to discover normative patterns of thought, the most valuable indicators are not the thoughts that people advocated, but the thoughts that they betrayed. Early American literature contains much information of that kind. Anne Bradstreet, for example, began one of her poems with a meeting of the "four ages of man," in which childhood, youth, and middle age all naturally "make way" for "wise old age":

    And last of all, to act upon this stage:
    Leaning upon his staffe, comes old age.
    Under his arme a Sheafe of wheat he bore,
    A Harvest of the best, what needs he more.
    In's other hand a glasse, ev'n almost run,
    This writ about: This out then I am done.
    His hoary haires, and grave aspect made way:
    And al gave ear, to what he had to say.

    Bradstreet, *The Tenth Muse* (London, 1650), p. 42.
11. Veneration and respect were not categorical alternatives. Veneration was a specific form of respect. Respect was general; veneration was particular.
12. Increase Mather, *Dignity and Duty of Aged Servants*, p. 63.
13. John B. Coolidge, "Hingham Builds a Meetinghouse," *New England Quar-*

terly, 34 (1961), 435–61. Robert Gross has also studied the Concord, Mass., meetinghouse list of 1774. People were seated first by age, then within age groups by wealth, and finally within wealth groups by social status. For example:

1st bench	70 & up	60–69	50–59	40–49
Richest 20%	5	5	0	0
Middle 40	5	1	0	0
Poorest 40	1	0	0	0
2nd bench				
Richest 20	1	3	3	0
Middle 40	0	6	0	0
Poorest 40	4	0	0	0
3rd bench				
Richest 20	0	0	3	7
Middle 40	0	0	0	6
Poorest 40	0	2	0	4

14. Mona Ozouf, "Symboles et Fonction des Ages dans Les Fêtes de l'Époque Révolutionnaire," *Annales Historiques de la Révolution Française*, 42 (1970), 569–93.
15. John R. Trumbull, *History of Northampton* (2 vols., Northampton, Mass., 1898–1902), I, 517; II, 74.
16. The practice of seating the meeting in Massachusetts was abolished by the following dates:

Watertown	1775	Townshend	1780	Ludlow	1797
Wenham	1765	Stow	1790	Newton	1800
Needham	1775	Weston	1791	Acton	1808
Amherst	1775	Middlefield	1791	Dover	1812
Topsfield	1780	Concord	1792	Deerfield	1820
Manchester	1780	Framingham	1794	Northfield	1830
Princeton	1780	Boxborough	1796	Pittsfield	1836

Source: Robert J. Dinkin, "Provincial Massachusetts: A Deferential or a Democratic Society," unpubl. Ph.D. thesis, Columbia, 1968, pp. 195–99; J. E. A. Smith, *The History of Pittsfield, Mass.* (2 vols., Boston, 1869–76), II, p. 312; Susan Kurland, "A Political History of Concord," unpubl. senior thesis, Brandeis, 1972, P. 148. Each town was apt to differ in detail. Some communities adopted seating assignments based explicitly on wealth, without having an auction. Others sold special pews to the wealthiest people in town, while at the same time distributing most seats in the traditional way.

17. William Bentley, Diary, II, 423.
18. Francis R. Gourgas, "Memoir of Abiel Heywood," *Memoirs of Members of the Social Circle in Concord. Second Series, From 1795 to 1840* (Cambridge, Mass., 1888). I owe this anecdote to the kindness of Robert Gross.
19. The word *cojer* may have meant the same thing as early as 1756.
20. See Mitford M. Mathews (ed.), *A Dictionary of Americanisms* (Chicago, 1951), p. 1153.
21. *Baldhead* (1535) is the only exception. Altogether, thirty-seven terms have been found for old men; thirty-six fit the same pattern.
22. In the eighteenth century *beldam* was an honorable title for grandmother. In the nineteenth century it became a pejorative, like *hag* or *virago*.
23. Samuel Richardson, *Clarissa Harlowe* (London, 1768), I, p. 331.
24. I. ii. 79.

25. Historians today sometimes offer three categorical objections to the use of literature and painting as evidence in social history: that it is elitist, that it reflects artists' conventions rather than societal customs, and that it is "impressionistic." All of those complaints (as caveats, at least) are incorrect. The first is empirically mistaken, for in Anglo-America formal culture was not restricted to a small elite. Literacy, book ownership, library membership, the social origins of artists, and the origins of their clientele show roughly the same pattern. From 1750 to 1850 the top 60 to 70 percent of the population (ranked by wealth) participated in cultural affairs. Only a minority was excluded. Intensity of participation was uneven, but not as much as one might expect. Undoubtedly, other societies were very different, but in America literary evidence is not necessarily "elitist." Second, the objections to an inference from "art" to "life" rest upon an error in logic—a fallacy of false dichotomy. Aesthetic conventions, after all, are the conventions of the culture in which they arise. A family painting is secondary evidence of that family's activities, but primary evidence of the artists's idea of the family. His idea is often highly conventional—but for our purposes conventionality is a strength, not a weakness, for it is the social convention that we wish to discover. Third, such evidence is not impressionistic if we clearly establish the boundaries of our inquiry in advance, and include all available evidence that falls within it, on both sides of the question.

26. A similar test might also be made of age relations in American drama and fiction—difficult because there was so little of it before 1790, but enough to be useful. The plays of Munford and Royal Tyler are full of references to age relations.

27. It was called "Borough English," or, in law, ultimogeniture. See George C. Homans, *English Villagers of the Thirteenth Century* (Cambridge, Mass., 1942), p. 123; Frederick Pollock and Frederic William Maitland, *The History of English Law Before the Time of Edward I* (2 vols., Cambridge, Eng., 1923), II, p. 280.

28. Smith tested the relationship by comparing the wealth of fathers and fathers-in-law of first and younger sons. He measured the advantages which birth order brought to chances for a fortunate and prosperous marriage. The results were as follows:

Date of tax list		Same wealth quintile as father		Higher wealth quintile than father		Lower wealth quintile than father		
Fathers	Sons	1st	Last	1st	Last	1st	Last	N
1647	1680	25	29	58	29	17	43	26
1749	1779	30	33	44	26	25	41	94
1779	1810	26	30	55	27	18	43	117
1810	1830	36	27	30	36	34	37	139
1830	1860	34	35	34	30	32	34	138

SOURCE: Daniel Scott Smith, "Parental Power and Marriage Patterns: An Analysis of Historical Trends in Hingham, Massachusetts," *Journal of Marriage and the Family*, 35 (1973), 424. Copyright 1973 by the National Council on Family Relations. Reprinted by permission.

29. Daniel Scott Smith has studied naming practices in Hingham, Mass., with the following results:

Marriage cohorts	Sons	Daughters
Pre–1700	14.0	3.5
1701–1720	18.7	17.8
1721–1740	11.8	18.5
1741–1760	6.2	19.7
1761–1780	11.3	16.2
1781–1800	15.0	13.8
1801–1820	10.8	13.0
1821–1840	7.6	6.8
1841–1860	8.1	12.0
1861–1880	8.5	8.3

SOURCE: D. S. Smith, unpubl. data.

30. Another fascinating test can be made by studying the changing taxonomy of age. When old age was more highly respected than youth, common conceptions of life-stages tended to be more elaborate at the end than at the beginning. On the other hand, in the modern world, where youth receives more attention than old age, those stages are more elaborate at the beginning than at the end of life. Two or three of Shakespeare's "seven ages of man" are devoted to the years before adulthood. The rest are reserved for maturity and old age. In our time the most widely cited taxonomy of age is Erik Erikson's "eight stages of man"—"oral-sensory," "muscular-anal," "locomotor-genital," "latency," "puberty and adolescence," "young adulthood," "adulthood," and "maturity." In that taxonomy, five stages out of eight are reserved for the years before adulthood; only one for advanced age.

The Status and Integration of the Aged in Japanese Society

ERDMAN PALMORE

Although Japan has achieved a high level of industrialization, the status of the aged has not declined as it has in other industrialized countries. The majority of elderly Japanese live with their children and have important household functions to perform. Well over half the men over age sixty-five continue to work, and there are many other indications that the aged are well integrated into community life. The vertical social structure of Japan and the tradition of filial piety have both contributed to the continued respect for the aged. Thus it is possible for a strong cultural tradition which promotes respect for older people to maintain high levels of status and integration for the aged, regardless of the degree of modernization.

Most of the research on modernization and aging has found that the status and integration of the aged tends to decline from a peak in stable agricultural societies to relatively low levels in modern industrial societies (Cowgill and Holmes, 1972; Palmore and Manton, 1974). This tendency has been attributed to many factors such as the decreased importance of land as a source of status, decreased importance of the extended family, increased geographical mobility, increased proportion of aged, urbanization, modern mass education, and rapidly changing technology, social structure, and cultural values.

However, it appears that Japan is an exception to this general rule. Japan is a modern industrialized society with 98.5 percent literate, 84 percent of the labor force in nonagricultural occupations, 68 percent in urban areas, and a per capita gross national product about the same as Great Britain's (Associated Press, 1973; U.S. Bureau of Census, 1973). Yet respect for the aged remains relatively high, and the aged are more integrated into the family, the work force, and the community than in other modern nations. This study documents the high status and integration of the aged in Japan and discusses the reasons for it. The statistics, observations, and interviews were gathered during the author's sabbatical leave in Japan during 1973. Most of the surveys referred to were based on national probability samples of 2,000 or more persons and used standard survey techniques of sample selection, interviewing procedures, and data processing.

SOURCE: Copyright 1975 by the Gerontological Society. Reprinted by permission from *The Journal of Gerontology*, Vol. 30, No. 2.

Integration in the Family

Perhaps the most striking difference between older Japanese and older Americans is that over three-fourths of Japanese aged sixty-five or more live with their children (Office of the Prime Minister, 1973), while only a quarter of Americans over sixty-five live with their children (Epstein and Murray, 1967). Furthermore, the typical household of the older Japanese contains not only his or her son, but grandchildren as well. Thus Japan is a clear exception to the generalization that "the three-generation household represents a structure which is rare in almost all industrial societies" (Shanas, et al., 1968). Of those older Japanese who do not live with their children, most live with other relatives and some live with nonrelatives. Thus it is rare to find an older Japanese living all by himself (only 5 percent of those over sixty-five), while in other industrialized countries about half the single aged live by themselves (Table 1).

However, many people discount this high proportion living with their children by assuming that the proportion is rapidly declining, that the majority of younger couples want to live separately from their parents, and that only economic necessity forces them to live with their aging parents. For example, a feature article in the *New York Times* stated,

> Although about 80 percent of the elderly still live with their children, that figure is rapidly decreasing. Young married adults in the cities prefer to live by themselves with their own children (Halloran, 1972).

Each of these assumptions is demonstrably false.

TABLE 1.   **Composition of Households of 65+ in Four Countries (Percentage Distribution)**

Composition	Japan M	Japan F	Great Britain M	Great Britain F	USA M	USA F	Denmark M	Denmark F
Couples:								
Alone	16	15	67	68	77	82	80	84
With child	79	79	29	28	18	15	17	14
With relatives	4	5	3	5	3	2	1	—
With nonrelatives	1	1	1	2	2	1	2	2
Total	100	100	100	100	100	100	100	100
Single:								
Alone	10	8	37	45	52	46	58	63
With child	82	84	41	37	38	37	20	21
With relatives	6	6	14	13	11	22	6	7
With nonrelatives	2	2	8	5	8	5	10	9
Total	100	100	100	100	100	100	100	100

SOURCES: For Japan, Nasu, 1973; for other countries, Shanas et al., 1968.

TABLE 2.   Percentage of Parents Wishing to Live with Children
by Age, Area, and Education

	% Wishing to Live with Children
Total	60
Age:	
20–29	52
30–39	56
40–49	60
60+	74
Area:	
Tokyo	50
6 large cities	53
Other cities of 100,000+	55
Cities less than 100,000	63
Rural	69
Parents' Education:	
Elementary school	79
Junior high school	66
High school	51
College	43

SOURCE: National Life Center, 1972. "Don't know" and no answer categories excluded.

In 1953 the proportion of Japanese over sixty living with their children was 81 percent (National Life Center, 1972) and in 1973 this proportion declined to 75 percent (Office of the Prime Minister, 1973). This is a decline of only 3 percent per decade. At that rate, over two-thirds of the aged will still be living with their children in the year 2000.

As for preference in living arrangements, a majority of parents at all age levels and in both cities and rural areas favor joint households and wish to live with their children when they retire (Table 2). The only exception is among college graduates who have a majority wishing to live separately from their children. It is true that more of the younger than older parents and more in the urban than rural areas wish to live separately from their children, which suggests a continuation of the present slow rate of decline in percentage of aged living with their children.

As for the assumption that most joint households are caused by economic necessity, the evidence is again to the contrary. I could find no national data on the attitudes of younger persons toward living with their parents, but one survey in the Tokyo metropolitan area found that most housewives in apartments (aged thirty to fifty-nine) who lived with parents favored a continuation of living in joint households. Only 3 percent wanted to live separately (Japan Housing Foundation, 1973). A survey of parents over age fifty asked those who said they wanted to live with their children upon retirement whether they would want to live together or separately if they had sufficient money and personal care for separate homes. Of those responding 91 percent said they would still prefer to live together with their children (Office of the Prime Minister, 1973). The same survey also found that 95 percent of those actually living with their children wanted to continue living with their children, and a third of those living separately would rather live with their children. Finally, only 20 percent gave "financial aid" as a reason for wanting to live with their children, while the rest gave reasons such as "It is natural to live with your children," "Companionship with children," and "Get care from children" (Table 3). Thus the joint household is not only the typical living arrangement, but is usually preferred for reasons other than economic necessity.

Furthermore, most of the aged in these joint households are well integrated in the daily routine and continue to perform many valued functions. For example, there is the function of the *rusuban,* or caretaker (literally "watcher during absences"). Because most Japanese houses have sliding wood and paper doors and are generally less burglar-proof than Western houses, it is usually considered necessary to have someone stay in the house most of the time as a caretaker to prevent burglary. This is an easy function for the aged, and one which most aged in joint households appear to perform frequently.

The grandmother appears to perform more important functions than the grandfather. Typically, she prepares meals, supervises younger children, does small gardening, and helps with the laundry.

> During the busy season everyone capable of active labor is indispensable. The grandmother, on the other hand, stays at home doing the housework or tending the babies, and sometimes acts as a liaison officer to the family (Koyama, 1961).

TABLE 3.   Reasons for Wanting to Live with Children

	% Giving Reason
Get care from children	38
It is natural to live with children	31
Companionship with children	30
Financial aid from children	20
Enjoyment of caring for children and grandchildren	9
Convenience	8
Children want me to live with them	6
Other reasons	2

Source: National Life Center, 1972. Percentages add up to more than 100 because some gave multiple reasons.

In addition, the grandmother is usually the perpetuator of religious affairs. It is she who makes offerings to the god of the kitchen and others and visits the shrines, making pilgrimages during the ceremonial days. Especially in rural areas, the grandmother often cares for the children to free the mother for field work.

> Criticism has often been directed at the fact that the grandmothers and not the mothers of the school children are present at the meetings of the parent-teacher association (PTA) in rural communities. From the standpoint of the farm families, the attendance of the grandmothers is taken for granted because the mothers are needed in the fields for doing the farm work (Koyama, 1961).

In urban areas also, the grandparents free the mother for outside work by caring for the children.

Grandfathers appear to be somewhat less active although there is considerable variability in this regard:

> [The retired grandfather] position is assumed gradually and has some variability. Retirement from a full work load and full authority to a routine of light tasks and advisor functions marks the step-by-step assumption of the role. . . . Skilled handicrafts, menial tasks, and some baby-tending become his main economic functions (Silberman, 1962).

An especially important function of both grandmothers and grandfathers is that of affectional support for the grandchildren. Grandparents appear to have less important functions than parents in the areas of task performance, discipline, and problem solving, but in the area of comfort and affectional support the grandparents are usually most important. In many cases, one child many be assigned to the grandmother and another to the grandfather. They bathe and sleep together and help each other (Vogel, 1967).

A survey of persons over sixty living with their children found help in the family business was the most frequent main role in the household for men, with gardening being second (Table 4). More than a third of the women specified housework as their main role, with help in family business and care of grandchildren running a close second and third place. Only 11 percent said they had no special role in the household. Another survey found that in a majority of households with a woman aged sixty to sixty-nine, the older woman had *primary* responsibility for housekeeping (National Life Center, 1972).

One of the most important functions of Japanese elders is that of senior advisor on family problems. Over two-thirds of Japanese over sixty report that they are consulted on family problems, and this proportion is even higher among the men and among the employed (Table 5). In earlier times the decision of the elder on all matters was final and usually accepted by all family members. These days the authority of the elders appears to be quite variable, depending on which matter is in question (the elders have more authority in "traditional" matters and less in regard

TABLE 4.   Main Roles in the Household (Percentage Distribution of Persons over 60 Living with Children)

	Total	Men	Women
Housework	26	14	36
Help in family business	21	27	16
Gardening	14	19	10
Care of grandchild	11	7	14
Other role	17	20	14
No special role	11	12	10
Total	100	100	100

Source: Ministry of Health and Welfare, 1972a.

to "modern" matters such as those involving technology), how much power and competence the elder retains, etc. Nevertheless, most elders are at least consulted on some family problems.

Considering all these functions, it is understandable why most of the normal aged living with their children are still considered valuable members of the household, rather than merely financial burdens.

Integration in the Work Force
Here, too, Japan is fundamentally different from other modernized countries. Well over half the aged men in Japan continue to work, compared to less than a third in the USA and Britain (Table 6). Despite Japan's high degree of industrialization, her labor force participation rate for men over sixty-five is about half again as high as the average for all industrialized countries. Also, the rate of employment among older Japanese is relatively high in all parts of the country, even though the proportion employed is about 5 percent higher in rural than in urban areas (Office of the Prime Minister, 1973).

This high rate of employment seems to have resulted from two

TABLE 5.   Percentages of Japanese over 60 Consulted by Their Children on Family Problems

	Total	Men	Women	Employed	Not Employed
Consulted	67	73	62	80	57
Not consulted	32	26	37	18	42
No answer	1	1	1	2	1
Total	100	100	100	100	100

Source: Ministry of Health and Welfare, 1972a.

TABLE 6. Percentage over 65 in the Labor Force by Country

	Men	Women
Japan	55	18
USA	32	13
Britain	28	8
Denmark	38	8
Average for countries that are:		
Industrialized	38	—
Semi-industrialized	61	—
Agricultural	70	—

SOURCES: Japan, Census Bureau, 1965; USA, Britain, and Denmark, Shanas et al., 1968; averages by industrialization, United Nations, 1962 (data for 1950s).

complementary traditions. One is the strong belief, even among the aged, that every able person should work as much and as long as possible (a belief similar to the Protestant ethic described by Max Weber). The other tradition is that of seniority and respect for the aged, which appears to prevent discrimination against the aged in employment such as is found in other countries. The aged in Japan appear to have more opportunities for employment. Less than 10 percent of employers surveyed said they were "dissatisfied" with the speed, skill, diligence, efficiency, or human relations of older workers (National Life Center, 1972).

These work traditions may appear to be contradicted by the fact that the customary retirement age in most businesses is around age fifty-five. But in Japan "retirement" at age fifty-five usually means simply switching to another company, to another job in the same company, or to self-employment. In fact, 96 percent of men aged fifty-five to fifty-nine continue to work (Office of the Prime Minister, 1973).

Over two-thirds of the older workers are self-employed or work in the family business. This is in contrast to the United States, where only a third are self-employed or unpaid family workers (Epstein and Murray, 1967). As for occupation, over half are farmers, lumbermen, or fishermen, in contrast to the United States, where only 20 percent of the men and 6 percent of the women are in agriculture (Epstein and Murray, 1967). Also, twice as many of the older Japanese than of the older Americans work in sales occupations. Thus in Japan there are many more opportunities for older persons to remain or become self-employed farmers or shopkeepers than in the United States. In rural Japan these older farmers are much in evidence, toiling in their little rice paddies or vegetable gardens with straw "coolie" hats to protect them from the weather. In urban Japan the older shopkeeper tending his or her little specialty shop is also a common sight. There are likewise many traditional occupations in which older persons are often at the peak of their career.

Painters, writers, actors, and certain highly skilled artisans often do not achieve full competence until their middle or late fifties, and many pursue active professional lives far into the seventies and even eighties. Great respect is accorded these people, even by the very young in the same profession (Smith, 1961).

These opportunities for older workers are another reason for the greater integration of the older Japanese in the labor force.

As for how much they work, some retire to part-time jobs and some increase their hours of work to make up for reduced earning, but the over-all average number of hours worked is about the same for wage and salary workers over age sixty as for other workers, i.e., about forty-eight hours per week (Table 7). It is probable that many self-employed workers do not work such long hours. Nevertheless, the Japanese older workers appear to put in more hours than in other industrialized countries. In the United States, Britain, and Denmark, the average number of hours for blue-collar workers over age sixty-five is less than forty hours per week (Shanas et al., 1968). Thus not only do more of the older Japanese continue to work, but they work longer hours as well.

Why do the older Japanese continue to work so much? How many continue to work because of financial necessity and how many work for other reasons? It is difficult to get valid and reliable data on this question because many people work for a mixture of motivations and the stated reasons are often influenced by rationalization and the social acceptability of various answers. Nevertheless, the findings of several surveys agree that less than half of all older workers continue to work primarily because of financial necessity. For example, one recent survey of all workers over sixty found that the most frequent reason given for working was "duty," while financial necessity was given by a little over one-third (Table 8). Even fewer of the workers in the primary industries gave financial necessity as the primary reason. Another survey which allowed multiple answers found similar percentages giving financial necessity but many more who said they wanted to continue working because it was enjoyable (28 percent) or because it was healthy (44 percent) (Office of the Prime Minister, 1973). Perhaps a more objective way to get at this is to ask whether the earnings are used for primary support or for secondary

TABLE 7. **Hours Worked per Month and Annual Earnings by Age**

	Average Hours Worked per Month	Average Total Annual Earnings (Yen)
All wage and salary workers	206	639,000
Wage and salary workers over age 60	207	579,000

Source: Ministry of Health and Welfare, 1970.

TABLE 8. Reasons for Working among All Workers over 60 (Percentage Distribution)

	Total	Primary Industries	Secondary Industries	Other Regular Workers	Day Laborers
Duty	41	47	31	36	38
Financial necessity	36	29	50	51	51
Enjoyable or healthy	17	20	17	8	5
Other	5	4	2	4	6
Total	100	100	100	100	100

SOURCE: Ministry of Health and Welfare, 1970.

support, luxuries, and such extras. The answers to this question indicate that less than half work to provide primary support, while the majority provide secondary support, luxuries, or other things (Table 9).

A survey which asked workers of all ages what their attitude toward work after retirement was found about half said that work after retirement is "normal" and only 7 percent said they would work only if it was financially necessary (National Life Center, 1972). A survey of men over age fifty found that 83 percent said that it is better to work as long as possible rather than retire from work, and there was little variation in this percentage by age, area, or education (Office of the Prime Minister, 1973).

I know of no comparable data in Western countries, but I expect that many more, perhaps most, American workers over sixty-five would say they work because of financial necessity. Most probably there would be few in America who would say they work because of duty, because it is healthy, or because it is "normal" to work after retirement. The fact that few Americans do work after retirement shows that most consider it "normal" to *stop* work at retirement. One piece of comparable evidence is

TABLE 9. Use of Earnings among Older Japanese Workers (Percentage Distribution)

	Total 60+	Men	Women
Primary support	43	54	23
Secondary support	33	27	45
Luxuries	8	6	10
Pocket money	6	5	9
Other	10	8	14
Total	100	100	100

SOURCE: Ministry of Health and Welfare, 1972a.

TABLE 10. Attitudes toward Work by Older Workers in Japan and USA (Percentage Distribution)

	Japanese Workers over 65	USA Workers over 65
Want to continue work	91	70
Want to stop work	4	19
Undecided	5	11
Total	100	100

Sources: Japan, Welfare Journal, 1971; USA, Epstein and Murray, 1967.

that most of the older Japanese workers want to continue working, while 30 percent of older American workers plan to stop working next year or are undecided (Table 10). In summary, the work ethic appears to be stronger among older Japanese than among the aged in other industrialized countries, and the majority in Japan continue to work for reasons other than financial necessity.

But what of the future? Is the present high level of integration of older Japanese in the work force a temporary phenomenon which will rapidly decline in the near future? Forecasting the future is a hazardous undertaking in any field, but based on recent trends it seems probable that there will continue to be only small declines in the employment of the aged.

Compared to the United States, the aged in Japan have experienced relatively little decline in labor-force participation since 1930 (Table 11). While the labor-force participation of older Americans was cut in half,

TABLE 11. Labor Force Participation Rates of Older People in Japan and the USA in 1930 and 1965

	% in the Labor Force	
	1930	1965
Japan: Total 65 +	38	34
Men	63	55
Women	19	18
Total 15–64	72	69
Men	88	86
Women	52	53
USA: Total 65 +	30	17
Men	54	27
Women	7	9
Total 15–64	55	67
Men	85	89
Women	24	44

Sources: 1930 and 1965, Japan Census; 1930 U.S. Census and 1965 Current Population Survey.

that of older Japanese declined only 4 percentage points, which is about the same decline experienced by the nonaged in Japan. It is true that older Japanese *men* experienced somewhat more decline (8 percentage points) than Japanese women, but this is much less than the precipitous drop experienced by older men in the United States (27 percentage points). Thus all the evidence shows that the Japanese elders have maintained a relatively high level of integration in the work force and will probably continue to do so in the foreseeable future.

Integration in the Community

The Japanese elders are also well integrated into their community life. About half of Japanese over age sixty-five belong to some kind of senior citizens' club (National Life Center, 1972). These clubs are usually organized and subsidized by the government. They usually meet at least once a month for lectures, gardening and landscaping the community, cleaning and repairing community centers, singing and dancing parties, going to an *onsen* (public hot bath) party, or study meetings. These clubs also occasionally participate in the demonstrations held to demand more government aid for the aged. Thus the elders' clubs serve multiple functions: community service, study and action aimed at helping elders, group recreation, group identification, and mutual support.

Japanese elders also frequently visit with their neighbors. A majority say they visit neighbors "often," and another third say they visit "occasionally" (Welfare Journal, 1971). Going on overnight trips to visit shrines, scenic spots, and relatives is another favorite activity of the majority of elders, especially among those aged sixty to seventy (Ministry of Health and Welfare, 1972a).

Respect for the Elders

Respect and affection are difficult concepts to measure, even within one culture. Comparable cross-cultural statistics on respect for the aged are nonexistent. However, we can describe many private and public practices which reflect the high respect for elders in Japan.

We have already described how most older Japanese continue to live with their children; how most of these arrangements appear to be motivated more by desire for companionship, for mutual aid, and by attitudes that it is "natural" than by the housing shortage or financial necessity; and how the aged perform many valued services in the household. We believe this is indirect evidence of a continuing high level of respect and affection for the elders by their families.

Perhaps the most pervasive form of respect for elders in the family (as well as outside the family) is the honorific language used in speaking to or about the elders. English and other languages have polite and impolite forms for some words, but Japanese is unusual in its extreme elaboration of different forms to show the proper degree of respect or deference. Differential respect is reflected not only in the different nouns, verbs, prefixes, suffixes, and other parts of speech, but is also reflected in the basic grammar and syntax of the language. And relative age of the speaker to the person referred to and the relative age of the listener is one of the basic dimensions determining the proper degree of deference and respect to be reflected in the language form used. Thus Japanese show respect for their elders every time they speak to or about them.

Another pervasive form of respect is that the elders are usually given precedence in all family matters. They usually get the best seat in the room, they are served first, they go through doors first and traditionally walk in front of younger persons. They are usually first to take the daily *ofuro* (hot bath shared by the family), and they get the best silks, decorations, and bedding.

There is a special family celebration to honor the elder when he or she reaches sixty-one years of age. On the sixty-first birthday the elder dons a bright kimono, such as those worn by children, to symbolize that he or she is no longer bound by the somber duties of middle age. Traditionally all the children and close relatives gather to help in the celebration of this transition.

In the United States there is usually little ceremony among members of the family. We often shed even the slight formalities of our etiquette when we come home. In Japan it is precisely in the family where respect for elders is learned and meticulously observed. When a younger person bows to his elder, the younger person bows lower and stays down longer than the elder. The elder may acknowledge the bow with a simple nod of his head.

There are popular sayings which illustrate family respect for their elders. One riddle says, "Why is a son who wants to offer advice to his parents like a Buddhist priest who wants to have hair on the top of head?" (Buddhist priests shave their heads.) The answer is, "However much he wants to do it, he can't" (Benedict, 1946). The following dilemma is often posed: If a man's mother and his wife were both drowning at the same time, whom should the man rescue first? In earlier times the answer usually given was his mother, because she is elder to his wife. These days the proper answer is not so clear, and there is considerable debate about whether a man's mother or his wife should take precedence. This may be contrasted with the United States, where the usual answer would clearly be his wife, because a man's primary loyalty should be to his wife.

The American reader may notice that we have often used the terms respect and affection together, and he may question whether these two different attitudes can go together or whether they are mutually incompatible. To contemporary Americans with their strong egalitarian values, it may seem unlikely that one could be truly affectionate toward one before whom he must bow and continually demonstrate his subservience. The Japanese do not usually view this as a problem. In fact, they tend to regard a vertical relationship, with authority and responsibility on one side and respect and subservience on the other, to be conducive to affection between the persons involved. They simply do not value independence and equality in personal relations the way we do, but rather value dependence and deference (Nakane, 1972).

It should be understood that the prerogatives of age are usually balanced by responsibilities and concepts of fairness.

> The prerogatives of generation, sex, and age in Japan are great. But those who exercise these privileges act as trustees rather than as arbitrary autocrats. The father or the elder brother is responsible for the household, whether its members are living, dead, or yet unborn. He must make weighty decisions and see that they are carried out. He does not, however, have unconditional authority. He is expected to act responsibly for the honor of the house. . . . The master of the house saddles himself with great difficulties if he acts without regard for group opinion (Benedict, 1946).

Thus the elder normally "earns" affection and respect from younger family members through his fairness, wisdom, and aid.

The amount of *public* respect in Japan for elders may be best documented by quoting from the 1963 National Law for the Welfare of the Elders (No. 133):

> The elders shall be loved and respected as those who have for many years contributed toward the development of society, and a wholesome and peaceful life shall be guaranteed to them. In accordance with their desire and ability, the elders shall be given opportunities to engage in suitable work or to participate in social activities.

This law also declares that "any person who is engaged in an enterprise which directly affects the life of the elders shall endeavor to promote the welfare of the elders in the management of that enterprise." Also, "the Central Government and local public bodies have responsibility to promote the welfare of the elders" (Article 4).

In contrast, the comparable law in the United States, the Older Americans Act of 1965 (US Public Law 89–73), nowhere contains any mention of love and respect for the aged. Nor does it even attempt to *guarantee* a "wholesome and peaceful life." Rather it only states that the duty of the government is to *assist* older people to secure equal opportunity to adequate income, health, housing, employment, etc. (Title 1). This obviously reflects a basically different attitude toward older people in Japan and the United States.

In order to fulfill its "guarantee" of a wholesome and peaceful life, the Japanese government has undertaken a series of programs for its elders:

1. Health Examination. Cities and towns hold annual health examinations for those who are 65 years of age or older. Individual guidance is then given to those who need further diagnosis or treatment.

2. Home for the Aged. For those 65 years or older who need to find a protective environment other than their homes, the following three kinds of institutions are provided by the law . . . Nursing home (*Yogo Rojin*); Special Nursing home (*Tokubetsu Yogo Rojin*) for those who are in need of constant medical supervision; and Home with Moderate Fee (*Keihi Rojin*) for those who have no family to live with.
3. Family Foster Care. For those who have no family to live with.
4. Grant of Medical Cost. Free medical care for most persons over age 70.
5. Home Helper. Housekeeping help for old people living alone.
6. Welfare Center for the Aged. To provide various education, recreation, and consultation services. In 1971 there were 233 such centers.
7. Other Programs. Including free "gadget-beds" for the bedfast, free employment service, home nurses, telephone centers to provide counseling service to the poor and the lonely, subsidies for sports meetings for the aged, and designation of September 15th as Old People's Day (Ministry of Health and Welfare, 1972b).

The last program mentioned, Respect for the Aged Day (*Keiro No Hi*), is one of the most dramatic expressions of respect and affection for the elders. Ceremonies in honor of the elders have been widespread for over three hundred years, but in 1963 Respect for Elders Day became a national holiday, and the law specifies that

> the governments of various levels should hold suitable activities to evoke the people's interest in and understanding of the welfare needs of the aged as well as to encourage old people to improve and enrich their own lives.

On each September 15 the Health and Welfare Ministry presents a silver cup and a letter from the premier congratulating each person who reached 100 during the past year. In Tokyo the Metropolitan Government presents a silver fan to those who became 100 during the year, a "respect for elders" medal to those who became 75, and gifts of 5,000 yen (about $17) to each of the more than 185,000 persons over the age of 75 in the city. Newspapers run feature articles on the aged and on the celebrations and rallies that are held in most cities. Even small hamlets usually have some kind of ceremony and celebration with gifts of honor for the elders in the community.

Respect for the elders has two main roots: the vertical society and filial piety. The vertical society establishes the right of all aged to general respect from younger persons, and filial piety specifies the obligations owed to one's own parents and grandparents.

The theory of Japan's vertical society has been most clearly elaborated by Nakane and most of the following description has been drawn from her recent book (1972). Put in its simplest form, this theory states that most Japanese interpersonal relationships are determined by a delicately graded hierarchy, or system of vertical relationships. Vertical relationships are those between superior and inferior, such as parent and child, master and servant, teacher and student, senior and junior persons. These are contrasted with horizontal relationships, which are those between equals, such as between colleagues and friends in our society. It is part of the theory that in Japanese society even relationships between colleagues and friends become vertical depending on age, sex, and other factors.

> Because of the overwhelming ascendancy of this vertical orientation, even a set of individuals sharing identical qualifications tend to create a *difference* among themselves. As this is reinforced, an amazingly delicate and intricate system of *ranking* takes shape.
>
> There are numerous examples of this ranking process. Among lathe operators with the same qualifications there exist differences of rank based on relative age, year of entry into the company or length of continuous service; among professors at the same college, rank can be assessed by the formal date of appointment; among commissioned officers in the former Japanese army the differences between ranks were very great, and it is said that even among second lieutenants distinct ranking was made on the basis of order of appointment (Nakane, 1972).

As is obvious from these examples, age and seniority are among the most important criteria for these vertical rankings. It is true that age may be superseded by other bases of status. For example, the head of a household, regardless of age, occupies the "highest" seat in the household, and his retired father retreats to a "lower" seat. Nevertheless, there is a residual respect which most older persons traditionally retain in relations with most younger persons.

The other root of this traditional respect is filial piety, which, in turn, goes back into both Confucian precepts and the even more ancient ancestor worship.

To appreciate the supreme importance of ancestor worship in ancient Japan, one need only consider the implications of the five basic beliefs of this religion:

> 1. The dead remain in this world—haunting their tombs, and also their former homes, and sharing invisibly in the life of their living descendants.
> 2. All the dead become gods, in the sense of acquiring supernatural power; but they retain the characters which distinguish them during life.
> 3. The happiness of the dead depends upon the respectful service rendered them by the living; and the happiness of the living depends upon the fulfillment of pious duty to the dead. . . .
> 4. Every event in the world, good or evil—fair seasons or plentiful harvests—flood or famine—tempest and tidal wave and earthquake—is the work of the dead.
> 5. All human actions, good or bad, are controlled by the dead (Hearn, 1955).

Because the ghosts of the ancestors were so powerful, it was most important that they be kept happy through reverence and nourishment.

> But, in spite of their supernatural power, the dead are still dependent upon the living for happiness. Though viewless, save in dreams, they need earthly nourishment and homage—food and drink, and the reverence of their descendants. Each ghost must rely for such comfort upon its living kindred;—only

through the devotion of that kindred can it ever find repose. Each ghost must have shelter,—a fitting tomb;—each must have offerings. While honorably sheltered and properly nourished the spirit is pleased, and will aid in maintaining the good fortune of its propitiators. But if refused the sepulchral home, the funeral rites, the offerings of food and fire and drink, the spirit will suffer from hunger and cold and thirst, and, becoming angered, will act malevolently and contrive misfortune for those by whom it has been neglected (Hearn, 1955).

Hearn may have exaggerated the importance of ancestor worship, but it was surely one of the bases for filial piety toward living parents and grandparents. Since reverence and devotion to dead ancestors was of great importance, respect and duty toward living parents and grandparents (who will soon become dead ancestors) became almost as important.

Oyakoko, or obligation to parents, was one of two unconditional and absolute duties (the other being *chu*, obligation to the Emperor, the law, and Japan). These two duties were so absolute and unconditional that there is a special word for them, *gimu*, to distinguish them from all lesser duties. *Gimu* are such unlimited obligations that it is said, "One never repays one ten-thousandth of *gimu*" (Benedict, 1946).

Much of this tradition is being questioned and rejected by the younger generations in modern Japan, and we do not have good longitudinal data to measure how much respect has declined (for a pessimistic view of the aged in Japan see Plath, in Cowgill and Holmes, 1972). But it should be clear by now that respect for the aged has strong roots growing out of both Japan's basic social structure and her fundamental religious beliefs.

Discussion

Some caveats to the main thesis of this paper are in order. It should be understood we are not claiming that there has been *no* decline in the status and integration of the aged in Japanese society. On the contrary, we have recognized that there are indications of relatively slow and small declines. Labor force participation of men over sixty-five has declined at about two-tenths of 1 percent per year since 1930. The percentage of the aged living with their children has declined about one-half of 1 percent per year since 1950. More of the younger and urban parents wish to live separately from their children. And although we do not have hard longitudinal data on how much respect for the elders has declined, it is clear that the young are questioning traditional values. Thus the trend is in the expected direction of *some* decline with modernization.

Furthermore, the concept of modernization is a complex and controversial one. It might be argued that despite Japan's high urbanization, industrialization, literacy, etc., she is still not as "modern" in some ways as Western nations. It is true that there are more small businesses in Japan, more self-employed shopkeepers and farmers, and that the paternalistic structures of Japanese corporations tend to be less impersonal than in the

West. Yet we contend that according to the usual objective indicators of modernization, Japan ranks at least among the ten or so most modern nations in the world and therefore should have low status and integration for their aged according to the standard theory. Therefore it seems clear that the standard theory needs revision in light of the relatively high status and integration that still persists for the elders in Japanese society.

Another possibility to consider is that the present low levels of pensions and social security payments may account for both the high proportions living with children and the high proportions in the labor force. One cannot be sure about the future effects of recent increases in pensions and social security, but our expectation is that these increases will not reduce proportions living with children and proportions in the labor force to levels as low as in Western societies, because of the strong cultural beliefs that parents should live with their children and should continue to work as long as possible.

A final point to consider is the high suicide rate among the Japanese aged. It might be argued that high suicide rates indicate low social integration. However, it appears that the main explanation is again cultural: suicide rates are higher in Japan at all age levels because suicide is a more accepted and honorable "solution" to problems ranging from "loss of face" to poverty and chronic illness.

Summary

Japan is an exception to the general rule that industrialization causes a sharp decline in status and integration of the aged. Despite a high level of industrialization, the status and integration of the aged in Japanese society has remained at relatively high levels compared to other industrialized countries. Most of the Japanese elders continue to live with their children and perform important functions in the household. The majority of men over sixty-five continue to be in the work force and this proportion has declined little since 1930. The elders are also well integrated into their communities through clubs and visiting neighbors. The high status of the aged is reflected in many private and public practices which give precedence to the elders. Respect for the elders has two roots: the vertical social structure and the tradition of filial piety.

Thus Japan demonstrates that the aged need not suffer from prejudice and discrimination in modern society. On the contrary, even in highly industrialized societies a culture which promotes respect for the aged can maintain high levels of status and integration for its older citizens.

NOTES

Much of the material in this paper is adapted from *The Honorable Elders* (Duke University Press, 1975). The study was supported in part by Grant HD

00668, NICHD, and by the Duke Bio-medical Sciences Grant 5-S05-RR07070-07. The Tokyo Institute of Gerontology provided office facilities and translators. Mr. Mikio Mori of the Dept. of Health and Welfare provided materials and assisted in many ways.

REFERENCES

Associated Press. *Almanac 1974.* Hammond Almanac, Maplewood, NJ, 1973.

Benedict, R. *The chrysanthemum and the sword.* Houghton Mifflin, Boston, 1946.

Cowgill, D., and Holmes, L. (Eds.) *Aging and modernization.* Appleton-Century-Crofts, New York, 1972.

Epstein, L., and Murray, J. *The aged population of the United States.* USGPO, Washington, 1967.

Halloran, R. Elderly Japanese seeking more government help, *New York Times,* Sept. 16, 1972.

Hearn, L. *Japan: An interpretation.* Charles E. Tuttle Co., Rutland, VT, 1955.

Japan Housing Foundation. *Apartment life and problems of the aged.* Japan Housing Foundation, Tokyo, 1973.

Koyama, T. *The changing social position of women in Japan.* UNESCO, Paris, 1961.

Ministry of Health and Welfare. *Summary results of survey of the conditions of old persons.* Ministry of Health and Welfare, Tokyo, (Sept.) 1972. (a)

Ministry of Health and Welfare. *Social welfare services in Japan.* Ministry of Health and Welfare, Tokyo, 1972. (b)

Ministry of Health and Welfare. *Survey of the aged.* Ministry of Health and Welfare, Tokyo, 1970.

Nakane, C. *Japanese society.* Univ. of California Press, Berkeley, 1972.

Nasu, S. *The aged and the development of nuclear families.* Metropolitan Institute of Gerontology, Tokyo, 1973.

National Life Center. *Fears about old age.* National Life Center, Tokyo, 1972.

Office of the Prime Minister. *Public opinion survey about problems of old age.* Office of the Prime Minister, Tokyo, 1973.

Palmore, E., and Manton, D. Modernization and status of the aged. *Journal of Gerontology,* 1974, 29, 205–210.

Shanas, E., Townsend, D., Wedderburn, D., Friis, H., Milhøj, P., and Stehouwer, J. *Old people in three industrial societies.* Atherton Press, New York, 1968.

Silberman, B. *Japanese character and culture.* Univ. of Arizona Press, Tucson, 1962.

Smith, R. Japan: The later years of life and the concept of time. In R. W. Kleemeier (Ed.), *Aging and leisure.* Oxford University Press, London, 1961.

U. S. Bureau of Census. *Statistical Abstract of the U.S.,* 1973. USGPO, Washington, 1973.

Vogel, E. *Japan's new middle class.* Univ. of California Press, Berkeley, 1967.

Welfare Journal. *Problems of older people.* Welfare Journal Co., Tokyo, 1971.

2

Theories of Aging

Social gerontology developed as a distinct field of research in the 1930s through a merging of concerns over the growing number and plight of aged persons in modern society. One major line of research involved the adjustment of older people to the employment and income problems generated by the Depression. Problems of adjustment were cast within the framework of developmental psychology, which tended to view old age as a period of declining abilities. Its approach involved questions of deceleration of and adjustment to decline, which was taken as more or less inevitable.

The pioneering study *Personal Adjustment in Old Age* (Cavan et al., 1949), using measures of adjustment, linked positive adjustment to continued activity, social interaction, and participation in institutional life. This led to a new focus on the question of optimal aging. From a concern with adjustment problems, research turned to understanding "normal" processes of aging. A major study which used a variety of indices to measure normal aging was conducted in Kansas City in the 1950s, a site selected because it represented a typical American city. The study focused on three concerns: the role performance of people between forty and seventy, the psychological states and characteristics of normal adults in the same age ranges, and the relationship between performance and characteristics. The results were inconsistent. One set showed no difference in interior states in spite of role changes like retirement or widowhood. The other set showed an increased withdrawal which accompanied these life changes. This withdrawal was termed the "interiorization" of the ego, a concept which set the stage for the development of disengagement theory.

Disengagement Theory
Disengagement theory is the only fully formulated theory of aging,

although it is no longer regarded as a valid explanation of aging. It was introduced in 1961 by Cumming and Henry.

The theory is based on the fact that death is inevitable. According to the postulates of disengagement theory, the inevitability of death forces the society and the aging individual to mutually sever many of their relationships. In this way the death of the individual will not disrupt the system. Although the extent and form of disengagement varies from person to person and from society to society, it is a universal phenomenon. Older people who gradually sever their social ties while at the same time turning psychologically inward are considered by disengagement theory to be the best adjusted and have the highest morale.

Almost as soon as disengagement theory was published, a number of criticisms arose. Many writers questioned whether it was truly a universal phenomenon, pointing to numerous examples of societies where older people maintain high status and remain fully engaged until death. Further, research studies showed that it was usually the engaged person, not the disengaged, who had the highest morale. A third criticism was that nonengagement may be a life-long personality characteristic of certain individuals and not an inevitable phase of the life cycle. These criticisms as well as many others eventually spelled the demise of disengagement theory as a satisfactory approach to the understanding of aging.

Activity Theory

At the same time that disengagement theory was being developed, an opposing approach which had provided the underlying framework for much early research existed. Termed "implicity" theory, and later known as activity theory, it has received attention largely as a critique of and response to disengagement theory.

Activity theory implies that, except for changes in biology and health, older people have essentially the same psychological and social needs as middle-aged people. From this perspective the decreased social interaction of the aged results from society's withdrawal from the aging person—a process which proceeds against the desires of most aging men and women. The older person who ages optimally is the one who remains active and manages to resist the shrinkage of his or her social world, maintaining the activities of middle age as long as possible and then finding substitutes for those losses which do occur (Brehm, 1968; Butler, 1976). In general, so far as activity theory suggests a positive relationship between morale and activity, the evidence favors this theory over disengagement theory.

In many ways, activity theory represents a value judgment rather than a theory of aging. While we might prefer to see older people remain active, preferences do not provide an adequate explanation of the relationship of the aged to society. In the 1960s sociologists began to attempt to explain aging in broader terms, and the emphasis shifted away from adjustment and optimal aging toward a concern with the position of the aged in society. The theory explaining the relationship between aging and modernization discussed earlier represents one of these attempts, and it has had a major influence on the development of the field. However, other theories have also been broached, and attempts are still being made to refine them.

Theories of Aging and Social Structure

Both subculture theory and minority-group theory were attempts to explain the increasing collective visibility and vulnerability of the aged in society. Minority-group theory emphasizes the outsider's view of the aged (Barron, 1953). According to this theory, the aged are a minority group because of three criteria: they are highly visible, they are discriminated against, and stereotypes exist about them (Breen, 1960). Minority-group theory was criticized on the grounds that the aged have no group consciousness but are merely a statistical aggregate. Further, membership in a true minority group is exclusive and permanent, whereas all people eventually become old (Streib, 1965). Subculture theory answers some of these criticisms by arguing that a sense of group consciousness can be expected to develop among the aged, since they do have common interests and are excluded from significant interaction with other groups in the population. Subculture theory is explained more fully in the article by Rose.

The article by Matilda White Riley subsumes both minority-group theory and subculture theory under a broader rubric, that of age stratification. According to Riley, it is useful to focus on society as a whole, recognizing that it is divided into various age strata, similar to the divisions of social class. Each age stratum has its own distinct subculture based on the fact that the people within it are at the same point in the life cycle and have a set of shared historical experiences. Riley also suggests that the aged may be considered a minority group if it can be shown that they have less access to power than younger age groups. On the other hand, it is also possible to argue that they control some kinds of power and refuse to yield it to the young. This is an empirical question which needs to be answered by examining relationships between age strata.

The most recent refinement of perspectives which attempt to explain the position of the aged in the social structure has been proposed by Dowd. In the final article he places the emphasis back on the aged per se. Taking as a given the decreased social interaction of the aged, Dowd suggests that this is due to the decrease in power resources possessed by the aged which forces them to exchange compliance, often their only resource, for sustenance by society.

In sum, recent theories have moved away from explanations of aging which include a value judgment as to which is the "best" way to age. The unresolved issue is whether it is more significant to study old age as one phase of the life cycle in a society divided into many age strata or whether the aged are unique in terms of their position in the social structure.

REFERENCES

Barron, Milton L. 1953. Minority group characteristics of the aged in American society. *Journal of Gerontology* 8:477–82.

Breen, Leonard. 1960. The aging individual. In Clark Tibbitts (ed.), *Handbook of social gerontology.* Chicago: Univ. of Chicago Press.

Brehm, Henry P. 1968. Sociology and aging: Orientation and research. *Gerontologist* 8 (Spring):20–23.

Butler, Robert. 1976. *Why survive?* New York: Harper & Row.

Cavan, Ruch, Ernest Burgess, Robert Havighurst, and H. Goldhammer. 1949. *Personal adjustment in old age.* Chicago: Science Research Associates.

Cumming, Elaine, and William E. Henry. 1961. *Growing old.* New York: Basic Books.

Streib, Gordon. 1965. Are the aged a minority group? In Alvin W. Gouldner and S. M. Miller (eds.), *Applied sociology.* New York: Free Press.

The Subculture of the Aging: A Framework for Research in Social Gerontology

ARNOLD M. ROSE

Two requirements must be met for a category of the population to develop into a subculture. First, the members of the category must have a positive affinity for each other. Second, they must be excluded to a significant extent from interaction with others in the population. Both criteria are met for a large number of the aged who have many common interests due to similar life experiences and who are age-segregated to an intense degree from the rest of society. The rising sense of group consciousness among the elderly, as indicated by the proliferation of organizations for the aged, indicates that they are in the process of changing from a category to a group with its own subculture.

This paper presents a theoretical framework for research in social gerontology which would parallel, but not necessarily be in opposition to, researches which are centered around the concepts of loss of social roles, social adjustment and maladjustment, and disengagement.

The Developing American Subculture of the Aging

A subculture may be expected to develop within any category of the population of a society when its members interact with each other significantly more than they interact with persons in other categories. This occurs under two possible sets of circumstances: (1) The members have a positive affinity for each other on some basis (e.g., gains to be had from each other, longstanding friendships, common background and interests, common problems and concerns). (2) The members are excluded from interaction with other groups in the population to some significant extent. In American society both sets of circumstances occur for a large and perhaps growing proportion of older people, although for some (who thereby become isolates) only the second develops with age, and these individuals never come to express an affinity with other older people. In

SOURCE: Reprinted from *Older People and Their Social World*, edited by Arnold Rose and Warren Peterson. Copyright 1965 by F. A. Davis Company. Reprinted by permission of the publisher.

other words, the aging subculture is developing and is, at the present moment, far from comprehensive in content or in coverage of older people.

The positive affinity which many older people feel for each other is based in some measure on their physical limitations, and hence common interests in a physically easy and calm existence, partly on their common role changes, and partly on having had common generational experiences in a rapidly changing society. The rejection by younger age groups is based to some extent on the same factors, but also on the low value given to inefficacy in our general culture. Retired people—who can no longer earn a living, whose physical abilities to "get around" and engage in sports are limited, and whose prospects for new achievements and success in competition are slim—experience a sharply diminished status. This is abetted by the absence of special marks of prestige attached to aging which are found in other societies—such as the attribution of special wisdom, the automatic accession to a higher political position, or the use of titles of respect (such as the title "U" in Burma, applied to all persons over forty years of age). Thus for both sets of reasons, the elderly tend to interact with each other increasingly as they grow older, and with younger persons decreasingly, and hence develop a subculture. The greater the separation of older people from other age categories, both as individuals and as a social group, the greater the extent and depth of subcultural development. In other words, older Americans are now historically in the process of changing from a category into a group, although the extent of this change varies from individual to individual. Every group has a subculture—a set of meanings and values which is distinctive to that group—although not every group is necessarily conscious of its distinctiveness or of the fact that it is a group. This chapter will consider some of the respects in which older people in the United States are developing a subculture, and will pose the question as to whether or not they are becoming conscious of themselves as a distinctive group.

There are certain trends occurring in our society which are tending to create some of the conditions necessary for the development of a subculture. These trends are of three types—demographic, ecological, and social organizational—and will merely be listed here with a minimum of discussion. First, there is the growing number and proportion of persons who live beyond the age of sixty-five, from 4.1 percent in 1900 to over 9 percent in 1960. This is relevant only in that there are more people eligible for creating an aging subculture, that is, there is more opportunity now than formerly for older people to interact with each other. Second, because of the advances in preventive medicine and in acute communicable disease control, and because of general progress in sanitation and increased use of birth control (reducing the age at which most women stop bearing children), there has been a tendency for a much larger proportion of the population to reach the age of sixty-five in physical vigor and health, and hence capable of creating a subculture. Third, the same causes have resulted in a larger proportion of older people attaining an advanced age, when they are likely to develop chronic illnesses [1] which cost a great deal more to treat than acute illnesses because of the long period of treatment. This is a new major common grievance to older people. It was a major source of the political battle in the Congress, beginning in 1957, over the Forand Bill and its successors in dealing with medical care for the aging, which has given many older people a sense of common lot and common interest.

Fourth, there have been some self-segregating trends among older people. "Retirement communities" in Florida and in other areas of good climate *to* which older people migrate are well-known examples of this self-segregation. Now there are studies showing that older people often do not follow general patterns of migration *out* of a rural county and so are left behind to form the dominant element in the population of the area.[2] This trend also seems to be operating *within* a metropolitan area: apparently it is the young adults, mainly, who move to the suburbs and the outlying sections of the city, leaving the older people concentrated in the inner section of the city.[3] Further, older suburbanites now show some tendency to move *back* to the central city. This ecological accessibility of older people to each other helps to create the conditions necessary for the development of a subculture.

Fifth, there has been an increase in compulsory and voluntary retirement, and a corresponding decline in self-employed occupations (at which a healthy older person could work as long as he wished past the age of sixty-five). The decline in employment of older people, independent of its other effects and values, has meant a loss of integration into the general society because an occupation necessarily obliges one to interact with others of various ages. Sixth, because of the long-run improvement in the standard of living and in educational level, an increasing proportion of people reach the age of sixty-five with the means (in terms of funds, knowledge, and leisure) to do something they consider constructive, and what they do often becomes part of their subculture. Seventh, the development of social welfare services for the elderly (particularly group work activities that bring older people together) serves to enhance their opportunities for identifying with each other and for developing a subculture. The increasing number of retirement homes, nursing homes, housing projects, specialized recreational facilities, and meeting places for the elderly—sponsored by churches, fraternal associations, and other private associations as well as by government—tend to separate older people from the rest of the society. Eighth, for various reasons associated with increasing migration and apartment dwelling, there has been less of a tendency for adult children to live in the homes of their parents, who retain their positions as heads of the household, and more of a tendency for older people to live by themselves, or for intergenerational dwelling together to take the form of the elderly parents living as dependents in the homes of their adult offspring.[4] This separation of vigorous older people from constant[5] contact with their adult offspring helps to create the conditions for the development of a subculture.

Not all of the distinctive behavior of the elderly can be attributed to the aging subculture; the following may also be involved: (1) biological changes and personal idiosyncrasies associated with physical aging; (2) general cultural norms for the behavior of the elderly held by all in the society (for example, conservative styles of clothing which are favored for the elderly by all age levels); (3) generational changes which cause older people to act out a "general culture" appropriate for an earlier period but which has become "old-fashioned" for contemporaries. This last-mentioned point brings out the fact that American society, like most others, is to some extent age-graded throughout. People tend to associate to a large extent with those of their own age level at every age. However, we shall be asserting throughout this paper that there are certain cultural trends which are making the elderly more segregated from other age categories than is true for the rest of the society.[6]

Since a person only gradually becomes old and must continue to play some role in the general society, the elderly retain a good deal of the general culture and some even carry on roles typical of younger age groups. The extent of isolation from the larger society—for example, through congregate living or through differential migration—varies from one older person to the next. Thus different old people have different degrees of involvement in the aging subculture. An age-graded subculture must necessarily be limited as compared to a subculture which has members who live most or all of their lives in it (e.g., that of an ethnic group, a class, a region). In an age-graded subculture, the time it takes to be socialized into it and out of it and the limited period for which it is expected to be followed by an individual are factors which prevent the subculture from becoming highly elaborate or enveloping most of its followers completely. This is true of the teen-age subculture and of the young marrieds' subculture, as it is of the subculture of the past-sixty-five.

There may even be categorical differences in involvement of older people in the aging subculture, for example, the possible tendency for the wealthy and educated elderly to retain more contact with the larger society than do the poorer and ill-educated, and hence to acquire less of a distinctive aging subculture. Perhaps one of the most important bases of differentiation among older people in regard to the extent to which they participate in an aging subculture is the type of community they live in. Those in retirement communities, in rural communities from which younger people are rapidly emigrating, and in the central parts of big cities are most age-separated and hence are most likely to develop a subculture. Those, on the other hand, who live in typical small cities, villages, and rural areas, and in suburbs and the outlying parts of large cities are probably least age-separated. In the former settings the elderly may so dominate the community that the culture of the entire community may be characterized by what we are calling the aging subculture: the commercial establishments, the recreational facilities, the newspapers, and many other local institutions may be marked by the domination of the elderly. This is more likely to be apparent in a small town than in a large city, even when the proportion of older people happens to be equally great in the latter. When there is a large proportion of the elderly in a large city, and the latter have developed a subculture, it is more likely to be segregated from the rest of the city. In a small town the aging subculture could more readily become dominant. If this differential does in fact exist, it could be a function of the class composition of the elderly as well as a function of the size of the community. In the large city it seems likely that the segregated elderly would include more lower-class persons, while in the small town they would include more middle-class persons who could more readily dominate the town.

The aging subculture is a general one that cuts across other subcultures—those based on occupation, religion, sex, and possibly even ethnic identification—which are characteristic of the middle-aged population.[7] Insofar as older people are somewhat more likely to unite on the basis of age than on the basis of these other divisions, relatively speaking, they are likely to weaken the other subcultures as they substitute a new one for them. On the other hand, for some of the elderly, perhaps for those who have been socially mobile, there may be regression to earlier ethnic and class characteristics of their childhood which had been temporarily superseded in middle age.

Influences which keep the elderly in contact with the larger society and thus tend to minimize the development of an aging subculture include: (1) The contacts with the family, which are not reduced by the parents getting older and in some respects may increase as the adult children settle down after marriage and as the older man after retirement has more time for association with his family. Declining health may also force closer dependence on, and hence more frequent contact with, adult children. (2) The mass media, which seem to play an increasing role in contemporary society and which have a tendency to cut across all subcultural variations. (3) Continued employment, even on a part-time basis, which keeps the older person in contact with a work group, an occupational association, and the economic standards of the general society. (4) The increasing number of contacts with social welfare agencies, both public and private, which "do" things for the elderly. The social workers themselves are generally not elderly, although they often put the older people into closer contact with each other and tend to separate them from the rest of the society. (5) An attitude of active resistance toward aging and toward participation in the aging subculture.

This might result from unusually good physical and mental health so that the person is biologically younger than his chronological years would indicate, from an opportunity to have a special identification with some younger group in the society, or from a rejection of the aging and the aging subculture. The latter alone, if not associated with some opportunity to have contacts with the general society beyond those afforded to most older people, will often result in isolation and group self-hatred.[8]

Characteristics of the Subculture of the Aging

Let us turn from a consideration of the general factors creating and influencing an aging subculture in our society to a consideration of some of the specific contents of that subculture. The areas of life chosen for analysis represent some of the variation in the facets of the aging subculture; they do not present a comprehensive picture. In one respect, a subculture may be said to mold the entire lives of those who participate in it, so that in singling out a few aspects of a subculture we are selecting only its more salient and distinctive ones. On the other hand, a subculture exists within a general culture, and the elderly whose subculture we are examining must also be understood to be Americans whose lives are dominated by a general American culture.

Just as the reasons for the formation of the aging subculture are both positive and negative, so the content of the subculture is both positive and negative. The positive things are those which older people enjoy doing together, or which the whole society encourages them to do together, or which they interpret as being a special opportunity for those with their status. The negative things are those which the elderly do together because they find themselves rejected or otherwise in opposition to the rest of the society. While it may not always be possible to specify that a given behavior pattern or way of thinking of older people is positive or negative, it should be recognized that to some extent the aging subculture is a contraculture—in opposition to the rest of the society. In some ways the contraculture of the aging is similar to that of other discriminated-against groups in the society, certain ethnic minorities, for example. But the aging are not distinguished from the rest of the society solely by discrimination and segregation, so that their subculture has a positive aspect even though distinctive from the general culture.

First, the status system of the elderly is only partially a carry-over of that of the general society.[9] Two kinds of status must be recognized for the retired elderly—one accorded them by the general society (which is generally markedly lower than that for a younger person of like wealth, education, achievement, and so forth), and one developed out of the distinctive values of the aging subculture. Certainly wealth carries over from the general culture as an important factor in status, with some significant exceptions: (1) With income from occupation gone, the variation in incomes from investments, pensions, and social security tends to be significantly less for most persons than were previous incomes from occupations, and the reduced variation probably tends to diminish the use of wealth for invidious distinctions of status. (2) Some of the attitudes toward wealth must develop of the type "you can't take it with you," and yet expenditures for night life, travel, and other expensive amusements must be curtailed for reasons of health, so that wealth must have somewhat less importance than it did at any earlier age. Possibly occupational prestige also carries over into old age, but its effect is probably less when the occupation is no longer practiced by the individual and the occupation itself is changing. The same is true of the prestige arising from the former holding of power. As previous holding of power and earlier achievement fade into the past, they are of diminishing influence in conferring prestige. General education probably carries over more since it is of current utility to the aging, but it, too, must have something of a dated quality. In preceding generations, youngsters were much less likely to be kept in school to the levels they are now likely to be, and the education they received is, in some respects at least, regarded as old-fashioned today.

These sources of status which carry over from the earlier years are probably of maximum influence for the elderly when they continue to live in the same community. If they have changed communities, occupational prestige after retirement must go down markedly, and the other factors be of reduced importance. If the aged individual is socially isolated, as sometimes happens, these factors in former status carry current prestige only as a sort of legend.

Two related factors may be hypothesized as having special value in conferring status within the subculture of the elderly. One is physical and mental health. This is not a highly significant value for most younger people (except for the relatively small percentage who do not have it, and they react as individuals, not as members of a group with a subculture).[10] But good health is sufficiently rare, and becomes rarer with advancing age, so that old people make much of it and exhibit a special admiration for those who remain healthy. A sickly old man who cannot take care of himself has little status among the elderly (or among any others in the society, except perhaps his family) even if he is wealthy, whereas a vigorous old man with keen senses will be accorded high status among his compeers even though he lives exclusively on a modest pension.

The second distinctive factor in the status system of the aging is social activity. This is, of course, partly based on physical and mental health, but it includes much more. Especially in recent years, many of the aging accord high status to those of their number who are willing and able to assume leadership in various associations of a social influence or expressive character composed primarily of the aging. We shall give more extended consideration to this in our later discussion of aging group consciousness. Here it may simply be noted that, because social activity among some of the elderly is based partly on physical and mental health, some of those who rise to prominence among the aging are persons of little previous eminence or skill and experience in group leadership.

There may be other distinctive factors in the status system in the aging subculture which deeper observation would reveal. One approach would be through an examination of the social participations and communications of the elderly. Little is known about this among social gerontologists, but there must be quantities of data in the commercial studies of audiences for the mass media and in other types of public opinion polls. A content analysis of the many magazines for the elderly, which have appeared during the last decade or so, should reveal much about the specific values of the aging subculture and suggest some of the processes through which that subculture is emerging.

Another important social value toward which the attitudes of the aging must differ markedly from those of the rest of the population is sex. While recent studies[11] suggest that older people are more capable of having sex relations and actually do have them than was formerly supposed, it seems likely that interest in sex declines with the years. Many older people in the United States today were raised in an era of sexual puritanism and the "double-standard," in which it was assumed to be natural that men had strong sex drives until they grew impotent in old age, while women naturally did not have significant sexual drives and they lost what they did have when they became older. This generational factor helps to keep interest in sex low. There are, of course, a few sexual radicals among older people, who keep up a high level of sexual interest and activity.

It was estimated for 1959 that about 2.4 percent of all marriages taking place in the United States were those involving a bride or groom, or both, over the age of sixty-five. Of these marriages, about one-third joined brides and grooms who were both over sixty-five. Of the approximately 16 million older people in the United States, about 7 percent got married during the typical recent year of 1959. Of course, the majority of older people were already married and hence not currently eligible for marriage. About 93 percent of the older brides and grooms had been married at least once before.[12]

After retirement, when men spend as much time around the house as do housewives and there is much less of a clear-cut difference in economic roles, the social and sexual distinctions between men and women are diminished. Many older men and women, particularly in the lower income groups, seem to seek sex differentiation by means of their social life. The unbalanced sex ratio among older people (121 women past sixty-five for every 100 men) must have some effect on their attitudes toward sex and sex differentiation. Perhaps it is simply that men are pampered and fussed over by their female associates; perhaps it is a woman-dominated social relationship in which men's wishes and interests are ignored because they are so greatly outnumbered.

There are many other areas of the aging subculture that could be analyzed and speculated about. Their self-conceptions, their attitudes toward death and marriage,[13] their interpersonal relationships and leisure activities,[14] their argot, their distinctive rituals,[15] their hobbies,[16] and scores of other important factors in their behavior and outlook must be significantly affected by the particular social settings in which they interact. There is perhaps less basis for speculation about these topics, in the almost complete absence of empirical data, than about the topics we have already considered. There is one topic, however, for which there is some empirical evidence available, one which is of growing significance for the aging. This is what I call "aging group consciousness," and to define it effectively I must first talk about the "aging self-conception." These concepts, as aspects of the aging subculture, will take up the remainder of this paper.

The Aging Self-Conception

The age of sixty-five has more or less come to be considered the age of entering "old age" in American society. It seems likely that the Social Security Act of 1935 did more to define this limit than any other single event. Most private pension schemes adopted or proposed since that date have taken the age of sixty-five as the date of retirement. Compulsory retirement requirements have become much more frequent since 1935, and they have often adopted sixty-five years as the age of effectuation. The double exemption on the income tax for those past the age of sixty-five did not become highly significant until the great increase of tax rates during the Second World War, but then it served to accentuate the importance of turning sixty-five. Thus a legal definition helped to differentiate more sharply a social category. But even today not all persons past the age of sixty-five are considered elderly. The exceptions among men are mainly those who are not retired, which is mainly among the self-employed and generally in the upper-status occupations. Among nongainfully employed women, for whom there is no definite age of retirement or who in effect retired much earlier when their youngest child left home, entrance into the social category of "the elderly" is not so clear-cut.

Regardless of precisely at what age they begin to think of themselves as elderly, for most Americans there tends to be a marked change in self-conception. This includes a shift in thinking of oneself: as progressively physically and mentally handicapped, from independent to dependent, and from aspiring to declining.[17] Because most of the changes associated with the assumption of the role and self-conception of being elderly are negatively evaluated in American culture, and because there is no compensatory attribution of prestige, as in other societies the first reaction of many older people is some kind of disengagement and depression. The disengagement is by no means completely voluntary.

The older person is *pushed* out of his occupations, out of the formal and informal associations connected with occupation, and even out of leadership roles in many kinds of nonoccupational associations. It is a matter mainly of social fact, not so much of natural inevitability, that many Americans reaching the age of sixty-five shift into a social role of disengagement.[18] The actual physical and mental decline is not generally very great under today's conditions of advanced medical science and social welfare, and in any case usually develops gradually rather than suddenly. But the culture defines the past-sixty-five person as elderly, and this definition is applied in a variety of ways. Some, of course, resist the shift to the new role and the negative self-conception; they try, whether successful or not, to hold onto the pre-sixty-five role and self-conception. When senility, feebleness, chronic illness, or mental illness sets in, of course, disengagement from the society is the only possible condition for all but the most unusual older person.

Aging Group Consciousness

During the past decade in the United States, we have been witnessing the growth of a new phenomenon which is greatly expanding the scope of the aging subculture. This is what may be called "aging group consciousness" or "aging group identification." Some older people have begun to think of themselves as members of an aging group. In their eyes the elderly are being transformed from a category into a group. Probably only a minority of the elderly have so far taken this social-psychological step, but their number is growing. One of the early manifestations of this attitude is for them to join some kind of recreational or other expressive association in which they can interact almost exclusively with persons of similar age. Then they begin to take some pride in the association, as evidenced, for example, by the titles of such organizations—"Golden Age Club," "Senior Citizens Club," or "Live Long and Like It" club. A social worker may have helped to get the club started, but the elderly sometimes take it over and the social-psychological transformation toward group pride is theirs. This group identification of the elderly may take place within organizations that are not age-graded—that is, the elderly members simply interact more with each other than with the other members because of their physical limitations or their common attitudes and interests. But they are more likely to develop group identification in organizations that are set up exclusively for the elderly. There their distinctive characteristics and interests are clearly made evident to them, and they can develop their distinctiveness unhindered by obligations to a non-age-graded group.

The next phase occurs when they begin to talk over their common problems in a constructive way. Probably elderly people have been complaining for some time about their reduced income, their inadequate housing, the difficulty of paying for medical care if they should be struck with a chronic illness, their reduced prestige and general social neglect. But recently some have come to talk about such problems not only with reference to themselves as individuals, but with an awareness that these things occur to them as a social group. Furthermore, they have begun to talk in terms of taking social action, not merely individual action, to correct the situation. Thus far, this advanced minority has supported certain government actions, both legislative and executive. Their current support of congressional bills for financing health care is to be seen in this context. It is all the more significant that they are radical supporters of this legislation for the benefit of the elderly when the majority of them are political conservatives on most other issues.[19] The elderly seem to be on their way to becoming a voting bloc with a leadership that acts as a political pressure group. Even the elderly who are organized into recreational groups sometimes shift naturally into political pressure groups. For example, in San Francisco and Los Angeles social clubs for the elderly formed a pressure group to get reduced bus fares for those past sixty-five, ostensibly so that their low-income members could afford to get to the meetings. It remains to be seen whether the future political activities of the aging become integrated into the existing political parties or whether they become segregated as in the McLain movement in California.[20]

The trends listed on an earlier page as contributing to the development of an aging subculture are also specifically contributory to an aging group self-consciousness. All these trends have combined to create new problems for the older population at the same time that they have given the aged a new, distinctive position in the society, set apart from those under the age of sixty-five. These are the conditions which enhance the likelihood that the elderly will develop a sense of group consciousness.

For the growing minority that has reacted against the negative self-conception characteristic of the aging in our society and has seen the problems of aging in a group context, there are all the signs of group identification. There is a desire to associate with fellow-agers, especially in formal associations, and to exclude younger adults from these associations. There are expressions of group pride and corollary expressions of dismay concerning the evidence of "moral deterioration" in the outgroup, the younger generations. With this group pride has come self-acceptance as a member of an esteemed group, and the showing off of prowess as an elderly person (for example, in "life begins at eighty" types of activities). There are manifestations of a feeling of resentment at "the way elderly people are being mistreated," and indications of their taking social action to remove their sources of their resentment. These are the signs of group identification that previous sociological studies have found in ethnic minority groups.[21] I do not mean to exaggerate this parallel, or to state that most older people today show most of these signs. But the evidence of the growing group-identification among older people in the United States today is available to even the casual observer.

Future Research on the Subculture of the Aging

Sociologists now need to get beyond casual observation and engage in systematic studies of this formation of group identification, of this transformation of a social category into a social group. The whole area of the subculture of the aging needs objective investigation, in the same manner in which sociologists have already studied ethnic, regional, and occupational subcultures. The opportunity to study these things in birth and in development should not be missed. One reason they have been neglected by sociological researchers thus far is that the aging have been a low-prestige segment of the population, and only those interested in social reform have been willing to study them. But the objective trends seem to point to a higher status for the aging in the future, so we can anticipate that even the sociologists will find it respectable to conduct research in this field.

In conducting this research, it is to be recalled that by no means all persons past the age of sixty-five participate in the subculture. There are those who retain the identifications and the cultural behavior patterns of middle-aged persons. It may be that, as the social movement of aging group consciousness gains more prestige for the elderly, the number of the past-sixty-five who are not forcibly disengaged from the general society but are allowed to continue their prestige roles in that society will increase. If this happens, the self-segregating aspects of the aging group-consciousness movement will decline and ultimately disappear, and the movement itself thus become automatically self-liquidating. Secondly, there are those elderly persons who "disengage" and become relatively isolated from all cultural patterns and all associations except those of the family, either by their own volition or as a consequence of rejection by the larger society, or because of physical and mental decline which forces disengagement. Thirdly, there are some who combine both of these sets of characteristics because they *never* were "engaged" in most of the institutional and associational structures of the society, and remain so after they reach the age of sixty-five. Those elderly persons who develop and participate in an aging subculture, such as we have described in these pages, are different from the individuals in these other three categories. We need to know something about the *characteristics* of these people and the *conditions* under which they form or participate in the subculture. We should also remember that individuals participate in the subculture to different degrees, and the factors associated with this *extent* and *form* of participation can be studied at the same time. Insofar as we approach the study of the aging subculture with these questions, the observations of this paper may be considered hypotheses for testing in order to develop nomothetic generalizations, rather than statements of empirical fact which contribute to a historical description of a single society at a given time.

The extent of participation in an aging subculture varies with types of communities—e.g., declining rural areas, central cities, retirement towns—and a delineation of characteristics of their residents and conditions under which they participate in an aging subculture will further add to our knowledge. We have hypothesized, too, that several significant trends now affecting American society will favor the conditions under which elderly people engage in a subculture. These trends need to be studied for their effect and for their relationship to the aforementioned conditions under which the aging are found currently to engage in subcultural behavior.

NOTES

1. Whereas in 1901 only 46.0 percent of deaths were caused by chronic illnesses, the proportion had risen to 81.4 percent by 1955. Source: Metropolitan Life Insurance Company, Statistical Bulletin no. 39 (August 1958), p. 9.
2. Jon A. Doerflinger and D. G. Marshall, *The Story of Price County, Wisconsin,* Agricultural Experiment Station, University of Wisconsin Research Bulletin no. 220 (1960).
3. This does not apply to certain minority groups who are prevented from moving freely to the suburbs.
4. This is here suggested to be a long-run trend, not necessarily as yet a dominant factor nor always a short-run trend. A study by Shanas suggests that most intergenerational dwelling together still takes the form of adult children living in the homes of their aging parents. See Ethel Shanas, *Family Relationships of Older People* (New York: Health Information Foundation, 1961), especially p. 12.
5. Many recent studies, by Marvin Sussman, Eugene Litwak, and others, show that there is a great deal of intergenerational *visiting*. As we have suggested elsewhere ("Reactions to the Mass Society," *The Sociological Quarterly* 3 [1962]:316–30), this is probably on the increase after a period (roughly 1880–1940) in which intergenerational visiting reached a low point.
6. Obviously the degree of age-group separation is a function of such mechanical factors as the number of age groups and the number of persons in each age group, as well as of cultural and demographic factors. In this paper, only the latter are considered.
7. For case evidence of this, see Gordon J. Aldridge, "Informal Social Relationships in a Retirement Community," *Marriage and Family Living* 21(1959):70–73.
8. By "group self-hatred" I mean a strongly negative attitude toward the self because one has a negative attitude toward the group or category which nature and society combine to place one in. The concept grew up in dealing with certain social and psychological phenomena in minority groups. See, for example, Arnold M. Rose, *The Negro's Morale* (Minneapolis: University of Minnesota Press, 1949), pp. 85–95.
9. For case evidence of this, see Aldridge, *op. cit.*, and G. C. Hoyt, "The Life of the Retired in a Trailer Park," *American Journal of Sociology* 59 (1954):361–70.
10. Cultural values have at least one characteristic in common with economic values: to have high value they must be relatively scarce. Thus younger people

do not gain much status merely by being healthy (because most of them are) unless they are prize specimens of good health.

11. Mainly the Kinsey studies: A. C. Kinsey, W. B. Pomeroy, and C. E. Martin, *Sexual Behavior in the Human Male* (Philadelphia: W. B. Saunders, 1948); A. C. Kinsey, W. B. Pomeroy, C. E. Martin, and P. H. Gebhard, *Sexual Behavior in the Human Female* (Philadelphia: W. B. Saunders, 1953).

12. These statistics are derived from "Cupid Comes to Older People," *Aging*, no. 93 (July 1962):8-9.

13. Robert W. Kleemeier, "Moosehaven: Congregate Living in a Community of the Retired," *American Journal of Sociology* 59 (1954):347-51.

14. Hoyt, *op. cit.*; L. C. Michelen, "The New Leisure Class," *American Journal of Sociology* 59 (1954):371-78; R. W. Kleemeier, ed. *Aging and Leisure* (New York: Oxford University Press, 1961).

15. Wayne Wheeler is undertaking a study of rituals among the aging.

16. Edwin Christ's study of hobbies among the aging is partially reported in chapter 6 of A. M. Rose and W. Peterson, eds., *Older People and Their Social Worlds* (Philadelphia: F. A. Davis Co., 1965).

17. These changes in social role and self-conception have been discussed more fully in my paper "The Mental Health of Normal Older Persons," *Geriatrics* 16 (1961):459-64. Also see Irving Rosow, "Retirement Housing and Social Integration," *Gerontologist* 1 (1961):85-91.

18. Compare Elaine Cumming et al., "Disengagement: A Tentative Theory of Aging," *Sociometry* 23 (1960):23-35; Elaine Cumming and William E. Henry, *Growing Old* (New York: Basic Books, 1961). Cumming's theory of disengagement applies to those elderly persons who are in good physical and mental health. Those in poor health are necessarily disengaged, of course, and thus their disengagement is not a matter of sociological theory but of biological fact. Cumming's theory also excludes family contacts from the definition of disengagement. With these qualifications, Cumming hypothesizes disengagement of the elderly to be a matter of "natural inevitability"— which places her theory in opposition to that presented in this paper.

19. Angus Campbell, "Psychological and Social Determinants of Voting Behavior" (paper presented at Fourteenth Annual Conference on Aging, University of Michigan, Ann Arbor, June 19, 1961).

20. F. A. Pinner, P. Jacobs, and P. Selznick, *Old Age and Political Behavior* (Berkeley: University of California Press, 1959).

21. Probably the first to note the minority group aspects of the aging was Milton L. Barron in "Minority Group Characteristics of the Aged in American Society," *Journal of Gerontology* 8 (1953):477-82. See also Milton L. Barron, "Attacking Prejudices against the Aged," in *Growing with the Years*, New York State Legislative Committee on Problems of Aging, Legislative Document no. 32, pp. 56-58, 1954; Leonard Z. Breen, "The Aging Individual," in *Handbook of Social Gerontology*, ed. Clark Tibbitts (Chicago: University of Chicago Press, 1960), especially p. 157; Samuel M. Strong, "Types of Adjustment to Aging," Proceedings of the Minnesota Academy of Science, 35-36, 398-405 (1957-58), especially p. 399; James H. Woods, *Helping Older People Enjoy Life* (New York: Harper & Row, 1953), pp. 1-2.

Social Gerontology and the Age Stratification of Society

MATILDA WHITE RILEY

It is possible to conceptualize society as divided by age as well as by social class. There are several ways to examine the meaning of age stratification. First, we can determine how an individual's location within the changing age structure of a given society influences his or her behavior and attitudes. There are two dimensions to this question, the life-course dimension and the historical dimension. People at the same stage of the life cycle have much in common, as do those born during the same historical period, such as the Depression. A second issue is the exploration of relationships *between* age strata, e.g., the generation gap, and *within* age strata, e.g., the tendency for the aged to prefer others of similar ages as friends. The third set of questions examines mobility between strata. While aging is a universal phenomenon, there are vast differences between age cohorts in the ways they age. The fourth consideration is the relationship between each of the first three issues and the changes that occur in society as a whole.

One decade after "the" White House Conference, and on the eve of another, the Gerontological Society and all of us involved in research in this field can survey with satisfaction the amount of information accumulated in these ten years and the impact of this information upon professional practice, public policy, and popular attitudes. That much remains to be done is patent to all gerontologists, but that the title of this symposium is "Research Goals and Priorities in Gerontology" suggests that we have reached a point where we can pick and choose among alternative strategies.

What we propose as a high priority for the future is a sociology of age stratification. Gerontologists working in the social science fields have amassed a remarkable body of facts on two main topics: being old and growing old.[1] Our immediate aim is not so much to add to these facts and ideas as to look at them from a fresh perspective. This perspective emphasizes not just old age, but all the age strata in the society as a whole; it emphasizes not just aging, but also the societal processes and changes that affect aging and the state of being old.

SOURCE: Copyright 1971 by the Gerontological Society. Reprinted by permission from *The Gerontologist*, Vol. 11, No. 1 (1971).

What do we mean by age *stratification*, which is only now emerging as a new field of sociology? A comparison with the well-established sociology of class stratification is provocative. In that field, two concepts, heuristically stimulating as analogous to our concepts of age strata and aging, have demonstrated their power in explaining diverse social phenomena. These concepts are *social class* (variously defined in terms of inequality of income, prestige, or power) and *social mobility* (consisting of upward or downward movement between lower and higher classes). These concepts of social class and social mobility, which any one of us can grasp intuitively from firsthand experience, have proved scientifically useful in defining and suggesting answers to many important questions. We shall list four sets of these questions briefly, as they may stimulate us to find answers to similar questions in relation to age and aging.

- *First*, how does an individual's location in the class structure channel his attitudes and the way he behaves? Here there is much evidence that, for example, a person's health, his desire to achieve, his sense of mastery over his own fate, or the way he relates to his family and to his job depend to a considerable extent upon his social class.
- *Second*, how do individuals relate to one another within and between classes? Within class lines many friendships are formed, marriages often take place, and feelings of solidarity tend to be widespread. Between classes relationships, even if not solidary, are often symbiotic, as people of unlike status live harmoniously in the same society. However, there seems to be greater opportunity between, than within, classes for cleavage or conflict, as in struggles over economic advantages or clashes in political loyalties.
- *Third*, what difficulties beset the upwardly (or downwardly) mobile individual, and what strains does his mobility impose upon the group (such as his parents of one class) whom he leaves behind and upon the new group (such as his wife's parents of a different class) who must now absorb him?
- *Fourth*, to the extent that answers can be found to these three sets of questions, what is the impact of the observed findings upon the society as a whole? If there are inequalities between classes, for example, what do these portend for the prosperity, the morality, or the stability of the overall structure of classes? What pressures for societal change are generated by differences, conflicts, or mobility between classes?

The literature on these four aspects of class stratification is impressive, pregnant with insights that might be extended to analyses of kindred phenomena. Our concern is to test the utility of the questions it evokes for understanding old age as just one stratum in a society stratified or differentiated, not by class, but by age. Thus we shall start by thinking of society as divided into strata according to the age of their members. *People* at varying ages differ in their capacity and willingness to perform social roles (of student, spouse, worker, or retiree, for example). Moreover, the age strata differ in the social *roles* members are expected to play and in the rights and privileges accorded to them by society. At any given period of time, old people must live as members of such a society, finding their place in relation to the other members who are younger than they and making choices among whatever opportunities are available to them. Over time, not only old people but people of different ages are *all* growing older, moving concurrently through a society which itself is undergoing change.

Age Stratification and the Individual

To ask our first question, then: How does an individual's location within the changing age structure of a given society influence his behavior and attitudes? (Mannheim, 1952). In the sociological literature generally it has been well established that individuals are conditioned by society. As Robert Merton puts it, "Structure constrains individuals variously situated within it to develop cultural emphases, social behavior patterns, and psychological bents" (Merton, 1957). Similarly, it has been well established in the literature of social gerontology that the state of old age reflects the structural context, showing wide variations (as well as some similarities) when primitive and modern societies are contrasted (Simmons, 1960), or even when modern Western nations are compared with one another (Burgess, 1960; Havighurst et al., 1969; Shanas and Associates, 1968). But how does it come about that, *within* a given society at any given time, individuals located in *different age strata* differ from one another? How are older individuals set off from the middle-aged and from the young?

The answer to such a question as this involves two distinct dimensions of time: a life-course dimension and a historical dimension. These two dimensions can be thought of as coordinates for locating the individual in the age structure of society. On the first dimension, individuals at the *same* state of the *life* course have much in common. They tend to be alike in biological development, in the kinds of roles they have experienced (such as worker, spouse, parent of dependent child), and in the sheer number of years behind and potential years ahead. People at *different* life course stages tend to differ in these very respects. The rough index of this life-course dimension is years of chronological age—we say that a person is aged twenty, or in the age category forty-five to sixty. But chronological age is of interest to us, not intrinsically, but only because it can serve as an approximate indicant of personal (that is biological, psychological, and social) experience—and this experience carries with it varying probabilities of behavior and attitudes. This life-course dimension is the familiar one that includes the age-related organic changes affecting physical and mental functioning and that links the biological and the social sciences.

But there is a second time dimension for locating an individual in the age strata that also affects his probability of behaving or thinking in particular ways. This dimension refers to the *period of history* in which he lives. People who were born at the *same* time (referred to as a cohort) share a common historical and environmental past, present, and future. For example, when Americans born in 1910 had reached the age of thirty, they had all (in one way or another) experienced World War I and the Great Depression, they were all currently exposed to World War II, and they all confronted the future of the 1940s through the 1970s. People who were born at *different* times (that is different cohorts) have lived through different intervals of history; and even when they encounter the same historical situation, they may, because they differ in age, experience it differently. Thus any one of us—just as we might be ethnocentric—is almost certainly (to add a needed term to our vocabulary) "*cohort-centric*." That is, we view old age, or any other stage of life, from the unique point of historical time at which we ourselves are standing. The rough index of this historical (or environmental) dimension is the date, or the calendar year. Here again our concern is not with dates themselves, but with the particular sociocultural and environmental events, conditions, and changes to which the individual is exposed at particular periods.

It comes as no surprise, then, that each of the age strata has its own *distinctive subculture.* By age differences in subculture we mean that a cross-section view of society shows, for myriad characteristics, patterns that are closely related to age. In our own society today, familiar instances of the differing subcultures among young, middle-aged, and old include such varied aspects of life as labor force participation, consumer behavior, leisure-time activities, marital status, religious behavior, education, nativity, fertility and childrearing practices, or political attitudes—to name only a few. Such age-related patterns differ from time to time and from place to place, as all the age strata in a society—not the old alone—display differences (or similarities) in behavior and attitudes on the two dimensions of life course and history.

If we want to go beyond a mere description of these age-related subcultures, however, we must examine them further, which leads to our next topic.

Age Stratification and Social Relationships

The second set of questions suggested by the analogy between class stratification and age stratification points to the utility of exploring *relationships* both *between* and *within* age strata. For not only the behavior and attitudes of discrete individuals, but also social relationships—people's positive or negative feelings and actions toward each other—are channeled through the age structure of the particular society. Thus a sociology of age stratification, by investigating these relationships, should help to illuminate the nature of old age.

Many aspects of the cleavages or the bonds *between* old and young, dramatized by philosophers and poets of the ancient past, are still widely discussed today. Is there an inevitable gap between generations? Do the elderly constitute a disadvantaged minority group, regarded with prejudice by the majority? Or do they control important centers of power, refusing to yield to the young? Are old people likely to form political blocs, seeking to solve their own problems with little regard for the rest of society? And if many conditions foster intergenerational conflict or exploitation, what other conditions foster relationships of harmony or reciprocity?

As a preliminary to addressing such momentous issues, one small illustration of the *sequential relations* among generations within the family will point out the interconnectedness of the age strata. If we start with the elderly generation of parents and their adult offspring, a well-known finding from the gerontological literature reports widespread exchanges of material support. This support varies in amount and kind, ranging from financial contributions and care in illness to baby-sitting and help with housework and home repairs. Contrary to previous notions of an upward flow of contributions *to* older people, the flow of support between aged parents and their adult offspring appears to be two-directional, either from parent to child or from child to parent as need and opportunity dictate (Riley, Foner, and Associates, 1968). Indeed (in the United States, at least), the proportions of older people who *give* help to their offspring appear to exceed the proportions who *receive* help from their offspring (Shanas, 1966; Streib, 1965; Streib and Thompson, 1960).

Let us now, however, include in the example still a third generation of the family, for it is our contention that many a commonplace observation about old people can take on new significance through extension to other age strata. Let us move from the flow of material assistance between aged parents and their middle-aged children to the flow between this middle generation and *their* young children. The principle can be illustrated by one small study (Foner, 1969) in which parents of high school students were asked what they would do with money unexpectedly received. Only 2 percent said they would use it to help their aged parents. But this was not because they would spend it on themselves or save it for their retirement; it was rather because, in the main, they would reserve it to help their children get started in life. Furthermore, the aged generation concurs; they do not expect repayment. The middle generation, then, does not neglect the old because of preoccupation with their own needs (in fact, they are far readier to offer help than are their aged parents to want or to accept it), but because of their preoccupation with the needs of their young children. In short, the flow of material support tends to be, not reciprocal, but sequential—with each generation (regardless of its means) attempting to aid the next younger generation.

As such a finding intimates, many middle-aged parents, by investing their resources in the future of their young children, are not only restricting any potential help they might give to the older generation; they are also restricting the accumulation of assets for their own later life. In this example, then, extension of the analysis from the oldest to the youngest generation in the family helps to clarify one aspect of the meaning of old age. Any lack of family support for aged parents now appears, not as willful indifference or neglect, but as an expression of normative agreement among all the generations about the direction in which aid should flow.

Many other conditions of the aged might similarly be better understood against the backdrop of the other strata with whom old people live and relate. Consider the work force data on older men as this might be compared with the differing circumstances of employment of younger people at various periods of history. In the early days of the Industrial Revolution in England, the father (or grandfather), as a skilled workman in his own right, could take his children with him into the factory, himself training the adult sons and supervising the little children throughout the long workday (Smelser, 1968). Thus his authority within the family could penetrate into the workplace, preserving traditional ties among the generations. If such an arrangement encouraged between-strata solidarity, then the subsequent changes in conditions of work may have undermined this basis. More recently, in the United States, quite another set of changes have marked the relative positions of older men and boys in the work force. Between 1900 and 1930, while the majority of older men remained economically active, the proportion of boys aged ten to fifteen who were fully employed declined from 25 percent to only 6 percent. Since World War II, as older men have been winnowed from the labor force, boys too are being extruded; the census no longer counts children under fourteen in compiling labor force statistics, and the participation rates of boys from sixteen through nineteen show slight but consistent declines. Thus older men today live in a society where the situation of both the old and the young must be interpreted in relation to the productivity and economic prestige of men in their middle years (Kalish, 1969).

Such examples suggest a general principle: Important increments to gerontological knowledge are obtainable by studying the entire age-differentiated society, not merely the old. The same principle holds when the research focus is on relationships *within* rather than *between* age strata. Here we shall simply allude to the concern of gerontologists with questions of age similarity as a basis for friendship, or age homogeneity as a feature of residential settings for older people (Madge, 1969; Riley, Foner, and Associates, 1968). It has been shown that, outside of family groups, older people tend (although by no means exclusively) to have friends who are similar to themselves in status characteristics—notably age—that signal mutuality of experiences, tastes, or values. However, as the sociological literature shows (Hess, 1971), such choice of age mates is only a special case of the widespread phenomenon of homophily (or similarity among friends in status or in values) (Lazarsfeld and Merton, 1954).

Age homophily, not only among the old but also at younger age levels, may be especially pronounced in the United States today as a number of factors converge to produce solidarity within age lines. Simply the rapidity of social change, for example, can sharpen the differences among strata and can thereby contribute to a sense of uniqueness among members of each single stratum. The expansion of education has extended the social (and often the physical) segregation of age-similars from children in the lower schools to older adolescents and even to young adults in colleges and universities (Parsons and Platt, 1971). Today's middle-aged people, too, many of whom have left the city to rear their children in the suburbs, have experienced long years of age-homogeneous neighborhood settings (Starr, 1971). And old people because of increasing longevity retain larger numbers of their age peers as associates (Spengler, 1969). In many respects, then, we live in an *age-graded* society, with a high potential for strong ties to develop within each age stratum.

However, the possible long-term consequences of such heightened conditions of within-stratum solidarity may be double-edged. On the one hand, homophily may be beneficial to the individuals involved. Age peers have long been recognized as easing the transition from childhood to adulthood (Eisenstadt, 1956); and they may perhaps aid adjustment in old age and at other points of transition in the life course as well. On the other hand, if age peers increasingly turn to each other for aid and comfort, detriments to relationships between strata may ensue as ties between generations may become attenuated or the potential for cleavage or conflict may be increased.

Aging and Cohort Flow

It is the third set of questions—those relating to the processes of *mobility* of individuals from one stratum to another—that brings into bold relief certain similarities, but also the essential differences, between class stratification and age stratification.

At points of similarity between the two processes, much can be learned about aging from the rich literature on class mobility. We tend to take aging for granted (much as before the development of physiology as a science, laymen took their bodily functioning for granted). Yet when aging (social, psychological, and biological) is viewed as mobility through the age strata, it is revealed as a process that entails many of the same tensions and strains as class mobility. Aging individuals must pass through key transition points in the society—from infancy to childhood, for example, from one school grade to the next, from adolescence to adulthood, or from work life to retirement (Clausen, 1971). And the degree of strain engendered by such transitions depends upon diverse social conditions—upon the continuity or discontinuity in the role sequences (Benedict, 1938); upon how fully institutionalized a particular role may be (Donahue, Orbach, and Pollak, 1960); upon the internal consistency of role expectations, facilities, and sanctions;[2] or upon how effectively people are trained or socialized at every stage of life (Brim, 1968; Brim and Wheeler, 1966). For example, consider the stress entailed in our society because we crowd formal education almost exclusively into the younger stages of life rather than spreading it over the life course as individuals require it. Since we do not regard students as full-fledged adults, what tensions must be endured by the young person who stays in the role of student beyond adolescence well into adulthood (tensions that are all too evident in universities today)? What difficulties beset the older person if, in order to obtain the further education he needs or desires, he must sacrifice his job? Like social mobility, too, aging places strains not only upon individuals but also upon the groups through which the aging individual passes. Thus a family must regroup itself after the marriage of its youngest child, or a community after the death of an elder statesman. Similarly, group adjustments are necessitated by the advent of new members like the birth of a child into a family, the entry of a new class of children into a school grade, or the move of a widowed old person into the household of her married daughter.

Despite such similarities, however, aging differs from class mobility in certain fundamental respects. Exactly because the analogy breaks down in these respects is age stratification revealed in its full uniqueness and in its intrinsicality to social change. In the first place, mobility across social classes affects only selected individuals, who can move either upward or downward and who can reverse direction at different stages of life. But mobility through the age strata is, of course, universal, unidirectional, and irreversible. Everybody ages. Everybody changes over his life course as personality develops, experience accumulates, and adjustments are made to new roles. Nobody can ever go back, although individuals may age in different ways and at different rates.

In the second place, knowledgeable as we are about the inevitability of aging, we take much less cognizance of the inexorability of birth and death, and of the endless succession of cohorts (or generations of individuals born at the same time)—for which there is no precise parallel in class mobility. Yet the sociology of age stratification requires examination of the fact that within a given society different cohorts can age in different ways. Each cohort is tied through its date of birth to societal history. Thus the aging of each new cohort is affected by the special situation of that cohort's particular era in history—by the changing cultural, social, and material conditions in the society and by events in the external environment. While all the members of one particular cohort move together over their life course through the same period of time, the various cohorts in the society can differ because they start at distinct times. Cohorts can also differ markedly in size and in composition (in the proportions of males and females, for example, or of blacks and whites, or of natives and foreign-born).

Consider a few examples of intercohort differences in the way people have aged in our own society in the *past*. Epidemiologists tell us that, in comparison with women born a century ago, today's women have experienced menarche at earlier ages and menopause at later ages (National Center for Health Statistics, 1966; Susser, 1969; Tanner, 1962). That is, the period of potential fertility has appreciably lengthened. In practice, however, *recent* cohorts spend fewer years of their lives in childbearing. Women have telescoped the phase of actual reproduction, having fewer and more closely spaced offspring nowadays than did their mothers or grandmothers (Glick and Parke, 1965). Moreover, the traumas of reproduction have been drastically reduced, as fewer women die in childbirth and fewer of their infants die.

Most striking of all the cohort differences, perhaps, are those in longevity—in the proportions of cohort members who outlive the ills of infancy, who escape maternal deaths and the other mortality risks of young adulthood, and who thus survive into the higher ages of the life span. The average lifetime (estimated at only two to three decades among cohorts born in ancient Rome or in medieval Europe) has risen in the United States from four decades among cohorts born in the mid nineteenth century to an estimated seven decades among those born in the mid-twentieth—a situation apparently unparalleled in human history.[3] The profound implications of such cohort differences in longevity can be intimated by just one of the many associated changes, the one called the "revolution in family structure" (Glick and Parke, 1965; Shanas, 1969).[4] The single nuclear household of a century ago (parents and their children, sometimes including a grandparent) has been replaced, because of increased joint survival, by several generations of related nuclear households: the young couple with their dependent children, the middle-aged parents, the aged generation of grandparents, and the great-grandparent who also often survives.

What do such differences between earlier and later cohorts presage for the people who will become old in the *future*? Speculation about many of these differences can prove fruitful of hypotheses. We might speculate, for example, about the extended period of husband-wife relationships in the middle years: the more recent couples have had more time to accumulate assets, or to learn independence from their offspring, or to prepare themselves for retirement. But not all predictions about future implications of cohort differences are entirely speculative, since everybody who will reach sixty-five during this century or during the early decades of the twenty-first century is already alive. Much information is already in hand about the size of existing cohorts, for example, or about their place of birth or their educational level. Thus, apart from unforesee-able changes (as through wars, depressions, or major shifts in migration or in values), fair estimates can be made about numerous characteristics of old people at particular dates in the future. The *size* of the aged stratum at the turn of the century will reflect the small number of babies in the Depression cohorts; but the size of the aged stratum will predictably increase again in the early decades of the coming century with the influx of the "baby boom" cohorts born after World War II (Spengler, 1969). In respect to *nativity*, the much-studied cohort who had passed age sixty-five or more by 1960 had contained a sizable proportion of early immigrants who were largely illiterate and unskilled, whereas the more recent cohorts who will reach old age in subsequent decades contain fewer and better-educated immigrants. Or in respect to formal *education*, we know that over 70 percent of the cohort aged seventy-five or more in 1960 had had less than nine years of school, contrasted with only 17 percent of the cohort aged twenty-five to twenty-nine, who will not reach age seventy-five before the year 2005 (Riley, Foner, and Associates, 1968). We are aware also of many changing societal or environmental conditions, not all of them salutary, that may influence in special ways the future life course of existing cohorts—as, for example, the spread of pollution might have the greatest effect on young cohorts subject to a full lifetime of exposure, or as the increase of smoking among women might bring female death rates more nearly into line with the currently higher male rates. We cannot overestimate the importance of charting such cohort differences for an understanding of old age.

Age and Social Change

We have been discussing the dual processes affecting individuals (or cohorts of individuals) in a society: aging as a social, psychological, and biological process; and the succession of cohorts which do not all age in exactly the same ways. We shall now ask how these processes relate to the macrocosm of the changing society (Ryder, 1965) of which the old people who concern us are one integral part.

Mannheim (1952) once proposed a tantalizing mental experiment. Imagine, he said, a society in which one generation lived on forever, and none followed to replace it. Let us, as social scientists, policy makers, and professional groups, make such an experiment! If everybody grows old together, what distinctions might remain between old and young? A few moments' thought are enough to suggest the ineluctable connections among the succession of cohorts, aging, and age stratification. For, in contrast to Mannheim's imaginary society, our own consists of successive cohorts, each with its own unique life-course pattern. It is clear that these cohorts fit together at any given time to form the age structure of young, middle-aged, and aged strata. And over time, as the particular individuals composing the particular strata are continually moving on and being replaced, the society itself is changing.

Certain connections now become apparent between the flow of cohorts and the age-related societal patterns and changes in individual behaviors, attitudes, and relationships (noted in the first sections of the paper). In the simplest case, because successive cohorts often age in different ways, some of these societal patterns and changes can be viewed as direct reflections of the differing cohorts that comprise the age strata at particular periods. Education is a noteworthy example of the significance of cohort flow for cross-sectional differences among age strata (Riley, Foner, and Associates, 1968). The rapid pace of educational advance over the century, leaving its mark on successive cohorts of young people, now sets the age strata clearly apart from one another. And these strata differences in education have incalculable importance for many aspects of behavior and attitude—for prejudice, feelings of powerlessness, narrow ranges of interest and friendships, and the like. Of course, such strata differences do not remain fixed. Not only do new cohorts come along, but society itself can change in its related institutions and practices. The age pattern of education today is a reversal of that in earlier societies where the old were honored for their greater knowledge. If one looks ahead from today's knowledge explosion, the information gap between the very young and even the not-so-young is deepening, creating pressures to change the entire structure of education if poeple beyond the earliest years are to maintain competitive equality.[5]

In another example, the cross-section age patterns for drinking or smoking have shown a general decline from younger to older strata; and these differences among strata are in part reflections of the past tendency for each new cohort to espouse these practices to an increasing degree (Riley, Foner, and Associates, 1968). Today's younger cohorts, however, may be introducing new habits that could, over the next decades, drastically change the cross-section age pattern. A recent campus interview elicited the student comment, for example, that

> upperclassmen still prefer beer, but a large majority of underclassmen prefer pot. Pot is big in the high schools, and it is very popular with freshmen who just came out of that environment. The trend is definitely away from beer (Cicetti, 1970).

Are these newcomers to the college likely to set the pace for the cohorts that follow?

In such instances, changes in societal age strata can be interpreted as the shifting composite of cohorts who, themselves affected by differing historical backgrounds, have aged in differing ways. In other instances, life-course differences among cohorts in one social sphere appear to stimulate further changes in other spheres. For example, far-reaching shifts in the relations between men and women at various ages—the decreasing differentiation between the sexes or the greater freedom of sexual behavior—might be traced in part to a reversal in cohort patterns of female participation in the labor force (Riley, Foner, and Associates, 1968; Riley, Johnson, and Foner, 1971). Many cohorts of women born during the late nineteenth century showed steadily declining rates of participation over the life course. Following World War II, a new pattern began to emerge, as many married women entered the labor force during their middle years, although work force participation of young women in the child-rearing ages remained low. The conjunction of these cohort trends meant that, for a considerable period, it was only the young mothers with little children whose labor force participation was low. This situation may have prompted a classic observation (foreshadowing the full force of the Women's Liberation Movement) that "for the first time in the history of any known society, motherhood has become a full-time occupation for adult women" (Rossi, 1964). Women at other times and places shared motherhood with demanding labor in the fields, the factory, or the household.

Can we expect that full-time motherhood is now institutionalized and will persist into the future? If so, we may be victims of our own "cohort-centrism"—one more proof that our understandings of society are influenced by our particular historical background. For this full-time preoccupation of American mothers with their young children seems already to be eroding as recent cohorts have developed a rather different pattern. Not only have the proportions of married women in the labor force during their middle years more than doubled, but there have been pronounced increases also among young married women, even those with little children (Manpower Report of the President, 1970). Thus it may appear to historians of the future that full-time motherhood was a peculiar phenomenon, existing in American society only for a few decades of the twentieth century. Whatever the future may actually hold, the example begins to suggest how the confluence of cohorts with differing life-course patterns in one respect (economic activity of women) can change society in other respects as well. Think, for example, of the mature women who no longer "retire" from major social roles many years before their husbands retire from work. Or think of the young husbands and wives who now share the work of homemaking and infant care. May such changing work habits result in entirely new modes of relationship in the family and—if only because of the widespread unavailability of working wives for daytime activities at home or in the community—in other social institutions?

In addition to the impress of cohort succession upon the history of society, it can sometimes happen that innovations emanating from a single cohort ramify rather quickly through the other age strata, without awaiting the lag over a long series of cohorts. Thus the excessive size of the "baby boom" cohort born after World War II has required drastic adjustments throughout a society unprepared to absorb it—from the initial requirements for obstetrical facilities through the successive pressures on housing, schools, the job market, the marriage market, and so on into the future. Among the many other widely discussed instances are the increased financial burden borne (through transfer payments) by the remainder of society because so many retired old people have inadequate incomes (Bernstein, 1969; McConnell, 1960); or the potential changes in the ethos surrounding work and leisure as large numbers of old and young no longer participate in the work force (Donahue et al., 1960; Riley et al., 1969). It has even been suggested that a completely revolutionary "consciousness," now informing the values and behaviors of many young people, may affect the entire society (Reich, 1970).

To return to the immediate topic of this essay, we offer a special challenge to the oncoming cohorts of social gerontologists—not merely to continue looking for new materials, but also to reexamine and fit together the existing materials in a new way. We suggest a review of old age as one ingredient in the societal macrocosm, inseparable from, and interdependent with, the other age strata. We suggest a review of aging and of the succession of births and deaths as integral parts of societal process and change that follow their own rhythm and that in themselves constitute immanent strains and pressures toward innovation. Such a sociological review can, we submit, help to explain old age and aging and can at the same time suggest potential solutions to some of the problems of great immediate concern.

In sum, the forces of social change, whether through deliberate intervention[6] or as an indirect consequence of existing trends, are not only constantly affecting the aging process, but are also bringing new influences to bear on the situation, on the characteristics of persons who are old, and on the younger age strata with whom old people are interdependent. Discovery and evaluation of the implications for old age of these forces for change constitute a whole new field of opportunity for social scientists, professional groups, and policy makers in gerontology.

NOTES

This paper was presented at a Symposium on Research Goals and Priorities in Gerontology, 23rd Annual Scientific Meeting of Gerontological Society, Toronto, Oct. 23, 1970. A more extensive treatment of this topic is contained in Riley, Johnson, and Foner, *A sociology of age stratification* (1971). This is the third volume of a series on *Aging and society*, published by Russell Sage Foundation, under a grant from The Ford Foundation. In addition to the authors of this third volume, the following persons have read earlier versions of this manuscript and made valuable criticisms and suggestions: Beth Hess, Robert K. Merton, Mary E. Moore, M.D., and John W. Riley, Jr.

1. A team of us at Rutgers required several years to gather, abstract, and organize this impressive body of knowledge before we were able to produce an inventory of research findings, roughly 600 pages of *selected* social science results, in Riley, Foner, and Associates, 1968.
2. Back (1969) claims ambiguity of retirement which, although socially defined as a right of the individual, offers low rewards and is socially undervalued.
3. To be sure, infant deaths weigh heavily in these averages. Moreover, the data are based on hypothetical, rather than true, cohorts. See Riley, Foner, and Associates, 1968.
4. Among couples born a century ago, the last child in the family was married, on the average, at about the same time as the death of one of the parents. But among recent cohorts, husbands and wives typically survive together as two-person families for a good many years after the last child has married and left home. Changes in family structure are associated with changes, not only in longevity, but also in childbearing and in household living arrangements; see Riley et al., 1968.
5. If such a change is not effected, we may expect increasing convergence of age and class stratification as education achieves preeminence among the distinguishing criteria of social class.
6. Many possibilities for intervention in the several professional fields are discussed in the series of essays in Riley, Riley, and Johnson, 1969, in which experts discuss the implications of social science knowledge for public policy and professional practice affecting older people.

REFERENCES

Back, K. W. The ambiguity of retirement. In E. W. Busse and E. Pfeiffer (Eds.), *Behavior and adaptation in late life.* Boston: Little, Brown, 1969.

Benedict, R. Continuities and discontinuities in cultural conditioning. *Psychiatry,* 1938, I, 161–167. (Reprinted in Kluckhohn, C., Murray, H. A., and Schneider, D. (Eds.) *Personality in nature, society and culture.* New York: Alfred A. Knopf, 1953.

Bernstein, M. C. Aging and the law. In M. W. Riley, J. W. Riley, Jr., and M. E. Johnson (Eds.), *Aging and society.* Vol. 2, *Aging and the professions.* New York: Russell Sage Foundation, 1969.

Brim, O. G., Jr. Adult socialization. In J. A. Clausen (Ed.), *Socialization and society.* Boston: Little, Brown, 1968.

Brim, O. G., Jr., and Wheeler, S. *Socialization after childhood: Two essays.* New York: John Wiley & Sons, 1966.

Burgess, E. W. (Ed.). *Aging in Western societies.* Chicago: University of Chicago Press, 1960.

Cicetti, F. Campuses revisited: New trend at Seton Hall. *Newark Evening News,* Sept. 30, 1970.

Clausen, J. A. The life course of individuals. In M. W. Riley, M. E. Johnson, and A. Foner, *Aging and society* Vol. 3, *A sociology of age stratification.* New York: Russell Sage Foundation, 1971.

Donahue, W., Orbach, H. L., and Pollak, O. Retirement: The emerging social pattern. In C. Tibbitts (Ed.), *Handbook of social gerontology.* Chicago: University of Chicago Press, 1960.

Eisenstadt, S. N. *From generation to generation: Age groups and social structure.* Free Press: Glencoe, Ill., 1956.

Foner, A. The middle years: Prelude to retirement? PhD dissertation, New York University, 1969.

Glick, P. C., and Parke, R., Jr. New approaches in studying the life cycle of the family. *Demography,* 1965, 2, 187–202.

Havighurst, R. J., Munnichs, J. M. A., Neugarten, B. L., and Thomae, H. (Eds.). *Adjustment to retirement; A cross-national study.* Assen, The Netherlands: Koninklijke van Gorcum, 1969.

Hess, B. Friendship. In M. W. Riley, M. E. Johnson, and A. Foner. *Aging and society.* Vol. 3, *A sociology of age stratification.* New York: Russell Sage Foundation, 1971.

Kalish, R. A. The old and the new as generation-gap allies. *Gerontologist,* 1969, 9, 83–89.

Lazarsfeld, P. F., and Merton, R. K. Friendship as social process: A substantive and methodological analysis. In M. Berger, T. Abel, and C. H. Page, *Freedom and control in modern society.* New York: D. Van Nostrand, 1954.

McConnell, J. W. Aging and the economy. In C. Tibbitts (Ed.), *Handbook of social gerontology.* Chicago: University of Chicago Press, 1960.

Madge, J. Aging and the fields of architecture and planning. In M. W. Riley, J. W. Riley, Jr., and M. E. Johnson (Eds.), *Aging and society.* Vol. 2, *Aging and the professions.* New York: Russell Sage Foundation, 1969.

Mannheim, K. The problem of generations. In P. Kecskemeti (Ed. & Trans.), *Essays on the sociology of knowledge.* London: Routledge and Kegan Paul (1928), 1952.

Manpower Report of the President, Mar., 1970. Washington: Government Printing Office.

Merton, R. K. *Social theory and social structure.* (Rev. ed.) Glencoe, Ill.: Free Press, 1957.

National Center for Health Statistics. Age and menopause, United States 1960–1962. *Vital and health statistics, 1966,* PHS Pub. No. 1000—Series 11, No. 19, Washington: Government Printing Office.

Parsons, T., and Platt, G. M. Higher education and changing socialization. In M. W. Riley, M. E. Johnson, and A. Foner. *Aging and society.* Vol. 3, *A sociology of age stratification.* New York: Russell Sage Foundation, 1971.

Reich, C. Reflections: The greening of America. *New Yorker,* Sept. 26, 1970, 42 ff.

Riley, M. W., Foner, A., and Associates. *Aging and society.* Vol. 1, *An inventory of research findings.* New York: Russell Sage Foundation, 1968.

Riley, M. W., Riley, J. W., Jr. and Johnson, M. E. *Aging and society.* Vol. 2, *Aging and the professions.* New York: Russell Sage Foundation, 1969.

Riley, M. W., Johnson, M. E., and Foner, A. *Aging and society.* Vol. 3, *A sociology of age stratification.* New York: Russell Sage Foundation, 1971.

Riley, M. W., Foner, A., Hess, B., and Toby, M. L. Socialization for the middle and later years. In D. A. Goslin (Ed.), *Handbook of socialization theory and research.* Chicago: Rand McNally, 1969.

Rossi, A. S. Equality between the sexes: An immodest proposal. *Daedalus,* Spring, 1964, 607–652.

Ryder, N. B. The cohort as a concept in the study of social change. *American Sociological Review,* 1965, 30, 843–861.

Shanas, E., and Associates. Family help patterns and social class in three countries. Paper presented at the meetings of the American Sociological Assn., Miami, 1966.

Shanas, E., and Associates. *Old people in three industrial societies.* New York: Atherton Press, 1968.

Shanas, E. Living arrangements and housing of old people. In E. W. Busse and E. Pfeiffer (Eds.), *Behavior and adaptation in late life.* Boston: Little, Brown, 1969.

Simmons, L. W. Aging in preindustrial societies. In C. Tibbitts (Ed.), *Handbook of social gerontology.* Chicago: University of Chicago Press, 1960.

Smelser, N. J. Sociological history: The industrial revolution and the British working-class family. In N. J. Smelser (Ed.), *Essays in sociological explanation.* Englewood Cliffs, NJ: Prentice-Hall, 1968.

Spengler, J. J. The aged and public policy. In E. W. Busse and E. Pfeiffer (Eds.), *Behavior and adaptation in late life.* Boston: Little, Brown, 1969.

Starr, B. C. The community. In M. W. Riley, M. E. Johnson, and A. Foner. *Aging and society.* Vol. 3, *A sociology of age stratification.* New York: Russell Sage Foundation, 1971.

Streib, G. F. Intergenerational relations: Perspectives of the two generations on the older parent. *Journal of Marriage & the Family,* 1965, 27, 469–476.

Streib, G. F. and Thompson, W. E. The older person in a family context. In C. Tibbitts (Ed.), *Handbook of social gerontology.* Chicago: University of Chicago Press, 1960.

Susser, M. Aging and the field of public health. In M. W. Riley, J. W. Riley, Jr., and M. E. Johnson (Eds.), *Aging and society.* Vol. 2, *Aging and the professions.* New York: Russell Sage Foundation, 1969.

Tanner, J. M. *Growth at adolescence.* (2nd ed.) Oxford: Blackwell, Davis Co., 1962.

Aging as Exchange: A Preface to Theory

JAMES J. DOWD

The sociology of age stratification provides an important new focus, but the emphasis on age per se rather than old age does not explain why decreased social interaction occurs in the latter phase of the life cycle. According to this selection, decreased social interaction of the aged is the result of a process of exchange between the aged and society. In modern postindustrial society older people have few power resources to exchange in daily social interaction. The process of disengagement which occurs in later life is the result of a series of exchange relations in which the relative power of the aged vis-à-vis the society increasingly deteriorates. The imbalanced exchange ratio which results forces many among the aged to trade compliance, their last resource, for societal sustenance.

Theoretical development within social gerontology has been limited to date to an almost exclusive preoccupation with the theories of *disengagement* and *activity*. The absence of alternative paradigmatic development in the study of aging is especially puzzling, since both of these approaches have been found wanting empirically. The tradition of life satisfaction researches within social gerontology—life satisfaction considered to be the correlational attribute *sine qua non* of both disengagement and activity theories—is illustrative of our lack of a reliable inventory of tested propositions.

The essence of activity theory has been stated to be the "positive relationship between activity and life satisfaction." Consequently, the "greater the role loss, the lower the life satisfaction" (Lemon, Bengtson, and Peterson, 1972). These hypotheses have been tested on numerous occasions with very little, if any, of the findings achieving even the most modest consensus. (For an overview of this controversy see, for example, Adams, 1971; Alston and Dudley, 1973; Cumming and Henry, 1961; Cutler, 1973; Edwards and Klemmack, 1973; Lemon et al., 1972; Martin, 1973; Tallmer and Kutner, 1970; Tobin and Neugarten, 1961; Youmans, 1969.)

What seems so obviously necessary, then, in this stage of development of social gerontological theory is a new beginning. The disengagement/activity paradigm which has guided research for almost fifteen years must be shelved—if at least only temporarily—in order to provide the

SOURCE: Copyright 1975 by the Gerontological Society. Reprinted by permission from *The Journal of Gerontology*, Vol. 30, No. 4.

opportunity for competing views of human behavior in the later stages of the life cycle to emerge. The developing sociology of age stratification represents an important and promising contribution in this regard; its focus, however, is less *old* age than it is *age per se*. What follows is an initial attempt at theory construction—a prolegomenon—which will hopefully anticipate a larger theoretical base within social gerontology. The intent is to draw upon the research tradition known as exchange theory, particularly the later developments of this theory which detail the nexus between exchange and power, in order to reconceptualize the relationship between age and social structure as—above all else—a process of exchange.

Disengagement and Activity Theories of Aging

In order to briefly summarize the essential postulates of the disengagement and activity theories of aging, it may prove beneficial to follow the lead of Rose (1964) and first describe what the theories are not. Disengagement theory, although consistent with, is not idential to the oft-observed generalizations that, as people get older, they become increasingly removed from their associations and social functions; or, as their health deteriorates and income becomes depleted, older persons are often forced to abandon these same associations and functions. What the theory of disengagement does refer to, as detailed in Cumming and Henry's *Growing Old* (1961), is the hypothesis that

> society and the individual prepare *in advance* for the ultimate "disengagement" of incurable, incapacitating disease and death by an *inevitable, gradual, and mutually satisfying process of disengagement from society* (Rose, 1964).

The disengagement postulate stresses the fact that the decreased rates of social interaction observed in the daily lives of older persons, in addition to being functionally advantageous to both the individual and the larger society, are often initiated by the older person himself. It is often, but not necessarily, a voluntary process satisfying to the individual because of the increased personal autonomy induced by decreased expectations of normative behavior and the opportunities for leisure time; it is functional for society as the disengagement of the older person releases his formerly held roles and statuses for the eventual occupancy by younger and presumably more efficient role incumbents (cf. Atchley, 1971; Cumming, 1964; Cumming, et al., 1960; Havighurst, Neugarten, and Tobin, 1964; Tissue, 1968).

Activity theory, often proffered as an alternative explanation of social aging supposedly contradistinctive to the disengagement hypothesis, actually assumes much the same behavioral phenomena in old age as disengagement theory. Neither theory argues that old age is characterized by anything but a generalized decrease in social interaction.

Although some advocates of activity theory have designed studies relating life satisfaction with degree of social interaction as a "critical test" of the disengagement/activity debate (a finding of life satisfaction positively associated with greater degrees of social interaction taken as supportive of activity theory), most statements of activity theory do not deny the disengagement theory postulate that old age is characterized by decreased social interaction. They too take as given the assumption that, vis-à-vis younger statistical aggregates, the rate of social interaction for older persons is just not as great.

The specific difference between the two theories concerns whether the observed negative association between aging and social interaction is voluntary and preceded by psychological disengagement on the part of the individual or imposed unilaterally on the individual by the structural requirements of the society (Havighurst, 1968; Lowenthal and Boler, 1965). Supporters of an activity theory of aging posit the latter and offer as proof the positive correlation often reported between higher levels of social interaction and life satisfaction (Carp, 1968; Lipman and Smith, 1969; Maddox, 1963; Prasad, 1964).

The conclusion often drawn is that neither theory is sufficient by itself to explain all of the myriad patterns of aging, many of which require further information of a sociological and social-psychological nature to elaborate meaningfully. Disengagement theory appears hopelessly anti-quated in its functionalist insistence on the necessity of social withdrawal for "successful aging" (read morale and sense of well-being). Activity theory, on the other hand, is less an actual theory complete with defined concepts and empirically verifiable propositions than it is a well-intentioned but thoroughly value-laden response to the less-than-ebullient characterization of aging attributed to the disengagement theorists. Neither theory, however, while focusing for the most part on descriptive accounts of the peculiar relationships between social interaction and life satisfaction, attempts to offer anything but the most perfunctory of explanations for the *decreased social interaction* itself. Rather, this phenomenon is given the status of a sociological given; that is, it is treated as something requiring no additional explanation. The fact of the de-creased interaction in old age, considered in this fashion as a nonprob-lematic given, may subsequently be included in a particular test of a theory—not as the problem itself—but merely as an empirical touchstone, a datum against which the conclusions from the major analysis are later measured. For some, the reasons appear all too obvious: decreased social interaction is "simply a matter of logic and has long been known to be a fact" (Rose, 1964).

The methodological difficulty which this assumption poses for both the disengagement and activity theories of aging (and, for that matter, theory construction in social gerontology generally) is that the answer to *why* social interaction decreases in old age can be so effortlessly produced as to effectively preclude further search for possible alternative responses. The reason is simple: older persons as a statistical aggregate suffer from lower income and poorer health than their more youthful counterparts (Palmore and Whittington, 1971). Consequently, they are physically and financially unable to be "engaged" to the same degree as when they were younger. Furthermore, the loss of role partners through the death of a spouse, friend, or relation—a frequent occurrence in old age—places additional limits on the range of possible interaction available to the aged individual.

It is upon this mutually shared perspective, then, that the activity and disengagement theories are built. I contend that the common-sense logic of this assumption, while compelling in its face validity, has functioned to divert more systematic analyses into its *why* component. No one can argue convincingly against the hypothesis that failing health or lowered income tends to stifle social interaction. But is it not possible that additional factors might also be operating to produce the same phenomenon and which, going unrecognized and hence not taken explicitly into account, preclude the construction of complete theory? This, it would seem, has been the case with previous attempts at theory construction in social gerontology. They have failed to recognize that decreased social interaction in old age is a result, not only of the previously mentioned conditions of widowhood, poor health, and lowered income, but also of an intricate process of exchange between society and the aged resulting from their power-dependent relationship. This is the alternative perspective of aging developed through an exchange-theory analysis of the problem.

The remaining pages will be an attempt to elaborate this exchange view of aging, beginning with the innovative notion of social behavior as exchange offered by Homans (1961) and further developed by Blau (1964) and Emerson (1962, 1972) in their analyses of exchange and power in social life and power-dependence relations.

Exchange Theory—Introduction

While very few social gerontologists continue to seriously espouse a disengagement view of the aging process, the theoretical void left by its discreditation leaves one to wonder whether the cure has been any more tolerable than the original ailment. That the disengagement postulate was very limited in its generalizability is a well-supported criticism. In its functionalist statements concerning the *mutual* process of disengagement between society and the individual, the theory clearly failed to recognize the implicit power advantage—and the consequent threat of future reprisal—society may utilize to achieve its desired ends. The disengagement theorists tacitly accept the functionalist dictum that because a certain structure exists, it is functional. Because the aging individual is observed to give up social roles and statuses, this disengagement is posited to be mutually desired and mutually benefiting for both the individual and the society. One advantage of an exchange-theory approach to social aging in our society would be a rejection of the functionalist-disengagement notion of reciprocity and an explicit analysis of both sides of each social transaction (or exchange) as problematic (cf. Wallace, 1969).

Exchange Theory: Concepts and Propositions

The basic assumption underlying much of the research collectively known as exchange theory is that interaction between individuals or collectivities can be characterized as "attempts to maximize rewards (both material and nonmaterial) and reduce costs (both material and nonmaterial)" (Knipe, 1971). Certain patterns of interaction among social actors (either groups or individuals) are sustained over time not, as the functionalists would have it, because there exist normative expectations specifying the maintenance of such an interaction or because such a pattern of interaction fulfills some socially required need; rather, interaction is maintained because men find such interaction rewarding—for whatever reasons. In the process of seeking rewards, however—whether the rewarding activity be intrinsic to the interaction itself such as love or extrinsic to the relationship such as an exchange of recipes among gourmet cooks—*costs* are inevitably incurred. Costs refer either to the negative value or unpleasantness actually experienced in the course of obtaining a reward or to the positive value associated with an alternative course of action which is forsaken to pursue the chosen rewarding activity. In effect, therefore, all behavior entails costs even if the cost involved is only the probability of rewards that are associated with activity other than the activity presently being pursued. As in economic exchanges, the profit one derives from social exchange is equivalent to the difference between rewards minus costs (Homans, 1961). A major proposition of exchange theory is that interaction between two or more social actors will most probably be continued and positively evaluated if the actors "profit" from the interaction. In other words, actors engaged in an exchange of behavior will continue their exchange only so long as the exchange is perceived as being more rewarding than it is costly (cf. Byrne, 1971; Shaw and Costanzo, 1970).

It is often the case that one of the participants in the exchange values the rewards gained in the relationship more than the other. It is in these situations that the variable of *power* enters the analysis. The exchange theorist's view of power is that it is derived from imbalances in the social exchange. From this perspective, power is synonymous with the dependence of Actor A upon Actor B. It is based in the inability of one of the partners in the social exchange to reciprocate a rewarding behavior. As we shall see in our analysis of the exchange relationship between the aged and society, whoever "commands services others need, and who is independent of any at their command, attains power over others by making the satisfaction of their need contingent on their compliance" (Blau, 1964). The compliance of the dependent partner in the exchange thus becomes an important source of rewarding, albeit costly, behavior which he can then exchange for continued rewards from the other partner in the interaction. Thus, for Blau, much of social life is

> an intricate exchange in which every participant in interaction approaches and withdraws in patterns that add to or subtract from his store of power and prestige. Everyone accumulates, by the judicious use of favors and services, a credit of power which he then invests in subsequent transaction (Bierstedt, 1965).

Aging as a Process of Social Exchange

Having elaborated the essential concepts and propositions of the exchange paradigm, we return now to the question raised earlier, namely, How do we account for the decreased social interaction frequently observed in the daily lives of older persons in our society? Acknowledging that the tremendous impact associated with impaired health, depleted income, and/or the loss of a spouse or associate is partially responsible for this phenomenon, it is our position that an exchange analysis of the problem would enable the researcher to discover additional—and heretofore untapped—sources of variation. The perspective discussed above, and in the pages that follow, emphasizes the concept of human behavior as an exchange of more or less rewarding behaviors between two or more social actors. Intrinsic to the concept of exchange is the notion of power. As discussed above, the partner in a social exchange who is less dependent on that exchange for the gratifications he seeks enjoys a *power advantage*. Such an advantage can then be utilized to effect compliance from the exchange partner.

In the case of the aged, decreased social interaction is the eventual result of a series of exchange relationships in which the relative power of the aged vis-à-vis their social environment is gradually diminished until all that remains of their power resources is the humble capacity to comply. Where once the now-retired worker was able to exchange expertise for needed wages, the final exchange required of most older workers would be their compliance (in the form of acquiescence to mandatory retirement) as exchange for sustenance (social security, medicare, etc.).

Disengagement theory's view of the problem, while objectionable in its functionalist view of disengagement as mutually satisfying, is nonetheless accurate in its identification of the problems of aging as those caused by the frequent lack of equilibrium between the individual's readiness to withdraw from his social world and the requirements of the social structure for continuous succession of role incumbents. We can formalize this general statement on personal versus societal readiness to disengage with the constructs of exchange theory.

From Table 1, one can see that the probability of continued engagement in social relationships is principally a function of the existing power relationships between the aging role incumbent and the society. In both instances of power imbalance included in this table (cells b & c), the power advantage favors society. This is the case in modern postindustrial society with its constant demand for current knowledge and technological innovation. The skills of many aged individuals become quickly outmoded, presuming they were sufficiently adequate in the first place. As power generally accrues from the prestige associated with higher-status occupations, the supply of power resources of the older worker frequently is meager from the start; hence the bargaining position of the aged social actor upon retirement quickly deteriorates as his supply of power resources becomes depleted.

This table, then, is obviously time- and culture-bound, representing the structural realities of twentieth-century industrial society. The aged of preindustrial society, for example, were able to accumulate a much larger share of power resources than their twentieth-century counterparts (cf. Adams, 1972; Cowgill and Holmes, 1972). They engaged in exchanges, more often voluntarily than not, of expertise gained from a lifetime of living in a much more stable society for deference and prestige. With the onset of the Industrial Revolution, however, and the concomitant specialization of knowledge, the aged have had less to offer. The actual craft or trade or the more general expertise of leadership and experience which sufficed as barter in exchanges of long ago are no longer considered rewarding. Consequently, whatever power advantage they once enjoyed

TABLE 1 Constructs of Exchange Theory

Readiness to Disengage	Society	
	POSITIVE	NEGATIVE
Individual — POSITIVE	a. Power balance: Mutually satisfying exchange.	b. Power imbalance: The individual with critical expertise is forced to remain engaged.
Individual — NEGATIVE	c. Power imbalance: The individual with little critical expertise is forced to disengage.	d. Power balance: Continued role incumbency is institutionally sanctioned, e.g., religious and political leaders.

gradually shifted to others in the society. And, as the growth rate increased in exponential leaps and bounds, the relative power of the aged decreased further as the resultant surfeit of available labor decreased their range of available employment opportunities.

This interpretation is supported by recent cohort analyses that suggest the difference between older and younger age cohorts is not so much the debilitating aspects of aging *per se* that result in the differential patterns of attitude constellations, cognitive functioning, task efficiency, etc., as it is the tremendous modal differences in the cohort-defining experiences of educational level, socioeconomic status of the family of origin, and occupational aspirations. From this view, the problem of the older worker is not only his diminished skills but also the fact that he was never trained initially in skills which are currently marketable (Cutler, 1974; Glenn and Zody, 1970; Riley, 1973; Ryder, 1965).

The institutionalization of *retirement*, where the older worker was mandatorily—and often involuntarily—released from the work force, was an inevitable outcome. In order to legitimate this forceful removal as an equitable exchange, the aged were allowed a much wider range for deviant behavior; the "role" of the retired older person in our society prescribes greater freedom to deviate from normative expectations based on the work ethic. In effect, society exchanges leisure time (and the financial burden thereof) for additional positions in the work force.

The difference between this view and that of disengagement theory is not that professional social scientists like Cumming and Henry fail to recognize that older members of society are regularly discarded to make room for the younger. Rather, it is a matter of ideological commitment. Like other structural-functionalists, Cumming and Henry are unable to accept the possibility that men are *forced* to act—not because that act is normatively governed—but simply because they have no other reasonable alternative. Disengagement theorists are well aware that the disproportionately large number of young adults who are competing for the jobs that are becoming more scarce as industry automates are forcing older workers from the job market. Their particular set of lenses through which they view the world allows them only to recognize what is functional for society. That certain institutions may not be "mutually satisfying" to the individual remains, for them, a source of wonderment (cf. Cumming, 1964).

The Nature of Exchange: Power-Dependence Relations

As Emerson (1962) has noted, power resides implicitly in the Other's dependence. Dependence of actor A on Actor B (notable as D_{ab}) is both directly proportional to actor A's motivational investment in the rewards offered by actor B, and inversely proportional to the availability of those rewards to actor A from sources other than B. If both parties in the exchange relation are equally dependent upon each other (that is to say, they both are equally desirous of the rewards offered by the other and have similar outside resources from which to obtain the reward), the relation is said to be *balanced*. When the exchange relation is unbalanced, the exchange partner who is the more dependent—hence less powerful— will attempt to rebalance the relation and thereby reduce the costs he incurs from the exchange. Emerson notes that the relation can be balanced through one of four possible *balancing operations*:

(a) *Withdrawal*, i.e., motivational investment in rewards offered by the Other is reduced. This is the balancing operation clearly descriptive of Cumming and Henry's disengaged individual.

(b) *Extension of power network*, i.e., alternative sources of the rewarding behavior are cultivated. Unlike the disengagement implied in the first example, this balancing operation resembles more activity theory's pro-testations supporting the development of new roles for the aged.

(c) *Emergence of status*, i.e., motivational investment in rewards offered by the less powerful partner is increased by the more powerful partner. The exchange relation could be balanced by the emergence of status of the less powerful partner as when, for example, revivals of formerly valued skills (e.g., the knowledge of construction of pot-bellied stoves during an energy crisis) serve to increase his power resources.

(d) *Coalition formation*, i.e., the more powerful member is denied alternative sources for achieving his goals. The interesting possibility of a coalition forming between older and younger cohorts is often hypothesized as a means of equalizing the power of the wage-earning middle-aged cohorts.

Should none of these options be exercised—which has been the case with the majority of older persons in our society—the less dependent and therefore more powerful participants in the relation (i.e., the middle-aged and young adult cohorts) are able to establish a rate of exchange favorable to them. The danger for the less powerful partner—the aged— is that once established, this unbalanced exchange rate becomes institu-tionalized and thereby provides a normative basis for future unbalanced exchanges (cf. Martin, 1971). As for the claims that the aged are not really powerless or that the relation between the larger society and the aged is one of balance, the evidence clearly indicates otherwise (Blau, 1973; Clark, 1972).

Positing, then, that the aged as a group *are* less powerful than younger age cohorts in our society, the next question to be answered concerns the actual use of power. In Emerson's (1972) scheme, power is not a discrete quantity of stuff which can be used or not used voluntarily or only at certain times. Rather, to have power is to use it. If A has a power advantage in his exchange relation with B, and if B has additional resources potentially rewarding to A, "A's use of power will increase, cutting further into B's resources, until its use is offset by incurred or anticipated costs to A." Only if the relation is balanced, where $P_{ab} = D_{ba}$ and $P_{ba} = D_{ab}$, will an increased use of power be unlikely.

The relationship between the aged and society, previously defined as an unbalanced exchange relation, is consequently one in which power is being exercised. Of course, the power being utilized in this case is not the power afforded by a superior military force or technological expertise; rather, it is the economic and social dependence of the elderly— legitimated by persistent social norms that specify many adult behaviors as inappropriate for those who have reached a certain age—which is the source of society's power. The younger worker who is promoted into a position left vacant by the retirement of its former occupant certainly does not perceive that power has been utilized in his behalf or that the retired role incumbent was in any way in competition with him. Yet we would only have to consider the probable sequence of events that would result should that older worker have refused to leave his particular machine or office to retire. Because most individuals have sufficiently internalized societal norms specifying institutions such as retirement as legitimate, the specter of society's sanctioning power is rarely realized. Yet in the individual relations between the aged and other groups in society, power *is* being used.

Many of these exchange relations between the aged and other age groups within society can be seen as a special case of the balancing operation described above as coalition formation. Blau (1964) notes that in any complex organization with given limited resources,

> it is only possible for management to balance one exchange relationship by unbalancing others. As one group gains a relative advantage, other groups are roused into opposition.

It is important, then, in attempting to understand the exchange between management and the older worker, we include in the analysis a consideration of the relationship between management and the remainder of the work force. Younger workers exchange their labor for wages and the implicit promise of job security and promotions. However, as the older worker remains on the job, he is blocking this path of career mobility for younger work cohorts. Hence the forced retirement of older workers or the decision of employers to divert more monies into increased wages than into employee pension plans reflect the changes within formal organizations that, Blau (1964) argues,

> tend to take a dialectical form as the intermittent refocusing of conflict and consensus is accompanied by realignment of internal exchange relationships.

Aging and the Decline of Power

Prerequisite to the exercise of power, however, is the possession of sufficient power resources. Resources are essentially anything which the exchange partner perceives as rewarding and which consequently renders him susceptible to social influence. Examples of power resources include money, knowledge, persuasiveness, and social position.

A frequent exchange entered into by most older people is the exchange of his position in the labor force for the promise of economic and medical sustenance in the form of social security and medicare. Or, the widowed woman living with her married children may be required to exchange compliance or approval for her room and board. The possible exchange situations are of infinite variety but, in general, the types of rewards (or power resources) are shown in Table 2.

From an exchange-theory perspective, then, the problems of aging are essentially problems of *decreasing power resources*. The aged have very little to exchange which is of any instrumental value. What skills they once had are often outmoded; the skills which remain can often be provided more efficiently and with less cost by others. Since the aged have no specific benefit—or power resource—to offer their exchange partner, they typically have no alternative but to offer some generally available response which is universally experienced as rewarding. In Blau's analysis of exchange and power, there appear to be four such generalized power resources: money, approval, esteem or respect, and compliance.

Money, even if the older retiree was able to afford parting with it, is "clearly inappropriate as a means of repaying diffuse social obligations" (Mulkay, 1971). A dinner invitation can hardly be repaid with a personal check. Approval would be an effective power resource were it not for the fact that approval is too plentiful and easy to obtain to be sufficiently rewarding. Consequently, esteem and compliance are the resources that generally tend to be utilized as social currency in exchange relations. Since esteem is the less costly of the two, it is the resource which is exchanged first. The older worker may attempt to exchange esteem for a lightened workload or his supervisor's tolerance of his decreased efficiency. However, esteem is a commodity the value of which decreases quickly in subsequent exchanges. Consequently, in exchanges of longer duration it is, as Mulkay (1971) indicates, "unlikely to prove an adequate incentive for those making particularly valuable contributions to the group." As a result, those exchange partners who are receiving valued benefits are obliged to reciprocate in some new and equally rewarding manner. It is at this stage that compliance, a very costly commodity, enters into the exchange ratio.

TABLE 2 Types of Rewards (or Power Resources)

	Intrinsic	Extrinsic	Unilateral
Spontaneous evaluation	Personal attraction	Social approval	Respect/ prestige
Calculated action	Social acceptance	Instrumental services	Compliance/ power

Source: From *Exchange and Power in Social Life* by P. M. Blau. Copyright © 1964 by John Wiley & Sons, Inc. Reprinted by permission of John Wiley & Sons, Inc.

When the esteem offered by the older worker no longer is sufficiently rewarding, he must resort to compliance, as when, for example, the older executive is forced to comply with management's wishes for him to "step down" to a less prestigious and responsible position or to suffer a decrease in salary. Eventually, the older worker must comply with management's demands for his resignation in the guise of retirement. Over the years, as this scenario has been repeated countless times, the process has become routinized, institutionalized, and legitimated. Indeed, the actual event known as retirement more accurately refers to a series of events—or exchange relations—in which the power advantage favors the employer:

> In this exchange relationship . . . the employee is more dependent than is the employer and accordingly more effectively controlled by the threat of negative sanctions (Mulkay, 1971).

Disengagement as Exchange

One answer, therefore, to why people disengage may not be because it is mutually satisfying for themselves and society to do so but rather because in the exchange relation between the aged and society, society enjoys a distinct power advantage. As to the question of how this unbalanced exchange relation evolved with society as the more powerful partner, the answer is that by being in the enviable position of "providing unilateral benefits to others (read the aged), . . . (society) accumulates a capital of willing compliance on which he can draw whenever it is to his interest to impose his will" (Blau, 1964).

Due to this legitimating function of social norms, the behavior of older persons is governed and restricted further by the sanctioning power of other older persons themselves. The older person who restricts his social life for fear of what his acquaintances would think is actually exchanging his compliance to their standards of acceptable conduct for their social approval. This exchange is interesting because it illustrates the double bind less powerful groups face when power is supported by social norms—they suffer possible reprisal not only from the group which possesses the power but also from within the boundaries of their own group as well. Mulkay (1971) explains:

> As power becomes mediated through legitimating norms, the processes of exchange involved become increasingly complex and indirect. Before power has been recognized as legitimate there is a relatively direct exchange between persons of high and low status. Those with high status provide valuable services while those with low status respond with esteem and compliance. Once power is supported by social norms, however, a new type of transaction develops among subordinates. For subordinates now receive approval from their peers, as well as from their leaders, for complying with the directives of those in authority. The act of compliance is no longer solely a means of rewarding one's superiors for valued services; it is also a request for approval from the collectivity at large. These transactions with peers introduce additional pressures for compliance. For they constrain individuals inclined to resist

particular directives to submit rather than forego the approval of their colleagues.

The pressure from his peers, together with the tremendous costs incurred by remaining engaged, offers a possible explanation of why some older persons seemed resigned to, even welcome, the opportunity to disengage. Because of their limited power resources, the costs of remaining engaged—that is, the costs in compliance and self-respect—steadily increase. Finally the point is reached beyond which additional costs become prohibitive. This is the phenomenon of disengagement.

It has been noted that disengagement from certain social institutions is inversely related to disengagement from other institutions (Carp, 1968). So, for example, the retired couple who interact less with their former friends and acquaintances often increase their frequency of interaction with their family. The explanation offered by Carp is that disengagement from either family or other significant reference or membership groups requires an increased dependence on the group(s) remaining. This very dependence, however, places the aged family member in another unbalanced exchange relationship with his increased dependence serving to again limit his potential power in the relationship.

A recent study of retirees in France lends support to this analysis. Focusing on the changes in family relationships resulting from retirement, the authors posit a direct relationship between power resources and degree of autonomy within the family:

> We should observe that the greater the retiree's economic and cultural patrimony to transmit to his children, the more he will actualize an organic and dominating familial solidarity. A situation of dispossession would lead him to contract organically solid familial exchanges, but which express a relation of dependence to the family. A medium level of resources would lead the retiree to maintain an autonomous relation with his family (Guillemard and Lenoir, 1974).

The cycle of exchange of esteem followed by compliance for the rewards of social acceptance, human interaction, and the satisfaction of his other human needs is repeated, following closely the pattern of exchange of the older worker (cf. Nord, 1969). The observations of Blau (1973) illustrate this point:

> The appearance of "mellowness" in many older people is a tactic to win acceptance and support. To protest their marginality would only alienate others, and this the person without any socially useful role cannot do because he lacks the opportunities for finding alternative social resources to replace his remaining social ties.

Propositions

Two basic propositions can be drawn from this exchange theory analysis of aging in contemporary industrial society. From a macrosocietal perspective, it can be observed that the amount of power resources possessed by the aged relative to other age strata is inversely related to the degree of societal modernization. Unlike the aged in more traditional societies, older people in industrialized societies have precious few power resources to exchange in daily social interaction. The net effect is an increased dependence upon others and the concomitant necessity to comply to their wishes. Mandatory retirement as a social policy is the most obvious result of this lack of power resources and consequent lack of power among the aged. A correlated hypothesis, stating an inverse relationship between societal modernization and status of the aged, has recently been tested and supported by various researchers (Palmore and Whittington, 1971; Cowgill and Holmes, 1972; Press and McKool, 1972; Bengtson, Dowd, and Smith, 1975).

The second proposition, reflecting a more micro-orientation, posits a curvilinear relationship between chronological age and the degree of power resources. Possession of power resources tends to be limited in youth, increasing through late middle age, and decreasing sharply in old age. More than any other social event, the phenomenon of retirement is directly related with the precipitous decline of power resources beyond middle age. A previous analysis by Abarbanel (1974) of ethnographic data from forty-seven societies supports the notion of a curvilinear relationship between age and control of power resources. Abarbanel found that control over most resources began before or immediately after marriage; peaked at the time termed middle family phase, that is, when the children are adolescents and the family labor force is most productive; and declined either in the latter part of the middle phase or in the late phase of the family cycle, when children marry and leave home. However, in terms of control of positions of political and spiritual leadership, Abarbanel reports that the peak control in preindustrial nonurban societies is not reached until the late family phase.

The relationship stated here between age and power resources reflects current realities and need not, therefore, be characteristic of aging in the future. Several trends, if continued, may anticipate a much less drastic decline in power resources in old age. Higher levels of education predicted for future aged cohorts, for example, would constitute a power resource of considerable significance. So, too, the growing public concern over pension funds and social security financing may lead to legislation promoting greater economic autonomy of older persons through regulated pension plans, increased social security benefits and, even, the reemployment of the older worker in a part-time capacity. The point is that there is nothing inherent in the aging process itself that necessitates a decline in individual power resources. The nature and degree of power resources possessed by any group of older persons is a function of shared cohort experience in addition to individual attributes.

The relationship between chronological age and possession of power resources must be further specified as to individual socioeconomic status and ethnicity. Those fortunate enough to possess considerable economic capital beyond retirement possess a power resource of undeniable importance. Socioeconomic status (SES) constitutes, in effect, a critical control variable in the relationship between age and power resources. The nature of the relationship, except in those rare cases of extreme wealth, does not change markedly with increased SES; it is more a case that, within a particular age stratum, the higher SES individuals will generally possess the greater power resources. Across age strata, however, the curvilinear relationship will tend to hold. The effect of SES is represented in Figure 1.

Summary and Conclusions

Exchange theory is a unique perspective of human behavior, one which views social interaction as basically an exchange of rewards between two social actors, be they individuals or groups of individuals. Similar to the economic transactions of, say, currency for either goods or services, it remains true in social exchange that "money talks." Whichever party in the exchange relation possesses the greater degree of social power (as with money) is the party which is able to control the rate of exchange and the distribution of rewards, or profits, among the parties to the exchange. So, unlike both disengagement and activity theories, an exchange theory of aging predicts outcomes of variable interaction and level of engage-

Figure 1 **Hypothesized relationship between control of power resources and age, within categories of socioeconomic status.**

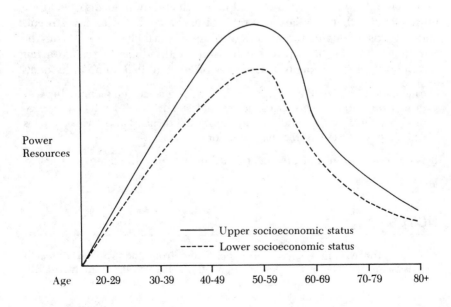

ment in old age depending upon the relative power of the individual older person or group of older persons vis-a-vis the source of the rewarding interaction, society.

Activity theory assumes the need for continued involvement throughout life; disengagement theory assumes that decline in involvement may be a phenomenon mutually desired by both individual and society. Exchange theory assumes neither but posits that the degree of engagement in old age is an empirical question, an outcome of a specific exchange relationship between an individual or group of individuals and the society in which the more powerful exchange partner dictates the terms of the relationship.

A serious limitation of the exchange approach summarized here has been recognized by Emerson (1972) as an inability to predict which of the four balancing operations (withdrawal, network extension, status-giving, or coalition formation) will be adopted at any one time. Although coalition formation appears to be the most potent alternative (the possibility of the aged coalescing with younger age groups is indeed intriguing, albeit improbable), the aged themselves have yet to develop any extensive awareness of their common social and economic plight, which is a necessary prerequisite to entering into coalitions. The aged have yet to display the emotional response to distributive injustice that Homans (1961) has so carefully operationalized as "anger."

Yet the fact that distributive justice is not being realized in the daily lives of many older persons is readily apparent. After a lifetime of investment in the forms of career, family, reputation, community service, etc., the aged are forced to endure the ignominy of prestige loss, social and economic discrimination, poverty-level subsistence, and social isolation. Blau (1964) acknowledges that although common norms develop in most societies that stipulate fair rates of exchange between investments and rewards, the going rates in many groups nevertheless depart from the fair rates, "making it impossible for some individuals to realize a fair return on their investments." Blau goes on to state that some individuals

> cannot even realize the *going* rate in their exchange transactions because factors other than these social norms and standards also affect exchange processes, notably the conditions of supply and demand in particular groups and the power relations that have developed.

It is our contention that this has been the case with the aged.

NOTES

Support for writing the present paper came from the Applied Research Division of the National Science Foundation's RANN Program (#GI-ERP-03496) and the 1907 Foundation, New York, NY. The author wishes to thank

Vern L. Bengtson and Pauline K. Ragan for their criticisms and comments on a preliminary draft of this paper. Any remaining errors of inference or interpretation are the author's sole responsibility.

REFERENCES

Abarbanel, J. S. Prestige of the aged and their control over resources: A cross-cultural analysis. Paper presented at 1974 annual meeting of the Gerontological Society (Portland).

Adams, D. L. Correlates of satisfaction among the elderly. *Gerontologist*, 1971, *11*, 64–68.

Adams, F. M. The role of old people in Santo Tomas, Mazaltepec. In D. O. Cowgill and L. D. Holmes (Eds.), *Aging and modernization*. Appleton-Century-Crofts, New York, 1972.

Alston, J. P., and Dudley, C. J. Age, occupation, and life satisfaction. *Gerontologist*, 1973, *13*, 58–61.

Atchley, R. C. Disengagement among professors. *Journal of Gerontology*, 1971, *26*, 476–480.

Bengtson, V. L., Dowd, J. J., and Smith, D. H. Modernization, modernity and perceptions of aging: A cross-cultural study. *Journal of Gerontology*, 1975, *30*, 688–695.

Bierstedt, R. Review of Blau's exchange and power in social life. *American Sociological Review*, 1965, *30*, 789–790.

Blau, P. M. *Exchange and power in social life*. John Wiley & Sons, New York, 1964.

Blau, Z. S. *Old age in a changing society*. New Viewpoints, New York, 1973.

Byrne, J. J. Systematic analysis and exchange theory: A synthesis. *Pacific Sociological Review*, 1971, *14*, 137–146.

Carp, F. M. Some components of disengagement. *Journal of Gerontology*, 1968, *23*, 382–386.

Clark, M. Cultural values and dependency in later life. In D. O. Cowgill and L. Holmes (Eds.), *Aging and modernization*. Appleton-Century-Crofts, New York, 1972.

Cowgill, D. O., and Holmes, L. D. (Eds.) *Aging and modernization*. Appleton-Century-Crofts, New York, 1972.

Cumming, E. New thoughts on old age. In R. Kastenbaum (Ed.), *New thoughts on old age*. Springer, New York, 1964.

Cumming, E., Dean, L. R., Newell, D. S., and McCaffrey, I. Disengagement: A tentative theory of aging. *Sociometry*, 1960, *23*, 23–25.

Cumming, E., and Henry, W. E. *Growing old: The process of disengagement*. Basic Books, New York, 1961.

Cutler, N. E. Aging and generations in politics: The conflict of explanations and inference. In A. R. Wilcox (Ed.), *Public opinion and political attitudes*. Wiley, New York, 1974.

Cutler, S. J. Voluntary association participation and life satisfaction: A cautionary note. *Journal of Gerontology*, 1973, *28*, 96–100.

Edwards, J. N., and Klemmack, D. L. Correlates of life satisfaction: A reexamination. *Journal of Gerontology*, 1973, *28*, 497–502.

Emerson, R. M. Power-dependence relations. *American Sociological Review*, 1962, *27*, 31–41.

Emerson, R. M. Exchange theory, Parts 1 & 2. In J. Berger, M. Zelditch, and B. Anderson (Eds.), *Sociological theories in progress*, Vol. II. Houghton Mifflin, Boston, 1972.

Glenn, N. D., and Zody, R. Cohort analysis with national survey data. *Gerontologist*, 1970, *10*, 233–240.

Guillemard, A. M., and Lenoir, R. *Retraite et échange social*. Centre d'Etude des Mouvements Sociaux, Paris, 1974.

Havighurst, R. J. Personality and patterns of aging. *Gerontologist*, 1968, *8*, 20–33.

Havighurst, R. J., Neugarten, B. L., and Tobin, S. S. Disengagement, personality, and life satisfaction in the later years. In P. From Hanson (Ed.), *Age with a future*. Munksgaard, Copenhagen, 1964.

Homans, G. C. *Social behavior: Its elementary forms*. Harcourt, Brace & World, New York, 1961.

Knipe, E. E. Attraction and exchange: Some temporal considerations. Paper presented at annual meeting of the Southern Sociological Society, Atlanta, 1971.

Lemon, B. W., Bengtson, V. L., and Peterson, J. A. An exploration of the activity theory of aging: Activity types and life satisfaction among in-movers to a retirement community. *Journal of Gerontology*, 1972, *27*, 511–523.

Lipman, A., and Smith, K. J. Functionality of disengagement in old age. *Journal of Gerontology*, 1969, *23*, 517–521.

Lowenthal, M. F., and Boler, D. Voluntary versus involuntary social withdrawal. *Journal of Gerontology*, 1965, *20*, 363–371.

Maddox, G. L. Activity and morale: A longitudinal study of selected elderly subjects. *Social Forces*, 1963, *42*, 195–204.

Martin, R. The concept of power: A critical defence. *British Journal of Sociology*, 1971, *22*, 240–257.

Martin, W. C. Activity and disengagement: Life satisfaction of in-movers into a retirement community. *Gerontologist*, 1973, *13*, 224–227.

Mulkay, M. J. *Functionalism, exchange, and theoretical strategy*. Schocken, New York, 1971.

Nord, W. R. Social exchange theory: An integrative approach to social conformity. *Psychological Bulletin*, 1969, *71*, 174–208.

Palmore, E., and Whittington, F. Trends in the relative status of the aged. *Social Forces*, 1971, *50*, 84–91.

Prasad, S. B. The retirement postulate of disengagement theory. *Gerontologist*, 1964, *4*, 20–23.

Press, I., and McKool, M., Jr. Social structure and status of the aged: Toward some valid cross-cultural generalizations. *Aging & Human Development*, 1972, *3*, 297–306.

Riley, M. W. Aging and cohort succession: Interpretations and misinterpretations. *Public Opinion Quarterly*, 1973, *37*, 35–49.

Rose, A. A current theoretical issue in social gerontology. *Gerontologist*, 1964, *4*, 46–50.

Ryder, N. B. The cohort as a concept in the study of social change. *American Sociological Review*, 1965, *30*, 843–861.

Shaw, M. E., and Costanzo, P. R. Theories of social psychology. McGraw-Hill, New York, 1970.

Tallmer, M., and Kutner, B. Disengagement and morale. *Gerontologist*, 1970, *10*, 317–320.

Tissue, T. L. A Guttman scale of disengagement potential. *Journal of Gerontology*, 1968, *23*, 513–516.

Tobin, S. S., and Neugarten, B. L. Life satisfaction and social interaction in aging. *Journal of Gerontology*, 1961, *16*, 344–346.

Wallace, W. L. Sociological theory. Aldine, Chicago, 1969.

Youmans, E. G. Some perspectives on disengagement theory. *Gerontologist*, 1969, *9*, 254–258.

3

Stereotypes of Aging

Research supports the notion that our society has a well-developed mythology regarding aging. Many people believe that the aged are isolated and lonely, that they have no interest in or capacity for sexual relations, that they cannot work as effectively as younger workers, and that they are set in their ways and unable to change (Palmore, 1977, p. 315).

Sources of Age Stereotypes

It is difficult to pinpoint the source of these stereotypes. Some writers have asserted that the phrasing of the questions in surveys affects the quality of the answers, making them overly negative. Asking people to agree or disagree with negative statements about old people gives respondents no opportunity to express positive opinions (Brubaker and Powers, 1976).

Butler (1969) believes these stereotypes have deeper roots. He suggests that the tendency to perceive aging in a negative fashion reflects a deep-seated uneasiness, a distaste for growing old, on the part of the middle-aged. These feelings arise partly from a fear of becoming powerless or useless, partly from a fear of becoming overburdened by the economically dependent part of the population, both the very young and the very old. Unfortunately, these negative feelings sometimes take the form of overt discrimination against the aged. Butler refers to age discrimination as "ageism," an insidious form of bigotry to which we must become alerted.

The Perpetuation of Age Stereotypes

While the sources of age stereotypes remain obscure, the means by which they are perpetuated are more readily identifiable. Television advertisements tell us how to hide "middle-aged spread" by wearing the proper girdle, or how to erase wrinkles and bags under the eyes through one easy application of facial cream. Magazine ads cry, "Why let ugly age spots make you look older than you really are?" "You're too young to look old." "You're not getting older, you're getting better." Even the lyrics to a popular song plaintively ask, "Will you still need me, will you still feed me, when I'm sixty-four?" Nearly everything we see in the media conveys the message that youth is beautiful, while wrinkles, gray hair, and irregularity must be eradicated along with spots on our glassware and rings around our collars. The first article, by Hess, suggests two reasons why the media portray the aged either negatively or not at all. First, the elderly are poor consumers because of low incomes, uncertainty about the future, and an unwillingness to invest in products they may not live long enough to enjoy. Second, old people are "poor copy," reminding the audience of role loss, deprivations, and death. In the second article, Francher provides a systematic analysis of the ways various age groups are portrayed in a random sample of television commercials.

Research on Stereotypes

A desire to obtain a scientific assessment of age stereotypes prompted the National Council on Aging (1975) to conduct a survey to determine how Americans as a whole perceive the aged, how the aged regard themselves, and how accurate these perceptions are. Participants in the study were men and women of all ages. The findings from the poll showed that young and old alike have negative perceptions of old age. Both groups believed that most older people were in poor health, did not have enough money to live on, were often lonely, did not have enough to do to keep busy, led sedentary lives, and spent most of their time in private and isolated activities. What was striking in the responses of those aged sixty-five or older was that while they agreed with the younger respondents that there were problems for "most people over sixty-five," they didn't see them as problems for themselves. They considered themselves exceptions. Some examples of findings from the poll indicate these discrepancies:

- Fifty percent of all respondents thought "poor health" a problem for the aging, but only 21 percent of older people cited it as a personal problem.
- Sixty-two percent of all respondents thought "not having enough money to live on" a problem for the aging, but only 15 percent of the elderly found it a personal problem.
- Sixty-seven percent of all respondents thought that most

people over sixty-five spend a lot of time watching television; only 35 percent of the older respondents reported doing so.

Thus the aged along with other Americans have accepted the negative stereotypes of aging in spite of contradictory personal experiences.

A variety of other studies have clearly shown that most of these beliefs regarding aging are false (Palmore, 1977). About two-thirds of the aged say they are never or hardly ever lonely, and most older people have frequent contact with close relatives, although this varies from area to area. In addition, they spend time socializing with friends, attending church or synagogue, and participating in organizational activities. Research by Masters and Johnson (1966) has shown that the capacity for satisfying sexual relations can continue for people into their seventies and eighties. The article by Rubin discusses some of the research on sexuality in later life, as well as the potentially harmful effects of the "sexless older years" stereotype.

Studies of older workers have shown that they perform as well or better than younger workers on most measures and that they have less job turnover, fewer accidents, and less absenteeism (Riley and Foner, 1968). Further, while the aged may become somewhat more fixed in their attitudes, most older people do change and adapt to major events such as retirement, widowhood, children leaving home, and chronic and acute illness.

Stereotypes of the aged are potentially harmful, because they induce anxiety about the aging process. They devalue aging and its associated characteristics and do not provide positive role models for older people. If these stereotypes become manifested in discrimination, then they are even more damaging. It is important for everyone to be aware of age stereotypes around them and to be capable of separating myth from reality.

REFERENCES

Brubaker, Timothy, and Edward Powers. 1976. The stereotype of "old": A review and alternative approach. *Journal of Gerontology* 31:441–447.

Butler, Robert. 1969. Ageism—another form of bigotry. *Gerontologist* 9:243–246.

Masters, William, and Virginia Johnson. 1969. *Human sexual response*. Boston: Little, Brown.

1975. Myths and realities of life for older Americans. *Myths and Realities: Perspectives on Aging*. Washington, D.C.: National Council on Aging.

Palmore, Erdman. 1977. Facts on aging: A short quiz. *Gerontologist* 17:315–320.

Riley, Matilda White, and Anne Foner. 1968. *Aging and society*. New York: Russell Sage.

Stereotypes of the Aged

BETH B. HESS

There are many stereotypes of older people which are not substantiated by research, yet as a society we tend to believe that these myths are true. It is important to examine the processes of communication to determine what and how information about old age is conveyed. While television and radio perform the positive service of keeping the aged informed, they do not program for old people, because broadcasters are dependent upon advertising revenues. Advertisers are not indifferent to the aged, but the elderly are not a primary market for many products. Those commercials that are aimed at older people usually promote products designed to minimize the effects of aging. The important question is whether these media portrayals of the aged become a self-fulfilling prophecy, limiting the adaptive capacities of the aged.

My qualifications as an expert on aging come from a three-year total immersion in the social science research literature as a member of the study group assembled at Rutgers–the State University under the direction of Matilda White Riley. Our first task was to assess the state of knowledge regarding aging and old people, to which end I searched out, read, abstracted, and evaluated the methodological reliability of hundreds of research papers in psychology and sociology dating from roughly 1950 to the present. This information was collated, codified, analyzed, and organized along with demographic, physiological, and medical data into Volume One of *Aging and Society: An Inventory of Research Findings*, by Matilda White Riley, Anne Foner, and associates.[1]

Having thus worked our way through thousands of pages of research, and having produced a volume of almost six hundred pages of carefully weighed and interpreted "findings," we were nonetheless distressed at how very little one could say for certain about any aspect of aging or the lives of old people today. Most studies were of limited value, the findings contradictory, the methodology faulty, and knowledge gaps abysmal. While the broad demographic data were reliable, comparisons were often more complex than they appeared, while reliance upon cross-sectional studies led to erroneous conclusions. More important, what we did find out about America's elderly frequently contradicted what we thought we knew about old people as a matter of common sense.

For instance, in our earlier, taken-for-granted world, old people were

SOURCE: Excerpted from "Stereotypes of the Aged" by Beth Hess in *Journal of Communication*, Vol. 24, No. 4. Copyright © 1974 by The Annenberg School of Communications. All rights reserved.

relatively unproductive workers, suffered precipitous declines in intelligence, were emotional and financial drags on their adult children, preferred to and actually did in large numbers live with their children, tended to be removed from active participation in the society, tended to have lost sexual capacities, were wracked by despair and anxieties, and tended to be ultimately dumped by uncaring kin into public institutions. In fact:

- Old people remaining in the labor force generally perform at comparable levels to younger workers; often better in tasks requiring experience, though somewhat poorer in those depending upon speed (10, p. 462 ff.).
- Declines in intelligence which are marked in cross-sectional data appear less so in longitudinal studies (10, p. 256 ff).
- Old people are as likely as not to have given help to adult children, while slightly more than one-third report receiving occasional gifts of money from their children (10, p. 542).
- Approximately 80 percent of men and women over sixty-five, in 1965, were living as heads of households or as wives of the head. Of the remainder, only 12 percent lived with their children, and only 4 percent in institutions (10, pp. 167, 172, 174). However, of those with living children, over one-fourth did live in the same household, while over 80 percent lived within one hour's distance from the nearest child (10, p. 169).
- While frequency of sexual intercourse declines with age (from age twenty on), many old people remain sexually active into their seventies, depending upon the availability of partners and willingness to utilize other outlets (10, p. 258 ff).
- Voting rates, in 1965, for persons seventy-five and over were *higher* than for those aged twenty-one to twenty-four (10, p. 461).
- Self-evaluations are positive across a range of traits, including body image (10, p. 290 ff).
- Institutionalization is typically a *last* resort for the families of the aged, and is usually preceded by a shift in the old person's ability to function or in the capacities of others to care for him or her (10, p. 583 ff).

Although the condition of the aged *is* indeed more deprived than that of younger cohorts, or even of the elderly themselves at earlier life stages, many negative stereotypes are clearly not supported by the research data.[2] That such myths (both positive and negative) are frequently shared by old people leads us to examine the process of communication: how and what information or misinformation about old age is conveyed and received by all age groups?

. . . .

With respect to entertainment, television per se, perhaps regardless of content, has been of invaluable service to old people. In an article addressed to retired persons, Davis (9) notes that television personalities can become substitutes for individuals no longer available to the viewer on a daily face-to-face basis, and that the afternoon soap operas "bring people into their lives." Television permits the old person, especially those who live alone, to maintain the illusion of being in a populated world, and to this extent must reduce feelings of isolation. Radio, similarly, brings the sound of life into an otherwise empty room.[3]

Regarding the dissemination of information, again, radio and television certainly keep the aged informed on what's happening to everyone else. But it is precisely information about old people themselves which we are concerned with in this paper, and here the track record is spotty. As Schramm (14) pointed out a few years ago (and little seems to have changed since), the media have overlooked the very fact of the emergence of old people as a major segment of the population, with as varied a range of characteristics as any age group. Indeed, the myths and stereotypes fail to capture the reality of old age in America precisely because there is no monolithic "aged" or any one successful way to age. Possibly, as Tuchman (17) notes, that which goes against common sense is simply not perceived as "fact" and the newsperson is loath to purvey it.

However, advertisers are by no means indifferent to those who form a large share of the audience for the early evening newscasts. Commercials for hair darkeners, laxatives, denture adhesives, and Geritol—products designed to minimize the effects of normal aging—are regularly seen with the early-evening newscasts.[4]

If we now attempt to "explain" media performance in the terms of our conceptual model,* clearly [those] most dependent upon advertising revenues cannot be expected to program for and about old people. The elderly are first of all "poor consumers" because of their low incomes, uncertainty about the future, and unwillingness to invest in products they may not live long enough to enjoy fully.[5] Second, old people are "poor copy": they remind us of role loss, deprivations, and ultimate demise, none of which is a helpful product association.

It is to the written mass media, more expensive and more difficult to procure, that young and old alike must turn for the kind of knowledge which would correct the stereotypes. Newsweeklies, *Reader's Digest*, women's magazines, and the "family-oriented" periodicals are important, if also infrequent, purveyors of up-to-date information on aging, while the *New York Times Magazine* (2, 4, 5) had three such articles within the space of a few months (on sexuality, longevity, and nursing homes). However, to convey a full range of information on a particular segment of the population often requires the production of a specialized periodical, which also serves an isolation-reducing, solidarity-enhancing function

---

Editor's note: The "conceptual model" refers to the relationship between the media, advertisers, and the audience.

(e.g., *Ebony* or *Ms.*), with emphasis on successful role models. The journal *Modern Maturity,* for the several million members of the American Association of Retired Persons (primarily teachers), is one such resource. The economics of mass distribution of specialized periodicals may effectively inhibit the emergence of a more broad-based, newsstand-type publication.

In the larger context, [advertisers] operate in a society in which youthfulness is the valued state of being, in which wrinkles, gray hair, lack of zap, and irregularity must be eradicated along with spotty glassware, grimy sinks, and dirty floors. Since we have never accepted gracefully the physical changes of middle age, how can the transition to old age be anything but stressful? And where are role models who could demonstrate avenues of successful aging? This question becomes crucial when we remember that today's old people are the first to survive in large numbers into an old age of retirement from work and family roles, in fair health, and with a good deal of confidence in their capacities for coping. Because this is a "new" stage in life, there are few models to follow and few institutionalized norms to guide them. Many, too, are inhibited in their enjoyment of leisure by the lingering effects of the work ethic: if productivity is good, nonproductiveness must be somehow sinful.

Turning now to the specific constraints on the old person as receiver of messages, we have already noted (a) the reliance upon and high consumption of media output, and (b) the unique characteristics of today's elderly. The salient variable, however, may be the degree of reference group imbeddedness. That is, a crucial condition for the maintenance of mythical representations is the *relative* structural isolation of the elderly. (Note "relative," since one myth concerns the abandonment of the aged by uncaring children, and another features grandma as a perpetual busybody.) Many exigencies of aging are at work here: death of spouse and friends, retirement and consequent loss of workplace contacts, declining vigor, lowered incomes, and higher probability of chronic illness. Old people are less likely than younger ones, or than themselves at younger ages, to be involved in ongoing webs of primary relationships; consequently they are more likely to receive media messages without the opportunity to test the validity of such inputs through conversation with others. Thus the "social construction of reality," whereby interacting individuals build a world of meaning which makes sense of their separate experiences and allows a degree of mastery over the environment, becomes more problematical for old people (or, indeed, for any isolated members of the society) than for those in a number of primary groups. We do know that the old people most cut off from daily intimate relationships are likely to have mental and physical disabilities, low self-esteem, high suicide rates, and so on (1, 6, 10, 15, 16). It is, however, often difficult to disentangle cause and effect: the isolation may be a consequence of impairment; or both isolation and impairment may be the consequence of absolute and relative poverty.[6]

. . . .

Clearly, these individuals [the aged, who are the media audience] know *they* are not like the stereotyped version of an old person, yet how is this cognitive dissonance resolved? Many, of course, do not perceive themselves as "old." It seems plausible, though I know of no conclusive study, that for others the phenomenon of "pluralistic ignorance" is operative, "the pattern in which individual members of a group *assume* that they are virtually alone in holding the social attitudes and expectations they do, all unknowing that others privately share them. This is a frequently observed condition of a group which is so organized that mutual observability among its members is slight" (7, p. 337). Pluralistic ignorance, complemented by the process of the self-fulfilling prophecy, suggests that some old people will come to behave in the stereotyped manner, while others believe that everyone else does. Either way, the stereotype remains untested. For example, Isadore Rubin (13) has written extensively on what he sees as the harmful self-fulfilling effect of the general belief that old age brings loss of sexual capacity. In a similar fashion, other myths may be limiting the adaptive capacities of the aged.

Figure 1 Family status of the elderly

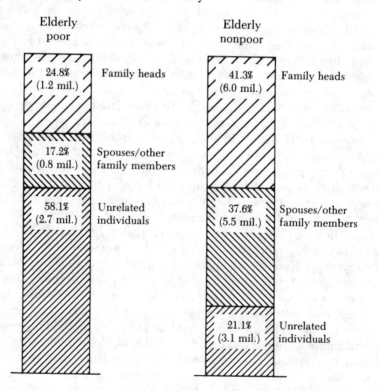

Elderly poor

24.8% (1.2 mil.)	Family heads
17.2% (0.8 mil.)	Spouses/other family members
58.1% (2.7 mil.)	Unrelated individuals

Elderly nonpoor

41.3% (6.0 mil.)	Family heads
37.6% (5.5 mil.)	Spouses/other family members
21.1% (3.1 mil.)	Unrelated individuals

In the absence of high levels of interpersonal contact, the burden of information dissemination falls upon the media.

Finally, what of [those] who are not elderly? If old age is as anxiety-producing as the attempts to suppress its manifestations indicate, it is doubtful that many younger persons would willingly expose themselves to media presentations of old age even when the tone is up-beat.[7] We are unlikely to want to find out more about what we refuse even to think of. More crucial, perhaps, is that the relative isolation of the elderly is also the relative isolation of other age groups from the elderly. Not that three-generation households were ever a typical form in the United States (another myth), but it was likely that relatives lived in close proximity and that intergenerational contacts were daily occurrences, even between nonkin. Young persons could hardly avoid learning by observation what lay ahead; anticipatory socialization was built into everyday life.

Without detailing the internecine conflict among sociologists of the family concerning the nature of contemporary intergenerational exchanges, the data show that while parent and grandparent generations are engaged in mutual gift- and service-giving, visit frequently, and feel psychologically close to one another, the overwhelming preference and actual choice of old people is to live alone (10, 16). If one is refuting the thesis of the isolated nuclear family system, these traits are cited as evidence of a "modified extended family." If, on the other hand, one emphasizes the independence of living units and the voluntary nature of exchanges, the contemporary structure is more accurately called a "modified nuclear family" system. What is at issue here is more than a semantic quibble, since periodic interaction, however intense, is different from extensive day-to-day exposure to the lives of the aged. Here again, the historical context and societal variables such as residential mobility patterns have an impact on personal life, in this instance the socialization opportunities and experiences of the different generations. And, once again, we must look to media representations to fill in knowledge gaps. . . .

NOTES

1. Volume Two, *Aging and the Professions*, edited by Matilda White Riley, John W. Riley, Jr., and Marilyn E. Johnson, appeared the following year, devoted to essays on applications of the research findings to the several professional fields concerned with old people: social work, nursing, architecture, law, and so forth. In 1972, the third and last volume was published: *A Sociology of Age Stratification*, by Matilda White Riley, Marilyn E. Johnson, Anne Foner, and associates.
2. Palmore and Whittington (8) recorded a widening gap between old and young age groups in economic, social, and residential terms. The decline in status and satisfactions of the aged, they note, is a feature of modern industrial societies.

The authors support the definition of the aged as a "minority group," due precisely to the negative stereotypes noted above, residential segregation, discrimination, and the development of a unique subculture.

3. However, for the downwardly mobile, formerly middle-class but currently recipients of old age assistance, Tissue (15) finds that "television, newspapers, books, hobbies, etc. may serve to pass the time, but they do not appear to provide a sufficient buffer against the combined shock of retirement, downward mobility, and poverty."

4. One notes some ambiguity in the images presented. On the whole, old age is to be minimized, but recent series of Sominex and Alka-Seltzer commercials feature old people as authority figures who attest to the time-proven reliability of the product—which clearly contradicts the "common-sense" belief that old people have outdated knowledge. Other advertisers are beginning to use similar promotions.

5. I am reminded of my grandfather, who I am sure is not atypical, who refused to buy a suit for the last decade of his life, feeling that he wouldn't get his money's worth out of it.

6. As Hochschild (3) neatly puts it: "Isolation is not randomly distributed across the class hierarchy; there is more of it at the bottom." Again: "The isolation of old people is linked to other problems. The old are poor, and poverty itself is a problem. The old are unemployed and unemployment, in this society, is itself a problem. The old lack community and the lack of community is itself a problem."

7. This must be a major problem for life insurance companies, as much of their advertising indicates. In a radio commercial I heard recently, a young husband announces that he has bought a policy during lunch-hour; his wife squeals her unwillingness to hear more about it. While reinforcing the stereotype of hysteria and fiscal irresponsibility in women, the ad does tap a basic reluctance of young people to think of death.

REFERENCES

1. Bock, E. Wilbur, and Irving L. Webber. "Suicide Among the Elderly: Isolating Widowhood and Mitigating Alternatives." *Journal of Marriage and the Family* 34:1, February 1972, pp. 24–31.

2. Cherry, Rona, and Laurence Cherry. "Slowing the Clock of Age." *The New York Times Magazine*, May 12, 1974, p. 20 ff.

3. Hochschild, Arlie Russell. "Communal Life Styles for the Old." *Society* 10:5, July–August 1973, pp. 50–57.

4. Jacoby, Susan. "Waiting for the End: On Nursing Homes." *The New York Times Magazine*, March 31, 1974, p. 13 ff.

5. Lobsenz, Norman M. "Sex and the Senior Citizen." *The New York Times Magazine*, January 20, 1974, p. 8 ff.

6. Lopata, Helena Z. "Loneliness: Forms and Components." *Social Problems* 17:2, Fall 1969, pp. 248–262.

7. Merton, Robert K. "Reference Groups and Social Structure." In Robert K. Merton, *Social Theory and Social Structure*. (Revised and Enlarged Edition.) Glencoe, Illinois: The Free Press, 1957.

8. Palmore, Erdman, and Frank Whittington. "Trends in the Relative Status of the Aged." *Social Forces* 50, September 1971, pp. 84–91.

9. Peterson, James A., quoted by Richard Davis "Guide to TV Viewing," *Modern Maturity*, April–May 1974, pp. 44–46.

10. Riley, Matilda White, and Anne Foner. *Aging and Society, Volume One: An Inventory of Research Findings*. New York: Russell Sage Foundation, 1968.

11. Riley, Matilda White, John W. Riley, Jr., and Marilyn E. Johnson (Eds.), *Aging and Society, Volume Two: Aging and the Professions*. New York: Russell Sage Foundation, 1969.

12. Riley, Matilda White, Marilyn Johnson, Anne Foner, et al. *Aging and Society, Volume Three: A Sociology of Age Stratification*, New York: Russell Sage Foundation, 1972.

13. Rubin, Isadore. "The Sexless Older Years." *The Annals of the American Academy of Political and Social Science* 376, March 1968, pp. 86–95.

14. Schramm, Wilbur. "Aging and Mass Communication." In Riley, Riley, and Johnson (11), pp. 352–375.

15. Tissue, Thomas, "Downward Mobility in Old Age." *Social Problems* 18, Summer 1970, pp. 67–77.

16. Troll, Lillian E. "The Family of Later Life." *Journal of Marriage and the Family* 33:2, May 1971, pp. 263–290.

17. Tuchman, Gaye. "Objectivity as Strategic Ritual." *American Journal of Sociology* 77:4, January 1972, pp. 660–679.

"It's the Pepsi Generation": Accelerated Aging and the Television Commercial

J. SCOTT FRANCHER

This study analyzes 100 randomly selected television commercials collectively, and the Pepsi commercial specifically, to illustrate how the youth complex serves to disenfranchise the aged. The threefold manifesto that emerges emphasizes the importance of the body, youth, and a life style based on action and sensory gratification. Some speculations concerning the possible effects of these youth-oriented commercials on the aged are made, particularly their potential for producing anxiety and hence inducing symptoms of senility. The author suggests that serious inquiry should be made into the role played by the mass media in shaping the self-image of the aged.

"You've got a lot to live and Pepsi's got a lot to give" are words that have reached all our ears via the medium of television advertising. The jaunty melody, which serves as the vehicle for the above Madison Avenue catch phrase, lures us into listening, and supposedly the majority of us are made to feel that we can become part of this "brave new world" simply by imbibing Pepsi-Cola. There are among us, however, those who no longer "have a lot to live"; namely, the aging and the elderly among us who are subtly, but surely, culturally disenfranchised by this message.[1]

External Stress

Now, it will come as a surprise to no one when one states that we live in an age that has placed unprecedented external stress on each and every individual. Our society dictates what we shall think, what we shall wear, when we shall attain maturity and responsibility, and yes—even when we shall grow old. This last societal dictate is perhaps the most damaging. The structure of our society forces the individual to assume a certain physical and mental attitude once he has acquired a prescribed number of years to his life. At an arbitrarily chosen point in the life cycle, individuals are put out to pasture, told they have become obsolete, and forgotten

SOURCE: Reprinted from the *International Journal of Aging and Human Development*, Vol. 4, No. 3. Copyright 1973 by Baywood Publishing Company, Inc.

about by those who will soon follow them (but would rather not think about it). Not only are these steps carried out, but within the system there are subtle reinforcers which condone these actions and dictate that we shall perceive them as the inevitable course of human existence. The commercial messages produced by the mass media are the reinforcers which foster individual images and attitudes of senility. Hopefully, an analysis of these media messages will bring a new awareness to the problem of the aging process in American society.

For the purpose of this article it was decided to limit the analysis of commercials to those seen on television. Because of the popularity of the television medium, commercials are almost universally seen in American society and have become a part of our visual culture. (Support for this contention can be found in the fact that the Federal Trade Commission has restricted tobacco manufacturers from advertising cigarettes on commercial television, whereas no such restriction has yet been imposed on other media—such as magazines.) Television, as a major part of our vast multi-media network, is constantly emitting messages which are geared to shaping, molding, and influencing the behavior of the individual in some way. It is therefore a potent and critical force in terms of its impact on the individual and his behavioral alternatives. The originality and novelty employed in their productions make them a highly popular and enjoyable quasi-art form. It is not unusual to hear audiences comment that they enjoyed the commercials more than the feature show! (This rise in popularity of the TV commercial is evidenced in this year's awards ceremonies at Carnegie Hall in New York for excellence in television advertising.) With such a wide audience and range of public appeal it can be assumed that the impact of these commercial message productions is as great as, or greater than, competing forms of advertising.

But what is the nature of the messages emitted in the television commercial? Above and beyond the manifest content, what relationship do these seemingly innocuous message productions have to one's self-image? Can any relationship be inferred between these message productions and the plight of the aged in American society?

Procedures Utilized

In order to answer these questions, the following set of procedures was utilized. First, 100 television commercials were randomly sampled and closely monitored. Second, a viewing schedule was devised and the following categories were noted for each commercial:

A. Type of product advertised.
B. Major characters—Here each character used in the message production was recorded and the physical characteristics such as age, sex, degree of attractiveness were quantitatively described.
C. Tone—How are the advertisers attempting to sell the product:

through serious advertising, humorous appeals, or some other form of attention-getting mechanism?

D. Target group—What age, sex, or interest group is the commercial directed toward?

E. Scene—What is the dramatic setting for the commercial message?

F. Promise implied by the commercial—What benefits can the user expect from the product?

Third, the verbal lines of the commercials were recorded verbatim.

It was hoped that the above procedures would offer some sort of evidence as to whether or not these television messages did affect the self-image of the aging person. Did the commercials reinforce the society's prescription of when to get old?

The commercials exhibited the following general characteristics:

A. *Type of product.* The range of products advertised was indeed impressive. Few tendencies regarding the products advertised and their bearing on attitudes toward the aging can be discerned at this time. Time of day, however, seems to bear some relationship to the products advertised. Midmornings and late afternoons evidence a large number of products intended for children. Toys, games, and foods with special appeal for youngsters seem to be especially popular during these hours. Afternoons show a tendency to emphasize the housewife as the target group. Detergents, beauty aids, and food products are especially popular during this time slot. Perhaps the widest range of products is seen in the evening hours. Presumably, this is the time when television is viewed by the working members of the population. Thus the most varied assortment of products are advertised during this time period.

B. *Characters.* Significant variation exists with reference to the characters used in the television commercial. When a single character carries the message of the advertiser, a young, attractive, modishly-attired, often sexy female is utilized. This trend was documented in 33 percent of the sample. More often than not, she is blonde and modishly attired. LaBarre[2] noted this tendency in 1946 when he stated:

> Advertisements, movies, popular fiction, and other vehicles of publicity, amusement, and fantasy unite in demonstrating to us that in our society it is the nubile young female who achieves the most attention, who is the cynosure of all eyes.

Next in order of frequency (14 percent) is the single character who is, to some degree, a celebrity. Age and physical attributes seem irrelevant here except when the product advertised is intimately associated with one of the sexes. Such is the case in the feminine hygiene products. It is assumed that the celebrity status is sufficient to lend weight to the product advertised. Single men account for 10 percent of the characters. Invariably they are young, handsome, and dressed according to contemporary canons of fashion. Age seems to be more flexible in the case of the male character, reflecting the inclination in American society of holding the woman more accountable for physically aging than the man. Men are permitted graying temples and a certain cragginess of face so long as the image of virility and sexual appeal are maintained.

Nine percent of the sample used no human characters, but instead relied upon animated figures or still photos. In these cases the voice describing the product becomes of prime importance. Invariably the voices can be identified as young.

Of those commercials using two characters (15 percent) either a couple or two members of the same sex were employed. Here the characters were young, attractive, and stylishly dressed. In only one instance is the couple older or middle-aged. It is significant that in this particular case the product advertised is a vitamin especially designed for older people, promising "a younger, more active you."

Eleven percent of the commercials viewed showed a number of people in montage fashion. In only two instances did the group contain any older characters. The general tone of these two commercials using the older characters was decidedly humorous.

What is significant here is that the overwhelming number of commercials utilize young, attractive people. Older people are used when a product especially designed for them makes more sense when advertised by a member of this age group or when the commercial is humorous in tone. It appears therefore that the tendency in America to elevate youth to a primary position is reflected in the primary visual position they enjoy in television advertising.

C. *Tone.* The tone of the commercial refers to the nature of its appeal to the viewing public. Although this category should ideally be based on the commercial as a total presentation, tone can refer to its relative seriousness or humor. Three distinct categories emerged: serious; serious imbued with a high degree of sexuality; and humorous. Significant differences exist between the three categories in terms of products advertised and the characters used in the commercial message. Serious commercials relied heavily upon celebrities or attractive young models (73 percent). Products in the serious category ran the gamut from breakfast cereals to automobiles. In the serious-sex-imbued category, 100 percent of the major characters could be characterized as young and attractive, while 45 percent of the products advertised in this category emphasized the body as their major focus. An interesting inversion exists in the humorous category. In 80 percent of these cases the characters were classified as average, man-in-the-street types, blatantly comical in some aspect of the presentation of self, or clearly middle-aged or old. In only one case did the character described as "older" advertise products for the body. They seem to be restricted to less personal products such as household detergents or food products.

D. *Target group*. In examining the data, no general characteristics can be attributed to this aspect of the viewing schedule. Suffice it to say that multi-various interests groups are reached—i.e., denture wearers, automobile owners, parents, women, housewives, etc.

E. *Scene*. The scene enacted in the commercial message proved to be too integral a part of the whole message production to be studied as a separate entity. What can be said at this juncture, however, indicates that the scene, pace, setting, drama, and motif provide an essential vehicle for the transmission of the commercial message.

F. *Promise implied*. The promise implied by the commercial is, of course, intimately bound up with the product itself. It is not surprising to learn that a popular laundry detergent promises a "cleaner, whiter wash." Yet important secondary messages or cues are implied by the age, sex, and physical attributes of the major character, the tone the message assumes, the setting in which the drama is acted, and the final outcome of the "commercial drama." Thus an otherwise neutral commercial for a popular soft drink which utilizes all youthful people engaged in action-oriented scenes such as tennis or hiking becomes restricted to a youthful, action-oriented population while at the same time promising to supply the energy needed for these activities. Fifty-seven percent of the commercials monitored pledged youth, youthful appearance, or the energy to act youthful. Often this pledge was coupled with the promise of increased sexual appeal and conquest, a phenomenon well documented in the history of American advertising.

Each commercial can be viewed as a system of interdependent parts. The group of messages which emerges from any commercial is dependent upon the juxtaposition and mutual interplay of these parts. A total message develops as the sum of these interacting messages.

Analysis of a Popular TV Commercial

The following analysis of a Pepsi-Cola commercial illustrates the principle and the method of analysis employed for each commercial monitored:

The commercial lasts for one minute. During its duration a number of short film clips are rapidly flashed upon the screen in a photo-montage fashion. In all, seven such clips appear. They are in the order of their appearance:

1. A handsome young man with modishly long blond hair is bending over a river bank drinking water from his cupped hands. The scene is one of bucolic isolation and peace. Private sensory gratification and delight in nature are highlighted here.
2. A handsome young couple are seen walking arm in arm along a river bank. The young man draws the girl closer to him and they embrace. They are laughing and enjoying both the physical and emotional closeness of the relationship.

3. A young, athletic-looking man is seen in a high dive. The camera angles beneath him revealing a perfection of physical form and adroit execution of a difficult physical maneuver. Here action-orientation, physical prowess, and the beauty of the body become cues suitable for emulation.

4. A group of young children are pictured at a birthday party. One jubilant youngster blows out the candles, and the other children gathered around him are caught up in the excitement of the group activity. Thus sociability, sharing and delight in group experience are of primary importance in this film clip.

5. A young, athletic-looking man is seen climbing down a mountain side. Action, youth, and physical prowess are lauded here.

6. A tall young man holding a toddler (female) on his shoulders is pictured walking down a long stretch of deserted beach. Father enjoying his child and the mutual closeness of the family are implied here.

7. The camera moves in for a close-up of a young, attractive girl in a group of young people. She is laughing and obviously enjoying herself. Joy, impulse release, and contentment within the group confines are expressed here.

8. A bottle of Pepsi-Cola fills the screen. The verbal message is carried by a youthful-sounding male chorus which sings the following song for the duration of the commercial:

There's a whole new way of living,
  Pepsi helps supply the drive.
It's got a lot to give for those who like to live,
  'Cause Pepsi helps them come alive.
It's the Pepsi generation,
  Coming at you, going strong.
Put yourself behind a Pepsi
  If you're living, you belong.

You've got a lot to live and
  Pepsi's got a lot to give.
You've got a lot to live and
  *Pepsi's got a lot to give.**

During the one-minute duration of the commercial the viewer is bombarded with a constant stream of cues. First, one notices that the pace of the commercial is lively, if not rapid. This effect is created by the photo-montage technique of rapidly changing visual images and the spirited rhythm of the musical line. Such an animated pace provides an appropriate setting for the action-oriented scenes in the film clip. The lyrics of the music line provide yet another reinforcement for action orientation as a major cue. Such phrases as "helps supply the drive," "coming at you, going strong," articulate what is implied by the pace and visual content of the scenes.

Notice too that all of the characters in the scenes are young and attractive. Youth as a major cue is reinforced by the lyrics which announce that "there's a whole new way of living" and "it's the Pepsi generation." Thus we are told that a new life style has displaced the no longer fashionable life style of the older generation. Indeed, the bearers of this new culture are the young who seek sensory gratification and impulse release either through private experience or under the aegis of the group. Action-oriented behavior is not only an end in itself but an indispensable means of attaining the pleasure of the "good life."

Triumph of New Over Old

Thus a threefold manifesto emerges based on the triumph of new over old, action over intellect, impulse over moderation. Through this edict a product otherwise general in its appeal and consumption becomes specifically directed toward youth as a target group and all those who aspire to emulate the youthful modes of behavior. The first part of this threefold manifesto may be called "emphasis on the body." The body is portrayed as young and svelte if female; lean and muscular if male. The variety of messages here charges the individual to pay close attention to the inevitable signs of aging of the body. One is instructed to maintain a youthful physique under all costs. If this fails, one is cued to mask the telltale indicators of aging. Face, hair, and hands become objects of special concern and are all-important indicators of aging. The second part of the manifesto is "the age phenomenon." Youth is depicted as the object of social concern and admiration. One is directed to measure both his body and the range of his activities by the barometer of age. A ready maxim emerges: What is or appears to be youthful is good and desirable; all that is otherwise is not. The third book completes the new canon: "You've got a lot to live." A life style based on action and sensory gratification is held up as the ideal pattern to follow. Here the "good life" is one both rich in material accouterments and symbols of youth. (Henceforth the "youth complex" will be used to refer to this threefold testament: emphasis on the body, emphasis on youth, and emphasis on action orientation and sensory gratification.)

It is perhaps not surprising to learn that in the Western world the disorganizing effects of aging on the human personality are physiologically defined and explained. Arteriosclerosis and chronic brain syndrome, two diseases commonly associated with the elderly, are credited with robbing the individual of viable social contacts with the outside world. The idea that senility and its attendant maladies are caused by actual physical changes and deterioration of the brain is deeply rooted in the American consciousness. Like the younger person defined as mentally ill, the older person labeled as senile is "cracked in the head."

Despite the fact that this notion persists, there are those who have transcended its limitations, providing us with unique insight into an otherwise tradition-bound area. One such innovator is Dr. Muriel Oberleder of the Bronx State Hospital, Bronx, New York, who believes the phenomenon which we label senility is not caused physiologically but is a function of the anxiety related to the cultural stresses placed on the aging in our society. Oberleder[3] states:

> In my belief, anxiety is the extra stress of aging; indeed, old age is anxiety. Old age occurs when external stresses overtax the older person's ability to function, and if you remove the stress, the person can again function. I feel that anxiety underlies all senile symptoms, and causes them. In old age you have more anxiety-evoking situations and fewer anxiety-reducing opportunities; that formula in itself could account for senility, or emotional breakdown in the aging.

It is of no small import that Oberleder identifies the fear of loss of sexuality, of loss of status, of loss of a sense of security, and the trauma caused by body changes as major foci of stress in the individual. She adroitly points out that these anxieties do not blossom into full flower at the age of sixty-five, but find their roots in the unresolved stresses of middle age. These anxieties not only have an incremental value for the individual, but when juxtaposed with the common life crises of older years (forced retirement, loss of spouse, loss of role, etc.) the individual often turns to the culturally prescribed role of senility. Quoting Oberleder,[4]

> I believe that people bring senility on themselves. . . . When you are really old and feeling stress, you grab at the senile symptoms to end the tension.

These factors which cause the anxiety, moreover, are largely cultural factors. No absolute cultural rule exists which determines sixty-five as the age of forced withdrawal from society. Indeed, even though the changes brought about by aging in the human body are inevitable, and part of the physical "program" to which all species are heir, society's attitude toward these changes is the crucial element—not the changes *per se*.

TV Commercials and Their Effect on the Aging

It is suggested here that an important causal relationship exists between the major messages which have been identified in television advertising and predispositions toward aging and the symptoms which are commonly called senile. These cues, I maintain, create anxiety and anger, two factors which Oberleder has identified as causal in the emotional breakdown of the elderly.

The major impact of [the Pepsi-Cola commercial] is undoubtedly a visual one. The viewer is presented with a rapidly changing series of scenes depicting young people in action poses or scenes depicting sensory gratification. The three elements which we have termed 'the youth complex' constitutes a message grouping. The messages charge one to take note of youth, action, and sensory gratification in a favorable way. This does not, however, operate on only the visual plane. It charges one to *feel* youthful, to *act* youthful, and to *believe* that youth, action, and sensory gratification as a focus has a universal validity, to hold youth in awe and to use youth as a role model.[5]

In the data gathered, youth is the model after which one is directed to measure one's self. Such culturally sanctioned role models constitute a crucial element in the socialization process. One can easily discern the functional character of such role models when observing the behavior of children. By imitating role models, children "practice" adult roles, modes of dress, and even styles of body deportment. Much has been written which illustrates how this imitative behavior facilitates the acquisition of appropriate cultural behavior. The data show that in 43 percent of the commercials monitored, the characters used were both young and attractive. Moreover, these youthful models are depicted in action postures, espousing sensory gratification. We can readily comprehend how this visual preoccupation with the youth complex serves the young. But what of the rest of the population which is no longer young, which can never again hope to realize the attributes of youth as depicted in the television commercial? Like the young viewer, the older one is charged through this message grouping to perceive, to feel, to do, to believe, to emulate, and to hold in awe—the youth complex. He is told that this is the cultural model *par excellence*, the self to which he must aspire. The gap between the physical and social self as experienced in reality and the television self, the model the viewer is directed to incorporate, may be so great that a loss of self-esteem is a natural consequence. Such occurrences as thinning hair, failing eyesight, dentures, and a more measured, less action-oriented life style are not accounted for by the social model; indeed, their very existence is met with denial.

The life works of George H. Mead and Charles H. Cooley have impressed upon us the importance of social validation in the development of the individual's self-esteem. When no appropriate means of social validation are made available to the individual, opportunities for the maintenance of self-esteem are severely jeopardized. Conceivably the individual responds with anxiety and anger, precisely those emotions which Oberleder has cited as germane to the emotional breakdown of the elderly.

The Youth Complex

The youth complex, a system of messages accentuating youth, action orientation, and sensory gratification, was identified as a major message grouping in television advertising. This message grouping directs the individual to invest positive emotion in these phenomena and, at the same time, further charges the individual to incorporate them into a variety of behavioral patterns. The individual is charged to see this youth complex favorably, to feel favorably disposed toward this perception, to perform in accordance with the dictates of this complex, to incorporate these values into his system of beliefs, and to reverently hold persons, objects, or events which symbolize or contain them. When the reality of one's physical person and social self roughly corresponds to the image projected by and contained within this youth complex, the possibility of conflict arising among the various aspects of this message system is markedly reduced, since an agreement is reached between the person's self-image and the projected image of the idealized self of the advertisement. Understandably, this conflict-free arrangement is most available to the young in our society. But what of the older person, the person who has long since passed the age when the attainment of this projected idealized self is no longer possible, the person whose body has long since passed the stage of the young, attractive model of the television screen? Speculatively, there can be little doubt that the older individual finds conflict, anxiety, and anger in this arrangement. For him the conflict lies at the very heart of this complex. On one hand he is directed through the message grouping to perceive the youth complex in a favorable fashion, while on the other hand it does not allow him the possibility or even the hope of bringing his own feelings and image of self in line with these perceptions.

The field of gerontology, having reached a point of increased awareness in the public consciousness, offers myriad possibilities for innovative research. We now know that the aged in our society are confronted with many anxiety-inducing and tension-provoking situations. This research suggests the necessity of our understanding the importance of the mass media and their role in shaping the aging person's awareness of self with respect to both social models and the rest of society. Until we know the extent to which popular heroes, celebrities, and fictional characters of the mass media influence the origin of life-style models, we cannot hope to fully understand or appraise their impact on the individual's image of self. Yet we do know more precise inquiry is needed in this significant area.

NOTES AND REFERENCES

1. Francher, J. Scott. American values and the disenfranchisement of the aged. *The Eastern Anthropologist*, XXII, *1* January–April, 1969, 29–36.
2. LaBarre, W. Social cynosure and social structure. In D. G. Haring (Ed.), *Personal character and cultural milieu.* Syracuse, N. Y.: Syracuse University Press, 1956, p. 535.
3. Oberleder, Muriel. Emotional breakdown in elderly people. *Hospital and Community Psychiatry*, July 1969, *20* (7), 191–196.
4. Ibid., p. 194.
5. Nelson, B. Actors, directors, roles, cues, meanings, identities: Further thoughts on "anomie." *The Psychoanalytic Review*, Spring 1964 (1), 135–160.

The "Sexless Older Years"—A Socially Harmful Stereotype

ISADORE RUBIN

The stereotype of the "sexless older years" has placed its stamp upon our entire culture. In many cases it acts as a self-fulfilling prophecy, causing older people to refrain from sexual relations for fear of appearing ridiculous. Our expectation that the aged remain asexual has done damage to the aging population, even though a growing body of research makes it clear that there is no automatic cutoff to sexuality at any age and that sex interests, needs, and abilities continue to play an important role in the later years. Older people will not be able to express their sexuality freely and without guilt unless society recognizes the normality of sexual expression in older persons.

It has been suggested that our culture has programmed marriage only until the child-raising period has been completed.[1] If this is true of marital roles in general, it is especially true of sexual roles in the later years. Society has not given genuine recognition to the validity of sexual activity after the childbearing years, creating a dangerous stereotype about the "sexless older years" and defining as deviant behavior sex interest and activity which may continue vigorously into these older years. Thus, for example, the opprobrious term "lecher" is never coupled with any age group but the old; the young are "lusty" or "virile."

A Self-Fulfilling Prophecy

This stereotype has until recently placed its unchallenged stamp upon our culture. In the late 1950s, undergraduates at Brandeis University were asked to take a test to assess their attitudes toward old people.[2] Those taking the test were requested to complete this sentence: "Sex for most old people. . . ." Their answers were quite revealing. Almost all of these young men and women, ranging in age from seventeen to twenty-three, considered sex for most old people to be "negligible," "unimportant," or "past." Since sex behavior is not only a function of one's individual

SOURCE: Reprinted from "The Sexless Older Years—A Socially Harmful Stereotype" by Isadore Rubin in volume no. 376 of *The Annals* of The American Academy of Political and Social Science. © 1968 by The American Academy of Political and Social Science. All rights reserved.

attitudes and interactions with a partner, but also a reflection of cultural expectations, the widespread belief about the older person being sexless becomes for many a "self-fulfilling prophecy." Our society stands indicted, says psychiatrist Karl M. Bowman, of grave neglect of the emotional needs of aging persons:

> Men and women often refrain from continuing their sexual relations or from seeking remarriage after loss of a spouse, because even they themselves have come to regard sex as a little ridiculous, so much have our social attitudes equated sex with youth. They feel uncertain about their capacities and very self-conscious about their power to please. They shrink from having their pride hurt. They feel lonely, isolated, deprived, unwanted, insecure. Thoughts of euthanasia and suicide bother them. To prevent these feelings, they need to have as active a sex life as possible and to enjoy it without fear.[3]

Most of our attitudes toward sex today still constitute—despite the great changes that have taken place in the openness with which sex is treated publicly—what a famous British jurist has called "a legacy of the ascetic ideal, persisting in the modern world after the ideal itself has deceased."[4] Obviously the ascetic attitude—essentially a philosophy of sex-denial—would have far-reaching effects upon our attitude toward the sexual activity of those persons in our society who have passed the reproductive years. Even so scientific a writer as Robert S. de Ropp, in his usually excellent *Man against Aging*, betrays the unfortunate effects of our ascetic tradition when he says:

> For sexual activity, enjoyable as it may seem in itself, still has as its natural aim the propagation of the species, and this activity belongs to the second not the third act of life's drama.[5]

In addition to our tradition of asceticism, there are many other factors which undoubtedly operate to keep alive a strong resistance to the acceptance of sexuality in older people. These include our general tradition of equating sex, love, and romance solely with youth; the psychological difficulty which children have of accepting the fact of parental intercourse; the tendency to think of aging as a disease rather than a normal process; the focusing of studies upon hospitalized or institutionalized older people rather than upon a more typical sample of persons less beset by health, emotional, or economic problems; and the unfortunate fact that—by and large—physicians have shared the ignorance and prejudices equally with the rest of society.[6]

It is significant, however, that centuries of derogation and taboo have not been successful in masking completely the basic reality that sex interest and activity do not disappear in the older years. Elaine Cumming and William E. Henry point out that our jokes at the expense of older people have revealed considerable ambivalence in the view that all old people are asexual.[7] The contradictory attitude which people possess about sexuality in the later years is also well illustrated by the history of the famous poem "John Anderson, My Jo," written by Robert Burns almost two centuries ago. In the version known today, the poem is a sentimental tribute to an old couple's calm and resigned old age. The original folk version—too bawdy to find its way into textbooks—was an old wife's grievance about her husband's waning sex interest and ability which makes very clear that she has no intention of tottering down life's hill in a passionless and sexless old age.[8] It is also interesting to note that sexuality in older women was an important part of one of Aristophanes' comedies. In his play *Ecclesiazusae* ("Women in Parliament"), Aristophanes described how the women seized power and established a social utopia.[9] One of their first acts was to place sexual relations on a new basis in order to assure all of them ample satisfaction at all times. They decreed that, if any young man was attracted to a girl, he could not possess her until he had satisfied an old woman first. The old women were authorized to seize any youth who refused and to insist upon their sexual rights also.

The Harmful Influence of the Myth

A British expert in the study of aging has suggested that the myth of sexlessness in the older years does have some social utility for some older women in our society who may no longer have access to a sexual partner.[10] However, the widespread denial of sexuality in older persons has a harmful influence which goes far beyond its effect upon an individual's sexual life.[11] It makes difficult, and sometimes impossible, correct diagnoses of medical and psychological problems, complicates and distorts interpersonal relations in marriage, disrupts relationships between children and parents thinking of remarriage, perverts the administration of justice to older persons accused of sex offenses, and weakens the whole self-image of the older man or woman.

A corollary of the failure to accept sexuality as a normal aspect of aging has been the tendency to exaggerate the prevalence of psychological deviation in the sexual behavior of older men and to see in most old men potential molesters of young children. Seen through the lenses of prejudice, innocent displays of affection have often loomed ominously as overtures to lascivious fondling or molestation. It is common, too, to think of the exhibitionist as being, typically, a deviation of old age.

Actually the facts indicate the falsity of both of these stereotypes. As research by Johann W. Mohr and his associates at the Forensic Clinic of the Toronto Psychiatric Hospital showed, "contrary to common assumption the old age group is the relatively smallest one" involved in child molesting.[12] The major age groups from whose ranks child molesters come are adolescence, the middle to late thirties, and the late fifties. The peak of acting out of exhibitionism occurs in the mid-twenties; and, in its true form, exhibitionism is rarely seen after the age of forty.

In relatively simple and static societies, everyone knows pretty much where he stands at each stage of life, particularly the older members of the group. "But in complex and fluid social systems," notes Leo W. Simmons, "with rapid change and recurrent confusion over status and role, no one's position is so well fixed—least of all that of the aging."[13] For many aging persons, there is a crisis of identity in the very sensing of themselves as old, particularly in a culture which places so great a premium upon youth. David P. Ausubel notes that, just as in adolescence, the transition to aging is a period where the individual is in the marginal position of having lost an established and accustomed status without having acquired a new one and hence is a period productive of considerable stress.[14] Under such conditions of role confusion, aging persons tend to adopt the stereotype which society has molded for them, in sex behavior as in other forms of behavior. But they do so only at a very high psychic cost.

For many older people, continued sexual relations are important not so much for the pleasurable release from sexual tension as for the highly important source of psychological reinforcement which they may provide. Lawrence K. Frank has said:

> Sex relations can provide a much needed and highly effective resource in the later years of life when so often men face the loss of their customary prestige and self-confidence and begin to feel old, sometimes long before they have begun to age significantly. The premature cessation of sexual functioning may accelerate physiological and psychological aging since disuse of any function usually leads to concomitant changes in other capacities. After menopause, women may find that continuation of sexual relations provides a much needed psychological reinforcement, a feeling of being needed and of being capable of receiving love and affection and renewing the intimacy they earlier found desirable and reassuring.[15]

The Growing Body of Research Data

Gathering data about the sexual behavior and attitudes of the aging has not been an easy task. To the generalized taboos about sex research have been added the special resistance and taboos that center on sexuality in older persons. For example, when the New England Age Center decided to administer an inventory to its members, they included only nine questions about sex among the 103 items.[16] The nine questions were made deliberately vague, were confined largely to past sexual activities, and were given only to married members. Leaders of the Center felt that if they had asked more direct questions or put them to their unmarried members, these people would not have returned to the Center. In California, a study of the attitudes of a sample of persons over sixty years old in San Francisco during the early 1960s included just one general open-ended question about sexual attitudes, apparently because of the resistance which many of the researchers had about questioning subjects in the area of sex.[17] Psychiatrists reporting on this research before the Gerontological Society noted that the people involved in research in gerontology are being hamstrung by their own attitudes toward sex with regard to the elderly in much the same way in which the rest of society is hamstrung with regard to their attitudes toward the elderly in such matters as jobs, roles, and those things which go into determining where a person fits into the social structure.

Fortunately, although no sample has yet been studied that was sufficiently broad or typical to present us with a body of norms, a sufficient amount of data now exists which leaves no doubt of the reality of sex interests and needs in the later years. While it is true that there are many men and women who look forward to the ending of sexual relations, particularly those to whom sex has always been a distasteful chore or those who "unconsciously welcome the excuse of advancing years to abandon a function that has frightened them since childhood,"[18] sexual activity, interest, and desire are not the exception for couples in their later years. Though the capacity for sexual response does slow down gradually, along with all the other physical capacities, it is usually not until actual senility that there is a marked loss of sexual capacity.

With the research conducted by William H. Masters and Virginia E. Johnson, who observed the anatomy and physiology of sexual response in the laboratory, confirmation has now been obtained that sexual capacity can continue into advanced old age.[19] Among the subjects whose orgasmic cycles were studied by these two investigators were sixty-one menopausal and postmenopausal women (ranging from forty to seventy-eight) and thirty-nine older men (ranging from fifty-one to eighty-nine). Among the women, Masters and Johnson found that the intensity of physiologic reaction and the rapidity of response to sexual stimulation were both reduced with advancing years. But they emphasized that they found "significant sexual capacity and effective sexual performance" in these older women, concluding:

> The aging human female is fully capable of sexual performance at orgasmic response levels, particularly if she is exposed to regularity of effective sexual stimulation. . . . There seem to be no physiologic reasons why the frequency of sexual expression found satisfactory for the younger woman should not be carried over into the postmenopausal years. . . . In short, there is no time limit drawn by the advancing years to female sexuality.

When it came to males, Masters and Johnson found that there was no question but that sexual responsiveness weakens as the male ages, particularly after the age of sixty. They added, however:

> There is every reason to believe that maintained regularity of sexual expression coupled with adequate physical well-being and healthy mental orientation to the aging process will combine to provide a sexually stimulative climate within a marriage. This climate will, in turn, improve sexual tension and provide a

capacity for sexual performance that frequently may extend to and beyond the 80-year age level.

These general findings have been supported by various types of studies which have been made over the course of the years. These studies include the investigation by Raymond Pearl in 1925 into the frequency of marital intercourse of men who had undergone prostatic surgery, all over the age of fifty-five;[20] Robert L. Dickinson and Lura E. Beam's studies of marriages and of single women, including a number of older single women and widows;[21] the Kinsey studies of the male and the female;[22] older men studied at outpatient clinics by urologists at the University of California School of Medicine at San Francisco;[23] extended study by Duke University psychiatrists of Negroes and whites living in the Piedmont area of North Carolina;[24] Joseph T. Freeman's study of older men in Philadelphia;[25] a study of patients attached to a geriatric clinic in New York;[26] a survey of veterans applying for pensions;[27] a questionnaire survey by *Sexology* magazine of men over sixty-five who were listed in *Who's Who in America*;[28] and a study of sex attitudes in the elderly at the Langley Porter Neuropsychiatric Institute in San Francisco.[29]

No Automatic Cutoff Date

All of these studies indicate the continuation of sex needs, interests, and abilities into the later years despite the gradual weakening that may take place. The Kinsey group, quite contrary to general conceptions of the aging process in sex, found that the rate at which males slow up sexually in the last decades of life does not exceed the rate at which they have been slowing up and dropping out of sexual activity in the previous age groups.[30] For most males, they found no point at which old age suddenly enters the picture. As far as females were concerned, the Kinsey investigators—like Masters and Johnson later—found little evidence of any aging in their capacities for sexual response.[31] "Over the years," they reported, "most females become less inhibited and develop an interest in sexual relations which they then maintain until they are in their fifties or even sixties." In contrast to the average wife, the responses of the husband dropped with age. Thus many of the younger females reported that they did not desire intercourse as often as their husbands. In the later years of marriage, however, many of the wives expressed the desire for coitus more often then their husbands were then desiring it.

The Duke University survey—reported by Gustave Newman and Claude R. Nichols—found that only those persons who were seventy-five or older showed a significantly lower level of sexual activity.[32] This study found that Negro subjects were sexually more active than white subjects; men were more active than women; and persons lower in the social and economic scale were more active than those in the upper-income group. A possible explanation of the greater activity reported by males lies in the fact that men and women of the same age were reporting on different age groups. The wives, on the average, would be reporting on sex activity with a husband who was perhaps four years older.

Despite the fact that masturbation has been usually considered an activity that ends with maturity, for many older persons this practice apparently continues to serve as a satisfactory form of release from sexual tensions when a partner is, for one reason or another, not available.[33]

Several of the studies suggest a correlation between early sex activity and a continuation into the late years. The Kinsey group found that, at age fifty, all of the males who had been sexually active in early adolescence were still sexually active, with a frequency about 20 percent higher than the frequency of the later-maturing males.[34] They report:

> Nearly forty years maximum activity have not yet worn them out physically, physiologically, or psychologically. On the other hand, some of the males (not many) who were late adolescent and who have had five years less of sexual activity are beginning to drop completely out of the picture; and the rates of this group are definitely lower in these older age periods.

They conclude:

> The ready assumption which is made in some of the medical literature that impotence is the product of sexual excess is not justified by such data as are now available.

Freeman[35] found that the sex urge of persons in advanced years correlated strongly with their comparative sex urge when young, and a similar finding was reported by the Duke University survey.[36]

Masters and Johnson report the same finding, with additional emphasis upon regularity of sexual expression as the essential factor in maintaining sexual capacity and effective performance for both males and females:[37]

> When the male is stimulated to high sexual output during his formative years and a similar tenor of activity is established for the 31–40-year range, his middle-aged and involutional years usually are marked by constantly recurring physiologic evidence of maintained sexuality. Certainly it is true for the male geriatric sample that those men currently interested in relatively high levels of sexual expression report similar activity levels from their formative years. It does not appear to matter what manner of sexual expression has been employed, as long as high levels of activity were maintained.

Factors Responsible for Declining Sex Activity

On the basis of present data, it is not possible to sort out the emotional element from the purely physiologic factors in the decline in sexual activity of the older male. Some animal experiments have shown that changes in the external environment can result in changes in sexual drive. When aging rats had the opportunity for sex activity with a number of partners, for example, the number of copulations increased considerably.[38] However, as soon as male rats reached a certain age, they failed to respond to females.[39]

Many men also find that, with a new partner, a new stimulus is given to their virility.[40] However, often these men return to their old level within comparatively short periods of time.[41] Present data lead us to conclude, with the Kinsey investigators:

> The decline in sexual activity of the older male is partly, and perhaps primarily, the result of a general decline in physiologic capacity. It is undoubtedly affected also by psychologic fatigue, a loss of interest in repetition of the same sort of experience, an exhaustion of the possibilities for exploring new techniques, new types of contacts, new situations.[42]

Masters and Johnson, on the basis of their clinical work with older males, describe six general groups of factors which they believe to be responsible for much of the loss of sexual responsiveness in the later years: (1) monotony of a repetitious sexual relationship (usually translated into boredom with the partner); (2) preoccupation with career or economic pursuits; (3) mental or physical fatigue; (4) overindulgence in food or drink; (5) physical and mental infirmities of either the individual or his spouse; and (6) fear of performance associated with or resulting from any of the former categories.

The most constant factor in the loss of an aging male's interest is the problem of monotony, described by the Kinsey group as "psychologic fatigue." According to Masters and Johnson, many factors may produce this: failure of the sexual relationship to develop beyond a certain stage; overfamiliarity; lack of sexual interest on the female's part; aging and loss of personal attractiveness of the female.

A major deterrent for many men is preoccupation with the outside world and their careers. Overindulgence in food and drink, particularly the latter, takes a high toll. According to Masters and Johnson, secondary impotence developing in the late forties or early fifties has a higher incidence of direct association with excessive alcohol consumption than with any other single factor.

As each partner ages, the onset of physical or mental infirmities is an ever-increasing factor in reducing sexual capacities. The harmful effect of this is sometimes multiplied by the negative or discouraging attitude of the physician. Once a failure in performance has occurred because of any of the factors, the fear of failure becomes an additional factor in bringing about withdrawal from sexual activity. "Once impotent under any circumstances," remark Masters and Johnson, "many males withdraw voluntarily from any coital activity rather than face the ego-shattering experience of repeated episodes of sexual inadequacy."

The very scanty data concerning the sexual attitudes of older persons suggest a more positive attitude toward sex among men than among women, with women being more "culture-bound" and still showing strong evidences of the effects of the Victorian age in which they acquired their attitudes toward sex.[43] A study of dreams of residents of a home for the aged and infirm, on the other hand, indicates a contrasting difference in emotional tone of the sexual content of the dreams of men and women: "Whereas in men sexual dreams revealed anxiety, failure, and lack of mastery, in women they usually depicted passive, pleasurable gratification of dependent needs."[44]

The Unmarried Have Sex Needs Too

It is not only the married who have sexual needs. Aging widows, widowers, and single persons, who make up an increasingly large segment of our population, face even greater problems in respect to sex than do the married. In the survey by Newman and Nichols, only seven of the 101 single, divorced, or widowed subjects reported any sexual activity with partners.[45] Apparently, the strength of the sexual drive of most elderly persons is usually not great enough to cause them to seek a sexual partner outside of marriage in the face of social disapproval and the difficulties of such an endeavor. Interestingly, however, thousands of older couples were reportedly living "in sin—or what they think is sin" because marriage would mean loss of social security payments.[46]

Dickinson and Beam reported that in their study of widows ranging from sixty to eighty years of age there was evidence of masturbation.[47] They reported that when these women underwent pelvic examinations, they showed such marked sexual reactions that they found that "it is desirable to relieve the patient's embarrassment by hurting her, lest she have orgasm." Since many older women are quite troubled by their practice of masturbation, marriage counselors have stressed the importance of helping older persons to accept this practice as a valid outlet when they feel the need for it.[48]

The Great Need for Information

Persons who have worked with "senior citizens" and "golden age" clubs have reported the great need for knowledge, the confusion, and the eager hunger for information about sex shown by persons in these clubs.[49] The many perplexing problems that they raise indicate the extent to which such information is needed to help people solve broader questions of remarriage and interpersonal relationships during their later years. The growing incidence of disease states in these years—each of which may require a difficult readjustment in sexual and other relationships—makes it essential that older people be provided with this information openly and consistently.[50]

It should be clear, however, that unless our entire culture recognizes the normality of sex expression in the older years, it will be impossible for older persons to express their sexuality freely and without guilt. Physicians are particularly crucial in this respect; unless they are convinced of the psychological importance of sexual functioning in the later years, they can do irreparable harm to their patients' sexuality.[51] Fortunately, at long last, medical schools and medical publications have begun to take steps to correct the glaring lacks in the education of medical students, which have in the past resulted in the creation of a body of medical practitioners who, by and large, shared the general prejudices of our society concerning sexuality in older persons.

NOTES

1. E. Cumming and W. E. Henry, *Growing Old* (New York: Basic Books, 1961), p. 155.
2. P. Golde and N. Kogan, "A Sentence Completion Procedure for Assessing Attitudes toward Old People," *Journal of Gerontology*, 14 (July 1959), 355–363.
3. K. M. Bowman, "The Sex Life of the Aging Individual," in M. F. DeMartino (ed.), *Sexual Behavior and Personality Characteristics* (New York: Citadel, 1963), pp. 372–375.
4. G. Williams, *The Sanctity of Life and the Criminal Law* (New York: Alfred A. Knopf, 1957), p. 51.
5. R. S. de Ropp, *Man against Aging* (New York: Grove Press, 1962), p. 252.
6. H. I. Lief, "Sex Education of Medical Students and Doctors," *Pacific Medicine and Surgery*, 73 (February 1965), 52–58.
7. Cumming and Henry, *op. cit.*, footnote, p. 21.
8. R. Burns, *The Merry Muses of Caledonia*, ed. J. Barke and S. G. Smith (New York: Putnam, 1964), pp. 147–148.
9. H. Einbinder, *The Myth of the Brittanica* (New York: Grove Press, 1964), p. 94.
10. A. Comfort, review of *Sexual Life after Sixty* by Isadore Rubin, *British Medical Journal*, II, March 25, 1967, 750.
11. Isadore Rubin, *Sexual Life after Sixty* (New York: Basic Books, 1965), chap. i.
12. J. W. Mohr, R. E. Turner, and M. B. Jerry, *Pedophilia and Exhibitionism* (Toronto: University of Toronto Press, 1964).
13. L. W. Simmons, "Social Participation of the Aged in Different Cultures," in M. B. Sussman (ed.), *Sourcebook in Marriage and the Family* (2nd ed.; Boston: Houghton Mifflin, 1963).
14. D. P. Ausubel, *Theory and Problems of Adolescent Development* (New York: Grune and Stratton, 1954), pp. 53 ff.
15. L. K. Frank, *The Conduct of Sex* (New York: Morrow, 1961), pp. 177–178.
16. E. B. Armstrong, "The Possibility of Sexual Happiness in Old Age," in H. G. Beigel (ed.), *Advances in Sex Research* (New York: Hoeber-Harper, 1963), pp. 131–137.
17. E. H. Feigenbaum, M. J. Lowenthal and M. L. Trier, "Sexual Attitudes in the Elderly." Unpublished paper given before the Gerontological Society, New York, November 1966.
18. W. R. Stokes, *Married Love in Today's World* (New York: Citadel, 1962), p. 100.
19. W. H. Masters and V. E. Johnson, *Human Sexual Response* (Boston: Little, Brown, 1966), sec. on "Geriatric Sexual Response," pp. 223–270.

20. R. Pearl, *The Biology of Population Growth* (New York: Alfred A. Knopf, 1925), pp. 178–207.

21. R. L. Dickinson and L. E. Beam, *A Thousand Marriages* (Baltimore: Williams & Wilkins, 1931), pp. 278–279, 446; and R. L. Dickinson and L. E. Beam, *The Single Woman* (Baltimore: Williams & Wilkins, 1934), p. 445.

22. A. C. Kinsey, W. B. Pomeroy, and C. E. Martin, *Sexual Behavior in the Human Male* (Philadelphia: W. B. Saunders, 1948); and A. C. Kinsey, W. B. Pomeroy, C. E. Martin, and P. H. Gebhard, *Sexual Behavior in the Human Female* (Philadelphia: W. B. Saunders, 1953).

23. A. L. Finkle *et al.*, "Sexual Function in Aging Males: Frequency of Coitus Among Clinic Patients." *Journal of the American Medical Association*, 170, July 18, 1959, 1391–1393.

24. G. Newman and C. R. Nichols, "Sexual Activities and Attitudes in Older Persons," *Journal of the American Medical Association*, 173, May 7, 1960, 33–35.

25. J. T. Freeman, "Sexual Capacities in the Aging Male," *Geriatrics*, 16 (January 1961), 37–43.

26. L. Friedfeld, "Geriatrics, Medicine, and Rehabilitation," *Journal of the American Medical Association*, 175, February 18, 1961, 595–598; and L. Friedfeld *et al.*, "A Geriatric Clinic in a General Hospital," *Journal of the American Geriatrics Society*, 7 (October 1959), 769–781.

27. L. M. Bowers, R. R. Cross, Jr., and F. A. Lloyd, "Sexual Function and Urologic Disease in the Elderly Male," *Journal of the American Geriatrics Society*, 11 (July 1963), 647–652.

28. I. Rubin, "Sex over Sixty-five," in H. G. Beigel (ed.), *Advances in Sex Research* (New York: Hoeber-Harper, 1963).

29. Feigenbaum *et al.*, *op. cit.*

30. Kinsey *et al.*, *Sexual Behavior in the Human Male*, pp. 235–237.

31. Kinsey *et al.*, *Sexual Behavior in the Human Female*, pp. 353–354.

32. Newman and Nichols, *op. cit.*

33. Rubin, "Sex over Sixty-five"; and Dickinson and Beam, *A Thousand Marriages*.

34. Kinsey *et al.*, *Sexual Behavior in the Human Male*, pp. 319–325.

35. Freeman, *op. cit.*

36. Newman and Nichols, *op. cit.*

37. Masters and Johnson, *op. cit.*

38. J. Botwinick, "Drives, Expectancies, and Emotions," in J. E. Birren (ed.), *Handbook of Aging and the Individual* (Chicago: University of Chicago Press, 1959), pp. 739–768.

39. L. F. Jakubczak, Report to the American Psychological Association, August 31, 1962.

40. J. Bernard, *Remarriage* (New York: Dryden, 1956), p. 188.

41. Kinsey *et al.*, *Sexual Behavior in the Human Male*, pp. 227–229; and A. W. Spence, "Sexual Adjustment at the Climacteric," *Practitioner*, 172 (April 1954), 427–430.

42. Kinsey *et al.*, *Sexual Behavior in the Human Male*, pp. 226–235.

43. Feigenbaum *et al.*, *op. cit.*

44. M. Barad, K. Z. Altshuler, and A. I. Goldfarb, "A Survey of Dreams in Aged Persons," *Archives of General Psychiatry*, 4 (April 1961), 419–424.

45. Newman and Nichols, *op. cit.*

46. *New York Times*, January 12, 1965.

47. Dickinson and Beam, *A Thousand Marriages*.

48. L. Dearborn, "Autoerotism," in A. Ellis and A. Abarbanel (eds.), *The Ency-*

clopedia of Sexual Behavior (New York: Hawthorn, 1961), pp. 204–215; and L. Hutton, *The Single Woman* (London: Barrie & Rockcliff, 1960), p. 58.

49. Feigenbaum *et al., op. cit.*
50. Rubin, *Sexual Life after Sixty*, chaps. xi–xiii.
51. J. S. Golden, "Management of Sexual Problems by the Physician," *Obstetrics and Gynecology*, 23 (March 1964), 471–474; and A. L. Finkle and D. V. Prian, "Sexual Potency in Elderly Men before and after Prostatectomy," *Journal of the American Medical Association*, 196, April 11, 1966, 139–143.

4

Adult Socialization and the Life Cycle

While social gerontology is generally perceived as the study of old age, other stages of the life cycle also come under its domain. Most social-psychological research has been focused on the extreme ends of the life cycle, childhood and old age (although even the emphasis on old age is relatively recent), but increasing attention has been directed toward the developmental concerns of middle age.

The traditional focus of social-psychological research has been on young children. Influenced by Freudian psychology, which emphasized the importance of early experiences on later behavior, most theories of development stopped with adolescence. It wasn't until theorists such as Erikson (1950) and Brim (1968) suggested that socialization continued throughout life and that adult socialization was different from socialization in childhood that other life-cycle stages came under scrutiny (Borland, 1978).

The Creation of Middle Age

Major historical changes have spurred an interest in studying middle age. Over the past two centuries we have witnessed the development of an increasing number of life periods. Middle age, or what has also been termed the postparental period, is a recent historical development caused by a decrease in the years spent in active parenthood. Through the eighteenth and nineteenth centuries parents had children well into their late thirties and early forties. In addition, average family size was greater than it is today. Child care and the launching of children extended through the period we now consider middle age and well into old age. It was not uncommon for a couple to have unmarried children still at home when they were in their late fifties or early sixties (Wells, 1971). Life expectancy was also much lower than it is today. The typical couple of two generations ago had a life expectancy which enabled them to survive together for thirty-one years after marriage, two years short of the time when their fifth child was expected to marry. The combination of increased life expectancy, lower fertility, and closer spacing of children created what we now define as middle age. By 1970 the average couple could expect to be alone without their children for at least thirteen years.

In addition to recognizing the impact of these demographic changes, researchers have come to realize that old age cannot be fully understood without understanding the period which preceded it. Each stage of life is influenced by prior experience and development. The style an individual develops to cope with changes in one stage of the life cycle affects the ability to either grow and develop or stagnate in subsequent stages.

The Concept of Age Norms

There are marked sex differences throughout the life cycle in terms of the significance and timing of specific events. For reasons that stem from both biology and socialization, the life course for women has traditionally been timed more in relation to family events— marriage, childbearing, and child rearing, while that for men is more tied to occupational events—career choice, advancement, and retirement. Thus men and women perceive different punctuation points across the life span that reflect contrasts in the structuring of their lives (Neugarten and Hagestad, 1976). These individually recognized differences in the timing of life-cycle events form a pervasive system of expectations concerning age-appropriate behavior that are generally recognized by all members of society. Age-related expectations, or age norms, often tend to be so subtle that we are unaware that they exist until they are violated. The girl who marries in her teens, the woman who has a child in her forties, the man who is still in school when he is thirty-five are all violators of age norms. Through social disapproval we sanction violators of age norms, for they cause disruptions in social relationships. The article by Neugarten, Moore, and Lowe describes how these age norms operate and how people are socialized to conform to them.

The Generation Gap

While different life-course concerns for men and women have been documented, there are indications that the traditional life cycle for women is disappearing. As more women enter the labor force as full-time employees early in life rather than following the traditional pattern of waiting until their children are beyond school age, the life-course sex differences become increasingly less relevant. The change in the life course for women is just one aspect of a broader issue, that of differences between generations or what has become popularly known as "the generation gap." Each generation, or age cohort, occupies a different position in historical time, and the members of that cohort share a collective mentality in the sense that they have common perspectives and concerns. Differences in perspective from one generation to the next can potentially create conflict, as each believes that its way of doing things is the right way. The article by Bengtson and Kuypers explores the factors that lead to differential perceptions across generations by comparing the views of students and parents as to the meaning and significance of the generation gap.

Events of Middle Age

The multiple changes that occur in youth and young adulthood are well known. Important decisions such as choosing a marriage partner or career must be made during this period. We also recognize that old age brings retirement, widowhood, and declining health. In contrast, a common belief has been that middle age is a relatively uncomplicated period when few major changes occur. No drastic decisions need be made; no drastic losses occur. Yet middle age is not devoid of significant life events, and it has the potential for both dissatisfaction and renewal.

For married couples the postparental period can be a time to rediscover the intimacy they enjoyed in the early years of marriage. Free from the constraints of child rearing, many couples experience an increase in marital satisfaction. On the other hand, couples who have stayed together for the sake of their children may find marital problems intensified as the focus turns increasingly to the quality of the marriage itself. Friends and relatives who have accepted a veneer of compatibility are often surprised when a couple separates after twenty years of marriage.

Like the timing of life-cycle events, the concerns which arise in middle age differ for men and women. Much of the research on middle-aged women has focused on the "empty nest" crisis—the period when women face a childless state for the first time in twenty or more years. The original belief was that this was a traumatic and difficult time for women who had devoted most of their lives to mothering. However, most research has not confirmed this perspective, and, in fact, it appears that many women perceive this time in life as one of increased freedom with many opportunities for self-renewal. Thus in middle age many women increase their involvement in an existing job or begin the search for a new career.

For men who have been involved in the work world for fifteen or twenty years, often defining their self-worth in terms of occupational success and achievement, mid-life becomes a time of judging and questioning. Have my choices been right? Were the sacrifices made along the way worth it? The excerpt by Levinson from *The Seasons of a Man's Life* illustrates some of the concerns and considerations for men in the mid-life transition.

Age structures our lives in more ways than we usually recognize. It determines to a large extent when we participate in different life-course events and how we feel about ourselves as we move through the life cycle. However, the age-related expectations which occur at a point in historical time are not sacred or unchanging but alter from generation to generation as each age cohort experiences a different social reality.

REFERENCES

Borland, Dolores Cabic. 1978. Research on middle age: An assessment. *Gerontologist* 18:379–386.

Brim, Orville. 1968. Adult socialization. In J. A. Clausen (ed.), *Socialization and society.* Boston: Little, Brown.

Erikson, Erik. 1950. *Childhood and society.* New York: W. W. Norton.

Neugarten, Bernice L., and Gunhild O. Hagestad. 1976. Age and the life course. In Robert H. Binstock and Ethel Shanas (eds.), *Handbook of aging and the social sciences.* New York: Van Nostrand Reinhold.

Wells, Robert. 1971. Demographic changes and the life cycle of American families. *Journal of Interdisciplinary History* 2:273–282.

Age Norms, Age Constraints, and Adult Socialization

BERNICE L. NEUGARTEN
JOAN W. MOORE
JOHN C. LOWE

Expectations regarding age-appropriate behavior form a pervasive system of rules which govern the timing of major life events and constrain social interaction. In attempting to determine how members of society vary in the degree of constraint they perceive with regard to age-linked expectations for behavior, the authors of this article conducted a series of interviews with middle-class people of various age groups. Respondents were asked to evaluate whether a specific behavior, such as wearing a two-piece bathing suit to the beach, was appropriate or inappropriate at each of three given ages. The authors found that while age norms were acknowledged to exist in the minds of "most people," the respondents believed that their own views were more liberal than those of other people. Older people tended to ascribe more importance to age norms than younger people. The authors concluded that personal belief in the relevance and validity of social norms increases through the adult life span, older people having learned that age is a reasonable criterion by which to evaluate others.

In all societies age is one of the bases for the ascription of status and one of the underlying dimensions by which social interaction is regulated. Anthropologists have studied age-grading in simple societies, and sociologists in the tradition of Mannheim have been interested in the relations between generations; but little systematic attention has been given to the ways in which age groups relate to each other in complex societies or to systems of norms which refer to age-appropriate behavior. A promising group of theoretical papers which appeared twenty or more years ago have now become classics,[1] but with the exceptions of a major contribution by Eisenstadt and a provocative paper by Berger,[2] little theoretical or empirical work has been done in this area in the two decades that have intervened, and there has been little development of what might be called a sociology of age.

SOURCE: Reprinted from the *American Journal of Sociology*, vol. 70 (May 1965) by permission of The University of Chicago Press. Copyright 1965 by The University of Chicago.

161

The present paper deals with two related issues: first, with the degree of constraint perceived with regard to age norms that operate in American society; second, with adult socialization to those norms.[3] Preliminary to presenting the data that bear upon these issues, however, a few comments regarding the age-norm system and certain illustrative observations gathered earlier may help to provide context for this study.

Background Concepts and Observations

Expectations regarding age-appropriate behavior form an elaborated and pervasive system of norms governing behavior and interaction, a network of expectations that is imbedded throughout the cultural fabric of adult life. There exists what might be called a prescriptive timetable for the ordering of major life events: a time in the life span when men and women are expected to marry, a time to raise children, a time to retire. This normative pattern is adhered to more or less consistently by most persons in the society. Although the actual occurrences of major life events for both men and women are influenced by a variety of life contingencies, and although the norms themselves vary somewhat from one group of persons to another, it can easily be demonstrated that norms and actual occurrences are closely related. Age norms and age expectations operate as prods and brakes upon behavior, in some instances hastening an event, in others delaying it. Men and women are aware not only of the social clocks that operate in various areas of their lives, but they are aware also of their own timing and readily describe themselves as "early," "late," or "on time" with regard to family and occupational events.

Age norms operate also in many less clear-cut ways and in more peripheral areas of adult life as illustrated in such phrases as "He's too old to be working so hard" or "She's too young to wear that style of clothing" or "That's a strange thing for a man of his age to say." The concern over age-appropriate behavior is further illustrated by colloquialisms such as "Act your age!"—an exhortation made to the adult as well as to the child in this society.

Such norms, implicit or explicit, are supported by a wide variety of sanctions ranging from those, on the one hand, that relate directly to the physical health of the transgressor to those, on the other hand, that stress the deleterious effects of the transgression on other persons. For example, the fifty-year-old man who insists on a strenuous athletic life is chastised for inviting an impairment of his own health; a middle-aged woman who dresses like an adolescent brings into question her husband's good judgment as well as her own; a middle-aged couple who decide to have another child are criticized because of the presumed embarrassment to their adolescent or married children. Whether affecting the self or others, age norms and accompanying sanctions are relevant to a great variety of adult behaviors; they are both systematic and pervasive in American society.

Despite the diversity of value patterns, life styles, and reference groups that influence attitudes, a high degree of consensus can be demonstrated with regard to age-appropriate and age-linked behaviors as illustrated by data shown in Table 1. The table shows how responses were distributed when a representative sample of middle-class men and women aged forty to seventy[4] were asked such questions as: "What do you think is the best age for a man to marry? . . . to finish school?" "What age comes to your mind when you think of a 'young' man? . . . an 'old' man?" "At what age do you think a man has the most responsibilities? . . . accomplishes the most?"[5]

TABLE 1   Consensus in a Middle-Class Middle-Aged Sample Regarding Various Age-Related Characteristics

	Age Range Designated as Appropriate or Expected	Percent Who Concur	
		MEN (N = 50)	WOMEN (N = 43)
Best age for a man to marry	20–25	80	90
Best age for a woman to marry	19–24	85	90
When most people should become grandparents	45–50	84	79
Best age for most people to finish school and go to work	20–22	86	82
When most men should be settled on a career	24–26	74	64
When most men hold their top jobs	45–50	71	58
When most people should be ready to retire	60–65	83	86
A young man	18–22	84	83
A middle-aged man	40–50	86	75
An old man	65–75	75	57
A young woman	18–24	89	88
A middle-aged woman	40–50	87	77
An old woman	60–75	83	87
When a man has the most responsibilities	35–50	79	75
When a man accomplishes most	40–50	82	71
The prime of life for a man	35–50	86	80
When a woman has the most responsibilities	25–40	93	91
When a woman accomplishes most	30–45	94	92
A good-looking woman	20–35	92	82

The consensus indicated in the table is not limited to persons residing in a particular region of the United States or to middle-aged persons. Responses to the same set of questions were obtained from other middle-class groups: one group of fifty men and women aged twenty to thirty residing in a second midwestern city, a group of sixty Negro men and women aged forty to sixty in a third midwestern city, and a group of forty persons aged seventy to eighty in a New England community. Essentially the same patterns emerged in each set of data.

The Problem and the Method

Based upon various sets of data such as those illustrated in Table 1, the present investigation proceeded on the assumption that age norms and age expectations operate in this society as a system of social control. For a great variety of behaviors, there is a span of years within which the occurrence of a given behavior is regarded as appropriate. When the behavior occurs outside that span of years, it is regarded as inappropriate and is negatively sanctioned.

The specific questions of this study were these: How do members of the society vary in their perception of the strictures involved in age norms, or in the degree of constraint they perceive with regard to age-appropriate behaviors? To what extent are personal attitudes congruent with the attitudes ascribed to the generalized other? Finally, using this congruence as an index of socialization, can adult socialization to age norms be shown to occur as respondents themselves increase in age?

The Instrument

A questionnaire was constructed in which the respondent was asked on each of a series of items which of three ages he would regard as appropriate or inappropriate, or which he would approve or disapprove. As seen in the illustrations below, the age spans being proposed were intended to be psychologically rather than chronologically equal in the sense that for some events a broad age span is appropriate, for others, a narrow one.

- A woman who feels it's all right at her age to wear a two-piece bathing suit to the beach:
  When she's 45 (approve or disapprove)
  When she's 30 (approve or disapprove)
  When she's 18 (approve or disapprove).

Other illustrative items were:

- A woman who decides to have another child (when she's 45, 37, 30).
- A man who's willing to move his family from one town to another to get ahead in his company (when he's 45, 35, 25).

- A couple who like to do the "twist" (when they're 55, 30, 20).
- A man who still prefers living with his parents rather than getting his own apartment (when he's 30, 25, 21).
- A couple who move across country so they can live near their married children (when they're 40, 55, 70).

The thirty-nine items finally selected after careful pretesting are divided equally into three types: those that relate to occupational career; those that relate to the family cycle; and a broader grouping that refer to recreation, appearance, and consumption behaviors. In addition, the items were varied systematically with regard to their applicability to three periods: young adulthood, middle age, and old age.

In general, then, the questionnaire presents the respondent with a relatively balanced selection of adult behaviors which were known from pretesting to be successful in evoking age discriminations. A means of scoring was devised whereby the score reflects the degree of refinement with which the respondent makes age discriminations. For instance, the respondent who approves of a couple dancing the "twist" if they are twenty, but who disapproves if they are thirty, is placing relative age constraint upon this item of behavior as compared to another respondent who approves the "twist" both at age twenty and at age thirty, but not at age fifty-five. The higher the score, the more the respondent regards age as a salient dimension across a wide variety of behaviors and the more constraint he accepts in the operation of age norms.[6]

The Sample

A quota sample of middle-class respondents was obtained in which level of education, occupation, and area of residence were used to determine social class. The sample is divided into six age-sex cells: fifty men and fifty women aged twenty to thirty, one hundred men and one hundred women aged thirty to fifty-five, and fifty men and fifty women aged sixty-five and over. Of the four hundred respondents, all but a few in the older group were or had been married. The great majority were parents of one or more children.

The only known bias in the sample occurs in the older group (median age for men is sixty-nine; for women seventy-two), where most individuals were members of senior citizens clubs and where, as a result, the subsample is biased in the direction of better health and greater community involvement than can be expected for the universe of persons in this age range. While senior citizens is a highly age-conscious and highly age-graded association from the perspective of the wider society, there is no evidence that the seventy-year-old who joins is any more or any less aware of age discriminations than is the seventy-year-old who does not join.[7] The older group was no more or less homogeneous with regard to religious affiliation, ethnic background, or indexes of social class than were the other two age groups in this sample.

Administration

To investigate the similarity between personal attitudes and attitudes ascribed to the generalized other, the questionnaire was first administered with instructions to give "your personal opinions" about each of the items; then the respondent was given a second copy of the questionnaire and asked to respond in the way he believed "most people" would respond.[8]

In about half the cases, both forms of the instrument were administered consecutively in personal interviews. In the remainder of the cases, responses on the first form were gathered in group sessions (in one instance, a parents' meeting in a school), and the second form was completed later and returned by mail to the investigator.

The two types of administration were utilized about evenly within each age-sex group. No significant differences in responses were found to be due to this difference in procedure of data-gathering.

Findings

The findings of this study can be read from Figure 1. The figure shows a striking convergence with age between the two sets of attitudes.

1. Age trends within each set of data are opposite in direction. With regard to personal opinions, there is a highly significant increase in scores with age—that is, an increase in the extent to which respondents ascribe importance to age norms and place constraints upon adult behavior in terms of age appropriateness.
2. With regard to "most people's opinions" there is a significant decrease in scores with age—that is, a decrease in the extent to which age constraints are perceived in the society and attributed to a generalized other.
3. Sex differences are minimal with the exception that young women stand somewhat outside the general trend on "personal opinions," with scores that differentiate them from young men but not from middle-aged women.

Discussion

The difference shown in these data between personal attitudes and attitudes attributed to the generalized other (a finding that holds true for all but the oldest respondents) implies that age norms operate like other types of norms insofar as there is some lack of congruence between that which is acknowledged to be operating in the society and that which is personally accepted as valid. It is noteworthy, on the one hand, that age norms are uniformly acknowledged to exist in the minds of "most people." While the data are not shown here, on each one of the thirty-nine behavioral items some 80 percent or more of all respondents made age discriminations when asked for "most people's opinions." In other words,

Figure 1 Perception of Age Constraints in Adulthood, by Age and Sex

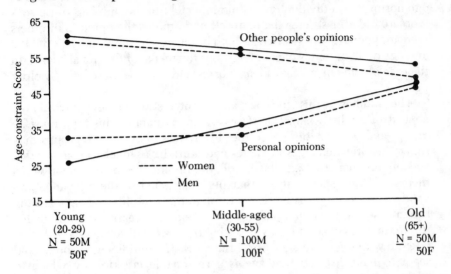

An analysis of variance for the data on "personal opinions" showed that age was a highly significant variable (F is statistically reliable beyond the .001 level); and the interaction between age and sex was significant (F is reliable at the .05 level). For the data on "other people's opinions," age alone is a significant variable (F is reliable beyond the .001 level).

general consensus exists that behaviors described in the test instrument are age-related. On the other hand, respondents uniformly attributed greater stricture to age norms in the minds of other people than in their own minds. This difference was reflected in the scores for every respondent as well as in the mean scores.

These findings indicate that there is an overriding norm of "liberal-mindedness" regarding age, whereby men and women consistently maintain that they hold more liberal views than do others. In many ways this situation is reminiscent of the phenomenon of pluralistic ignorance, in which no respondent's personal view of the attitudes of others is altogether correct.[9] In other ways, however, this may be a situation in which respondents tend to exaggerate, rather than to misconstrue, the opinions of others. A young person who says, in effect, "I am not strict about age norms, but other people are," is indeed correct that other people are stricter than he is (as shown in these data on "personal opinions"); but he exaggerates, for other people are not so strict as he thinks. Similarly, when an old person says, in effect, "I think this is the norm, and other people think so, too," he is also partly correct that other old people agree with him, but he ignores what *young* people think.

These partial misconceptions have at least two implications: first, when a person's own opinions differ from the norms he encounters, he may exaggerate the differences and place the norms even further away from his own opinions than is warranted. Second, it may be that in considering age norms, the individual gives undue weight to the opinions of persons who are older or stricter than himself and ignores the opinions of others who are younger or less strict. In both instances, the norm image is not the average of all opinions encountered but the image of the "ideal" norm. In the case of age norms, the "ideal" norms may well be those held by older persons.

The findings of this study are also of interest when viewed within the context of adult socialization. Cross-sectional data of this type must be interpreted with caution since the differences between age groups may reflect historical changes in values and attitudes as much as changes that accompany increased age itself. Still, the findings seem congruent with a theory of adult socialization: that personal belief in the relevance and validity of social norms increases through the adult life span and that, in this instance, as the individual ages he becomes increasingly aware of age discriminations in adult behavior and of the system of social sanctions that operate with regard to age appropriateness. The middle-aged and the old seem to have learned that age is a reasonable criterion by which to evaluate behavior, that to be "off-time" with regard to life events or to show other age-deviant behavior brings with it social and psychological sequelae that cannot be disregarded. In the young, especially the young male, this view is only partially accepted; and there seems to be a certain denial of age as a valid dimension by which to judge behavior.

This age-related difference in point of view is perhaps well illustrated by the response of a twenty-year-old who, when asked what he thought of marriage between seventeen-year-olds, said, "I suppose it would be all right if the boy got a good job, and if they loved each other. Why not? It isn't age that's the important thing." A forty-five-year-old, by contrast, said, "At that age, they'd be foolish. Neither one of them is settled enough. A boy on his own, at seventeen, couldn't support a wife, and he certainly couldn't support children. Kids who marry that young will suffer for it later."

Along with increased personal conviction regarding the validity of age norms goes a decreased tendency to perceive the generalized other as restrictive. The over-all convergence in the data, a convergence which we have interpreted in terms of adult socialization, may reflect status and deference relationships between age groups in American society, where high status is afforded the middle-aged and where social enforcement of norms may generally be said to be vested in the mature rather than the young. The young person, having only recently graduated from the age-segregated world of adolescents, and incompletely socialized to adult values, seems to perceive a psychological distance between himself and "most people" and to feel only partially identified with the adult world. This is evidenced by the fact that when asked, "Whom do you have in mind when you think of 'most people'?" young adults tended to answer, "Older people."

Only for old people is there a high degree of congruence between personal opinions and the opinions ascribed to others. This may reflect not only the accumulated effects of adult socialization and the internalization of age norms, but also a certain crystallization of attitudes in the aged. Older respondents volunteered the most vehement and the most opinionated comments as they moved from item to item, as if to underscore the fact that their attitudes with regard to age and age-related behaviors are highly charged emotionally. Under these circumstances, there is likely to be a blurring of distinctions between what the respondent himself regards as right and what he thinks other people would "naturally" regard as right.

With regard to sex differences, the fact that young women perceive greater constraints regarding age-appropriate behavior than do young men is generally congruent with other evidence of differences in socialization for women and men in our society. Young women are probably more highly sensitized to the imperatives of age norms than are young men, given the relatively more stringent expectations regarding age at marriage for women.

It should be recalled that the present study is based upon quota samples of middle-class respondents and that accordingly the findings cannot be readily generalized to other samples. Nevertheless, the findings support the interpretation that age norms are salient over a wide variety of adult behaviors and support the view that adult socialization produces increasingly clear perception of these norms as well as an increasing awareness that the norms provide constraints upon adult behavior.

NOTES

This article is adapted from the paper "Age Norms and Age Constraints in Adulthood," presented at the annual meeting of the American Sociological Association, September 1963. This study has been financed by research grant No. 4200 from the National Institute of Mental Health (Bernice L. Neugarten, principal investigator). The authors are indebted to Mrs. Karol Weinstein for assistance in the collection and treatment of the data.

1. Following the classic article by Karl Mannheim ("The Problem of Generations," *Essays on the Sociology of Knowledge* [New York: Oxford University Press, 1952], pp. 276–322), these include Ralph Linton's discussion in *The Study of Man* (New York: Appleton-Century, 1936); Ruth Benedict, "Continuities and Discontinuities in Culture Conditioning," *Psychiatry*, I (1938), 161–67; Kingsley Davis, "The Sociology of Parent-Youth Conflict," *American Sociological Review*, V (1940), 523–35; and Talcott Parsons, "Age and Sex in the Social Structure of the United States," *American Sociological Review*, VII (October 1942), 604–16. Anthropological classics include Arnold Van Gennep (1908), *The Rites of Passage* (Chicago: University of Chicago Press, 1960); Robert H. Lowie (1920), *Primitive Society* (New York: Harper & Bros., 1961). More recently, A. H. J. Prins, *East African Age-Class Systems* (Groningen: J. B. Wolters, 1953) has presented a critical analysis of concepts and terms in use among anthropologists.

2. S. N. Eisenstadt, *From Generation to Generation* (Glencoe, Ill.: Free Press, 1956); and Bennett M. Berger, "How Long Is a Generation?" *British Journal of Sociology*, XI (1960), 10–23.

3. With some exceptions, such as the work of Robert K. Merton, *Social Theory and Social Structure* (Glencoe, Ill.: Free Press, 1957), sociologists have as yet given little attention to the broader problem of adult socialization.

4. The sample was drawn by area-probability methods (a 2 percent listing of households in randomly selected census tracts) with the resulting pool of cases then stratified by age, sex, and socioeconomic status. Using the indexes of occupation, level of education, house type, and area of residence, these respondents were all middle class. The data were gathered in connection with the Kansas City Studies of Adult Life, a research program carried out over a period of years under the direction of Robert J. Havighurst, William E. Henry, Bernice L. Neugarten, and other members of the Committee on Human Development, University of Chicago.

5. For each item in the table, the percentages that appear in the third and fourth columns obviously vary directly with the breadth of the age span shown for that item. The age span shown was, in turn, the one selected by the investigators to produce the most accurate reflection of the consensus that existed in the data.

   The way in which degree of consensus was calculated can be illustrated on "Best age for a man to marry." Individuals usually responded to this item in terms of specific years, such as "20" or "22," or in terms of narrow ranges, such as "from 20 to 23." These responses were counted as consensus within the five-year age range shown in Table 1, on the grounds that the respondents were concurring that the best age was somewhere between twenty and twenty-five. A response such as "18 to 20" or "any time in the 20's" was outside the range regarded as consensus and was therefore excluded.

6. For each item of behavior, one of the ages being proposed is scored as the "appropriate" age; another, the "marginal"; and the third, the "inappropriate" (the age at which the behavior is usually proscribed on the basis of its transgression of an age norm). A response which expresses disapproval of only the "inappropriate" age is scored 1, while a response which expresses disapproval of not only the "inappropriate" but also the "marginal" age receives a score of 3. The total possible score is 117, a score that could result only if the respondent were perceiving maximum age constraint with regard to every one of the thirty-nine items. A response which expresses approval or disapproval of all three ages for a given behavior is scored zero, since for that respondent the item is not age-related, at least not within the age range being proposed.

   The "appropriate" age for each item had previously been designated by the investigators on the basis of previous findings such as those illustrated on Table 1 of this report. That the designations were generally accurate was corroborated by the fact that when the present instrument was administered to the four hundred respondents described here, more than 90 percent of respondents on successive test items checked "approve" for the "appropriate" one of the three proposed ages.

7. On the other hand, members of senior citizens are more likely to be activists and to regard themselves as younger in outlook than persons who do not join such groups. If this is true, the age differences to be described in the following sections of this paper might be expected to be even more marked in future studies in which samples are more representative.

8. The problem being studied here relates to problems of conformity, deviation, and personal versus public attitudes. As is true of other empirical research in

these areas, the terms used here are not altogether satisfactory, in part because of the lack of uniform terminology in this field. For example, while age norms are in some respects related to "attitudinal" and "doctrinal" conformity as posed by Robert K. Merton ("Social Conformity, Deviation, and Opportunity Structures: A Comment on the Contributions of Dubin and Cloward," *American Sociological Review*, XXIV [1959], 177–189), these data do not fit that analytical framework because age norms are less clear-cut than the norms Merton discusses, and the realms of attitudinal and doctrinal conformity are less prescribed.

Similarly, the projection of personal attitudes upon the generalized other has been studied by Jacob W. Getzels and J. J. Walsh ("The Method of Paired Direct and Projective Questionnaires in the Study of Attitude Structure and Socialization," *Psychological Monographs*, Vol. LXXVII [Whole No. 454, 1958]); but their theoretical model is not altogether applicable because in the present research the phenomenon of projection cannot be demonstrated. The same lack of fit exists with the concepts used by Milton Rokeach, *The Open and Closed Mind* (New York: Basic Books, 1960); and with the concepts of social norms, norms of common consent, and personal norms as used by Elizabeth Bott, *Family and Social Network* (London: Tavistock, 1957). The *self, generalized other* terminology is therefore regarded as the most appropriate for describing the present data.

9. Floyd H. Allport, *Social Psychology* (Boston: Houghton Mifflin, 1924).

Generational Difference and the Developmental Stake

VERN L. BENGTSON AND
JOSEPH A. KUYPERS

While there are many reasons for the dissimilarities and conflicts between generations, the emphasis in this selection is on the role played by the differing developmental stakes the young and middle generations have in each other—that is, their need for each other. Because the older generation has a stake in continuity and the validation of their lives and values, and the young have a stake in just the opposite, in discontinuity and the freedom to develop their own life styles, they perceive their interactions with each other differently. The older generation tends to minimize the generation gap, believing that differences are mainly a matter of life status and maturity. The younger generation tends to maximize the differences, which it sees as arising from opposing values and morality. Both sides fear the loss of something they cherish. The authors suggest that an awareness of the arbitrariness of these fears can help reduce intergenerational conflict.

There is drama in the continuing succession of one generation by another. This drama begins with the differences in behavior and attitudes exhibited by emerging generations; it develops with the reaction of older generations to these innovations; and it reaches a climax with the changes in configuration of culture which result. And then the drama begins anew, with yet another cast of actors.

In today's society something new seems to have been added to the drama: a sense of urgency, of concern that the magnitude of differences between age groups has outstripped the continuity of plot that holds culture together. One wonders about those differences. What causes significant behavioral contrasts between generations? Why do such differences seem so stridently obvious today? Are they, perhaps, more apparent than real? What accounts for the anxiety surrounding generational differences? What explains the contrasting responses of youth and their elders to the manifestation of such differences; why are they welcomed by youth, and perceived with dismay or indignation by parents?

SOURCE: Reprinted from the *International Journal of Aging and Human Development*, Vol. 2, No. 4. Copyright 1971 by Baywood Publishing Company, Inc.

A growing number of analyses have contributed much to understanding the causes of dissimilarity between generations in behavior (see, for example, Cain, 1967, 1970; Elkind, 1970; Neugarten, 1970; Thomas, 1971; Troll, 1970; Hill, 1970). However, social scientists have not been as successful in identifying those factors affecting the quality of *interactions* and the element of *threat* in intergenerational interchanges. Perhaps prior analyses have focused too little on the issue of attribution—the *perceptions* generational actors have of each other and the bases for these perceptions. The purpose of this paper is to examine some critical factors which may determine perceptions across generations, under the central assumption that *cross-generational perceptions are just as determinative of the quality of intergenerational relations as are the actual differences* in philosophy, attitude, and action between cohorts.

Our argument is as follows: The perceptions one generation has of another in interaction are related less to the state of the *perceived* than to the state of the *perceiver*. We will suggest that the individual's personal history, his position in society, and his state of development substantially color his perceptions and expectations of the other generations. Further, we will argue that cross-generation perceptions of their mutual interaction are often based on two processes: the *fear-of-loss mythology* ("If I don't watch out, I'm going to lose. . . .") and the *developmental-stake mythology* ("If the young reject my values, my life has come to nothing"). We submit that these mythologies contribute substantially to the experience of anxiety in the drama of generations, because they work to increase the gap between what is perceived and what is real in generational differences. We will argue, in conclusion, that differences between age groups need not be tinged with such fear, for the drama of generational evolution contains the potential for adaption to, and mastery of, social ills.

In discussing our own perceptions of the drama of generations, we will draw from two ongoing studies at the University of Southern California and the University of California, Berkeley. The first is a large survey of youth, their parents, and grandparents, focusing on attitudinal aspects of differences and continuities between cohorts. The second study is an extension of the long-term longitudinal project begun in Berkeley in 1928, in which the aged parents of the original sample are being interviewed in order to examine continuities through time and between generations in aspects of personality and social functioning. These studies are, of course, still in progress and we will be using our impressions gathered from as yet incomplete data to support the argument.

Some Data on Differences in Perception Across Generations

We begin with some data from a study of students and their parents more fully described elsewhere (Bengtson, 1969). These data suggest considerable differences in perception between the youthful and mature generation when both look at their common interaction.[1]

Perceptions of Generational Social Distance

First we will review previously reported findings regarding what may be called "social distancing" between generations. Perceptions of within-family interaction were overwhelmingly favorable; for example, on the summary measure of intergenerational integration, a very high proportion of each generation (78 percent of the students and 87 percent of the parents) reported "close" or "very close" relations. Similar reponses were elicited by the questions concerning global evaluation of the quality of communication and understanding between parents and students. Even given this favorable assessment, some differences in perception emerge. Parents consistently overestimated the degrees of closeness, understanding, and communication, compared to their children's responses. Perceptions of generational interaction outside the family showed the same pattern. When asked if they thought a "generation gap" existed, over 80 percent of the students said yes, while only 40 percent of the parents responded affirmatively. Further, when asked if this gap is inevitable, 70 percent of the students said yes, compared to only 58 percent of the parents (percentages based on those cases responding yes to the preceding question).

What these data seem to indicate is, first, that in terms of their own family, both parents and students tend to minimize the scope of the "generation gap." In the second place, however, there is a consistent difference between parents and children, with the students consistently emphasizing a greater distance and the parents minimizing the distance. These data, admittedly tapping surface perceptions and broad generalizations concerning intergenerational relations, indicate that youth and parents indeed display a different perception of the nature and evaluation of intergenerational relations, both within and outside the family.

Perceptions of Family Discussion and Disagreement

Respondents were also asked to report the extent of discussion between themselves and their parent (or child) on eleven topics selected on the basis of pilot studies as of greatest import for families of young adults. The topics, ranging from religion and politics to sex and dating, were each rated as to the frequency of discussion and then the amount of disagreement. The results of the comparison between the students' reports and those of the parents is presented in Table 1.

It can be seen from this table that there is a statistically stable difference between the amount of discussion reported by the parents and that reported by the children. For both the mother and the father, the estimate of the parent is higher than that of the child. In terms of disagreement perceived in these eleven issues, the obverse pattern emerges. Students report considerably higher disagreement than do the parents.

TABLE 1   Differences in Amount of Discussion and Disagreement on Eleven Topics as Reported by Parents and Children[1]
(N = 312 students, 371 parents)

	Students' perception		Parents' perception			
	$\overline{X}$	s.d.	$\overline{X}$	s.d.	t	p
Discussion:						
With father	27.07	6.40	30.37	6.17	5.42	.001
With mother	29.36	6.60	33.69	4.71	7.72	.001
Disagreement:						
With father	19.89	5.47	17.72	4.16	4.37	.001
With mother	19.56	5.21	17.32	3.15	5.20	.001

[1] Scores are summed means on reported discussion or disagreement on eleven issues, such as values, politics, religion, sex, money, dating, friends, etc. Scores on each item range from 1 (never discuss, never disagree) to 4 (discuss very often, very often disagree).

Why should such differences in the definition of mutual interaction exist? Part of the answer must be found in the *expectations* brought to the interaction by the two generations.

Perceptions of the Nature of Generational Difference

We asked about the specific nature of generational differences as experienced by the Ss. One would expect youth and parents to be concerned with different aspects of the relationship and thus to attend to different factors as being problematic.

A content analysis was carried out on the open-ended responses to several questions: In what ways is there a generation gap in your society, in your opinion? What is it that you disagree about most with your parents (child)? In what ways would you like to see the relationship with your parents (child) changed?

These questions ask for the content of the respondent's perceptions of the generations and, therefore, his own personal concerns as he looks at the drama of generational differences. The issues that parents identify as sources of friction between themselves and their children may be considered as evidence not so much of the student's behavior, but of the dominant concern that the parents have.

With regard to the first question, that of the personal definition of the "gap," it is clear (Table 2) that both parents and students agree on three major areas as basic issues dividing the generations: issues of value and morality; issues of interpersonal interaction, such as tolerance, understanding, and closeness; and the age-status issues having to do with responsibility and freedom. However, there is a difference between the generations regarding the emphasis placed on the different categories. Students maintained that issues of values and morality are the essential definers of the "gap" (35 percent), while parents saw the greatest cause in

TABLE 2 In what ways is there a generation gap? In your own words, define the "gap."

	Students		Parents		Both (total)	
	%	N	%	N	%	N
1. Personal habits and traits (grooming, empathy, stubbornness, underachieving)	4.0	10	4.8	16	4.5	26
2. General personal orientations (use of time, leisure, hypocrisy)	2.8	7	1.8	6	2.2	13
3. Values and morality (life goals, philosophy of life, sex, religion)	34.8	88	19.7	64	26.2	152
4. Age-status and generational issues (maturity, responsibility, freedom, independence, age, diff. life exper.)	19.8	50	25.9	85	23.3	135
5. Politics and social relations (social consciousness, patriotism, law and order, race relations, politics)	2.8	7	.6	2	1.6	9
6. Interpersonal interaction (tolerance, understanding, closeness, family rules, choice of friends)	25.0	63	29.0	95	27.2	158
7. Economic issues	0	0	.3	1	.2	1
8. No gap: gap is a myth	4.0	10	8.6	28	6.6	38
9. Other and noncategorizable	7.1	18	9.5	31	8.4	49
SUBTOTAL		253		278		581
10. No response	18.9	59	11.6	43	14.9	102
TOTAL	100.0	312	100.0	371	100.0	683

the area of breakdowns in interaction between the generations (29 percent). Over twice as many parents as students maintained that "there is no gap" or that "the gap is a myth" (4 to 9 percent).

This basic difference in theme becomes even more apparent in the respondents' attempts to define the gap as it most applies to their own families (Table 3). Parents responded in two major areas: grooming, housekeeping, empathy (22 percent), and lack of tolerance, understanding, and closeness (19 percent). Again, the students identified as a primary source of disagreement issues relating to values and philosophy of life (22 percent). Problems of interpersonal relations (23 percent) ranked high for the students, as for the parents; but the issues of politics and social relations, while cited as important areas of disagreement by the students

TABLE 3 What is it you disagree about most with your parents (child)?

	Students		Parents		Both (total)	
	%	N	%	N	%	N
1. Personal habits and traits (grooming, empathy, stubbornness, underachieving)	6.8	21	21.6	72	14.7	93
2. General personal orientations (use of time, leisure, hypocrisy)	6.6	20	9.0	30	7.9	50
3. Values and morality (life goals, philosophy of life, sex, religion)	21.6	65	9.3	31	15.2	96
4. Age-status and generational issues (maturity, responsibility, freedom, independence, age, diff. life exper.)	7.2	22	5.1	17	6.2	39
5. Politics and social relations (social consciousness, patriotism, law and order, race relations, politics)	13.4	40	8.1	27	10.6	67
6. Interpersonal interaction (tolerance, understanding, closeness, family rules, choice of friends)	22.9	69	18.6	62	20.8	131
7. Economic issues	9.0	27	8.7	29	8.9	56
8. No, nothing much	6.7	20	15.6	52	11.4	72
9. Other and noncategorizable	5.0	15	3.6	12	4.3	27
SUBTOTAL		299		332		531
10. No response	4.3	13	10.5	39	7.6	52
TOTAL	100.1	312	100.0	371	99.9	683

(13 percent), were not defined as one of the top three areas of discord by the parents (8 percent). Sixteen percent of the parents said that there is no disagreement whatsoever, compared with 7 percent of the children.

The pattern of responses by the two generations to these and other questions seems consistent. Both parents and students identify disagreement in the dimensions of interpersonal interaction (lack of respect, tolerance, family rules, etc.). From this point the generations diverge. Students point to issues of values, morality, politics, and life goals as major points of friction between generations, while parents attend to the personal habits and traits. Parents tend to minimize the philosophical, abstract, ideological component of differences, while the students maximize these differences. Parents attend to issues of personal habits and traits and the age-status differences and personal maturity.

It is as if the parents were saying, "Yes, there are differences between the generations, but these are not intrinsic; they are simply due to difference in life status and maturity." The students, by contrast, are saying, "The contrasts we see are in values and basic orientations to life. There are differences, and they are important."

These data suggest (a) that there is a consistent pattern of solidarity and warmth between the generations, and (b) that there are also differences in the interpretation each has of their interaction. There must be therefore some *expectational processes related to the other generation that color perception.* What are these processes? One has to do with *one's own experiences as members of an age group rooted in time,* time measured in both historical and personal terms. Another has to do with *one's own need for the other generation:* it may be termed the "developmental stake."

Objective Roots of Generational Difference: History, Power, Maturity

To understand the differences, both real and perceived, between age groups, it is necessary to recognize the historical, social, and personal factors that influence the experiencing of each generation. In some ways a discussion of such factors may seem premature, because of the frequently overlooked fact that the nature, extent, and consequences of differences between generations are still very much open to a variety of interpretations (see Feuer, 1969; Adelson, 1970; Bengtson, 1970; Kalish, 1969; Mead, 1970). In this paper we have chosen not to focus on the degree to which actual differences in philosophy, action, or moral judgment exist (or do not exist), for we have commented on these elsewhere (Bengtson, 1969, 1970; Birren and Bengtson, 1969; Kobrin and Bengtson, 1970; Kuypers, 1970). Rather, we intend to emphasize the critical factors that determine perceptions across generational lines, under the assumption that one foundation for intergenerational action is its perceptual base. There are four factors which are readily observable (hence "objective") that account for such differences. We will mention these briefly before considering two additional "subjective" factors.

The first factor concerns the different *historical settings* in which different generations find themselves. As much as we are a product of our *zeitgeist,* displacement in historical time will contribute to differences in value, attitude, life style (see, among others, Mannheim, 1952; Berger, 1960).

A second factor concerns the point of contact an individual has relative to the historical evolution of *social institutions.* Social systems change; their component parts evolve with the passage of time. It is easy to see that young men of twenty years of age in 1900, in 1940, and in 1970, equated in every other way, would face quite a different spectre of military life, because of the transformations of that institution within our society.

A third factor involves *age-status differentials* and social system positions. Persons at different points along the life cycle typically exhibit differential penetration into, and identification with, the social institutions of their culture. This relates to the succession to higher and higher status with the passage of personal time, and to the differential commitment persons have in maintaining social institutions and personal investments. The picture is abundantly clear in terms of the middle generation having its major involvements and identities defined by the running, governing, educating, parenting, guiding roles in society. The power differential that this social system identification creates becomes a major source of clash between generations (see Feuer, 1969; Musgrove, 1969).

Fourth, there is the critically important factor of differential life tasks and psychological concerns patterned by *psychological development*. While it is clear that society changes over time, that behaviors and orientations of youth and middle age are partly conditioned by the historical context impinging on them, it is also clear that the individual experiences and adapts differently along his life line because of developmental changes. If one could, for the moment, hold constant personal history and vary only stage of psychological development, different concerns and interests would be evidenced. The dominant concerns, characteristic needs, or cognitive mechanisms of forty-year-olds are different from those of twenty-year-olds (see Birren, 1969). A recent dissertation by Weimer (1970) demonstrated age-related shifts in dominant psychological concerns from psychophysiological data. The variation in "developmental tasks" (Havighurst, 1953), "ego-developmental crises" (Erikson, 1950, 1959), "decelerated socialization" (Davis, 1940), or "increased interiority" of personality (Neugarten, 1968), between one stage of life and another, leads inevitably to significant differences in interaction and perspectives between cohorts. Or, in the words of one of our respondents, a forty-three-year-old mother:

> The younger generation cannot feel or think as an older person who has had a myriad of experiences, responsibilities, joys, disappointments, and sadness to color his thinking, perspectives, values, and reactions. Likewise, it is difficult to remember how *we* felt and thought when we were younger—the plain joy of living, the things we considered important, etc.

Many scholars have commented that differences in value, philosophy, and ego involvements are likely over time. Erikson and Neugarten for example, have noted that the *intimacy* concerns of a young adult have quite a different impact on the person than do the *generative* concerns of the middle-aged man or woman. These concerns, for the young person, are likely to lead to a primary interest in the development and establishment of personally meaningful relationships with peers, the development and establishment of personal philosophies and value systems on which to base action. The middle-aged person, by contrast, is likely to be critically concerned with the maintenance of already developed commitments and value systems and with the development of what might be called *personal heirs*. The concern is not with personal relationships with peers, but with the development and growth of social and personal heirs to extend one's personal history into the future.

These psychological concerns have quite different implications regarding the saliency one generation has relative to another. Youth, for example, is likely to experience the parenting generation, in part, as relatively expendable objects. Their role of parenting and socializing is past, from the youth's point of view. Attempts of the parenting generation to guide and direct, to control or instruct, may be experienced with mild toleration or more dramatic irritation. The parenting generation, on the other hand, is likely to invest a good deal of energy in the progress and development of youth. Great concern and personal meaning is attached to their behavior. In short, they are high saliency objects.

Thus the condition is set in which middle generation adults need to orient, socialize, and direct youth, a direction which, itself, is antithetical to the personal concerns of youth. And so we now have the elements which create a *differential of intentionality* between generations. While youth presses for minimization of external controls, the press of the middle generation is just the opposite, to guarantee generational continuity through influence on the youth.

It is interesting to note that Erikson views the grandparenting generation as concerned with personal issues of meaningfulness of life, of personal integrity, and with life review. In this view, other persons of younger generations may be relatively low saliency objects, regardless of age. This is similar to an element in Charlotte Buhler's theory of phases in life goals (see Buhler, 1967). Buhler emphasizes that the fourth phase of the life cycle (forty-five to sixty-five) involves self-assessment regarding attained or failed goals; while the fifth (after sixty-five) centers on the tendency to establish inner order.

Up to this point we have adhered relatively faithfully to reasoning introduced by scholars of the stature of Erikson, Havighurst, Buhler, and Neugarten. By now a departure is required to examine the foundations for middle and young generational developmental concerns, the relation of these concerns to perception, and their essential mythological character.

Subjective Roots of Generational Perception: The Developmental Stake and the Fear of Loss Myth

David Elkind (1970) has called attention to the contractual agreements entered into by parents and children. He emphasizes that the terms of the contract must change with the increasing maturity of the child, as the nature of the investment each bases in the other shifts. Bettelheim (1963) has noted that some parents may view as their child's main task in life the justification of a parent; the child is to provide the parent with what was lacking in his (the parent's) own life. Some children may view their goal in life as that of surpassing the parent—socially, economically, or intellectually. These examples focus on our central concern in explaining differences in cross-generational perception: the nature of *interactional expectations* as each generation views the other.

What is it in an individual's condition that determines how he sees another? When one has an investment in the fortunes of another, the expectation is often summarized by saying, "I've got a stake in him." What is the nature of the stakes the generations have in each other, and the roots of these stakes?

For the middle generation, evidence points to the high saliency of issues centering around the meaning, the justification, and, as Haan (1970) has pointed out, the validation of their life and the commitments they have made to it. This is especially true in times of rapid social change when previously assumed cultural values are called into question. At a time when the middle generation may be confronting the realization of their personal mortality, the glimmering realization of the finitude of their own personal history, questions about the essential worth, meaning, and even judgment of their life come to the foreground. Neugarten has suggested that a shift in time perspective occurs in middle age, when time left to live becomes the life-cycle yardstick.

We maintain that many in the middle years seek resolution to these issues in the development of the young generation. An experienced continuity with the next generation—which is one's personal extension into the future—becomes the experiential answer to the questions What is my life all about? Where will it lead to? Does it make any sense?

An interesting example of this concern is found in the long history behind inheritance litigation. Recently Back and Baade (1966) presented a social-psychological analysis of "the social meaning of death and the law." They argued that the use of the law and its inheritance restrictions are designed to be safeguards against man's tendency, especially in the wealthy and powerful, to extend his control and influence well past his death. To quote from Back and Baade (p. 316),

> the urge to control the conduct of future generations through conditional or limited testamentary dispositions in favor of natural persons and of charities is deepseated, especially in Great Britain and in the United States.

The developmental stake which the middle generation has in the young, therefore, creates a view of the young as social heirs, that is, as (*a*) extension of the self and (*b*) continuous with the older generation's personal-social order. This developmental concern colors the perception the elders have of the emerging generation. It explains why the middle generation would *minimize the essentiality* of differences perceived between the generations. In the face of behavior which, in reality, reflects both difference and continuity, the middle generation is constrained to believe and perhaps to fabricate the continuity.

The developmental stake of the young is quite different. They have high investment in establishing their personal life styles, in forming their attitudes toward major issues and institutions. As based on their developmental concerns, they are more concerned with the *establishment*, as opposed to the *validation*, of values and strategies. Such issues imply freedom to experience and develop.

In other words, youth is at a point of attempting to establish its existence and its style, to throw off the *stake* of the parenting generation. An oppositional stake is created, a stake which colors youth's view of the middle generation. The young are pressed to see discontinuity across generations, and they tend to *maximize the essentiality* of differences. For them, those of the middle generation are low saliency objects. Thus they react with the anticipation of differences and with the tendency to view the differences as essential.

Cross-Generational Differences and the Fear of Loss

We now have before us the array of influences which explain the fear-of-loss mythology; the backdrop for interpreting the intergenerational drama. For the middle generation, the feared loss is, indeed, quite dramatic. If not one's existence, certainly one's validation is at stake. The completion of our earlier statement is "If I don't watch out, I'm going to lose my identity, reason for being, and value." Difference is indicative of loss. Loss is feared, hence the demand to counteract the feared loss.

There exists in the middle generation a ready vocabulary of motive to explain away the youth revolt. Phrases such as the following are used often these days—and often by those in highest offices—as adults attempt to explain the violence of youthful confrontation: only a passing phase . . . a radical minority . . . outside agitators . . . only a bystander . . . a communist plot to undermine . . . breakdown of discipline . . . a function of college administrative spinelessness . . . simply youthful experimentation . . . certainly not true in my family. The message of such euphemisms may be the following: My stake in the oncoming generation is so great that there cannot be any basic disruption between us. To so disrupt will seriously question the validity of my own beliefs.

The same fear of loss exists in the younger generation. The fear here is related to powerlessness, to the perceived meaninglessness of the social order into which one is moving, and to the blurring of distinctiveness between oneself and the parenting generation. There exists a ready vocabulary of motive to explain the essentiality of revolt: You can't trust *anyone* over thirty . . . nonnegotiable demands . . . so up-tight . . . irrelevant . . . off the pigs. The message here is: My stake in the future is being cataclysmically endangered by the controls put on by the middle-aged Establishment. My stake in the freedom the older generation wants to deny me is so great that there cannot be any continuity between us. To see continuity is to seriously question the validity of my own beliefs about the nature of man, environment, wealth, and interpersonal affairs.

The Relation of Perception to Control

While identifying the mythological bases for intergenerational perceptions (mythological in the sense that their validation is nonexistent), it is at once apparent that they serve as very real bases for action, especially action in the form of control and influence. As noted earlier, the developmental stake implies differential control of the generations: the middle is more likely to control the destinies of the young, being in command of information, monies, and other resources, and being concerned with generational continuity. The young are predisposed to seek dissociation between themselves and the generation of those in command. The difficulty comes in the extent to which the young experience the forces on them as controlling and whether these controls violate philosophical roots of life, such as freedom, openness, justice. The middle-aged see youth resenting the legitimate demands for order and continuity, while youth experiences arbitrary expression of control and authority.

For the young generation, therefore, the fear of loss involves loss of freedom—the freedom to choose and establish personal controls. As with the middle generation, the anticipated fear of loss across the generations is quite dramatic for the young. The stakes are high on both sides of the generational theater.

Conclusion

In this paper we have explored the influences, real or mythological, of those factors that lead to differential perceptions across generations. Our analysis has centered on the assumption that perceptions are one foundation for action between generations. We explored the historical, social, and personal causes of differential perception across generations. We concluded by suggesting the existence of a basic contrast in expectations concerning generational interaction, rooted in the developmental stakes each generation has in each other and the mythological bases for these perceptions.

To recapitulate, our argument has been this: For the middle generation, the backdrop for perceiving generational relations concerns the establishment and maintenance of *continuity* over time. Experienced *conflict* arises from their anticipation that youthful emergence, unless guided and controlled, will create disruptive discontinuity. For the young generation, the perception backdrop rests on their focus on individuation, change, and *emergence*. Experienced conflict arises from their anticipation that middle-generation influence will delimit their development. For both, perceptions across generations are characterized by *fear*: fear of losing the ability to emerge, on the one hand, and to establish continuity, on the other.

The question naturally arises, after having argued for the sources of fear in the generational drama, of how to reduce the defensive, protective, and what seems to be the self-defeating conflict between generations. While not pretending to approach an inclusive answer to this critical question, we do nurture the hope that *awareness* of the arbitrariness of the essential fear across generations will help. To realize that the perspectives, urgencies, and criticisms of youth, for example, do not intrinsically forecast social dissolution, but rather offer energy and commitment for constructive change will, itself, be helpful. To realize that the power and influence of the middle generation does not automatically predict generational control, but rather offers the mechanism for rapid social change, will, itself, be helpful. While the middle generation may be essentially concerned with *continuity* and validation, the emergence of youth is not intrinsically oppositional. Nor is the young person's struggle for emergence intrinsically antithetical to a quest for continuity.

Ultimately, all members of the generational drama must acknowledge that there is a moral error in behavior that seeks to control and externally determine the form of another's life, no matter what the reason. *To seek validation for the self through control of another is an error*, for individuals and for generations. Rather we must evaluate the worth of our social order and its institutions by the experiential meaning they have for people. The meaningful answer to the question of meaning rests not in the continuation through time of currently operative policies and structures, but in the effect they have on the condition of man. A shift is required in which we look not across generations, fearing what is to be lost and preparing to defend against that loss, but in which we seek what can be gained from the constructive utilization of the perspectives of youth and the executing abilities of the middle generation.

NOTES

An earlier version of this paper was presented at the symposium on "The Generation Gap: Real or Contrived?" American Psychological Association 78th Annual Convention, Miami Beach, September 4, 1970. We acknowledge the assistance of Marijo Walsh, Rosemary Sundeen, and Chris Lovejoy. Preparation of this paper was supported by Grant MH HD 18158 from NIMH.
1. This material derives from a survey of college students and their parents at a large private university. The study was later replicated with three other samples drawn from public institutions in the same area. A total of 312 students and 371 of their parents provided data in this study. This report was published in V. L. Bengtson, Inter-age differences in the generation gap, *Gerontologist*, 1971, Part II: 85-90.

REFERENCES

Adelson, J. What generation gap? *New York Times Magazine*, 1970 (Jan. 18), 10–13.

Back, K., and Baade, J. The social meaning of death and the law. In J. McKinney and F. De Vyver (Eds.), *Aging and social policy*. New York: Appleton-Century-Crofts, 1966.

Bengtson, V. L. The "generation gap": Differences by generation and by sex in the perception of parent-child relations. Paper presented at Pacific Sociological Association meetings, 1969.

Bengtson, V. L. The "generation gap": A review and typology of social-psychological perspectives. *Youth and society*, 1970, 2 (1).

Bengtson, V. L. Generation and family effects in value socialization. *American Sociological Review*, 1975, 40: 358–71.

Bengtson, V. L., and Black, K. D. Intergenerational relations and continuities in socialization. In P. Baltes and K. W. Schaie (Eds.), *Life-Span Developmental Psychology: Personality and Socialization*. New York: Academic Press, 1973.

Berger, B. How long is a generation? *British Journal of Sociology*, 1960, *II*, 10–23.

Bettelheim, B. The problem of generations. In E. Erikson (Ed.), *Youth: Change and challenge*. New York: Basic Books, 1963.

Birren, J. E., and Bengtson, V. L. The problem of generations: Emotions vs. reality. Paper presented at hearings before the Senate Subcommittee on Aging, held at the Center for the Study of Democratic Institutions, Santa Barbara, Calif., October 17, 1968. Condensation in *The Center Magazine*, 1969, 2 (2), 84–87.

Birren, J. E. Age and decision strategies. In A. T. Welford and J. E. Birren (Eds.), *Decision making and age*. Basel, Switzerland: Karger, 1969.

Buhler, C. Human life as a whole as a central subject in humanistic psychology. In J. Bugehtal (Ed.), *Challenges of humanistic psychology*. New York: McGraw-Hill, 1967.

Cain, L. D. Age status and generational phenomena: The new old people in contemporary America. *Gerontologist*, 1967, 7 (2), 83–92.

Cain, L. D. The 1916–1925 cohort: Their contribution to the "generation gap." Paper presented at the American Sociological Association meetings, September 2, 1970.

Davis, K. The sociology of parent-youth conflict. *American Sociological Review*, 1940, 5 (4), 523–534.

Elkind, D. P. The youth revolt and parental exploitation. *Mental Hygiene*, 1970, *54* (4), 490–497.

Erikson, E. H. *Childhood and society*. New York: W. W. Norton, 1950.

Erikson, E. Identity and the life cycle. *Psychological Issues*, 1959, 1 (1).

Feuer, L. *The conflict of generations: The character and significance of student movements*. New York: Basic Books, 1969.

Haan, N. The generation gap as moral redefinition in families. Paper presented at the American Psychological Association meetings, 1970.

Havighurst, R. Flexibility and the social roles of the retired. *American Journal of Sociology*, 1953, *59*: 309–11.

Hill, R. The three-generation technique as a method for measuring social change. In R. Hill and E. Konig (Eds.), *Families east and west*. Paris: Mouton, 1970.

Kalish, R. The young and the old as generation gap allies. *Gerontologist*, 1969, *9* (2), 83–90.

Kobrin, S. and Bengtson, V. L. Generational contrasts in the attribution of legitimacy. Paper presented at the American Sociological Association meetings, 1970.

Kuypers, J. Generational continuities and contrasts in personality: Effects on family interaction. Paper presented at Gerontological Society meetings, Toronto, October 24, 1970.

Mannheim, K. The problem of generations. In K. Mannheim, *Essays in the sociology of knowledge*. London: Routledge, Kegan Paul, 1952.

Mead, M. *Conflict and commitment: A study of the generation gap*. New York: Basic Books, 1970.

Musgrove, F. The problem of youth and the structure of society in England. *Youth and Society*, 1969, *1* (1), 39–58.

Neugarten, B. L. The awareness of middle age. In B. L. Neugarten (Ed.), *Middle age and aging: A reader in social psychology*. Chicago: University of Chicago Press, 1968.

Neugarten, B. L. The young and the old in modern societies. *American Behavioral Scientist*, 1970, *12*, 43–57.

Thomas, L. E. Family correlates of student political activism. *Developmental Psychology*, 1971, *4* (1), 58–73.

Troll, L. The generation gap: Conceptual models. *Aging and Human Development*, 1970, *1*, 199–218.

Weimer, A. S. Shifts in psychological concerns from adolescence to later maturity. Unpublished doctoral dissertation, University of Southern California, 1970.

The Mid-life Transition

DANIEL LEVINSON

Hypothesizing that adult life proceeds through a series of stages, Levinson studied forty men between the ages of thirty-five and forty-five who differed in terms of social class, racial, and religious background in order to specify the characteristics of these life stages. He and his colleagues interviewed these men who included hourly workers in industry, business executives, university biologists, and novelists over many months. This selection concerns the life stage termed the mid-life transition which occurs for a man between the ages of thirty-eight and forty-three. It is a time when a man begins to take an accounting of his life, to judge himself as a success or failure. At this point he is likely to question the choices he has made, asking himself "What have I done with my life?" Some of this turmoil may be manifested by drastic changes in his external life structure. He may get divorced and remarry or make a major occupational shift. However, the critical aspect of the mid-life transition is the way in which a man comes to grips with his internal self. He must continue the process of individuation begun earlier in life and come to terms with his own mortality. If he is unable to accomplish these tasks successfully, he is likely to experience a withering of the self in later life.

The late thirties mark the culmination of early adulthood. At around forty a man can make some judgment regarding his relative success or failure in meeting the goals he set himself in the enterprise of becoming one's own man. Success here means that the enterprise has flourished: he has achieved the desired position on his "ladder"; he has been affirmed within his occupational and social world; he is becoming a senior member of that world with all the rewards and responsibilities seniority brings.

Often a man looks forward to a key event that in his mind carries the ultimate message of his affirmation by society. This "culminating event" takes on a magical quality in his private fantasy. If it goes the right way, he will know that he has truly succeeded and is assured of a happy future. A poor outcome, on the other hand, will mean that he has failed in a profound sense, that not only his work but he as a person has been found wanting and without value.

When a man experiences a developmental crisis in the late thirties, it stems from the overwhelming feeling that he cannot accomplish the tasks of becoming one's own man: he cannot advance sufficiently on his chosen

SOURCE: From *The Seasons of a Man's Life*, by Daniel J. Levinson. Copyright © 1978 by Daniel J. Levinson. Reprinted by permission of Alfred A. Knopf, Inc.

ladder; cannot gain the affirmation, independence, and seniority he wants; cannot be his own man in the terms defined by his current life structure. Whatever the degree of his success or failure—no matter whether he is advancing brilliantly or in the depths of crisis—as long as a man is concerned primarily with these questions he has not yet emerged from the period of becoming one's own man.

At around forty, a new period gets under way. The mid-life transition ordinarily has its onset at age forty or forty-one and lasts about five years. For the fifteen men in our sample who completed this period, the average age at termination was forty-five and a half, the range forty-four to forty-seven. We doubt that a true mid-life transition can begin before age thirty-eight or after forty-three.

The mid-life transition is a bridge between early adulthood and middle adulthood. As in all transitions, a man must come to terms with the past and prepare for the future. Three major tasks must be worked on. One task is to terminate the era of early adulthood. He has to review his life in this era and reappraise what he has done with it. A second task is to take his first steps toward the initiation of middle adulthood. Although he is not yet ready to start building a new life structure, he can begin to modify the negative elements of the present structure and to test new choices. A third task is to deal with the polarities that are sources of deep division in his life. Let us consider the three tasks in turn.

Reappraising the Past

The initial focus in the mid-life transition is on the past. The major task is to reappraise the life structure of the settling-down period within the broader perspective of early adulthood as a whole and even of preadulthood. A man's review of the past goes on in the shadow of the future. His need to reconsider the past arises in part from a heightened awareness of his mortality and a desire to use the remaining time more wisely. Past and future coexist in the present, but he suffers from the corrosive doubt that they can be joined.

Now the life structure itself comes into question and cannot be taken for granted. It becomes important to ask: What have I done with my life? What do I really get from and give to my wife, children, friends, work, community—and self? What is it I truly want for myself and others? What are my central values and how are they reflected in my life? What are my greatest talents and how am I using (or wasting) them? What have I done with my early dream and what do I want with it now? Can I live in a way that combines my current desires, values, and talents? How satisfactory is my present life structure—how suitable for the self, how viable in the world—and how shall I change it to provide a better basis for the future?

As he attempts to reappraise his life, a man discovers how much it has been based on illusions, and he is faced with the task of *de-illusionment*.

By this expression I mean a reduction of illusions, a recognition that long-held assumptions and beliefs about self and world are not true. This process merits special attention because illusions play so vital a role in our lives throughout the life cycle.

The profound human ambivalence toward illusion is reflected in our everyday language. On the one hand, illusion has a negative connotation. It is associated with magic, sleight of hand, enchantment, errors of perception and belief. In a culture highly committed to science, technology, and rationality, illusion is generally regarded as inappropriate or even dangerous. The word itself derives from the Latin *ludere*, to play. While playful illusions can be accepted as part of the imaginative world of childhood, an adult is expected to be more realistic, practical, down to earth. The loss of illusions is thus a desirable and normal result of maturity.

On the other hand, our culture recognizes that illusions have their value even in adult life and that giving them up is often painful. We enjoy magic as a game of illusion. We use the term "disillusionment" to refer to a painful process through which a person is stripped of his most cherished beliefs and values. To be disillusioned is not merely to have lost one's illusions; it is to become cynical, estranged, "unable to believe in anything." This is one possible outcome of the loss of illusions, but not the only one.

To identify the broader process which is so important in the mid-life transition, I use the term "de-illusionment." The process of losing or reducing illusions involves diverse feelings—disappointment, joy, relief, bitterness, grief, wonder, freedom—and has diverse outcomes. A man may feel bereft and have the experience of suffering an irreparable loss. He may also feel liberated, free to develop more flexible values and to admire others in a more genuine, less idealizing way.

Illusions can be tremendously harmful; but they can also inspire works of great nobility and accomplishment. They play a crucial, helpful, and hurtful part in the lives of most persons during early adulthood. Some reduction in illusions is now appropriate and beneficial, but it is neither possible nor desirable to overcome *all* illusions in the mid-life transition or even by the end of middle adulthood. Illusion continues to have its place—a mixed blessing, or a mixed curse—all through the life cycle. The best way to avoid illusions is not to want anything very much. And that is hardly a prescription for a full life.

Early adulthood provides a fertile ground for illusions. Individual capabilities and drives are at their peak. A man must "believe in" himself—even in the face of reality, if need be—and in significant persons, groups, and ideologies, so that he can shape a course toward a better life for himself and others, according to his lights. "Good enough" development in early adulthood means that he has aspirations, makes commitments to persons and enterprises, and strives with some enthusiasm and discipline toward valued goals.

Modifying the Life Structure

As the mid-life transition proceeds, the emphasis gradually shifts from past to future. A man must make choices that will modify the existing life structure and provide the central elements for a new one. He must begin planning for the next phase. As he makes a commitment to these choices and embarks upon a new pattern of existence, the transition is over and a new period—entering middle adulthood—begins.

Some men make significant changes in the *external* aspects of the life structure during the mid-life transition. The more drastic changes involve divorce, remarriage, major shifts in occupation and life style, marked decline in level of functioning, notable progress in creativity or in upward social mobility.

Other men make fewer and less visible external changes. They tend to "stay put" during the mid-life transition, remaining in the same marriage and family, the same surroundings, occupation, and even work place. If we look more closely, however, we find that important though less obvious changes have occurred. A man's marital relationship is different, for better or worse. His children are growing up and family life is taking new forms. His parents have died or have become more dependent, and this has considerable impact upon his role as son and family member. Even if he is in the same work place, the character of his work has been altered as a result of changes in technology, in organizational structure, or in him. Seemingly small promotions or demotions have greatly affected his work activities, his position in the work world, and the personal meaning of work for him. Finally, he has been influenced by changes in the nation and the world, such as war, depression, and social movements of all kinds. This changes affect everyone in some way, but the effects are mediated by a man's age and period of development.

The mid-life transition also brings significant changes in the *internal* aspects of a man's life structure. He works on various developmental issues that have special urgency at mid-life. He may change appreciably in social outlook, in personal values, in what he wants to give the world, in what he wants to be for himself. The inner changes may be highly conscious and openly expressed, or subtle and hidden. They may come out in dramatic external changes. Even if the changes merely color the fabric of his life without grossly altering it, they give it a substantially different meaning.

A primary task of the mid-life transition is to modify the life structure of the thirties and to create the basis for a new structure appropriate to middle adulthood. The final test of the developmental work done here, as in all transition periods, is the satisfactoriness of the life structure emerging from it. Whatever the nature of the developmental work done, and however modest or profound the structural changes wrought, the individual's life in the mid-forties will differ in crucial respects from that in the late thirties. . . .

The Individuation Process

Throughout the life cycle, but especially in the key transition periods such as infancy, pubescence, and the mid-life transition, the developmental process of *individuation* is going on. This term refers to the changes in a person's relationship to himself and to the external world. The infant, leaving his mother's womb, must gain some idea of his separate existence. He must decide where he stops and where the world begins. He must separate himself from his mother, yet maintain a tie to her. He must form a sense of "reality" that allows him to accept his surroundings as having an independent existence not necessarily subject to his control. The child's world gradually expands to include his family, neighborhood, and friends; and his self becomes more complex through his relationships with other persons and institutions.

These changes are part of the individuation process. In successive periods of development, as this process goes on, the person forms a clearer boundary between self and world. He forms a stronger sense of who he is and what he wants, and a more realistic, sophisticated view of the world: what it is like, what it offers him and demands from him. Greater individuation allows him to be more separate from the world, to be more independent and self-generating. But it also gives him the confidence and understanding to have more intense attachments in the world and to feel more fully a part of it.

Every developmental transition, as I have said, involves termination and initiation: the termination of an existing life structure and the initiation of a new one. In order to accomplish this, a person must reappraise and modify the existing life structure. This is a challenging and difficult job; it would perhaps be impossible if individuation were not simultaneously playing a role. In a transition period, individuation is the underlying process that links termination and initiation. It prepares the inner ground, laying an internal basis on which the past can be partially given up and the future begun.

In the early adult transition, a boy-man begins his novitiate in the adult world and takes an important step in the individuation process. He must loosen his ties to the pre-adult world and the pre-adult self. Depending in large part on how well individuation goes at this time, he forms a valued adult identity and becomes capable of living with a greater degree of autonomy. He has more responsibility for himself and others and gains competence in his various social roles.

At best, however, a man in his mid-twenties is but a step beyond adolescence. His pre-adult self, with its ties to parents and the pre-adult world, operates with great force throughout early adulthood. Although some developmental gains may be made in the age thirty transition, he will not be much more individuated in the late thirties than he was at twenty-five. After the early adult transition, the next great opportunity for developmental work on individuation is the mid-life transition. In this period, a man must modify the early adult self (including, as it does, the baggage of unresolved problems from childhood and adolescence) and the life structure of the late thirties. Greater individuation is needed if he is to form a life structure more appropriate for middle adulthood.

What are the most significant changes to be made in mid-life individuation? Most investigators emphasize a single facet of the process. Erikson gives primary emphasis to generativity vs. stagnation as a stage of ego development in the middle years.[1] According to Jaques, the central issue at mid-life is coming to terms with one's own mortality: a man must learn now, more deeply than was possible before, that his own death is inevitable and that he and others are capable of great destructiveness.[2] In her biographical study of Goya, Martha Wolfenstein proposes that the reworking of destructiveness was the basic process in his transformation, during his forties, from an excellent court painter to an artist able to deal with the universals of human tragedy.[3] Bernice Neugarten identifies the basic mid-life change as a growing "interiority": turning inward to the self, decreasing the emphasis on assertiveness and mastery of the environment, enjoying the process of living more than the attainment of specific goals.[4]

Jung first proposed the distinction between the first and the second half of life, with the years around forty as the meridian. He showed that a new effort at individuation begins at mid-life and continues through the remaining years. Unlike many later writers who adopted his term but not his complex understanding of its meaning, he distinguished many facets of the individuation process.

Steering a course somewhere between the single-factor emphasis of some investigators and the tremendously complex approach of Jung, we shall discuss four tasks of mid-life individuation. For a given individual some of these may be more problematic or more conspicuous than others, but all of them are present and all must be considered in a general understanding of adult development. Each task requires a man to confront and reintegrate a polarity—that is, a pair of tendencies or states that are usually experienced as polar opposites, as if a person must be one or the other and cannot be both. As he becomes more individuated in middle adulthood, a man partially overcomes the divisions and integrates the polarities.

Four Tasks of Mid-life Individuation

The four polarities whose resolution is the principal task of mid-life individuation are: (1) young/old; (2) destruction/creation; (3) masculine/feminine; and (4) attachment/separateness.

Each of these pairs forms a polarity in the sense that the two terms represent opposing tendencies or conditions. Superficially, it would appear that a person has to be one or the other and cannot be both. In actuality, however, the paired tendencies are not mutually exclusive. Both sides of each polarity coexist within every self. At mid-life a man feels young in many respects, but he also has a sense of being old. He feels older than the youth, but not ready to join the generation defined as "middle-aged." He feels alternately young, old, and "in-between." His developmental task is to make sense of this condition of in-between and to become young/old in a new way, different from that of early adulthood.

The destruction/creation polarity presents similar problems of conflict and reintegration. The mid-life transition activates a man's concerns with death and destruction. He experiences more fully his own mortality and the actual or impending death of others. He becomes more aware of the many ways in which other persons, even his loved ones, have acted destructively toward him (with malice or, often, with good intentions). What is perhaps worse, he realizes that he has done irrevocably hurtful things to his parents, lovers, wife, children, friends, rivals (again, with what may have been the worst or the best of intentions). At the same time, he has a strong desire to become more creative: to create products that have value for himself and others, to participate in collective enterprises that advance human welfare, to contribute more fully to the coming generations in society. In middle adulthood a man can come to know, more than ever before, that powerful forces of destructiveness and of creativity coexist in the human soul—in my soul!—and can integrate them in new ways.

Likewise, every man at mid-life must come more fully to terms with the coexistence of masculine and feminine parts of the self. And he must integrate his powerful need for attachment to others with his antithetical but equally important need for separateness.

All of these polarities exist during the entire life cycle. They can never be fully resolved or transcended, though some utopian thinkers have held out this promise and some great religious prophets have been seen by others (though rarely by themselves) as having done so. They are not specific to the mid-life transition, but they operate here with special force.

Every developmental transition presents the opportunity and the necessity of moving toward a new integration of each polarity. To the extent that a man does this, he creates a firmer basis for his life in the ensuing phase. To the extent that he fails, he forms inner contradictions that will be reflected in the flaws of his next life structure. It is human both to succeed and to fail in these tasks: even as we resolve old conflicts and reach new integrations, we also create the contradictions that will in time stimulate further change and development.

The individuation process and the integration of polarities are ultimately internal and must be carried out within the person. I want to emphasize, however, that a polarity is not solely an inner matter. It is part of a man's life. The opposing tendencies exist both within the self and in the external world. As individuation progresses, a person not only becomes internally more differentiated and complex; he also develops more effective boundaries that link him to the external world and enable him to transact with it more fully. Moreover, the factors that influence how he deals with a polarity are external as well as internal. The splitting of young and old or of masculine and feminine occurs in our culture and social institutions as well as in each individual personality. We can understand a man's struggles to reintegrate a polarity only if we place these struggles within the context of his life and take account of both self and world. . . .

The Mid-life Transition as Developmental Crisis

Some men do very little questioning or searching during the mid-life transition. Their lives in this period show a good deal of stability and continuity. They are apparently untroubled by difficult questions regarding the meaning, value, and direction of their lives. They may be working on such questions unconsciously, with results that will become evident in later periods. If not, they will pay the price in a later developmental crisis or in a progressive withering of the self and a life structure minimally connected to the self.

Other men in their early forties are aware of going through important changes, and know that the character of their lives will be appreciably different. They attempt to understand the nature of these changes, to come to terms with the griefs and losses, and to make use of the possibilities for growing and enriching their lives. For them, however, the process is not a highly painful one. They are in a manageable transition rather than in a crisis.

But for the great majority of men—about 80 percent of our subjects—this period evokes tumultuous struggles within the self and with the external world. Their mid-life transition is a time of moderate or severe crisis. Every aspect of their lives comes into question, and they are horrified by much that is revealed. They are full of recriminations against themselves and others. They cannot go on as before, but need time to choose a new path or modify the old one.

Because a man in this crisis is often somewhat irrational, others may regard him as "upset" or "sick." In most cases, he is not. The man himself and those who care about him should recognize that he is in a normal developmental period and is working on normal mid-life tasks. The desire to question and modify his life stems from the most healthy part of the self. The doubting and searching are appropriate to this period; the real question is how best to make use of them. The problem is compounded by the fact that the process of reappraisal activates unconscious conflicts—the unconscious baggage carried forward from hard times in the past which hinders the effort to change. The pathology is not in the desire to improve one's life but in the obstacles to pursuing this aim. It is the pathological anxiety and guilt, the dependencies, animosities, and vanities of earlier years, that keep a man from examining the real issues at mid-life. They make it difficult for him to modify an oppressive life structure.

A profound reappraisal of this kind cannot be a cool, intellectual process. It must involve emotional turmoil, despair, the sense of not knowing where to turn or of being stagnant and unable to move at all. A man in this state often makes false starts. He tentatively tests a variety of new choices, not only out of confusion or impulsiveness but, equally, out of a need to explore, to see what is possible, to find out how it feels to engage in a particular love relationship, occupation, or solitary pursuit. Every genuine reappraisal must be agonizing, because it challenges the illusions and vested interests on which the existing structure is based.

The life structure of the thirties was initiated and stabilized by powerful forces in the person and his environment. These forces continue to make their claim for preserving the status quo. A man who attempts a radical critique of his life at forty will be up against the parts of himself that have a strong investment in the present structure. He will often be opposed by other persons and institutions—his wife, children, boss, parents, colleagues, the occupational system in which he works, the implicit web of social conformity—that seek to maintain order and prevent change. With luck, he will also receive support from himself and from others for the effort to examine and improve his life.

Why do we go through this painful process? Why should a crisis so often be our lot at mid-life? [There are] several sources of difficulty stemming from the era shift between early and middle adulthood. Moreover, we need developmental transitions in adulthood partly because no life structure can permit the living out of all aspects of the self. To create a life structure I must make choices and set priorities. In making a choice I select one option and reject many others. Committing myself to a structure, I try over a span of time to enhance my life within it, to realize its potential, to bear the responsibilities and tolerate the costs it entails.

Every life structure necessarily gives high priority to certain aspects of the self and neglects or minimizes other aspects. This is as true of the settling-down structure of the thirties as of all others. In the mid-life transition these neglected parts of the self urgently seek expression. A man experiences them as "other voices in other rooms" (in Truman Capote's evocative phrase). Internal voices that have been muted for years now clamor to be heard. At times they are heard as a vague whispering, the content unclear but the tone indicating grief over lost opportunities, outrage over betrayal by others, or guilt over betrayal by oneself. At other times they come through as a thunderous roar, the content all too clear, stating names and times and places and demanding that something be done to right the balance. A man hears the voice of an identity prematurely rejected; of a love lost or not pursued; of a valued interest or relationship given up in acquiescence to parental or other authority; of an internal figure who wants to be an athlete or nomad or artist to marry for love or remain a bachelor, to get rich or enter the clergy or live a sensual carefree life—possibilities set aside earlier to become what he now is. During the mid-life transition he must learn to listen more attentively to these voices and decide consciously what part he will give them in his life.

. . . .

NOTES

1. *Erikson* Erikson's theory of Generativity vs. Stagnation is presented in "Identity and the Life Cycle," *Psychological Issues*, 1 (1959), 1–171. His fullest biographical example of this stage is *Gandhi's Truth* (Norton, 1969).
2. *destructiveness* See Elliott Jaques, "Death and the Mid-Life Crisis," *International Journal of Psychoanalysis*, 46 (1965), 502–14, reprinted in Elliott Jaques, *Work, Creativity and Social Justice* (International Universities Press, 1970).
3. *Goya* Martha Wolfenstein, "Goya's Dining Room," *Psychoanalytic Quarterly*, 35 (1966), 1, 47–83.
4. *"interiority"* Bernice L. Neugarten, "A Developmental View of Adult Personality." in James E. Birren, ed., *Relations of Development and Aging* (Charles C Thomas, 1965).

5

Living Environments

When discussing living environments for older people, the two most important questions are *where* and *how*. Where do the aged live? How many live in cities, in rural areas, in retirement communities? And how do the aged live compared with people of other ages? Do they have special problems which result from inadequate conditions in their immediate environment? Are older people more satisfied living among age peers or do they thrive on contact with people of all ages? What kinds of support systems are they able to mobilize to fulfill various needs? Researchers have investigated all these questions. This part will provide some of the answers.

Urban and Rural Environments

The issue of where older people live is somewhat more complex than it seems. In general, older people live in the same places that younger people live—in cities. The urbanization that accompanied industrialization caused a population shift from rural to urban areas among all age groups. In 1900 over 75 percent of those sixty-five and older lived on farms or in small towns and villages; by 1970 this figure was just slightly more than 25 percent. This process of urbanization created some unique problems, particularly for the elderly poor, who tend to be concentrated in inner-city zones. As younger, more affluent people abandoned inner cities, the aged become victims of urban decay. Often living in substandard housing, their reduced mobility forced them to rely on resources in their immediate neighborhood. Further, many of the urban aged are inexperienced in urban living. Having grown up in small towns and villages, they can best be described as "urban villagers." As Lopata points out in her article, they have limited access to primary kinship networks, and they underutilize other, formal sources of support.

The trend of urbanization does not entirely convey the complexity of the living situation of the aged, for they do tend to be more highly concentrated in certain regions. In terms of raw figures the greatest number of older people live in the six most populous states: California, Illinois, New York, Ohio, Pennsylvania, and Texas. However, when we look at which states have the highest proportion of people over sixty-five, a somewhat different picture emerges. For the United States as a whole, slightly over 10 percent of the population is sixty-five or older. Therefore any state or area which has an older population of more than 10 percent is disproportionately old. Two regions in the United States—the central Midwest and the Sunbelt—can be described as disproportionately old. In states like Kansas, Missouri, Oklahoma, Arkansas, Nebraska, and South Dakota, more than 12 percent of the population is aged sixty-five and older. The reason these states have such comparatively high proportions of older people is one of attrition. With fewer jobs in farming, younger people have migrated out of these states, leaving older, less mobile people behind. Even this does not completely explain the situation, for in many isolated small towns in these states, it is not uncommon to have as much as 20 percent of the population sixty-five or older; in a few areas this figure is over 30 percent. These rural communities have become retirement communities by default.

The problems of the rural aged are different from those of city dwellers. They tend to have lower incomes than their aged counterparts elsewhere and are more likely to be in poor health. Transportation is also a major problem for older people living on farms, and they are often forced to leave the farm and move into a nearby town for the sake of convenience, even though this is a difficult transition for some. On the other hand, the rural aged are more likely to own their own home and to be living with a spouse. The article by Youmans describes various aspects of being old in a rural environment.

In other parts of the country a very different process is operating. In Florida over 16 percent of the population is sixty-five or older, and the proportion of aged is also high in Arizona. In this case the pleasant climate acts as a draw, attracting streams of retirees from other, less desirable areas. Pockets of retirees can also be found in quasi-resort areas such as the Ozarks of Missouri or the coastal region of Virginia. Those who move tend to be more affluent and often choose areas where friends and relatives have migrated before them.

Age Integration versus Age Segregation

Special settings such as resort areas or retirement communities tend to attract the attention of researchers, because there the aged are concentrated and highly visible. Thus there have been many studies which have focused on aging in age-segregated housing. In part this focus arose from a debate over whether age-integrated or age-segregated housing provided a more satisfactory situation for the aged. Some argued that it was better for older people to live in environments where there were people of all ages in close proximity. According to this perspective, contact with young people is stimulating and beneficial to the aged. Others argued that in a society such as ours, where most people interact with others of the same age, an age-segregated environment would enhance the ability of older people to make friends and participate in social activities.

Several researchers have attempted to determine whether older people are, in fact, less isolated in housing which has a high proportion of other people of similar ages. Rosow (1967) did the pioneering work on this subject. He interviewed 1,200 older people in several apartment buildings in Cleveland with different proportions of older residents. He divided the apartments into three types: normal, having less than 15 percent aged; dense, with 33 to 49 percent older residents; and concentrated, having more than 50 percent aged. Rosow found that residential proximity did not stimulate friendships between generations and that older people who lived in age-concentrated neighborhoods had more friends. Further, those who lived in an age-integrated neighborhood still selected friends from among others of their own age. Rosow's research strongly supported the age-segregation argument.

In another study Carp (1966) compared two groups of older people, one that was accepted for residence in a new public housing facility for the aged called Victoria Plaza and a second group that was not. Her main concern was the effect of an improved social environment on feelings of happiness, number of activities, number of friends, and health. She found that on each variable, the scores of residents showed improvement after living in Victoria Plaza, while those of nonresidents remained the same or decreased slightly. Her research provided additional support for retirement housing and age-segregation.

Living among age peers does seem to facilitate friendships and increase the likelihood of participation in activities for the aged. This apparent tranquility is enhanced by the fact that most planned retirement communities are privately owned and tend to be composed of residents who are both white and middle class. In contrast, in federally financed retirement housing, where racial integration is a requirement, the predominantly low-income residents have concerns of a different nature. The article by Quadagno, Kuhar, and Peterson demonstrates that issues other than the number of friends become salient in integrated retirement housing. Maintaining an even racial balance among the tenants is a source of tension, and intimate friendships between residents of different races are often discouraged through subtle means of structuring social interaction.

Despite the large amount of research on retirement communities and the like, it is important to recognize that only 3 percent of the older population live in special settings of this sort. Most elderly persons live in ordinary houses or apartments in their own communities (Carp, 1976). In any case, housing is only one aspect of a complex issue which includes large-scale demographic patterns and concerns for the general well-being of the aged in all phases of life.

REFERENCES

Carp, Francis M. 1966. *A Future for the aged*. Austin: The Univ. of Texas Press.
———. 1976. Housing and living environments of older people. In Robert H. Binstock and Ethel Shanas (eds.), *Handbook of aging and the social sciences*. New York: Van Nostrand Reinhold, pp. 244–270.
Rosow, Irving. 1967. *The social integration of the aged*. New York: The Free Press of Glencoe.

Support Systems of Elderly Urbanites: Chicago of the 1970s

HELENA ZNANIECKI LOPATA

They lack two essential ingredients for successful urban life: an upbringing in an experienced urban household and an education above a minimal level in urban schools. A large proportion of these elderly have been found to be unaware of or unwilling to use the services and programs created to fill their needs. Nor do they have ready access to supports extending from primary relationships, made difficult by urban barriers, such as unsafe neighborhoods, or by lack of personal resources, such as the ability to seek and engage in new roles and relations. Lopata suggests that urban planners must find ways to help these "urban villagers" to overcome their isolation from society.

The Chicago metropolitan area contains many people, particularly many elderly people, who are not leading "urban lives," not utilizing many of its vast resources to develop and modify complex support systems. A *support system* is a set of relations involving the giving and receiving of objects, services, social and emotional supports defined by the giver and the receiver as necessary or at least as helpful in maintaining a style of life (see Lopata 1971, 1972a, 1972b). Traditionally most support systems of human beings grew out of primary relations, ascribed automatically at birth or available throughout the life span and replaceable upon loss from a relatively small pool of familiars. Gradually, as societies became urbanized, industrialized, and complex (Winch and Blumberg, 1968), they created and became increasingly dependent upon secondary sources for support systems of members, involving relations which are formalized and depersonalized, organized around specific functions, often transitory but always demanding structured entrance and exits and tested performance. The participants in a secondary support system give and/or receive these supports as part of their job or other social role, or as an officially sanctioned function within bureaucratized and increasingly large social organizations. The distinction between primary, or personal, support systems involving individuals in mutual exchanges of total personalities and secondary, or functionally structured, supports is not a dichotomous one, actual relations falling into niches along a continuum

SOURCE: Copyright 1975 by the Gerontological Society. Reprinted by permission from *The Gerontologist*, Vol. 15, No. 1 (1975).

between the ideal types; and complex societies have evolved many means of converting one type of relation into another, training their members to move voluntaristically into different forms and levels of social engagement, containing different supports systems, as their life circumstances change. Such societies, typified by urban America, require different personal resources of members than do societies able to provide satisfactory support systems automatically at birth, through long-term relations or replacements guaranteeing engagement. It is the thesis of this paper that many metropolitan Chicago elderly residents lack the abilities to voluntaristically engage in supportive relations, while the society's complexity and mobility have removed many of the ascribed, or at least long-standing, primary support systems.

The theoretical framework for the examination of variations in the support systems of Chicago-area urban elderly and the factors contributing to these variations comes from two studies of metropolitan widows and the examination of data contained in the Chicago Needs Assessment Survey.[1] It is based on the theses that voluntaristic action requires individualistically built ability to analyze the resources, choose desired ones, plan and carry out steps necessary for social engagement, engage, and then turn to new resources as the definition of needs is modified by events or changes in the life cycle; and that current residents of urban centers vary greatly in these personally developed resources. A subthesis is that these resources are based on more than one generation's socialization into urban life, early urbanites laying a foundation for new generations to effectively utilize the formal schooling system by which modern societies attempt to prepare their members for participation (Jencks et al., 1972). The recency and the rapidity of urbanization in American society and its dependence upon rural in-migrants and rural immigrants from a variety of foreign lands mean that a relatively small segment of its elderly population have experienced those two background conditions for urban life: growing up in households of experienced urbanites and being educated beyond the minimal literacy levels in American urban schools. For the remaining of the elderly the city is not a very viable environment in that they remain "urban villagers" (Gans, 1962), living in geographically and social-space restricted areas surrounded by limited levels of familiar, primary supports, or become social isolates as the supports they passively accepted become less available or less viable. All current evidence indicates that people who are best able to live in cities, to utilize their complex resources for building support systems, have lived in the upper rungs of the American social-class ladder for a relatively long time, are located in the WASP contingent of the society, are middle-aged, well educated, male, etc. This leaves out all those older residents of its cities who never fit into the cosmopolitan urbanite category in adulthood, as well as those whose health or financial restrictions prevent continued engagement at this level of supports.

Chicago: History and 1970 Characteristics

The city of Chicago is located in an extended Standard Metropolitan Statistical Area which, like all such SMSAs,

> included at least one city of 50,000 inhabitants or more, the county in which it is located and contiguous counties which are essentially metropolitan in character and are socially and economically integrated with the central city (Kitagawa and Taeuber, 1963).

The Chicago SMSA included in 1960 "six counties, 249 incorporated suburban municipalities, the City of Chicago, and around 3,000 square miles of unincorporated areas" (Opperman, n.d.). Only 48 percent of the total SMSA population lived in 1970 in the city of Chicago, while almost half resided in urbanized areas around it, the remaining very small proportion being in rural areas. This distribution makes Chicago a highly urban complex and one heavily dominated by the central city itself. Two of the counties are actually in the state of Indiana.

Farr (1973) explains its "Americanness" as due to several characteristics: its location near the center of the country; its function as a hub of transportation and communication; the diversity of its economic base; the extent to which it has drawn its population from a variety of nations and areas of the United States; its socioeconomic, racial, and religious heterogeneity; and its long-lasting image as the "melting pot" *par excellence*. Chicago's own anthem, "There she stands, besides the inland sea, with outstretched arms to welcome you and me . . . ," makes reference not only to its location but to the fact that it recruited a variety of migrants. As late as 1930, 25.3 percent of its white population was foreign-born, and 39.6 percent were native-born of foreign or mixed parents, for a total of 65.0 percent of foreign-stock identity. The most prevalent foreign-stock nationalities in Chicago in 1930 were the Poles, Germans, Russians (mostly Russian Jews), Italians, and Swedes. Only 6.9 percent of Chicago's population was black and only 0.2 percent was identified as "other" races in 1930. The heavy influx of blacks occurred during and after World War II so that by 1970 they formed 32.7 percent of the residents, but the other races expanded very slightly into 1.7 percent of the total. In spite of the immigration of recent years of Spanish-speaking people, mostly from Mexico and Puerto Rico, the death of older European immigrants decreased the percentage of foreign-born (Puerto Ricans are not included in this category) to 11.0 percent of the white population so that the total native-born count for whites increased to 89.0 percent.

The new migrants into Chicago, that is, the blacks and the Spanish-speaking peoples, tend to be younger, with more numerous offspring than true of the city in 1960, thus dropping the median age from 32.9 to 29.6 by 1970. The drop is somewhat reflected in the changes in the proportion of elderly. The city tends to be populated by the very young adults and the very old of the white native-born and by the adults with children of the newcomers. The suburbs tend to be inhabited by established white families, native-born of native-born parents. The median number of school years completed by Chicagoans has increased from 8.5 in 1940 to 11.25 for males and 11.9 for females in 1970. The last named median is less than the national of 12.2. Chicago has been a city with a relatively large proportion of single-family detached dwellings, together with the "two" and "three flats" judged typical by its observers.

In 1930 and 1940 the city was divided into seventy-five "natural" community areas by University of Chicago teams of sociologists. Wirth and Bernert (1949) defined these in their introduction to the second *Local Community Fact Book*:

> The modern metropolis is a city of cities, a mosaic of little worlds and aggregate of local communities, each one differentiated from the others by its characteristic function in the total economy and cultural complex of city life. . . . [Chicago is] made up of seventy-five component local communities, each of which has a history of its own and is marked off from the others by distinctive physical and social characteristics and by natural boundaries.

Ernest Burgess (quoted by Gist and Fava, 1964) organized the city into five concentric zones, distinguished from each other by distance from the center, concentration of activity, and density of people, industry, and other resources. The first zone was the central business district:

> This is where skyscrapers, department stores, cheap variety emporia, hotels, restaurants, theaters, and motion-picture houses are concentrated to meet the needs of downtown shoppers or transients. The inner zone is essentially an area of retail trade, light manufacturing and commercialized recreation. In Chicago it is called the "Loop."

The term, the "Loop," comes from the circle created by the elevated tracks, but the zone extends beyond this business district to include some nighttime residents. There is still a high concentration of the elderly in this zone.

The second zone of modern cities, modeled by Chicago, was the zone of transition. This encompassed a heavy concentration of lower-income people, being inhabited by pre-World War II years,

> by Old World immigrants and rural migrants, by unconventional folk, and by social outcasts such as criminals and prostitutes. Typically, the zone of transition also contains some high-cost living—the Gold Coast (Gist and Fava, 1964).

The contrasts of the zone of transition attracted sociologist Zorbaugh (1929). This zone, in fact, drew a great deal of sociological attention, in several studies preceding, within, and following the 1920s.

The other zones of Burgess theory have generally been neglected in sociological research. Zone III contained workingmen's homes, of upper-lower and lower-middle-class flavor. Zone IV is inhabited by middle-class dwellers:

> professional people, owners of small businesses, the managerial group, clerical forces and the like. There are hotels and apartment houses here, and detached residences with spacious yards and gardens (Gist and Fava, 1964).

Zone V of commuters forms the "outer periphery of the city." It includes suburb-like city neighborhoods and community areas as well as the suburbs and exurbs (Spectorsky, 1955).

The combined picture of Chicago as it was forming itself into a metropolitan center indicates a history of immigration, first of Europeans, especially those from rural eastern and southern parts, followed by black and Spanish-speaking people of young age and relatively low education, streaming first into the central city and then, barring discrimination and failure to move up the American status ladder, moving to its suburbs with increasing acculturation.

By the 1970s Chicago had built itself into the second largest city of America, and it has changed considerably since the years documented by the Chicago writers and the University of Chicago sociologists, although much of its older population still remembers those years. The city is no longer the "hog butcher of the world"; its stockyards were closed years ago. Although steel mills still operate on the far south side of the city and in the industrial northwest of Indiana, a smaller proportion of the total SMSA's population works in them than in prior decades. The city's area around the Loop is also changing, as slums are razed by urban renewal and replaced by high rises, usually inevitably shifting the composition, since old-time residents cannot afford the new housing. Economic life is moving out, generally skipping the intermediary zones and settling in the formerly "bedroom"-stereotyped suburbs. The industrial plants are becoming decentralized and moving in smaller units beyond city limits, on the heels of their white workers, creating transportation problems for their black and other minority employees still basically confined to the inner city. Traffic out of Chicago in the morning and into it in after-work hours is now almost as heavy as in the opposite direction. There are over a hundred business and shopping districts in and surrounding Chicago. The post-World War II suburban housing boom has been accompanied by a vast expansion of shopping malls and other complexes. These are now being followed by apartment complexes, almost self-sufficient in the services they provide, insuring work-free and safe environments and "freedom from loneliness" in suburbs rather than the city, designed for the young with small children and the retired or almost retired who no longer need detached homes.

The history and structure of Chicago have usually insured a greater concentration of the elderly in the inner-city zones. This is particularly true of two categories of the elderly. The first category includes the ethnics of European or other backgrounds and the blacks, those people who are restricted by their lack of personal resources, by prejudice, and by discrimination to residence in ghetto or near-ghetto communities. The second type is limited to middle- and upper-class dwellers of the expanded Gold Coast. Chicago's skyline has witnessed a dramatic boom in high rises, placed in a strip along the lake, both south and north of the Loop. Some of the lake has even been filled in to create more desirable land space for the high rises which are built as far north as the 6400 block. These buildings, besides housing the very wealthy in apartments which are converting from rentals to condominiums at a rapid pace, often contain small units designed to attract young singles (Starr and Carns, 1973), retired couples, or the widowed and divorced. Farther west, sometimes within two blocks of this strip, are found the slums or the near-slums. These are now extending as far as Uptown, much farther north than the original zone of transition, but now occupied by such a variety of problem-ridden people of different backgrounds as to be selected as a Model City area for the focusing of problem-solving community resources. Uptown, like the Loop, contains a disproportionate number of elderly, the not-so-impoverished residents living nearest the park bordering the lake and the very poor, often socially isolated, in blocks stretching west. A number of the elderly now live in Chicago Housing Authority buildings in the area, in middle-income apartment buildings and in a variety of retirement hotels, purposely designed as such or becoming such by their very age and lack of transients. The same is true of several areas near the lake on the south side of the city. Chicago's Housing Authority has also built complexes housing the elderly, in isolation from other age groups, or as part of low-rental housing for different age groups, within the black belt, or belts, extending south and west from the Loop.

The suburban elderly are concentrated in older communities, such as Oak Park where those aged sixty-five and over total 5.7 percent of the male and 10.6 percent of the female segments of the population; in centers of more heterogeneous suburbs such as Evanston, where they are only 4.8 percent of the male and 9.2 percent of the female population because of the size of this town bordering Chicago on the north; or in the specially designed apartment or other housing combinations made attractive to people with their needs or tastes located in younger communities. A major problem of the elderly living in suburbs has been transportation, since these communities are built upon the premise of automobiles and therefore ignore public transportation other than the trains radiating out of the city for commuting workers. People lacking cars must live within walking distance of services or these commuting spokes.

Within the city of Chicago, however, public transportation is extensive, reputedly one of the best in the country. Its use by the elderly has been facilitated by a reduced fare, recently expanded to a "24-hour around-the-clock basis" (Mayor's Office for Senior Citizens, July, 1973) by the efforts of the Mayor's Office for Senior Citizens after it discovered through a Chicago Needs Assessment Survey that transportation is one of the major problems facing the city elderly. Chicago also provides its residents with an extensive park system with numerous activity programs, many of which are specifically directed toward the elderly. The city resources also consist of extensive medical and health-maintaining facilities, with numerous hospitals, although many are congregated into complexes in certain areas of the city. These complexes are often connected with medical schools and so have numerous clinics. Since they are themselves old, they tend to be located in the older areas of the city. This means that some are almost becoming geriatric centers simply because of the nature of the surrounding population. On the other hand, the areas are often of high-crime rate so that an undetermined but possibly high proportion of the population underuses them as health resources.

Other features of Chicago on the negative side of the ledger, as far as quality of life and social life space are concerned, directly affect the elderly. One of these is Chicago's weather, which is often uncomfortable enough to prevent leisurely activity and social contact with others living nearby by those who do not have norms for invitational visiting. A second feature of Chicago which is detrimental to social interaction is the high rate of mobility and the disintegration of the local community areas (Stein, 1960). The minority groups who are now becoming increasingly dominant in the city have visible physical divergence from the older population, a divergence against which there is a great deal of prejudice and fear (Novak, 1971). Many of the foreign-stock groups, as well as the native-born of native parents who still remain in the city, are openly resentful of, and resisting, the city, state, and federal government's efforts to provide more resources to the racial minorities than they feel were provided to them when they were at the bottom of the socioeconomic ladder. They have made it partly up this ladder, and they want to rest on their laurels without competition from below.

Underutilization of Secondary Support Systems by the Older Metropolitan Chicago Residents

The combination of the background characteristics of many metropolitan Chicago residents aged sixty and over, their current location within the community, and the characteristics of the city itself, have resulted in a gap between the societal resources for support systems and the actual supports in which the elderly are involved. The city of Chicago has developed a number of programs designed to aid its elderly population, to provide services solving problems or creating links to social roles and relations. According to a summary of the Chicago Needs Assessment Survey (CNAS) conducted and analyzed by Kirchner Associates (1972), most elderly scored low on a "functioning-in-society index" which measured "perception of the availability of selected services or programs as well as the ability to confront and resolve problems which might be encountered in dealing with a person or agency." The services or programs available in Chicago to its elderly population about which knowledge was tapped included the meal delivery programs, group dining facilities, information centers, free food, food stamps, medicare, the "friendly visitor," and medical and dental clinics and reduced transportation rates. Many who were aware of the services did not use them even when they defined their own monetary, health, nutritional, or transportation situation as inadequate. An example of an extreme lack of awareness refers to information centers which assist in the location of urban resources. Only 9.9 percent of the 1001 respondents knew of such centers and only 36.6 percent of those who knew of them actually used them. Of the 87 percent who did not know of such centers, 84.5 percent thought it would be a useful service for the city to develop.

Chicago's elderly not only lack awareness of, and even when they have necessary information, show unwillingness to use, the resources created especially to meet their specific needs, but they tend to be underusers of other resources for support systems involving any but primary relations. Thus the social life space of only about half of the CNAS respondents includes attendance at a church or a synagogue, and only 21.4 percent attend once a week or more. "Club attendance is an activity of only 30 percent of the total sample" (Steiner, 1972). Although there are numerous recreational indoor and outdoor areas in the city, many of the elderly do not know of them and fewer make use of them. In fact, there is a tendency to constrict the vast and complex city into a limited number of streets traveled regularly in meeting daily needs and the homes of friends and relatives.

The primary relations which form part of the support systems of Chicago are, however, somewhat constricted through the weakening or difficulty of reaching traditional sources of such supports: the "safe" and stable neighborhood, long-time friendships, the sibling and even the offspring homes, made difficult by barriers created by the city. Thus, although 74 percent of the CNAS respondents visited with friends, neighbors, or relatives during the week preceding the interviewing, 25.8 percent saw no one and an additional 14.5 percent visited only once. Neighboring can be a fulfilling source of support systems, but the widowhood studies showed that the widows, much as the CNAS elderly, tend to limit themselves to only casual contacts outside of the residences. Thus, although 39 percent of the elderly of both sexes talk to one of their neighbors "longer than just saying 'Hello' every day," 55.5 percent felt that people in their neighborhood keep to themselves and only 37 percent that people around them visit often. A third have not reached a satisfactory level of neighboring. The widows who were asked about forms of neighboring in greater detail confirmed that the contacts are limited, in that 70 percent never lend or borrow, 30 percent never drop over informally, 34 percent never visit by invitation, 78 percent never go together to club meetings, and 73 percent never go out of the neighborhood together for other purposes (Lopata, 1973a).

In spite of the fact that most of the Chicago-area elderly of all marital status have contact with at least one offspring with relative frequency, the relations are not symmetrical with all children, nor are many people able to fill their lives with such support systems. Although available in emergency situations across household lines, children and siblings operate independently. The elderly living in independent households, as most of them do, may not be isolated from their relatives (Sussman, Litwak, and Shanas chapters in Shanas and Streib, 1965), but their relations are often not reflective of a full support system. The most supportive is the living spouse, and widowhood or divorce usually brings increased social isolation on the part of people unaccustomed to reengaging in societal roles.

In sum, the studies under consideration in this paper indicate that the elderly of the Chicago area, although not generally completely isolated, are not strongly societally engaged. "It would appear as though the number of social relations and contacts established by the elderly is below a 'desirable' level" (Kirchner Associates, 1972). Except for their primary relations, often made difficult to sustain consistently by several characteristics of the city, such as its size, density, mobility, and heterogeneity of population, and the lack of personal resources such as time, financial comfort, health, and habit, or voluntaristic action, the urban elderly are generally not involved in a complex support system or social life space. The remaining part of this short paper will argue that the social engagement in multidimensional support systems is dependent mainly on personal resources.

Variations in the Use of Secondary and Primary Resources in the Development of Support Systems by the Elderly

Five major variables affect the involvement of Chicago-area elderly in social life spaces and support systems of varying size and composition, according to the studies under consideration. All of these relate to the individual's background as an urbanite. The distribution of these characteristics within the studied population reflects the reality of life in Europe and America during the years when the elderly were growing up and learning to live in a particular environment, and the reality of Chicago's life at the present time. The variables influencing life style and support systems are: place of birth, sex, race, education, and age. Of course, there is an interdependence between education and the other four variables. Chicagoans by birth, particularly younger white men who received several years of schooling, have the lowest probability of being socially isolated, of underusing secondary and even of inadequately using primary resources for building support systems than are other segments of the elderly population. Marital status is a facilitating factor in social engagement because a couple has each other and two resources for social engagement, but the other variables operate irrespective of the marital status.

The underusers of societal resources are first- or second-generation urbanites with little formal education (see also Lopata, 1973b). They are also apt to lack all forms of personal and societal resources. Birth outside of the city tends to be associated with socialization into folk, rural, and structurally simplistic life, often in cultures very foreign from that developed in Chicago. Males, particularly white males, tend to be more aware of both indoor and outdoor recreational resources than females and to make more use of them. Nonmembership in voluntary organizations tends to increase by age but to be sex and race related. For example, younger (aged sixty to sixty-four) white and black males tend to have similar incidence of nonmembership, but the gap between them increased with age, the elderly whites being much more apt to belong to a group than the blacks. This is probably largely due to the differences in education. Among the women, and in spite of the picture developed out of the Moynihan (1967; see also Rainwater and Yancey, 1967) report of the matrilocal elderly black woman surrounded by numerous relatives and active in her church, the inadequacy of the lower-class black woman's social contact in widowhood is strong and reflects her own educational achievement. As documented elsewhere (Lopata, 1973a), the uneducated black widows do not have any advantages over their white counterparts in being able to prevent social isolation. In fact, since they are apt to have had a less adequate education if brought up in the south, they are more apt to be isolated. In the CNAS, black females did have a higher membership rate than did white women but only in the very oldest age group of seventy-five and over. Only church attendance was higher among the black than the white women, but even that distribution covers only half of the former. In fact, both the CNAS and the widowhood studies document the many ways the elderly blacks are disadvantaged by their past socialization into nonurban life and lack of formal education, but they are simply the extreme examples of the failure of modern urban social systems to offset the disadvantages of all the elderly who did not have the benefits of many generational urban and educated environments.

Summary and Conclusions

Much of what is said and written about the quality of life in modern cities for the elderly fails to grapple with the fact that many of these people are simply not urbanites. They are socialized into primary support systems of long standing, and when these fall away due to many life events, they do not have the personal resources to reengage into new roles and relations. Thus in much of metropolitan Chicago there is a mismatch between the personal resources provided for social engagement and the expectations of connecting lines to societally developed resources. Modern cities increasingly require voluntaristic social engagement, flexible to the extent of being built and rebuilt as life circumstances change with children's marriages, widowhood, retirement, and other events. Such engagement is dependent upon personal resources, health and money being very important ones, but also the self-confidence and competence, knowledge, and ability, to first work out problems in the abstract and then to carry on plans of action which facilitate real urban life. The quality of life in the city seems to be most strongly affected by personality-developed resources, since the societally developed ones are increasingly apt to require voluntaristic engagement. How long the lag between the social system and personal abilities and resources will last in American society is hard to determine. In the meantime, however, it is the task of social scientists and urban planners to find ways of assisting the urbanites, in their attempts to increase their social life space, by providing personalized resources out of secondary agencies, bringing them to those people who do not have initiating behavior habits, or by providing bridging personnel to facilitate their going out to seek new ways of social engagement. We must either help those types of elderly people, mostly of minority background, to lead a more urban life, or assume that the city is viable only for other age groups, or for no age group. As social scientists we must not confuse what has happened when cities haphazardly expanded through the absorption of rural people in the past with what can be true of cities in a more rationally planned future.

NOTES

1. A current study of the support systems of widows of all ages is funded through a contract with the Social Security Administration (#SSA-71-3411) and Loyola Univ. of Chicago. I am grateful to Mr. Robert Ahrens and Mr. Clarence L. Fewer of the Mayor's Office for Senior Citizens, who cooperated in my obtaining the data collected in the "Chicago Needs Assessment Survey, 1973." Tabular data may be obtained from the author.

REFERENCES

Farr, F. *Chicago*. Arlington House, New Rochelle, NY, 1973.
Gans, H. *The urban villagers*. Free Press of Macmillan, New York, 1962.

Gist, N. P., and Fava, S. F. *Urban society* (5th ed.). Thomas Y. Crowell, New York, 1964.

Jencks, C., Smith, M., Acland, H., Bane, M. J., Cohen, D., Gintis, H., Heyns, B., and Michalson, S. *Inequality: Reassessment of the effect of family and schooling in America.* Basic Books, New York, 1972.

Kirchner Associates. *The Chicago needs assessment survey,* final report for the Mayor's Office on Senior Citizens, Chicago, 1972.

Kitagawa, E. M., and Taeuber, K. E. *Local community fact book, Chicago metropolitan area, 1960.* Univ. of Chicago, Chicago, 1963.

Lopata, H. Z. Support systems involving widows in nonagricultural areas: A comparative study. A research proposal for the Social Security Administration, 1971.

Lopata, H. Z. The influence of historical events upon the life styles of widows in an American urban area. Paper presented at the 9th International Congress of Gerontology, Kiev, 1972. (a)

Lopata, H. Z. Societal factors affecting the support systems of widows. Paper presented to the Committee on Family Research Seminar, Moscow, 1972. (b)

Lopata, H. Z. *Widowhood in an American city.* Schenkman Publishing, General Learning Press, Cambridge, MA, 1973. (a)

Lopata, H. Z. Effects of schooling on social contacts of urban women. *American Journal of Sociology,* 1973, 79, 604–619. (b)

Mayor's Office for Senior Citizens. Chicago needs assessment survey, 1973. (unpublished)

Moynihan, D. P. *The Negro family: The case for national action.* MIT Press, Cambridge, MA, 1967.

Novak, M. *The rise of the unmeltable ethnics.* Macmillan, New York, 1971.

Opperman, P. Note to the reader. *Suburban factbook.* Northeastern Illinois Metropolitan Area Planning Commission, Chicago, n.d.

Rainwater, L., and Yancey, W. C. *The Moynihan report and the politics of controversy.* MIT Press, Cambridge, MA, 1967.

Shanas, E., and Streib, G. F. (Eds.). *Social structure and the family: Generational relations.* Prentice-Hall, Englewood Cliffs, NJ, 1965.

Spectorsky, A. C. *Exurbanites.* Lippincott, Philadelphia, 1955.

Starr, J. R., and Carns, D. E. Singles in the city. In H. Z. Lopata (Ed.), *Marriages and families.* D. Van Nostrand, New York, 1973.

Stein, M. *The eclipse of community.* Harper & Row, New York, 1960.

Steiner, P. L. R. Understanding social isolation among the aged in Chicago. Thesis, Dept. of Social Sciences, Univ. of Chicago, Chicago, 1972.

Winch, R., and Blumberg, R. L. Social complexity and family organization. In R. Winch and L. Goodman (Eds.), *Selected studies in marriage and the family.* Holt, Rinehart & Winston, New York, 1968.

Wirth, L., and Bernert, E. H. *Local community fact book of Chicago.* Univ. of Chicago Press, Chicago, 1949.

Zorbaugh, H. W. *The gold coast and the slum.* Univ. of Chicago Press, Chicago, 1929.

The Rural Aged

E. GRANT YOUMANS

Older people in rural areas have smaller incomes, are restricted in mobility because of inadequate transportation, report poorer health, and express a more negative attitude toward life than their urban counterparts. They also have less frequent contact with children. One approach to rural problems in general has been to encourage small industries to locate in rural towns, but the research indicates that local industrialization may have a negative impact on the financial situation of the rural aged. The author concludes that more research is needed to help solve some of these problems.

In recent decades public attention has been directed to the conditions of life of older people in American society. Awareness of these conditions has been augmented by the increasing number and proportion of the aged in the population and their consequent greater visibility to the rest of society. In 1850 about 3 percent of the population was aged sixty-five and over; 100 years later, it was 8 percent; and in 1975 persons aged sixty-five and over constituted 10 percent of the population, representing 9.2 million men and 13.1 million women. It is estimated that the present percentage will increase slightly during the remainder of this century, but the absolute numbers of persons aged sixty-five and over will increase to 40.6 million by the year 2000. Slight improvements in mortality are anticipated. Average life expectancy at birth is predicted to increase to 69.9 for men and 78.0 for women by the year 2020.[1]

The U.S. Bureau of the Census reported 5,431,906 persons aged sixty-five and over as living in rural areas of the nation in 1970. Of these, 4,533,714 were rural nonfarm and 898,192 lived on farms. In the rural nonfarm population, the females exceeded the males in number, but in the rural-farm population there were more older men than older women.[2] Demographic data indicate a growing concentration of aged persons in small towns of the United States. This increase is partially explained by the out-migration of young people and the in-migration of retired farmers from the open country and elderly people from urban centers.[3]

The growing attention to problems of the elderly has been accompanied by an enormous volume of literature about aging. During the first half of the century (1900–1948), about 18,000 publications on aging were reported,[4] but in the twelve years following, over 34,000 publications

SOURCE: Reprinted from "The Rural Aged" by E. Grant Youmans in volume no. 429 of *The Annals* of The American Academy of Political and Social Science. All rights reserved.

appeared.[5] It is reasonable to assume that research on a topic of such vital concern as human aging will continue to expand.

In such a rapidly growing research field, there has been a notable defect—the limited number of studies of older persons living in rural environments in the United States. Yet such a deficiency is not too surprising. It is characteristic of American society that new fields of inquiry emerge in urban centers and then gradually spread to rural areas. Social gerontology, a late arrival to the disciplines concerned with aging, has followed this pattern. Almost all social gerontologists are urban dwellers, and their research efforts have been directed mainly to studies of human aging in city environments.

The objective of this chapter is to present information on the objective and subjective conditions of life of the sizable number of older persons who live in rural areas of the United States. It is recognized that standards for assessing the life of the rural elderly do not exist in either the objective or subjective domain. In the absence of such criteria, it is assumed that comparisons of data on the rural aged with data on the urban aged will be useful.

The observations that follow are organized around selected questions that are assumed to have an important bearing on the lives of the rural aged in the United States. What is the nature of "rurality" in the United States: What are the income levels of the rural aged? Does industrialization of rural areas benefit older people? What is the nature of the social life of the rural elderly? What is the health status of older persons living in rural areas? How adequate is the subjective life of the rural aged? What are the implications of the answers to these questions for older rural Americans?

Rurality

The status and well-being of any large category of persons is inextricably interrelated with the social, economic, and cultural conditions of the society in which they live. The term "rural" suggests an agricultural economic base, low population density, and relative isolation from large population centers.[6] As a social-psychological concept, "rurality" suggests a continuum. At one extreme is a complex of behavior and mental outlook characteristic of what anthropologists call a folk[7] or *gemeinschaft*[8] society. At the other end of the continuum are found the orientations characteristic of contemporary large urban centers. Both types of orientation obtain in any given region, area, village, town, or city, and the degrees of commitment to one or the other pose important problems for the inhabitants.

The traditional or folk type of society and culture places strong emphasis on conventional behavior and conformity to traditions and customs and values strong adherence to kinship control of behavior.

Persons living in societies predominantly of the folk type tend to have few interpersonal contacts, and such contacts tend to be primary in nature and of long duration and limited to a small geographic area. Sacred and religious beliefs play an important role in the orientations of people in the folk type of society.

In contrast, the modern orientations of contemporary urban life emphasize more individualistic behavior, a rejection of custom and tradition, and weakened kinship control. The typical urbanite engages in many social contacts of a secondary nature and of short duration. In the urban centers, one finds strong adherence to secular values and beliefs and a tendency to reject sacred and religious orientations.

In recent decades most rural areas in the United States have undergone substantial changes. There has been a notable shift from the older folkway of life to a more modern and technologically advanced type of society. Trends toward modernization in most rural areas are reflected in increased productivity, fewer farms, and more part-time farming; in more specialized and increasingly efficient agricultural businesses; in more complex social organizations, such as schools, churches, and business enterprises; in improved transportation and communication facilities; and in greater movements of rural people from place to place.[9]

The conflicts between allegiance to the folk or to the modern urbanized type of culture and society pose critical problems for many older Americans who live in small cities, towns, villages, and the open country, or on farms. The older population in these areas, most of whom were born before 1910, undoubtedly internalized orientations toward life that are characteristic of a folk type of society. The young adults, born mostly in the 1950s, tended to adopt a way of life more typical of an industrialized type of society.

The intergenerational differences that ensue are acutely painful for many olders persons. The differences in outlook, the variances in behavior, and the conflicts are especially troublesome to older people who are members of minority groups. These older persons, such as rural black Americans, rural American Indians, and rural Spanish-speaking people, experience the trauma of witnessing the disappearance of the cultural ways that gave meaning and significance to their lives.[10] Rejected, lonely, and out of touch with contemporary values and behavior, many of them have little to look forward to and little to live for. They tend to be the forgotten and neglected people passed by in the modernization process.

Income

An adequate annual income is probably the most important indicator of the economic well-being of persons at any stage of the life cycle. It is assumed that annual incomes received by men and women living in urban centers of the United States reflect the economic rewards derived from an industrialized society and that such incomes may be used as a standard of comparison.

Data on annual incomes in the United States by age, sex, and place of residence are provided by the U.S. Bureau of the Census for 1959 and 1969. An examination of these income figures indicates the economic position of various rural age groups in the nation relative to that of urban persons age fourteen and over for that decade.

Table 1 places in salient perspective the disadvantaged economic position of the rural aged males relative to that of other male age groups in the nation in 1959 and 1969. Throughout the decade the annual median incomes of the rural aged males were markedly less than those of all urban males age fourteen and over, substantially less than those of all rural nonfarm and farm males age fourteen and over, and less than those of urban males age sixty-five and over.

The relative economic position of the rural aged males was fairly constant over the decade. In 1959 and 1969 the respective annual median incomes of rural nonfarm males age sixty-five and over were $1,351 and $2,205, only 30 and 32 percent, respectively, of that of all urban males age fourteen and over. For the rural-farm males age sixty-five and over, the respective annual median incomes were $1,417 and $2,514, only 31 and 37 percent, respectively, of that of all urban males age fourteen and over. The disparity for the urban aged over the decade was not as great;

TABLE 1 Annual Median Income by Sex, Age Group, and Place of Residence in the United States, 1959 and 1969

	1959		1969	
AGE GROUP AND RESIDENCE	($)	%	($)	%
Male				
Urban age 14 and over	4,559	100	6,860	100
Rural nonfarm age 14 and over	3,330	73	5,591	82
Rural farm age 14 and over	2,105	46	4,509	66
Urban age 65 and over	1,961	43	3,188	46
Rural nonfarm age 65 and over	1,351	30	2,205	32
Rural farm age 65 and over	1,417	31	2,514	37
Female				
Urban age 14 and over	1,606	100	2,514	100
Rural nonfarm age 14 and over	951	59	1,838	73
Rural farm age 14 and over	823	51	1,534	61
Urban age 65 and over	844	53	1,562	62
Rural nonfarm age 65 and over	662	41	1,104	44
Rural farm age 65 and over	632	39	887	35

SOURCE: Computed from U.S. Bureau of the Census, *Census of Population, 1960 and 1970: Detailed Characteristics*, Final Reports PC(1)-D1 and PC(1)-D1, United States Summary (Wasington, D.C.: Government Printing Office, 1962 and 1973), tables 219 and 245.

respective annual incomes were $1,961 and $3,188, or 43 and 46 percent of that of all urban males age fourteen and over.

The annual median incomes of female age groups in the nation showed trends similar to those for the men from 1959 to 1969. Over the decade, the annual median incomes of the rural aged females were substantially less than those of all urban females age fourteen and over, much less than those of all rural nonfarm and farm females age fourteen and over, and less than those of urban females age sixty-five and over (Table 1).

The relative economic position of the rural aged women, like that of the rural aged men, was fairly constant over the ten-year period. In 1959 and 1969, the respective annual median incomes of rural nonfarm females age sixty-five and over were $662 and $1,104, only 41 and 44 percent, respectively, of that of all urban females age fourteen and over. For rural farm females age sixty-five and over, the respective annual median incomes were $632 and $887, only 39 and 35 percent, respectively, of that of all urban females age fourteen and over. Again, the income of elderly urban females compared more favorably ($844 and $1,562; 53 and 62 percent respectively) than did that for rural females (Table 1).

Rural Development

Many rural communities in the United States, while retaining characteristics of traditional and folk societies, have undergone considerable industrialization. The Rural Development Act of 1972 was designed to encourage and accelerate economic growth in rural areas of the nation. Implementation of the act involved developing strategies whereby rural communities could attract industrial enterprises. It was assumed that such enterprises, if established in rural areas, would increase employment and services, increase incomes, inject new money into the community, and, in general, improve the quality of life.

Many rural communities have painfully discovered that the expected benefits from industrialization have not been achieved. Preliminary evidence suggests that the process of industrialization in many rural areas of the nation has had a differential impact upon various categories of persons. Some groups in the communities have benefited while other groups have experienced detrimental effects.[11]

A five-year longitudinal study in rural Illinois offers evidence of the negative impact of industrialization upon the economic well-being of the elderly in the area studied.[12] The hypothesis examined in the study was that the "industrial development of small communities is directly associated with a decline in the relative economic status of the elderly residents of the communities." The hypothesis was subjected to empirical tests in what the authors called a "natural experiment." Two communities of comparable social, demographic, and economic characteristics were selected. One community, designated the experimental area, had witnessed the construction of a heavily capitalized, ultra-modern cold rolling mill in the five-year period. The second community, used as a control area, had not experienced industrial development.

The findings in the study suggest that neither the economically active rural aged nor the retired rural residents of the experimental area benefited from industrial development. The study did not attempt to assess the impact of industrial development upon other aspects of life of the older residents, such as the cost of living, mental and physical health, local tax structure, and community facilities and services.

Social Life

An important indicator of well-being is the freedom and opportunity to interact with persons and groups of one's choice. Many older rural persons are limited in their social activities, and an important factor in these restrictions appears to be the lack of adequate transportation facilities.[13] Older rural women apparently are more restricted in social life than older rural men.[14] A low socioeconomic level and retirement are salient factors in the reduced social participation of many older rural men.[15] Further, according to Walter McKain, the present generation of older rural people grew to maturity when the family provided the dominant form of social life.[16] Today the traditional social function of the family has almost disappeared in many rural areas of the nation, and no satisfactory social organization has been developed to replace it.

A comparative study of older persons living in an urban and a rural environment provides some detailed data on their family relationships, their community participation, and their leisure-time hobbies and pastimes.[17] In both rural and urban areas, proximity was an important factor in the frequency of visits between the older person and his or her children and siblings. The children and siblings of the urban aged were somewhat more widely dispersed than those of the rural elderly; despite this distance factor, urban older persons visited with their children and their siblings more often than did the rural older persons. In addition, the rural older people said they depended more on their children and siblings to initiate visits than did the urban aged. These rural-urban differences in family visiting patterns probably reflected the more limited financial resources of the rural elderly as well as the poorer transportation facilities available in the rural area.

Slight differences were found between older rural and urban persons in the average number of reported community activities (rural 1.5 and urban 1.7). In both areas the most popular community activity was church related, and for the great majority this was the only activity reported. A greater proportion of the urban than rural aged took part in service and welfare organizations, in social clubs and lodges, and in Golden Age clubs. As might be expected, a larger proportion of the rural aged were members of farm organizations. Informal social activities played a slightly more important role in the lives of the older rural persons, and a greater proportion of the rural than of the urban elderly said they knew people in the community well, offered help to their friends and neighbors, and visited with friends and neighbors.[18]

Older rural persons engaged in slightly fewer hobbies and pastimes than did the older urban persons (average number 2.5 and 2.7, respectively). A slightly larger proportion of rural older persons engaged in fishing and hunting, while a larger proportion of urban aged engaged in playing cards, woodwork and crafts, dancing, and collecting. More than one-fourth of the persons in the study said they would like to take part in more activities, but there was little difference between the rural and the urban older persons in this desire. A slightly larger proportion of the rural than urban aged said that their lives could be more useful and that time was a burden.[19]

Health

It is commonly believed that rural living in the United States offers distinct health benefits to older people. It is alleged that the rural elderly enjoy the advantages of abundant fresh air and sunshine, out-of-doors activities, a slower-paced life style, and strong emotional support of close family and friends. It appears that such an idyllic picture of rural America is the product of popular writers. Careful studies do not substantiate the pastoral fantasy that glorifies rural communities as a paradise for older persons.[20]

Two studies in Kentucky offer systematic data on the comparative health status of rural and urban older persons. In both studies, each person interviewed was asked if he or she had any ailments or health conditions that bothered the respondent either all the time or periodically. Those who answered "yes" were then asked to name the ailments or health conditions. In the 1959 study 74 percent of the rural aged reported one or more ailments, compared with 61 percent for the urban aged; the rural older persons reported a higher prevalence of arthritis and rheumatism, high blood pressure, urological difficulties, and ailments of the respiratory system.[21]

In the 1971 study, responses to the question on physical health were placed in eight substantive categories.[22] On seven of these categories, the older rural men and women reported a greater proportion of ailments than did the urban aged; the rural elderly reported double the proportion of persons afflicted with cardiovascular difficulties and slightly greater proportions having respiratory, sense organs, endocrine, urinary, and psychiatric problems.

Available data on self-reported health ratings provide some clues about the health of rural and urban older men. Rural older men consistently rated their health as poorer than did the older urban men. Only 15 percent of the rural elderly men rated their health as "good," compared with 47 percent for the older urban men. Of the rural aged men, 75 percent said their health was worse than at age 50, compared with only 51 percent of the urban older men; 56 percent of the aged rural men said they had serious health problems, but only 24 percent of the urban aged men made such a statement; and 76 percent of the rural aged men compared with only 40 percent of the urban older men reported that their health conditions had obliged them to cut down on their activities.[23]

The comparatively poorer health of older rural persons undoubtedly reflects a variety of social and economic conditions. Among these are the characteristically lower economic and educational levels of the rural people, which inhibits their benefiting from health programs and knowledge. In addition, in the United States, the distribution of medical and health care services has favored urban locations, as is evidenced by the concentration of research centers, clinics, medical specialists, dentists, and various ancillary medical personnel in the more populated areas of the nation.[24]

Subjective Life

For most persons, old age brings limitations of one kind or another. The cumulative effect of these decrements tends to have a negative impact upon the subjective life of many older persons. Each person has within his life span a potential for developing a positive outlook, depending on a variety of biological, psychological, and sociological forces influencing his behavior. Available evidence suggests that rural environments have less potential than urban settings for producing a favorable mental outlook among older people.

A study of value orientations offers some clues about the subjective life of older rural and urban persons.[25] In a Kentucky study, nine scales were used to assess orientations toward selected values in American society, such as authoritarianism, religion, achievement, dependency, and pessimism. Respondents in the rural and urban samples agreed or disagreed with three statements on each scale. Responses to the statements indicated that the rural older people tended to have a more negative outlook on life than did the urban older people. The rural aged were also more authoritarian in viewpoint, more fundamentalistic in religious outlook, less motivated toward achievement, evidenced a greater dependency on government, and revealed greater hopelessness and despair.

An attitudinal study of rural and urban older persons revealed findings similar to the previous report on values.[26] In this study each person in the rural and urban samples responded to 72 agree-disagree statements constituting 24 attitude scales about economic well-being, self-image, morale, community life, family relationships, and general outlook. Comparison of mean scores on the 24 attitude scales yielded 17 statistically significant differences between the older rural and urban persons studied; of these, the urban aged scored more favorably than the rural elderly on 12, and the rural aged scored more favorably than urban older persons on 5, resulting in an overall ratio favoring the urban aged of 2.4 to 1.

The findings of the study indicated that the rural elderly, compared with the urban aged, worried more about their financial conditions, revealed less satisfaction with their housing, and maintained they had greater need for more money; revealed a more negative view of themselves and a poorer self-evaluation of their health; found their lives more dreary and were more concerned about their inability to lead useful lives; rated their communities less favorably in terms of visiting patterns, neighborliness, and general benefits; and reported greater alienation and more worry.[27]

In contrast, the rural aged, compared with the urban aged, revealed a greater sense of general happiness, greater family pride, stronger family support, and stronger feelings of personal gratification, as well as giving more favorable ratings to their neighborhoods as places in which to live.[28]

Implications

The disadvantaged position of older persons in urban environments in the United States has been previously documented.[29] Older persons in rural environments of the nation appear to be even more disadvantaged. Available information suggests that many rural older persons have extremely small incomes, inadequate means of transportation, a restricted social life, and poor physical and mental health. Many suffer from triple jeopardy: they are old, poor, and isolated in communities lacking organizations to serve the aged.[30]

The conditions of life of rural older persons in the United States strongly suggest the need for research and application in nonmetropolitan gerontology. Reliable information is needed on all aspects of life of older persons living in smaller cities, towns, villages, the open country, and on farms. Of special importance is the need for regional comparisons and for careful longitudinal studies conducted at strategic locations. Periodic assessments at these locations could provide public and private agencies with reliable data on demographic and migratory trends; on income, employment, housing, taxation, transportation facilities, and the industrialization process; on physical and mental health and nutritional levels; and on public safety, crime, social welfare, family and community life, and recreational and leisure-time facilities.

A feasible organizational structure to serve the interests of the rural and nonmetro aged is the concept of the Area Agency on Aging as outlined in the 1973 amendments to the Older Americans Act.[31] Such a client-centered agency could serve as an advocate of the interests of older persons, as a planner and coordinator of services for the aged without actually providing services, and as a catalyst and innovator in finding and pooling untapped resources and information needed for comprehensive programs and services for the older people.

NOTES

1. *Interchange*, vol. 1, no. 1 (Washington, D.C.: Population Reference Bureau, Inc., January 1976).
2. U.S. Bureau of the Census, *Census of Population 1970: Detailed Characteristics*, Final Report PC(1)-D1, United States Summary (Washington, D.C.: Government Printing Office, 1973), Table 199.
3. Donald O. Cowgill, "The Demography of Aging in the Midwest," in Arnold M. Rose and Warren A. Peterson, eds., *Older People and Their Social World* (Philadelphia: F. A. Davis, 1965).
4. Nathan W. Shock, *A Classified Bibliography of Gerontology and Geriatrics* (Stanford, Calif.: Stanford University Press, 1951).
5. Nathan W. Shock, *A Classified Bibliography of Gerontology and Geriatrics, Supplement One, 1949–1955* (Stanford, Calif.: Stanford University Press, 1957); and *A Classified Bibliography of Gerontology and Geriatrics, Supplement Two, 1956–1961* (Stanford, Calif.: Stanford University Press, 1963).
6. Robert C. Atchley, *Contemporary Conceptions of "Rural"* (Oxford, Ohio: Scripps Foundation at Miami University, prepublication manuscript, 1976), pp. 1–14.
7. Robert Redfield, "The Folk Society," *American Journal of Sociology*, 52 (1947), 293–308.
8. Charles P. Loomis and J. Allan Beegle, *Rural Social Systems* (New York: Prentice-Hall, 1950), p. 784.
9. Everett M. Rogers and Rabel J. Burdge, *Social Change in Rural Societies* (New York: Appleton-Century-Crofts, 1972).
10. Jerold E. Levy, "The Older American Indian," Olen E. Leonard, "The Older Rural Spanish People of the Southwest," and Stanley H. Smith, "The Older Rural Negro," in E. G. Youmans, ed., *Older Rural Americans* (Lexington: University of Kentucky Press, 1967).
11. Mary Jo Grinstead, Bernal L. Green, and J. Martin Redfern, *Rural Development and Labor Adjustment in the Mississippi Delta and Ozarks of Arkansas* (Fayetteville, Ark.: Agricultural Experiment Station, Bulletin 795, 1975).
12. Frank Clemente and Gene F. Summers, "Industrial Development and the Elderly: A Longitudinal Analysis," *Journal of Gerontology*, 28 (1973), 479–83.
13. Ira Kaye, "Transportation Problems of the Older American" in J. B. Cull and R. E. Hardy, eds., *The Neglected Older American* (Springfield, Ill.: Charles C Thomas, 1973).
14. Carl V. Patton, "Age Groupings and Travel in a Rural Area," *Rural Sociology*, 40 (1975), 55–63.
15. Philip Taietz and Olaf F. Larson, "Social Participation and Old Age," *Rural Sociology*, 21 (1956), 229–38.
16. Walter C. McKain, Jr., "Community Roles and Activities of Older Rural Persons," in E. G. Youmans, ed., *Older Rural Americans* (Lexington: University of Kentucky Press, 1967).
17. E. Grant Youmans, *Aging Patterns in a Rural and an Urban Area of Kentucky* (Lexington, Ky.: Agricultural Experiment Station Bulletin 681, 1963). In 1959

data were collected from 1,236 men and women age sixty and over, half of whom lived in a metropolitan center and half in a rural county of Kentucky.

18. Ibid.

19. Ibid.

20. Walter C. McKain, Jr., "Aging and Rural Life," in W. Donahue and C. Tibbits, eds., *The New Frontiers of Aging* (Ann Arbor: University of Michigan Press, 1957).

21. E. Grant Youmans, *Aging Patterns in a Rural and an Urban Area of Kentucky*.

22. E. Grant Youmans, "Age Group, Health, and Attitudes," *The Gerontologist*, 14 (1974), 249–54. The older persons studied were age sixty and over.

23. E. Grant Youmans, "Health Orientations of Older Rural and Urban Men," *Geriatrics*, 22 (1967), 139–47. The younger men were age sixty to sixty-four and the older men age seventy-five and over.

24. Bert L. Ellenbogen, "Health Status of the Rural Aged," in E. G. Youmans, ed., *Older Rural Americans* (Lexington: University of Kentucky Press, 1967).

25. E. Grant Youmans, "Perspectives on the Older American in a Rural Setting," in J. B. Cull and R. E. Hardy, eds., *The Neglected Older American* (Springfield, Ill.: Charles C Thomas 1973).

26. These findings are based on a survey this author conducted in 1971 of 803 persons age twenty and over living in a metropolitan center and a rural county of Kentucky. Aged persons were age sixty and over. The study was carried out jointly by the Economic Development Division, Economic Research Service, U.S. Department of Agriculture, and the Kentucky Agricultural Experiment Station, Lexington, Ky.

27. Ibid.

28. Ibid.

29. Matilda W. Riley and Anne Foner, *Aging and Society*, vol. 1: *An Inventory of Research Findings* (New York: Russell Sage Foundation, 1968).

30. *Triple Jeopardy: Myth or Reality* (Washington, D.C.: National Council on the Aging, 1972).

31. U.S. Bureau of the Census, Social Statistics for the Elderly, Area Level System, Stage 1, Omaha (Washington, D.C., 1975).

Maintaining Social Distance in a Racially Integrated Retirement Community

JILL S. QUADAGNO
RUTH G. KUHAR
WARREN A. PETERSON

This study was conducted in a racially integrated public housing retirement community. The methods used for data collection were extensive, informal fieldwork and structured questionnaires. While there were no significant differences between the black and white residents in terms of income, education, or marital status, the black residents tended to be a more diverse group. From the field data it was determined that residents redefined the formal, task-oriented activities going on in the community as work, while perceiving other less structured activities as leisure. In the work activities there was no interracial tension. However, in the leisure-oriented activities considerable tension between black and white residents was expressed. Residents who attempted to develop interracial friendships were censored, and white residents expressed concern about maintaining an equal balance of blacks and whites in the community. Using the concept of social distance developed by Bogardus, it appears that both black and white residents were comfortable interacting in a setting defined as work, supporting the premise that occupational settings are least likely to be characterized by negative racial attitudes.

In 1933 Bogardus developed what he termed a "social distance" scale to measure the hierarchical arrangement of discriminatory attitudes, and he followed this scale with a series of studies examining racial attitudes over time by region and sex (Bogardus, 1933, 1958, 1959a, 1959b). In the 1940s Myrdal pursued the subject of social distance in a detailed analysis of American society by incorporating the recognition that whites organized their relations with blacks according to a "rank order of discrimination." According to Myrdal (1944, p. 60), the two strongest prohibitions were, first, those relating to "intermarriage and sexual intercourse involving

SOURCE: Copyrighted, 1978 by *Journal of Minority Aging* (formerly *Black Aging*); reprinted with permission.

white women" and, second, those which concerned "behavior in personal relations." As Myrdal elaborated the meaning of the latter, it included "barriers against dancing, bathing, eating, drinking together, and social intercourse generally." Least likely to be problematic and therefore last on the "rank order of discrimination" was discrimination in jobs or other means of earning a living.[1]

Several studies since the 1940s have incorporated the concept of social distance in various ways. Minard (1952) examined race relationships in a Pocahontas, West Virginia, coal field using a combination of participant-observation and interviewing. He found strong solidarity between black and white workers within the mines but segregated patterns of interaction maintained outside of the work situation. Minard (1952, p. 30) noted, "A spirit of general good will has been fostered within the mine among the white and colored workers. The community outside, however, constitutes a negative influence and the spirit of integration dissolves under its impact." Confirming what Myrdal had noted earlier, discrimination was least on the job and most in the area of personal life.

In another study Harding and Hogrefe (1952) interviewed white department-store employees to determine if contact with black co-workers would reduce prejudiced attitudes. Using a form of a social distance scale, they found that there were no significant differences between those who were working in an integrated work situation and those who were not. Both groups were equally likely to have few objections to working with blacks but to have reservations about blacks as neighbors or personal friends. Thus this study implied that contact did not affect attitudes.

More recently Caditz (1975) interviewed white liberals regarding attitudes toward several items, such as busing, residence, and occupation. Her framework was conceptually similar to a measure of social distance. Caditz (1975, p. 23) noted that "the situations most easily handled by the respondents are the occupation and hiring situations." She concluded that "the closer to the individuals' family setting and primary responsibilities for significant others, the more difficult the situations are to resolve" (1975, p. 29). Her reasoning to explain these findings was that:

> White liberals experience the least difficulty in expressing attitudes consistent with integration in longstanding situations which are clearly defined in the culture. The area of employment of minorities holds clear-cut "definitions of the situation" for those adopting integration as a solution to interracial inequities. White liberals are familiar with expected behaviors and ideological positions with respect to their roles.

Again, the concept of social distance was confirmed as a factor affecting attitudes of whites toward interaction with blacks. Interaction in the work sphere is less affected by prejudice than interaction in the interpersonal spheres of life.

What is problematic with all these studies is that they have only dealt with attitudes and behaviors of whites toward blacks. By narrowing the concept of social distance to one that is created and maintained by whites, researchers have granted whites the power, theoretically, to define and control all interracial situations. The hidden assumption is that blacks do not have any reciprocal desire to maintain social distance, nor do they have the power to do so. Thus the attitudes and behaviors of blacks are ignored as insignificant, and a subtle form of intellectual racism is perpetuated.

Several studies have been done of race relations in interracial housing situations. Most of these studies have focused solely on friendship and intimacy rather than the broader concept of social distance. Many of these studies also perpetuate the bias described above. For example, Wilner, Walkley, and Cook (1952) examined attitudes of white women living in integrated housing projects, hypothesizing that increased contact with blacks would reduce prejudice. In this study women living in integrated projects reported more positive contacts and attitudes toward blacks than women in segregated housing projects. Similarly, Festinger and Kelley (1951) found that when a town had a black housing project forced upon it, attitudes toward blacks in general and project residents in particular were negative. However, community action programs which put people in close proximity improved the attitudes of whites residing in the town.

However, some researchers have been concerned with reciprocal concerns of blacks and whites. In 1951 Deutsch and Collins did a study of interracial housing. They found that close physical proximity to members of another race under conditions of residential equality enhanced attitudes toward members of the other group. More recently, Lawton has done several studies of friendships in public housing. In a study of older tenants in public housing, Lawton and Simon (1968) found that blacks and whites tended to choose friends of the same race and that this tendency was increased for whites when the number of blacks was disproportionately high. However, cross-racial friendships appeared to be more frequent among the elderly than among young people. Lawton and Simon noted that "one gets the very strong impression of relative tranquility in interracial relations, as compared with those in public housing for younger people."

In a more recent study Nahemow and Lawton (1975) investigated friendships in middle-income public housing which was both age-integrated and racially integrated. They found that racial barriers began to break down when individuals shared daily living space. Proximity proved to be the critical factor in the selection of friends. However, 72 percent of all reported friends were of the same race. Nahemow and Lawton (1975, p. 210) concluded that "not only did whites tend to make friends with whites, blacks with blacks, and Puerto Ricans with Puerto Ricans, but they would go farther from home base to do so." In summary,

it appears that interracial friendships are facilitated by integrated housing, but that people still prefer friends of their own race.

There has been a recent and continued expansion of the proportion of
the population over age sixty-five. This population increase has been
accompanied by a concern for adequate retirement housing. Most
privately developed retirement housing caters to the middle class and
tends to be racially segregated. To date no studies of integrated *private*
middle-income retirement communities have been reported (Christopherson, 1972; Hochschild, 1973; Sherman, 1973; Jacobs, 1974; Marshall,
1975; Heintz, 1976). This situation is quite different for residents of public
retirement housing, since housing authority regulations require that public
housing be racially integrated. As described above, Lawton has done
some work on integrated middle-income *public* retirement housing, but
no one has investigated the increasingly predominant lower-income
retirement communities. Further, Lawton has focused mainly on the
numbers of friends rather than the quality of friendships or the social and
structural basis of friendship maintenance. In spite of the suggestion that
tranquility exists, no research has investigated in depth the ways in which
interracial relationships are sustained in integrated housing situations.

In retirement communities, as in other situations where individuals are
set apart in some way from the wider society, internally defined social
orders tend to arise which contribute to a redefinition of the traditional
delineation of activities. Several researchers have confirmed that in
retirement communities residents who are no longer formally connected
to the world of work create work by redefining ongoing activities. For
example, in her study of the residents of Merrill Court, Hochschild (1973)
found that the widows, who had lost some previously held roles, developed new ones defined within the context of social relationships in the
community. Activities which occurred on a regular basis and which had a
specific goal were defined as work. In describing the "beehive of
activity" apparent in Merrill Court, Hochschild (1973, p. 39) notes:

> All this activity had a special meaning for the widows. Through it they defined
> what was work and what was leisure. . . . All the women were living on social
> welfare, social security, or pensions, and in the eyes of society they were not
> workers. They earned no pay and had no employer, paid no taxes, and
> punched no time clocks. They came to the Recreation Room voluntarily, and a
> decision to come downstairs to work was a decision about what to do with
> their leisure. But if you asked them, they would tell you they were working.
> They jokingly talked about being on "company time" and talked about what
> they would do when they were "free" to attend to their own affairs.

Other less organized activities that had no clear task-like purpose continued to be defined as leisure. What is important to recognize is that to the
outside observer all the activities appeared to be leisure. It was Hochschild's intimate acquaintance with the social definitions of the situation
that enabled her to separate the work activities from the leisure activities.

In another participant-observation study of a retirement community, Sequin (1973) also found that the residents "generated social structures that established alternative family roles, work-type roles, etc." Neither of these studies was concerned with race relationships. However, it is possible that these internal worlds which create work and leisure out of activities that appear to the outside observer to be only leisure could be a means for maintaining the social distance between blacks and whites confirmed in earlier studies. The purpose of this study is to examine race relations in a racially integrated public housing retirement community to determine if the tranquility discussed earlier does, in fact, exist, and to evaluate how relations between blacks and whites are structured.

Method and Sample Description

This study was conducted in a public housing retirement community for low-income people. The research site, which will be referred to as Horizon Heights, is an urban high-rise located in a working-class, predominantly black neighborhood of a midwestern city. Horizon Heights is the first of seven high- and low-rise apartment buildings built in 1968. The city officials put up and sold bonds and awarded the bid to HUD. The original plan was to construct only one high-rise. Later, the Housing Authority initiated plans to build the remaining six units. HUD subsidized the rent, which is 25 percent of a resident's adjusted income, and will continue rent subsidies until the bonds are paid off. Afterwards the Housing Authority will maintain the buildings. The buildings are maintained with rent revenue. Horizon Heights was built specifically as retirement housing.

Method

Two methods were employed in the data collection process. First, extensive fieldwork was conducted for a period of a year. The fieldworker spent many hours in the community talking to people informally, conducting open-ended interviews and attending meetings, activities, and social events. The field data were collected at different times during the day and night, including weekends and holidays, so that a full portrait of life at Horizon Heights could emerge. Some of the interviews and proceedings were tape-recorded, while other data were transcribed later from extensive notes taken by the fieldworker. The field data were then organized and analyzed by topics which were central to the ongoing life in the community.

Subsequent to the fieldwork, a structured questionnaire was administered to a random sample of residents in Horizon Heights. To introduce the survey to the residents of the community, the fieldworker explained the survey to the people at some of the activities in the community. Then interviewers telephoned the residents and made appointments to administer the questionnaire. Of the approximately 312 residents of the community, a sample of 159 interviews was completed.

Description of the Physical Setting

Horizon Heights is a sixteen-story rectangular building with public space on the first floor. An adjoining one-story building houses the Midwest City Housing Authority. There are eighteen apartments on fifteen floors, totaling 270 apartments. Nearby there is an area of low-rise or one-story apartments totaling thirty-three apartments. Presently, approximately three hundred persons over age sixty-five are residents. Horizon Heights is located adjacent to the Midwest City downtown shopping area.

The first floor consists of an entry hallway, a business office, postal mailboxes, a lobby, a community center room, a health clinic and waiting room, a dining room, a few miscellaneous offices, elevators, restroom facilities, and hallways. There are several places for announcements in the lobby and in the hall area, such as a bulletin board near the elevator and an easel containing a large newsprint pad where daily announcements are placed.

On the upper floors a central hallway runs the length of the building. All apartments open onto this hallway. There are three types of apartments: studio, one bedroom, and two bedroom. Studio apartments have an accordion door between the living room and the bedroom. There is a picture window in each, and the walls are painted in muted tones. Each apartment has a kitchenette, living room, bath, and bedroom. The doors of the apartments are quite close to one another and the halls are not well lighted. Each floor has a laundry room equipped with washer, dryer, a small table, sink, and counter space.

The central lobby is a large room equipped with well-worn synthetic upholstered chairs, indistinctive in color and shape, placed in a random order throughout the room. Sitting in the lobby, a person has direct visibility to the entrance, the elevators, and the hall. A guard sits between the entry and the elevators and conscientiously requests all nonresidents entering the building to register and declare the nature of their business. About three-quarters of the way into the lobby are some free-standing screens which divide the sitting area from a small game-table area and kitchenette facilities.

Description of the Residents

The residents of Horizon Heights are working- and lower-class black and white retirees recruited largely from the surrounding neighborhood, drawn by the prospect of inexpensive, relatively attractive housing. Sixty-three percent of the residents are black and 37 percent white, and most had previously lived in largely segregated neighborhoods. As shown in Table 1, most of the residents have incomes under $5,000. White males tend to have the highest incomes, with 57 percent having incomes

TABLE 1   Income Distribution by Race and Sex

Income distribution	White		Black	
	Male (N = 7)	Female (N = 57)	Male (N = 19)	Female (N = 76)
$1,000–1,999	0.0	0.0	0.0	1.4
$2,000–2,999	14.3	7.3	5.9	18.1
$3,000–3,999	14.0	50.9	41.2	38.9
$4,000–4,999	0.0	36.4	11.8	18.1
$5,000–5,999	14.3	1.8	29.4	15.3
$6,000–6,999	57.1	3.6	5.9	5.9
$7,000–9,999	0.0	0.0	5.9	1.4
$10,000–14,999	0.0	0.0	0.0	1.4

Chi sq. = 4.87, d.f. = 7, N.S.

between $6,000 and $6,999.[2] Overall, both black and white men have higher incomes than the women, although there are a few notable exceptions. What is notable is that while blacks are most likely to have the extremely low incomes, they are also most likely to have extremely high incomes. It appears that in terms of income level, the black residents are a more diverse group than the white residents.

As is true for most people over sixty, women are much more likely to be widowed than men. Table 2 reports marital status by race and sex. Sixty-nine percent of the white women and 76 percent of the black women are widowed, whereas 85 percent of the white men are married and none are widowed. Black men are much more likely to be widowed than white men (52 percent), which explains why the statistics reported in this table approach the level of significance.

In regard to education, over 57 percent of the white males had finished the eighth grade or less, and the others had some high school or graduated high school. None had any college or vocational training. Both black and white women were more likely than men to have completed high school and have some college. What is again distinctive is that blacks not only show the lowest educational levels (less than third grade), they also are

TABLE 2   Marital Status by Race and Sex

Marital status	White		Black	
	Male (N = 7)	Female (N = 57)	Male (N = 19)	Female (N = 76)
Married	85.7	8.9	31.6	10.5
Divorced	14.3	14.3	10.5	11.8
Widowed	0.0	69.6	52.6	76.3
Single	0.0	7.1	5.3	1.3

Chi sq. = 6.91, d.f. = 3, N.S. (p<.07).

TABLE 3 Education by Race and Sex

Last year school completed	White		Black	
	Male (N = 7)	Female (N = 57)	Male (N = 19)	Female (N = 76)
No formal school	0.0	0.0	0.0	1.3
Kindergarten–third	0.0	0.0	15.8	7.9
Fourth–sixth	14.3	10.5	31.6	13.2
Seventh–eighth	42.9	27.4	31.6	25.0
Ninth–tenth	28.6	14.1	10.5	19.8
Eleventh–twelfth	14.3	28.1	0.0	18.4
Some college	0.0	10.6	0.0	10.5
College graduate	0.0	0.0	5.3	1.3
M.A. degree	0.0	0.0	0.0	1.3
Vocational training	0.0	8.8	5.3	1.3

Chi sq. = 15.15, d.f. = 17, N.S.

most likely to have advanced educational training. A similar pattern was exhibited by black women, including one woman holding a master's degree. Thus the black residents were more diverse in education as well as income than the white residents. This may be an indication that minority status in our society tends to compress diversity, making race a master status which is more significant than income or education.

Data Analysis

In Horizon Heights a variety of activities occur on a daily, weekly, and monthly basis. Some of these are formal, organized activities while others are informal kinds of gatherings which meet various needs. It was important for the fieldworker to observe both types of activities, since participation in formal activities was relatively low. As shown in Table 4, more than half of the residents, regardless of race, did not participate in any activities of a formal nature.

Of those formal activities available to the residents, some took place in Horizon Heights and were organized by the management or members of the community. Others took place in the wider urban area. While the difference between black and white residents in terms of participation in formal activities in the community was not statistically significant, it did approach the level of significance. In Table 5 it can be seen that the white women were somewhat more likely than black women to participate in formal activities in Horizon Heights. Nearly 30 percent of the white women participated in one or more formal activities in the community, as

TABLE 4 Number of Formal Activities Participated in by Race and Sex

Number of activities listed	White		Black	
	Male (N = 7)	Female (N = 57)	Male (N = 19)	Female (N = 76)
None	57.1	49.1	57.9	55.3
One	42.9	17.5	26.3	19.7
Two to five	0.0	28.1	15.8	23.4
Six or more	0.0	5.3	0.0	1.1

Chi sq. = 1.72, d.f. = 6, N.S.

opposed to only about 19 percent of the black women. In contrast, there was no difference in regard to participation in activities in the wider community.

From the fieldworker's observations, it was apparent that the critical variable was not participation within or outside the community, but *how* the activities came to be defined by the residents. While all activities, formal or informal, appeared to be leisure activities initially, the participant-observation data revealed that they were redefined by the residents. Thus some activities were considered work, whereas others continued to be considered leisure. These redefinitions were influential in affecting race relations in the community.

Work Activities

Those activities which are defined as work are characterized by racial integration and harmony. In these activities there is a clear task to be accomplished, and role relationships are specified. One of these activities is the cancer volunteer group, which meets on a weekly basis. This group is composed entirely of women. They prepare cancer bandages and pads for hospital patients as well as construct lap robes. They divide the jobs and work very effectively as a group. Weekly attendance is between

TABLE 5 Number of Formal Activities Participated in inside the Community by Race and Sex

Number of activities inside Horizon Heights	White		Black	
	Male (N = 7)	Female (N = 57)	Male (N = 19)	Female (N = 76)
None	71.4	70.2	68.4	80.3
One	28.6	15.8	26.3	7.9
Two or more	0.0	14.1	5.3	11.8

Chi sq. = 7.85, d.f. = 4, N.S. (p<.09).

TABLE 6 Number of Formal Activities Participated in outside the Community by Race and Sex

Number of activities outside Horizon Heights	White		Black	
	Male (N = 7)	Female (N = 57)	Male (N = 19)	Female (N = 76)
None	85.7	64.9	89.5	64.5
One	14.3	12.3	0.0	21.1
Two or more	0.0	22.9	10.6	14.5

Chi sq. = 5.70, d.f. = 4, N.S.

twenty and thirty persons, and the women appear very dedicated to this work. They are eager to display the various plaques they have received honoring their years of service. Since this group meets on a regular basis with a specific goal, it is similar to and, in fact, is equated with work. In this activity black and white women work together with no tension. Some field notes illustrate the situation:

> The field director had requested that I pay particular attention to the seating arrangement at the various activities at the Heights. That morning at the cancer group, I noticed that the black women were really randomly seated throughout the group. There were some groups of two or three black women, but then there were some who were sitting mixed in with the whites. The group seemed evenly distributed between blacks and whites. This morning I worked at the table with four black women, most of whom were either cutting or stuffing gauze bandages. One lady was stitching lap robes. Most of the conversation that morning consisted of comments about making quilts.

The residents are involved in the administrative functioning of the community, and the Resident's Council is a political group which is formal and task oriented. The council consists of elected officers, committee chairpersons, and elected floor representatives as well as low-rise representatives. Meetings are held monthly and are open to any interested resident. Some of the activities of the council are to manage many of the social activities of the community, to send cheer messages to the ill, to raise money for various needs such as equipment, and to handle complaints from the residents. Blacks and whites participate equally in council affairs, and there is no racial tension evident at council meetings. While several explosive issues have arisen at Residence Council meetings, they have centered on resident-management tensions and internal political matters, not race.

Leisure Activities

Activities which are social in nature and not associated with an instrumental goal include shopping trips on the Horizon Heights bus, sitting in the lobby chatting, eating at the congregate meal site which is located in the building, and attending Vespers services. These activities are not defined as work by the residents, since they are not task oriented and role relationships are not specified. These activities tend to be racially segregated in terms of who participates and the style of participation. For example, many of the residents sit in the lobby every morning to chat, plan their daily activities, and watch the passers-by. Generally the white men do not sit in the lobby at all. The black men sit in a group in the center of the lobby with the white women sitting in chairs on one side of the men and the black women on the other side.

A similar situation exists at the nutrition site which is located in the first floor of the building. Most residents eat there daily, and blacks and whites generally sit at separate tables. On bus trips to shopping centers and other events in the local area, groups also tend to remain racially segregated. For example, if there is a preponderance of black residents who sign up in advance for a particular trip, white residents may refuse to ride the bus at all. The following excerpt from the field notes relates a situation in which this occurred:

> In the hall I ran into Mrs. Marshall, who took me aside and whispered that she wanted to tell me something. She said in a tone of voice of almost outrage that she didn't participate in anything anymore. For example, there was a trip yesterday that only blacks attended on the bus with the exception of one white woman. She said, "Can you imagine, there were white women who went, but they drove down separately in a car, and they didn't even invite the other white lady to go along with them." This conversation was prompted by an announcement on the chalkboard telling about a trip in the future which people were required to sign up for at the present.

Vespers services also tend to be racially segregated. Black and white residents attend different services outside the community, and white residents do not attend Vespers services held at Horizon Heights.

Sources of Tension

While the initial impression of the state of affairs at Horizon Heights is one of relative tranquility, similar to reports of other cited research, there are obviously strong existing tensions, as indicated by the in-depth field research. An attractive, integrated living situation cannot erase the impact of years of racial tensions, and the effects of past attitudes and beliefs still affect the lives of many residents. The following story told by one black resident illustrates this point:

> She noted that her father had an intense hatred of white people due to the way he had been treated throughout his life, and when they were children always told them horrible stories about how whites would treat a black person. She said she now has nothing to do with whites, except perhaps a passing "hello," unless she feels she must.

Similarly, a white resident related attitudes toward blacks illustrating a lack of previous experience with interracial living or even interracial contact.

> She pointed out that she had never had any contact with black people before she moved into the Heights. She used to live in the country, and after her husband's death decided to move into the city to be closer to her children. She reemphasized that she had never known black people before and that she felt there was a lot of hatred between the two races.

The result of the past experiences of both black and white residents leads to an occasional incident of open hostility, but, more generally, intimate contacts are just avoided. It is clear from the field notes that close friendships are generally discouraged, and social pressures are brought to bear on those who attempt to maintain them:

> Mrs. Horton was an extremely well-dressed black woman, outgoing and articulate. After explaining further what I was doing there, she related part of her history. She has lived there from the very beginning. She likes it all right but feels the relations racially are quite strained. She related in long detail how she had had a white friend named Ida who also lived there from the beginning. They had been friends before moving in. They liked to visit back and forth and go places together. They received harassment from both races, and Ida got more and more upset about it and finally moved out after some vulgar names about her were exchanged one evening in the lobby.

Since past interracial experiences of most residents had been either negative or nonexistent, the few residents who did form cross-racial friendships found these friendships difficult to maintain.

At times the desire on the part of some residents to maintain a segregated life style erupted into an outright rejection of the forced integration policy mandated by the housing authority. As one black resident told a fieldworker:

> She was happy living at Horizon Heights, though she related an incident where she was forced to move to a different floor because "some old white lady from the South" constantly harassed her.

In spite of the rather negative portrait presented, it is important to recall that formal relationships such as those involved in activities defined as work where clear role prescriptions are apparent do not present any difficulty for residents, and daily activities are generally carried on harmoniously.

The issue of maintaining a racial balance between black and white residents crops up frequently as a major source of tension, particularly for white tenants. They are not only concerned about the racial balance at activities as in the incident described earlier, but are also fearful of becoming a minority on their own floor and in the building as a whole. According to one white resident:

She said that her biggest objection is that there are so many blacks. There are fourteen on her floor alone, and she objects to that. She said they circulated a petition about a year ago and nothing was done about it, that Mr. Milford said the whites who circulated the petition were discriminating against the blacks.

Although residents do not have access to information regarding the number of tenants of each race occupying the building and calculations are difficult to make on an informal basis due to the turnover of residents, whites are quite preoccupied with this issue.

Later it got to be time for me to leave, and I stopped back in the health clinic to get my coat. Mrs. Wilfred came in and rather dramatically said to Joan, the nurse, "I'm going home. I need to go home." She threw up her arms above her head and stated that she just had to get away. She stated that Mrs. Flory had stopped her in the lobby and said she had heard that three more people had moved in, and she wanted to know whether they were black or white. She said Mrs. Flory actually demanded to know whether they were black or white. Mrs. Wilfred said that she resented her attitude and was not about to answer her question, that these people were legitimately living in the building and that it was none of her business.

As substantiation of some of the impressions from the field data, a concern with racial balance also appeared unexpectedly on the survey responses. In answer to the question "What are the things that you find least satisfying about living here?" six white residents mentioned a concern about the proportion of black residents in relation to the number of whites. Only one black resident brought up the question of race, and this was described as a concern about feeling discriminated against.[3]

Feeling Comfortable in the Community

In spite of the expressed tensions which exist, most residents feel that Horizon Heights is a comfortable place to live and that people, in general, are friendly. This can be illustrated by responses to two questions on the questionnaire. People were asked, "Do most people here visit with each other or do they keep to themselves?" Table 7 reports the results of the statistical analysis of the responses to this question. The overwhelming majority of both black and white residents feel that people visit and do not keep to themselves. In addition, when asked "Is this home for you?"

TABLE 7 Perceived Neighborliness of Community by Race and Sex

Perceived neighborliness	White		Black	
	Male (N = 7)	Female (N = 57)	Male (N = 18)	Female (N = 76)
Visit	85.7	64.9	77.8	67.1
Keep to selves	14.3	35.1	22.2	32.1

Chi sq. = 0.36, d.f. = 1, N.S.

TABLE 8   The Community as Home by Race and Sex

Is this home for you?	White		Black	
	Male (N = 7)	Female (N = 57)	Male (N = 19)	Female (N = 76)
Yes	100.0	98.2	89.5	90.8
No	0.0	1.8	10.5	6.6
Sometimes	0.0	0.0	0.0	2.6

Chi sq. = 0.82, d.f. = 2, N.S.

an even higher percent of the residents responded positively. The responses to this question are illustrated in Table 8. Both black and white residents feel that Horizon Heights is "home."

Conclusion

It is clear from the survey data that few differences exist between black and white residents in this retirement community. While blacks tend to be somewhat more diversified in terms of income and education, these differences are not statistically significant. Blacks and whites tend to participate equally in activities, both in the retirement community and outside it in the wider community. They tend to feel the same about their living situation. In spite of this similarity of background, behavior, and feelings, racial tension does exist. This tension appeared slightly in the survey data, but was really only obvious after extensive fieldwork.

The expressed satisfaction of the residents seems to contradict the concern about racial issues. However, these findings are not really contradictory. Residents maintain tranquility by artificially creating a means of maintaining social distance. By defining formal structured activities as work, they are able to interact comfortably in these situations. It is only in leisure-type activities where the potential for intimate friendships exists that tensions interfere with daily interaction. The implications of these findings suggest that an increase in formal activities in integrated housing may reduce racial tension and segregated patterns of interaction.

NOTES

This article is a revised version of a paper presented to the Gerontological Society, San Francisco, 1978. This study was supported by Grant #HEW SRS 10P 90151 from the Social Security Administration, U.S. Department of Health, Education, and Welfare, Washington, D.C. We would like to thank David

Oliver and Henry Brehm for comments on an earlier draft of this paper and Linda Phelps for preparation of the data analysis.

1. It should be pointed out that Bogardus's scale was concerned with measuring attitudes, whereas Myrdal's analysis applied to actual behaviors or actions. Bogardus was describing prejudice, and Myrdal was describing discrimination.
2. The reported incomes are family income rather than individual income. Since most of the white men are married, this would account for their relatively high income levels.
3. Both black and white interviewers were used to administer the questionnaire.

REFERENCES

Bogardus, E. S. 1959a. Racial reactions by regions. *Sociology and Social Research*, 54 (March–April):286–290.

——. 1959b. Race reactions by sexes. *Sociology and Social Research*, 43 (July–August):439–442.

——. 1958. Racial distance changes in the United States during the past thirty years. *Sociology and Social Research*, 43 (November–December):127–135.

——. 1933. A social distance scale. *Sociology and Social Research*, 17 (January):265–271.

Caditz, Judith. 1975. Ambivalence toward integration: The sequence of responses to six interracial situations. *Sociological Quarterly*, 16 (Winter):16–32.

Christopherson, Victor A. 1972. Retirement communities: The cities of two tales. *Social Science*, 47:82–86.

DeFleur, M. L., and F. R. Westie. 1958. Verbal attitudes and overt acts. *American Sociological Review*, 23 (December):667–673.

Deutsch, M., and M. E. Collins. 1951. *Interracial housing: A psychological evaluation of a social experiment*. Minneapolis: University of Minnesota Press.

Festinger, L., and H. H. Kelley. 1951. *Changing attitudes through social contact*. Ann Arbor: University of Michigan Press.

Harding, John, and Russell Hogrefe. 1952. Attitudes of white department store employees toward Negro co-workers. *Journal of Social Issues*, 8:18–28.

Heintz, Katherine. 1976. *Retirement communities: For adults only*. New Brunswick, N.J.: Center for Urban Policy Research.

Hochschild, Arlie. 1973. *The unexpected community*. Englewood Cliffs, N.J.: Prentice-Hall.

Jacobs, Jerry. 1974. An ethnographic study of a retirement community. *Gerontologist*, 14:483–487.

Kutner, B., C. Wilkins, and P. Yarrow. 1952. Verbal attitudes and overt behavior involving racial prejudice. *Journal of Abnormal and Social Psychology*, 47 (October):649–652.

Lawton, M. Powell, and B. B. Simon. 1968. The ecology of social relationships in housing for the elderly. *Gerontologist*, 8:108–115.

Linn, L. S. 1965. Verbal attitudes and overt behavior: A study of racial discrimination. *Social Forces*, 43 (March):353–364.

Lohman, J. D., and D. C. Reitzes. 1954. Deliberately organized groups and racial behavior. *American Sociological Review*, 19 (June):342–344.

Marshall, Victor W. 1975. Socialization for impending death in a retirement village. *American Journal of Sociology*, 80:1124–1144.

Merton, Robert K. 1949. Discrimination and the American creed. Pp. 99–126 in Robert M. MacIver (ed.), *Discrimination and national welfare*. New York: Institute for Religious and Social Studies.

Minard, Ralph D. 1952. Race relationships in a Pocahontas coal field. *Journal of Social Issues*, 8:29–44.

Myrdal, Gunnar. 1944. *An American dilemma*. New York: Harper & Row.

Nahemow, Lucille, and M. Powell Lawton. 1975. Similarity and propinquity in friendship formation. *Journal of Personality and Social Psychology*, 82:205–213.

Sequin, M. M. 1973. Opportunity for peer socialization in a retirement community. *Gerontologist*, 13:184–188.

Sherman, Susan. 1973. Methodology in a study of residents of retirement housing. *Journal of Gerontology*, 28:351–358.

Wilner, Daniel M., Rosabelle Price Walkley, and Stuart W. Cook. 1952. Residential proximity and intergroup relations in public housing projects. *Journal of Social Issues*, 8:45–72.

6

Aging and Family Relationships

In studying the family in later life, one area of concern has been the ways in which the family is affected by changes in society. Specific attention has been paid to the effects of industrialization on both family structure and interpersonal relationships. A second research focus has looked inside the family itself to see what kinds of changes occur as people move through the life cycle. From newly married couple to the postparental phase, a husband and wife undergo many changes in relation to each other and other family members.

Postindustrial Family Structure

A myth about family life which was commonly believed until recently is that people used to live in three-generation households. Supposedly industrialization broke up extended family households, and the nuclear family structure gained priority. We now know that true three-generation households existed only rarely and that modern family ties are quite extensive (Shanas et al., 1968). Most family theorists now speak of a modified extended nuclear family structure, meaning that family members do not necessarily live in the same household but do maintain contact through an interchange of visits (Shanas, 1973). The article by Streib looks at the older family from two points of view: the makeup of the family households themselves and the kin networks to which family members belong. Streib discusses the amount of contact between older parents and their children and attempts to anticipate the changes which might occur in older families in the future.

Marriage in Later Life

As couples move through the life cycle, the quality of marital interaction changes. Some researchers believe it changes for the better, others for the worse. In one study which dealt with this question, husbands and wives of all ages were interviewed. Of all the age groups, the middle-aged women were the most critical of their husbands and most prone to report difficulties in getting along with them (Lowenthal et al., 1975). Four-fifths of all newly wed and older women evaluated their spouses positively, but only two-fifths of the middle-aged women did so. Interestingly, men of this age stressed their wives' virtues but felt they were not meeting their wives' expectations, particularly their wives' desires for attention and companionship. Other research has shown that there also tends to be a decrease in sexual satisfaction for couples at this point in the life cycle, with wives expressing slightly more dissatisfaction than husbands (Burr, 1970). The increase in the divorce rate which occurs for middle-aged couples after their children leave home indicates that this is a period of strain. In general, studies show that marital satisfaction tends to be high among those recently married, lower during the child-rearing years, and high again toward the latter portion of the life cycle.

In contrast to the tensions of middle age, marriage in old age is best characterized by a feeling of peacefulness and a lack of stress. Long-married couples tend to emphasize loyalty and emotional security over all other important characteristics of marriage. Further, married people facing retirement express renewed interest in the personalities of their spouses (Lowenthal et al., 1975). Both men and women tend to give positive descriptions of their spouses, and many see improvement in their marriage after the departure of children.

Marriages characterized by equality between partners tend to be happier than those where traditional sex-role distinctions are maintained (Clark and Anderson, 1967). In part this is because the retirement of the husband in a traditional marriage can cause strain. One study found that husbands tended to become more involved in household tasks after retirement, sometimes in spite of themselves. If their marriage was companionate, they tended to be comfortable doing these tasks. However, if their main role had been as provider, the transition from the work world to the home was difficult, and their wives found their presence an intrusion (Kerckhoff, 1964).

It is almost inevitable that one spouse, usually the husband, will precede the other in death. Widowhood is usually a permanent status for women. Only 5 percent of women who become widowed after age fifty-five remarry (Cleveland and Gianturco, 1976). There is great variation in reactions to widowhood. In one study of widows in Chicago, 48 percent said they had recovered from their husband's death within a year, partly perhaps because of strong support networks of other older widows (Lopata, 1973). Widowhood is less common for men, and it appears that adjusting to being alone may be more difficult for them. The article by Berardo discusses the problems of the aged widower.

New Family Roles in Old Age

Just as marital relationships change as people move through the life cycle, so other family relationships change as well. Children who were once dependent establish their own households. However, family ties remain strong. Most older people have at least one child living less than an hour away, and they visit frequently with those who live farther (Shanas et al., 1968). The preferred living arrangement is to have children nearby but not in the same household. Nearly every survey shows that older people would rather live in their own home but near their children. They value their independence and move into their children's homes only when health or financial circumstances make independent living impossible (Troll, 1971).

In addition to changing relationships with children, people acquire other family roles as they age. Although we tend to associate grandparenting with old age, it is actually more likely to occur in middle age. Earlier marriage, earlier childbirth, and longer life expectancy are producing grandparents in their forties (Troll, Miller, and Atchley, 1979, p. 108). Further, as middle-aged women return in greater numbers to the work force, there is an increasing tendency for both grandmothers and grandfathers to be employed. The rocking-chair image of grandparents is no longer accurate. In the final article Robertson analyzes the significance of grandmotherhood and examines different types of grandmothers. She finds that grandmotherhood is often enjoyed more than parenting, because it provides the pleasure of children's company without the responsibilities of being a parent.

The existing literature is rather sparse on relationships with other relatives. Little attention has been paid to sibling relationships, although brothers and sisters provide a potential source of support in old age. Six out of seven women over age sixty-five have a living sibling, while only slightly more than half have a husband alive (Shanas et al., 1968). This is a resource which will become less common in the future, since younger people now have fewer brothers and sisters due to the lower birth rate.

The family is ultimately the major resource for the aged in society. Older married couples have each other for companionship and help in times of crisis; and when the elderly are single, they turn to children and other relatives for mutual support. While family relationships have changed, they have not lost their meaning, and it seems unlikely that any future changes will destroy the importance of family ties.

REFERENCES

Burr, Wesley. 1970. Satisfaction with various aspects of marriage over the life cycle: A random middle-class sample. *Journal of Marriage and the Family* 32:29–37.

Clark, Margaret, and Barbara G. Anderson. 1967. *Culture and aging.* Springfield, Ill.: Charles C Thomas.

Cleveland, William P., and Daniel T. Gianturco. 1976. Remarriage probability after widowhood: A retrospective method. *Journal of Gerontology* 31(1):99–103.

Kerckhoff, Alan. 1964. Husband-wife expectations and reactions to retirement. *Journal of Gerontology* 19:510–516.

Lopata, Helena Z. 1973. *Widowhood in an American city.* Cambridge, Mass.: Schenkman.

Lowenthal, Marjorie F., Majda Thurner, David Chiriboga, and Associates. 1975. *Four stages of life.* San Francisco: Jossey-Bass.

Shanas, Ethel. 1973. Family–kin networks and aging in cross-cultural perspective. *Journal of Marriage and the Family* 35:505–511.

Shanas, Ethel, Peter Townsend, Dorothy Wedderburn, Henning Friis, Poul Milhhoj, and Jan Stehouver. 1968. *Older people in three industrial societies.* New York: Atherton Press.

Troll, Lillian. 1971. The family of later life: A decade review. *Journal of Marriage and the Family* 33:263–290.

Troll, Lillian, Shelia J. Miller, and Robert C. Atchley. 1979. *Families in later life.* Belmont, Cal.: Wadsworth.

Old Age and the Family: Facts and Forecasts

GORDON F. STREIB

In this article the author has three main concerns. First, he attempts to clarify the categories of family types which occur in the later phase of the life cycle. Second, he discusses the major known facts about the family in later maturity and analyzes which will persist to the end of the twentieth century. Third, he considers what changes in the family might occur if the political and economic system of the United States were radically restructured. He concludes that the older family of the future will not be isolated but will continue to exchange support with adult children. Among the present trends which will increase are age-segregated housing, early retirement, and improved pension and social security benefits.

There has been an increasing interest among scholars, scientists, and journalists in what life will be like in the year 2000 (Winthrop, 1968). It is surprising how little attention is given in this growing literature to family structures and relations, especially those of the latter part of the life cycle.

Why has the older family been ignored? First because the study of old age is not as popular and interesting as predictions of technological advances. It is concerned with decline, deceleration, and death and thus tends to be avoided or ignored. In our youth-oriented culture, old age is not considered a captivating topic to study.

Some of the older utopian societies, such as the Shakers of the Oneida community, were concerned with the roles of older people (Nordhoff, 1875; Carden, 1969). However, in the descriptions of new forms of family relationships which one reads so often these days in the popular press, the entire emphasis is placed on the family relationships of young people. There is no mention of the problem of "Grandma in the commune."

Finally, the family is regarded as a dependent social form which is influenced by technological and economic factors; thus it can respond to change but cannot stimulate or influence it.[1]

In this paper we will be concerned with three major topics. First, a clarification will be made of the social groups or family categories which constitute the major units of analysis for the study of the family in the latter part of the life cycle.

SOURCE: "Old Age and the Family: Facts and Forecasts" by Gordon F. Streib is reprinted from *Aging in Contemporary Society*, Sage Contemporary Social Science Issues, Volume 6, Ethel Shanas, editor, pp. 25–39 by permission of the Publisher, Sage Publications, Inc. © 1970.

Second, a discussion will treat the major facts known about the family in later maturity, followed by a prognosis as to which of these characteristics of older families will probably persist as social trends into the next generation—that is, until the end of the present century.

Finally, consideration will be given to the possible consequence for older families if a restructuring should occur of the United States from a democratic, capitalistic, industrialized society to some other political or economic type.

The major information base which will be drawn upon for our discussion and analysis will be the United States. We assume, however, that many if not most of our observations, particularly the facts and the forecasts which we make, would apply to other Western industrialized countries. The primary reason for assuming the basic similarity of family structures and relations in Western industrialized societies is the fact that the detailed, careful, cross-national study of Denmark, Great Britain, and the United States by Shanas et al. (1968) has shown strikingly similar findings for these three societies.

It should be stressed that the forecasting of family structures and relations for a generation ahead is not a scientifically well-grounded operation (Goode, 1968). The fragmentary body of knowledge which we possess is based upon limited samples of information gathered with the use of crude instruments. Moreover, the theories of social change pertaining to the family—as well as to other social institutions—are rudimentary, and this is particularly true about the future of industrialized societies.[2]

Our major approach is through analysis of trends and extrapolation from known information, and is essentially intuitive in nature. Our role as forecaster is well described by W. J. Goode (1968: 337):

> To predict the social structural problems with which the next generation will try to cope, and thus to suggest which data will be most significant, is to assume the mantle of prophet. But with the entrance of so many prophets on the stage at this time, one more can hardly be a burden.

The Family in Old Age—Diverse Structures

It is important to clarify and specify what is meant by the family in old age. There has been a tendency in discussion to consider old age as beginning at some arbitrary point—sixty or sixty-five years of age. This approach to understanding family structure and relations can be quite deceptive because the family must be viewed in a much more realistic social context than is suggested by simply splitting the life cycle into neat age cohorts as is done in census tables.

It is more accurate and useful to consider the family in terms of stages or phases which are correlated in a crude way with age, but which must be considered in relation to a number of other very significant variables: sex, marital status, family-cycle stage, and place of residence. The life-cycle, or developmental, approach to family studies is particularly important in the last part of life because this is the disengaging period—it may begin in the forties and with some degree of regularity move in a unidirectional way towards break-up and final dissolution. At all stages of the life cycle, there are a variety of families varying in the demographic characteristics of age, sex, and numbers, plus having variations resulting from different combinations of roles and relationships which are associated with social-psychological characteristics, such as feelings of solidarity, familism, and the like.

Definitions of Family in Old Age

A major distinction which must be made is that between (1) the residential family, or the kind of family in which one lives, and (2) the modified extended family, or kin network, to which a person belongs. In Table 1 we present data summarizing the distribution of one-, two-, three-, and four-generation families to which older persons belong in three industrialized societies. The overall pattern shows a similar distribution for the three countries, for about three out of four older persons belong to kin networks of three or four generations. The United States has an even larger proportion of four-generation families than Denmark and Great Britain.

When we examine the kinds of residence patterns or households which one finds among sixty-five-year-olds and older in the three societies, we note that the household types encompass the most frequent living arrangements. The two most frequent kinds of household type in old age are the married couple and the widowed person living alone. They account for about two-thirds of all old families having persons over sixty-five years of age. Thus, in specifying the family in old age, we see that there is a substantial proportion of "single-person families," or, as the Internal Revenue Service calls them, "heads of households." Many of these older "families," while maintaining separate residences from their children or relatives, keep in close contact through frequent visiting or telephoning.

TABLE 1 Percentage of Older Persons Whose Kinship Networks Include Different Numbers of Generations

Number of Generations in Family	Denmark	Britain	United States
One	18	24	18
Two	7	9	6
Three	56	51	44
Four	19	17	32
N =	2,435	2,485	2,436

Source: Shanas et al. (1968: 143). Reprinted by permission.

These two major aspects of family life—the residential family and the extended family as described above—are essentially static views—a snapshot—at one point in time. What is more interesting, more important, and much more difficult to study are the dynamics of the family and the effects on the kinship networks. When we examine families in the latter part of life, we must be concerned with the fact that the distribution of various kinds of kin structures and the living arrangements are changing. This is striking even when one looks at cross-sectional data for a broad age spectrum over a thirty-year span (Thompson and Streib, 1961: 186–187). For example, the modal pattern of living arrangements in the period beyond age sixty-five declines tremendously from what it was about twenty years earlier. Census data for the United States show that almost 80 percent of males forty-five to fifty-four years of age and slightly more than 70 percent of the females in the forty-five to fifty-four age category live with a spouse in their own household. There is a steady decline in this kind of living arrangement with a drop at about age sixty-five. There is an increasing differential over time between men and women, so that at age seventy-five and over, more than 40 percent of all men are still living with a spouse in their own household in contrast to less than 15 percent of the women.

Forecasts for the Family in Old Age

In this section we will outline some of the major facts and trends concerning the family and old age, and on the basis of this knowledge we will forecast the characteristics of family life and family structures pertaining to later maturity in the year 2000. For the sake of clarity we have assigned these trends to three broad categories: (1) biosocial, (2) sociocultural, and (3) social-psychological. There is obviously some degree of overlap in these categories, but they can be regarded as constituting three distinct analytical levels.

Biosocial

These characteristics are rooted primarily in biological phenomena.

TABLE 2   Distribution of Household Types of Elderly Persons 65 and Over In 3 Industrialized Societies

---

1. Living alone, never married (4–8%)
2. Married couple (35–45%)
3. Married couple and married or single children (7–14%)
4. Widowed (or divorced or separated) parent and married or unmarried children (9–20%)
5. Widowed (sometimes divorced or separated) living alone (22–28%)

SOURCE: Shanas et al. (1968: 218). Reprinted by permission.

Social and cultural factors impinge upon them, and social scientists consider them usually as demographic factors or variables.

1. The life expectancy for white males is approximately sixty-eight years and for white females about seventy-five years (Riley et al., 1968: 28–29). We forecast that the length of life will not be greatly extended for most persons (Kahn and Wiener, 1967: 51–57). Major scientific discoveries may well be made in the biological and medical sciences which will alter this possibility. However, some investigators seem to be rather conservative in their expectations about major scientific breakthroughs regarding major causes of death for older persons such as heart disease, cancer, and stroke. Medical gimmickry, involving such things as heart transplants, may contribute to our knowledge of human anatomy and physiology, but major organ transplants will not be widely practiced and therefore will not affect the longevity of very many older persons.

2. Women live longer than men. The life expectancy of men and women has increased over a long period of years, but since the turn of this century, the differential in the expectancy of life between the sexes has steadily increased (Riley et al., 1968: 28–29). The universal fact that throughout the animal kingdom the female of the species is longer-lived appears to be a persistent biosocial trend. The continuation of this trend implies that the present tendency for many more women than men to become widowed should be a stubborn fact of family life for at least a generation and probably longer.

Sociocultural

These facts and trends are more closely linked to social and cultural components of society than those listed under biosocial. They are more closely related to the norms, attitudes, and values shared and transmitted by most members of the society.

1. About nine out of ten persons eventually marry. The trend for most adults to marry at least once will continue to be a major cultural pattern.

2. Men marry women who are on the average three or more years younger than themselves. The tendency of men in most cultures, and specifically in the United States, to choose younger women for marital partners will not change. This culturally influenced pattern will continue to accentuate the larger proportion of widows than widowers in the older population.

3. We anticipate that the increasing concern with environmental problems—many of which are highly correlated with population pressures—will result in smaller families. More families will have one, two, or no children than in the present older generation. The smaller family will result in fewer grandchildren.

Social-psychological

These trends can be conveniently classified under three kinds of family role relationships: husband-wife, parent-child, and sibling.

Husband-wife relationships

1. The basic family unit in old age is the marital dyad, for among persons sixty-five and older, 53 percent are married couples (Riley et al., 1968: 159). A broad picture of all persons over age sixty-five in the United States shows that 71 percent live in families with other persons to whom they are related and 22 percent live alone (Riley et al., 1968: 167). Only about 12 percent of older married couples live with their children (Riley et al., 1968: 168). "Initmacy at a distance" will continue to be preferred by both old and young as the living arrangement for older persons. Unless there is a radical decline in the standard of living—which might necessitate some doubling up in housing—married olde couples will prefer to live separately from their children.

2. American society has more permissive sexual norms than a generation ago. The forecast for the next generation is that there will be an increased understanding of the fact that sexual activity is normal in older persons. The fuller understanding of man's sexuality and the greater permissiveness in which the present generation has been reared will result in more tolerance of older persons having platonic and sexual liaisons than is common at the present time.

3. Mid-life divorce is on the increase in American society. This trend will continue into the next century. Marriages may be continued for the sake of children, but when children reach maturity, there will be a greater proneness to terminate a marriage. Greater numbers of divorces among the old will probably be associated with more remarriage. There will also be more remarriage of widowed persons (McKain, 1969: 123). The remarriage of older persons will have repercussions for parent-child relations (McKain, 1969: 108–122) because of the problems related to the transfer and disposition of property, visiting patterns, and family assistance patterns.

Parent-child relationships

1. Contrary to some of the stereotypes about the rejected old person, there is considerable contact between old parents and their adult children. Even though the residential family may consist of only one person, the modified extended family remains an important part of the older person's life.

   In the study of three industrialized societies (Shanas et al., 1968: 174) it was reported that most older parents (over three-fifths) had seen at least one child the same day of the interview or the previous day, and another fifth had seen a child within the previous week. The percentage of older persons who had not seen a married child in the previous year was very small (3 percent). This existence of an extended kin network in which parents and children are in regular and frequent contact with one another will continue and may increase in the decades ahead. The assertion by some theorists that the isolated nuclear family is the modal pattern in American society is not supported by a variety of studies in the contemporary situation, and isolation will not characterize modal family patterns in the future.

2. Reciprocity patterns are evidenced; adult children and their parents maintain a viable kin network involving mutual patterns of assistance. Small services are rendered reciprocally by each generation. In the United States more than half the older persons reported they helped their children (Shanas et al., 1968: 204-205). Moreover, the aged are independent of regular monetary aid from their children. In the United States only 4 percent report receiving regular financial aid.

The reciprocity of help—shopping, housework, baby-sitting, home repairs, and so on—as a form of kin assistance will continue as a family pattern into the next century. The overwhelming percentage of the old now report receiving no regular financial aid from children. This pattern will persist, unless there is a major economic depression, a catastrophe, or a major social restructuring.

3. The postparental period is not a traumatic and negative experience for most families, in spite of gloomy reports of the "empty nest" syndrome (Deutscher, 1964: 52-59; Gurin et al., 1960: 92-93, 103). A number of cultural trends will tend to perpetuate this pattern in American older families. The fact that more women will be employed outside the home suggests that their lives will have other foci than child rearing. Furthermore, the increasing emphasis on the dangers of overpopulation and the desirability of small families, coupled with the pronouncements from women's liberation groups that women have a destiny other than as breeding machines, will encourage women to have broader interests. Opportunities for travel and other leisure pursuits also suggest that parents will be able to find substitute interests for family-centered activities. With the problems of the "generation gap" and the increasing cost of higher education for children, many families will find the "empty nest" period a time of contentment and fulfillment.

Sibling relationships

1. Living with siblings will not be an important form of living arrangement except for the single—never married—person. Even the widowed or divorced do not live with siblings. This pattern will continue into the generation ahead.

Societal Trends

The following trends are more remote from the family itself, but they will have profound effects upon family structures and relations. These trends are an integral part of the larger trends in postindustrial American society.

1. Most older persons will live in their own homes, but there will be more specialized communities and residences which will be age segregated (Walkley et al., 1966).
2. The average age for retirement of men is about sixty-five. There are an increasing number of retirement plans which permit an early retirement option. The retirement age will decline in the years ahead as a result, in part, of economic benefits received by a person when he elects to retire early. The probable consequences of more persons retiring early will be that a larger proportion of older persons will change their residence for climatic reasons, kinship consideration (to be near children or other kin), or to have a smaller and more comfortable home. However, the large majority of retirees will continue to live in their long-term place of residence.
3. There will be improved health and medical-care provisions which will release the immediate family from some of the health-care costs which it assumed in the past.
4. Assuming no major restructuring of the economic and political systems, there will be improved pension and social security benefits. More persons will be able to retire earlier on special early retirement plans. Despite these gains and also assuming some moderate growth in the economy, the aged in general will continue to be an economically underprivileged segment of the society.

Qualifications and Variations from the Major Patterns

These generalizations must, of course, be qualified for subgroups and subcategories of the population. The importance of major variables which have been found to influence social relations and human behavior in the past may be changed to some degree in the next generation. But it seems probable on an intuitive basis, projecting past trends into the future, that ethnic, religious, racial, residential, occupational, and educational factors and variables will be significant in qualifying, modifying, or accentuating most of the above generalizations. We believe that the struggle for racial, religious, and social justice will continue and will probably accelerate in the decades ahead. Moreover, there will be definite positive changes in the social, economic, and political situation of the underprivileged and those groups and categories of the population which suffer discrimination.

The major ethnic and racial minorities—blacks, Mexican-Americans, and the American Indians—will receive more opportunities than in the past, yet a pragmatic forecast suggests that substantial numbers of these minorities will continue to be underprivileged compared to the majority of white Americans. The most difficult and unresolved internal social problem will be the situation of black Americans. The matrifocal family continues to be a significant pattern among lower-class blacks (Frazier, 1939: Billingsley, 1968), and it is forecast that increased social insurance benefits will alleviate somewhat the stringent economic situation of the lower-income black family in their gerontological phase.

Among lower-income and less-educated white Americans, one can also expect that socioeconomic differences will continue to be observed concerning the latter period of life. For example, Kerckhoff (1964) found that professional and managerial couples welcome retirement and have a more favorable experience in retirement while lower occupational levels tend to be more passive in advance of retirement and they report their retirement experience more negatively.

Radical Restructuring of the Society and the Family

Social scientists do not have a very high batting average in predicting the broad course of human affairs, and it is probably risky to make prognostications about these matters. However, with all of the hazards that such activity entails, we propose the following possibilities.

We believe that there is a low probability of radical restructuring of American society. The general institutional structures will continue to be organized in about the same way—government, the economy, education, and so on. There will be modifications, of course, but it is unlikely that in the next decade or two the capitalistic economic system with government intervention in some sectors will be changed in its major contours.

How will this affect the family? Even if there should be a major restructuring of the society—for example, governmental ownership and control of major industries, banks, utilities, and the like—the family as an institution and as an interacting group will tend to operate basically in the ways which are familiar to contemporary Americans, with emotional and mutual help patterns of prime importance. We note that in other countries having undergone drastic change—Communist China and the Soviet Union—family structures, because of their resiliency and tenacity, are not quickly altered. There may be some adaptations to meet the exigencies of possible inefficiencies which might result from the drastic alteration of the political and economic systems, but the family members will continue to interact as a primary group.

If a radical restructuring of the society does occur in the next generation, the likelihood of the present middle-age cohort faring better under the restructured society is not great. First, the radical restructuring is more likely to be initiated and carried out by young people, and if successful, younger persons would tend to be the power wielders in the new system, such as has occurred in Cuba. Second, assuming even the most orderly radicalization and smoothest transition, there are likely to be periods of strain and areas of neglect. Even if the reorganization should be carried out with a minimum amount of force and violence, the old are likely at best to find themselves in a state of "benign neglect" unless the new regime can maintain a high level of productivity equal to that of the old order. The care and treatment of the old is rather highly correlated with the general level of economic development and social security of the society as a whole. Hence, it is unlikely that the aged will receive any special consideration.

In this connection, it is interesting to observe the situation of the aged in Russia since the time of the complete restructuring of that society with the goal of more humane treatment of all Soviet citizens. One of America's leading students of the Soviet family reported in 1968 that a half century after the Bolshevik revolution, only about half of the Soviet population is covered by social security (Geiger, 1968: 204). Coverage is provided only to those who have worked for an extended period. Geiger also reported that only 38 percent of the women over the legal retirement age of fifty-five were receiving pensions in 1959. The Soviet family has adapted to the lack of adequate pensions for the aged and the shortage of homes for the aged by the use of a three-generation extended family form. Geiger (1968: 205) summarized the situation in these words:

> In the marketplace of mutually desired services it has been a good bargain; in exchange for a home, the aged have taken over, according to capacity, the functions left undone by the working wife and mother. In past years this arrangement has been such a standard practice that it was defined as desirable. In the words of a worker: "It is good when both spouses work and have someone to do the laundry and cooking, etc." All benefit from this arrangement, including the Soviet regime itself, which saved itself the expense for many years of becoming a true welfare state.

New Family Structures on a Micro-scale

We have asserted that there is a low probability there will be a major alteration of the political and economic structure of the United States in the next generation. Further, if a major restructuring should occur, its immediate chief effect upon many older families will be a decline in the standard of living.

There is another way in which *some* American families might be changed in their basic structure and relationships and that is by the creation of collectivities, enclaves, cultural islands, and settlements which would foster or develop family forms which would differ from the modal pattern found in the larger society. The number of persons who might live in collectivities would probably be relatively small in proportion to the total population, but their influence might be greater than their sheer numbers might suggest.

Historically, the United States has been the haven for the settlement of peoples from abroad who desired to pursue a way of life which might be variant from that of their neighbors. The United States has also spawned a variety of indigenous groupings with norms and values which differ from those of the larger society. Some of these ethnic, religious, or cultural enclaves survive, while others have been short-lived. Among those from abroad which have maintained their cultural identity for a long period have been pietistic groups like the Amish, who have lived in the United States for over two centuries (Hostetler, 1968).

Broadly speaking, these American communities can be dichotomized into those which were (or are) organized on the basis of private property or those in which property is collectively held—communal societies. The study of these communities indicates that those in which property is held privately by individuals or by blood relatives are longer-lived than those which have the communal ownership of property.

In this connection, it is pertinent to study the communes of Israel. The kibbutzim have had to confront and cope with the problem of an aging and aged population. To my knowledge, the communes now being organized in this country have given no attention to gerontological issues. This is, of course, quite understandable because their major concerns are ideology, membership recruitment, internal tensions, and sheer survival in many cases. However, if any remain viable long enough, at the turn of the century they will face similar problems to those which the kibbutzim of Israel have encountered. One of the interesting facts found in the perceptive report by Talmon (1961) is that Israeli communes have a form of benign disengagement in which persons disengage gradually, and probably with less strain than may be true of older persons in the larger Israeli and American society. However, what is more significant from the standpoint of the family in old age is that parents of the members who move into the kibbutzim in later life are happier and more contented than the aging members who have lived in the commune for long periods, for the latter are often very critical. Moreover, the parents of the members, as new residents, do not have the ideological commitment to youth, work, and productivity, and are not pressured by group norms and behavior as are the older members. They are grateful to be there and do not suffer the decline in status and power which the older members must face. The aging member who has had an integral position in the settlement and adheres to its values must face more pressure and strains.

There is a marked increase in retirement communities in the United States (Walkley et al., 1966), and it is instructive to compare them in terms of structure and ideology with the communal settlements of Israel and of this country. This comparison offers valuable clues about some family and community issues in the decades ahead. The retirement village or retirement home usually requires the payment of a substantial fee for the purchase of an apartment or house, or for lifetime lodging. The terms, conditions, and housing may vary considerably, but our concerns here are not real estate and economics but family structures and relations. The person who moves into a retirement community buys his home or apartment as an individual private investment and pays for it and the community facilities which are involved. It is primarily an individual economic decision and occurs because the person or his family can pay the cost involved. There are few if any political or ideological aspects involved. By contrast, young people who join communes (this was and is true of the Israeli kibbutzim) have strong and deep ideological reasons in almost all cases. Idealism is high and the economic considerations are rather low in the priorities. It must be pointed out that while ideological motives can be very powerful, they have a certain fragility and instability and are subject to alteration due to shifts in beliefs and also because of the economic and social pressures which arise internally and in the larger society. Hence in the long run the ideologically organized commune faces a different set of problems from those of the retirement community which is established primarily for economic reasons.

It is predicted that retirement villages, based on economic considerations combined with community of interest, will continue to flourish in the United States. However, they will remain a middle-class phenomenon and will not involve any real sharing of resources, but will continue as contractual arrangements based on the ability of the person or his family to buy this style of life.

Conclusions

In the future old families will find that they are increasingly in competition with other groups in the society, such as militant youthful racial or ethnic minorities who will be seeking a larger share of the community's funds. There will continue to be a struggle for federal and local funds and resources. Unless the old become more militant, which is doubtful, they will never get as much concern and attention in American society as they would like. Furthermore, there are three inescapable problems over which they have little or no control: inflation, declining health, and for the women, widowhood.

Yet there are many optimistic aspects to the forecast of life ahead for the family in old age. With increasing social benefits, improved medical insurance, and more widespread pension plans, more older families can look forward to declining years of comfort and fulfillment. If they are adaptive, they will be able to find meaningful lives with their own resources and those of their families and peer groups. The bulk of evidence in American society is that they will be able to maintain their own residences, as they overwhelmingly prefer, and still remain in close emotional contact with their kin networks.

NOTES

1. William J. Goode (1963: 18) is one sociologist who has stressed that the family may be an independent factor influencing the process of industrialization. William F. Ogburn in his early work stressed the impact of technology upon other institutions. In Ogburn's (see Ogburn and Nimkoff, 1955) later work, his approach was much more intricate, for he analyzed technology linked in complex ways to other causes of changes in the family. The statement of Fred Cottrell (1960: 92) would probably be accepted by many as a summary of the issue: "There is probably nothing on which social scientists agree more completely than upon the thesis that, to a very great extent, social change is tied up with technological change."
2. Goode (1968) has offered an excellent analysis of both the major theoretical questions concerning social change and the family and also the kinds of data required to obtain some tentative answers.

REFERENCES

Bell, D. (1967) "Introduction," pp. xxi–xxviii in H. Kahn and A. J. Wiener (eds.), The Year 2000. New York: Macmillan.

Billingsley, A. (1968) Black Families in White America. Englewood Cliffs, N.J.: Prentice-Hall.

Carden, M. L. (1969) Oneida: Utopian Community to Modern Corporation. Baltimore: Johns Hopkins Univ. Press.

Cottrell, W. F. (1960) "The technological and societal basis of aging," pp. 92–119 in C. Tibbitts (ed.), Handbook of Social Gerontology. Chicago: Univ. of Chicago Press.

Deutscher, I. (1964) "The quality of postparental life: Definitions of the situation." J. of Marriage & the Family 26 (February):52–59.

Frazier, E. F. (1939) The Negro Family in the United States. Chicago: Univ. of Chicago Press.

Geiger, H. K. (1968) The Family in Soviet Russia. Cambridge: Harvard Univ. Press.

Goode, W. J. (1968) "The theory and measurement of family change," pp. 295–348 in E. B. Sheldon and W. E. Moore (eds.), Indicators of Social Change. New York: Russell Sage Foundation.

———. (1963) World Revolution and Family Patterns. New York: Free Press.

Gurin, G. et al. (1960) Americans View Their Mental Health. New York: Basic Books.

Hostetler, J. A. (1968) Amish Society. Baltimore: Johns Hopkins Univ. Press.

Kahn, H. and A. J. Wiener (1967) The Year 2000. New York: Macmillan.

Kerckhoff, A. C. (1964) "Husband-wife expectations and reactions to retirement." J. of Gerontology 19 (October):510–516.

McKain, W. C. (1969) Retirement Marriage. Storrs, Conn.: Storrs Agricultural Experiment Station.

Nordhoff, C. (1875) The Communistic Societies of the United States. New York: Schocken Books.

Ogburn, W. F. and M. F. Nimkoff (1955) Technology and the Changing Family. Boston: Houghton Mifflin.

Riley, M. W. et al. (1968) Aging and Society. New York: Russell Sage Foundation.

Shanas, E. (1973) Family-Kin Networks and Aging in Cross-cultural Perspective. J. of Marriage and the Family 35 (August):505–511.

―――― et al. (1968) Old People in Three Industrial Societies. London: Routledge & Kegan Paul.

Talmon, Y. (1961) "Aging in Israel, a planned society." Amer. J. of Sociology 67 (November):284–295.

Thompson, W. E. and G. F. Streib (1961) "Meaningful activity in a family context," pp. 177–211 in R. W. Kleemeier (ed.), Aging and Leisure. New York: Oxford Univ. Press.

Walkley, R. P. et al. (1966) Retirement Housing in California. Berkeley: Diablo Press.

Winthrop, H. (1968) "The sociologist and the study of the future." Amer. Sociologist 3 (May):136-145.

Survivorship and Social Isolation: The Case of the Aged Widower

FELIX M. BERARDO

The impact of widowhood is more severe for the male than it is for his female counterpart. He is less likely to be experienced at housekeeping; to live with, be close to, or exchange favors with his children; or to have or be satisfied with social relationships. His problems are compounded by retirement, which not only deprives him of his occupational role, but also removes him from meaningful contact with friends and co-workers. Social isolation among aged widowers leads to a precarious condition which is reflected in unusually high rates of mental disorders, suicides, and mortality.

The rapid social change which has characterized American society since the late nineteenth century has been accompanied by significant modifications in family organization and structure, with important implications for aged family members. Unfortunately, however, scholars are not agreed about the consequences of these changes. For example, the changes alleged to have brought about the isolation of older persons from their children and the development of feelings of neglect and loneliness among them are also cited as having produced closer affective ties between the older person and his children (Brown, 1960, 170). Research concerning the relationship between the social isolation of the aged and their personal adjustment has similarly resulted in contradictory interpretations. Thus, while the findings of some investigators indicate that a decrease in contacts with friends accompanies deteriorating social adjustment, others have found no relationship between adjustment and the frequency of interaction with friends, relatives, and children (Morrison and Kristjanson, 1958).

One of the reasons suggested for the discrepancies in research findings and interpretations in this area is the tendency for investigators to treat "the aged" as a homogeneous population. Thus,

> data on the aged often are not distinguished with respect to widowhood status; consequently exact information concerning the widowed becomes difficult to ascertain. Moreover, in most of the research that has been done, differences in levels of functioning as well as differences in backgrounds and experiences are

overlooked or ignored; social class and cultural values are typically not differentiated nor considered; and a host of important socioeconomic variables are submerged under the all-inclusive homogeneous category of "the aged" (Berardo 1968, 199).

Widowhood and the Aged Male

In order to illustrate the heterogeneous character of the older population and to provide insight into the nature of their adaptations to a changing status, this paper concentrates upon one segment of that population, namely, the aged survivor. More specifically, it seeks to examine the environmental conditions surrounding the aged *male survivor* and to assess his accommodation to widowhood status. As such, this paper forms a companion piece to an earlier work dealing with the social adaptation of female survivors (Berardo, 1968).

Widowhood Status and Aging

That widowhood status[1] presents rather serious problems for both individuals and families has long been recognized. This fact is perhaps most dramatically illustrated by periodic demographic analyses and other research which have consistently demonstrated that widows and widowers exhibit higher rates of mortality, mental disorder, and suicide than married persons of the same age (Berardo, 1968). These findings are particularly relevant to the older population, who experience more disruption of marital status through death of spouse than any other age group.

The aged person in American society finds himself in a phase of the life cycle which requires certain economic and sociological adaptations if he is to execute successfully an acceptable pattern of daily living which is not detrimental to his self-concept. For the aged married, the requirements for accomplishing this transition are eased by a variety of circumstances, including the benefits of mutual planning and sharing, reciprocal socio-emotional support, and the psycho-social buttress of a lengthy and continuous period of paired interaction and activity. On the other hand, for the aged widowed the requirements for satisfactory living are confounded by the absence of a significant role partner. Both the social and psychological supports necessary for maintaining a balanced existence are frequently diminished and, in some instances, almost totally absent.[2]

Widowhood: A Neglected Aspect of the Family Life Cycle

It would seem that the large and growing population of elderly people, a significant proportion of whom are widowed, would provoke systematic study of their lives, problems, and individual-familial modes of adaptation to survivorship. However, a recent review of the literature has revealed that for a variety of reasons the special problems that confront the widowed both at the time of bereavement and later have received little attention from social scientists. Moreover, with respect to those investigations which have been carried out,

> researchers have generally concentrated on the bereavement processes, *per se*. Consequently, they have approached their subject matter primarily, if not exclusively, from a psychological (including social-psychological and psycho-analytical) frame of reference. The personal, intrapsychic reactions to the shock of "dismemberment" have been particularly stressed. Within this context, case history analyses of individual conflict and adjustment to annihilation—with specific emphasis on the phenomena of grief, sorrow, and other components of the mental-emotional mourning process—predominate (Berardo, 1968, 198).

It has been noted that this type of orientation is characterized by a general lack of concern with the social life of the widowed and their long-term adjustments (Gorer, 1965, 150). Apparently, very few investigators have attempted to develop the sociological implications of widowhood status or to discover the social and environmental factors associated with the adaptive behavior of the bereaved.[3] Indeed, it appears that the majority of sociological research on widowhood has focused on individual reactions to the immediate crisis event, with little attention given to the adaptation of survivor families over time (Berardo, 1968, 198).

Widowhood must be viewed as a social and emotional crisis situation[4] involving increasing numbers of older people and their families. It requires the development of alternative patterns of behavior if the individual is to maintain satisfactory relations with his family, kin groups, and the community, and if the survivor is to sustain a minimum level of personal equilibrium. Sociologically, widowhood status requires the reintegration of roles suitable to a new status. The diverse ways in which this is accomplished and the extent to which the aged male survivor is able to make a satisfactory transition will be considered in the remainder of this paper.

Male Survivorship More Problematic

Some sociologists have suggested that, from an individual as well as familial standpoint, the problems of a surviving husband are more serious than those which confront a surviving wife. It has been noted, for example, that a large proportion of aged widows are capable of living alone and taking care of themselves, whereas an aged widower is more likely to need someone to prepare his meals and provide him with other kinds of general care. "Moreover, the aged mother is more likely to be invited to live in the family of a son or daughter because she can be very useful in the household and pay her way in services rendered in the home" (Smith, 1955, 267-69). The point is that the female survivor is more numerous (the widows currently outnumber widowers by more than four to one), her economic problems perhaps more difficult and, moreover, she is more likely than the aged widower to be welcomed into the home of her adult married offspring and to find a useful place there.

In this connection, the lot of the aged widower has been graphically portrayed as follows:

> The elderly widower is less numerous in the population than is the widow. He may be as acutely stricken by his wife's death as the widow by that of her husband. A lifetime of close association with a woman whose complementary activities form the basis of a home now requires the most basic revision for which the widower may be wholly unprepared. If the wife was the homemaker-housekeeper, all those things upon which he depended and could anticipate in the management and upkeep of their mutual affairs devolve wholly upon him. The economy of convergent interests, the mutual resolution of each other's basic needs, the reciprocity of activities establishing well-ordered roles which is a bulwark of marriage are supplanted by a solitary and often disjointed independence. The viniculum that is marriage is disengaged by death, and the widower may find himself incapable of remaking his life into an integrated whole (Kutner et al., 1956, 63).

Thompson and Streib similarly contend that for the widow, unlike the widower, housekeeping tasks usually do not represent any marked change of patterns and problems of adjustment. In their view, for a large proportion of widows who live alone, daily household tasks "constitute a very important variety of meaningful activity, and ability to maintain certain standards of good housekeeping often represents a challenge and a test of the degree to which the older woman is avoiding "getting old" (Thompson and Streib, 1961, 177-211). In this same connection, it has been suggested that the role of grandfather probably includes a much narrower range of meaningful activities than the role of grandmother, and on this account may be another important factor in the life adjustment of the elderly male survivor (Cavan, 1962, 526-36). An additional factor favoring the female is her preference for the type of recreation that can be engaged in during old age, such as knitting and hobby crafts; in contrast, the elderly male is often not vigorous enough to carry on his former outdoor activities (Landis, 1942; Berardo, 1967b, 19-20).

On the other hand, there are sociologists who suggest that it is the woman and not the man who faces the greatest difficulty in returning to the single status. Bell (1963, 412-16), for example, feels that the role of the widow may be socially and psychologically more difficult than the role of the widower for a variety of reasons. He argues that in American society (1) marriage is generally more important for the woman than the man and, therefore, when it is terminated by death she loses a role more basic to the wife than may be the case for the surviving husband; (2) the widow is more apt to be forced to "go it alone" because, in comparison to the widower, she receives less encouragement from family and friends to remarry; (3) the widow faces much more difficulty in providing and caring for herself and her children because her financial resources usually are considerably less than those of a widower; and (4) because there are far greater numbers of widows than widowers, and because the majority of them are widowed at advanced ages, it is much more difficult for a surviving wife than for a surviving husband to change her status through remarriage.

Actually, there is little consistent evidence that survivorship status demands more drastic role changes for either sex. The following examination of the available comparative evidence concerning their relative adaptive patterns may be a step toward illuminating the problem.

Recent Evidence on Social Adaptation of the Aged Widowed

Some recent empirical information concerning the status of the aged widower comes from a study conducted in Thurston County, Washington (Berardo, 1967b). This study focused on the critical problems confronting the aged married and widowed population and involved a comparative sociological analysis of the ways in which these problems were resolved. Findings revealed that the most isolated subjects in the Thurston County sample were the aged widowers. This was especially true among those respondents who were older, relatively uneducated, and living in a rural environment. Another factor that led to social isolation was poor health, which sometimes caused a widower to be confined to his home and consequently limited his social contacts.[5] In addition, it was noted that, in comparison with other marital statuses, widowers were least likely (1) to be living with children, (2) to have a high degree of kin interaction or be satisfied with extended family relationships, (3) to receive from or give to children various forms of assistance, or (4) to have friends either in or outside of the community or to be satisfied with their opportunities to be with close friends. Further, they were least likely to be church members or to attend church services, or to belong to and participate in formal organizations or groups. Apparently, the overall consequences of all this is an insufficient amount of stimulating and rewarding social interaction.

There are, however, less easily identifiable factors which may be associated with the social isolation of the aged widower in American society. Such factors are cultural in nature and have to do with sex-role definitions and expectations. We have already noted the consensus among some sociologists that the role of the female remains relatively unchanged upon the death of her spouse. The assumption is that a woman will continue to perform her household duties, such as cleaning and cooking and other tasks, in much the same way as when her husband was alive. Consequently, many aged widows can maintain separate living quarters and care for themselves. The aged widower, on the other hand, is confronted with a series of practical problems as a result of the death of his wife. He finds himself faced with accomplishing additional and traditionally female tasks, such as keeping house. Consequently, he is likely to need someone to prepare his meals, maintain the household, and provide him with general care. At the same time, however, there is a general societal expectation that males should fend for themselves and avoid taking on a dependency status. This is an expectation which the aged widower is not always able to live up to. But his awareness of that expectation may lead to a certain hesitation or reluctance to seek assistance. In fact, in certain instances this awareness may make the widower feel compelled to sustain a public image of self-sufficiency in the face of a burdensome existence. It is quite possible that the isolation and loneliness of some widowers are the consequences of this reluctance to admit an inability to maintain a rewarding independent existence.

Other findings from the Thurston County study are informative. The rather low degree of social participation observed on the part of the widowers was not due to a lack of available free time. On the contrary, widowers in the sample generally had a greater surplus of leisure hours than other marital groups. Nevertheless, they had much more difficulty in occupying themselves with meaningful activity.

The lower degree of kinship interaction among aged widowers is partially explained by the central role assigned to females in maintaining kinship obligations. In American society the female has assumed responsibility for integrating the kindred, whether through direct contact or via other communicative processes (Berardo, 1967a). Thus women generally exhibit a much greater involvement in the kinship system than men (Farber, 1964, 206–214). Moreover, it has been observed that the greater participation of females in the performance of duties imposed by kinship provides them with many opportunities for exhibiting a preference for the maternal side of the family. "In those activities with relatives which are not clearly obligatory, a woman is able to express her preference for her own blood relatives, and in doing so increase their contact with her children as compared with her husband's relatives' contact" (Robins and Tomanec, 1962, 340–46). The consequences of the emphasis on the maternal line are eventually reflected in widowhood. Thus, in some recent research on extended family relations it was found that when the surviving parent was the mother, kinship interaction remained almost as high as when both parents were alive. On the other hand, when the surviving parent was the father, the frequency of interaction with extended family members was nearly as low as when both parents were deceased.[6]

Social Consequences of Widowhood Status

In examining the changes in status and age identification (i.e., conceptions people have of themselves as being young, middle-aged, or old) that occur over the life span, Blau (1956) analyzed data gathered from a representative sample of respondents sixty years of age or older residing in Elmira, New York. She notes that although the loss of one social status is generally accompanied by entry into another, in the case of retirement or widowhood, such transitions are particularly difficult. Both of these transitions are major status changes which typically occur in old age and which denote the permanent loss of two crucially important social roles as well as the activities and relationships that define them.

It was hypothesized that such changes in social status among the aged would be associated with shifts in their age identification. However, analysis revealed only partial confirmation of this hypothesis. Although retirees of each age level considered themselves old more frequently than those who were still employed, this was less true of the widowed. At each age level, the widowed considered themselves old only slightly more often than those who were still married. This differential effect of retirement and widowhood on age identification was explained in terms of the differential perceptions and consequences of the two statuses. More specifically,

> Retirement is a *social* pattern which implies an invidious judgment on the part of others in the society about the lack of fitness of *old* people to perform a culturally significant role, whereas the death of the marital partner, being a natural event, and not a socially induced one, does not have such implications in our culture. Thus, the retired individual, but not the widowed one has reason to believe that he is socially defined as old (Blau, 1956, 200).

Moreover, retirement abruptly removes a person from his occupational peer group and either drastically reduces or completely eliminates his participation in those informal but meaningful social relations developed on the job. The death of a spouse, on the other hand, eliminates only a single crucial social relationship. Blau concluded that perhaps "loss of membership in a peer group has more pronounced effects on the self-image of older people than the loss of an intimate interpersonal relationship, and that this helps to explain the differential effect of retirement and widowhood on age identification" (Blau, 1956, 200).

Effects of Widowhood on Friendship Patterns

Blau's study also revealed that death of spouse was more apt to precipitate "old age" if the aged individual failed to participate in a friendship group. That is to say, the presence of a friendship group was found to be less effective in preventing the age identification consequence of retirement than of widowhood. Apparently, group memberships are more influential than intimate dyadic relations in delaying the tendency of a person to conceive of himself as old and to identify with the old.

Indeed, there is good evidence that major shifts in social status which occur as a result of widowhood and retirement significantly affect friendship patterns. Blau found that the maintenance of friendship ties was an important mechanism of adjustment among older people following either retirement or widowhood. More specifically, it was found that while the extent of friendship participation generally declines with age, "a change in either marital status or employment status tends to have an adverse effect on friendships" (Blau, 1961, 430).[7] A closer examination of the data, however, revealed that a change in marital status from married to widowed had different consequences for the individual's social participation depending on whether the person was under or over seventy years of age. For those persons seventy years of age and older, widowhood had no detrimental effects on their social participation, whereas the friendships of those still in their sixties were adversely affected. This finding is explained in terms of the greater number of widowed persons available at the older age levels:

> Widowhood appears to have an adverse effect on social participation only when it places an individual in a position different from that of most of his age and sex peers. People tend to form friendships with others in their own age group, and to the extent that this occurs, the widowed person under seventy is likely to be an "odd" person at social gatherings, since most of his associates are probably still married and participate with their spouse in social activities. This difference in his marital position may very well have a detrimental effect on his participation. But after seventy, married couples who continue to participate jointly in social activities become the deviants, since most of their friends in this age group are likely to be widowed (Blau, 1961, 431).

In terms of sex differences, this analysis showed that among older persons under seventy, the loss of a spouse had a more adverse effect on the social participation of widowers than on that of widows. Again, a structural explanation is offered to account for these differences. In the age group under seventy there was a much larger proportion of female survivors (43 percent) than male survivors (13 percent). Given this imbalance with reference to his age and sex group, the aged male widower occupies a more deviant position than his female counterpart. This means that most of the friends of the male widower in his sixties are still married. Although widowhood status is likely to decrease an older woman's social participation with married friends, the overall decrease will not be as great as that observed among widowers, since widows under seventy are more likely to have associates who also are widowed.

In the age group over seventy, however, the proportion of widowers increases substantially with the result that the earlier differences observed between married and widowed men practically disappear. At that point widowhood status ceases to have an isolating effect upon aged male survivors. When a widower enters his seventies, he discovers that many more of his friends have also lost their wives. In short, he encounters a larger pool of male survivors with whom he can interact in terms of social companionship. These and other findings led to the conclusion that "widowhood tends to exert a detrimental effect on friendships in those structural contexts where it is relatively rare but not in those where it becomes more prevalent" (Blau, 1961, 433).

Loss of Occupational Role and Social Isolation of Widowers

The evidence seems fairly clear that the adjustment of older males to widowhood status is rather directly linked to two major factors, namely, their health and occupational status, with the latter playing the more dominant role (Kutner et al., 1956, 66–67). During most of his working life the American husband engages in sharply differentiated roles from that of the wife. From a sociological point of view, it is primarily by virtue of his significance in the occupational sphere and attendant social roles of family breadwinner that the husband manages to develop and sustain a satisfactory self-image and status both in society and in the home (Lipman, 1962, 475, 85).

With the onset of retirement, however, traditional sex-differentiated roles and the self-concepts which derive from them frequently undergo various degrees of strain and alteration, especially in the case of males. Whereas many wives of retirement families are able to satisfactorily continue their traditional role as homemakers, a similar pattern of role continuity is denied the husband: "The role of wage earner, which he had conceived as his primary role, is suddenly withdrawn; structurally he is isolated from the occupational system and this shock often has grave effects upon his entire existence" (Lipman, 1962, 476). Thus if an older man becomes unemployed through retirement, suffers ill health, and loses his wife as well, it would no doubt be a gross understatement to suggest that the groundwork is laid for some rather damaging consequences.[8] For example, Kutner and his associates (1956, 67) found that while the morale of widowers remained fairly high, it was severely affected by the subsequent loss of employment and good health. However, the onset of poor health was not as detrimental to morale as was retirement or unemployment. Interestingly, when married and widowed men who are employed and in good health were compared, no differences in morale were observed.

Widowhood, Mortality, and Social Isolation

Townsend's (1957) analysis of social isolation among the aged in London led him to conclude that while it was generally difficult for older persons to adapt to new situations, those forced to adjust their lives following the death of a spouse faced particular difficulties. In this connection, he was impressed by the expressions of loneliness voiced by the widowed respondents in his sample.[9] This led him to hypothesize that the aged widowed were likely to exhibit higher mortality rates than married or single persons, including their age peers who had been widowed when younger (Townsend, 1957, 178). While Townsend was unable to obtain systematic data about the influence of bereavement upon death rates, he did examine mortality rates, by age and marital status, for England and Wales. His analysis showed higher death rates among older widowed people than others, with the highest death rates occurring among the aged widowers. Townsend noted that the higher mortality of males, and widowers in particular, could not be explained entirely by biological and physiological differences. Instead "the social and especially the family circumstances of individuals are a major determinant of the rate of decline in the power of self-adjustment and self-defense in later life" (Townsend, 1957, 181–82). On the basis of evidence from his own study Townsend suggests that aged persons who are socially isolated or desolated will not survive as long as those older persons functioning within a secure family system.

Analyses of national vital statistics and census data for the United States by Kraus and Lilienfeld (1959) revealed that the widowed have significantly higher mortality rates than married persons of the same age, and that mortality rates are particularly high among young widowed people.[10] They suggest three possible explanations for the higher death rate among the widowed: (1) individuals with a short survival potential tend to choose mates like themselves; (2) the widowed and his deceased spouse share the unfavorable environmental factors which led to the death of the first spouse; and finally, (3) the grief, new worries, responsibilities, and alterations in daily routine that follow bereavement have a damaging effect upon the surviving spouse.

Young, Benjamin, and Wallis (1963) similarly suggest that the shock of widowhood might weaken the resistance to other causes of death. In order to test this notion, they examined the "duration effect" of being widowed, that is, how long people had been widowed when they died. Their analysis of the duration effect of widowhood on the mortality of 4,486 widowers aged fifty-five and over showed that widowhood *increased* the mortality rates of these male survivors by about 40 percent in the first six months following bereavement. This initial increase in widower mortality was eventually followed by a return to the level for married men in general.

Additional investigations in the United States as well as abroad have supported the general finding regarding the higher mortality of the widowed and, in particular, the widower. Moreover, recent research by Rees and Lutkins (1967) has provided rather dramatic statistical confirmation of the long-standing hypothesis that a death in the family produces an increased postbereavement mortality rate among close relatives, with the greatest increase in mortality occurring among surviving spouses.

During the first year following bereavement, deaths among the bereaved close relatives were seven times as frequent as among a control group. The mortality rate for male relatives was found to be significantly greater than for female relatives and the rate for widowers was considerably higher than that for widows.[11]

At present, precise knowledge is lacking concerning the primary causative agents underlying this association between bereavement and mortality. Homogamy (the tendency for the fit to marry the fit and the unfit to marry the unfit), common infection (both spouses dying from the same disease), joint unfavorable environment (unfavorable environmental circumstances that cause one spouse to die also causes the other to die), and loss of care (i.e., care formerly provided by the deceased spouse) have all been suggested as possible influence (Young, Benjamin, and Wallis, 1963). Still others subscribe to the so-called "broken heart" syndrome. In the latter connection, British studies have found that the great increase in mortality among widowers is largely attributable to death from coronary thrombosis and arteriosclerotic heart disease (Parkes and Benjamin, 1967, 232).

Finally, a number of researchers have suggested that the emotional stress associated with grief may lower physical resistance to disease and even a person's "will to live." In this connection, several investigators have contended that Western culture is more stressful to males, since it permits women to overtly express their emotions but encourages men to suppress similar feelings. Thus, for example, a study of older survivors who had lost their spouses less than five years previously found that they were much more likely to be lonely and were more disposed toward social isolation than married or single older people. While the investigator found no clear-cut differences between widows and widowers of various age levels regarding loneliness and social isolation, he nevertheless suggests that aged male survivors are more apt to be affected by the demise of their wives because "the psychological position is very different for men, since widely accepted norms of emotional and social behavior in our society makes it more acceptable for women to weep, to express grief, and to receive comforting and consolation—but less acceptable for men" (Tunstall, 1966, 153).

Clearly then, a number of factors are capable of affecting widower adaptability to the loss of his most significant interpersonal tie. Moreover, it has been observed that:

> When the bereaved person is supported by a united and affectionate family, when there is something left to live for, when the person has been adequately prepared for the loss, and when it can be fitted into a secure religious or philosophical attitude to life and death, there will seldom be much need for professional help. When, however, the bereaved person is left alone in a world which is seen as hostile and insecure, when the future is black and the loss has not been prepared for, help may be needed (Leading Article, 1967, 3).

Widowhood and Suicide

Durkheim is generally recognized as the first well-known sociologist to stress the connection between widowhood and suicide. He felt that those suicides which occurred at the crisis of widowhood were "really due to domestic anomie resulting from the death of husband or wife. A family catastrophe occurs which affects the survivor. He is not adapted to the new situation in which he finds himself and accordingly offers less resistance to suicide" (Durkheim, 1951, 259). Numerous investigators have since demonstrated that within a given age group the suicide rates of the widowed are consistently higher than the married, and *the rate of completed suicides is significantly higher for males*. A recent review of these studies indicates that suicide—whether attempted or successful—frequently tends to be preceded by the disruption of significant social interaction and reciprocal role relationships through the loss of a mate (Rushing, 1968). Moreover, these studies further reveal that the death of one or both parents in childhood is common among attempted and actual suicide victims and that the incidence of suicide among such persons when they attain adulthood is much greater than that for comparable groups in the general population.

Although a great deal of research has been conducted on the etiology and social correlates of suicide, investigators frequently ignore or fail to report the details concerning the differential rates of widows and widowers. Durkheim (1951, 171–216) was exceptional in this respect in his attempts to specify the conditions under which widowhood would be more disastrous for males or females. Among other things, he showed that widowers with children were more prone to self-destruction than widowers without children. It was Durkheim's contention that the presence of children tends to intensify the crisis through which the widower is passing. Forced to shoulder a double burden and to perform a variety of maternal functions for which he is unprepared, the male survivor with children finds his life acutely disrupted. "It is not because his marriage is ended but because the family which he heads is disorganized. The departure, not of the wife but of the mother, causes the disaster" (Durkheim, 1951, 188). Thus in a more recent study of the adjustment of children in motherless homes it was found that widowers generally were unable to communicate effectively with their children in a manner that led to the smooth operation of the family from both an emotional and a practical viewpoint. The basic reason for this was the father's inability to understand and compensate for the deceased mother's functions. "Yearly physical check-ups, recognizing the child with a fever, tending the child with measles, comforting the one with fears of the dark, knowing what is a reasonable curfew time, or what to advise the youngster to wear on a date, etc. are all second nature for a mother, and then becomes an area of knowledge and functioning to be developed by the father" (Wargotz, 2968, 5–6).

In the above-mentioned study, the investigator felt that professional help would have been beneficial to almost all of the fathers interviewed, as well as the children.[12] Such help is apparently even more of a necessity in those instances in which the loss of the mother has occurred through suicide (Cain and Fast, 1966). As one might suppose, the impact of an individual's suicide upon his spouse is rather profound. To begin with, there is the usual social embarrassment engendered by a spouse's self-annihilation, including feelings of intense guilt and shame, and other distorted postsuicide bereavement reactions. Moreover, the surviving spouse typically must undergo questioning and probing by the police, the coroner's office, insurance representatives, and other personnel, and such encounters tend to be extremely trying. Finally, it has been observed that "they find in their extended family, neighbors, and community not the emotional support and practical assistance usually offered the bereaved, but rather ambivalent avoidance, flurries of gossip, and downright accusations" (Cain and Fast, 1966, 878). Such reactions not infrequently lead the survivor to withdraw from social interaction and become inaccessible to those societal agents which might be of assistance in supporting their attempts to reorganize their lives.

Widowhood and Mental Illness

That a high correlation exists between marital status and mental illness has been repeatedly noted in the scientific literature. While considerable professional controversy prevails over identification of the exact sequence of the antecedent-consequent conditions which predispose individuals toward various forms of organic and psychogenic disorders, the evidence is quite consistent that widowed persons experience a substantially higher rate of mental disorders than the still-married, particularly among the older populations and among the widowed males (Adler, 1953).

The association between marital status and mental disorders has been shown to be a function of several intervening factors, including age, socioeconomic status, physical condition, and the degree as well as duration of social isolation (Adler, 1953; Bellin and Hardt, 1958; Lowenthal, 1964, 1965). Problems of social isolation, often accompanied by distressing loneliness, are especially germane to the personal adjustment of aged survivors, a very high proportion of whom are residing alone as occupants of one-person households (Belcher, 1967).

A large-scale survey (Gurin et al., 1960, 236–38) which attempted to assess the mental health of the American public found that widows and widowers were different from other marital statuses and from each other in the following ways: (1) The widowed said they worry "all the time" more frequently than any other group except the divorced and separated women. Female survivors reported extreme worrying more often than widowers. (2) Again, with the exception of divorced or separated women, the widowed were unusually low in their reported feelings of present happiness. This was especially true of male survivors. (3) Widows and widowers were most pessimistic, with more anticipation of unhappiness and death in the near future than any other group. Widowers were more pessimistic than widows. (4) The widowed had the lowest "immobilization" scores,[13] with widowers scoring lowest of all. Analysis revealed that these differences were affected little by age, and the investigators concluded that "the picture of the widowed status is a bleak one; with divorce, it seems to be the solitary status which holds the greatest threat to positive adjustment . . . the widowed group—the only clearly *nonvoluntary* solitary status—reports particularly intense feelings of distress, both in the present and in anticipation of the future" (Gurin et al., 1961, 238).

A number of studies have found higher gross rates of psychiatric impairment among the widowed (as well as the separated, divorced, and single) than among the married (Bellin and Hardt, 1958). The relationship between widowhood status and mental disorder, however, often appears to be contingent upon other variables. For example, Lowenthal and Berkman's (1967) study of the mental health of the aged in San Francisco showed that the relationship between widowhood and psychiatric impairment was both inconsistent and conditional upon the pattern of socioeconomic status, physical condition, and other factors. Among those aged respondents in good physical condition the differences in rate of psychiatric impairment between the widowed and married were either small or nonexistent, regardless of socioeconomic status. On the other hand, among those subjects in poor physical condition but high in socioeconomic status, the differential rate of psychiatric impairment between the widowed and married was large. These and other findings led the investigators to suggest that "poor physical condition is more closely related to mental disorder among the aged than is socioeconomic status; for regardless of socioeconomic status, the highest impairment rates . . . occur in conjunction with poor physical condition" (Lowenthal and Berkman, 1967, 74–75).

This conditional relationship of marital status (widowhood in particular) to psychiatric difficulties was further demonstrated when a comparison was made between rates of impairment by sex and age, deprivation (measured by poor physical condition, low social activity, and complaints about living arrangements), and marital status. This comparison showed little difference in rate of psychiatric impairment between married and widowed respondents who were "relatively nondeprived," but a pronounced difference in favor of the married among those respondents exhibiting a high deprivation score. The investigators concluded that the rather sizeable differences observed indicate that the "vulnerability to the stresses of widowhood is especially contingent on the incidence of other deprivations present; the greater the latter, the fewer would be the resources to withstand the additional stresses of widowhood" (Lowenthal and Berkman, 1967, 75).

Concluding Remarks

The transition from agrarian to urban and industrial society in America was accompanied by the emergence of a conception of the aged which stressed the involuntary structural isolation of older couples from their children and relatives (Parsons, 1959). In this perspective the young were seen as giving priority and allegiance to the norms of occupational achievement and this, along with the high mobility of the labor force, was said to isolate older people from their families. Consequently, there developed a view of the aged family as rejected, lonely, and a liability. To a considerable extent, this stereotype continues to prevail in both the popular mass media and scientific literature. As one gerontologist has commented, "most theories of aging are couched in the language of despair" (Kutner et al., 1962, 6).

In recent decades, however, empirical evidence has accumulated which cast considerable doubt upon what Shanas has termed this "myth of alienation" (Shanas, 1963). Her analysis of national census data on persons sixty-five years and older showed that the majority of the noninstitutionalized aged in the United States who had children were in close proximity to at least one of them and saw them often (Shanas, 1961). Cross-cultural comparisons reveal that in Britain, Denmark, and the United States (Shanas, 1967) as well as in other industrialized societies a similar pattern prevails, that "where distance permits, the generations continue to shoulder their traditional obligations of elders toward their children and the children to the aged" (World Health Organization, 1959).

Within the above context, the situation of the aged widower in America would appear to represent an anomalous case. The evidence presented in the preceding pages strongly suggests that the aged male survivor encounters rather severe difficulties in his efforts to adapt to the single status; that he experiences a different impact from the loss of a spouse than that experienced by his female counterpart. Thus, for example, "while some widowers manage to organize themselves domestically with great efficiency, others indeed fall into domestic anarchy and confusion" (Tunstall, 1966, 153).

In addition to the practical necessity of becoming proficient in domestic roles, the widower must find an adequate substitute for the intimacy of that primary relationship once provided by his wife, and this is perhaps the most difficult task of all. For some, remarriage provides a partial solution, but the courtship opportunities of the aged are of a limited nature in American society. Even if an older male is successful in locating a potential second mate, he will still have to overcome certain obstacles induced by a cultural bias which often frowns upon such unions.

McKain has commented recently on the social sanctions which prevail against elder marriages as follows:

> One solution for the widowed person who wishes to live in a family environment is to remarry and have a home of his own. The older person, independent and financially secure, vigorous and in good health, needing and appreciating companionship, is in a good position to remarry. However, at this point a barrier has been erected between what he wishes to do and what society expects him to do. His friends, his children, and the community at large rise up and condemn his remarriage. He is regarded as "too old for that." The wagging fingers, the knowing smiles, the raised eyebrows, and the cruel tongues are set in motion. Marriage is for the young in age, not the young in heart. Our ideas of marriage have lagged behind important changes in the family as a social institution. Attitudes have not kept pace with practices. Social conventions are not consistent with social realities (McKain, 1969, 6).

McKain contends that such conditions have had the effect of curtailing the number of older marriages and, in fact, of forcing many elderly couples to marry in secret. Apparently, many such couples who desire to marry in spite of family and community pressure do so by crossing state lines in order to avoid public opinion and public censure (McKain, 1969, 6–7).

We have seen that the widower's problems of adjustment are further compounded by the loss of his occupational role. For most of his adult life his work has been a principal source of his identity and self-conception. Retirement severs that identity, often in an abrupt fashion, and removes the male survivor from meaningful contact with friends and co-workers. The combined retiree-widower status places him in a position of structural isolation, leading to reduced communication and interaction with significant others. The culture provides little in the way of guidelines concerning steps that must be taken if he is to successfully reorganize his life and avoid succumbing to the process of alienation.

Finally, it should be noted that in American society separation and isolation are intimately associated with death in a variety of contexts.[14] To some extent this is a consequence of certain aspects of our sociocultural system. For example, our modal funeral customs in many ways dramatize the separation process; the activities surrounding the burial, the religious ceremonies, etc. all tend to emphasize the loss. Moreover, the emphasis on the nuclear family and the narrow circle of significant others which characterizes the network of interpersonal relationships in our culture often produces an exaggerated sense of social isolation and generates considerable anxiety among the bereaved.

> Most individuals live within a tight security circle, relying upon only a few people for emotional gratification. This tends to produce intense rather than diffuse affective relationships, rendering separation from only a few people a potentially critical emotional experience. The possibility of finding adequate

substitutes for significant others is remote. As a consequence, the whole self-image of an individual is under maximum risk when he is faced with separation (Howard and Scott, 1966, 163).

Indeed, it has been argued that in American society separation from significant others is tantamount to social isolation.[15] The analysis presented in this paper would lead one to conclude that, at least in the case of the aged male survivor, such an argument has considerable validity.

NOTES

This article is an expanded version of one originally prepared for a book edited by Howard M. Bahr in preparation under the tentative title of *Social Isolation, Alienation, and Homelessness*. Scientific Paper No. 3285, College of Agriculture, Washington State University. Work conducted under Project 1900. The author wishes to thank Professors Athol A. Congolton and Howard M. Bahr for reading the original manuscript and for their many constructive suggestions.

1. Unless otherwise specified, the term widowhood as used in this paper will have reference to *male* survivors only.
2. Most sociologists would no doubt agree that "few events in the life cycle require more extensive changes in activities, responsibilities, and living habits (or cause greater alterations in attitudes, reranking of values, and alterations of outlook on life) than does a change from one marital status to another" (Bogue, 1959, 212).
3. As Hilton (1967, 183) reminds us: "Intrapsychic events, whatever their explanation, do not pursue their course regardless of current happenings in the world about. Mourning is enacted in society. The bereaved will receive some comfort and help from others. After the loss of a person, new patterns must be established with the family and with friends and in a wider society that expects individuals to show a balance of personal dependence and independence. Mourning cannot be complete unless the bereaved succeed in making an adequate worldly adjustment without the one they have lost."
4. In recent decades, social scientists and caseworkers have shown increasing interest in examining family crises and exploring various modes of crisis intervention. For a review and elaboration of both the clinical and social definitions of the crisis concept as it applies to widowhood, see Hill (1958), Parad and Caplan (1960), Miller and Iscoe (1963), Parad (1965), and Mackey (1968).
5. A comment by Rose (in Rose and Peterson, 1965, 10) is relevant here: "Good health is sufficiently rare, and becoming rarer with advancing age, so that old people make much of it and exhibit a special admiration for those who remain healthy. A sickly old man who cannot take care of himself has little status among the elderly (or among any in the society, except perhaps his family) even if he is wealthy, whereas a vigorous old man with keen senses will be accorded high status among his compeers even though he lives exclusively on a modest pension."
6. It should be noted that interaction with kin on the part of the husband need not necessarily be decreased as a result of the death of the wife. For example,

there is nothing, in principle, to prevent the surviving husband from initiating and promoting extended family interaction. He may, for example, write letters and make telephone calls, as well as actually visit with married offspring families and other relatives.

7. It will be recalled that the Thurston County study also revealed that married persons had more friendship ties than widowed persons. Moreover, widowers were most likely to have no friends at all. In addition, the widowed were more likely than the married to prefer friends of their own age group, and widowers were most likely to state such a preference (Berardo, 1967b, 25–26).

8. Sociologists have stated this as a more general principle: "The more life disruptions a person had had, the greater the probability that he would have a low morale" (Montgomery, 1965, 41).

9. Of importance here is the useful conceptual distinction between isolates and desolates in old age. Townsend suggests that isolates are persons who have become secluded from their families and from society, whereas desolates are persons who have been recently deprived of the company of a loved one (Townsend, 1957, 182). It is his contention that desolation rather than isolation is the major reason for loneliness in old age.

10. More specifically, their analysis shows that the poorest risk is the white, male survivor between the ages of twenty-five and thirty-four, whose chances of dying were 4.31 times as great as his married counterpart. Among the age groups beyond thirty-four the preponderance of the death rates of the widowed over those of the married decreased steadily with age.

11. Rees and Lutkin's analysis suggests that young and middle-aged men whose wives died outside of the home are particularly vulnerable. For the total sample, there was five times the risk if the original death occurred some place other than home or hospital, probably because deaths at "other sites" were invariably sudden and the shock to relatives presumably greater.

12. For a detailed examination of the consequences of parental suicide on the surviving parent-children relationship, including the psychological impact of parent suicide upon the young child, see Cain and Fast (1966). For an analysis of the effects of widowhood status on the mental health of children, see Langner and Michael (1963). The latter study also examines the effects of widower remarriage on the mental health of children. For pertinent research on the widowed who become stepparents, see Bernard (1956).

13. Immobilization was defined in terms of psychological incapacity and inertia, a lack of psychological integration or psychological dysfunction (Gurin et al., 1960, 181–191).

14. Indeed, it has been observed that several factors operate in American society to prevent a direct confrontation with the reality of death itself as well as its consequences (Krupp and Kligfeld, 1962; Srub, 1966).

15. Howard and Scott also comment on the reciprocal relationship between death and social isolation, noting that persons who are undergoing the process of becoming socially isolated frequently in turn become overly concerned about death: "The individual experiencing separation from others may become obsessed with the idea of death. Ordinary values, those previously associated with primary groups or with society in general, may pale into insignificance when they are no longer shared with significant others. As these values lose their saliency, behavior patterns once structured by culturally shared imperatives may come to be based upon only the grossest considerations of life and death. As a result, the fear of death may come to outweigh the fear of dying, and the person may be motivated toward ego-destructive behavior" (Howard and Scott, 1966, 164).

REFERENCES

Adler, Leta M. The Relationship of Marital Status to Incidence and Recovery from Mental Illness. *Social Forces*, 1953, 32, 185–194.

Belcher, John C. The One-Person Household: A Consequence of the Isolated Nuclear Family? *Journal of Marriage and the Family*, 1967, 29, 534–540.

Bell, Robert R. *Marriage and Family Interaction*. Homewood, Illinois: Dorsey, 1963.

Bellin, Seymour S., and Robert H. Hardt. Marital Status and Mental Disorders among the Aged. *American Sociological Review*, 1958, 28, 155–162.

Berardo, Felix M. Kinship Interaction and Communications among Space-Age Migrants. *Journal of Marriage and the Family*, 1967a, 29, 541–554.

——. Social Adaptation to Widowhood among a Rural-Urban Aged Population. *Washington Agricultural Experiment Station Bulletin 689*. College of Agriculture, Washington State University, 1967b.

——. Widowhood Status in the United States: Perspective on a Neglected Aspect of the Family Life-Cycle. *The Family Coordinator*, 1968, 17, 191–203.

——. Death, Bereavement, and Widowhood: A Selective Bibliography. Department of Sociology, Washington State University. Mimeographed. 1969.

Bernard, Jessie. *Remarriage: A Study of Marriage*. New York: Dryden, 1956.

Blau, Zena S. Changes in Status and Age Identification. *American Sociological Review*, 1956, 21, 198–203.

——. Structural Constraints on Friendships in Old Age. *American Sociological Review*, 1961, 26, 429–439.

Bogue, Donald T. *The Population of the United States*. Glencoe, Illinois: The Free Press, 1959.

Brown, Robert C. Family Structure and Social Isolation of Older Persons. *Journal of Gerontology*, 1960, 15, 170–174.

Cain, Albert, and Irene Fast. Children's Disturbed Reactions to Parent Suicide. *American Journal of Orthopsychiatry*, 1966, 36, 873–880.

Cavan, Ruth S. Self and Role Adjustments during Old Age. In Arnold M. Rose (Ed.), *Human Behavior and Social Processes: An Interactionist Approach*. Boston: Houghton Mifflin, 1962, pp. 526–528.

Durkheim, Emile. *Suicide: A Study in Sociology*. Glencoe, Illinois: The Free Press, 1951.

Farber, Bernard. *Family: Organization and Interaction*. San Francisco: Chandler, 1964.

Freud, Sigmund. Mourning and Melancholia. In *Collected Papers of Sigmund Freud, IV*. London: The International Psychoanalytic Press, 1924, 1949, pp. 152–170.

Gorer, Geoffrey. *Death, Grief, and Mourning*. Garden City, New York: Doubleday, 1965.

Gurin, Gerald, Joseph Veroff, and Sheila Feld. *Americans View Their Mental Health*. New York: Basic Books, 1960.

Havighurst, Robert J., and Ruth Albrecht. *Older People*. New York: Longmans, Green, 1953.

Herzog, Elizabeth, and Cecelia E. Sudia. Fatherless Homes. *Children*, 1968, September–October, 177–182.

Hill, Reuben. Social Stresses on the Family. *Journal of Social Casework*, 1958, 39, 139–150.

Hilton, John. *Dying*. Baltimore: Penguin Books, 1967.

Howard, Alan, and Robert A. Scott. Cultural Values and Attitudes toward Death. *Journal of Existentialism*, 1965–66, 6, 161–174.

Kraus, Arthur S., and Abraham M. Lilienfeld. Some Epidemiological Aspects of the High Mortality in the Young Widowed Group. *Journal of Chronic Diseases*, 1959, 10, 207–217.

Kutner, Bernard, David Fanshel, Alice M. Togo, and Thomas S. Langner. *Five-Hundred over Sixty*. New York: Russell Sage, 1956.

Krupp, George R., and Bernard Kligfeld. The Bereavement Reaction: A Cross-cultural Evaluation. *Journal of Religion and Health*, 1962, 1, 222–246.

Landis, Judson T. Hobbies and Happiness in Old Age. *Recreation*, 1942, 35, 607, 641–42.

Langner, Thomas S., and Stanley T. Michael. *Life Stress and Mental Health*. New York: The Free Press, 1963.

Leading Articles. Broken Hearts. *British Medical Journal*, 1967, 4 (October–December), 2–3.

Lindemann, Erich. Symptomatology and Management of Acute Grief. *American Journal of Psychiatry*, 1944, 101, 141–148.

Lipman, Aaron. Role Conceptions of Couples in Retirement. In Clark Tibbetts and Wilma Donahue (Eds.), *Social and Psychological Aspects of Aging*. New York: Columbia University Press, 1962, pp. 475–485.

Lowenthal, Marjorie F. Social Isolation and Mental Illness in Old Age. *American Sociological Review*, 1964, 29, 54–70.

———. Antecedents of Isolation and Mental Illness in Old Age. *Archives of General Psychiatry*, 1965, 12, 245–254.

Lowenthal, Marjorie F. and Paul L. Berkman. *Aging and Mental Disorder in San Francisco*. San Francisco: Jossey-Bass, 1967.

McKain, Walter. *Retirement Marriage. Storrs Agricultural Experiment Station Monograph 3*. University of Connecticut, 1969.

Mackey, Richard A. Crisis Theory: Its Development and Relevance to Social Casework Practices. *The Family Coordinator*, 1968, 17, 165–173.

Miller, Kent, and Ira Iscoe. The Concept of Crisis: Current Status and Mental Health Implications. *Human Organization*, 1963, 22, 195–201.

Montgomery, James E. Social Characteristics of the Age in a Small Pennsylvania Community. *College of Home Economics Research Publication 233*. Pennsylvania State University, 1965.

Morrison, Denton E., and G. Albert Kristjanson. Personal Adjustment among Older Persons. *South Dakota Experimental Station Technical Bulletin 21*, 1958.

Parad, Howard J., and G. Caplan. A Framework for Studying Families in Crisis. *Social Work*, 1960, 5, 5–15.

Parad, Howard J. (Ed.). *Crisis Intervention: Selected Reading*. New York: Family Service Association of America, 1965.

Parkes, C. Murray, and B. Benjamin. Bereavement. *British Medical Journal*, 1967, 3, 232–233.

Parsons, Talcott. The Social Structure of the Family. In Ruth N. Anshen (Ed.), *The Family: Its Function and Destiny*. New York: Harper, 1959, pp. 241–274.

———. The Aging in American Society. *Law and Contemporary Problems*, 1962, 27, 22–35.

Phillips, Bernard S. A Role Theory Approach to Adjustment in Old Age. *American Sociological Review*, 1957, 22, 212–217.

Rees, W. Dewi, and Sylvia G. Lutkins. Mortality of Bereavement. *British Medical Journal*, 1967, 4 (October), 13–16.

Robins, Lee N., and Miroda Tomanec. Closeness to Blood Relatives outside the Immediate Family. *Marriage and Family Living*, 1962, 24, 340–346.

Rose, Arnold, and Warren A. Peterson (Eds.). *Older People and Their Social World*. Philadelphia: Davis, 1965.

Rushing, William. Individual Behavior and Suicide. In Jack P. Gibbs (Ed.), *Suicide*. New York: Harper and Row, 1968, pp. 96–121.

———. Deviance, Interpersonal Relations, and Suicide. *Human Relations*, 1969, 22, 61–76.

Shanas, Ethel. Living Arrangements of Older People in the United States. *The Gerontologist*, 1961, 1, 27–29.

———. The Unmarried Old Person in the United States: Living Arrangements and Care in Illness, Myth, and Fact. Unpublished paper prepared for the International Social Science Research Seminar in Gerontology, Makaryd, Sweden, 1963.

———. Family Help Patterns and Social Class in Three Countries. *Journal of Marriage and the Family*, 1967, 29, 257–266.

Smith, T. Lynn. *Social Problems*. New York: Crowell, 1955.

Srole, Leo, Thomas L. Langner, Stanley T. Michael, Marvin K. Opler, and Thomas A. C. Rennie. *Mental Health in the Metropolis*. New York: McGraw-Hill, 1961.

Stub, Holger R. Family Structure and the Social Consequences of Death. In Jeanette R. Forta and Edith S. Deck (Ed.), *A Sociological Framework for Patient Care*. New York: Wiley, 1966, pp. 191–200.

Thompson, Wayne E., and Gordon F. Streib. Meaningful Activity in a Family Context. In Robert W. Kleemier (Ed.), *Aging and Leisure: A Perspective Into the Meaningful Use of Time*. New York: Oxford University Press, 1961.

Townsend, Peter. *The Family Life of Old People*. Glencoe, Illinois: The Free Press, 1957.

Tunstall, Jeremy. *Old and Alone: A Sociological Study of Old People*. London: Routledge and Kegan Paul, 1966.

Wargotz, Helen. The Adjustment of Children in Motherless Homes. *The Single Parent*, 1968, 11 (May/June), 4–10.

World Health Organization. *Mental Health Problems of the Aging and the Aged, Technical Report, Series No. 171*. Geneva: World Health Organization, 1959.

Young, Michael, Bernard Benjamin, and Chris Wallis. The Mortality of Widowers. *The Lancet*, 1963, 2 (August), 454–456.

Grandmotherhood: A Study of Role Conceptions

JOAN F. ROBERTSON

Stereotypes of grandmothers range from jolly old ladies who spoil their grandchildren to meddlesome intruders in family life. This article tries to separate fact from fiction by examining the way in which grandmothers themselves view the grandparenting role. Four main groups are identified. One does little with their grandchildren and has an independent life centered on friends their own age. A second category is concerned primarily about what is morally good or right for their grandchildren. A third type views grandchildren as a source of great personal satisfaction, while the final category places little emphasis on either social or personal aspects of grandparenthood. Grandparent types appear to be predicted by life style, particularly the degree of involvement in family as opposed to friends, community, or occupation. Contrary to some earlier findings, the majority of grandmothers report actively enjoying their role.

Grandmotherhood is a topic which evokes considerable interest and speculation among researchers and the general public, but few facts exist to verify most of the speculation. The information that is available comes from four distinct sources: (1) informal norms as reported in such places as the "Dear Abby" column, *Ladies' Home Journal*, and popular myths; (2) studies detailing aspects of grandmotherhood *ex post facto* from data collected for other purposes; (3) clinical literature based on problem-oriented families; and (4) sources that focus on the topic directly but yield questionable evidence because of their absence of a theoretical perspective, the ambiguity and contradictory nature of their findings, and the fact that they are not particularly definitive about the significance of the role to the adults who assume it.

Throughout the centuries, informal norms and myths have prevailed and have influenced stereotypic impressions about women and their roles (Cinderella and fairy godmother myths, "Dear Abby" tales). In these stories grandmothers often play a central role.

Traditionally grandmothers have been portrayed as jolly, white-

Source: Reprinted from *Journal of Marriage and the Family*, February 1977, pp. 165–174. Copyright 1977 by the National Council on Family Relations. Reprinted by permission.

thatched, bespectacled old ladies who lavish goodies and attention on their grandchildren. Not infrequently, the media allude to grandmothers as happy-go-lucky, meddlesome intruders in family life who are politely tolerated because they add a unique dimension to family interaction.

A second source of information on the topic involves a number of studies which focus on selected aspects of grandmotherhood *ex post facto* on the basis of data collected for other purposes. In these sources, grandparents are believed to voluntarily engage in the bargaining and exchange of helping behaviors with their children and indirectly with their grandchildren in an attempt to secure love and attention. Grandmothers, for example, often act as babysitters (Lajewski, 1959); parental surrogates (Townsend, 1957); interveners in times of crises and disaster (Young, 1954; Von Hentig, 1945; Hill, 1970); bearers of family history and tradition (Boyd, 1967); household caretakers when parents are ill, giving birth, or on vacation (Sussman, 1962, 1953; Sheldon, 1949); and supplementers of family income through giving gifts to grandchildren or by helping with educational expenses (Sussman, 1953, 1963). In a somewhat different vein, grandparents also act as companions and confidants to grandchildren (Neugarten and Weinstein, 1964), and perform tension-reliever roles for families by acting as arbitrators in conflicts between parents and children (Schorr, 1960).

Also, because grandparents have neither authority nor responsibility for their grandchildren, they are able to interact more freely with them than are parents. An open exchange between parents and children is often inhibited by the feeling of duty and/or obligation that is built into the respective roles. Both parent and child can interact with the grandparent without these restraints and thus relieve tensions created by the duty/obligation relationship (Radcliffe-Brown, 1952).

A third source of information about grandmotherhood is the bulk of clinical literature based on problem-oriented families. In these reports, grandmothers have been said to exert both positive and negative influences on family functioning.

On the positive side, Spark and Brody (1970) have portrayed grandmothers as "crucial ingredients in family practice," and Lidz et al. (1957) and Meissner (1964) have called them stimulators of growth in all phases of family life. Other researchers have said that grandmothers are role models which strengthen families when parents themselves are inadequate role models (Lidz, 1957; Smith and Loeb, 1965). Also on the positive side, Hader (1965) states that grandmothers can act as modulating influences in family life because of their objectivity and life experiences. The value of grandparenting also has been demonstrated by the success of foster grandparent programs (Saltz, 1970).

On the negative side, Ackerman and Franklin (1965) have described grandmothers as stimulators of conflict. Rappaport (1958) says grandmothers are prone to reduce parents to childlike status in the eyes of their children, often creating feelings of omnipotence in grandchildren if the grandparent is also weak. Grandparents also have been referred to as carriers of excessive hostility which gets transmitted to grandchildren and sometimes precipitates antisocial behavior in adolescents (Strauss, 1943). In addition, they are sometimes considered to be overindulgers of grandchildren (Fried and Stern, 1948); excessive users of parental time, thus interfering in parent-child relationships (Fox, 1937); and usurpers and dominators of the mother's role (Vollmer, 1937; Borden, 1946).

The final source of information regarding grandmotherhood is a small number of studies that focus directly on the role (Albrecht, 1954; Kahana and Coe, 1969; Neugarten and Weinstein, 1964). In studying a sample of institutionalized and community-residing grandparents, Kahana and Coe revealed that as a source of gratification, grandparenthood had little salience for 59 percent of an institutionalized sample as compared to 21 percent of a community-residing grandparent sample. They posited that community-residing grandparents resorted to grandchildren to anchor themselves in the social structure on which they were losing hold. Institutionalized grandparents, on the other hand, having already disengaged from the social system, had little use for the social roles provided by grandparenthood. By contrast, Neugarten and Weinstein found, from interviewing both grandmothers and grandfathers in seventy middle-class families, that grandparenting allowed many people to fulfill biological continuity and emotional self-fulfillment needs, whereas for others the role had little impact on the self.

Albrecht, employing a representative sample of old people in a small midwestern community, found that grandparents neither had nor desired the responsibility for grandchildren, but they basked in reflected glory when grandchildren achieved success. Radcliffe-Brown (1952) suggested that friendly equality between grandparents and grandchildren existed as a relieving reaction to the tension caused between parents and children by parental authority and by the obligations each had toward the other. Nadel (1951) hypothesized that informality between grandfather and grandson is associated with the lack of family authority by the grandfather. The latter hypothesis was put to test by Apple (1956) using ethnological reports on seventy-five societies. She concluded that closeness between grandparents and grandchildren is not universal in kinship behavior, but confirmed Nadel's hypothesis that an indulgent, close, and warm relationship was fostered by disassociation of grandparents from family authority.

The primary objective of the present research was to develop a typology from which it would be possible to examine the significance of grandmotherhood by focusing upon the conceptions of grandmothers with regard to the meaning and behaviors they associate with the role. What do grandmothers think and feel about grandmotherhood as detailed from their descriptions of the role? What specific behaviors do grandmothers engage in with grandchildren? What is the frequency of these behaviors? Who initiates the behaviors—grandparents, parents, or grand-children? *A second objective of the research was to test the hypothesis that grandparenting types are predicted by life style, that is, factors such as age of grandmother, marital or work status, education, number of grandchildren, satisfaction with life, and level of involvement with friends and in community associations.*

Method

Sample

Using U.S. Census Tract Information, a three-stage area probability sample of housing units in a section of Madison, Wisconsin (population 170,000), was drawn. Specific census tracts were selected because they contained a high proportion of middle-age and older persons as well as a wide range of socioeconomic statuses. Other than sex, the only restrictive criteria of the sample were that a grandchild could not be living in the home with the grandmother and that the grandmother could not be a parental surrogate to the grandchildren. A total of 751 households were screened to produce the final sample size of 125 grandmothers. The completion rate for households that had a grandmother was 91 percent. Researchers at the Wisconsin Survey Research Laboratory drew the sample, assisted in the development of the instrument, and conducted the interviews in the spring and summer of 1970. The instrument was composed of a series of open-ended and highly-structured items which were developed from two pilot studies with a combined sample of 300 or more.

Subjects

About 38 percent of the 125 respondents were age seventy or over in contrast to 9 percent who were in their forties. Almost one-half (47.2 percent) were married, whereas 41 percent were widowed. Close to two-thirds of the subjects had not graduated from high school and, of these, more than one-half had only an eighth-grade education or less. About one-tenth of the subjects had some college education. The relatively low educational background reflects the large number of individuals aged seventy and over. The subjects were predominantly Lutherans and Catholics of Germanic and Scandinavian backgrounds. The income for close to one-half of the subjects ranged between $3,000 and $9,000. More than one-fourth reported an income of less than $3,000, whereas an equal proportion reported an income of $9,000 or over, undoubtedly reflecting the differences between the married and the widowed or between the retired and the employed, both factors which are related to age. The average number of grandchildren was three. Less than one-third had great-grandchildren, but for this group the average number of great-grandchildren was seven. The average age at which one became a grandmother was forty-six.

Procedures

Meaning of grandmotherhood: using interaction theory (Mead, 1934), it was posited that role meaning is distinct from and precedes behavior. Role meaning is a product of anticipatory socialization, and an individual assumes the grandparent role with a host of preconceived attitudes and expectations regarding the role. These attitudes and expectations are either borne out or not by the individual's active experiences in the role, and they are derived from two major sources: those which are determined almost exclusively by social or normative forces and which meet the needs of society, and those which stem from personal forces within the individual and which meet his or her personal needs. Therefore, the meaning of the role was examined within the context of two independent, but not mutually exclusive, dimensions. One was labeled a *personal dimension* (Factor I) and the other a *social dimension* (Factor II). A grandmother could reflect one of four general role types. For example, grandparents scoring high on both dimensions were assigned to the *apportioned* role-meaning type; those low on both dimensions were assigned to the *remote* type. Individuals who were high on the personal but low on the social dimension were seen as being the *individualized* type while the opposite—individuals high on social but low on the personal dimension—were seen as *symbolic* types.

In order to determine each subject's role-meaning type, the subjects were administered a battery of ten Likert-type items for each dimension. As an example, a woman who agreed with the statement, "I would tell my grandchildren to always remember that love and companionship are more important to a successful marriage than money," would score high on the social dimension. A woman who agreed with the statement, "One of the most important things about having grandchildren for me is that they make me feel young again," would score high on the personal dimension.

. . . .

In addition to the above items, the subjects were asked to respond to a series of structured items asking how they felt when they learned for the first time they were going to be a grandmother; which role was easier—parenting or grandparenting; in what ways did they enjoy the former role most; in what ways was the role easier; and, what was their conception of a *good* grandparent.

Behavior of grandmothers: using the available literature on the topic and the action-theory perspective (Parsons and Shils, 1962), a battery of fourteen highly structured items was devised to examine a variety of expressive and instrumental behaviors. Nine of the items refer to instru-

TABLE 1 Role Meaning°

No.	Item	Social dimension (Factor I)	Personal dimension (Factor II)
33	I would tell my grandchildren to always remember that love and companionship are more important to a successful marriage than money.	.701	.056
30	Going to visit a friend for Christmas is more enjoyable than having Christmas with one's family.	.606	.090
29	The greatest happiness is found in a family where all members work together as a group.	.562	.119
37	I feel I should do what is morally right to set a good example for my grandchildren.	.499	.186
31	One of the most important things I want from my grandchildren is for them to "respect their elders."	.456	.250
38	I feel that my grandchildren should be encouraged to choose their own occupation whether their parents agree or disagree with their choice.	.426	.113
34	Life would be very lonely for me without my grandchildren.	.267	.543
43	The most important thing about having grandchildren for me is that they have brought a deep sense of emotional satisfaction to my life.	.222	.526
41	One of the most important things about having grandchildren for me is that they make me feel young again.	.118	.455
44	If one of my grandchildren had the opportunity to take a pleasure trip around the world, I think he should take the trip first and see life while he is still young and worry about going to college and getting a job later.	-.075	.412
40	I think I should be able to give my grandchildren whatever I can and not be worried about spoiling them.	-.002	.349
26	One of the most important things about having grandchildren is that they provide me with a way to see my blood line carried on for another generation.	-.009	.393

°N = 125

mental behaviors and four are expressive types. The subjects were asked to respond "yes" or "no" to whether or not they engaged in each specific behavior. They were given a score of one point for each behavior they engaged in, with a possible range of scores from 0–14. Subscores for expressive behaviors (possible range: 0–4) and for instrumental behaviors (possible range: 0–9) were also obtained.

After detailing the types of behaviors they engaged in, the subjects were asked to indicate how often they engaged in the behavior. They were scored on frequency responses ranging from seven points for behaviors engaged in daily to one point for those performed less than a few times a year. The subjects were then asked, "Who suggests this?" to which they could respond, "mostly me," "mostly my grandchildren," or "mostly my children."

Results

Types of Grandparenting

Meaning of grandmotherhood: analysis of these data indicated that three variables were statistically significant in differentiating role meaning—education, satisfaction with life, and the frequency of behaviors. Age of the grandmother was also a significant factor, but it was not as significant as predicted (see Table 2).

The meaning of grandmotherhood can best be described by an examination of the four profiles of each role type.

The first role-meaning group, the *apportioned*-type grandmothers, comprised 29 percent of the sample, with an N of 36. These women were as likely to be concerned about doing what was morally right for their grandchildren as they were about feeling that grandparents should feel free to indulge grandchildren and not worry about spoiling them. Illustrative of this type was Mrs. A, who said in describing her relationship with her grandchildren:

> I do love them. I'm always glad to see them come, but just as glad to see them go—it's sort of a relief to be able to stretch out and relax. . . . I've often criticized my granddaughter about her short dresses, but it has no effect. . . . I'm busy with friends, too.

These data revealed an interesting profile for this group. Of the four role-meaning types, these grandmothers had the second highest educational attainment, the second highest frequency of friendship associations, and the highest frequency of community involvements. The life-satisfaction scores for this group were lower than the *symbolic* or *remote* types, falling slightly above the mean for the sample as a whole. This was the second youngest group of grandmothers with a mean age of sixty-four. The majority of these women were widowed and unemployed as

TABLE 2   Role Types by Life Style°

Life-style variables	Appor- tioned N = 36	Sym- bolic N = 33	Individu- alized N = 21	Remote N = 35	Signifi- cance level
			Role types		
Age of grandmother	64.27	61.63	69.33	65.37	.10
Education	4.03	4.58	3.47	3.68	.007
Number of grandchildren	7.83	5.84	8.19	5.57	.10
Satisfaction with life	9.22	9.72	9.47	7.77	.04
Friendship associations	34.66	35.84	31.91	33.54	—
Community associations	1.94	1.45	.95	1.60	.20
Behavior					
Frequency of expressive behavior	1.33	.78	1.61	.68	.01
Frequency of instrumental behavior	6.44	5.42	6.09	5.17	.03
Frequency of combined behaviors	7.77	6.21	7.71	5.85	.006
Family size:					
Number of children	3.41	3.03	3.47	3.17	—
Number of great-grand- children	1.19	2.30	4.85	1.17	.19

°Analysis of variance, group means; N = 125

indicated in Table 3. This group was the most involved with their grandchildren in terms of behavior.

The second group of grandmothers, the *symbolic* type, comprised 26 percent of the sample, with an N of 33. These women were more concerned about doing what was morally good or right for grandchildren. They placed little, if any, emphasis on the sources of satisfaction which characterized the personal dimension items. Instead, their primary focus was on what is normative. Illustrative of this type was Mrs. B. In referring to her grandchildren she stated:

> We want our grandchildren to get a good education, to be good, clean people, good workers as they grow up . . . there are things they could help me with, but they don't offer and I'm too proud to ask. A good grandparent is to be a real Christian, set examples, practice what you preach.

The profile for this group indicated that they were most like the *apportioned*-type grandmothers. They held the highest educational attainment in that most had completed high school or attended some college. These grandmothers were the most involved with their own friends, had low community involvement, but were very satisfied with life. They were the youngest group of grandmothers having a mean age

TABLE 3 Role-Meaning Types by Marital and Work Status Percentage Distribution

Variable	Apportioned	Symbolic	Individualized	Remote
Marital status				
Married	47	55	38	46
Single°°	53	45	62	54
Totals	100	100	100	100
Work status				
Employed	44	52	33	43
Nonemployed	56	48	67	57
Totals	100	100	100	100

°°Includes 12 percent who are divorced or separated, 8.8 percent and 3.2 percent respectively, and 88 percent who are widowed.

of 61.6 years. The majority of the women were married (55 percent) and employed (52 percent). This group scored the second lowest with regard to behaviors they engaged in with grandchildren. In terms of behavior, they were most like the *remote* role meaning type.

The third role-meaning group, the *individualized* type, comprised 17 percent of the sample, with an N of 21. These women responded positively to those items which placed a heavy emphasis on the *sources of satisfaction* which characterized the personal dimension. They expressed very little, if any, regard for normative expectations from grandchildren. They were more concerned that grandchildren help them curb loneliness, keep them young, and carry on the family blood line than they were about respect, marrying for love and companionship, or doing what is morally right for grandchildren. An example of this type of grandparent is illustrated in the remarks of Mrs. C, a fifty-nine-year-old woman who said of her grandchildren:

> They've helped me forget I'm getting older—they keep me from getting lonesome . . . they help me forget my problems.

The fourth role-meaning group, the *remote* type, comprised 28 percent of the sample, with an N of 35 grandmothers. These individuals placed little emphasis on either social or personal aspects of grandparenthood. Generally, they were not very involved with, or concerned about, the elements of any relationship with their grandchildren. They held no strong attitudes or expectations regarding grandchildren, suggesting indifference or limited meaning of the role for them. This group was below the average for the sample as a whole in regard to education, and they scored second lowest in friendships and community involvements. They were the second oldest group of grandmothers, their mean age being sixty-five. They scored the lowest on both life satisfaction and frequency of behaviors with grandchildren. The majority of these women were widowed (54 percent) and unemployed (54 percent). Clearly, these grandmothers responded to grandparenting in a distant, impersonal, and ritualistic manner.

For the overall sample, grandmotherhood is a role which is actively enjoyed. Nearly 80 percent of the respondents indicated that they were elated, proud, excited, thrilled, happy, etc., when they learned, for the first time, that they were going to be a grandmother. This is in contrast to 5 percent who had mixed emotions about it, 3 percent who were unaffected, and only 4 percent who were unhappy. The remaining 8 percent felt they were either too young or too old to be a grandmother and had no further reactions. Interestingly, 86 percent of these women indicated that their feelings about grandmotherhood had not changed over the years. When asked which role they enjoyed most, parent or grandparent, 37 percent preferred grandparenting, 32 percent parenting, and 25 percent equally enjoyed both roles. On the whole, grandmothers report that grandparenting is an easier role. Seventy-nine percent of grandmothers state that, "as a grandmother you are free from upbringing responsibilities . . . you have more time to spend with and enjoy grandchildren than when your children were young . . . and you can see and enjoy grandchildren, then send them home." According to 80 percent of the grandmothers interviewed, a *good* grandmother is one who does the following: loves and enjoys grandchildren; sets good examples (religion, honesty, right versus wrong), helps grandchildren when asked or needed; does not interfere too much in grandchildren's lives; is a good listener; doesn't interfere with parental upbringing or spoil grandchildren; and can use discipline with grandchildren if it is needed.

Behavior of Grandmothers

A precise picture of the grandmothers' behaviors with grandchildren is reflected by an analysis of the fourteen behavioral items listed in Table 4. Although grandmothers reported they engaged in all fourteen activities with grandchildren, evidence indicated that they did so in only three out of the fourteen with a high frequency. These behaviors were babysitting, home recreational activities such as reading stories and playing games, and spontaneous drop-in visits for leisure and fun. Whereas grandmothers may desire to engage in certain behaviors with grandchildren (as reported by their statements that they did engage in those behaviors), in reality they failed to carry through the behavior very frequently. Elsewhere, Robertson (1975) has reported that one of the reasons for this discrepancy relates to grandmothers' fears that parents may view attempts at a high frequency of behavior with grandchildren as meddlesome, intrusive, or inappropriate. In ten of the fourteen behaviors, grandmothers indicated that they initiated the behavior. The two exceptions, babysitting and home recreation, were initiated by the parent and grandchildren, respec-

TABLE 4 Role Behaviors with Grandchildren (N = 125)

Role behavior	Activity			Frequency°°			Initiator			
	Yes	No	Inapp.°	High	Low	Inapp.°	G/P	G/C	Ch.	Inapp.°
Provide gifts	97.6	1.6	.8	23.2	72.0	4.8	97.6	—	—	2.4
Babysit with grandchildren	92.0	7.2	.8	55.2	33.6	11.2	35.2	3.2	52.8	8.8
Home recreation	79.2	19.2	1.6	49.6	24.2	26.4	30.4	47.2	—	22.4
Zoo and shopping trips	69.6	29.6	.8	21.6	44.8	33.6	61.6	6.4	30.4	1.6
Drop-in visits	64.8	33.6	1.6	46.4	13.6	40.0	57.6	1.6	3.2	37.6
Relate family history	47.2	50.4	2.4	4.0	40.0	56.0	25.6	18.4	1.6	54.4
Teach sewing	42.4	55.2	2.4	10.4	27.2	62.4	13.6	27.2	.8	58.4
Help with emergencies	39.2	59.2	1.6	7.2	28.8	64.0	23.2	9.6	6.4	60.8
Take grandchildren on vacations	28.4	60.8	.8	2.4	34.4	62.3	22.4	8.8	6.4	62.4
Take children to church	37.6	60.8	1.6	5.6	32.0	62.4	33.6	3.2	.8	62.4
Provide advice on personal problems	29.6	68.0	2.4	5.6	21.6	72.8	16.8	12.8	—	70.4
Provide advice regarding work	24.0	72.8	3.2	4.0	18.4	77.6	17.6	6.4	—	76.0
Provide advice regarding religion	13.6	84.8	1.6	4.8	8.0	87.2	9.6	3.2	.8	86.4
Teach native language	1.6	96.8	1.6	—	1.6	98.2	.8	—	.8	98.4

°Inappropriate refers to those cases in which age, sex, residential proximity, health, etc., preclude such behaviors.
°°High Frequency: Subjects engaged in behavior once a month or more.
Low Frequency: Subjects engaged in behavior a few times a year or less often.

tively. These findings uphold Lajewski's (1959) findings that grandmothers often act as "built-in babysitters" and other evidence indicating that grandparents often serve parental-surrogate and household-caretaker functions (Sheldon, 1949; Sussman, 1953, 1962, 1963; Townsend, 1957). They also substantiate Radcliffe-Brown's (1952) thesis that friendly equality prevails between grandchildren and grandparents. This same theme emerges with regard to ethnic influence. Similar to Boyd's (1967) data, nearly half of the subjects (47.2 percent) acted as bearers of family history and tradition. Though this behavior occurred infrequently, when it did occur it was initiated by either the grandparent or the grandchildren, not by the parents. This supports Boyd's perspective that the third generation sometimes attempts to revive family history through elders.

It is significant to note that the only behaviors which grandmothers engaged in with a high frequency were those which were initiated by the parent or grandchild. This suggests that parents may affect the frequency of role behavior with grandchildren in that grandmothers become involved only in those behaviors which are sanctioned by parents as indicated by their initiation of the behavior.

Grandparenting Types by Life Style

The relationship between grandparenting types and life style is indicated in tables 2 and 3. As illustrated by the four role types, grandmotherhood holds a different significance for different individuals. The most important factor affecting role salience is life style: that is, the extent to which grandmothers are involved in work, friendship, and community associations. As indicated in tables 2 and 3, women who are younger (mean age for sample sixty-one), married, more educated, and have the highest number of friendship associations (while not statistically significant from other types) score highest in life satisfaction and have the second lowest frequency of behavior with grandchildren (only the remote or distant-type grandparent has a lower frequency). Generally, these women were more involved in extrafamilial activities and espoused attitudes and expectations regarding the role which were socially or normatively oriented. These activities were their primary source of satisfaction and their grandchildren were viewed as secondary sources of satisfaction. This is not meant to imply that grandmotherhood is not a prominent aspect in the lives of these women, but rather it signifies where they place their priorities. A clear illustration of this were the *symbolic*-type grandmothers who were involved in a number of other social roles. This was indicated in the comments of a fifty-four-year-old married employed woman, who said, when asked about the meaning of grandmotherhood:

> I really wasn't too happy at first because I felt I was much too young for that. But, now as I look back, my grandchildren have enriched our lives . . . I'm glad to be young and healthy enough to do things with them when I can; I don't

have much time though . . . I work and we have so many things to do ourselves and so do the kids these days . . . they don't have time for us either.

In contrast, a number of grandmothers attached primary significance to the role. These were the *individualized* types (mean age for sample sixty-nine) who have more of a familial life style. They had few friends, low frequency of community associations, and were unemployed. They were the oldest grandmothers and had the least education. Interestingly, they had the highest frequency of both expressive and instrumental behaviors, suggesting that grandparenthood may be one of the few roles available to them. These women clearly espoused attitudes and expectations which indicated that grandmotherhood provided them with emotional gratification, and that grandchildren helped alleviate the loneliness and isolation associated with increasing age and disengagement from the social milieu.

The importance of grandchildren in alleviating loneliness is evidenced in the remark of Mrs. D, a seventy-year-old retired widow who, in describing ways in which she would like to have her grandchildren help her, said:

> I'd like to have them come and see me often. I'd like them to take me for rides, to visit with me and help me keep up my morale. They are good grandchildren, I know they will come.

This same theme is echoed in the words of another grandmother in her seventies who, when asked the same question, commented:

> I'd be awfully unhappy not to have my grandchildren. As I look at some of my friends who have no one, it's terrible. There are so many people alone. . . . The more people you have to think about, the less you worry about yourself.

The only group of individuals that attached little or no significance to the role of grandparenthood was the *remote* type who the researcher believed are unique and generally dissatisfied personality types, as shown in their substantially lower life-satisfaction scores.

Summary and Conclusions

This paper addresses a number of issues relevant to the significance of grandmotherhood. First, it describes the development of a typology which is useful in delineating the meaning and behavior associated with four distinct types of grandparenting. Grandparenthood is seen as a role which has a different meaning for individuals. Some grandmothers talk about the meaning of the role from the context of normative or social orientations. These are labeled the *symbolic* types. Others speak of grandmothering in highly personal tones and have more of an inner-directed orientation. They talk almost exclusively about the joys and pleasures of grandparenting with little, if any, emphasis on normative expectations. These are labeled the *individualized* types. Many grandmothers espouse a blend of normative and personal meanings regarding the role. These are labeled the *apportioned* types. On the other hand, some grandmothers attribute little meaning to the role and view grandparenting in a distant sense. Accordingly, these are labeled the *remote* types.

Second, the research indicates that grandparent types are predicted by life style. Grandparenting types are a reflection of role salience, which is the meaning and behaviors grandmothers associate with the role. Grandmothers view grandparenting in relation to their degree of involvement with their families. This is associated with a number of factors, such as the age of the grandmother, whether she works, marital status, education, number of grandchildren, satisfaction with life, and the frequency of friendship and community ties. These factors, particularly the influence of age, interact with one another to produce two contrasting grandmother life styles—one which is extrafamilially oriented and the other which is intrafamilially oriented. It is this life style which predicts grandparenting types. For example, younger grandparents fall into the *symbolic* role type. These women attach a normative meaning to the role. Generally, they are very involved in extrafamilial activities. This appears related to the fact that they are the most educated, and most are married and working. They also have a great many friendships and community ties and score high on life satisfaction. While grandmothering is described as a joyous role, it is clear that they are more involved in their own lives and place less emphasis on grandparenting. This is corroborated by their low frequency of behavior with grandchildren. Conversely, the older grandmothers fall into the *individualized* role types. These women were the least educated; undoubtedly a function of age. As expected, most were widowed and nonemployed. They had the lowest number and frequency of friendship and community ties. They speak of grandmotherhood in highly laudable and personal or affective tones. Grandchildren are viewed as important to their daily lives because they help fill lonesome hours. This is evidenced in the fact that these women have the highest frequency of interaction behavior with grandchildren—an interesting finding in view of their age.

In reference to family development theory, it is hypothesized that the role of grandmotherhood changes over time with the age of the grandmother and the age of the grandchild. The writer also believes that family relationships change over time—a point that Bengtson and Black (1973) make in their analysis of intergenerational relations and socialization and which is also reflected, to some extent, in Reuben Hill's (1970) family consumer theory.

Third, these data also provide unique information about grandparenting behavior and role enjoyment. In terms of the former, it is clear that grandparent behaviors, that is, actions carried out in acting the grandmother role, revolve primarily around babysitting, home recreation, and drop-in visits—mostly those initiated by the parent or grandchild. Finally, grandmotherhood is a role which is actively enjoyed by grandmothers, a finding which is in contrast to some of the previously cited findings.

NOTES

This research was used as a basis for a paper presented at the Gerontological Society Meetings, Toronto, Canada, October 21–24, 1970. The author is especially grateful to Dr. Vivian Wood for advice and assistance while conducting this research and in the preparation of this manuscript.

REFERENCES

Ackerman, Nathan, and P. F. Franklin. 1965. "Family dynamics and the reversibility of delusion formation: A case study in family therapy." P. 286 in I. Boxzormenyi-Nagy and J. L. Framo (Eds.), Intensive Family Therapy. New York: Harper & Row.

Albrecht, Ruth. 1954. "The parental responsibilities of grandparents." Marriage and Family Living 26 (August):201–204.

Apple, Dorian. 1956. "The social structure of grandparenthood." American Anthropologist 58 (August):656–663.

Bengtson, Vern, and K. D. Black. 1973. "Intergenerational relations and continuities in socialization." Pp. 207–234 in Paul Baltes and K. W. Schaie (Eds.), Life Span Developmental Psychology: Personality and Socialization. New York: Academic Press.

Borden B. 1946. "The role of grandparents in children's behavioral problems." Smith College Studies in Social Work 17 (December):115–116.

Boyd, Rosamonde. 1967. "The emerging social roles of the four-generation family." Pp. 11–21 in Charles G. Oakes (Ed.), Our Elderly Americans: Challenge and Response. Spartanburg, S. C.: Converse College.

Fox, F. 1937. "Family life and relationships as affected by the presence of the aged." Pp. 1–13 in Committee on Mental Hygiene, Family Welfare Association of America (Eds.), Mental Hygiene and Old Age. New York: State Charities Aid Association.

Fried, Edrita G., and K. Stern. 1948. "The situation of the aged within the family." American Journal of Orthopsychiatry 18 (January):31–53.

Hader, M. 1965. "The importance of grandparents in family life." Family Process 4 (March):228–240.

Hill, Reuben. 1970. Family Development in Three Generations. Cambridge, Mass.: Schenkman.

——. 1949. Families under Stress. New York: Harper & Brothers.

Kahana, Eva, and R. M. Coe. 1969. "Perceptions of grandparenthood by community and institutionalized aged." Proceedings of 77th Annual Convention of the American Psychological Association 4:735–736.

Lajewski, Henry C. 1959. "Working mothers and their arrangements for the care of their children." Social Security Bulletin 22 (August):8–13.

Lidz, Theodore, A. R. Cornelison, S. Fleck, and Dorothy Terry. 1957. "The intrafamilial environment of schizophrenic patients II: Marital schism and marital skew." American Journal of Psychiatry 114 (September):241–248.

Mead, George H. 1934. Mind, Self and Society. Chicago: University of Chicago Press.

Meissner, W. W. 1964. "Thinking about the family: Psychiatric aspects." Family Process 3 (March):1–40.

Nadel, S. F. 1951. The Social Foundations of Social Anthropology. Glencoe: Free Press.

Neugarten, B., and Karol Weinstein. 1964. "The changing American grandparent." Journal of Marriage and the Family 26 (May):199–204.

Parsons, Talcott, and A. Shils (Eds.). 1962. Toward a General Theory of Action. New York: Harper Torchbooks.

Radcliffe-Brown, A. R. 1952. Structure and Function in Primitive Society. London: Cohen and West.

Rappaport, E. A. 1958. "The grandparent syndrome." Psychoanalytic Quarterly 27 (October):518–537.

Robertson, Joan F. 1971. "Grandparenthood: A study of role conceptions of grandmothers." Unpublished doctoral dissertation, University of Wisconsin-Madison.

———. 1975. "Interaction in three-generation families, parents as mediators: Towards a theoretical perspective." International Journal of Aging and Human Development 6 (2):103–110.

Saltz, Rosalyn. 1970. "Evaluation of a foster grandparent program." Pp. 512–517 in A. Kadushin (Ed.), Child Welfare Services: A Source Book. New York: Macmillan.

Schorr, Alvin L. 1960. Filial Responsibility in the Modern American Family. Washington, D.C.: Social Security Administration, U.S. Department of Health, Education and Welfare.

Sheldon, J. H. 1949. "Old age problems in the family." Milbank Memorial Fund Quarterly 27 (April):119–132.

Smith, Imogene W., and Dorothy Loeb. 1965. "The stable extended family as a model in treatment of atypical children." Social Work 10 (July):75–81.

Spark, Geraldine M., and Elaine Brody. 1970. "The aged are family members." Family Process 9 (March):195–208.

Strauss, C. A. 1943. "Grandma made Johnny delinquent." American Journal of Orthopsychiatry 13 (April):343–346.

Sussman, M. B. 1953. "The help pattern in the middle-class family." American Sociological Review 18 (February):22–28.

———. 1962. "Kin family network: Unheralded structure in current conceptualizations of family functioning." Marriage and Family Living 24 (August):231–240.

———. 1963. "The isolated nuclear family: Fact or fiction?" Pp. 89–95 in M. B. Sussman (Ed.), Sourcebook in Marriage and the Family. Boston: Houghton Mifflin.

Sussman, M. B., and Lee Burchinal. 1962. "Parental aid to married children:

Implication for family functioning." Marriage and Family Living 24 (November):320–332.

Townsend, Peter. 1957. The Family Life of Older People. London: Routledge and Kegan Paul.

Vollmer, H. 1937. "The grandmother: A problem in child rearing." American Journal of Orthopsychiatry 7–8 (July):378–382.

Von Hentig, Hans. 1945–1946. "The sociological function of the grandmother." Social Forces 24 (March):389–392.

Young, Michael. 1954. "The role of the extended family in a disaster." Human Relations 7 (August):189–204.

7

Work, Retirement, and Leisure

Retirement is a relatively new phenomenon, both in the United States and in other countries around the world. It is the creation of modern industrial society. Although older people may stop work or may change the nature of the work they perform in nonindustrialized societies, no formal mechanism exists for providing needed resources in old age. Rather security is obtained through property ownership or reliance on family members.

The History of Retirement in the United States

The advent of the first public pension programs in the United States occurred in the eighteenth century. They were applied to police, firemen, and other hazardous occupations and were later extended to include most categories of public and civil service. Private pension programs emerged in the latter part of the nineteenth century in a few new large-scale corporate enterprises such as the railroads. The first general social insurance laws providing for all the population were not passed until the mid-1930s in the United States, although they had begun as early as 1883 in Germany and other European countries (Friedmann and Orbach, 1974, p. 611).

The delay in the organization of large-scale pension programs in the United States until well into the twentieth century has been attributed to two factors. First, our value system, which evolved from Calvinistic Protestantism, defined work as central to life itself, with leisure being considered somewhat sinful. As Friedmann and Or-bach (1974, p. 612) state:

> A society that has for so long stressed only work-related values seems to be reluctant to accept without doubt or recrimination the possibility of acquiring a large leisure class in the form of the retired aged.

The second factor is that some of the stigma attached to disability and indigency or welfare payments was also attached to pension programs, making even those aged most likely to benefit from them somewhat resistant to the idea of formalized payments to the retired.

In 1937 the Old Age, Survivors, and Dependents Insurance Act was passed, providing regular income for the retired. The basic idea was that people would contribute from their earnings. This money would be supplemented by funds from their employers and would become available to contributors on their sixty-fifth birthday. Because each successive wave of workers was expected to include more people than the previous one, the incoming payments were expected to always exceed the amount being paid out to retirees. However, legislators did not anticipate either the decreasing birth rate or the expansion of early retirement plans, which reduced the number of contributing workers and simultaneously increased the number of retired being supported. The present crisis in social security is a result of these factors, and the system is now in the process of being amended to take into account the changing situation. The article by Withers discusses some of the arbitrary aspects of our retirement system as well as some mistaken beliefs about older workers.

The Decision to Retire

Several factors affect an individual's attitude toward retirement. One of the most important is the meaning which work has held for that person. Social scientists, who are often highly committed to their own jobs, have often made the mistaken assumption that all workers find their jobs equally meaningful. This has led to a very negative conception of retirement. Testimony given by a witness speaking to the U.S. Senate Special Committee on Aging (1967) summarizes the opinion of many workers:

> One thing that really disturbed me was a remark made here a short time ago by one of the witnesses about factory workers, if they really know whether they want to retire or not. Another remark that quite shook me up was the fact that maybe some of these people love their work. Now I could understand a person in a chosen profession—and most of the witnesses have been professional people—I could understand them

having a love for their work, but I think that the gentlemen on the platform understand as I do, that working in a factory, which includes about 95 percent of the people on social security, is not a matter of choice. When you go into a factory, it is a matter of assignment. They say, "Do this," and you are assigned to a machine and this is what you do and you repeat it over and over and over, the same little routine operation. There is no diversification and absolutely no opportunity for knowledge or exchange or anything else—you just stand there all day long, day after day, year after year, for a lifetime. And then somebody asks you, "Do you really want to retire?"

Practically every person working in a factory today wants to retire. The only deterrent to people retiring from factories is whether they are going to get a pension on which they will be able to live and support their wife or other dependents in the mode or manner in which they have been accustomed. That is the only deterrent.

Most studies which have systematically examined the relationship between the meaning of work and orientation to retirement have found great variation according to the type of work in which a person is engaged. Generally, professionals and executives are reluctant to leave work and find it difficult to anticipate retirement. In contrast, most skilled or semiskilled workers would prefer to retire as early as possible, but are most concerned about financial security after retirement (Simpson, Back, and McKinney, 1966). The article by Quadagno examines the attitudes of a group of professional men and women toward retirement.

Anticipated income in retirement is the second major factor affecting a person's readiness for retirement. The original act which defined the criteria for social security was not supposed to provide a "pension at the level of comfort and decency for all Americans. Instead, it was to provide a floor below which they could not fall" (Cottrell, 1974, p. 26). The level of income provided by social security is meager at best, and for many it is significantly below the amount necessary to provide necessities.

Some people planning to retire have additional income from private or public pensions. However, these other pensions are still much less common than is generally believed, and many provide only a meager supplementary income to social security. This is because most private pensions were designed after social security came into being and were primarily intended as supplements to social security rather than as major sources of income in and of themselves. Further, they are not necessarily a secure source of income, and it is possible for a person to count on a pension which never materializes. As one economist warns:

In all too many cases, the pension promise shrinks to this: If you remain in good health and stay with the same company until you are sixty-five years old, and if the company is still in business, and if your department has not been abolished, and if you haven't been laid off for too long a period, and if there is enough money in the [pension] fund, and if that money has been prudently managed, you will get a pension (Schulz, 1970, p. 39).

While new laws have been passed to protect individuals' rights to pensions, the effectiveness of these laws is still unclear.

Some people find that the decision to retire is out of their hands. The issue of mandatory retirement is controversial. Those who argue in its favor state that older workers need to be systematically phased out of the work force to create opportunities for younger workers. Others believe that mandatory retirement rules unjustly discriminate against older people, who are prevented from exercising talents and skills in the work world solely on the basis of age. Being forced to retire may make a person feel useless, signaling to that person that he or she may no longer be as free to make other life choices as well.

After retirement other activities take on new significance. Those who have reduced family life and other relationships to appendages of the work world throughout their lives find the adjustment to retirement difficult. However, this is not typical of most retirees. In general, there appears to be high continuity in family and other relationships after retirement, and it is not seen as a major crisis (Streib, 1965). The final article by Atchley questions the view that retirement creates an unfillable void and suggests that leisure activities play an important role in bridging the gap between pre- and post-retirement life.

While there are problems associated with retirement, they are generally not caused by people being unable to adjust to increased leisure and the absence of work. Rather the major problems are lack of sufficient income to enjoy this leisure and the loss of self-esteem which accompanies forced retirement. If people have adequate financial provisions when they retire and are allowed to retire when they feel ready, this time of life can be as interesting and satisfying as any other.

REFERENCES

Cottrell, Fred. 1974. *Aging and the aged.* Dubuque, Iowa: Wm. C. Brown Co.
Friedmann, Eugene, and Harold Orbach. 1974. Adjustment to retirement. In S. Arieti (ed.), *American handbook of psychiatry.* New York: Basic Books, pp. 609–645.
Schulz, James H. 1970. *Pension aspects of the economics of aging: Present and*

future roles of private pensions. Washington, D.C.: United States Special Committee on Aging.

Simpson, Ida, Kurt Back, and J. C. McKinney. 1966. Attributes of work, involvement in society, and self-evaluation in retirement. In I. Simpson and J. C. McKinney (eds.), *Social aspects of aging*. Durham, N.C.: Duke University Press, pp. 55–74.

Streib, Gordon. 1965. *Longitudinal study of retirement*. Ithaca, N.Y.: Cornell University.

Some Irrational Beliefs about Retirement in the United States

WILLIAM WITHERS

The arbitrary nature of our retirement system and the many irrational and mistaken beliefs about older workers make retirement problems difficult to solve. The retirement irrationalities dealt with in the following article include the sacrosanct age of sixty-five for retirement, erroneous assumptions about productivity and age, and the idea that the aged consume less and hence need less income. The trauma of retirement comes not simply from decreased income but also from societal institutions and values which make the retiree a social reject.

For many people retirement is a traumatic experience. It usually occurs prematurely and involuntarily at ages well below the proverbial three score and ten. Income is drastically reduced when it happens. At least 40 percent of all employees are not covered by private pensions, and many who supposedly are never receive a penny: they change jobs prior to eligibility, or the funds are dissipated. Social security benefits and savings seldom compensate for loss of the income they had when working or for the lack of a private pension.

But the trauma of retirement comes not simply from decreased income, although many regard it as the prime factor. Society has created institutions and values which make the retiree a social reject. Since he no longer works, he is relegated to an inferior social status. Such social downgrading was caused by the Industrial Revolution, which placed prime value on work rather than leisure (Jones, 1968).

Deprived of work, the social basis of self-respect, it becomes difficult for the individual to justify his leisure. Bravely he insists that his golf score, assisting his wife with the household chores, and volunteering for work with the Red Cross are adequate substitutes for being a business executive or a well paid blue-collar worker. He tries to rebel against the mores, but the attempt is made at an age when he has lost much of his capacity for rebellion.

The arbitrariness of our retirement systems and the many irrational attitudes and mistaken beliefs about older workers make the problems of

SOURCE: "Some Irrational Beliefs about Retirement in the United States" by William Withers is reprinted from *Industrial Gerontology*, Volume 1, Number 1, Winter 1974, published by The National Council on the Aging, Inc.

retirement difficult to solve. For example, consider the following assumptions for which there is little if any solid supporting evidence.

- The right age for retirement is sixty-five.
- Work capacity always declines with age.
- Older workers cannot be retrained.
- It does not pay to retrain older workers, because they retire so soon afterward.
- It is futile to retrain older workers, because no one will hire them.
- Older workers cannot be hired by companies with insurance programs, because it is impossible to fit them into these programs.
- It is undesirable to hire older workers as a group; they are so poorly educated.
- In retirement, income can be greatly reduced because old people consume less per person and need less income than young people.
- Older workers should be retired because in our advanced technological economy their labor is not needed. They should make room for younger workers.

The Sacrosanct Age

For many people, age sixty-five has been regarded as the right age for retirement, at least for men. It was legally sanctified in 1935 by the social security law. One fails to uncover any significant reason for this choice, except the fact that by then sixty-five had become common as a cut-off point in business. Moreover, life expectancy was approaching seventy, and a five-year prior retirement must have seemed logical.

It should not be implied here that a higher age should have been chosen due to the subsequent improvements in the health and productive capacity of older people. Rather, the difficulty with age sixty-five comes from the rigidities it introduced into our retirement systems. An obvious illustration is the involuntary retirement of persons at fifty-five or less with no social security for seven or ten more years. At the upper end of the age scale, still-capable people are forced to retire at sixty-five; if they go on working, their earnings are arbitrarily limited.

The meaninglessness of age sixty-five is evinced by the deviations from it. In reducing the eligibility for social security to sixty-two, first for women and then for men, even the federal government departed from the original plan. But the main deviation occurred in private business, seen in the decreasing participation rates for male workers in the labor force aged fifty-five to sixty-four from 83.4 percent to 80.5 percent between 1950 and 1973.

In many private and public pension systems, retirement may occur after twenty or twenty-five years of service without regard to age at the time of retirement, except that in many plans a person must be at least fifty-five. Thus in some pension systems age has become less of a qualification for retirement than years of employment. Where employees are not in jobs covered by pensions, separation from employment often occurs without a specific age related to it.

One man may be thrown out of work at forty-five simply because the business that employed him failed and he cannot find other work for which he is suited. The age at which people are considered too old for a job varies widely. In one occupation it may be forty-five; in another, sixty. In fact, age often is not so much a determining factor in the discharge of older workers as the pressure to employ younger people or management's effort to reduce or avoid large pension obligations.

Systems More Flexible in Europe

In some European countries, age requirements in public and private pension systems are more flexible than in the United States. Specific ages do not have the sanctity we bestow on age sixty-five. Public insurance plans are less uniform and varied to suit different types of employment. Austria, for example, has separate systems for wage earners, farmers, self-employed workers, and miners. Although the normal retirement ages for men and women are usually sixty to sixty-five, pensions may be received as much as five years earlier (Organization of Economic Cooperation and Development, 1970).

Also in European systems, a variety of circumstances permits workers to receive pensions prior to the specified retirement age. Austria, Italy, and Luxembourg allow a lower pensionable age when insurance payments have been made for thirty-five or forty years. In Austria and West Germany, the pensionable age may be reduced if a worker is currently unemployed and has been involuntarily so for one year. In Greece, Spain, and Italy, earlier retirement is allowed in unusually tiring or unhealthful employment. Austria, Denmark, and Turkey permit earlier retirement in case of chronic illness. In twelve countries, workers receiving pensions may continue to work and earn any amount. (These countries include France, Germany, Iceland, Ireland, Italy, Luxembourg, the Netherlands, Norway, Sweden, and Switzerland.)

Only three countries, Belgium, Greece, and Sweden, follow our practice of limiting the amount of pensions granted before a fixed retirement age to the reduced actuarial value of contributions, and only the United States and Great Britain restrict the amount a pensioner can earn after retirement.

Fixing retirement universally at a given age is irrational because it (1) bears no strict relationship to work capacity; (2) is not adapted to the conditions or practices of different industries or occupations; (3) limits older people's potential earnings even though security benefits fail to supply them with enough income; (4) creates an artificial reason for the premature discharge of older workers; and (5) if the pension system is based strictly on an actuarial basis, the number of years worked and contributions made, *not the retirement age*, should determine the eligibility of an employee to receive a pension.

Productivity Assumptions Are Erroneous

Irrationality about retirement age is closely associated with irrationality about older-worker productivity. If workers produce progressively less as they grow older, surely by sixty-five they should be put out to pasture. If the regression in capacity accelerates due to technological advancement, the argument for retirement at sixty-five becomes stronger. Closely related is the lesser degree of formal schooling of the present forty-five-to-sixty-five group, since it is assumed that the kinds of jobs that become available as technology advances require more education. If true, can the older worker be retrained as he is forced out of the labor market by technology? The answer is often negative, on the assumption that aging causes a decline in learning capacity.

Let us first consider the relevance of formal schooling. To begin, it is largely irrelevant except for a few professional occupations. Modern technology, by and large, does not require that the average worker have more formal schooling (Berg, 1970; Jaffe and Froomkin, 1968).

Secondly, older workers in the next couple of decades will have much more formal schooling than at present. For persons aged twenty-five to thirty-four the median number of years of school completed will increase from about 12.5 in 1970 to 13.0 in 1990; for those aged forty-five to fifty-four the median will rise from 12.1 to about 12.6; and for the age group fifty-five to sixty-four, from 10.6 to 12.5 (Johnston, 1973).

As to retraining, available evidence indicates that (1) older people can be retrained as readily as the young provided the training methods are suitable to them (McFarland, 1973), and (2) that intelligence, a factor in retraining, does not decline with age (Jamieson, 1968; Haberlandt, 1973). Longevity studies of intelligence, which at one time tended to prove its decline with age, more recently have demonstrated the opposite when tested groups are differentiated by educational and environmental background (Green and Reimanis, 1970).

Contentions such as the inadvisability of training older workers because they will soon retire, or that no one will hire them after retraining, are also fallacious (Mullan and Gorman, 1972). They assume inhibiting conditions which do not necessarily exist. If a worker, age sixty, is retrained at a cost of $1,000, this expenditure is similar to a capital investment. If the annual yield on an investment is high enough and spread over sufficient time, the pay-back point is reached and profits are earned. If the worker in our example were retired in a year, obviously it might not pay to retrain him, but why retire him in a year? Contradictory reasoning is involved in the no-hiring assumption.

As for the argument that labor productivity decreases with age, the evidence is contradictory; it depends on the individual and the job (Arvey and Mussio, 1973).

Do Old People Need Less Income?

Pensions and retirement income, including social security benefits, are far less on the average than preretirement incomes. Lower retirement income is rationalized by the assumption that people sixty-five and over need less to live on, explicitly stated in the U.S. Department of Labor's *Retired Couple's Budget for a Moderate Living Standard* (1966). They have no go-to-work expenses; they need less entertainment money; less clothes replacement; less furniture and so on. But a percentage decrease in need is seldom cited, nor are most fully aware of the amount of the decrease in income that occurs.

Jaffe (1972) found that the median annual incomes of families with sixty-five-year-old heads were 49 percent of those with heads fifty-five to sixty-four. The percentage has declined steadily from 56 percent in the period 1950 to 1954. Those over sixty-five living alone, in 1969 about two-fifths of the upper-age population, had an even greater percentage of income reductions.

But the assumption that "need is less" is wrong. A number of investigations reveal that older people's consumption needs increase. Even with such belt-tightening as they can and do manage, their legitimate needs cannot be reduced by 50 percent. Jaffe compared per-capita expenditures of cohorts of family heads of the same income class at ages sixty-five to seventy-four with those fifty-five to sixty-four. Total expenditures of the older heads were 9 percent higher. Clothing expenses were 5 percent less, but all other types of spending were greater.

In recent years the areas where old age expenditures increase, such as rent and medical care, have been inflated most. Notions about the reduced consumption of old people are a throwback to the early nineteenth-century rural life, when grandmother lived at home with her children and grandchildren in the family farmhouse and ate only porridge because she had lost her teeth. The landlord did not raise her rent, and her clothing and medical costs were negligible.

Even if we could assume that old people are able to reduce their standard of living drastically, the question remains, Why should they? Are they not entitled to live as well as anyone else? One suspects social rejection of the aged or a belief that only the young can enjoy life. Also involved is the work ethic labeling persons who don't make money inferior and unworthy of much income. They should be happy to get anything; they are "through," and society is through with them.

Aren't Older Workers Needed?

Has technology so increased productivity that we can produce all we need with a smaller and smaller labor force? A common belief is that we can. If true, there *is* a strong case for retiring people earlier.

We have been producing much more from year to year, with shorter hours and longer vacations. In real terms, the gross national product (GNP) has increased greatly since World War II; we are still growing, although at a rather slow rate. Thus mathematical calculations can be made which seem to prove that fewer and fewer workers are needed, that older workers will find it increasingly difficult to obtain jobs, and that the average retirement age will be further reduced.

Jaffe (1972) makes such calculations. He estimates, for example, that with a work year of 1,560 hours, a 3 percent average annual increase in output per man-hour and an average annual increase in the GNP of 4 percent, only 106 million workers will be needed in the year 2000, although the total minimum labor force will amount to 123 million in that year. His projections may come true because of our economic system's restrictive character, but his method of projection may be incorrect.

Output per man-hour is a physical figure which cannot really be compared with GNP growth, a monetary figure, even if converted for price change. In modern income flow analysis, full employment equilibrium is a parity of consumption and investment spending with incomes (wages, interest, rent, and profits) at a level that will employ everyone seeking work, whatever the output per man-hour. At income levels near full employment, output per man-hour declines. Whether we can or will employ everyone in the labor force depends on our willingness *to pay everyone*, and this in turn depends upon what we are willing *to pay for*.

Millions of Citizens Impoverished

If we consider our present economic system, we find millions of people at or below the poverty level. They lack adequate food, clothing, housing, education, social services, recreational facilities, and medical care. If we set aside all theoretical and statistical analysis, we are bound to conclude that we still have too much poverty. We do not produce enough despite our great economic progress; much of what we need to produce requires more manpower. It cannot be produced through machines that increase output per man-hour alone.

Can we mechanize doctors, teachers, entertainers, social workers so that one worker produces as much as three or four did before? The future picture of labor needs would seem different if seen from the standpoint of physical input and output. In money terms, we may need less labor; in physical terms, we need more.

The immediate question is: Can we expect the future economy to shift money demands so that it results in a fuller satisfaction of our physical needs? Though no one knows, must we assume that it cannot or will not? Ever since the New Deal, the distribution of income has been altered in the direction of greater public welfare.

The future need for older workers will depend in part on the population's age distribution and its absolute size. A stationary population appears to be in the offing; the chart of age distribution is changing from a pyramid into an oblong (U.S. Bureau of the Census, 1972). Assuming a stationary population and a growing economy, is it not reasonable to expect an increase in the demand for labor? If there will not be enough twenty-one-to-forty-four-year-old workers in the labor force to meet the accelerating demand for labor, employers will be forced to turn to those in the forty-five-to-sixty-five age group.

Irrationality Bases Are Multiple

The programs to cope with old-age problems in this country amount to a confused and jerry-built structure of social security and public assistance, resulting from conflicts with older beliefs and new social values which have emerged since World War II. In the early days of the New Deal, when the federal government assumed great responsibility for relief through the Federal Emergency Relief Administration (FERA) and the Works Progress Administration (WPA), a controversy developed in Washington over *need* and *right*. The FERA distributed millions of dollars in terms of need, but a public reaction soon developed against giving money "for nothing." In part the WPA was a response to this objection by making token work the basis of relief. Subsequently the social security system was established to provide pensions after sixty-five *as a right* created through payroll tax deductions from wages during the working lives of the claimants.

Aid to those with low incomes continued and also increased on both the local and national government levels. We compromised. Persons with insufficient income receive supplements partly based on need and partly on right. Since neither is enough to eliminate poverty in old age, it continues to be a serious national problem.

The concept of *right* stems from the nineteenth-century work ethic. Payment is made for work, and one has a right to an old-age income only if he has worked and saved for it. He saves either voluntarily or through compulsion in the social security system of saving. Consequently, to give people in their old age, or at any age, money which they have not earned or saved seriously violates the work ethic. Our social security system, originally (and which largely remains) actuarial in theory, is founded on the work ethic. Every major increase in benefits requires an increase in payroll deductions.

The concept of right may be questioned now just as it was in the early

New Deal days. If a person works hard all his life, does he have a right only to a substandard living merely because he could not save enough to provide an annuity that will pay better? Many of our public pension systems for teachers, policemen, firemen, and other civil servants have abandoned the actuarial basis. If civil servants have a right to a reasonable pension whether or not their payroll deductions are adequate to pay for it, why is the same not true for the great mass of social security recipients? What, then, is meant by *right*? Is it the right to receive what an individual saved or the right to a decent standard of living in his old age?

Several objections have been raised to discarding the actuarial basis for social security. Some say it would cost too much, but actually the country could afford it. The fact is we are not sure that we want to discard it. Basically that *is* the reason, and it leads us right back to the work ethic and to another element in the situation—derogation of age. In our time, Youth is King.

A wave of youthism has had a counterpart in the derogation of age since World War II. Few societies today place such high value on youth and so little value on age as does the United States. No doubt the results of studies by sociologists and anthropologists will show the value system is due partly to the war, which caused a veneration of power and youth and widespread rejection of older ways of thinking. Its emergent attitudes and values were related to youth. Emphasis on strength and the "looks" of things are all associated with youth. As youth was upgraded, naturally age went down. So some of our irrationalities about retirement and older workers are the rationalizations used to derogate age.

We cannot solve the problems of older workers, retirement, and old-age poverty unless we think straight about these matters. The removal of old-age poverty should be a prime national objective. Higher incomes for older people should be mandated. They can be provided if we have a higher rate of economic growth, fuller employment of those over forty-five, and public and private pensions based on need, far higher than those we have now.

Admittedly, all this will require more careful national planning than we now have and also basic revisions in our social values and priorities. But fundamental changes will not be possible if we cling to our retirement irrationalities.

NOTES

Dr. A. J. Jaffe suggested to the author that the subject of retirement might be explored from the standpoint of its irrationalities, which thus form the basis for this article.

REFERENCES

Arvey, Richard D. and Stephen J. Mussio, "Test Discrimination, Job Performance and Age," Industrial Gerontology, no. 16, pp. 20–29, Winter 1973.

Berg, Ivar. *Education and Jobs: The Great Training Robbery*, New York, Praeger Publishers for Urban Education, 1970.

Green, Russel F. and Gunars Reimanis, "The Age-Intelligence Relationship—Longitudinal Studies Can Mislead," *Industrial Gerontology*, no. 6, pp. 1–16, Summer 1970.

Haberlandt, Karl F. "Learning, Memory and Age," *Industrial Gerontology*, no. 19, pp. 20–37, Fall 1973.

Jaffe, A. J. "Retirement: A Cloudy Future," *Industrial Gerontology*, no. 14, pp. 1–88, Summer 1972.

———, and Joseph Froomkin. *Technology and Jobs*, New York, Praeger Publishers, 1968.

Jamieson, G. H. "Age, Speed, and Accuracy: A Study in Industrial Retraining," *Occupational Psychology*, 40 (4):237–242, 1968.

Johnston, Denis F. "Education of Workers: Projections to 1990," *Monthly Labor Review*, 96 (11):22–31, 1973.

Jones, H. A. "The Elderly Person," *Quarterly Journal of the National Old Peoples Welfare Council*, 81:2–8, June 1968.

McFarland, Ross A. "The Need for Functional Age Measurements in Industrial Gerontology," *Industrial Gerontology*, no. 19, pp. 1–19, Fall 1973.

Mullan, Cathal and Liam Gorman. "Facilitating Adaptation to Change: A Case Study in Retraining Middle-Aged and Older Workers at *Aer Lingus*," *Industrial Gerontology*, no. 15, pp. 20–39, Fall 1972.

Organization for Economic Cooperation and Development, *Flexibility of Retirement Age*, Paris, 1970.

U.S. Bureau of the Census. "Projections of the Population of the United States by Age and Sex: 1972 to 2020," *Population Estimates and Projections*, series P-25, no. 493, December 1972.

U.S. Department of Labor, Bureau of Labor Statistics. *Retired Couple's Budget for a Moderate Living Standard*, bulletin no. 1570-A, Autumn 1966.

Career Continuity and Retirement Plans of Men and Women Physicians: The Meaning of Disorderly Careers

JILL S. QUADAGNO

Few studies have been done on the retirement of women. This article examines three assumptions about women and work through interviews with men and women physicians who were approaching retirement or who had already retired. Older men and women physicians were equally likely to have had irregular work histories. For men these were due to historical circumstances, such as war, whereas the career interruptions of women were related to their basic social identity as wives and mothers. It was also shown that both male and female physicians derive their ideas about the meaning of work from the medical culture which defines intrinsic rewards as most satisfying. This in turn affects the ability to make realistic plans for retirement, since being active and being dedicated are both values that conflict with assumptions physicians make about retirement.

If we use the concept in this way, the proposition that commitment produces consistent lines of activity is tautological, for commitment, whatever our intuitions about its independent existence, is in fact synonymous with the committed behavior it is supposed to explain. It is a hypothesized event or condition whose occurrence is inferred from the fact that people act as though they were committed (Becker, 1960, p. 35).

Becker observed that in order to avoid this tautological error, it was necessary to "specify the characteristics of being committed independent of the behavior commitment [serves] to explain."

Unfortunately, studies of careers and achievement seem to have ignored Becker's warning by assuming that an irregular work history signifies a lack of serious career commitment. For example, Ginzberg

SOURCE: "Career Continuity and Retirement Plans of Men and Women Physicians: The Meaning of Disorderly Careers" by Jill S. Quadagno is reprinted from *Sociology of Work and Occupations*, Vol. 5, No. 1 (Feb. 1978), pp. 55–73, by permission of the publisher, Sage Publications, Inc.

(1966, p. 101), who found a high correlation between continuous work history and achievement, goes so far as to state that "a continuous work history is almost a prerequisite for high, or even good, achievement. A woman cannot reach the top in her field unless she is willing to devote a major portion of her life to work. Continuity is a necessary factor but not, of course, the only factor." In contrast, Holmstrom (1973, p. 56), who did in-depth interviewing on twenty professional women, found that they achieved professional success through untraditional routes, frequently working part-time at various points in their lives, but still managing to attain professional acclaim and recognition for their work.

If women have been marginal to the labor force,[1] then it is possible that they will have different but not nonexistent career orientations. One way to measure the career orientations of women is to explore the meaning which work has for them and to see if it differs from the meaning which men attach to work.

The Meaning of Work

The meaning of work has been found to be a crucial variable in predicting attitudes toward retirement. Friedmann and Orbach (1974) distinguish between intrinsic meanings of work deriving from the performance of the task itself and the extrinsic significances of work which structure an individual's participation in other spheres of life activity. Studies investigating the relationship between meaning of work and orientation to retirement have found a strong connection between these two variables. Those who stress extrinsic meanings of work are more likely to favorably anticipate retirement, while those who emphasize the intrinsic meanings which work holds view retirement unfavorably (Friedmann and Havighurst, 1954; Morse and Weiss, 1955; Simpson, Back, and McKinney, 1966).

Generally, these studies have compared meaning of work for those in different occupational categories, such as blue-collar, white-collar and professional, but they have not included women in their samples. The one major longitudinal study, including a national sample of nearly 2,500 subjects, which did compare the retirement attitudes of men and women across a broad range of occupational categories did not confirm the assumption that work is relatively meaningless to women (Streib and Schneider, 1971). In analyzing the relationship between occupational status and retirement patterns, Streib and Schneider (1971, p. 56) found a different work commitment according to occupational status.

> Upper white-collar and professional workers are generally more committed to their work and derive more satisfaction from it than do blue-collar workers. Thus we would anticipate that those who have higher-status occupations would be more reluctant to retire because of the importance of the role attached to the position. The "cost" of retiring would be too great.

They found that among all professionals, both men and women, there was a greater tendency to remain working or to retire and then return to work, while those in other occupational categories were more likely to retire earlier and remain retired. However, this pattern was not as clear for women as it was for men.

One problem with making comparisons between men and women within even a single census category such as professional is that significant internal labor market trends are not visible. For example, use of the category professional obscures the fact that professionals such as dentists, physicians, and engineers are predominantly male, while those occupations defined as semiprofessional such as nursing and teaching (excluding college-level teaching) are predominantly female (Grimm and Stern, 1974; Quadagno, 1976). Both nursing and teaching have entry and exit patterns that differ from those occupations classified as professions, and thus are not really comparable in terms of retirement orientations. A more meaningful measure would be to compare the retirement orientations of men and women within a single occupation.

Women in Medicine

Until very recently, few women have been employed in those occupations classified as "professional." Among physicians, an occupation which is assumed to require a high degree of career continuity, women have been a decided minority. From 1910 until 1970, less than 7 percent of all physicians were female[2] (Epstein, 1970; Sullivan, 1974). Women physicians who are presently age fifty-five or older began their careers at a time when they were not only a minority among women in the labor force in general,[3] but were even more deviant in that they chose an occupation that was traditionally male. In this sense, they were truly pioneers. Even if it is true, as Payne and Whittington (1976) suggest, that women are socialized to gain their identity from their roles as wives and mothers, it is not a necessary corollary that "the idea of commitment to a professional or work role appears inconsistent with the older women's image of the female role" (Payne and Whittington, 1976, p. 493). Again, this is a vague usage of the concept of commitment based on an assumption not confirmed by empirical investigation. The real meaning of careers for women can only be ascertained by disentangling the concept of commitment from the requirement of continuity. Only if this is done can attitudes toward retirement be understood, since retirement is not a static event but a process evolving out of a lifelong orientation to work. This study compares the career patterns of men and women physicians who are in the preretirement phase of life and measures both their orientation to work and retirement plans.

This study will examine three related assumptions about women and work which are prevalent in the gerontological literature:

1. Women have more irregular career patterns than men.
2. Due to irregular career patterns, women are less committed to work than men and attach different meanings to work.
3. Since work has a different meaning for women than it does for men, the transition to retirement is easier for women.

Methodology

This study of the work and retirement orientations of older physicians was a part of a larger study of career decisions of physicians throughout the life cycle. The method of quota sampling was used with subjects being selected on the basis of age and sex. The original study included one hundred physicians, fifty males and fifty females. This study deals only with those forty physicians between the ages of fifty-five and seventy-two, twenty men and twenty women, who could be classified in a preretirement category.[4] Approximately half the doctors practiced in small towns and half in large metropolitan areas. Two-thirds of those sampled had private practices, while one-third were connected with teaching hospitals, university clinics, or public health. No more than four physicians of any single specialty were interviewed.

The interview, which lasted for approximately one hour, consisted of a series of open-ended questions encompassing several topics, including the collection of life histories, information on the meaning of work, and plans for retirement. In regard to the life histories, specific work history information was collected. Subjects were asked to list each work experience from medical school to present occupation, including any interruptions, the reason for the interruption, and the amount of time of the interruption. Meaning of work was assessed by analyzing the responses to the question "What do you find to be the single most satisfying aspect of your work?" The responses were then categorized as "intrinsic" or "extrinsic" using the categories established in three other studies of the orientation to work of physicians (Becker et al., 1961; Coker, 1966; Back, 1958). Intrinsic reasons are those derived from the occupational culture of medicine[5] as opposed to lay definitions of occupational success. Intrinsic satisfactions defined by a subcultural value system are a type of side-bet referred to by Becker (1960, p. 39) which explain consistent lines of activity independent of the activity itself. In other words, adherence to subcultural definitions of success is an indicator which should help to explain continuity. In this sample intrinsic satisfactions included exercising active medical responsibility, interest in the subject matter, intellectual problem solving, patient contact, altruism, and enjoyment of the technical skills required. Extrinsic rewards corresponded to lay definitions of success and included such factors as money, prestige, hours, amount of time for self, and residence (type of town). The subjects were also asked a series of questions about retirement in terms of whether or not they were making active plans to retire and what these plans were.

TABLE 1 Career interruptions by sex of respondent

No. of times career interrupted	Male physicians (%) (N = 20)	Female physicians (%) (N = 20)
Never	15.0	25.0[a]
One	70.0	45.0
Two or more	15.0	30.0

Chi square = 2.59, d.f. = 2, N.S.

a) These women were all unmarried.

Findings

Assumption 1: If the assumption that women have more irregular careers than men is true, then women should have more career interruptions than men. This assumption is derived from the idea that women take time out from work for the demands of marriage and child rearing. As shown in Table 1, this assumption did not prove to be true. While the distribution of career interruptions differed for men and women, the overall number was not significantly different. Men were most likely to have one career interruption. Married women were also most likely to have one career interruption, but many had two or more career interruptions.

A second related assumption is that women have longer periods of time away from work. From Table 2, it can be seen that women do spend longer periods of time away from work than men but that this difference is small.

Assumption 2: If women are less committed to work than men, they should attach different meanings to work. Less commitment should mean less attachment to intrinsic meanings derived from medical culture and more attachment to extrinsic meanings derived from lay definitions of satisfaction, since acceptance of subcultural values is one side-bet confirming commitment. As illustrated in Table 3, this did not prove to be the case. There was no significant difference between men and women on the meaning attached to work. In fact, women physicians were somewhat more likely to emphasize the intrinsic rewards of medicine derived from the definitions of the medical culture rather than lay definitions of success.

Assumption 3: If the retirement transition is easier for women than it is

TABLE 2 Length of interruption by sex of respondent

Average length of interruption	Male physicians (N = 20)	Female physicians (N = 20)
Total time in years	3.1	4.3

316 WORK, RETIREMENT, AND LEISURE

TABLE 3 Meaning of work by sex of respondent[6]

Meaning of work	Male physicians (%) (N = 20)	Female physicians (%) (N = 20)
Intrinsic	75.0	85.0
Extrinsic	25.0	15.0

Chi square = .625, d.f. = 1, N.S.

for men, then they should be more willing to think about retirement as a viable life option and make definite plans to retire. Table 4 shows that most of the physicians in this sample, regardless of gender, were not making any plans for retirement. This is consistent with other literature on retirement among professionals who find intrinsic satisfactions in work (Friedmann and Havighurst, 1954). What is unique in this case is the inclusion of women in these findings.

Discussion

It was demonstrated above that female physicians did not have more disorderly careers than male physicians in terms of number of career interruptions, although they were likely to have had somewhat longer interruptions in their careers. What was the nature of these interruptions and what effects did they have on individual career paths? For the male physicians the main career interruption was war. Nearly all the male physicians were affected in some major way by World War II, and one of the younger physicians in this group was in the Korean War. For many these career interruptions had a serious effect on careers and medical practices. This was particularly true for those in mid-career at the outbreak of World War II. Many of the physicians in this age cohort graduated from medical school during the 1930s. This meant that they began their careers during the Depression. Many who were just beginning to get private practices established, after years of near poverty, either volunteered or were drafted at this critical point. An elderly surgeon describes the effects of a four-year interruption on his career:

Well, my two young men [two resident physicians] came along, and they got

TABLE 4 Plans for retirement by sex of respondent

Retirement plans	Male physicians (%) (N = 20)	Female physicians (%) (N = 20)
Yes	30.0	25.0
No	70.0	75.0

Chi square = .124, d.f. = 1, N.S.

started before I got back and out of the army and all my jobs had just disappeared. The schools, the railway job disappeared, and all those jobs that I had had were through when I got back. And some of the others I turned over to my young men. See, the disruption came just at the wrong time, from the time I was thirty-eight until I was forty-three. See, things were very slow during the Depression, and I almost stopped doing surgery. Then I just got going again from 1935 to 1940 and had to take off again. Then I was gone during the war and had to get going all over again.

In another case an obstetrician experienced two interruptions, one during the war when he was just beginning his career and a second interruption when he was in his early fifties due to illness. The first interruption retarded the development of his practice, while the second caused him to alter the course of his career completely.

The academic side of medicine always interested me. If it weren't the middle of the Depression, I probably would have been a medical school teacher rather than a medical practitioner. But I did a little general practice at first merely because everyone was destitute at that time and then went into ob-gyn privately up to the time of the war. During the war I did very largely ob-gyn. As a matter of fact, I was in the army in a general hospital. When I came back, it was not easy to begin all over again, but I did and practiced until 1956 when I became ill and wasn't able to work for two years. Then I came to the health service.

In contrast to the men, the women were likely to be pulled from their careers by the expected factors of marriage and child rearing, particularly the latter.[7] A typical pattern was to finish medical school, do an internship or residency, and then drop out of medicine for a few years to take care of small children. Some returned to medicine gradually, working part-time first and then reentering the profession on a full-time basis as their children grew. Others waited longer and then perhaps returned to school for some additional training before returning to full-time work. Their methods for working out their careers tended to be idiosyncratic. With other female physicians nearly nonexistent for this age cohort, no role models were present to guide their decision making. As one successful pediatrician in private practice and mother of four noted:

When I started, there weren't many women so there weren't a lot of people I could go to and say, How did you do it? Because the one woman I was working with was not married, she had no children, so she didn't have these problems. The ones I knew the best were not married.

As with the men, the effect which these disruptions had on their careers varied. Some women managed easily to return to medicine and had successful practices. Others made compromises for their families so great that they could never be reconciled with a successful medical practice. For example, one woman who was trained in obstetrics and gynecology at a prestigious medical center describes the effects of marriage and child rearing on her career:

I had practiced about three years when I got married and practiced ob-gyn for two years after that shortly before my first baby was born. Then I mostly stayed home for about three years, since there was about eighteen months between my two children. And then after that I did school health while my kids were growing up. Women raising children will do jobs that no one else will take. I also did health examinations for the Y and preschool roundup and all the other jobs that doctors who have offices don't have time for.

She never returned to her original specialty, obstetrics-gynecology, due to the difficulty of reconciling the irregular hours with the demands of raising a family. When she was widowed at age forty-five, she took a job with a college health service.

My main motivation to switch from school health to something else was I had two kids in college. School health pays $2.50 an hour. It wasn't anything that was particularly attractive. It was a semivolunteer job—not for me because it was largely what I was supporting the family on—but I certainly couldn't support two kids in college with it.

Both men and women in this sample experienced major career disruptions. For some they were merely an inconvenience, while for others they drastically changed the course of the individual's career. It should be noted that although there was no quantitative difference between men and women in regard to career interruptions, there was a qualitative difference. Men who interrupted their careers for war remained practicing physicians, while women temporarily abandoned the work role for the wife-mother role. However, neither were in a position to build private practices, so that this difference may be relatively insignificant for this age cohort.

Meaning of Work

The insignificance of the differences in type of career interruption of men and women becomes apparent when examining specific satisfactions associated with work. The single most important value expressed by both men and women was being "active," being able to exercise medical responsibility, a value derived directly from medical culture. For example, one surgeon noted, "What I find most satisfying about medicine is doing surgery, being able to do something besides ordering tests and giving medication, to be able to do something decisive." As one anesthesiologist in private practice stated,

One of my favorite courses in medical school was physiology, and anesthesiology is essentially applied physiology and applied pharmacology, and it's very much like a dog lab. You inject some atropine and you listen and the heart rate speeds up or you give a medication and you paralyze. So it's very much like that and that's something I've always enjoyed. It's almost like you're in a laboratory.

In contrast, a few expressed extrinsic satisfactions with medicine more reflective of lay definitions of success. For example, one surgeon who had been chief of surgery at a small hospital and was planning to retire soon stated, "I was a poor little farm boy and being a doctor gave me a chance to be somebody, and I had some pretty high-class people coming to me at one time."

The assumption that work means something different to women than it does to men is false in this instance. While women are sometimes forced to place themselves in less desirable work situations due to family demands and the lack of institutionalized means of handling these demands, their feelings about work come from values learned in medical school and through collegial association. Men may also find themselves in undesirable work situations due to personal difficulties or historical circumstances which affect career paths, and these irregularities may appear to an outsider to signify a lack of commitment. However, these factors are independent of the values placed on work. The woman quoted earlier who had had a very irregular career and had at one time worked for $2.50 an hour said, "You have to love medicine and be dedicated. It's your whole life." A male physician echoed her sentiments: "If you embark on a thing like medicine, there is no half way point. People speak of slowing down, limiting practice. This is nonsense. You either do medicine or you don't, one of the two. You take care of the people when they need you." In contrast, a male gynecologist who had had a very successful private practice expressed disillusionment with the value of commitment. When asked if he would do anything differently if he had his life to lead over, he replied:

> Yes, I'd work in the basic sciences as a teacher and not do clinical medicine. I think the amount of effort you put into it is not commensurate with the results. An obstetrician never knows whether he'll be home for a meal. He probably won't. I used to work twenty to twenty-one hours a day without taking my clothes off, day in and day out. I never knew my children. I could never go to a movie and sit through a whole show without the phone ringing. I think I would rather be a tramp or a teacher, I don't know what.

It is the acceptance of the value system rather than the regularity of the career path that is the critical indicator of commitment, and researchers who assume that consistency is synonymous with commitment are missing an important theoretical linkage. A physician may maintain consistency without commitment or may be highly committed without showing consistency.

Retirement

While the subject of retirement was obviously a matter of considera-tion for most of the physicians, it was generally treated in a rather idealistic or unrealistic manner. For example, one woman physician stated:

> Well, I hope to retire from here, but I don't plan to retire from being a doctor.

Down near Branson, there is the School of the Ozarks which has a very beautiful infirmary and one nurse to run it. And I would like to get down there and teach part-time if necessary. If not that, why perhaps the Peace Corps or some sort of a mission project.

Similarly, a sixty-six-year-old former chairman of pediatrics at a large medical center expressed ambivalence when questioned about plans for retirement.

Q. How do you feel about retirement?
A. Retiring from the job of being chairman is great because that's a terrible headache.
Q. How about retiring permanently? Do you have any plans?
A. No, I don't know what I'm going to do when I have to get out. I can't imagine myself being idle. I don't think I'm cut out for sitting on my hands and doing nothing. I'm sure I'll find something to do but just what it will be, I don't know.

Thus for many the intrinsic rewards attached to work which signified idealistic commitment to medicine prevented them from being able to formulate clear plans for retirement. The value of remaining active and the ideal of dedication were frequently greater determinants of life choices than the fulfillment of personal needs.

Conclusion

Three related assumptions concerning the relationship of women to work and retirement shown to be prevalent in the literature were examined among a sample of practicing physicians between the ages of fifty-five and seventy. None of them were shown to be valid assumptions for this particular sample. One of the most important issues discussed dealt with the assumption that there is a relationship between regular work histories and commitment to work. Since women have traditionally been employed in lower-paying, lower-status occupations where career interruptions are common, it has been assumed that women in general have less commitment to work than men. However, when an occupation such as physician is examined, men and women show similar degrees of work commitment and are also equally likely to have irregular career patterns. The real issue is that the career interruptions of men occur for different reasons than they do for women, and these reasons are evaluated differently by society. As Holmstrom (1973, p. 54) notes:

Career interruptions are also partly a matter of perception. There is a difference between how different interruptions are defined. Men often interrupt their careers for military service. Women often interrupt their careers for child rearing. . . . And these interruptions, at least up to now, have been perceived very differently by employers and educators. In a curious paradox of human values, men have been criticized only slightly for career interruptions in which their task was to kill off other members of the human race; but women have been severely criticized for taking time away from their profession in order to raise the next generation.

Equally significant was the discovery that these career interruptions are relatively meaningless in terms of predicting career commitment and attitudes toward retirement. Physicians learn a set of values from the occupational culture of medicine which override externally derived attitudes. Intrinsic rewards of work are viewed as most satisfying. This in turn affects the ability to make realistic retirement plans, since being active and being dedicated are both values that conflict with assumptions physicians make about retirement.

Sociologists have defined a professional career as a full-time, all-consuming activity. This static and rigid picture of the occupational structure is not only inaccurate but is harmful both to women whose nurturant activities are denigrated and to older individuals who accept a set of values which makes it difficult for them to extricate themselves from the labor force.

The small sample size of this study made it impossible to control for some potentially relevant variables, such as type of practice, specialty, and location site. In this sense, the assumptions were not truly tested in terms of generalizing the findings to the retirement situation of all physicians. However, this was not the purpose of the study. The orientation was exploratory in nature, an attempt to examine individual perceptions of the retirement process and to define problem areas which could then be more systematically tested on a larger sample.

The career interruptions of the men and women physicians were qualitatively different, since the men continued to practice medicine while the women moved into an entirely different sphere of activity. One could argue that in different historical times when there is not a military emergency, the differences in career interruptions for men and women physicians would be great. On the other hand, it is equally possible to argue that younger women physicians may be less likely to interrupt careers for child rearing and may rear children while continuing to work full time. The real issue is whether women will define career success in terms of the male model, or whether they will in the future renegotiate the definitions of success inherent in the occupational culture as it presently exists. The increasing number of women in medicine should eventually alter the way in which a career in medicine is defined and judged.

NOTES

I would like to thank David Mangen, Helena Lopata, and Harold Orbach for comments on an earlier draft of this manuscript. Support for this project was provided by a predoctoral fellowship from the Midwest Council for Social

Research in Aging, and thanks are also due to Warren Peterson for his sponsorship.

1. When the work histories of women have been analyzed, they have been shown to be more irregular than those of men. A study by the U.S. Department of Labor Women's Bureau (1969, p. 55) showed that "only 42 percent of the women who worked at some time in 1967 were employed full time the year round. In contrast, 70 percent of all men with work experience in 1967 were full-time year-round workers." Similar findings were reported by Lopata and Steinhart (1971). However, a major difficulty in making generalizations about the work consistency of women in comparison with men is that it may be a status difference rather than a true difference in work patterns that is being measured. Women, in general, tend to be employed in lower-status, lower-paying occupations than men, particularly being clustered in white-collar clerical work (Kreps, 1971, p. 37).

2. This is rapidly changing as women enter medical schools in increasing numbers. Women represented 12.3 percent of all medical students in 1972, 16.8 percent in 1973, and this figure is still increasing (Duke, 1973; Sullivan, 1974).

3. Although approximately 40 percent of all women in this age cohort had worked at some time in their lives, the typical pattern for most women was to work during their early twenties before marriage and children and then drop out of the labor force entirely (Riley and Foner, 1968, p. 44).

4. The mean age for male physicians was 62.3, and the mean age for female physicians was 61.6.

5. Becker et al. (1961) refer to an occupational culture as an esoteric set of standards shared by colleagues for judging, among other things, occupational success.

6. These figures closely correspond to the findings of other studies investigating the meaning of work to physicians. Most physicians emphasize the intrinsic rewards of work (Becker et al., 1961).

7. All the men and fifteen of the women had been married for at least twenty years. Five of the women had never married. Four of the men and five of the women were presently widowed. There were no divorces among this sample. The mean number of children was 2.7 for the married males and 2.5 for the married females. One woman physician had five children.

REFERENCES

Atchley, Robert C. 1973. *The social forces in later life: An introduction to social gerontology.* Belmont, Cal.: Wadsworth.

Back, Kurt W. 1958. Public health as a career of medicine: Secondary choice within a profession. *American Sociological Review* 23 (October):533–541.

Becker, Howard S. 1960. Notes on the concept of commitment. *American Journal of Sociology* 66 (No. 1):32–40.

Becker, Howard S., Blanche Geer, Everett Hughes, and Anselm Strauss. 1961. *Boys in white: Student culture in medical school.* Chicago: Univ. of Chicago Press.

Coker, Robert E. 1966. Medical students' attitudes toward public health. *Milbank Memorial Fund Quarterly* 44 (April):155–180.

Cumming, Elaine, and William Henry. 1961. *Growing old.* New York: Basic Books.

Duke, William F. 1973. Women students in U.S. medical schools: Past and present trends. *Journal of Medical Education* 48 (February):186–190.

Epstein, Cynthia Fuchs. 1970. *Women's place: Options and limits in professional careers.* Berkeley: Univ. of California Press.

Friedmann, Eugene A., and Robert Havighurst. 1954. *The Meaning of work and retirement.* Chicago: Univ. of Chicago Press.

Friedmann, Eugene A., and Harold Orbach. 1974. Adjustment to retirement. Pp. 609–645 in S. Arieti (ed.), *American handbook of psychiatry.* Vol. 1, 2nd ed. New York: Basic Books.

Ginzberg, Eli. 1966. *Life styles of educated women.* New York: Columbia Univ. Press.

Grimm, James W., and Robert N. Stern. 1974. Sex roles and internal labor market structures: The female semiprofessions. *Social Problems* 21 (June):690–705.

Holmstrom, Lynda Lytle. 1973. *The two-career family.* Cambridge, Mass.: Schenkman.

Kreps, Juanita. 1971. *Sex in the marketplace: American women at work.* Baltimore: Johns Hopkins Press.

Lopata, Helena Z., and F. Steinhart. 1971. Work histories of American urban women. *Gerontologist* 11(4):27–36.

Morse, N.C., and R.R. Weiss. 1955. The function and meaning of work and the job. *American Sociological Review* 20:191–198.

Payne, Barbara, and Frank Whittington. 1976. Older women: An examination of popular stereotypes and research evidence. *Social Problems* 23 (April): 489–504.

Quadagno, Jill. 1976. Occupational sex-typing and internal labor market distributions: An assessment of medical specialties. *Social Problems* 23 (April):442–452.

Riley, Matilda, and Anne Foner. 1968. *Aging and society.* New York: Russell Sage Foundation.

Simpson, I.H., Kurt W. Back, and J.C. McKinney. 1966. Attributes of work, involvement in society, and self-evaluation in retirement. In I.H. Simpson and J.C. McKinney (eds.), *Social aspects of aging.* Durham, N.C.: Duke Univ. Press.

Streib, Gordon F., and Clement J. Schneider. 1971. *Retirement in American society.* Ithaca: Cornell Univ. Press.

Sullivan, Margaret A. 1974. A new era: Challenges for the woman physician. *Journal of the American Medical Women's Association* 29 (January):9–11.

U.S. Department of Labor, Women's Bureau. 1968. *Part-time employment of women.* WB 68–151. Washington, D.C.: Government Printing Office.

Retirement and Leisure Participation: Continuity or Crisis?

ROBERT C. ATCHLEY

Recreation and leisure fill people's needs for relaxation, entertainment, and personal development. As people age, they spend more time in leisure pursuits. A question has been raised as to whether leisure roles can fill the void created by the absence of work. Some researchers believe it cannot. According to this perspective, a person's occupational identity pervades all aspects of life, so that leisure activities cannot provide the self-respect that comes from being gainfully employed. However, other studies show that anxiety and depression do not accompany retirement, indicating that retired people do not feel a loss of identity. Continuity in other roles, including family relationships and leisure activities, helps to maintain self-esteem. In fact, one-third of those who retired voluntarily did so to devote more time to leisure pursuits. It appears that a distorted view of the meaning of work may exist in the literature.

Recreation and leisure are institutions that are different yet closely related. *Recreation* refers to activities such as sports, games, the vacation, hobbies, and the like that aim to renew mind and body by either relieving them of tension or delivering them from boredom. Recreation is thus primarily a reaction to some state of body or mind. *Leisure* activities, on the other hand, are pursued as ends in themselves. They are unplanned and unrequired. Leisure is primarily *action*, directed generally toward self-development.

Leisure and recreation share one prime characteristic: both are reserved for time periods not already set aside for working at a job, sleeping, performing domestic tasks, or meeting family obligations.

Recreation and leisure aim primarily at relaxation, entertainment, and personal development. As such, they are institutions that are oriented around the needs of individuals, particularly the needs for tension management, enhancement of self-esteem, and identity (Atchley, 1970).

For simplicity we will lump recreation and leisure together under the general label of leisure.

Information about patterns of leisure among older people is essential in examining the nature of growing old. People gradually expand the time

SOURCE: Copyright 1971 by the Gerontological Society. Reprinted by permission from *The Gerontologist*, Vol. 11, No. 1 (1971).

they spend in leisure roles as age increases (Riley and Foner, 1968). Upon retirement, leisure pursuits occupy a great deal of the individual's time, and there is a question as to whether leisure roles can fill the void left by work. There is little doubt that leisure can fill the *time* formerly occupied by work, but the problem is whether leisure is capable of giving the individual the kind of *self-respect* and identity that he got from the job.

The Identity Crisis Theory

Perhaps the most articulate and repeatedly quoted spokesman on the negative side is Miller (1965), who has taken the following position:

1. Retirement is basically degrading because although there is an implication that retirement is a right that is earned through lifelong labor, there is also a tacit understanding that this reward is being given primarily to coax the individual from a role he is no longer able to play.
2. Occupational identity invades all of the other areas of the person's life. Accordingly, the father and head of household roles, the friend role, and even leisure roles are mediated by the individual's occupational identity.
3. The identity that comes from work is related to deeply ingrained values as to which roles can give a legitimate identity.
4. Leisure roles cannot replace work as a source of self-respect and identity because it is not supported by norms that would make this legitimate. That is, the retired person does not *feel justified* in deriving self-respect from leisure. Leisure is simply not defined as a legitimate source of self-respect by the general population.
5. Beyond the simple need to be doing something there is a need to be engaged in something that is defined by most people as utilitarian or gainful in some way. Thus the stamp collector must emphasize the financial rewards, paintings are offered for sale, or woodworking is confined to immediately "useful" objectives. In short, the only kinds of leisure that can provide identity are work-substitutes.
6. There is a stigma of "implied inability to perform" that is associated with retirement and carried over into all of the individual's remaining roles and that results in an identity breakdown.
7. Identity breakdown involves a process whereby the individual's former claims to prestige or status are invalidated by the implied inability to perform, and this proves embarrassing for the stigmatized person. Miller calls this result "the portent of embarrassment."
8. Embarrassment leads to the individual's withdrawal from the situation or prevents him from participating to begin with.
9. The answer lies not in inventing new roles for the aging, but rather

in "determining what roles presently exist in the social system
... offering vicarious satisfactions, that can reduce the socially
debilitating loss accompanying occupational retirement."
10. Miller implies that creating an ethic which would make full-time
leisure an acceptable activity for a worthwhile person is a possible
way to resolve the dilemma of the retired leisure participant.

Miller's analysis of the situation is an insightful one. Nevertheless, it
rests on the assumption that prior to retirement the individual derived
his identity primarily from his job. Also implied in Miller's identity crisis
theory is the assumption that most people want to stay on the job, since
this is their main identity, and that therefore most retirement is involuntary. This is no doubt related to the fact that Miller leaves out of his
discussion those who retired voluntarily. Miller also implies that he
subscribes to the activity theory of adjustment to aging since he assumes
that lost roles need to be replaced (Havighurst, 1963).

Evidence Concerning Identity Crisis

There are several sets of questions which thus emerge from an examination of the identity crisis theory presented by Miller. First, is his portrayal
of the relationship between involuntary retirement and leisure an accurate
one? Second, is the pattern, even if accurate, typical of most older leisure
participants? Third, what is the pattern among those who are voluntarily
retired? Data from recent studies of retired people can shed some light on
these questions.

Some of these data will be drawn from the Scripps Foundation Studies
in Retirement, a series that has produced several published reports
(Atchley, 1967, 1969; Cottrell, 1970; Cottrell and Atchley, 1969) and which
is still continuing.[1]

1. Retirement has been found to result in a loss of a sense of involvement, *but this was unrelated to other self-concept variables of optimism and autonomy* (Back and Guptill, 1966).

Disengagement theory tells us to expect some withdrawal from
involvement, and it is noteworthy that this loss of involvement does not
appear to have adverse results for other aspects of the self-concept. This
leads to skepticism concerning Miller's "portent of embarrassment."

2. Strong work-orientation *is* frequently found among retired people,
but this is *not* accompanied by anxiety, depression, dislike of retirement,
or withdrawal from activity (Cottrell and Atchley, 1969).

Our findings indicate that a strong positive orientation toward work
"*exists* apart from the job itself but . . . has no *import for the individual*
apart from the job itself." In terms of adjustment, there was apparently *no*
negative result from carrying a positive orientation toward work into
retirement.

3. When men retired from upper-white-collar, middle-status, and semiskilled jobs were compared, it was found that the upper-white-collar people had internalized occupationally oriented norms. Middle-status workers were oriented toward specific tasks and situations often resulting in the acquisition of skills that were transferable to leisure situations. Semiskilled workers were engaged mainly in activities oriented about things (Simpson, Back, and McKinney, 1966).

Of these occupational strata, the upper-white-collar stratum comes closest to Miller's model of the retired person. These are work-oriented people. However, neither of the other two strata fit the work-oriented model. Middle-status people develop skills on the job that carry over into other roles. Thus the salesman may carry his smooth-talking style over into his leisure roles. Semiskilled people are oriented around the job, but not necessarily because they have any deep abiding commitment to the job. For them it may be purely a matter of not having been trained for anything *other than* a job.

4. The *style* of work activities tends to remain dominant in retirement.

Simpson et al. (1966) found that upper-white-collar jobs were oriented about *symbols*, middle-status jobs were oriented around *people*, and semiskilled jobs were oriented around *things*. The middle-status people showed the greatest continuity in style from pre- to post-retirement. This suggests that retirement, and leisure roles in particular, offer greater opportunities for practicing interpersonal skills than for practicing skills oriented around symbols or things.

The implication of this finding is that it is not so much the *ethic* learned on the job that interferes with successful pursuit of leisure in retirement but rather the skills. Those who learn job skills that cannot be readily used in leisure pursuits have a hard time adjusting to an increase in leisure unless they have had the opportunity to learn these skills elsewhere. This concept is reinforced by the finding that in terms of retirement activities middle-status people who had thing-oriented jobs resembled the semi-skilled more than they did their middle-status peers.

5. In addition, data from retired railroaders indicate that there are continuities in the situations people face that minimize the impact of retirement (Cottrell, 1970). Family, friends, church, and other roles continue despite retirement. Cottrell's data suggest that the portent of embarrassment and loss of identity is minimized by the tendency to select friends on the job from among those of one's own age. The end results of this process is to create *retirement cohorts* of people who have known each other on the job and who retire together. In the Scripps Foundation studies of retirement this phenomenon has been observed among those retired from occupations as diverse as teacher, railroader, and telephone operator (Atchley, 1967; Cottrell, 1970; Cottrell and Atchley, 1969). It results in a group of retired friends who have known each other for years and whose concepts of each other involve a great deal more than the mere

playing of an occupational role. Nevertheless, this group is also capable of sustaining the prestige gained on the job because they know all about how this prestige was generated.

To the extent that older people are geographically mobile, they might tend to lose these continuities, but most retired people, particularly the semi- or unskilled, do not move away from their place of long-term residence (Riley and Foner, 1968).

6. Cottrell's data (1970) also indicate that as the concept of retirement is incorporated into the culture, the tendency to look upon work as a temporary part of life increases.

The implication here is that if work is not a permanent part of life, then one puts greater emphasis on other parts of life that are more permanent. For example, if a man knows the day he begins working that he will work twenty-five years and then quit, he is very likely to avoid letting work become an all-consuming part of his life.

7. In terms of ethic, it is not at all clear whether most people regard work as a necessary prerequisite for making leisure legitimate or simply as a necessary economic function which interferes with the pursuit of leisure. It *is* quite clear that our heritage has always included those who did not work because they could afford not to. Accordingly, legitimacy of leisure may rest not so much on work as on the idea that the money used to sustain leisure came from a legitimate source, that is, it was either earned by working or inherited. In the Scripps Foundation studies of retirement many middle-income retired people have shown not the slightest reluctance to embrace leisure roles, given the fact that their income was secure (Atchley, 1967; Cottrell and Atchley, 1969). Perhaps if most retired people were not pauperized by retirement, the "portent of embarrassment" mentioned by Miller would fade away.

8. Nearly two-thirds of retired men retired as a result of their own decision. *Less than one in five* was retired involuntarily as a result of reaching retirement age (Cottrell and Atchley, 1969; Riley and Foner, 1968).

By leaving out those in poor health and those who voluntarily retired, Miller (1965) effectively limited the group he was talking about to less than a third of the retired men and an even smaller proportion of the retired women.

Identity Continuity Theory

It may seem that we have dwelt too long and too deeply with the relation between leisure and retirement. Nevertheless, if we are to understand the nature of leisure among older people, it must be put in its proper context. Miller's position is a very common one and is constantly being used as a basis for decisions that influence older people's lives. Our detailed examination of this approach has shown it to be at least questionable and very possibly false.

To begin with, there is evidence in the Scripps Foundation studies and elsewhere that the adjustment problems sometimes associated with retirement are *not* the result of the loss of work and the identity it provides. In fact, a highly positive orientation toward work had little influence on retirement adjustment. There is no indication that highly work-oriented people are unable to take up leisure roles; in fact, just the opposite. We could find no concrete evidence that retirement in and of itself negatively influences the *quality* of one's family life, friendships, or associations.

Accordingly, an alternative to Miller's identity crisis theory of the relationship between retirement and leisure might contain the following points:

Many people are never highly work-oriented and thus they may very well provide a model for others concerning what it would be like to derive self-satisfaction from leisure. In addition, the ethic of the system allows this as long as the money used to lead a life of leisure is legitimately earned.

Self-respect *can* be gained from leisure pursuits in retirement if (*a*) the individual has enough money, and (*b*) he has a cohort of retired friends who will accept his full-time leisure as legitimate and help him to negate the stigma of implied inability to perform, if such a stigma exists. As retirement becomes more and more an expected part of the life cycle, this orientation should spread beyond the cohort of friends. In any event, the retired individual will continue to see *himself* as a railroader, teacher, etc. even though he no longer plays the role. Thus the crux of this alternative theory is *identity continuity*.

Wide occupational differences exist in the concept of the usefulness of an activity. There are many people for whom interpersonal interaction *was* their occupational skill, and it is this *activity* that is useful rather than some abstract goal. In this sense, then, leisure can act as a work-substitute where it needs to and provide identity continuity.

Very few people rest their entire identity on a single role. If they did, there would surely be far more suicides than there are now. The only thing that makes failure bearable is that we seldom fail in all our roles at once.

Each person generally has several roles that he stakes his identity on. Work may be at or near the top, but not necessarily so. There simply is not the kind of homogeneous consensus on the value of work that would keep it at the top for everyone. In fact, the many systems of competing values in a complex society *insure* that there will be a wide variety of self-values. Thus the probability that retirement will lead to a complete identity breakdown is slight, and there may be just as many people who rely on leisure pursuits for self-respect as there are who rely on work, particularly among those with unsatisfying jobs.

Some decline of involvement may be natural as the individual adjusts to declining energy, but most people expand their leisure involvement when they retire. Nevertheless, this change is not regarded negatively by most retired people. In fact, most people voluntarily retire, and many of these volunteers cite a preference for leisure as their reason for retiring.

Conclusion

There is no doubt that there are some people for whom Miller's identity crisis pattern is a grim reality, but it does not appear to be a typical pattern, even among the minority of older people who are forced to retire. Among voluntary retirees, a third retired to devote more time to leisure. The ethical issue may be difficult for some to resolve, but not for the majority, even among the highly work-oriented.

The identity continuity theory and the data which give rise to it suggest that leisure can have a great deal of positive value as a bridge between pre- and post-retirement life and that this value will increase in the future.

Between the two of them, the identity continuity and crisis theories probably account for the majority of cases. Nevertheless, to settle the inevitable question as to the proportions of retired people who fit each model, studies are needed that are broader in scope and wider in range than any thus far brought to bear on the question. One of the intriguing but often infuriating aspects of studying aging in the United States is the sometimes overpowering geographic, social, and psychological diversity of the older population. Perhaps further probing will uncover still other patterns of relationship between retirement and leisure participation.

While the research that has been done seems to support the identity continuity model more than Miller's identity crisis model, there is still a great deal of work that needs to be done before either model can be used with a high degree of confidence.

NOTES

1. The research in this series has been partially supported by grants AA-66-4-012 and AA-4-67-012-02 from the Administration on Aging, U.S. Department of Health, Education, and Welfare.

REFERENCES

Atchley, R. C. Retired women: A study of self and role. PhD dissertation, American University, Washington, 1967.

Atchley, R. C. Respondents vs. refusers in an interview study of retired women: An analysis of selected characteristics. *Journal of Gerontology*, 1969, 24, 42–47.

Atchley, R. C. Recreation and Leisure. In *Understanding American Society: The dynamics of social institutions*. Belmont, Calif.: Wadsworth, 1970.

Back, K. W., and Guptill, C. S. Retirement and self-ratings. In I. H. Simpson, K. W. Back, and J. C. McKinney (Eds.), *Social aspects of aging*. Durham: Duke University Press, 1966.

Cottrell, F., and Atchley, R. C. *Women in retirement: A preliminary report*. Oxford, Ohio: Scripps Foundation, 1969.

Cottrell, F. Technological change and labor in the railroad industry. Lexington, Mass.: D. C. Heath, 1970.

Havighurst, R. J. Successful aging. In R. H. Williams, C. Tibbitts, and W. Donahue (Eds.), *Processes of aging*. Vol. I. New York: Atherton, 1963.

Miller, S. J. The social dilemma of the aging leisure participant. In A. M. Rose and W. A. Peterson (Eds.), *Older people and their social world*. Philadelphia: F. A. Davis, 1965.

Riley, M. W., and Foner, A. *Aging and society*. New York: Russell Sage Foundation, 1968.

Simpson, I. H., Back, K. W., and McKinney, J. C. Continuity of work and retirement activities. In *Social aspects of aging*. Durham: Duke University Press, 1966.

8

Minority Groups and Aging

An unfortunate bias in much research in social gerontology—one which is only now in the process of being corrected—is the tendency to focus on the needs and problems of the white middle class. Certainly there is some overlap in the problems that affect all aged, regardless of race or ethnicity. However, members of various minority groups may have different and perhaps unique concerns, and attention is now being directed specifically toward determining just what these concerns are and how they can be solved.

Issues in Studying Minority Aged

A focus on the minority aged brings up two issues. First, what are the general characteristics that all minority groups have in common and that can help us understand the problems of their aged members? Second, what are the special characteristics of each minority population which make that group of older people culturally unique?

In regard to the first issue, five characteristics can be identified which are particularly relevant to aged minority group members (Moore, 1971). First, each minority group has a special history which entails some degree of subordination to the dominant culture. Thus there is a shared collective experience which has placed its members in their present position in American society. Second, this special history has been accompanied by outright discrimination as well as the development of negative stereotypes. Third, each minority group has developed its own distinct subculture with varying norms and values which affect attitudes of that group toward aging and the aged. Fourth, these subcultures have institutionalized "coping structures" to support the minority group member in dealing with hostility and exclusion from the wider society. Finally, rapid change is occurring in minority communities both internally and in terms of their relationship to the rest of society. These changes have both positive and negative features. Discrimination and prejudice is being attacked, but at the same time some of the characteristics which make minority group's culturally unique are being lost.

The ultimate question which was raised by the National Urban League in *Double Jeopardy* is whether minority group status compounds the problems of aging in general. Does the subordinate status suffered by minority group members cause them to have additional problems related to income and health, beyond those associated with aging for all people? The article by Dowd and Bengston attempts to test the double jeopardy hypothesis in terms not only of income and health but of family relationships and life satisfaction as well.

The Black Aged

After examining issues of relevance to all minority aged, it is important to look at those characteristics which are unique to particular minorities. The situation of the black aged is complex. On the one hand, incomes for aged blacks are substantially lower than they are for whites. In 1974 the median income for families with heads sixty-five years of age and older was $7,315 for whites, but only $5,075 for blacks. On the other hand, aged blacks are more likely than whites to be living in an extended family situation. Four times as many families headed by older black couples compared to white couples take younger relatives into their household. Further, nearly half of the black families headed by older women have related children living with them, in contrast to only 10 percent for comparable white families (Hill, 1971). Older blacks are also not likely to be institutionalized. As shown in Table 1, 96.9 percent of all black males aged sixty-five to seventy-four and 97.6 percent of all

TABLE 1   Living Arrangements of Aged Blacks by Sex and Age, 1970

	Males		Females	
Living arrangement	65–74	75+	65–74	75+
% in households	96.9	94.7	97.6	94.0
% in group quarters	3.1	5.3	2.4	6.0

SOURCE: Jackson 1977.

black females in the same age group were living in a household in 1970. Only 3.1 percent of the males and 2.4 percent of the females were living in group quarters, either mental hospitals or institutions.

It is also important to recognize that the aged black population is as internally heterogeneous as the white population and that myths must be separated from reality in determining priorities in service provision and programming to the black community (Jackson, 1977). The article by Davis discusses both the history of the black community and the present-day consequences of that history on aged blacks.

Hispanic-American Aged

While relatively few systematic studies have been done on older black Americans, even less is known about Spanish-speaking older persons. As is true for blacks, the incomes of Hispanic aged tend to be lower than those of whites of similar age. The 1970 census shows that the median income was $2,038 for Hispanic males sixty-five or over and $1,113 for females. Further, in this same year 87 percent of all Spanish-speaking aged had only eight years or less of formal education (Bastida, 1979). The research which has been conducted has emphasized the importance of the extended family in maintaining the integration and status of the aged person within the community. A recent study has confirmed the importance of the family among a sample of older persons of Mexican, Puerto Rican, and Cuban origin. Although few of the aged Hispanics in this study lived with their children while their spouse was still alive, there was a strong tendency for children, particularly sons, to fulfill family obligations by bringing an elderly widowed parent into their household (Bastida, 1979). However, the assumption that the family can provide sufficient support for its aged members no longer holds for many Hispanics. The article by Maldonado suggests that urbanization is beginning to break down the traditional extended family ties and that outdated conceptions of Chicano culture are working to the disadvantage of aged Mexican-Americans.

The Indian Aged

In 1976 the National Tribal Chairmen's Association met to discuss specific problems of the Indian aged (National Indian Conference on Aging, 1976). The president of the organization, Wendell Chino, described the importance of the elderly to the community:

The elderly Indian, down through the years, has been the preserver of the Indian race, Indian culture, Indian history. . . . Being the heart and the center of [the] Indian family, they bring into that family unit an experience, maturity . . . knowledge, wisdom. One of the greatest values of the Indian elderly is that they represent to us a repository. All that we like to claim and talk about as Indian . . . came to us from the Indian elderly.

The cultural isolation of the Indian aged from the wider society intensifies their problems. The association identified a series of concerns specific to the Indian aged and advocated remedial action to serve their needs. Among their concerns was the fact that the sole source of income for many elderly Indians is welfare, with few being eligible for social security. To combat this problem they suggested that "social security benefits be extended to all male and female elderly upon reaching the age of eligibility regardless of their participation during previous periods of employment" (National Indian Conference on Aging, 1976, p. 11). They advocated that nursing homes be built on reservations, close to family members, and that they be organized in such a way as to preserve Indian culture and reduce the shock of institutionalization. Perhaps the most radical suggestion was that the minimum age for eligibility for programs for the elderly be lowered to forty-five for Indians, since their life expectancy is only forty-five.

One writer suggests that few of the provisions of the Older Americans Act, first passed in 1965 and subsequently amended and extended in 1975, have been activated in the Indian community because a cultural ethnocentrism pervades all aspects of the law. According to John (1977, p. 5), a "lack of understanding of Indian culture effectively diminishes the success to which the programs authorized by the Older Americans Act can aspire. Until this problem is surmounted, the Indian elderly will remain in need of remedial efforts to satisfy critical needs." The issue of low life expectancy is just one aspect of the biases in the act, which defines age sixty as old. Another is that income from native crafts is sometimes considered in determining eligibility for welfare programs. This has the effect of discouraging elderly Indians from using their skills, thus depriving them of employment and heightening their sense of isolation and loss of purpose (John, 1977, p. 7)

Not only do minority group aged suffer from problems of poorer health and lower income than their white counterparts, but they are often additionally penalized due to biases in the ways in which services are organized. Correcting lifelong deprivations will only solve part of the problem for the minority aged, for specific cultural variations must also be considered in the design and implementation of programs.

REFERENCES

Bastida, Elena. 1979. *The aging of Hispanic-Americans*. Unpublished Ph.D. dissertation. University of Kansas.

Hill, Robert B. 1971. The black elderly. In U.S. Senate Special Committee on Aging, *The multiple hazards of age and race: The situation of the aged black in the United States*. Washington, D.C.: Government Printing Office.

Jackson, Jacquelyne J. 1977. "The black aging: A demographic overview." In Richard A. Kalish (ed.), *The later years*. Monterey, Cal.: Brooks/Cole.

John, Robert. 1977. The status of the elderly Native-American. Unpublished manuscript.

Moore, Joan W. 1971. Situational factors affecting minority aging. *Gerontologist*, 11 (Spring): 30–35.

National Indian Conference on Aging. 1976. *Summary report*. Phoenix, Ariz.: National Tribal Chairmen's Assoc.

Aging in Minority Populations: An Examination of the Double Jeopardy Hypothesis

**JAMES J. DOWD AND
VERN L. BENGSTON**

Being old in an industrialized society is burden enough; being old *and* a member of a minority group is seen by many as constituting double jeopardy. Not only do the minority aged experience a decline in status, income, and health, but they also suffer from the effects of living in a discriminatory society. Some researchers have contested the double jeopardy perspective, noting that while some disparities between white and minority groups are marked, age tends to act as a leveler, obscuring group differences. The study described in this article confirmed the double jeopardy hypothesis for health and income, both of which decreased disproportionately for black and Mexican-American aged. However, the minority aged tended to be more similar to whites in frequency of contact with relatives and in life satisfaction, confirming that a leveling effect did occur in these areas.

The plight of the minority aged has been characterized by many as one of "double jeopardy" or "multiple hazards" (Jackson, 1970; 1971a; National Council on Aging, 1972; National Urban League, 1964; U.S. Senate Special Committee on Aging, 1971). These descriptions refer to the additive negative effects of being old *and* black (or any other racial/ethnic minority) on frequently cited indicators of quality of life, such as income, health, housing, or life satisfaction.

The minority aged are said to bear, in effect, a double burden. Like other older people in industrial societies, they experience the devaluation of old age found in most modern societies (Cowgill and Holmes, 1972). Unlike other older people, however, the minority aged must bear the additional economic, social, and psychological burdens of living in a society in which racial equality remains more myth than social policy. It

SOURCE: Copyright 1978 by the Gerontological Society. Reprinted by permission from *The Journal of Gerontology*, Vol. 33, No. 3.

has been noted in this regard that, compared to the white aged, most of the minority aged "are less well educated, have less income, suffer more illnesses and earlier death, have poorer quality housing and less choice as to where they live and where they work, and in general have a less satisfying quality of life" (U.S. Senate Special Committee on Aging, 1971).

The implications of double jeopardy for both social policy and social gerontological research are many. For social scientists with research interests in the field of gerontology, the awareness of the double jeopardy situation has been reflected in an increased concern with the methodological biases imposed by sample composition and a consequent call for more cross-ethnic research (Ehrlich, 1973; Jackson, 1971b, c; Kalish, 1971; Kent, 1971a, b). By restricting sampling to populations of aging whites, the risk of compositional effects is greatly increased. That is, the varying racial composition of different age strata may confound interpretation of findings should race be related to the dependent variable of interest (Douglas et al., 1974). Rather than continue to *exclude* minority aged from ongoing gerontological research, a growing number of social gerontologists have criticized prior research for its failure to *control* for variables such as ethnicity, education, locale of residence and SES [socioeconomic status] (cf., Bengston et al., 1977; Reynolds and Kalish, 1974).

Related to this methodological issue is the policy issue of whether racial or ethnic identity alone constitutes sufficient basis for differential treatment. Several have argued affirmatively, suggesting that racial contrasts are so great as to require a social policy that reflects those differences (Jackson, 1971b; National Urban League, 1964). The U.S. Senate Special Committee on Aging (1971), for example, has expressed concern that if the characteristics of the minority aged are indeed different from the general older population, social policy must be modified to reflect such differences. Others have disagreed, noting that while differences among ethnic groups are frequently observed and incontestable, it also is true that the aging individual, regardless of ethnic background, is subject to a variety of influences which cut across racial lines and may mediate or level differences in patterns of aging (Kent and Hirsch, 1969). The relative numbers of minority *aged* having good health and adequate income, for example, may well be less than those of aged whites. If, however, the percentage differences between middle-aged blacks or Mexican-Americans and their white counterparts are greater *yet*, a characterization of the minority aged as being in double jeopardy would be an incomplete description. Viewed from a different perspective, it may also be said that age exerts a *leveling* influence on the ethnic differences found among the younger cohorts.

To address this issue, we will present data on a series of selected dependent variables (ranging from economic and health indicators to social interaction and life satisfaction items) in order to identify the nature of age differences within different ethnic groups. The analysis will focus on the two apparently contradictory perspectives on ethnicity and aging identified above. The first perspective suggests that the minority aged suffer from a situation of double jeopardy, that is, the experience of both race *and* age discrimination combine to make their relative status more problematic than that of either the aged or racial minorities considered separately. The second perspective views *advancing age as a leveler* of racial inequalities that existed in mid-life. To what extent either of these perspectives can be said to characterize the lives of the minority aged is the central question to be answered in this paper.

Sample and Methods

The data to be analyzed in this research were collected as part of a larger survey with a probability sample of 1,269 residents of Los Angeles County stratified by age and SES within race groups (see Bengston et al., 1976). The sampling universe of the research included all black, Mexican-American, and Anglo residents of Los Angeles County, aged 45 to 74. The sample drawn from this universe was divided into nine age-by-ethnicity cells, formed by the cross-classification of the three ethnic categories and three age strata (45-54, 55-64, and 65-74). The sample design further specified equal distribution within the three race groups between two socioeconomic strata. SES was operationalized using the Duncan Socioeconomic Index; the score of 31 on this index was established as the dividing point between the two strata during the sampling phase.

Respondents were identified through a multistage sampling procedure, the initial stage of which involved screening more than 15,000 households chosen from 184 census tracts in Los Angeles County to identify eligible respondents. Final interviews were conducted between July 1974 and January 1975 by a team of interviewers matched with the respondents on race/ethnicity. Interviews were conducted either in English or Spanish, depending upon the respondent's preference. Response rates averaged approximately 80 percent during both screening and final interviewing.

Table 1 presents the final distribution of 1,269 respondents by age and ethnicity.

Although the present sample was not part of a longitudinal panel, which would ideally be necessary for proper analysis of the "leveling" properties of age, the design does facilitate at least an initial investigation of this issue as it allocates cases equally into three age strata and three ethnic groups. Thus while we cannot follow one birth cohort through time and determine whether increased age "levels" any ethnic variation that may exist, we *can* compare three different age strata and determine the extent of the ethnic variation within each stratum. If the ethnic differ-

TABLE 1 Sample Composition by Age and Ethnicity

Age	Ethnicity			Total
	BLACK	MEXICAN-AMERICAN	WHITE	
45–54	134	146	137	417
55–64	135	149	135	419
65–74	144	154	135	433
Total	413	449	407	1269

ences among the 65–74-year-old individuals are not as great as those among the 45–54-year-old, there would be an indication that age exerts a leveling influence.

Double jeopardy, on the other hand, would be indicated should the following conditions obtain: (1) significant differences exist between minority and white respondents over 65 on a dependent variable that *favor* the white respondents; (2) within the particular minority group being studied, a significant decline in the dependent variable with increasing age can be observed; and either (3a) significant differences do *not* exist between younger (45–64) minority and white respondents; or (3b) significant differences exist between younger minority and their white counterparts that favor the white respondents but which are not larger than the differences observed between the *older* minority and their white counterparts; or (3c) significant differences exist between *younger* minority and white respondents that favor the *minority* respondents. In other words, a condition of double jeopardy will be said to characterize the minority aged should the relative disadvantages of the minority *aged* vis-à-vis the white aged in any of the dependent measures included here (income, health, life satisfaction, and primary group interaction) be equal to or greater than the relative disadvantage of *middle-aged* minority respondents vis-à-vis middle-aged white respondents.

Measurement

The *dependent* variables chosen for this analysis include: (1) total family income for 1973; (2) self-assessed health; (3) a series of social-interaction items (e.g., frequency of interaction with children, grandchildren, friends, and relatives); and (4) two measures of life satisfaction. The two life-satisfaction measures were derived from a factor analysis of a battery of eleven items selected primarily from the Philadelphia Geriatric Center Morale Scale (Lawton, 1975). The principal components factor analysis indicated that two factors underlie the eleven life-satisfaction items. The construction of these two measures is detailed in Appendix B. Actual items used to measure each of the dependent variables are listed in Appendices A and B.

The analysis that follows will compare *mean* scores for the nine age/race categories studied here on each of the four major dependent variables. F-tests for the significance of any observed differences among means will be conducted for both age and race groups. Rather than presenting separate pair-by-pair comparisons of the age strata or race groups, the F-test allows a more parsimonious, single comparison which addresses the question of whether or not all three age strata or race groups differ among themselves sufficiently to cause one to reject the hypothesis of equal population means (Blalock, 1960).

In addition to reporting the *simple* means for each of the nine categories of the predictor variables, multiple classification analyses (MCA) will be run to determine the extent of change in the simple means produced when controls are introduced into the analyses. In effect, MCA distinguishes *net* means from simple, or gross, means. In order to preclude attributing to race or age differences that which more accurately should be attributed to the effects of sex or SES, for example, F-tests will be run for the differences in *net* means as well as the differences in gross, or simple, means. Only the uncontrolled, or simple, means are actually presented in the tables, however. The results of the F-tests for differences among controlled (net) means are indicated in tables 2–5 by asterisks. One asterisk (located above and to the right of the results of the F-tests for differences among simple means) indicates the probability of Type 1 error to be less than .10; two asterisks indicate $p < .05$; and three asterisks indicate $p < .001$. In either case, the logic of the analysis remains the same: If the aging process can be said to level in old age the differences found to exist between ethnic groups in middle age, the means (either simple or net) of the white and minority respondents on the dependent variable under consideration should become more similar with older age strata. The controls to be entered into the analysis are two variables frequently reported to be distributed differently within different racial/ethnic groups: sex and occupational prestige (SES). Occupational prestige is measured here using Duncan's Socioeconomic Index for all occupations. Respondents are coded according to the occupation they held *most* of their lives. Housewives are coded according to their spouse's occupation. Widowed, separated, or divorced women are also coded according to their late/former spouse's occupation unless they have been widowed, separated, or divorced for more than five years, in which case their (the respondent's) *current* occupation is used.

Additionally, income and health are included as controls in the analysis of life satisfaction and primary group interaction; income also is included as a control variable in the analysis of *health;* and, vice versa, the measure of health is entered as a control into the analysis of income. Each of the four control variables utilized here (sex, occupational prestige, income, and health) was selected because of the differing nature of its distribution by both race and age.

Analysis

When the double jeopardy hypothesis was initially stated by the National Urban League in 1964, the focus of concern was in the areas of income and health. Analyzing the income and health data in the present research, one is led to conclude much as did the National Urban League, viz., in terms of their relative income and health, the minority aged do indeed suffer double jeopardy.

Income

The data presented in Table 2 show that, while the income of both white and minority respondents declines with age, the mean income reported by older black and Mexican-American respondents is considerably lower than any other group in the sample (3.49 and 3.36, respectively). Further, the relative *decline* in income between the thirty-year age span studied here is much greater for minority respondents than it is for whites. The mean income reported by blacks, for example, declined 55 percent (7.80 to 3.49) across the three age strata. Mexican-Americans showed an even larger drop in mean income, 62 percent, across the three age strata.

The income of older white respondents, by contrast, declined only 36 percent (from 10.941 to 6.891). Thus the rather large income "gap" that exists between middle-aged minority and white respondents, becomes an even larger one among the respondents aged sixty-five or older. These differences in income cannot be explained merely by invoking the SES, sex, or health differences that exist between white and either Mexican-Americans or blacks. Even with these variables held constant, the net incomes of the respondents over sixty-five (these figures are not included in the tables) are *3.89* for blacks, *3.89* for Mexican-Americans, and *5.84* for whites, a finding that remains significant ($p < .001$).

Health

In response to the question "In general, would you say your health is very good, good, fair, poor, or very poor?" older minority respondents were significantly more likely to report poorer health than white respondents even with the effects of SES, sex, and income held constant. The differences in health among the three ethnic groups were less apparent among younger respondents, particularly those aged fifty-five to sixty-four. While the mean health scores of blacks and Mexican-Americans across the three age strata dropped, respectively, 13 percent and 19 percent, the mean score of white respondents declined less than 9 percent (from 4.271 to 3.911). As was the case with income, the self-assessed health of whites is greater than that of minority respondents at each age stratum with the greatest disparity occurring among those aged sixty-five or older.

While it is possible that the poorer health reported by the minority aged may reflect a bio-genetical difference between whites and non-

TABLE 2 Age and Race Effects on Income and Health

Dependent variable	Age range	Ethnicity of respondent			F-test race diffs.
		BLACK	MEXICAN-AMERICAN	WHITE	
Income[a]	45–54	7.80	8.87	10.94	$p < .001$°°°
	55–64	5.75	6.82	9.35	$p < .001$°°°
	65–74	3.49	3.36	6.89	$p < .001$°°°
	F-Test Age Diffs.	$p < .001$°°°	$p < .001$°°°	$p < .001$°°°	
Self-assessed health[b]	45–54	3.80	3.86	4.27	$p < .001$
	55–64	3.45	3.48	3.80	$p < .05$
	65–74	3.28	3.11	3.91	$p < .001$°°°
	F-Test Age Diffs.	$p < .001$	$p < .001$	$p < .001$°°°	

[a]The income data reported in this table are *not* raw income scores in thousands of dollars but rather the mean score computed from 15 income *categories* (see Appendix A). However, since the categories used here approximate very closely raw income (reported in thousands of dollars), the figures in this table can be interpreted as *estimates* of actual dollar income.
[b]Health data were coded from 1 to 5 with higher scores indicating better health.

whites that is also manifest in the different life expectancies at birth for each group, the more probable explanation for these health differences is a sociological one. Because of past and present policies of racial discrimination in our society, nonwhites have had less income, inadequate nutrition, and consequently poorer health and a lower life expectancy at birth than whites.

The relative life expectancies of different race or ethnic groups tend to converge, however, as individuals age. Although older blacks and Mexican-Americans report poorer health than older white respondents, estimates of the additional life expectancy of persons already fifty years of age differ by less than three years for whites and nonwhites (Bengston et al., 1976). This suggests that while racial discrimination may indeed be largely responsible for the lower life expectancy at birth of blacks and others classified as nonwhite, it does not adequately explain the increased proportions of *older* blacks and Mexican-Americans who report their health to be poor. *Age* discrimination is implicated as well in the health problems experienced by our society's minority aged. Consequently, the descriptive label, double jeopardy, is certainly appropriate when analyzing the health status of older blacks or Mexican-Americans.

Life Satisfaction

Life satisfaction is a concept that, while directly affected by both income and health, is related to age in ways that suggest income and health to be only imperfect predictors at best. For, while the transition to old age is generally associated with declines in income and health, life satisfaction—particularly as measured by tranquility—remains relatively stable over the thirty-year span analyzed here.

Considering tranquility, this pattern of stability is less characteristic of Mexican-Americans than it is of either blacks or whites. While the tranquility scores of black respondents remain virtually the same at each age level and the scores of whites show small *increases* with age, the tranquility scores reported by Mexican-Americans in our sample decline slightly with increasing age (this decline is not statistically significant). Consequently, although the mean level of tranquility reported by forty-five to fifty-four-year-old Mexican-Americans is somewhat higher than that reported by whites of similar ages, this pattern is reversed among the older (65–74) respondents. In this oldest age group, Mexican-Americans have significantly lower tranquility scores than either whites or blacks ($p < .05$). However, from our earlier definition, this pattern cannot be said to constitute a case of double jeopardy for the Mexican-American respondents, since no statistically significant decline *with age* is observed.

Considering the second measure of life satisfaction included in the present analysis, optimism, the situation of Mexican-Americans *does* meet the definitional criteria for double jeopardy specified earlier. The data in Table 3 show that for Mexican-Americans: (1) there is a significant

TABLE 3 Age and Race Effects on Life Satisfaction

Dependent variable	Age range	Ethnicity of respondent			F-test race diffs.
		BLACK	MEXICAN-AMERICAN	WHITE	
Tranquility	45–54	2.15	2.08	1.95	$p > .10$***[a]
	55–64	2.16	2.08	2.14	$p > .10$
	65–74	2.17	1.93	2.17	$p < .05$
	F-Test Age Diffs.	$p > .10$*	$p > .10$**	$.10 > p > .05$***	
Optimism	45–54	1.60	1.29	1.47	$p < .01$***
	55–64	1.39	1.25	1.38	$p > .10$
	65–74	1.31	0.98	1.43	$p < .001$***
	F-Test Age Diffs.	$p < .05$	$p < .01$	$p > .10$	

[a] The three asterisks indicate that, when sex, SES, income, and health were controlled, the differences among ethnic groups in the 45–54-age group were found to be significant ($p < .001$). The reader should note that, without controlling on any variables ethnic differences were not apparent ($p > .10$), a finding which points to importance of introducing test factors (or controls) into the analysis.

decline in optimism with age; (2) their optimism scores in old age are significantly lower ($p < .001$) than the scores of older whites (0.981 vs 1.431); and (3) their dissimilarity from white respondents (as measured by differences in group means) is greater among older respondents than it is among younger respondents. White respondents have higher optimism scores than Mexican-Americans at every age considered here; and the difference in mean scores is greater in old age as whites show a decrease in mean optimism of only 2 percent between the youngest and oldest strata, while Mexican-Americans evidence a *decline* of 23 percent.

No such double jeopardy characterizes black respondents on either tranquility or optimism. In each case, the differences that exist between *younger* blacks and whites become *smaller* with increasing age. On tranquility, for example, there is almost no difference between black and white respondents sixty-five to seventy-four years old, while a small difference is observed among younger respondents.

On optimism, black respondents do evidence a decline with age, although at none of the three age strata studied are the differences between blacks and whites substantially different. This point becomes more clear when one considers the differences in *net* means (not reported in the tables) for black and white respondents after income, SES, health, and sex are held constant. Among the older (sixty-five- to seventy-four-year-old) respondents, blacks have a net Optimism score of 1.37 and whites have an almost identical score of 1.38. For blacks, then, particularly on the tranquility component of life satisfaction the age-as-leveler hypothesis receives moderate support, while the double jeopardy hypothesis is not supported by the data.

Primary Group Interaction

Different measures of primary group interaction are included in the analysis in order to obtain estimates of the degree of social integration and group cohesion of the three ethnic groups under investigation. While primary group interaction may not be as critical an indicator of relative status as income or health, it does indicate a source of reward available to the individual in the course of their daily lives that contributes significantly to overall "*quality* of life." The reliable presence of other people may constitute an important resource that enables the older individual to insulate himself from the breakdown in self-esteem and diminution of skills often associated with the transition to old age in our society.

Primary group interaction was measured here by asking the respondent when was the last time he or she had seen (a) children (b) grandchildren; (c) other relatives; and (d) friends and neighbors. On the first two measures, frequency of contact with children and grandchildren, the data in Table 4 indicate that, generally, it is the white respondents who report the *lowest* frequency of contact. Mexican-Americans at every age report the most frequent contact with their children and grandchildren. Even

TABLE 4   Age and Race Effects on Frequency of Interaction with Children and Grandchildren

Dependent variable	Age range	Ethnicity of respondent			F-test race diffs.
		BLACK	MEXICAN-AMERICAN	WHITE	
Frequency of contact with children	45–54	4.31	4.56	4.18	.10 > p > .05**
	55–64	4.16	4.38	3.94	p < .05
	65–74	3.91	4.25	4.09	.10 > p > .05*
	F-Test Age Diffs.	p > .10	.10 > p > .05	p > .10	
Frequency of contact with grandchildren	45–54	3.99	4.28	3.90	p > .10*
	55–64	4.07	4.44	3.79	p < .001***
	65–74	3.87	4.37	3.76	p < .001***
	F-Test Age Diffs.	p > .10	p > .10	p > .10	

when controls such as income, occupational prestige (SES), health and sex are introduced, the unique cultural heritage of Mexican-Americans in our society remains very evident in the data as the differences between Mexican-Americans and blacks and whites continue to be statistically significant in all but one case. Consequently, when one considers frequency of primary group interaction as an important personal resource, the relatively advantageous position of Mexican-American respondents (and, to a lesser extent, black respondents) vis-à-vis white respondents persists into old age.

Table 5 presents the data for the final two measures of primary group interaction, frequency of contact with (a) other relatives and (b) friends and neighbors. Considering the *contact with relatives* variable first, a variation of the age-as-leveler pattern can be identified. In this case, a significant ethnic difference is observed among 45- to 54-year-old individuals, although the difference is one which favors the minority respondents. Whites in this age group have significantly lower contact with their relatives than either blacks or Mexican-Americans ($p < .01$). This difference becomes smaller with increasing age, however, as the pattern of contact with relatives among minority respondents declines, while the levels of contact reported by whites remains stable across age strata. The result is the *leveling* of ethnic differences in contact with relatives in old age. The F-test for the oldest age group shows no significant ethnic differences either with or without statistical controls. As with the two previously discussed measures of primary group interaction, Mexican-Americans report a higher mean frequency of contact with relatives than either blacks or whites at all three age ranges included in the analysis. The extent of this difference among the older respondents, however, is not sufficient to warrant claims of significance.

Focusing attention on the frequency of interaction the individual social actor has with friends, neighbors, or other non-related acquaintances, an interesting shift in the pattern of ethnic differences occurs. Whites report *higher* levels of contact with friends and neighbors than blacks or Mexican-Americans at all ages. Further, the differences among ethnic groups are significant at each age level *with* the inclusion of control variables ($p < .05$) as well as without controls ($p < .001$).

While the contact with friends and neighbors for white respondents increases in small increments with each age stratum, there are no apparent age differences in contact with friends or neighbors among black and Mexican-American respondents. As a result, the differences in old age (over sixty-five) between groups are the most visible of all. We do not characterize the lower contact of the minority aged with friends and neighbors as being a double jeopardy situation, however, for the following reason: for the minority respondents, the observed *lower* interaction on this variable is not explained to even a minimum degree by their *age*. Younger blacks, for example, are not substantially different than older

TABLE 5 Age and Race Effects on Frequency of Interaction with Relatives and Friends

Dependent variable	Age range	Ethnicity of Respondent			F-test race diffs.
		BLACK	MEXICAN-AMERICAN	WHITE	
Frequency of contact with relatives	45–54	3.52	3.53	2.97	p < .01***
	55–64	3.10	3.31	2.74	p < .01**
	65–74	2.80	2.99	2.81	p > .10
	F-Test Age Diffs.	p < .001°	p < .01	p > .10	
Frequency of contact with friends	45–54	2.32	2.06	2.69	p < .001**
	55–64	2.26	2.04	2.77	p < .001***
	65–74	2.43	2.04	2.98	p < .001***
	F-Test Age Diffs.	p > .10	p > .10	p < .05°°	

black respondents on this variable. While ethnic differences, then, are certainly present in frequency of contact with friends and neighbors, the lower mean contact reported by the minority aged does not constitute double jeopardy.

The greater frequency of *familial* interaction (i.e., interaction with children, grandchildren, and relatives) among the minority respondents, particularly Mexican-Americans, suggests that the primary-group needs of the minority aged *are* being satisfied within the extended family. However, the fact that Mexican-Americans also report the *least* amount of interaction with nonrelated individuals, such as friends, neighbors, or acquaintances, suggests a certain amount of social isolation for the minority respondents as well.

These data also suggest the possibility that individuals seek, and generally find, an optimum level of social interaction. The need to maintain at least a minimum level of primary-group interaction requires individuals to seek new patterns in their social exchange networks should death, for example, steal from them a spouse or relative (cf. Acock et al., 1974). This phenomenon appears particularly salient for white respondents, whose interaction with children, grandchildren, and relatives is generally less than either blacks or Mexican-Americans yet whose frequency of interaction with friends and neighbors is considerably greater than either Mexican-Americans or blacks.

Summary and Conclusion

Utilizing data from a large (N = 1,269) multistage probability sample of middle-aged and aged blacks, Mexican-Americans and Anglos living in Los Angeles County, indicators of relative status and primary-group interaction were analyzed to determine the degree and nature of any ethnic variation. It was found that differences among the three ethnic groups do exist and, in some cases, particularly on income and self-assessed health, constitute a case of double jeopardy for the minority aged.

But while double jeopardy was found to be an accurate characterization of the black and Mexican-American aged on several variables, the data also suggest that age exerts a leveling influence on some ethnic variation over time. Variables such as frequency of interaction with relatives as well as, for black respondents, the life satisfaction factors of tranquility and optimism all evidence a certain decline in the extent of ethnic variation across age strata. While cross-ethnic longitudinal research designs would be necessary to definitively explore the age-as-leveler hypothesis, the present analysis offers some support for the earlier cross-sectional work of Kent (1971a) in this area. His perspective on the issue of the relationships among ethnicity, age, and social problems bears careful consideration:

The problems older people face are very similar regardless of ethnic background. This is not to say that the same proportion of each group faces these problems; obviously they do not. The point, however, is that if we concentrate on the group rather than on the problem, we shall be treating symptoms rather than causes.

Put differently, to presume that ethnic differences are alone sufficient to understand the personal and social situation of the aged ignores tremendous variation both *across* ethnic boundaries and *within* ethnic categories (as has been underscored, for example, by Jackson, 1970, 1971a). Data discussed here only partially support those who argue that the world of the minority aged is one of double jeopardy. Differences in old age across race lines on income or health, for example, do suggest that older blacks and Mexican-Americans suffer from a double jeopardy. However, on variables measuring frequency of familial contact, the mean figures for black and Mexican-American respondents indicates fairly stable interaction—not less—across each age strata. The existence of double jeopardy, therefore, is an empirical, not a logical, question. To assume otherwise would be to ignore the warning of Kent (1971c) that "age may be a great leveler with regard to both racial and social influences."

NOTES

The development of this paper was supported by grants from RANN program of the National Science Foundation (#APR 75-21178), the UPS Foundation of the United Parcel Service (Vern L. Bengston, Principal Investigator; Pauline K. Ragan, Project Director), and AOA (#90-A-1010/02). James J. Dowd, Principal Investigator. Thanks also to members of the Community Research Planning Committee (Alicia Noriega and Carnella Barnes, Chairpersons of the Chicago and Black caucuses, respectively). None of these individuals or agencies, however, bears any responsibility for the analyses or interpretations presented here.

REFERENCES

Acock, A. C., Dowd, J. J., and Roberts, W. *The primary group: Its rediscovery in contemporary sociology.* General Learning Press, Morristown, NJ, 1974.

Bengston, V. L., Kasschau, P. L., and Ragan, P. K. The impact of social structure on the aging individual. In J. E. Birren and K. W. Schaie (Eds.), *Handbook of the psychology of aging.* Van Nostrand Reinhold, New York, 1976.

Bengston, V. L., Cuellar, J., and Ragan, P. K. Stratum contrasts and similarities in attitudes toward death. *Journal of Gerontology,* 1977, 32, 76–88.

Blalock, H. M. *Social statistics.* McGraw-Hill, New York, 1960.

Cowgill, D. O., and Holmes, L. D. *Aging and modernization.* Appleton-Century-Crofts, New York, 1972.

Douglas, E., Cleveland, W. P., and Maddox, G. L. Political attitudes, age, and aging: A cohort analysis of archival data. *Journal of Gerontology,* 1974, 29, 666-675.

Ehrlich, I. F. Toward a social profile of the aged black population in the United States: An exploratory study. *Aging and Human Development,* 1973, 4, 271-276.

Jackson, J. J. Aged Negroes: Their cultural departures from statistical stereotypes and rural-urban differences. *Gerontologist,* 1970, 10, 14-145.

Jackson, J. J. Compensatory care for the black aged. In *Minority aged in America,* Occasional Paper #10, Institute of Gerontology. Univ. Michigan-Wayne State Univ., Ann Arbor, 1971, 15-23. (a)

Jackson, J. J. Negro aged: Toward needed research in social gerontology. *Gerontologist,* 1971, 11, 52-57. (b)

Jackson, J. J. Sex and social class variations in black and parent-adult child relationships. *Aging and Human Development,* 1971, 2, 96-107. (c)

Kalish, R. A. A gerontological look at ethnicity, human capacities, and individual adjustment. *Gerontologist,* 1971, 11, 78-87.

Kent, D. P. Changing welfare to serve minority. In *Minority aged in America,* Occasional Paper #10, Institute of Gerontology. Univ. Michigan-Wayne State Univ., Ann Arbor, 1971, 25-34. (a)

Kent, D. P. The elderly in minority groups: Variant patterns of aging. *Gerontologist,* 1971, 11, 26-29. (b)

Kent, D. P. The Negro aged. *Gerontologist,* 1971, 11, 48-51. (c)

Kent, D. P., and Hirsch, C. Differentials in need and problem solving techniques among low-income Negro and white elderly. Paper presented at the 8th International Congress of Gerontology, Washington, 1969.

Lawton, M. P. The Philadelphia Geriatric Center morale scale: A revision. *Journal of Gerontology,* 1975, 30, 85-98.

National Council on Aging. *Triple jeopardy: Myth or reality.* National Council on Aging, Washington, 1972.

National Urban League. *Double jeopardy: The older Negro in America today.* National Urban League, New York, 1964.

Palmore, E., and Manton, K. Ageism compared to racism and sexism. *Journal of Gerontology,* 1973, 28, 363-369.

Reynolds, D. K., and Kalish, R. A. Anticipation of futurity as a function of ethnicity and age. *Journal of Gerontology,* 1974, 29, 224-232.

United States Senate Special Committee on Aging, Lindsay, I. B. *The multiple hazards of age and race: The situation of aged blacks in the United States.* Washington, 1971.

Appendix A: Operationalization of Dependent Variables

A. 1973 family income:
   "Now, please look at the Income Card and give me the letter of the income group that includes the total income for you (and your spouse) for last year, 1973 (before taxes). That figure should include salaries, wages, dividends, interest, profits, pensions, and support from children and all other income."

01.	0 −1,999	(A)		09.	$ 9,000– 9,999	(I)
02.	$2,000–2,999	(B)		10.	$10,000–10,999	(J)
03.	$3,000–3,999	(C)		11.	$11,000–11,999	(K)
04.	$4,000–4,999	(D)		12.	$12,000–14,999	(L)
05.	$5,000–5,999	(E)		13.	$15,000–19,999	(M)
06.	$6,000–6,999	(F)		14.	$20,000–24,999	(N)
07.	$7,000–7,999	(G)		15.	$25,000 or over	(O)
08.	$8,000–8,999	(H)				

B. Self-assessed health:

"In general, would you say your health is . . . very good (5), good (4), fair (3), poor (2) or very poor (1)?"

C. Primary group interaction:

1. "When did you last see . . . (a) any of your adult children who do not live with you? . . . (b) any of your grandchildren? . . . (c) any of these (previously specified) relatives?"

    01. more than a year ago
    02. within the last year
    03. within the last month
    02. within the last week
    01. today or yesterday

2. "Now, how often do you visit with *other people*, such as friends, neighbors, or acquaintances?"

    01. less than once a month
    02. at least once a month
    03. at least once a week
    04. daily

Appendix B: Varimax Rotated Factor Matrix of Life Satisfaction Items[a]

	Tranquility	*Optimism*
1. Do you have a lot to be sad about?	.613	.243
2. Do you feel that life isn't worth living?	.420	.324
3. Do you worry so much that you can't sleep?	.664	.150
4. Do you feel afraid?	.476	.169
5. Do you feel bored?	.576	.208
6. Do you feel lonely these days?	.577	.217
7. Do you get upset easily?	.450	.134
8. Do you feel that things keep getting worse as you get older?	.381	.494
9. Do you feel that you have as much pep as you did last year?	.062	.307

10. As you get older, do you feel
    less useful?   .221   .697
11. Do you feel that life is hard for you?   .539   .440

---

[a]Items 1 thru 8, 10 and 11 were all recoded such that positive scores indicate life *satisfaction*, not dissatisfaction, and the greater the score, the greater life satisfaction. A response of "hardly ever" to item #5 above, for example, is coded to indicate positive life satisfaction.

Note: The indices representing each of the two factors were constructed by repeatedly multiplying the factor-score coefficient of each item by the standardized score corresponding to the appropriate item and then summing the results of these operations for *each* of the variable items. The labels applied to the factor variables, *Tranquility* and *Optimism*, were suggested by a description of the individual variables that loaded highest on the particular factor.

Growing Old Black
DONALD L. DAVIS

Beginning with World War I blacks migrated from areas in the rural South to the cities of the North. They now comprise a high proportion of the elderly poor in the inner cities, where they are more likely than whites to live in overcrowded housing. Only 15 percent of all blacks over age sixty-five have completed high school, and this inadequate educational background has confined them to labor or service work. Older black men are particularly likely to be employed in occupations which are seasonal or have high turnover, while low-paid domestic work has been the most common employment open to older black women. Part of the deprivation suffered by the aged black is due to low social security benefits resulting from the accumulated effects of unstable employment and low wages. Thus in retirement the percentage of blacks living below the poverty level is almost twice that of whites. The effects of poverty are directly related to health. Aged blacks have disproportionately high death rates and lower life expectancy than whites. Inferior educational opportunities have created a cycle of unsteady work and high rates of unemployment. These factors with their accompanying problem of poor pay lead to disproportionate rates of poverty in old age.

The People

Many aged black people live on tenaciously, in urban ghettos and the recesses of rural areas all over America. They learned years ago to live within prescribed arenas—physical, social, economic—that limited their full participation in the American social scene. This paper describes these barriers and how they relate to the anguish and the frailties that are, many times, inseparable from the pain of aging in a youth-oriented society.

The National Urban League has recently completed a study, *Double Jeopardy*, which states that: "Today's Negro is different from today's aged white because he is Negro . . . and this alone should be enough basis for differential treatment."

Consequently, while many persons and agencies involved in the field of aging recognize the responsibility of a complete network of services to meet the individualized needs of our aged, we often fail to realize that we may have very few relevant programs for the black segment of the aged population. For, as W. E. B. DuBois cited in his classic 1899 study of *The Philadelphia Negro*:

SOURCE: U. S. Senate Special Committee on Aging, *The Multiple Hazards of Age and Race: The Situation of Aged Blacks in the United States* (Washington, D.C.: Government Printing Office, September 1971), pp. 53–64.

The existence of certain social problems affecting Negro people is plainly manifest. Here is a large group of people . . . who do not form an integral part of the larger social group. This in itself is not altogether unusual; there are other unassimilated groups. . . . And yet in the case of the Negro, the segregation is more conspicuous, more patent to the eye and so intertwined with a long historic evolution, with particularly pressing social problems in poverty, ignorance, crime, and labor that the Negro problem far surpasses in scientific interest and social gravity most of the other race or class questions.

Black Americans, for the most part, are people who have spent their prime working years contributing to the growth of large central cities where they now live. Of this group, three out of every ten persons, sixty-five years or over, live in four of the most populous states—New York, California, Pennsylvania, and Illinois—each of which has more than 1 million such persons.

These people, for the most part, are now confined to some of the most decaying areas of the inner cities in these states. Current inflation, coupled with the inability to find work, continues to increase the despair of these aged citizens.

It has been stated by Kent and Hirsch,[1] in their recently completed study, that our current lack of knowledge in the field of gerontology applies primarily to noninstitutionalized, low-income, elderly white and black persons. Despite the high percentage of these groups living in our central cities and who comprise a large percentage of the client populations of health and welfare agencies, neither racial group had undergone an extensive study prior to the Kent and Hirsch study.

The Pathway of Black People to the Cities

In most decades since 1860 the black population has increased less rapidly than that of whites. However, in the last forty years the black population has reversed its earlier trend and has shown more growth than the white population. Since 1860, blacks have formed the following percentages of the U.S. population:

1860	14.1	1920	9.9
1870	13.5	1930	9.7
1880	13.1	1940	9.8
1890	11.9	1950	10.0
1900	11.6	1960	10.6
1910	10.7	1969	11.0

SOURCE: U.S. Department of Commerce, Bureau of the Census.

These statistics reveal that the black population decreased from 14.1 percent in 1860 to 9.7 percent in 1930. But in 1969 the black population significantly increased to 11.9, and totaled a little above 22 million people. The recent rapid increase in the proportion of blacks within our population is largely due to an increase in life expectancy among blacks. Although the birth rate has long been higher among blacks than whites, a higher death rate decreased or held constant the proportion of blacks in the population. For instance, the life expectancy of blacks in this century has increased at a faster rate than that of whites: 38.4 years for nonwhite as compared with 20.7 for white men, and 32.7 years for nonwhite as compared with 25.2 for white women. Although life expectancies for nonwhites have increased at significant rates in recent years, their life expectancy continues to be lower than that for whites.

The black population appears proportionately greater nationwide than it really is, largely because massive migration of blacks into the central cities of large metropolitan areas has been accentuated by out-migration of whites from the cities to the suburbs. The percentage of blacks within the total population has shown minimal change in this century. However, the black population has instead been characterized by rapid migration from the South and farms into central cities of metropolitan areas, where 55 percent of all blacks lived in 1969.

The black migration from South to North and from country to city has probably been one of the most massive population changes in the history of our country. Sixty years ago, in 1910, approximately eight of ten blacks lived in one of the eleven states of the "Old Confederacy." As Silberman stated:

> Over 90 percent of these Negroes, moreover, lived in rural areas. Negroes began moving to the North during World War I and continued to move during the 1920s, when restrictive legislation slowed down the flow of immigrants from southern and eastern Europe. By 1940, the Negro population in the Old Confederacy had increased by only 12 percent, whereas in the same period the Negro population elsewhere in the U.S. had more than doubled, from 1.9 to 4 million.[2]

In the half century ending in 1960, the black population of the United States had increased 92 percent, but less than 3 percent of this increase occurred in the five southern states which had the greatest black population in 1910. In contrast, almost half of the increase took place in the states of New York, Illinois, California, Pennsylvania, and Ohio. Among these states, in 1960, for instance, were located the first three cities with greatest concentration of black population. In 1969 the six cities with largest black population were as follows:

- New York, 1,087,931
- Chicago, 812,637
- Philadelphia, 529,240
- Detroit, 482,223
- Washington, 411,737
- Los Angeles, 334,916

As a result of the significant population growth shown in the above table, it would appear that the aging black population will expand at a very rapid rate in these states and, therefore, should receive close attention from state, local and federal agencies. The extent of migration and urbanization is best illustrated in observing the population composition of those ten northern and western cities with the greatest black concentration. We found that nearly one-half of the black residents were not born in the city of residence, since most of this group was born in the South.

Why did such a rapid migration occur among the black population during the fifty-year period from 1910 to 1960? Primarily to find better opportunities for employment in the North. After World War I reduced immigration from Europe, northern employers were forced to meet some of their needs for unskilled and semiskilled workers among the black population. Closely related to these circumstances is the fact that the wages paid for unskilled and semiskilled work—the type of employment for most blacks at that time—were and remain higher in the North than in the South. In addition, living conditions were not as oppressive in the North. Although the North was characterized by extreme prejudice, discrimination, and de facto segregation, cities outside the South were not committed to the pervasive and rigid system of legal segregation which limited job opportunities for blacks.

It has been mentioned that the increased life expectancy for blacks has resulted in a larger overall black population group with a similar significant increase of aged blacks in the total population. In 1969, for instance, "Negro and other" composed 12.3 percent of the total population; 9.6 percent of the 45–64 age group, and 7.9 percent of the age 65 and above group. By 1969 Brotman[3] reported that 60.7 percent of the black population aged 65 and above lived in metropolitan areas compared to 61.2 percent of the white population aged 65 and above living in the same area. Of the black total, a significant 47.5 percent resided within the central city compared to only 33.4 percent whites who lived in the central city. Further, the Committee for Economic Development has estimated that the nonwhite elderly population (65 and over) living within our central cities will more than double during the period 1960–1985, rising by a total of 600,000 (108.7 percent) or 24,000 per year. In contrast, the estimated growth of the white population age 65 and above in the central cities will rise only 3 percent in this same period (155,000 or 6,200 per year). Future growth of the aged white population, it appears, will occur primarily in suburban areas.

If this estimated growth in the elderly nonwhite central city population does occur, they will comprise a much greater proportion of all elderly poor in those cities, perhaps one-fourth rather than one-sixth as in 1968. Further, the increased growth of the nonwhite elderly population could be much more significant because the Committee for Economic Development based its estimated population expansion upon census data which contained a reported undercount of at least 10 percent in some black inner city areas. Based upon these criteria, we can probably expect the nonwhite elderly population in our central cities to expand as fast as our nonwhite age group under age fifteen living in the same area. This rapid expansion of these age groups will pose grave problems for the future, since the same age groups now comprise a large percentage of the poor people in our central cities. Both of these age groups now and for the foreseeable future represent essentially a drain on the economic resources of the community unless and until appropriate planning and actions occur.

Family Living Patterns

We are told in *Double Jeopardy*, which studied approximately 2.5 million old-age recipients, that a higher percentage of elderly blacks than whites were heads of households, but that most of the blacks lived under deprived conditions. For example, nearly the same percentage, 30 percent, white and black household heads lived alone, but 20 percent of the blacks and only 12.5 percent of the whites had other persons besides husband or wife living with them.

Although overcrowding seldom appears to be an obstacle among the general aging population, a 1963 study by the U.S. Housing and Home Finance Agency found that among elderly nonwhite renters, 9 percent did live under extremely overcrowded conditions with more than $1\frac{1}{2}$ persons per room, while 5 percent of home owners were living in similar conditions. In contrast, among the total population, only 3 percent of the aged renters and 1 percent of the owners lived in these same conditions. Older blacks are more apt to live in large family groups than the aging population in general. Again, *Double Jeopardy* identified a larger proportion of black Old Age Assistance recipients than whites living in someone else's household—28 percent as compared with 23 percent. This same study also cited that approximately 5 percent of all elderly blacks resided with nonrelatives, as compared with a 2 percent average of all elderly persons.

As a result of this tendency of older blacks to live in someone else's household,

> It means . . . they must carry on the energy-consuming household work for large families and care (for) younger children at an age when the older person's health is poorest, energies lowest and the need for less stress is greatest.

A larger proportion of older blacks than whites are not living with their spouses. In testimony before the Special Committee on Aging, Miss Jeweldean Jones of the National Urban League commented that the higher percentage of older black males and women who are single can be attributed to greater broken marriages, shorter life expectancies of black males, and family patterns. According to Miss Jones' testimony, the present public welfare laws encourage the male to leave the family, which results in family separations while blacks are in early adulthood. Consequently, the chances of blacks becoming old and single are much greater than their white counterparts. This same welfare system helps to perpetuate feelings of helplessness and dependency which the poor black youth carries with him throughout his life and into old age.

Although living alone without a spouse is accepted as a common experience of older persons regardless of race and economic characteristics, Kent and Hirsch found that over half of their low-income inner-city respondents living alone had been without their spouses for fifteen years or more. As we know, the problem of adjusting to aging is apparently magnified by the loss of spouse. If this assessment is characteristic of most urban inner-city elderly populations, the Negro aged fares less well than the white, since at all levels in both sex groups, more blacks than whites have been without a spouse for fifteen years.

Since the aged black in our inner cities does not have as long a residency in these areas as the aged white, we can expect that among blacks, the proportion without living kin will increase with age. Among whites, on the other hand, fewer can be expected to be without living kin at an advanced age. We learn from the Kent and Hirsch study that 11 out of every 100 blacks had no living kin, in contrast with 6 out of every 100 whites who had no living kin.

It is unlikely that there will be dramatic changes in the family patterns of the black aged population rapidly enough to modify the trend of a large proportion of black aged households composed either of persons living alone or many persons living together.

Social and Economic Conditions

The Senate Committee on Aging heard much about the inadequate financial resources available to elderly poor black people. Miss Jeweldean Jones testified at these hearings that it was "bad enough to be black in our society . . . also bad to be old in a youth-oriented culture. But to be old and black is indeed to be in double jeopardy." In this testimony Miss Jones commented:

The pitifully low incomes of elderly people, especially elderly Negroes, is reflected in terms of daily bread and medical care. The $3,010 minimum annual income set by the Bureau of Labor Statistics as a modest but adequate budget for an elderly couple provides not quite an egg a day per person, about a half pound of meat and no provision for special diet or the expensive kinds of medical care all too often associated with the terminal illness that strikes one in ten aged couples every year.

Seven out of every ten elderly Negro couples have less than $3,000 a year; one in two couples, less than $2,000; and one couple in ten must live on less than $1,000 a year.

The older Negro man or woman who lives alone faces a daily existence even more bleak than that of married couples. $1,800 is the figure set by the BLS for a minimum sustenance budget for the lone elderly person, a budget which does not cover such basic items as medical care, car fare to the clinic, replacement of worn-out clothing.

Yet, 76.6 percent of the older men and 96.5 percent of the women have less than $2,000 a year; 45.7 percent of these men and 68.5 percent of lone older Negro women must try to get along on less than $1,000 a year.

Retirement for the aged black is primarily a logical sequence of the deprivation which faced him prior to retirement. Accordingly, the black in retirement usually suffers because of his unstable employment and low wage background which result in smaller social security benefits. In 1962, for instance, black retired couples averaged about two-thirds of white retirement income, and fully half of them had less than $1,960 for the year. Further, . . . for the year 1966, in those families headed by individuals sixty-five and over, 47 percent of the nonwhite families were poor as compared with 20 percent of the white families.

Work and Black Men

Although we have observed an improvement in the employment status of blacks during the last decade, black men of all ages are still less likely than white men to find full-time employment. In 1964 little more than half of all nonwhite males who worked had full-time, year-round jobs, compared with two-thirds of all white males. Moreover, long-term unemployment is quite prevalent among older nonwhite men, as they tend to have relatively less education and training than whites of the same age group, and are likely to be employed in heavy manual labor and in occupations particularly subject to seasonality or high turnover. During the period 1948–1964, labor force participation rates in the 55–64 age group dropped more among nonwhite males than white males. In 1948, for example, nearly 89 percent of all black males aged 55–64 were in the labor force, but by 1964 their labor force participation had dropped to almost 79 percent. In contrast, the labor force participation during this same period for white males in the same age group dropped from nearly 90 percent to only 87 percent.

In 1969, among those over sixty-five, both white and black males had relatively sharp declines in employment, as both groups together average only about 26.5 percent labor force participation rates—25 percent for blacks and 27 percent for whites. With reference to the proportion of older black males who do not participate, Beattie pointed out that:

> The aged and aging Negro faces a difficult, if not impossible situation in trying to remain in or re-enter the labor market . . . the Urban League has been able to place only one Negro male applicant who was beyond 45 years of age, in a St. Louis industry . . . the Negro is still the last hired and the first fired.[4]

Work and Black Women

Aged black women work outside their homes more often and longer than white women. In 1965 only 9.7 percent of white women aged sixty-five and over were in the labor force, whereas 12.9 percent of black women were still working. As we have pointed out previously, the black aged male is forced into early retirement; in contrast, his spouse may continue in the labor force, but her employment is usually confined to domestic work. These differences in labor force participation are highly significant because they imply that the black aged male is not the breadwinner and thus enters old age without a defined social function, since the black aged female's continued participation in the labor force means that she will be head of the household. Kent and Hirsch, in their study, for instance, found that after age sixty-five, black women and white men were most likely to be employed. Although these roles are not radically different from those family patterns that existed for today's aged black families in their early adulthood years, they still mean that the aged black male's problems in adjusting to retirement are much different from those of the white aged male.

Occupational Diversity of Black Workers

Although the proportion of nonwhite workers has increased in fields from which they have previously tended to be excluded such as professional and technical jobs, approximately two-fifths of these workers were still engaged in service, laborer, or farm occupations in 1969, which was more than twice the proportion of whites in these same occupations. Regardless of improvement in the overall occupational situation for blacks, most older blacks are likely to be engaged in labor or service work which is unskilled and subject to low pay or unstable seasonal employment. Of all employed blacks in 1969, only 6 percent were employed in professional or technical occupations whereas more than half were employed as farm laborers, domestics, and service workers. Furthermore, in 1969, 20 percent of all employed black females were private household or domestic workers compared to only 3 percent white females involved in similar work. A large percentage of the domestic female workers are middle-aged and elderly blacks, and, according to the President's 1970 Manpower Report, half of all families headed by domestic workers were considered poor.

Today's aged black population has entered old age with a wide gap between their retirement income and that of whites. In 1968, the median income of black families for those age sixty-five and above was only 65 percent of that for white families in the same age group. In its 1969 report on *Developments in Aging*, the U.S. Senate Special Committee on Aging cited that although about one of every four persons age sixty-five and above is poor, the percentage among black aged is practically twice as great since almost one of every two—47.7 percent—blacks sixty-five and older can be considered poor. Furthermore, the efforts of the aged black to escape from poverty are frequently multiplied by prejudices in our society, which, according to Dr. Inabel B. Lindsay means that the family head cannot look forward to increased earning potential through better education, job training, and decreases in employment discrimination.

As Berkowitz and Burkhauser stated,[5] for the older worker who is also a black man, or poorly educated, or not highly skilled, the chances of becoming unemployed are more likely than that of the white older worker who is also unskilled and poorly educated. These same authors commented that if the older black worker has skills that have become technologically inefficient or if he is caught in a stagnant industry, his unemployment probability is further compounded.

Work and Educational Attainment

If present economic policies of this country continue, we can expect the aging black population in our inner cities to comprise a large "underclass" depending on government assistance for daily existence. Even if every racial barrier were immediately eliminated for the aged black worker, the mass of aged blacks would still face a disastrous economic future. Their limited educational attainment in part was the starting point of a vicious cycle which failed to prepare them for skilled jobs or for upgrading opportunities. Although we have observed a higher educational attainment of young adult blacks in recent years, the educational levels of middle-aged and elderly blacks are very low.

The Manpower Report to the President, 1970, indicated that approximately three of every five blacks, age 25 to 29, have completed high school—which is almost twice the proportion among those blacks age 45 to 54 and four times that for the 55-to-64 black group. When educational achievements are compared between black and white middle-aged and older persons, the results reveal significant gaps in the two age groups. In the 45-to-54 group, for instance, 59 percent whites had completed high school whereas only 29 percent blacks completed similar educational levels. Further, in the group 55 to 64, only 15 percent blacks had completed high school compared to 45 percent whites who had done likewise. In 1969 the percent distribution by median years of school completed for persons aged 20 years and above was as follows:

| | Median years of school completed | |
AGE	BLACK	WHITE
20 and 21	12.2	12.8
21 to 24	12.2	12.7
25 to 29	12.1	12.6
30 to 34	12.0	12.5
35 to 44	10.6	12.4
45 to 54	9.1	12.2
55 to 64	7.6	10.9
65 to 74	6.1	8.9
75 and over	5.2	8.5

As we can readily observe from the above statistics, the aged black's inferior educational attainment has probably contributed to his few job opportunities, less steady work, a high rate of unemployment, and low pay scales, which make inevitable the insecurity and poverty of aging Negroes. There appears to be a close relationship between the aged black's meager education and his poor socioeconomic conditions. Lumber observed the same relationship and commented that "poverty feeds inferior education; inferior education feeds poverty."

Social Security Benefits

The result of the aged black person's employment in most low-level occupations is a marked differential in the incomes of black and white social security beneficiaries, even though liberal amendments have been added to the Social Security Act since 1955. Dr. Lindsay submitted a statement to the U.S. Senate Committee on Aging which stated that the benefits gained for women and children through these liberalizations were of considerably greater significance than those for retirees. Of this latter group only 8 percent were nonwhites at the end of 1967, as compared with a mere 6 percent in 1955—the average benefit for nonwhites than whites age 65 and over (on the basis of the number of recipients per 1,000 population of this age). For instance, public assistance in 1962 accounted for 70 percent of the income received by nonwhite married women, who seldom owned any income-producing assets such as private individual annuities and so forth. In contrast, among the white aged, two-thirds of the couples and about half of the nonmarried reported such income. Although the necessity for public assistance may be a new experience for most whites, many elderly blacks merely retire from general public assistance to Old Age Assistance at the age of 65. For instance, the Kent and Hirsch Pennsylvania study found some highly significant differences between their low-income black and white sample with reference to public assistance:

Over 20 percent of the black respondents received Old Age Assistance benefits whereas only 10 percent of the white respondents received this type of aid.

Although many factors contributed to the difference in recipients of Old Age Assistance, the basic underlying factor appeared to result from the average social security benefit being smaller for the blacks than for whites, thus permitting more blacks to be eligible for supplementary assistance.

In addition to having more frequent dependence on Old Age Assistance, in the two lowest age groups (65–74 and 75–84), more blacks than whites also implied they were once welfare recipients.

Among those respondents either receiving welfare assistance or who applied for welfare since age 65, 20 percent of the respondents reported that they felt they needed welfare assistance since reaching age 65. The difference between races was highly significant as almost one-fourth of the black respondents implied a felt need, whereas only slightly more than one-tenth of the whites in each age group indicated such need.

When asked why they did not apply for Old Age Assistance benefits, the group who responded specified that they failed to apply because of reasons including the following:

1. Felt an imposition on personal life and children;
2. Fear of losing their owned home; and also,
3. Aspects of delivery of service which indicate that the aged have difficulty coping with both travel to the district welfare office and the "red tape" of intake procedures.
4. Aspects of delivery of service which imply that there is a lack of accurate information concerning eligibility among the potentially eligible aged groups.

We can conclude from this Pennsylvania study that large numbers of aged blacks are forced to retire to being an Old Age Assistance recipient, to climax a lifetime of social and economic indignities.

Health Conditions

Although we have observed that the elderly black is often handicapped economically and educationally, his health needs also pose serious problems in adjusting to old age. Despite the fact that there has been a significant increase in life expectancies for blacks, their death rate continues to be disproportionately high, and the morbidity rates for blacks exceed that of whites in comparable age groups.

In 1967, at birth, whites could expect a life expectancy of 71.3 years compared to only 64.6 years of life expectancy among blacks. In this same year, the white male at birth could expect to reach his 68th birthday whereas the black male could only expect to live 61 years. However, Beattie reported that after age 75 nonwhite mortality is lower than white. Thus, although fewer nonwhites survive to reach 75, those who do may, on the average, expect a remaining lifetime of about 2.5 years longer than the whites.

According to *Double Jeopardy*, the incidence of death from the leading killers—heart disease, cancer, brain hemorrhage, and accidents—is proportionately greater for older blacks than older white people. It has been cited also that deaths of nonwhites age 65 and over from tuberculosis account for 15 percent of all deaths; those from influenza and pneumonia, 8 percent of all deaths—16 percent of all patients in tuberculosis hospitals are nonwhites.

Although the reasons why men are not in the labor force are similar for both nonwhites and whites, a much larger proportion of nonwhite males than white males are not working because they are ill and disabled. In 1969, in the age group 55 to 64, the number of nonwhite males who were unable to work was 38 percent compared to only 28 percent of white males. Among the age group 65 and over, the ratio was quite similar as the number of nonwhite males unable to work was 19 percent compared to 9 percent in the white male group.

During the period 1961–1963, nonwhite persons after age 25 reported a higher rate of restricted activity, bed disability, and a greater number of days lost from work than white persons. In spite of their greater need for medical attention, blacks of all ages visit physicians less often than white persons and go to the dentist about one-third as often.

Institutional Care and Medicare

In Miss Jones' testimony about the plight of our black aged, she cited the lack of skilled nursing-home care as a national disaster for the country and an intolerable situation for blacks, since few nursing homes have been willing to admit aged black patients. Chronically ill Negroes in many states have been condemned to live out their lives in custodial-care mental hospitals because there is literally no place for them to go.

> Most Negroes cannot afford . . . costs of medical care and must either do without or settle for that which the community provides at nominal or no cost—care which, more often than not, is offered with indifference, at best, and frequently in a way calculated to humiliate.

These problems reflect both the inadequacy and unavailability of preventive and remedial health services for our increasing aged black population. The cost of food and drugs in inner-city ghetto areas is much higher than it is in the rest of the metropolitan areas. The income of the aged black buys relatively fewer of the items needed to sustain normal health. Health and housing are closely related, and substandard housing adversely affects those who must live in these dwellings. Of all the housing occupied by nonwhites in the United States in 1968, 24 percent of these occupied by blacks were substandard, as compared to 6 percent for whites. In both races, it can be assumed that a disproportionate share of such housing is occupied by the aged. As we have earlier mentioned, aged blacks—to a much greater extent than whites—are forced to share housing with relatives or friends.

Social Services

In addition to the shortage of health practitioners who are working in inner-city black areas, there is also a lack of related social services. The social or welfare worker for many aged black persons is their only contact and source of information regarding public health services. We all are aware of the scarcity of such workers, who too seldom are able to actively serve this segment of the population.

Conclusion

Given the history and the reality of the lives of elderly black Americans, imperative action is clear. Their future, like the future of the Mexican-American and the American Indian, is inextricably linked to efforts of this society to discharge its responsibility to all of its members. The dysfunction in the society endemic to the life space of elderly black Americans increasingly demands attention and contributes to the deepening crisis of the aged in our country. Facts and statistics notwithstanding, growing old black is a peculiar and perilous experience.

Their history usually reflects low-paid employment, a disproportionate amount of unemployment and underemployment, inadequate health care with resulting high death rates, greater necessity to depend on public assistance, and, for most aged blacks, family situations which offer little aid.

The deprived socioeconomic conditions of the elderly black population are rather complex and also require that we understand the need of special reaching out in order to motivate older blacks to participate in and utilize existing aging programs and services.

Since so many older blacks live in poverty and need additional income, but cannot gain entry to the labor force, we suggest the creation of an employment program based on human service jobs. We believe such a program would be helpful to both the elderly black population and the community, because it would permit the older blacks to realize their potential, maintain themselves economically, and bring meaning to their lives while enriching the services of the community. It would seem especially advantageous to involve elderly blacks in cases where, conditioned by a heritage of segregation to resist free interchange with whites, they might participate more freely with other blacks to help provide some of the substantial service needs that exist within the black community, as well as in other communities.

NOTES

1. Kent, Donald P., and Carl Hirsch. *Social, Economic, and Health Conditions of Negro and White Aged and Their Utilization of Community Resources*. Final report submitted to the Administration on Aging. Grant AA-4-68-028-01. 1971.
2. Silberman, Charles E., "The City and the Negro," *Fortune*, March 1962.
3. Brotman, Herman, "The Older Population: Some Facts We Should Know" (draft), *Administration on Aging*, HEW, April 1970.
4. Beattie, W. M., Jr., "The Aging Negro: Some implications for Social Welfare Services," *Phylon*, 21:131–135, 1960.
5. Berkowitz, Monroe, and Richard Burkhauser, "Unemployment and the Middle-Aged Worker," *Industrial Gerontology*, 3 (October 1969).

The Chicano Aged

DAVID MALDONADO, JR.

Aged Mexican-Americans are commonly assumed to hold high status and to be well cared for by their extended families. This generalization can be misused to avoid providing necessary services. Moreover, it does not take into account the vastly changed conditions of Chicano life. Since World War II the Mexican-American community has experienced a transformation from a rural community to an urban one. Most of the Mexican-American aged grew up in rural areas, yet they now find themselves residing in a city or a small town far from their children. While efforts are made to maintain traditional family relationships and to care for the aged in spite of urbanization, the task is becoming increasingly difficult. Nevertheless, the old assumptions persist, and as a result the needs of the Chicano aged are often unrecognized and unmet.

Social scientists, both within the Mexican-American community and without, have created sociological and psychological theories that supposedly explain and describe the elderly Chicanos (*los viejitos*). Some of the theories have been based on factual data and on observation at some point in history and formerly were justified. This was especially true of the concepts of the extended family and of the patriarchal or matriarchal structure, which refers in this instance to the high status and the roles of the family's older members. However, it is becoming questionable whether these theories now describe this particular segment of the Chicano community. (In this article, the terms "Chicano" and "Mexican-American" are used interchangeably.)

The Chicano population has experienced rapid and dramatic social change since World War II. Today's elderly Chicanos have seen in their lifetime a phenomenal degree of social change that has greatly affected individuals, their family, their society, and the manner in which each relates to the other. Yet, in general, society's attitudes toward them are more applicable to previous generations of older Chicanos than to those of the present generation, especially if they have lived most of their lives in the United States. The result is a population living today who are treated as if they belonged to a past generation.

Nevertheless, it is important to recognize that there is a constant flow of immigrants from Mexico. Thus there are some elderly Chicanos who have not gone through this drastic social change and who therefore more closely maintain the traditions expected of them. The variety that is evident among the present older generation makes the stereotyping all the more unjust and invalid.

Back of popular sociological theory is the assumption that aged Mexican-Americans are properly cared for because of the extended family pattern. It is also assumed that the aged have the emotional and social support they need to maintain a positive self-esteem and a positive relationship with their environment because of their role and status as the older family members.

These popular viewpoints, although they may be based on historical fact, may today be incomplete and misleading notions. They may well work to the disadvantage of aged Mexican-Americans rather than have positive implications for their well-being. For example, public and private social agencies may find it convenient to use these generalizations to cover their inadequate services to older Mexican-Americans and their lack of understanding of these people. Governmental social agencies, in "respecting the culture," may be avoiding their responsibility to provide services since they place responsibility on the Chicano family. At the same time, the agencies are not providing the family with the resources for making needed services available to the aged. Social scientists, in their delight at discovering a social theory that contains some truth, seem content to perpetuate the theory without vigorously following it through the extreme social changes that occurred in the last decades.

The Extended Family

The Mexican-American family has traditionally been characterized by its pattern of extended relationships. The relationships go beyond the nuclear family to include adult relatives (cousins, uncles, or aunts), other dependent children (orphans or children of divorced parents), and the grandparents or even the great-grandparents.[1] The extended family may live within one household or in a cluster of homes around its older members, either on a farm or in a *barrio*. The important elements are the interpersonal and intergenerational relationships and the interdependence, rather than the strictly physical or geographical proximity, of family members. As Sotomayor notes:

> It is a supportive and flexible structure assuming functions in dealing with the environment and with the emotional and psychological aspects of the family unit and individuals.[2]

The extended family bends to the needs of the group or its individual members. The group may care for the children of working or unemployed parents and may provide emotional and social support when its adult members need it, either in times of development or in times of stress.

Such a family pattern especially affects the aged. The larger group shares the physical or emotional needs of any member. Thus aging Mexican-Americans within the extended family structure face no threat to their physical survival. Biological change, especially loss of physical strength, does not present a threat to the aged; the family will care for them. The group increasingly supports the male when he gradually loses his instrumental role (employment for wages) and the female when she just as gradually becomes limited in her ability to continue her household chores. The conclusion implied is that the aged, regardless of physical or mental capability, will continue to be part of the extended family. Such a pattern does not permit the isolation of older men and women but retains them within both the physical and social life of the family.[3] It is common to see a very old man, bedridden at home, but surrounded daily by his children or grandchildren. And it is equally common to see a very old woman in such a situation. In a way, that bedridden person even becomes the center of the family's life.

The aged person in the extended family holds high status and commands the respect and obedience of the younger family members. To quote Sotomayor, "The aged are greatly respected among Mexican-Americans; positions of authority are assigned to them regardless of their sex."[4] Within the extended family structure, the aging person grows in prestige and respect. He holds high rank and has influence in the life of the group.

A myth that has developed and has been perpetuated is that the Mexican-American family is a patriarchal structure.[5] The oldest male, either son or father, is pictured as playing the dominant role. Closer observation reveals that the woman plays an even more active role as she grows older, to the point that the grandmother plays quite a dominant role in the extended family. This does not mean that the elderly male is playing a lesser role; it probably indicates the high early death rate among the men. But more important, it indicates that the surviving older parent, whether man or woman, continues as head of the hierarchy; the oldest son does not become head merely because he is male.

Many Anglo-Americans assume that aging Chicanos, since they supposedly are growing in respect and status, do not face emotional or psychological stress on reaching old age. These people take it for granted that the patriarchal pattern of the extended family provides the support and the roles that help the individual avoid such stress. Thus the popular view is that the aging Chicano has few special problems either physically or emotionally. The extended family is expected to provide for the elderly. Meanwhile, those planning the research studies about the aging and those responsible for considering the distribution of resources to the needy aged in both the public and private welfare sectors tend to exclude the Chicano.

Changing Patterns

Just as myths about the Chicano aged maintain images that no longer reflect true conditions, so some stereotypes about them are themselves based on other stereotypes. The popular view is based on conditions that have changed or are rapidly changing; the false image is based on a myth of the Mexican-American family, which is making social adjustments as it reflects the changing situation of the Chicano community in the larger society.

The Chicano community today appears to be transforming the basic social structure of its extended family. There seems to be a gradual movement toward developing and strengthening the nuclear family. The basic need of survival, rather than purposeful planning or modified Chicano values, is probably bringing this about. It would appear that the more deeply Chicanos participate in the urbanized industrial society of the United States, the greater is the social and economic pressure to adapt their social structures to the society or to accept structures that the system produces. The nuclear family seems to be a product of the modern society.

Kooy has described the effect that a changing social environment has on the family and its older members.[6] In a study of the transformation of the town of Achterhoek in the Netherlands from a rural agrarian society to an industrial urban system, he pointed to the increased importance of the nuclear family, the accompanying breakdown of the extended family, and the dwindling status and role of the elderly. Thus a connection was indicated between urbanization, the nuclear family, and the role of the aged. Along with greater modernization came increased physical and social needs of the aged because of their isolation, loss function, and loss of status.

Agrarian societies produce social structures that are functionally appropriate to them. The extended family is an example of a social structure that is functional in an agrarian society. Such a family provides the society with a balanced distribution of manpower and the persons who can perform the roles necessary for surviving in the system. The family unit in its extended form provides workers (mature men, youths, some younger women), persons having knowledge based on experience (the aged), those who engage in child care (older women), and those who perform other supportive roles (housewives). Together all make it possible for families and individuals to survive.

Such a system provides for individuals of all ages and conditions and develops roles for them. To a considerable degree, the extended family in an agrarian society is self-supporting and independent. Because of its independence from the rest of society and because of the way that work needed for survival is distributed within the group, the family tends to develop a strong sense of group identity and of interdependence. The young workers depend on others for supportive services (for example, meals); the old, when they cannot work, depend on the young. Thus, in an agrarian society, one can readily see how an extended family pattern develops, in which the aging members continue to perform functional roles and even attain higher status than they had when they were younger.

Attachment to the Land

The Mexican-American community, since World War II, has been experiencing a transformation from a rural to an urban society. A brief historical survey of Mexican-Americans reveals an initial agrarian experience. The Chicano culture was established on certain fundamental principles of land distribution, land usage, and love for the land. The Indian reverence for the land and the Spanish methods of land distribution (land grants, communal rights, and so on) blended to give birth to a people deeply attached to the land. The cries of revolution have been *tierra o muerte* (land or death) from the early struggles for independence to the present.

Mexican-Americans living in the United States have maintained a history and culture close to the land. For as long a time as they could and as much as possible, they built their lives close to the land. In short, Chicano history is a history of the land.

At the start, most Mexican-Americans were in the rural areas of the Southwest. Their survival depended on farming. During the transitional period (from independence, to the Mexican War, to the time Mexican-Americans became a minority group in the country) they continued to work the land and maintain the extended family, which proved to be a fairly stable social system encouraging their survival. The extended family, in turn, kept alive the roles and relationships involved in such a pattern. For example, in this system respect for the aged was maintained, useful roles for the elderly were assured, and the immediate family provided for their needs. This pattern is still found in rural areas, among migrant farm workers, and even in some urban *barrios* where families tend to cluster around the older parents.

But Chicanos have not remained on the farm; they have moved into the city. Their migration into the urban areas began with World War I, although its largest thrust was during World War II. Chicanos moved to the city to man the machines; they also left the farm for military service, and they never returned. They left the Rio Grande Valley in Texas to move into San Antonio, Houston, Dallas, Fort Worth; they left rural communities to form *barrios* in Albuquerque, Phoenix, Tucson; they moved into Los Angeles and Denver, even Detroit and Chicago. Chicanos have become urban.

This movement into the city has had its effect on life style. It has thrust young Chicanos into an urban and industrial environment in which the pressure to survive challenges their old ways. Their aged parents probably remained on the farm or in the rural community. Their brothers and sisters similarly moved into the city, although some may have remained near their parents.

But Chicanos, like all people bred in a particular culture, cannot discard their culture by merely moving away from its source to new surroundings. Cultural forms and values continue. When the parents become too old or too isolated, they may move into the city to be closer to their children. Efforts are made to maintain what has been functional and what has traditional value. But the modern setting exerts strong pressure to change those within it, if they are to survive. The extended family is no longer functional. Despite the great value that its members place on it, the extended family may actually impede their well-being.

Just as Chicanos left the farm for the city, they left farmwork for more skilled jobs, higher wages, and education. Social mobility also exerts pressure. Children are earning more than their parents ever dreamed of earning; their social status has risen with their education or skills. The children have risen higher on the social ladder than their parents, uncles, or even older brothers and sisters.

These phenomena have created pressure to break up the extended family and strengthen the nuclear unit. Young Chicanos have become independent of their parents and their brothers and sisters. Interdependence is decreasing. The young Chicano family is increasingly becoming more distant physically from relatives. It is mobile.

Implications for the Aged

The physical and social mobility of their children has had an equally dramatic effect on aged Mexican-Americans. Rapid and dramatic changes for the young have often placed the elderly in an awkward and difficult position. Their social environment has completely changed within their lifetime. Although they were reared within one culture (in a purer form), they now find themselves in a situation for which their early socialization did not prepare them. Tension and disjointedness seem to describe the relationship between this new social environment and the one in which they developed their values, attitudes, and expectations.

Most aged Mexican-Americans grew up in a rural community or on a farm. They had a function to perform then, and knew that when they reached old age they would still have a role, because they had seen their grandparents carry important roles in the extended family on the farm. Today the aged Chicanos find themselves in a city, surrounded by a system that does not need their knowledge and skills. Or they find themselves in a small town far from their children. They had prepared themselves for and looked forward to roles in old age that have never materialized.

Thus aged Chicanos are increasingly without a role. They find also that, since their children have moved upward socially and educationally, their own status and respect have relatively decreased. Their children do not need their knowledge to survive today. The values of the aged relate to an agrarian society; their children are living today in an urban industrial setting. The expectations of the aging Chicano do not always coincide with those of the younger generation.

The total effect is a population that may be misunderstood by both the general society and by its own culture. The general society, by having a dated understanding of Chicano culture, believes that the Chicano family can and will provide for its older members. The younger Chicano generation is having an increasingly difficult time in doing so. This does not mean that young Chicanos do not appreciate their parents. It is rather that they must adjust and pay a price for surviving and participating in such a mobile, urban, and industrial society as that in the United States today.

Both the older and younger Chicanos are recognizing the tension and transition. The young will not abandon the elderly for the sake of mere progress. Neither will the elderly cling to the young and demand care. Recent studies have shown that both generations are making adjustments, both are maintaining a strong sense of family, and the young are keeping their respect for the elderly.[7] The aged Chicano is independent.[8] He does not want to be a burden. He cherishes ownership of his home. The younger generation does much to keep the elderly close by and to provide personal attention. In San Antonio, for example, aging Chicanos did not want to go into a home for the aged, not only because of their strong sense of autonomy, but also because their children did not favor their going into an institution.[9]

As the Chicano family adjusts to the mobility and urbanization of the younger generation, the changes and adjustments in family patterns have serious implications for the welfare of the older generation. Yet the old myths of the extended family have blinded both the social scientists who formulate theories and the practitioners who provide social services so that they fail to understand the present crisis of the Chicano aged. Thus all too often elderly Chicanos are limited in the roles they are able to perform, and those who are in need may not receive the services provided to the aged who belong to other cultures.

NOTES

1. William Madsen, *The Mexican-Americans of South Texas* (New York: Holt, Rinehart & Winston, 1964), pp. 46–47.
2. Marta Sotomayor, "Mexican-American Interaction with Social Systems," *Social Casework*, 5 (May 1971), 321.
3. Margaret Clark and M. Mendelson, "Mexican-American Aged in San Francisco: A Case Description," *The Gerontologist*, 9 (Summer 1969), 90–95.
4. Sotomayor, op. cit., 321.
5. Arthur J. Rubel, *Across the Tracks—Mexican-Americans in a Texas City* (Austin: The University of Texas Press, 1966), pp. 60–70.
6. G. A. Kooy, "Social Systems and the Problem of Aging," in Richard Williams et al., eds., *Processes of Aging*, vol. 2 (New York: Atherton Press, 1963), pp. 43–60.
7. Francis M. Carp, *Factors in Utilization of Services by Mexican-American Elderly* (Palo Alto: American Institute for Research, 1968).
8. W. C. Steglich et al., "Survey of Needs and Resources among Aged Mexican-Americans" (Lubbock: Texas Technological College, 1968); and Carp, op. cit.
9. *See* Carp, op. cit.

9

The Politics
of Aging

The increased proportion of older people in our society has led to considerable speculation regarding their political impact. Some writers have suggested that the aged will become aware of their mutual interests and problems and form an effective voting bloc, while others point to the diversity of the aged population as a whole as an inhibitor of group consciousness. Regardless of whether or not older people share an awareness of their common identity, there is little question that government agencies and political bodies have increased the amount of attention directed to concerns of the aged. How these shifts in policy arise is examined in this part.

The Political Consciousness of the Aged

The notion of large groups of older people organizing politically to exercise "senior power" is intriguing. The aged make up only 10 percent of the nation's population, yet they vote in large numbers, forming a disproportionate share of the electorate. Persons sixty-five years of age and older constitute as much as 16 percent of the voting population (Binstock, 1972). In spite of their numbers, there is little evidence to suggest that the aged vote as a bloc in any systematic age-related fashion. Instead they continue the voting patterns established earlier in life, with social and economic rather than age-related factors being the chief consideration (Ragan and Dowd, 1974). Traditional affiliations based on social class, religion, area of residence, and political party continue to be the influential factors. Certainly instances can be identified in which the percentage of older people voting for a party or particular candidate has switched markedly from one situation to the next. However, these switches are reflections of those that occur among middle-aged and younger voters and cannot usually be attributed to age. The article by Foner discusses the potential for age-based intergenerational conflict arising from differential access to political power. After describing the mechanisms which reduce conflict, the author concludes that people will continue to unite on the basis of social class rather than age, except for those issues calling for sweeping social changes.

The Political Impact of Senior Power

Most evidence points to the unlikelihood of all older people ever forming a cohesive voting bloc, and this should not be surprising. Even if it could be affirmed that older people identify themselves as old, the identity itself is rather new, negative in effect, and only one among many competing and usually stronger identities. Several studies have shown that a high proportion of people over age sixty-five do not perceive of themselves as old or aged. Most of these people are economically advantaged, of high socioeconomic status, and in good health. Even the poorer aged, who are more likely to identify themselves as old, do not tend to attribute their problems specifically to age. Problems related to income, health, housing, and transportation have been, to some extent, life long concerns which merely become exaggerated with age (Riley and Foner, 1968). On the other hand, older people do coalesce on some issues that involve their self-interest as an age group. For instance, they are generally opposed to greater tax support for public schools (Binstock, 1974). However, these issues tend to arise on the community level, and this type of political momentum has not as yet been mobilized at the national level.

The article by Riemer and Binstock questions the importance politicians place on the "aged vote." Using the Carter presidential campaign as an example, the authors conclude that age-related issues played only a minor role in Carter's overall campaign strategy.

While the aged may never form a cohesive voting bloc, they are not devoid of political influence. Through organizations which appeal to a variety of subgroups of older persons, the aged are able to clearly articulate their interests. The precedent for interest-group associations for the aged in national politics was set by the Townsend movement, which began in California in 1933. Townsend, a Long Beach physician, proposed a tax on all business transactions to finance a $200-a-month pension for every person over age sixty. At one time it was widely believed that the Townsend movement was decisive in the passage of the Social Security Act, but recent analysis indicates that its major impact was rather to speed up legislation which was already overdue (Binstock, 1972).

Presently there are hundreds of organizations that lobby for programs affecting the aged, but most of these are ad hoc groups, mobilizing only when an aging-related legislative proposal happens to affect their interests in more than a passing way (Binstock, 1972). Only ten organizations that actively engage in national politics are more or less exclusively involved with issues related to the aged. Most of these organizations represent special interest groups, but three are mass membership organizations which support a wide variety of senior citizen concerns (Pratt, 1974). They are the National Retired Teachers Association (NRTA), the American Association of Retired Persons (AARP), and the National Association of Retired Federal Employees (NARFE). Through effective organization and lobbying efforts, these groups have been able to exert some discernible impact on the national political scene. The combined NRTA-AARP has a dues-paying membership of over six million persons. Through membership dues, travel plans, and insurance plans, these organizations and others like them have substantial operating revenues and are bureaucratically organized to pursue clear goals. In contrast, the most visible but least bureaucratically organized old-age organization, the Gray Panthers, relies on the charisma of its leader, Maggie Kuhn, and ideals of radical political activism to gain support for its programs, which are generally concerned with grassroots organization and the meeting of local needs. The final article, by Jacobs and Hess, describes both the ideals and the problems faced by the Gray Panthers.

Although the aged are politically limited as a voting bloc, they do exercise considerable influence on the political scene through effective organizational skills and lobbying for specific programs.

REFERENCES

Binstock, Robert H. 1972. Interest-group liberalism and the politics of aging. *Gerontologist* 12 (Autumn): 265–280.

———. 1974. Aging and the future of American politics. *Annals of the American Academy of Political and Social Science*, 415 (September): 199–212.

Pratt, Henry J. 1974. "Old age associations in national politics." *Annals of the American Academy of Political and Social Science*, 415 (September): 106–119.

Ragan, Pauline K., and James J. Dowd. 1974. The emerging political consciousness of the aged: A generational interpretation. *Journal of Social Issues* 30 (3): 137–158.

Riley, Matilda White, and Anne Foner. 1968. *Aging and society: A sociology of age stratification.* New York: Russell Sage Foundation.

Age Stratification and Age Conflict in Political Life
ANNE FONER

Age is a basis of structured social inequality, for age strata are
unequal in their access to positions of political power. Given this
existing inequality, the question arises why age conflict, which
occasionally occurs, is not a constant feature of society. There are
several factors which serve to reduce age conflict. First, people have
multiple group affiliations, so that they form cross-cutting allegiances to family, church, and work organizations. Second, the
inevitability of aging means that younger people are oriented
toward future as well as present roles. These conflict-reducing
mechanisms are more likely to be effective if the issues are material,
concerning the distribution of economic resources, rather than ideal,
concerning questions of freedom and justice.

The political rebellion of youth in the 1960s and early 1970s has generated
a great outpouring of commentary and analysis. Although this outpouring
has heightened awareness of age as an important influence on social life,
there has been as yet relatively little systematic attention to age in its own
right as a source of social inequalities, values, group loyalties, and societal
conflict. This paper focuses on this last point, going beyond the recent
youth protests to explore age generally as a basis of political cleavage in
modern society.

A few writers have sought through historical and comparative analysis
to broaden our perspective on contemporary youth movements. For
example, it has been noted that youth movements emerge periodically,
tending to develop around such broad social issues as peace and the rights
of oppressed or deprived groups (see, for example, Altbach and Peterson,
1972; Feuer, 1969; Laqueur, 1969; Lipset, 1971). Apart from the reputed
idealism of youth, however, there is no general agreement about the
conditions giving rise to youth protests. In fact, Lipset (1971:743–4) seems
to interpret youth movements not primarily as an expression of age
conflict, but rather as unrestrained action to realize the ideals to which
young people have been socialized. Conversely, Laqueur (1969:33–41)
detects in youth revolts a rejection of ideas received from the older
generation. He also remarks, without explaining his assertion, that these
rebellions prosper only against a background of rising affluence. Thus a
number of questions have been raised about the general phenomenon of

Source: Reprinted with permission from *American Sociological Review*, Vol. 39,
1974, pp. 187–196.

age as a basis of political dissension, questions that invite further analysis.

It is the thesis of this paper that such analysis can be brought into focus from the perspective of age stratification. The emerging theory of age stratification, outlined by Riley, Johnson, and Foner (1972), treats age as a centrally important characteristic—like class, sex, or ethnicity—influencing individual behavior and societal structure. In particular, this paper addresses a few broad issues: First, what is the potential for age conflict in political life? What are the age-related roots in the social structure of such conflict? Second, if there is a high potential for age cleavage, why do sharp political struggles between young and old erupt only sporadically? Third, what conditions are likely to foster political conflicts along age lines?

Age Stratification and Sources of Age-related Conflict

Several concepts and assumptions are germane to understanding age as a base of stratification and those age-related processes which may lead to clashes between age strata.

Some Elements in the Theory of Age Stratification

The theory of age stratification (Riley, Johnson, and Foner, 1972: chap. 1 especially) assumes that age "locates"[1] individuals or groups of people in the social structure. Age strata are viewed as layers which cut across the whole society, just as class strata do, but which order people and roles by age rather than economic position. Thus each age stratum is composed of people similar in age or life stage, who tend to share capacities, abilities, and motivations related to age. Age is also a criterion for entering or leaving roles and for the different rewards and obligations associated with these roles. In short, age is a basis of "structured social inequality."[2] Of particular relevance for political conflict, age strata are unequal in access to positions of political power. In most societies, young adults are less likely to be political leaders than middle-aged and older adults. Moreover, younger and older people often differ markedly in their political attitudes and ideologies (Riley and Foner, 1968: chap. 19).

The age-related differences in behavior and orientations at any given period are linked to two independent processes: (1) aging, as the individual changes psychologically and physiologically over the life course from birth to death, passes through role sequences, and acquires experience in these roles; and (2) cohort flow, as one cohort (generation) succeeds another, each having lived through a different historical period. In political terms, aging differentiates age strata insofar as people may become more conservative as they age or may gain greater access to political power. And differing cohort experiences can distinguish age strata because each cohort starts its political career in a different social climate or experiences unique events which have a lasting impact on its members' political views (Mannheim, 1952; Cain, 1964; Ryder, 1965).

These dynamics of aging and of cohort succession can lead to sharply polarized age strata, though such an outcome is clearly not ineluctable. Much depends on the direction and strength of changes with age and on the particular impact of new cohorts entering the polity. For, while the two processes of aging and cohort succession are analytically independent of one another, in any given period their joint operation influences the similarities or differences between age strata.

The Impact of Aging and Cohort Succession—An Illustration

An empirical example,[3] drawn from a fuller analysis by Agnello (1973), illustrates how aging and cohort succession are each involved in age-related changes in political attitudes over a sixteen-year span. As Table 1 shows, repeated national surveys reveal a marked decline (from 80 percent in 1952 to 49 percent in 1968) in overall agreement with the statement, "Voting is the only way that people like me can have any say about how the government runs things." These figures suggest not only a general decline in an exclusive reliance on electoral politics, but a change in the relations among age strata. In 1952 there were only minimal cross-section age differences; but by 1968 the differences between the youngest and the oldest strata had become pronounced.

Let us consider how aging and cohort succession may have contributed to these changing patterns in the above attitudes toward voting. (Table 1 alone, based like most cohort tables only on the two independent variables of age and date, does not permit one to disentangle the "effects"

TABLE 1 Percentage Agreeing with the Statement, "Voting is the only way that people like me can have any say about how the government runs things."

	Election year (age in parentheses)		
Year of birth	1952	1960	1968
1940–1947			37% (21–28)
1932–1939		69% (21–28)	41% (29–36)
1924–1931	79% (21–28)	69% (29–36)	44% (37–44)
1916–1923	74% (29–36)	67% (37–44)	49% (45–52)
1908–1915	81% (37–44)	74% (45–52)	56% (53–60)
1900–1907	82% (45–52)	74% (53–60)	62% (61+)
1892–1899	84% (53–60)	78% (61+)	
Before 1892	80% (61+)		
Difference between oldest and youngest strata	+1	+9	+25
Total electorate	80%	72%	49%
Total sample	1,899	1,954	1,557

SOURCE: Adapted from Thomas Agnello, 1973:257. Data for his analysis, originally compiled by the Michigan Survey Research Center, are drawn from comparable cross-section probability samples of the United States.

of these two processes from many other aspects of social change [see, for example, Riley, 1973].[4] Such a table does, nevertheless, provide invaluable clues to the two processes as these are intertwined with complex historical trends.) First, with respect to aging, the rows in Table 1 show how, within each cohort, there is a change over the life course toward less agreement with the statement. Thus aging is not necessarily associated with inflexibility of attitude, although the decreasing acceptance in the earlier cohorts (born before 1924–1932) lags behind the sixteen-year trend in the total electorate.[5] Second, with respect to cohort succession (seen in the diagonals of Table 1), the differences among cohorts are even more noticeable than the life-course differences as each more recent (younger) cohort is less likely to agree with the statement (especially at the start of the political career, age twenty-one to twenty-eight). Combining both processes, one might imagine a situation in which life-course and cohort differences offset each other exactly, resulting in the persistence to 1968 of the similarity among all age strata observed in 1952. In fact, however, the life-course changes, though tending to counteract, are not strong enough to offset the differences in cohort succession. Such findings indicate that both aging and cohort succession are implicated here in the societal trend.

Aging, Cohort Succession, and the Political Context

In this one illustration, then, one could attribute the gap between young and old in good part to the influx of new cohorts with decidedly less traditional orientations than older cohorts. But on other political questions, age strata may align quite differently. Life-course change does not always lag behind the general societal trend (see, for example, Evan, 1965). And new cohorts are sometimes less liberal than earlier ones, as is hinted in various cross-section data that show, for example, postrevolutionary Cuban workers, aged twenty-one to twenty-seven, as less favorable to the revolution than the (now older) rebel generation of Castro (Zeitlin, 1967:227); or young southern whites (under twenty-five) as less liberal on racial issues than their slightly older counterparts (Sheatsley, 1966:226).

As data are forthcoming, and more detailed theories aid the analysis of many specific issues and of the people's general political stance, it should become possible to specify the political circumstances in which aging and cohort succession work jointly to sharpen or minimize age differences in political attitudes and behaviors. There are some fragmentary clues already about political changes accompanying the process of aging. Contrary to widespread assumptions about growing rigidity with age, certain studies, like the Agnello example in Table 1, indicate that people do change political attitudes as they grow older, often becoming more liberal. Data on various specific issues—for example, attitudes toward trade unions, United States participation in a world organization, or equal pay for equal work for men and women—show that changes with age tend to be in the same direction as the general trend in the society (Evan, 1965, adapted by Riley, Johnson, and Foner, 1972:133–7). Such clues suggest that people, as they age, can respond to a changing political climate.

An intriguing hypothesis is suggested by one set of questions that contrasts specific attitudes with overall political stance (Evan, 1965, adapted by Riley, Johnson, and Foner, 1972:133–7). While on several specific issues the changes with age follow the societal trend (sometimes conservative, sometimes liberal), the life-course pattern of a general political orientation was quite different. Thus when people were asked whether they viewed themselves as conservative or liberal in politics, there was a net shift with age toward a more conservative position in every cohort for which there are data, even though in the society as a whole there was no similar trend. This apparently growing inclination to consider oneself conservative in some general sense suggests a wish not to rock the boat. Perhaps the influx of new, more liberal cohorts prompts the desire of established cohorts to make haste slowly. One can also interpret such responses as commitment to the existing institutions and associated values with which people are familiar and to which they have made an adjustment (Foner, 1972:139; cf. Becker, 1960; Ryder, 1965:858). The finding does not mean that, as they age, people cannot accept piecemeal changes; for the data on specific issues indicate that many do adapt to specific changes they can evaluate in the light of their own experience. In view of the hypothesized commitment to the fundamental social structure, such piecemeal changes are probably accepted because they seem to fit into, rather than threaten, existing social institutions.

In short, whether changes occur with age seems to depend on the issues being debated. If future analysis bears them out, these interpretations suggest that calls for sweeping changes in the society are most likely to provoke sharp age rifts by heightening the general resistance to change among people as they age.

Scattered clues are also at hand to suggest how the political climate affects cohort succession. It is often assumed that young cohorts, in "fresh contact" (Mannheim's phrase) with the political world, whose political ideas are just being formed, will be especially responsive to new political trends (Mannheim, 1952; Heberle, 1951:118–22; Lipset, 1963:279–83; cf. Ryder, 1965:848–51). Agnello's data (see Table 1) give an illustration of this process. In this instance, the new cohorts' lesser acceptance of voting as the only means to political influence would seem to mirror the wave of civil disobedience and protests in which young people participated in the 1960s. It has also been suggested that major events like wars and economic crises not only have a special impact on young cohorts, but that youthful responses tend to influence political views and behavior throughout the life course. One recent analysis, for example, points to the Depression years as strongly influencing the political views of the undergraduates of that period. Lipset and Ladd (1972) reanalyze Gallup data to show that the generation in college from 1929–1933 was consistently more liberal in its voting behavior in the elections of 1956, 1964, and 1968 than both older and younger cohorts.[6]

Such examples, though limited, suggest how the political context may affect the direction in which people change (or fail to change) their political views with age, and how it can influence the character of new cohorts. Certain political occurrences appear to impinge on both aging and cohort succession to heighten age disagreements, as, for example, foreign policy crises or sharp economic fluctuations, which may prompt young cohorts to espouse radically new ideas, the very kinds of ideas likely to raise the hackles of the old. Thus, especially in periods of rapid social change, the potential for age cleavage in political life seems far-reaching.

Age Stratification and the Potential for Reducing Age-related Conflict

Although our society has undergone dramatic changes over the century, it has not always experienced concomitant age-youth struggles—as the "silent generation" of the 1950s reminds us. Why is it that age differences, seemingly omnipresent beneath the surface of social life (Sorokin, 1969:193), do not regularly erupt in sharp political conflicts?[7] And when these conflicts emerge, why are the issues so often related to peace, morality, or justice? I propose that, just as there are age-related roots in the social structure precipitating age conflict, there are age-related mechanisms for reducing conflict. I shall first suggest how these conflict-reducing mechanisms are likely to operate and then consider how they may relate to the ebb and flow of issues of central political concern in the society. In discussing the possibilities of containing or preventing age conflict, I consider factors which may either minimize age-related political differences or, if such differences do emerge, forestall the outbreak of sharp and bitter struggles. Two features of social life that hold promise for reducing open conflict seem particularly age-related: membership in age-heterogeneous groups and age mobility.[8] These two features can serve to forge ties across age strata or reduce the possibility of enduring solidarity within strata.

Age-heterogeneous Groups

Multiple group affiliations often serve to reduce conflict in highly differentiated societies, with their many groups and potential bases of conflict. For the individual, membership in several groups may loosen his commitment to the values and goals of a single group; and for the society, conflicts within the various groups can sometimes offset each other. As Edward A. Ross (Coser, 1964:76) noted many years ago:

> A society . . . which is ridden by a dozen oppositions along lines running in every direction may actually be in less danger of being torn with violence or falling to pieces than one split just along one line.

Age strata seem particularly subject to cross-cutting allegiances. Unlike class stratification, where it is possible to conceive of members of particular classes having few contacts with people in other classes, members of age strata nearly always belong also, at critical points in their lives, to at least one age-heterogeneous group—the family. What, then, are the mechanisms by which age-heterogeneous memberships reduce political conflict? Under what conditions are these mechanisms most likely to work?

For one thing, members of such age-heterogeneous groups as a church or work organization often have common goals and interests that may override age differences on political matters. On the job, workers of all ages may unite to improve working conditions, especially where individuals of different ages hold similar jobs. In addition, association with people of other ages in primary groups tends to bring about feelings of mutual loyalty and responsibility and to forge close emotional bonds among all members. Such ties heighten the incentive to avoid political actions that might weaken or sever mutual attachments. Finally, interaction among age-heterogeneous members in these groups enables persons of differing political persuasion to socialize each other. It is no accident that children in the United States so often follow the party identification and voting patterns of their parents, so much so that, reminiscent of the Gilbert and Sullivan lyric, Hyman (1959:74) remarks that individuals may well be born into a political party. While this observation stresses the impact of parental ideas on children, children also teach their parents— or, at least, children, as they become politically aware, reactivate their parents' long-held but possibly latent views (cf. Riley et al., 1969). There was journalistic speculation, for example, that many prominent political figures in the United States were greatly influenced in their anti-Vietnam war positions by their college-age children.[9]

People of different ages in particular social groups are often held together, then, by common interests, shared sentiments, feelings of allegiance to one another, and sometimes affection. Such ties can transcend political disagreements among age strate and check extreme polarization. And where political cleavage tends to follow the divisions between age strata, these cross-age relationships can minimize the likelihood that cleavage will erupt in open conflict.

But what if these groups themselves are subdivided by age conflicts? If the issues dividing age strata within these groups are not the bases of political struggles, then intragroup age rifts seem unlikely to become politicized, to spawn political conflict in the larger society. In such circumstances, moreover, struggles in societal subsystems may serve as a safety valve by restricting to nonpolitical arenas the expression of resentments and frustrations that might otherwise erupt in the larger society. By contrast, should the issues dividing age strata in the various societal groups coincide with those involved in the age conflicts in the polity, then the age cleavages are likely to reinforce each other.

The Inevitability of Aging

The process of aging also holds promise for reducing age conflict although, like membership in age-heterogeneous groups, its effectiveness is related to current issues. Aging *is* mobility—that special type of mobility of individuals from one age stratum to the next. Unlike mobility between class strata, aging is inevitable and universal. Because of its unique characteristics, aging can serve in special ways to minimize conflict among age strata. Consider the class analogy again. Those in the lower classes who seek membership in a higher class often take on the values and ideas of the class to which they aspire (Merton, 1957:262–80), thereby losing a sense of identification with their class of origin. Is not this outcome more likely when mobility is inevitable? That is, young people, especially those on the threshold of adulthood, are undoubtedly oriented to their future adult roles as worker, spouse, or parent and thus to the roles, with their associated attitudes, of older strata. This process may involve merely becoming more tolerant of the differing views of older people; or it may even involve adopting the viewpoint of more mature people—a type of "anticipatory socialization" or "false consciousness." Older people, on their part, may sympathize with the young because they "have been there" themselves. To the extent that such reciprocal orientations exist, they can weaken the incentive or the capacity to struggle. Young people's acceptance of the norms of older strata can dissipate the feeling of "we-ness" among age peers that is so important an aspect of group solidarity. And sympathetic understanding of each other's views among both old and young breeds mutual accommodation.

But even if the young remain hostile to the views of older people, the inevitability of aging can undermine in other ways their motivation to participate in militant protests. Many youths are unwilling to risk future rewards by engaging in activities that could lead to disciplinary measures, even arrest or expulsion from school or job. Alternatively, young people may be quite willing to accept subordinate status or other deprivations, if they view these as temporary. Indeed, many dissatisfactions with their current status may seem trivial, as long as improvement in the future can be realistically expected.

Certain issues do impel young people to action. Yet even here the inevitability of aging may operate—at least as it can hamstring the effectiveness of their struggles. Aging sets limits to the period of youth, which may be nearly ended before political awareness fully develops. Youth movements may have difficulty maintaining continuity of membership and leadership as particular members move on to the next age stratum (cf. Lipset and Altbach, 1967:240). And in the transition to adulthood, people united earlier may lose their sense of common fate, as the concerns of youth lose their relevance, or as their relative impotence is gradually replaced by the power and influence given adults.

Like membership in age-heterogeneous groups, however, aging can sometimes work to kindle militant struggles. This seems particularly likely if an issue—like a war in which the young person must participate— requires prompt resolution. Or, if the individual's future appears to hinge on an immediate outcome. Then the short period of youth that remains to him may heighten his sense of urgency and involve him in struggles seeking instant results. If the issue remains unresolved, the boundaries of age cleavage may merely move forward over the life course. Indeed, in such instances aging may become the instrument for change by disseminating new beliefs across the threshold of an older stratum.

I have proposed, then, that mechanisms which weaken bonds in an age stratum, or those which strengthen ties between age strata, can reduce age conflict. For, if weak solidarity in an age group limits its capacity to confront other age groups, solidarity ties across age lines lessen the motivation to struggle. But whether cross-cutting group affiliations or the inevitability of aging do in fact limit age conflicts in political life appears to depend on the nature of the issues at stake and on the degree to which issues coincide among the many subsystems of society. Let us now consider types of issues that might respond to the conflict-reducing mechanisms I have discussed.

Reduction of Conflict and the Political Context

It is my hypothesis that age-related conflict-reducing mechanisms are most likely to be effective when the major issues of political controversy are material rather than ideal, that is, concern the way economic resources are distributed rather than questions of freedom and justice, the rights of all people, or ethical principles.[10] Thus, beyond the youthful idealism noted by poets and philosophers, the propensity of the young to challenge the old—especially around ideal issues—may be deeply rooted in the structure and dynamics of age stratification.

Material Issues and Conflict-reducing Mechanisms

Material issues bring into play class interests involving people of all ages. Many material issues are not clearly age-related. Rather they are likely to bear upon and to activate economic class interests that cut across age lines, thereby reducing the salience of age differences. Where class interests dominate, individuals in a class, whatever their age, will tend to unite in pressing their demands. For example, in a shop or a union, although young and old may differ about how to distribute benefits— present pay increases versus pension increments—they will nevertheless work together to fight a wage freeze or legislation which restricts unions.

Even where such economic issues as taxes or expenditures that favor particular age categories may divide the public along age lines, polarization between age strata is often avoided since the issues also divide along cross-cutting class lines. Within a particular class, people belong to age-heterogeneous groups where benefits designed for one age stratum indirectly accrue to people of other ages. Consider the family where public health care for the aged lightens the burden for younger family members, or where government financing of young people's college education reduces the financial obligations of middle-aged parents (cf. Riley, 1971). Or, consider the shop whose younger workers may support legislation providing liberal pensions for older workers to open up jobs for themselves.

The inevitability of aging with its potential for increased financial rewards may also allay young people's discontent with their relatively poor economic status. How great, after all, is the incentive to struggle over economic issues as long as the future holds promise of improvement?

In sum, it appears that membership in age-heterogeneous groups and age mobility can operate to reduce conflict around material issues by superseding age cleavages, or reducing the immediacy of these issues.

Ideal Issues and Conflict-reducing Mechanisms

Ideal issues seem less readily subject to such mechanisms. To be sure, few issues are purely "ideal" or "material." There may well be economic components in issues of war and peace, for example, or ideal components in the unequal distribution of wealth in an affluent society. As pure types, however, the two are distinct; and many specifically ideal issues seem more likely than material issues to drive a wedge between generations.

Ideal or moral issues involving justice or equality for society as a whole do not ordinarily bring into play cross-cutting solidarities. They tend to be broad, general questions touching all major spheres of social life which call forth differences between young and old everywhere. Further, if an age stratum is rebuffed on such an issue, its status and power become issues, reinforcing the basis of age cleavage (cf. Gusfield, 1966:173). Nor is age mobility likely to reduce the dissensions. Self-interested anticipation of improvement at the next stages of their own lives, which might otherwise induce young people to postpone struggle, is irrelevant when the struggle is for justice or equality for all. And to the extent that the issues seem urgent, youth's right to be heeded now becomes more crucial than the possibility of higher status in the future. Finally, for youth these may be all-or-nothing issues requiring sweeping social changes.[11] It is such basic changes that older people see as a threat to their way of life and are especially likely to oppose.

The characteristic immediacy of many ideal issues and the inability or unwillingness of older people to change for them prompt young people (at least important segments of the youth) to resort to militant political methods.[12] Their sense of urgency is in keeping with the strong emotional overtones of ideal issues and the fact that some of these—like war—raise doubts about the very shape of their future or whether there will be a future at all. This impatience of youth is exacerbated by slow-paced government agencies, dominated by mature strata unable, even when willing, to make such rapid changes. But older people are often not willing. When youth demand fundamental changes, the resistance of the old is aroused, and the militancy of youth increased.

For such reasons, ideal issues seem less amenable than material issues to processes that might reduce age conflict. It is controversies over such broad issues that seem so threatening to the old, so pressing to the young.

In sum, this paper has emphasized age in its own right as an important base of societal stratification. Because of the dynamic processes leading to an age-stratified society—with different strata often having unequal power and opposing political views—there is a high potential for political conflict along age lines. At the same time there are age-related mechanisms for reducing sharp age struggles. I have hypothesized that these conflict-reducing mechanisms are least effective when ideal issues predominate in political life. The fact that these types of issues are not always paramount in the polity helps explain the sporadic nature of sharp age conflicts. And since it is likely that these issues will be most prominent during periods of affluence, age conflicts may well prosper in the best of times.

NOTES

1. This term is borrowed from Karl Mannheim (1952), one of the first to formulate certain similarities and differences between age and class.
2. Heller (1969) uses this term as a title for her reader on social stratification. For a discussion of social inequality based on age, see Riley and Johnson (1971).
3. Full data for such analyses are not readily available. They must include information about several cohorts at the start of their political careers, when political orientations are first being formed. In addition, comparable data for each cohort for several periods of time after entry into the political system are necessary for disentangling cohort differences from life-course differences. A growing number of cohort studies deal with such political topics as party identification, voter turnout, and various political attitudes (for example, Crittenden, 1962; Cutler, 1968; Evan, 1965; Glenn and Grimes, 1968; Glenn and Hefner, 1972; Klecka, 1971). Such studies vary in their approximation of the "optimum" form of cohort analysis, facing many difficulties in achieving comparability of sampling or question wording, in allowing for mortality and migration, and in the knotty problems of analysis. (For a discussion of such possible pitfalls and a general overview of the problems, assumptions, and principles underlying cohort analysis, see Riley, Johnson, and Foner, 1972:22–90, 583–618, and, especially relevant to analysis of political data, 115–59.)

4. In the growing literature on this "identification problem" in cohort analysis, see Cohn (1972) and, as one of the special instances for which relevant solutions have been developed, see Mason et al. (1973). Another procedure is exemplified in a further analysis of Table 1, in which Agnello (1973:258) "controls" on education as one factor in social change which, highly correlated with age, might confound the effects of age. (In fact, this control does not change his original finding. And, of substantive interest, is the possibility that the large size of the educated sector of the young cohort might itself serve to stimulate attitude change.)
5. Methodological issues involved in comparing life-course changes in cohorts with changes over time in the total sample are discussed in Riley, Johnson, and Foner (1972:72–3); Cutler (1969-1970); Crittenden (1969–1970); and Glenn and Hefner (1972).
6. However, the finding does not hold for the earliest period examined, 1948; and the authors note that other survey data do not show comparable behavior for the Depression cohort. Further, in 1964 and 1968, each entering (youngest) cohort was even more likely to support the Democrats than the Depression cohort (Lipset and Ladd, 1972:75–8).
7. Feuer (1969:8) claims, for example, that revolutionary change in modern times has often been unaccompanied by a younger generation in conflict with an older one. See also Lipset and Altbach (1967:240) for comments on cycles in student political action, and Reinhold (1970) for examples of varying patterns of age conflict in antiquity.
8. Parallel factors, such as cross-pressures and social mobility, have been examined as they affect class polarization in the polity. Discussions of status inconsistency are also pertinent to age (as in Riley, Johnson, and Foner, 1972:413–14).
9. Such hypothesized effects of membership in age-heterogeneous groups are, of course, likely to be attenuated to the extent that actual contact and interaction between people of different ages are reduced, as in the case of young people living away from home.
10. The distinction is based on Weber's analysis (Gerth and Mills, 1958:180–94) and its later elaborations by Gusfield (1966:13–24, 172–88) and Hofstadter (1964a:84–5, 88, 1964b:98–100). Cf. Berelson, Lazarsfeld, and McPhee (1966:183–4) and their general discussion relating these types of issues to cleavages in political life (194–214).
11. In 1970, a period of vigorous student dissent, a survey of college students, for example, found 75% agreeing that "basic changes in the system will be necessary" to improve the quality of life in America (Keniston and Lerner, 1970:56).
12. Evidence that many young people did not look askance at nonconventional politics at a time when student protests were flourishing is suggested, for example, by late 1970 surveys of eighteen- to twenty-year-olds (both college and noncollege) which found that 54% regarded student protests as a healthy sign (Harris Survey, 1971).

REFERENCES

Agnello, Thomas J., Jr. 1973. "Aging and the sense of political powerlessness." Public Opinion Quarterly 37 (Summer):251–9.

Altbach, Philip G. and Patti M. Peterson. 1972. "Before Berkeley: Historical perspectives on American student activism." Pp. 13–31 in Philip G. Altbach and

Robert S. Laufer (eds.), The New Pilgrims: Youth Protest in Transition. New York: David McKay.

Becker, Howard S. 1960. "Notes on the concept of commitment." American Journal of Sociology 66 (July):32–40.

Berelson, Bernard R., Paul F. Lazarsfeld, and William N. McPhee. (1954), 1966. Voting: A Study of Opinion Formation in a Presidential Campaign. Chicago: University of Chicago Press.

Cain, Leonard D., Jr. 1964. "Life course and social structure." Pp. 272–309 in Robert E. L. Faris (ed.), Handbook of Modern Sociology. Chicago: Rand McNally.

Cohn, Richard. 1972. "Mathematical note." Pp. 85–8 in Matilda White Riley, Marilyn Johnson, and Anne Foner, Aging and Society. Volume III, A Sociology of Age Stratification. New York: Russell Sage Foundation.

Coser, Lewis A. (1956), 1964. The Functions of Social Conflict. New York: The Free Press.

Crittenden, John. 1962. "Aging and party affiliation." Public Opinion Quarterly 26 (Winter):648–57. 1969–1970. "Reply to Cutler." Public Opinion Quarterly 33 (Winter):589–91.

Cutler, Neal E. 1968. The Alternative Effects of Generation and Aging Upon Political Behavior: A Cohort Analysis of American Attitudes toward Foreign Policy, 1946–1966. Oak Ridge, Tennessee: Oak Ridge National Laboratory, 1969–1970. "Generation, maturation, and party affiliation: A cohort analysis." Public Opinion Quarterly 33 (Winter):583–8.

Evan, William M. 1965. "Cohort analysis of attitude data." Pp. 117–42 in James M. Beshers (ed.), Computer Methods in the Analysis of Large-Scale Social Systems. Cambridge, Massachusetts: Joint Center for Urban Studies of the M.I.T. and Harvard University.

Feuer, Lewis S. 1969. The Conflict of Generations. New York: Basic Books.

Foner, Anne. 1972. "The polity." Pp. 115–59 in Matilda White Riley, Marilyn Johnson, and Anne Foner, Aging and Society. Volume III, A Sociology of Age Stratification. New York: Russell Sage Foundation.

Gerth, H. H., and C. Wright Mills (eds.). 1958. From Max Weber. New York: Oxford University Press.

Glenn, Norval D. and Michael Grimes. 1968. "Aging, voting, and political interest." American Sociological Review 33 (August):563–75.

Glenn, Norval D. and Ted Hefner. 1972. "Further evidence on aging and party identification." Public Opinion Quarterly 36 (Spring):31–47.

Gusfield, Joseph R. 1966. Symbolic Crusade. Urbana, Illinois: University of Illinois Press.

Harris Survey. 1971. Reported in New York Post, January 7.

Heberle, Rudolph. 1951. Social Movements. New York: Appleton-Century-Crofts.

Heller, Celia S. (ed.). 1969. Structured Social Inequality. New York: Macmillan.

Hofstadter, Richard. 1964a. "The pseudo-conservative revolt (1955)." Pp. 75–95 in Daniel Bell (ed.), The Radical Right. New York: Doubleday, Anchor Books. 1971. "Youth and politics." Pp. 743–91 in Robert K. Merton and Robert Nisbet (eds.), Contemporary Social Problems. New York: Doubleday, Anchor Books.

Hyman, Herbert H. 1959. Political Socialization. Glencoe, Illinois: Free Press.

Keniston, Kenneth and Michael Lerner. 1970. "The unholy alliance against the campus." New York Times Magazine (November 8):28–9, 56–86.

Klecka, William R. 1971. "Applying political generations to the study of political behavior: A cohort analysis." Public Opinion Quarterly 35 (Fall):358–73.

Laqueur, Walter. 1969. "Reflections on youth movements." Commentary 47 (June):33–41.

Lipset, Seymour Martin. (1960), 1963. Political Man. New York: Doubleday, Anchor Books. 1971. "Youth and politics." Pp. 743–91 in Robert K. Merton and Robert Nisbet (eds.), Contemporary Social Problems. New York: Harcourt Brace Jovanovich.

Lipset, Seymour Martin and Philip G. Altbach. 1967. "Student politics and higher education in the United States." Pp. 199–252 in Seymour Martin Lipset (ed.), Student Politics. New York: Basic Books.

Lipset, Seymour Martin and Everett Carll Ladd, Jr. 1972. "The political future of activist generations." Pp. 63–84 in Philip G. Altbach and Robert S. Laufer (eds.), The New Pilgrims: Youth Protest in Transition. New York: David McKay.

Mannheim, Karl (1928). 1952. "The problem of generations." Pp. 276–322 in Paul Kecskemeti (ed. and tr.), Essays on the Sociology of Knowledge. London: Routledge and Kegan Paul.

Mason, Karen Oppenheim, William M. Mason, H. H. Winsborough, and W. Kenneth Poole. 1973. "Some methodological issues in cohort analysis of archival data." American Sociological Review 38 (April):242–58.

Merton, Robert K. 1957. Social Theory and Social Structure. The Free Press of Glencoe.

Reinhold, Meyer. 1970. "The generation gap in antiquity." Proceedings of the American Philosophical Society 114 (October):347–65.

Riley, Matilda White. 1971. "Social gerontology and the age stratification of society." The Gerontologist 11 (Spring, Part 1):79–87, 1973. "Aging and cohort succession: Interpretations and misinterpretations." Public Opinion Quarterly 37 (Spring):35–49.

Riley, Matilda White and Anne Foner. 1968. Aging and Society. Volume I, An Inventory of Research Findings. New York: Russell Sage Foundation.

Riley, Matilda White, Anne Foner, Beth Hess, and Marcia L. Toby. 1969. "Socialization for the middle and later years." Pp. 951–82 in David A. Goslin (ed.), Handbook of Socialization Theory and Research. Chicago: Rand McNally.

Riley, Matilda White and Marilyn E. Johnson. 1971. "Age stratification and the society." Presented at the Annual Meetings of the American Sociological Association, Denver, Colorado.

Riley, Matilda White, Marilyn Johnson, and Anne Foner. 1972. Aging and Society. Volume III, A Sociology of Age Stratification. New York: Russell Sage Foundation.

Ryder, Norman B. 1965. "The cohort as a concept in the study of social change." American Sociological Review 30 (December):843–61.

Sheatsley, Paul B. 1966. "White attitudes toward the Negro." Daedalus (Winter):217–38.

Sorokin, Pitirim. (1947), 1969. Society, Culture, and Personality. New York: Cooper Square Publishers.

Zeitlin, Maurice. 1967. Revolutionary Politics and the Cuban Working Class. Princeton, New Jersey: Princeton University Press.

Campaigning for "The Senior Vote": A Case Study of Carter's 1976 Campaign

YOSEF RIEMER AND
ROBERT H. BINSTOCK

The authors of this article wanted to determine if politicians behave on the premise that there is an "aged vote." They used the campaign of Jimmy Carter to examine the role that votes of older people play in electing candidates to office. The coordinators of Carter's "Senior Citizens Desk" identified and developed positions on the major concerns of the elderly. Ford and the Republicans were portrayed as indifferent to aged people's interests. However, the campaign funds actually expended on senior issues were relatively low, and Carter did not emphasize the issues in his speeches. Examined in isolation, the data on the seniors campaign make it appear that a concerted effort was made to appeal to the aged vote. But from an examination of the issue in the context of the entire campaign effort, it could be argued that the chief strategists did not see the aged as a constituency that could be influenced by emphasizing age-related issues.

The November 1978 elections have brought forth familiar assertions concerning the role that the votes of older persons may have played in electing some candidates and defeating others. Yet, to date, systematic research on the political attitudes and behavior of the aging has not yielded any evidence that old-age-based election campaign efforts cause older persons to shift voting allegiance from one candidate to another (Hudson and Binstock, 1976). Perhaps the continuing efforts of self-styled "political gerontologists" (Cutler, 1977) to find evidence of such a phenomenon will produce results, especially as new age cohorts, subject to new combinations of period effects, join the growing ranks of the chronologically old.

Even if the conventional beliefs regarding the voting behavior of older persons are unsupported by evidence, however, the beliefs in themselves may be powerful political factors. If politicians believe in the commonly

SOURCE: Copyright 1978 by the Gerontological Society. Reprinted by permission from *The Gerontologist*, Vol. 18, No. 6 (1978).

purveyed images of the aged as a potentially cohesive and decisive voting bloc, then they may be influenced by those beliefs in their allocation of election campaign resources, in their public commitments to policy positions, and in their approaches to the adoption and implementation of policy. Regardless of whether there is an "aged vote," the belief that there is may importantly shape electoral campaign and public policy decisions.

Do politicians behave on the premise that their campaign efforts and their policy-related activities can shift the votes of older persons from one candidate to the other? While it is conventional to assume that they do, we are unaware of research literature that attempts to examine this premise in a systematic fashion.

The central purpose of this article is to emphasize the need for systematic research on politicians' perceptions of "the senior vote," and on how those perceptions may affect electoral campaign and policy-related behavior. Our vehicle for accomplishing this purpose is a case account of the 1976 campaign of Jimmy Carter for the presidency of the United States.[1] In presenting this case we do not simply wish to add to the accumulation of reports on senior campaign efforts, although that is a useful objective. Instead, the objective is to place the senior campaign activities within the context of the overall Carter campaign effort, and thereby point up some issues for further examination. The data from this case study may be sufficient to illuminate these issues, if not to resolve them.

The Senior Campaign

Jimmy Carter, like all presidential candidates since the New Deal, took public positions on issues affecting older persons. And, as in all Democratic campaigns since 1960, a special Senior Citizens Desk within the Carter campaign organization worked to secure the votes of older persons for the candidate.

Carter's Positions on Senior Issues

As a backdrop against which Carter could present his positions on issues regarding older persons, the 1976 Democratic Presidential Campaign Committee (DPCC) often attacked sharply both Ford's and the Republican party's records on aging-related issues. Typical was a press release entitled "Carter Details GOP Neglect of Elderly,"[2] with excerpts from a speech the candidate had delivered in Miami. Carter characterized the Republican response to "the needs of older Americans" as a "callous, disgraceful record," charging that the Ford Administration had "proposed cutbacks in social security benefits, reductions in food programs for the elderly, and increases in the cost of Medicare." In addition, the candidate claimed that the incumbent administration had cut back housing for the elderly and was responsible for "extremely high inflation that robs every elderly person living on a fixed income." With an additional attack on Ford's record as a congressman, Carter concluded, "This is the kind of record Gerald Ford is running on. It is a shocking, disgraceful record, and he ought to be running from it instead of on it."

To contrast Carter's position with this portrayal of Ford and the Republicans, the DPCC issued a circular entitled "Carter and Ford on Aging in America,"[3] in which the Democratic candidate declared, "Americans have the right to expect in their later years that they will have an adequate income, comfortable housing, access to expert and affordable health care, and adequate transportation." In this and other campaign documents, Carter addressed senior citizen issues by stating more specific positions on income, health, housing, transportation, nutrition, and crime.

Regarding income for the aged, Carter pledged to "preserve the present cost-of-living benefits of the social security program."[3] He promised "to restore the fiscal integrity" of the social security system "by raising the wage base, rather than by raising the contribution rates."[4] He also favored "moving toward liberalization of the social security earnings test,"[5] but opposed complete elimination of it. To deal with problems of health, the candidate advocated "a national health care program" that would "promote early preventive and diagnostic care" and "allow for home health alternatives to institutionalization."[6] In the area of housing he called for "more rapid implementation of the rental housing program, and strong federal protection for persons threatened with displacement by landlords seeking to convert to condominium ownership."[6] He also declared himself "committed to a rapid increase in the Section 202 housing program for the elderly."[7] To deal with crime against the aged, Carter felt that "the federal government can help by encouraging state criminal justice agencies to plan crime prevention and victim assistance programs for the elderly, and by encouraging the development of swift and efficient criminal justice to insure certain punishment of those who prey on the helpless."[8] And, in addressing programs authorized by the Older Americans Act, he promised to "put an end to delay in implementation of nutrition programs for the elderly" and to "give a high priority to a transportation policy for senior citizens."[9]

Beyond these positions set forth as purported contrasts to those of Ford and the Republicans, Carter advanced two additional views. Taking a stand against age-based mandatory retirement, he observed a "need to change the laws and policies that force retirement on older people who are willing and able to work."[10] And to "take command of the Executive Branch to make it function . . . in response to the needs of the elderly," he promised "to appoint a Counselor on Aging in the Office of the President."[11] In a position paper explaining this pledge, he said he would "give this counselor full authority to coordinate existing programs and to develop new initiatives" so that the federal effort to serve the aged would be "efficient, manageable, and most of all comprehensible to, and usable by, those for whom it is intended."[12]

The "Seniors Desk"

In addition to the candidate's speeches and a dozen or so press releases and "position" documents issued by the campaign press office, the DPCC created two mechanisms specifically structured to focus on senior citizens. One of these was a National Senior Citizens for Carter/Mondale Advisory Committee, linked to similar campaign advisory councils on aging that were established in the states. The state councils were created to distribute campaign literature and to carry out senior citizen campaign activities in response to suggestions made by Democratic mayors and congressmen. The National Advisory Committee, jointly chaired by Congressman Claude Pepper, the Reverend Martin Luther King, Sr., Senator Frank Church, Governor Milton Shapp, and former Governor Pat Brown, was composed with an eye to the publicity it might attract through the fame of its members. The only specific request made of this group, however, was to attend a committee meeting on October 9 in Atlanta. Media coverage of this event was limited to a story in *The Colony Square Town Crier*, a publication issued at the residential complex in which the committee's meeting was held.

The primary mechanism for focusing efforts toward senior citizens was the DPCC's "Seniors Desk," one of the eleven such desks created to concentrate on specific campaign concerns. Most of these desks were expected to mobilize support from mass electoral constituencies such as seniors, blacks, Jews, and women; but a few were established for liaison with politicians—mayors, governors, congressmen, and the Democratic National Committee.

The Seniors Desk was under the joint direction of two Carter supporters from Georgia, H. Oliver Welch and Frank Newton. These co-coordinators and the rest of the desk's staff were unpaid. During the closing weeks of the campaign, twelve full-time volunteers were working for the Seniors Desk. Some were representing senior organizations: Roy and Doris Purdy for the National Council of Senior Citizens (NCSC); and Dave Dunning for the American Association of Retired Persons (AARP). Others were there because of long-time interest and involvement in the field of aging (Bob Weiner, staff director of the Subcommittee on Health and Long-term Care, U.S. House of Representatives Select Committee on Aging; Yosef Riemer, research assistant with that subcommittee; and Dick Kennedy, a former director of an Area Agency on Aging). Four others were ardent Carter supporters: Bill Lamkin, Bob Lohse, Ed Dougherty, and Rachelle Tarbutton.

The Seniors Desk undertook a variety of activities. One of the first was to write a pamphlet called "Jimmy Carter on the Elderly" which contrasted a critical portrayal of Ford and the Republicans with Carter's campaign promises and positions on aging-related issues. One million copies of this brochure were printed and then distributed to persons designated as senior campaign coordinators in each state.

A continual activity of the desk was to arrange for speakers to address large groups of seniors on behalf of the candidate. These speakers included Nelson Cruikshank, then on leave from the presidency of the National Council of Senior Citizens, and Congressman Claude Pepper, who was then Chairman of the Subcommittee on Health and Long-term Care of the House Select Committee on Aging. In addition, the distinguished anthropologist Dr. Margaret Mead was invited to tour the eastern United States, speaking about a project she called the "Senior-Junior Political Partnership." Her message was that the young and old should join together and realize their common interests. In immediate terms of the campaign, the goal was for seniors to "take nonvoting juniors to the polls to show them how the cornerstone of democracy works, and juniors to assist seniors who are in need of transportation or a strong arm to lean on."[13]

In addition to these speakers recruited primarily for senior citizen audiences the desk was also able to make use of the less specialized Carter campaigners for appearances before senior groups. Rosalynn (Jimmy's wife) and particularly Miz Lillian (his mother) made a number of appearances at senior rallies, housing projects, nutrition sites, senior centers, and nursing homes throughout the country.

Along with its efforts to arrange these appearances, the seniors unit worked to build audiences of older persons to hear the speeches. Even when a campaign appearance was not geared specifically to the aging, the seniors staff would try to turn out a large contingent of older persons. For instance, if Jimmy were scheduled to speak at an airport rally, the desk would attempt to have a sizable group of local senior citizens present.

Another activity was to encourage organizations in the field of aging to join in with the Carter campaign, in one fashion or another. The nature of the cooperation that was sought and the success of these efforts varied substantially. At one extreme, the seniors staff was able to contact local chapters of NCSC and AARP and get their help in building crowds for Carter campaign appearances. At the other extreme, the staff sent a telegram comprised of Carter/Mondale greetings and positions on senior issues to the national meeting of the Gerontological Society, an organization of some 5,000 researchers and practitioners in aging; but the telegram was not read to the meeting.

The Seniors Desk also undertook several projects to "get out the vote" by making it easier for older persons to get to the polls. The staff tried, but failed, to persuade the International Taxicab Association to provide rides to the polls for senior citizens at a fixed rate of fifty cents. Similarly, unsuccessful attempts were made to have Greyhound Lines and National Trailways provide low-cost bus transportation.

The culmination of the Seniors Desk activities was planning and organizing "National Senior Citizens for Carter/Mondale Day" on October 28, five days before the election. Designed to focus as much attention as possible on the candidate's commitment to older persons issues, the day began with Carter giving a breakfast speech to a group of seniors in Pittsburgh. Then, throughout the day, sixty-seven congressmen, thirty-four candidates for Congress, twenty-seven mayors from a roster of the fifty largest cities in the country, and other leaders of civic and senior organizations were committed to appear in their own communities at a variety of events geared toward seniors. These events included speeches at nursing homes, senior rallies, and nutrition program sites; news conferences; intensive distributions of campaign literature on Carter and the elderly; and, uniquely, a lawn bowling party for seniors that took place in a public park.

Assumptions behind the Seniors Campaign

Obviously the prime objective of the Seniors Desk in undertaking these activities was to get the largest possible number of older persons to vote for Carter and the fewest possible to vote for Ford. But what connections did they see between this objective and the activities they undertook to achieve it?

At the outset, the seniors staff recognized that "getting out the vote" of older persons would not, in itself, be a desirable strategy. They knew that the voting participation rate of older persons is relatively high, and stated explicitly in their "National Senior Citizens Campaign" manual that "70 percent of sixty-five and over vote" and that in the 1972 presidential election "15 percent of voters were sixty-five and over."[14] Moreover, the Seniors Desk volunteers were well aware of historical patterns through which the percentages of older persons' votes cast for the two major parties have fluctuated, but tended to favor Republicans. In contrast, for example, the Minorities (blacks) Desk of the Carter campaign worked with the assumptions that black voters have a relatively low voting participation rate and have been predisposed to vote for Democratic candidates in recent presidential elections. Consequently, that desk primarily stressed a "get out the vote" strategy in its campaign activities. But the Seniors Desk assumed that a primary emphasis on getting seniors to the polls would be fruitless unless something were done to maintain and increase the constituency's predilection to vote for Carter. Indeed, they were concerned that if nothing were done to switch some senior votes to Carter, a very high turnout of older voters might be beneficial to Ford.

Assuming that the votes of a substantial, unspecified number of older voters could be swung from one candidate to the other, the seniors campaign operated on the premise that the way to bring about such a swing would be through effective use of senior issues. This issue strategy involved several steps. First, the desk co-coordinators identified the "major concerns of elderly" as "income, health care, transportation, housing, personal security (crime, unemployment, etc.),"[14] and developed positions for Carter on these issues which they believed would appeal to older persons. Second, they developed a portrayal of Ford's record on these concerns which they believed would be unappealing. Third, they got Carter to state publicly many of the positions they developed as well as attack Ford's record. Fourth, they were able to distribute approximately one million copies of releases, position papers, and speeches focused on senior citizen issues. And finally, they made these issues the main focus of National Seniors Day, of the meeting of the National Advisory Committee, and of their numerous efforts with the aging organizations and the campaign advisory units in the states.

In short, the primary strategy of the Seniors Desk was to develop a favorable contrast between Carter's and Ford's positions on senior issues, and to convey that contrast to as many older persons as possible. However, some of the assumptions implicit in this strategy were not explicitly confronted by the co-coordinators of the seniors campaign.

One conventional assumption, of course, was that voters are swayed more by issues favoring their self-interest than by altruistic issues, party attachments, or images of the candidate. How does one speech on senior issues compare with one speech on justice, or with one loving interlude between Miz Lillian and her son in prime time?

Even accepting the assumption that self-interest issues are most important in swinging votes, another implicit assumption was that older voters primarily identify themselves, and hence their self-interest, in terms of aging. When a person reaches sixty-five, or enters retirement status, he or she does not suddenly lose all prior self-identities—sex, race, education, peer group and community ties, and so on—and the self-interests that can be derived from them (Binstock, 1972). Take the case of a seventy-three-year-old Caucasian, Catholic widow in Chicago, living comfortably on income from capital gains and dividends, who is deeply involved in advocacy for children's programs. Given a candidate who takes positions on race relations, abortion, urban affairs, tax reform, day care for children, and on senior issues, which self-interest or interests are decisive in influencing the vote of this "senior citizen"?

Similarly, the seniors campaign strategy assumed that the elderly are a homogeneous group of persons. No strategy was developed to differentiate among the chronologically aged for conveying Carter's positions on specific issues to subgroups within the mass constituency that could be viewed as most likely to respond to the message being delivered. The one dimension that was used to differentiate among older voters was political geography. That is, an explicit idea of the Seniors Desk co-coordinators was to emphasize delivery of Carter's message to senior citizens in 15 states that comprise a total of 315 electoral votes.[14]

In summary, the Carter seniors campaign was based on a series of assumptions: that older persons were a constituency that could be swung from one candidate to the other; that the means of converting them was their self-interest as derived from a primary identity as senior citizens; that they would respond, in self-interest, to a series of campaign promises on issues presumed to concern seniors in the aggregate. The strategy was to make sure that as many as possible of the chronologically old knew what the candidate stood for. This basic framework of assumptions and strategy used by the Seniors Desk was largely the same as those in other presidential senior campaigns over the last several decades (Pratt, 1976).

The Larger Context of the Carter Campaign

The evidence available to us on the total Carter campaign effort does not suggest that the top echelon of Carter campaign officials necessarily shared the assumptions of the Seniors Desk. While we cannot quote direct statements from campaign leaders that would convey their assumptions explicitly, we can report on a number of indications which suggest that the overall campaign did not place high priority on efforts to convert, and on efforts to not lose, the votes of older persons.

One of the firmer indications of low priority for the seniors campaign can be found in a comparison of the funds that were allocated among the eleven campaign desks. The Seniors Desk requested $40,228 for personnel and travel and hoped to employ four persons.[15] But as Table 1 shows, the $6,500 total it had for those purposes was the lowest of any desk, and the Seniors Desk was one of two that had no paid staff at all.

Less firm as data, but interesting to explore, are the transcripts of two nationally televised debates between the presidential candidates in which they had many open-ended opportunities to project their positions on domestic issues, but a limited amount of time in which to do so. (A third televised debate, October 6, 1976, was confined to issues of foreign policy.) There is little to be gained from undertaking a quantitative comparison between the number of times Carter mentioned senior-related matters, and the times he mentioned other interest areas reflected by the desks listed in Table 1. One could argue, for instance, that a discussion of inflation was just as much—or more, or less—a labor or an urban issue as it was a senior issue. What we have done, however, is to read the two transcripts carefully for any discussion of older persons (inclusive of all variant terms such as "the aged," "the aging," "seniors," and so on) or of programs that are widely identified with older persons (e.g., Medicare). In this fashion it is at least possible to see what the candidate did do, or did not do, to use these two debates as vehicles for identifying himself with senior issues.

In the two debates that included domestic issues, Jimmy Carter said four things that pertain to older persons or older persons' programs. In our view, it would be difficult to interpret any of these comments as strong attempts by the candidate to win votes, or to not lose votes, of older persons.

In the first debate, September 23, Carter was asked at the outset what

TABLE 1   Paid Staff and Expenditures for Specialized "Desks" of the 1976
Democratic Presidential Campaign Committee, Inc.[a]

Name of desk	No. of paid staff	Expenditures[b]
Conservationists	2	$ 11,295
Democratic National Committee Liaison	2	10,000
Jewish	1	16,762
Labor	2	10,800
Minorities (blacks)	15	80,000
Political Relations (governors & congressmen)	2	12,000
Rural	0	11,635
Senior Citizens	0	6,500
Urban (mayors)	1½	10,741
Urban Ethnic (Catholics, including Spanish-speaking minorities)	4	18,000
Women	5	17,000
TOTALS 11	34½	$204,733

[a] For the period of July 15–Nov. 2, 1976.

[b] These direct "desk" expenditures are for personnel and travel; overhead costs for WATS lines, space, supplies, equipment, etc. were available equally to all desks on a pooled basis.

    SOURCE: Campaign finance records of the 1976 Democratic Presidential Campaign Committee, Inc., as reported by Frank Newton, Co-coordinator, Carter Seniors Desk.

he would do to reduce unemployment. In the context of a nearly 500-word answer he said,

> a very small investment of taxpayers' money in the housing field can bring large numbers of extra jobs, and the guarantee of mortgage loans, and the putting forward of "202" programs for housing for older people, and so forth, to cut down the roughly 20 percent unemployment now existing in the construction industry.[16]

A few minutes later, in an attempt to portray Ford and all Republicans as consistently opposed to programs that help people, the Democratic candidate said:

> I remember when Herbert Hoover was against jobs for people, I remember when Alf Landon was against social security, and later President Nixon, sixteen years ago, was telling the public that John Kennedy's proposal would bankrupt the country and would double the cost.[16]

At the close of this September debate, Carter was given an open-ended opportunity to summarize his views. In his closing statement of about 450 words he listed the elderly as one in a series of constituencies to which the public sector should be responsive:

We need to have a government that's sensitive to our people's needs, to those who are old and poor, who don't have adequate health care, who have been cheated too long with our tax programs, who've been out of jobs, whose families have been torn apart.[16]

In the other debate on domestic subjects, held October 22, the candidate attacked the Republican record on civil rights and mentioned the elderly as one of the constituencies that had suffered while Nixon and Ford had been in the White House:

There was a time when there was hope for those who are poor and downtrodden and who are elderly, or who are ill or who were in minority groups, but that time has been gone.[16]

While noting these four comments that had some relevance to senior issues, it is also important to report that Carter had dozens of opportunities throughout the debates to bring senior issues into his presentations, but chose other issues—mental health, drug addiction, etc.—instead. Even in his final summary at the end of the third debate, when he touched on twelve domestic policy issues (reform of the tax structure, cost of health care, infant mortality, cancer, quality of health care, unemployment, education, secrecy in government, housing, balancing the budget, inflation, and reform of the bureaucracy), no statement emerged that seemed directed at older persons as a constituency of voters.[16]

The Seniors Desk, though disappointed with the amount of attention and emphasis given to old-age issues in the debates, was not surprised. The seniors staff had continual difficulty in getting Carter scheduled to give speeches on issues related to older persons. Prior to National Seniors Day they were able to arrange for the candidate to make but one major senior address, in Miami on October 19. Carter's participation in National Seniors Day was arranged only after the Seniors Desk had obtained commitments from well over one hundred congressmen, mayors, and candidates for Congress to make speeches throughout the country. At that, Carter gave just one speech at a breakfast in Pittsburgh during the entire Seniors Day.

Throughout the election campaign the seniors unit was generally frustrated in its persistent requests to have the top echelon of the Carter campaign pay more attention to older voters. Despite repeated lobbying from the seniors staff, older persons issues were mostly ignored in the candidate's speeches and press conferences and in campaign advertisements in the media. Carter's positions on old-age issues were largely disseminated through the direct arrangements for speakers to local seniors groups and for distribution of flyers, pamphlets, and brochures.

While Carter did take positions on a number of older persons issues, there were still further positions suggested by the Seniors Desk that did not surface in the campaign. For instance, the seniors staff was not able to get the candidate to come out in favor of "circuit breaker" legislation through which the states would exempt the chronologically old from paying more than a fixed percentage of income for property taxes.

The frustrations felt by the Seniors Desk staff—in its efforts to have old-age issues receive higher priority in debates and speeches, in campaign advertising and press releases, in schedules for the candidate's personal appearances, and in the number and importance of senior issues to which the candidate was committed—do not tell us much in themselves about the Carter campaign leadership's perception of the relative importance of the senior effort. Perhaps the staffs of the other desks felt as much, or greater, frustration regarding the amount of attention paid to their interest areas. It might be instructive to make quantitative comparisons regarding the proportions of advertisements, press releases, candidate appearances, and "minor" and "major" issue commitments, as they were distributed among the interest areas reflected by the specialized desks; but no data available from this case would reliably provide either interest-area breakdowns or even totals on these activities for the overall Carter campaign.

Implications of the Case

Although nothing definitive can be inferred from this case account of the Carter campaign, we do think that the evidence presented is sufficient to convey the need to look at senior campaign efforts within a larger context of political activity. An examination of the Carter seniors campaign in isolation—the candidate's official positions on old-age issues, and the activities of the National Advisory Committee and the Seniors Desk—might lend itself to an interpretation that an attempt to maintain and/or shift the allegiance of older voters was a major activity of the Carter campaign. But a look at the data available on the broader context of the campaign effort could well lend itself to contrary interpretations.

It would not be unreasonable to argue from the data reported above that the top echelon leadership of the Carter campaign: (1) did not wish to offend older voters or organizations in the field of aging; (2) wanted to have Carter identified as a supporter of the aged, but not at the expense of scarce resources or other identifications; (3) did not share the assumptions of the Seniors Desk that older persons were an important constituency that could be swung from one candidate to another through a campaign based on old-age policy issues.

Whether or not one agrees with these interpretations is immaterial, for the central purpose of this case has been to emphasize the value of systematic research on politicians' perceptions of "the senior vote," and on how those perceptions may affect electoral campaigns and policy activities. Journalists are telling us almost every day that the changing demographics of American society have made older persons into a powerful electoral force. Those of us concerned about the well-being of older persons, and who have yet to see firm evidence of this phenomenon called "the senior vote," have remained relatively silent. Perhaps some of us have assumed that it could not hurt to fool the politicians, to let them think that 22 million voters are ready to rise up in wrath at the slightest misstep.

Or, have some politicians been fooling us by going through the motions? By giving less money, staff, time, and publicity to the aging than to any other citizen-based constituency? We believe that the case of the Carter campaign raises enough doubts to underline the importance of research on this topic. Knowledge of the politician's perception of who has what kind of power over him or her is an important point of entry for gaining a more sophisticated understanding of how older voters and aging-based organizations influence politics and public policy.

NOTES

This article is a revised version of a paper prepared for presentation at the XIth Int. Congress of Gerontology, Tokyo, Japan, Aug. 25, 1978.

1. Primary data on the campaign were gathered by Y. Riemer from campaign documents, interviews, and direct participant-observation while a staff member of the Carter campaign.
2. 1976 Democratic Presidential Campaign Committee, Inc. (1976 DPCC), "Carter Details GOP Neglect of Elderly," *The Daily Bulletin*, Oct. 19, 1976.
3. 1976 DPCC, "Carter and Ford on Aging in America," 1976.
4. 1976 DPCC, "Carter Details GOP Neglect of Elderly," *op. cit.*
5. 1976 DPCC, "Carter and Ford on Aging in America," *op. cit.*
6. 1976 DPCC, "Jimmy Carter on the Elderly," 1976.
7. 1976 DPCC, "Carter and Ford on Aging in America," *op. cit.*
8. 1976 DPCC, "Carter Details Neglect of Elderly," *op. cit.*
9. 1976 DPCC, "Carter and Ford on Aging in America," *op. cit.*
10. 1976 DPCC, "Carter Details GOP Neglect of Elderly," *op. cit.*
11. 1976 DPCC, "Carter Would Appoint Counselor on Aging to Assure Basic Rights for the Elderly," Oct. 19, 1976.
12. 1976 DPCC, "Jimmy Carter on the Elderly," *op. cit.*
13. Dick Kennedy, "Memo to the Seniors Desk Staff," 1976.
14. H. Oliver Welch and Frank Newton, *National Senior Citizens Campaign*, 1976 DPCC, 1976.
15. 1976 DPCC Senior Citizens Desk, "Budget, Elderly Citizens for Carter," 1976.
16. *1976 Congressional Quarterly Almanac* (Washington, DC: Congressional Quarterly Service, 1976), 919–944.

REFERENCES

Binstock, R. H. Interest-group liberalism and the politics of aging. *Gerontologist*, 1972, 12, 265–280.

Cutler, N. E. Demographic, social-psychological, and political factors in the politics of aging: A foundation for research in "political gerontology." *American Political Science Review*, 1977, 71, 1011–1025.

Hudson, R. B., and Binstock, R. H. Political systems and aging. In R. H. Binstock and E. Shanas (Eds.), *Handbook of aging and the social sciences*. Van Nostrand Reinhold, New York, 1976.

Pratt, H. J. *The gray lobby*. Univ. of Chicago Press, Chicago, 1976.

Panther Power: Symbol and Substance

RUTH HARRIET JACOBS AND BETH B. HESS

The Grey Panthers demonstrate some of the opportunities and difficulties in the political organization of the aged. They have drawn national attention from the news media because they upset conventional expectations of the elderly; militant senior citizens came as a newsworthy surprise. Organized into grassroots "packs" affiliated with a national headquarters, the Panthers' public image is as an old-age movement. Yet from the beginning they have been a coalition of old and young, and they have often aligned themselves with other aggrieved groups. These alliances have helped maintain the militancy of the movement but have troubled those members who joined because of age-related problems rather than general societal concerns. To continue successfully, the organization must broaden its membership base without compromising its principles of political activism.

High on the list of political organizations whose influence belies actual membership is the Gray Panthers, a loose alliance of over seventy local "networks" or "packs" with about five thousand dues-paying members. The success of the Panthers in becoming synonymous with political action on behalf of the aged can be related to a variety of factors which illustrate both the recurring dilemmas of radical social movements in America and the ambiguities of a "Politics of Aging."

The Panthers as a Social Movement

Role of the Media

In much the same manner as the National Organization for Women (NOW), the Panthers benefited early on from the attentions of the mass media, and for much the same reason: reversal of role expectations. That women and old people should become proponents of militancy, engage in street theater, criticize capitalism, and otherwise bite the hands which so patronizingly fed them was "newsworthy." The degree of exposure which NOW and the Panthers have enjoyed has given both organizations

SOURCE: Reprinted from *Long Term Care and Health Services Administration Quarterly* (Fall 1978), Panel Publishers, Copyright September 1978.

the appearance of greater strength than either events or membership warrant, but each has become symbolic of widespread discontent.

In serving as lightning rods, these organizations also become targets of ridicule and "backlash" politics, more apparent thus far in the case of women than of the elderly, perhaps because the latter are taken less seriously as menaces to the status quo—indeed, their activities may be perceived simply as "cute." And what the media giveth, the media can also take away, through the withdrawal of coverage—nothing is as stale as yesterday's news—or a belated application of the "fairness doctrine" in which the opposition must be heard from. While there is no well-organized opposition to the Panthers as there is to the women's movement, most television coverage of the recent social security tax rise emphasized the burden which this places on younger wage-earners rather than the benefits to older people.

Problem of Leadership

An additional reason for media attraction to the Panthers was the existence of a most articulate and charismatic leader: Maggie Kuhn, surely the antithesis of the "little old lady in tennis shoes." Kuhn's appeal to talk-show audiences probably has the same roots as that which made an enormous success of the play "Arsenic and Old Lace," which may lead some to discount the basic message she brings: a radical critique of our values and stratification system.

Maggie Kuhn's energy and personality have been largely responsible for the publicity received by the Panthers. But her centrality poses a problem, as Weber has pointed out, for any movement originally based on charisma, and even more so in an organization whose leaders are in their sixth and seventh decades. Further, the "routinization of charisma" is doubly troublesome for social movements which eschew hierarchical organization as a matter of principle. The same issue has racked the women's movement, leading one feminist leader to speak of "the tyranny of leaderlessness" as at least as dangerous a trap as reliance upon either the charismatic leader or a bureaucratic cadre.

Problem of Structure

In the case of the Panthers, the original aim was to organize at the grassroots level into "packs" sensitive to local needs but affiliated as a network whose headquarters would be responsible for maintaining contact and a sense of direction through a newsletter. Lack of central organization, however ideologically satisfying, has probably reduced the effectiveness of the Panther movement. Recognition of this came during the 1977 convention when a dues structure was imposed for the first time. Hitherto, income was a haphazard proposition, relying mainly on Kuhn's speaking fees and the sale of literature or T-shirts.

Since the membership is itself financially strained, outside sources are now being solicited. Taking money from foundations, industry, or the

United States government, of course, has its own hazards for an organization which stands in opposition to all three. The charge of hypocrisy can be raised, antiestablishment fervor dampened if not compromised; and cooptation is a real danger. Nonetheless, receiving a $16,000 Administration on Aging (AoA) grant for its most recent convention did not inhibit the Panthers from adopting resolutions deeply critical of federal agencies.

In another effort to establish a degree of order to the movement, regional coordinating councils were formed to keep track of state and local caucuses, and the four regions were brought into a working relationship with a National Steering Committee. While not all Panthers agreed on this course, the lack of coordination, even of knowledge of what others were doing, was perceived as too great a cost for doctrinal purity.

Problem of Principles

This dilemma, principle versus practical efficacy, emerged most clearly at the 1977 convention when delegates discussed a proposed position paper, "Economic Rights—Economic Democracy." Essentially, the paper was an attack on the free enterprise system written by a task force advised by Professor David Gordon of the New School for Social Research. Among the convention delegates were many elderly attracted to the Panthers as a means of enhancing the image and power of old people, but not necessarily committed to all the positions espoused by the founders, many of whom had been leftist activists all their lives. If the Panthers were to broaden their support and membership base, clearly they would have to take into consideration the views of less radical members.

Some hint of this problem was given at the 1975 convention when several delegates walked out after a vote favoring the legalization of marijuana. Indeed, the political conservatism of today's cohort of older people is well documented, but this is the major pool from which recruits must be drawn at this time. And for many at their first Panther convention, such ideas as nationalization of transportation were too much to contemplate with equanimity.

Sensing that the passage of the economic position paper would split the fragile unity recently forged among diverse delegates, the proponents withdrew their motion for its consideration. In this, the Panthers have acted in a manner very different from the new feminists or the 1930s socialists, placing broad-based solidarity above doctrine. It remains to be seen whether such tactics will in fact make the organization more attractive to large numbers of the elderly.

The Panthers as an Age-based Organization

The second set of issues which the Panthers illustrate are those of an age-based politics.

Young and Old

The Panthers began as a coalition of the old and the young; they maintain this as their basis and goal. But their public image is as an old-age movement, and it is difficult to tell how much attraction the Panthers retain for the type of college youth who first supported it during that period in the late 1960s when civil rights activism and the antiwar movement transformed the campuses. Some of those whose political consciousness was honed during that period are still active in the Panther network along with a few current college students, but most new recruits are people in their sixties and seventies.

That the bulk of membership is this old sets some limits on the energies and finances of the organization. On the other hand, the Panthers offer an opportunity for activity, comradeship, and purpose to many who feel that they've been "put on the shelf." Nonetheless, sustained action and continuity of leadership will be more problematic than in other political associations. When the "cohort effect" is also taken into account—that many of today's elderly are products of traditional, rural, or small-town socialization, often foreign-born, and primarily high-school educated— one can realize the difficulties in mobilizing individuals to become political gadflies: this is not their style or value orientation.

Local Action

Organizing the elderly at the grassroots is also extremely arduous. Problems of time and place and transportation must be overcome, but most difficult is the raising of consciousness so that potential participants see themselves as sharing an overriding set of interests. It has been suggested that the diversities among the aged are too many and too powerful to be submerged in an old-age identity, and many others have remarked on the denial mechanisms which operate to keep this consciousness at bay.

In spite of these drawbacks, several local actions have been very successful, both in capturing attention and in effecting change. Addressing the 1977 convention, Professor Robert Binstock, past president of the Gerontological Society, characterized the Panthers as the one group with power to make a difference because they "could make a nuisance of themselves." Binstock warned against getting together with such establishmentarian organizations as AARP and NCSC, but, rather, to concentrate on their own mission. "You have to have local militant action," he advised. "If, in the process of developing an organization here in Washington, you lose action at the local level, the battle is lost. You need a sense of crisis in the local community." And so the Panthers have done:

- In Los Angeles, in 1977, Panthers set up a tent city on an empty lot near City Hall and the *Los Angeles Times* Building, to protest lack of affordable housing.

- The Panthers have succeeded in organizing tenants of all ages into a political force in Washington, D.C.
- In Chicago, Panthers sponsor an hour-and-a-half weekly radio program.
- In Boston, a $15,000 grant was awarded for an interdependent living project.
- Cincinnati Panthers have introduced courses on normal aging into the public schools, while in San Diego they have joined the fight for better food in school cafeterias.
- In Oregon, Panthers won a lawsuit against a freeze in welfare funds, and in Washington, D.C., stopped the District from cutting 40,000 recipients from the Medicare rolls.

Alliances

In many of the above instances, Panthers have obviously had to join with other aggrieved parties: the poor, the ill, renters, even schoolchildren. On other issues, they have allied themselves with those opposing military spending, nuclear weapons, racism, and sexism. The Steering Committee has supported the needs of the handicapped, the Equal Rights Amendment, national health insurance, full employment, an end to mandatory retirement at any age, and the boycott of J. P. Stevens.

Possibly, this tactic of "floating alliances" will be the most effective for the Panthers. On purely age-based issues, these others will have an obligation to reciprocate the support of the Panthers. Additionally, the recognition that some interests are not necessarily limited by age will speed the recognition of a common fate among both old and young. This was the thrust of Michael Harrington's remarks to the 1977 delegates: "The movement you represent is one of the most important and dynamic movements that has ever come. Your movement is not a movement apart but is a movement relating to many other constituencies."

Yet there is a source of tension here. Many become Panthers out of personal concerns, or at least those related to age status. This energy, already limited, could become dispersed among too many goals for either personal fulfillment or organizational success. But if the sources of age-based problems are in the larger social structure, then the social critique is an essential component of the Panther mission. This is hardly a novel dilemma, and no resolution has yet improved upon Hillel's framing of the question: "If I am not for myself, who will be? But if only for myself, what am I?"

Misalliances

The Panthers, as have others representing relatively powerless groups, are aware of the potential for exploitation by those whose professional interests intersect those of the disadvantaged. In the case of the aged, certainly large numbers of old people have benefited directly from legislation at the federal and state levels, and from many of the services mandated by the Older Americans Act. But so have others: nursing-home operators and physicians, from Medicare; local politicians, from the network of Area Agencies on Aging; university administrators and researchers, from the allocations for research and training; insurance companies attached to voluntary senior citizen organizations; and the employees of emergent federal and state bureaucracies. There is a growing constituency of service providers, administrators, researchers, and lobbyists whose careers now depend upon continued funding for the aged.

But the Panthers are there to monitor. For example, the most recent meeting of the Gerontological Society was leafleted by Panthers asking such questions as: "Is the profession of gerontology a parasite feeding on the expanding population of older people? Does the Society exist primarily to acquire research and training funds for universities and to advance the goals of its members?" A hastily convened debate between Maggie Kuhn and the president and president-elect of the Society was one of the best-attended sessions of the annual meetings.

The broader question here will undoubtedly remain on the agenda of the Panthers and other activists: Once formal organizations have formed around the needs of a special group, do they develop a momentum of their own, leading to goal displacement? Is there a vested interest in perpetuating social problems by those whose livelihoods depend upon the continued existence of such conditioning? Cui bono?

The Future of the Panthers and the Politics of Age

It is probably not too dramatic to say that the Panthers are at the crossroads—the question is how many crossroads. The need for broader-based membership is paramount, but who shall these new members be? Many would applaud the increased participation of other disadvantaged or politically marginal persons—blacks, poor ethnics, Hispanics—but almost by definition these are not near the centers of power. Yet, again almost by definition, the types who could fill the movement coffers or lean heavily on policymakers are not likely to be attracted by the aura of radical quixotism which is part of the Panther mystique.

If the Panthers were able to broaden their membership base, what compromise in principles might ensue? The argument has also been made the other way around: that the persistence of the Panthers has led other, more conservative old-age-based associations to adopt more militant tactics and radical goals. In yet another perspective, if membership needs are placed above doctrine, the new recruits could easily find themselves radicalized over time and through experience.

As for the question of cooptation, certainly the $16,000 from Administration on Aging for a convention was cheap compared to the costs of fully-covered medical insurance, or any other major need of the elderly.

The greater danger, it seems to us, lies in the apparent success of the *mainstream* proponents of "gray power." To the extent that this concept is given coverage and thereby credence, most Americans will perceive the aged as essentially taken care of—indeed, as almost piggy in their demands on the public purse. We are witnessing something very like this in the current move to lower the social security taxes just levied. In this scenario, the Panthers will be seen as representing a lunatic fringe, and one without any real grievance. Thus trivialized, or even continuing to be patronized by the media, the Panthers could become one more of the exotic social movements to have flashed briefly across the American sky before confronting the reality that the great majority of citizens do not want radical change.

In the meantime, the Panthers continue to symbolize the possibilities of old-age activism, serving as a goal to those who would stop short of the best, seeking to consolidate the concerns of young and old, raising consciousness, questioning the most sacred of American values, and ultimately giving us an example of effective aging: to care enough to fight, to risk being thought silly, to work for those goals which will enhance the quality of life throughout the life course.

10

THE ECONOMICS
OF AGING

The issue of providing adequate financial security for the aged members of our society is complex and subject to constant shifts in government policy as well as changes in the composition of the aged population. One area of interest is the relationship between the economic situation of the aged and that of other members of society. Of equal importance is the impact that changes in this broad relationship have on individuals' lives. Aside from general societal concerns, there are specific concerns regarding control over pension funds, or variations in the financial security of subgroups of older people such as women and minorities. This part touches upon all these issues.

Family Relations in a Bureaucracy

The formalization of the social security system in the United States in the 1930s signified a shift in the means of provision for the elderly. It represented a movement away from personal, informal arrangements by family members and local communities to impersonal arrangements under the jurisdiction of large bureaucracies. By formalizing financial resources to the aged through collective means, the economic situation of the retired improved substantially. At the same time, people were not willing to accept social security for what it was, a form of income transfer from workers to the retired. Instead it was defined as an insurance program. This definition freed it from the stigma of welfare but led to a misunderstanding of how social security is funded and a fear of the system "going broke." In fact, the issue boils down to this: Do the people of the nation want a higher standard of living in their middle years at the expense of a lower standard during their retirement years? (Schulz, 1973, p. 156). Each society must determine how willing it is to transfer income from workers to the retired. The article by Hollister explains how the social security system works and discusses the apparent need to maintain the myth that it is an insurance program rather than a form of income transfer between generations.

In addition to concerns about financing, some scholars have been concerned with the possible effects of this shift on family relationships. Two opposing consequences have been suggested. The traditional view has been that increased bureaucratization of services would lead to a serious weakening of relationships between parents and children. Since independent retirement incomes enable the aged to maintain their own homes, often distant from their children, this could have the effect of weakening family ties and increasing dependence on the bureaucracy. Other scholars have suggested that old people have difficulty in coping with the complexities of large organizations and that their children serve as a link to them, providing a buffer against the bureaucracy and a means of entry into the social order.

Evidence from both the past and present supports the latter point of view. An interesting historical example is provided by the Poor Laws of nineteenth-century England. One indicator of the willingness of family members to help aged relatives is the proportion of older people who are institutionalized. All evidence suggests that given the choice, most old people consider an institution an undesirable place to live. In late nineteenth-century England prior to the introduction of old-age pensions, the proportion of aged in institutions rose dramatically as relief to the aged outside of the workhouse was tightened by conservative Poor Law administrators (Anderson, 1977, p. 45). After old-age pensions were introduced, the number of institutionalized elderly fell from a high of 6 percent in 1909 to 2.2 percent by 1931. Anderson suggests that when the aged are not financially dependent on children, they are more readily able to maintain harmonious relationships based on mutual interdependence. A pension enables an older person to bring cash resources into the household, providing a positive incentive for cementing family relationships. One ninety-year-old man who lived with one of his children was asked to describe his reaction to the pension of 1909. He said that before the pension:

> Often 'ave we thought as 'ow it would be a-best for us to go, and sometimes a'most 'ave prayed to be took; for we was only a burden to our children as ke'p us. . . . But now we wants to go on livin' forever, 'cos we gives 'em the ten shillin' a week, and it pays 'em to 'ave us along with 'em (Anderson, 1977, p. 51).

The article by Kreps provides a more contemporary perspective, addressing the issue of intergenerational relationships within a bureaucratic structure.

Present Sources of Economic Security in Old Age

Social security is basically a very secure form of income for the aged. Workers are guaranteed payment when they retire. However, problems of inequities of payment have been built into the system. Retirement benefits are calculated on the basis of preretirement contributions, and some groups in society, particularly women and blacks, have been systematically underrepresented in secure, higher-paying jobs. In 1970 black workers received pensions averaging $250 per year below the average for whites. Single women have also been penalized by the system. Of those who receive the minimum benefit, half are retired single women (Atchley, 1977, p. 129). This group includes women who have been working in jobs with low earnings, those whose careers were interrupted for child rearing, and widows who do not receive the full value of their deceased husband's benefits. The article by Burks discusses some of the many ways older women are particularly vulnerable to weaknesses in the system.

Pension plans in the private sector are less secure than social security, and some of them never materialize at all. One tragic example illustrates some of the problems of private pension funds. A teamster drove a truck for more than twenty-two years, faithfully paying his dues to the pension fund. Forced to retire due to a severe cataract condition in 1973, he received the shattering news that because he had been laid off for a few months in 1960 and 1961, the "break in service" disqualified him from a $400-a-month pension (*Newsweek*, 1979, p. 67).

This man's story is not unique. Many pension programs are scarred by poor financing and management and uncertain "vesting"—the workers' right to collect all the pension money set aside. In 1974 Congress made a comprehensive attack on the pension problem and passed the Employee Retirement Income Security Act. Under this act most workers who are covered by private pension plans are guaranteed some benefits after ten years on a job unless a "break in service" lasts more than a year. While this act has provided more security in the private pension system, it has had the unintended negative consequence of encouraging many smaller employers to completely drop their pension plans for fear of not being able to comply with the law's tougher standards. Further, workers who change jobs frequently, remaining on one job less than ten years, still have no protection.

People who retire do so with the possibility of many pleasant years free from work responsibilities. However, for many the constraints of poverty offset the benefits of this freedom. Dramatic changes have occurred in the last fifty years in terms of providing adequate financial protection for the aged, but there are still many inequities in the system and many issues to be resolved.

REFERENCES

Anderson, Michael. 1977. The impact on the family relationships of the elderly of changes since Victorian times in governmental income-maintenance provision. In Ethel Shanas and Marvin B. Sussman (eds.), *Family, bureaucracy, and the elderly*. Durham, N.C.: Duke Univ. Press.

Atchley, Robert. 1977. *The social forces in later life*. Belmont, Cal.: Wadsworth.

Newsweek magazine. 1979. The pension mess. February 26.

Schulz, James. 1973. The economic impact of an aging population. *Gerontologist* 13:111–117.

Social Mythology and Reform: Income Maintenance for the Aged

ROBINSON HOLLISTER

This article explains how the social security system works and criticizes the contradictions within the system. Although one function of the system is to reduce poverty, the supporters of the system have maintained the myth that social security is an insurance program so that people will not attach the stigma of welfare to it. Unfortunately, this means that lower-income people are disproportionately taxed. Those alarmists who fear that the system is an economic time bomb due to the increasing proportion of the population that is over age sixty-five forget that there will also be fewer dependents under the age of eighteen who have to be supported from federal revenues. While we need a more realistic assessment of the costs of supporting both the young and the aged, it may be that the misperception of the system is necessary for its perpetuation. Though figures have changed since 1974, when this article was written, the author's argument remains valid today.

Herman Melville's little-read, and even less appreciated, novel *The Confidence Man*[1] begins:

> At sunrise on a first of April, there appeared suddenly . . . a man in cream-colours, at the waterside in the city of St. Louis.

> His cheek was fair, his chin downy, his hair flaxen, his hat a white fur one, with a long fleecy nap. He had neither trunk, valise, carpetbag, nor parcel . . . he stepped aboard the favourite steamer *Fidele*, on the point of starting for New Orleans.

The man works his way through the crowd on the boat and comes next to a placard announcing a reward for the capture of a mysterious impostor.

> Pausing at this spot, the stranger so far succeeded in threading his way, as at last to plant himself just beside the placard, producing a small slate and tracing some words upon it, he held it up before him on a level with the placard, so that they who read the one might read the other. The words were these:

> "Charity thinketh no evil"

SOURCE: Excerpted from "Social Mythology and Reform: Income Maintenance for the Aged" by Robinson G. Hollister in Volume no. 415 of *The Annals* of The American Academy of Political and Social Science. © 1974 by The American Academy of Political and Social Science.

419

The crowd around the placard jostles him aside.

> . . . the stranger quietly turned, and writing anew upon the slate, again held it
> up:
>
>   "Charity suffereth long, and is kind."

Illy pleased with his pertinacity, as they thought it, the crowd a second time thrust him aside, and not without epithets and some buffets, all of which were unresented.

The lamb-like man is a mute.

> The stranger now moved slowly away, yet not before altering his writing to
> this:
>
>   "Charity endureth all things."

Shield-like bearing his slate before him, amid stares and jeers he moved slowly up and down, at his turning points again changing his inscription to—

>   "Charity believeth all things."

and then

>   "Charity never faileth."

The word charity, as originally traced, remained throughout uneffaced, not unlike the left-hand numeral of a printed date, otherwise left for convenience in blank.

At this point, nearby, the ship's barber opens his shop:

> . . . jumping on a stool, he hung over his door, on the customary nail, a gaudy
> sort of illuminated pasteboard sign, skilfully executed by himself, gilt with the
> likeness of a razor elbowed in readiness to shave, and also, for the public
> benefit, with the two words not unfrequently seen ashore gracing other shops
> besides barbers':
>
>   "No Trust"

The mute is, perhaps, the first guise, or masque, of the confidence man. As the novel progresses, other figures appear who inspire confidence or distrust among the crowd. We are never sure who is the impostor, who the victim, which the confidence man and which the exposer of confidence men. This, according to some Melville critics, is his comic commentary on the role of religion in society. Is religion an ultimate form and source of trust among men or is it a confidence game?

Trust and Confidence

I would like to use these images in discussing the debate over the reform of the social security system in the United States. Is the social security system a form and source of trust among men or is it a confidence game? Are the supporters of the social security system as currently structured—

persons I shall refer to as the priests of social security—confidence men or are they the purveyors of trust and charity? There are those—whom I will call Johnny-come-lately reformers—who, like the barber, would post the sign "No Trust" over the social security system. Are they unveilers of confidence men or destroyers of social trust?

Schema

The issues I wish to raise are really quite simple, but the social security system to which I wish to apply them is quite complex, as are most social institutions of trust or most confidence games. Thus I must spend a good deal of time on technical details in order to make some simple points. Therefore, in order to motivate—or obviate—the reader's task of working through technical details, I will make my simple basic points at the outset in the abstract:

(1) there are dangers in building a social institution around a consciously conceived myth;

(2) in recent years, as the program matures, the inherent contradictions in the social security myth have been coming into sharper relief;

(3) thus the price paid for the social myth is rising;

(4) in spite of points (1) through (3), one must seriously consider whether—as the priests of social security warn us—social myth is not the necessary cement with which to hold together social institutions.

In the sections which follow I will first sketch out the features of the system as it existed prior to the major Social Security Amendments of 1972 and will provide the standard positive and negative critique of the system at that stage. Then I will describe the developments in the system embodied in the 1972 amendments and indicate their great importance. This consideration of the system will facilitate the analysis of both the technical and the philosophical arguments between the priests of social security and the Johnny-come-lately reformers which is presented in the final section of the paper.

In what follows I will focus on the debate about the aspects of the social security system which relate to retirement benefits. The system also includes elements involving benefits for survivors of covered workers, for disability and blindness, and for medical care. There are equally important issues to be discussed concerning these features, but the limits of space preclude taking them up here.

Features of the Social Security System
Prior to the 1972 Amendments

In order to discuss the debate over reform it is necessary for me to sketch out a few of the details of the system which existed—and which persist in the present—prior to the 1972 amendments to the Social Security Act. Since I wish to discuss primarily the retirement system, I will omit most details relating to survivors, disability, and medical care provisions of the system.

Description

From the outset the system has been financed through a payroll tax. In 1937 the tax was paid on the first $3,000 of each covered worker's earnings, and the amount was 1 percent taken from the employee and 1 percent paid by the employer. As the coverage of persons and the type and level of benefits have risen, this tax has been increased slowly, but steadily, so that at present the first $13,200 of earnings are taxed and the employee pays 5.85 percent and the employer 5.85 percent. The funds from the payroll tax are paid into a trust fund. However, the trust fund is just large enough to cover current benefits; it does not represent the sum of accumulated assets for workers who have been paying over the years.

In order to receive retirement benefits a worker now entering the system will have to have forty quarters of covered employment by the time he or she retires. Naturally, those who were older when the system started have different eligibility limits, and the provisions for covering survivors and disabled are different.

Another feature of eligibility for benefits for those between sixty-five and seventy-two deals with earnings; it is often called the retirement test. Individuals between sixty-five and seventy-two may earn up to $2,400 per year without penalty; if they earn more, their benefits are reduced by fifty cents for each dollar earned. "This provision . . . is included in the law to assure that monthly benefits will be paid to a worker only when he has substantially retired."[2] Those over seventy-two receive their full benefits regardless of their annual earnings. Property—or unearned—income does not affect benefits.

The amount of benefits a retiree receives is related to the average of his covered earnings, with the average determined after subtracting the five years of lowest earnings. Covered earnings are earnings which have been subject to the payroll tax—for example, the first $13,200 are currently taxed, so earnings over $13,200 are not covered. Some jobs are not covered by social security—at the outset about four out of ten workers were not covered, now the figure is one out of ten—so that earnings in such jobs are neither taxed nor included in the average of covered earnings used in determining benefits.

The relationship of monthly benefits received after sixty-five to the average monthly covered earnings prior to sixty-five varies with the level of earnings. Table 1 gives some examples for benefits under the 1971 law. Those with lower monthly average earnings receive benefits which are a higher percentage of their past average earnings than those with high monthly past earnings; benefits are skewed so as to redistribute benefits toward lower earners. Also, workers are now allowed to retire at the age

TABLE 1 The Relationship of Retirement Benefits to Average Covered Earnings under Social Security, 1971

	Monthly benefits	
Average monthly earnings	Single	Couple
$250	$145	$218
$750°	$293	$443

°In 1971 no retired worker could have average covered earnings any greater than $432. This was so because the income limit to the payroll tax was substantially lower than at present.

of sixty-two rather than sixty-five as required in the past. If they elect to do so, their benefits are permanently reduced on an actuarial basis to reflect the fact that they will be paid benefits over a longer period than if they had retired at sixty-five.

Evaluation of pre-1972 features

With these bare outlines of the system in mind, we can turn to the evaluation of the system's features as they existed prior to the 1972 amendments. I will deal first with the positive aspects and then turn to the shortcomings.

The designers and supporters of the system as it stands have emphasized several interrelated virtues of the program. First, it is a contributory system—many like to call it social insurance. The contributory essence is highlighted by the clearly identifiable social security tax which allows the worker to have the feeling that he is paying something now which will in some sense determine what he will receive in the future. Second, the sense of the system as being contributory is reinforced by the fact that the benefits are graduated so that, in general, those who have had higher earnings and paid more in the past will get higher benefits than their lower-earning cohorts who paid less in social security tax. Third, the system is compulsory in the sense that all—in covered industries—must pay the payroll tax; however, as a result of compulsory participation, it yields "benefits as a right." Fourth, the retirement test is an important part of the system in that it emphasizes that the system is meant to replace earnings.

Fifth, many of the above-mentioned features are similar to those of private insurance or pensions, but social security is to be differentiated from private insurance in that it is shaped by considerations of public needs as well—indeed, for this reason it is referred to as social insurance. These public needs are reflected in the fact that people with lower past earnings have greater unmet needs and, therefore, that they receive benefits at a higher percentage of their average past earnings than do those with high past earnings. In addition, unlike private insurance, retirement benefits under social security are periodically increased across the board as average needs rise with the rise in average living standards.

A sixth key feature is the effect of social security on the extent of poverty among the aged. For example, in 1966—a date chosen because of the availability of detailed data—60 percent of the social security benefits went to people whose income without social security would have been below the poverty line and, of this group, 90 percent were lifted from poverty by virtue of the social security payments. Finally, it is important to point out that social security is the largest income maintenance program. In the fiscal year 1973 it paid out $42 billion dollars to 25 million recipients.

Yet, while the social security system is generally recognized as the most successful social program in the history of the country, a number of shortcomings—even as it stood prior to the 1972 amendments—are widely noted. The most fundamental criticism is that two incompatible functions have been bound into one system, with the result that neither function is adequately performed. One function is to provide a social transfer mechanism so that individuals may have income in their older years which exceeds any earnings they may have for those years.[3] The second function is to redistribute income within cohorts of the aged so that some sort of income floor is provided for the poorest. Putting these two functions in a single program means that each is compromised by the constraints imposed by the other.

The income redistribution—or poverty reduction—function is compromised by the necessity of tying benefits to past earnings. If a person was poor before the age of sixty-five and if his benefits are less than 100 percent of his average past earnings, he will, of necessity, be poor after sixty-five. At best, the system as it stands yields about 80 percent of earnings averaged over the working lifetime. Moreover, since earnings in the early working years are lower due to youth and to a lower economy-wide wage level, benefits are usually less than 50 percent of earnings just prior to retirement. The ineffectiveness of social security as a poverty support is illustrated by the fact that whereas 12 percent of all persons are poor, 19 percent of those over sixty-five are poor. Alternatively, one can note that 16 percent of the aged who receive social security benefits are poor in spite of their social security income—that is, their income including social security falls below the poverty line.

The functioning of the system as a social mechanism for transferring income toward older age is impaired by the redistributive features of the system. It is not a federalized annuity-type system, since the amount one receives relative to one's age cohort is only roughly related to the amount one has paid in social security taxes.[4] The ratio of benefits to past payroll tax paid is generally higher for low wage earners.[5]

A second major shortcoming of the system which has been pointed out is that it discourages work among the aged. The retirement test feature of benefits amounts to placing a 50 percent tax on earnings within a certain range for workers sixty-five to seventy-two. For example, in 1970 the law stated that a beneficiary could earn up to $1,680 without having benefits reduced. From $1,680 to $2,880 benefits would be reduced by fifty cents for each additional dollar earned—that is, the recipient's net income would go up by only fifty cents for each additional dollar earned, resulting in a reduction equivalent to a 50 percent tax rate. Any earnings over $2,880 caused benefits to be reduced by one dollar for each dollar earned, up to the point where benefits were reduced to zero[6]—that is, the equivalent of a 100 percent tax rate on earnings.

To some it may seem a relatively trivial point that there may be some discouragement of work effort among those sixty-five to seventy-two. In fact, the retirement test was originally included in the system when it was designed during the 1930s in order to encourage older workers to retire to make more jobs available for the many unemployed nonaged workers. This rationale makes little sense today.

In any case, earnings are not a trivial matter as a source of income for the aged. This is illustrated in Table 2. In 1972 the poverty line was approximately $2,500 for a couple aged sixty-five and over and $2,000 for a single individual aged sixty-five and over. Thus the divisions according to these income cut-offs in Table 2 provide an approximate, but not exact, separation according to poor and nonpoor within families with aged heads and within aged unrelated individuals. For families with aged heads it is evident that the difference in earnings between those below $2,500 total income and those above is by far the largest difference in income by source. If those in poor families had, in fact, earnings anywhere near those of nonpoor families, they would clearly escape poverty. For unrelated individuals the differences in earnings between the low-income and high-income groups is not as substantial. Even so, if individuals with incomes below $2,000 had earning opportunities as great as those available to individuals with incomes above $2,000, they would have had average income sufficient to lift themselves from poverty.

The potential effect of the retirement test built into social security may well go beyond its direct effect of discouraging work effort in the range where benefits are reduced because of earnings. This is so due to the possible influence of social legislation in setting standards for retirement which the private sector quickly adopts. The labor force participation rate of males sixty-five and over has fallen from 45.8 percent in 1950 to 24.4 percent in 1972. Many attribute this decline to older persons' increasing income which allows them to enjoy the luxury of retirement. However, there is an important question about the proportion of retirements which are involuntary, forced by increasingly severe private sector retirement rules. It is noteworthy, for example, that the sharpest declines in aged male labor force participation occur when the unemployment rate is high. In fact, for the period 1966 to 1969, when unemployment rates were at their lowest point since 1953, the labor force participation of males over sixty-five actually increased. After 1969, as unemployment

TABLE 2 Sources of Income for Families with Head of Household 65 and Over and for Unrelated Individuals 65 and Over, 1972

Income	ERN ($)	SS ($)	DIV ($)	PA ($)	UI ($)	PRV ($)	ATI ($)
			FAMILIES				
Below $2,500 (N = 1,132,000)	131	1,569	131	218	131°		2,179
Above $2,500 (N = 6,458,000)	4,461	2,468	1,329	95	475	664	9,492
All families (N = 7,590,000)	3,759	2,340	1,170	84	418	585	8,356
			INDIVIDUALS				
Below $2,000 (N = 2,238,000)	28	1,050	70	154	70	28	1,400
Above $2,000 (N = 3,943,000)	892	1,688	1,313	94	328	375	4,690
All individuals (N = 6,181,000)	586	1,447	827	103	241	241	3,445

SOURCE: Unpublished tabulations from Current Population; survey conducted by the United States Bureau of the Census.

Definitions: ERN: average income from earnings; SS: average social security and railroad retirement income; DIV: average income from dividends, interest, net rental, estates, trusts, net royalties; PA: average income from public assistance or welfare payments; UI: average income from unemployment compensation, workmen's compensation, veteran's benefits, government employee pensions; PRV: average income from private income from private pensions, annuities, alimony and so on; ATI: average total income.

Note: Of those 65 and over, 69 percent were in families, while 31 percent were unrelated individuals.

°Since the number of families receiving PRV income in this income class is less than 75,000, total UI + PRV is given.

began to rise again, the aged male labor force participation rate resumed its long term decline.

Other evidence suggestive of considerable involuntary retirement among the aged is provided by the data on the characteristics of those persons taking advantage of the early retirement provisions under social security—that is, retirement at sixty-two rather than sixty-five, with permanently lowered benefits. In general, these early retirees have had considerably more spells of unemployment and lower wages than those who retire with full benefits at sixty-five.[7] The early retirees hardly conform to the picture of persons with higher income taking the opportunity to indulge in the leisure of early retirement. The opportunity for the aged to work is important not only for its pure economic return, but also because work is the most important force for social integration in the society. If the example of social legislation encourages the private sector to lower retirement age, to stiffen retirement standards and thereby to increase the extent of involuntary unemployment, then it has indirectly contributed to the increased social isolation of the aged.[8]

A third major shortcoming of social security created prior to 1972 is that its method of financing is regressive. A worker subject to the payroll tax with earnings just at the maximum level—the maximum of $12,000 in 1972 and of $13,200 at present—pays the same absolute amount of social security tax as a man with earnings ten or twenty times that amount. Thus the social security tax is a higher proportion of income for those with low incomes than for those with very high incomes.

In addition, it is argued by many that the tax which is nominally paid by the employer is, in fact, shifted to the worker.[9] The employer tax raises the price of a manhour of labor. Therefore the employer will hire the same amount of labor as he would if there were no tax only if the workers will accept a wage lower by the amount of the tax. Whether the employers' portion of the tax is fully or only partially shifted to the employee is a matter of some dispute. However, the myth that the employer pays the tax disguises the full extent of the true tax on low incomes.

Finally, the most broadly stated complaint is that the originators and supporters of the system have misused the analogy with insurance in order to disguise many of the above-listed shortcomings. The critics argue that, unlike private insurance or annuities, benefits do not reflect the accumulated value of payments in a fund—in addition to accrued interest—but rather are set by the changes in legislation over time. The benefits, in fact, reflect a transfer from the younger generation to the older generation in each period. The benefits of each individual bear only a very rough relationship to the value of social security taxes paid over the past lifetime (see, for example, footnote 3). One analyst concludes:

> The insurance analogy constitutes a "pre-emptive strike" against potential taxpayer and legislative resistance to payroll tax increases: the budget-minded legislator in particular may be soothed by the conception that each prospective recipient will pay his own way under the system instead of living off the taxpayers in general.[10]

The 1972 Amendments and Related Developments

Major increases in social security benefit levels and shifts in its structure began to take place with legislative action in the fall of 1969. Moreover, they were more or less continuously under debate in the process of enactment or under revision until the culminating action of the 1972 Social Security Amendments. Some minor adjustments have been made since the 1972 amendments, but they stand as the major landmark in a period of extraordinary activity in the area of social security legislation.[11] These legislative changes covered a wide variety of provisions; however, I will sketch out just a few of the most important ones in order to set the background to the new debate between the priests of social security and the Johnny-come-lately reformers.

Benefits

The statutory benefit levels were sharply increased: from December 1970 to December 1973 the minimum benefit was increased by 54 percent and the maximum by 66 percent. During the same period the consumer price index went up by 23 percent. The increase in benefits was clearly more than enough to offset inflation during this period. These changes were sufficient to improve the real income of those over sixty-five relative to the real income of the rest of the population. A further increase in benefits of 11 percent across the board, signed into law at the end of 1973, was to be accomplished in two steps: 7 percent in March 1974 and the remainder in July 1974. By July of 1974 the minimum benefit for a worker sixty-five and over was $93.80 per month and the maximum $295.37.

Indexing

Starting in 1975 benefits were automatically increased by the same percentage amount as the increase in the consumer price index. In addition, the threshold at which the retirement test takes effect—the level of annual earnings permissible before benefits are reduced—will be increased automatically at the rate of increase in the average wage level for all employees in the economy.[12]

Financing

In order to finance the increase in benefits and some extensions in coverage, the payroll tax was increased substantially both by extending the base of taxable earnings—from $7,800 in 1969 to the current $13,200—and by increasing the tax rate for both employees and employers. These changes were only the last and most dramatic stage of a long history of increases in the payroll tax.

The payroll tax has risen much faster than other federal taxes. As a percentage of all federal tax receipts it has risen from 4 percent in 1949 to 30 percent in 1973. Now, the revenue from the payroll tax is equal to about 50 percent of the revenue from the federal income tax. Moreover, if one includes both the employer and employee portion of the payroll tax—on the grounds, argued above, that the employer portion is in fact shifted to the employee—over half the population pays more in payroll taxes than it does in federal income taxes.

Finally, given the regressivity of the payroll tax, the effects of the increases since 1969 have worked to shift the combined burden of the payroll—again assuming the worker pays both employer and employee tax—and federal income tax toward lower-income families. For example, for families with incomes below $3,500 and for those with incomes between $9,000 and $13,000, the combined effect of changes in the payroll tax and reductions in the income tax have actually been to increase the total federal tax burden.[13] For the poorest—that is, those with incomes below $3,500, who pay no federal income tax—the increases in the payroll tax have amounted to a 22 percent increase in their federal tax burden since 1969.

It should also be noted that the base earnings limit for the payroll tax will also be increased automatically with increases in the average wage level for all employees. In addition, the law has scheduled increases in the payroll tax rate for both employer and employee to 6.05 percent in 1978, to 6.30 percent in 1981 and to somewhat higher levels further in the future.

Supplemental Security Income

The most revolutionary shift in the social security structure was the creation of a new national program, starting in 1974, of financial assistance to low-income persons sixty-five and over, the blind, and the disabled. The program is called Supplemental Security Income (SSI). This program replaces federal and state programs of aid to the aged, blind, and permanently and totally disabled. For an eligible person with no other income it will pay, as of July 1974, $146 a month—$1,752 annually—and $219—$2,628 annually—for a couple. The structure of benefits approximates that of a negative income tax in that, after a certain amount of excluded income, benefits are reduced by fifty cents for each additional dollar of income. The provisions for determining eligibility are related to financial need, but are somewhat complex. The definition of what shall be counted as income is also complex.

The program will be fully federally administered by the Social Security Administration and will be federally financed from general revenues. States will be allowed to add supplementary payments to the SSI benefits; furthermore, those state supplements will not be counted as income in determining the SSI benefits. Those who received SSI benefits may not participate in the federal food stamps program.

The SSI program represents a major step forward in income maintenance for the aged. Its major strong points are:

(1) In general, SSI will yield an increase in cash income for the aged poor.
(2) A national minimum income standard will be set for aged, blind, and disabled. Under the previous federal and state programs minimum cash assistance levels were set by the states and varied considerably from state to state.
(3) Eligibility conditions for the program will be uniform across the nation. In the federal and state programs these conditions also varied across state lines.
(4) Administration of welfare programs for the aged will be simplified by consolidation in the single, national administrative structure. States may also opt to have the Social Security Administration administer their state supplement programs.

. . . .

The Importance of the 1972 Developments

The revisions in the social security program from 1969 through 1972 have had a profound effect on the character of the debate about the future of income maintenance for the aged. Several features of the changed context stand out.

The Explosive Burden of Welfare

The conjuncture of rapid expansion of social security in the last few years and increased sensitivity to demographic trends has caused alarm in some quarters about the future costs of the social security system and the burden it will place on future workers. One analyst estimated: "[if inflation continued at 2.75 percent and average wage levels grew at 5 percent per annum] and if Congress never again sweetens the program, the maximum retirement benefit will rise to $7,236 in 1980 and will top $30,000 by the year 2010. Meanwhile the maximum contribution per worker will reach $8,288 with income up to $66,300 then subject to social security tax." The analyst does not, however, mention that if those projections are correct, the average income level will also have risen over five times by the year 2010. She goes on to conclude:

> The practice of providing retirees with far larger benefits than they contrib-
> uted cannot continue indefinitely. At some point, the growing burden on the
> labor force will become both an economic and political time bomb. . . . The
> whole history of social security is a good example of how government adopts
> policies that encourage consumers to spend while disregarding their effect on
> production and investment.[14]

Clearly, part of what motivates this sort of concern is the sharp increases in benefit levels in the last few years and the awareness that declining birth rates will have effects on the age structure of the population such that the ratio of persons over sixty-five to those in the working ages will increase. Some estimates of the age structure and labor force are presented in Table 3. The aged dependency ratio is the ratio of those over sixty-five not in the labor force to the total labor force. The figures give a

TABLE 3   Dependency Ratios

	1972	1980	2000	2020
Aged dependency°	.18	.19	.20	.25
Total dependency°	1.36	1.19	1.10	1.12

SOURCE: The underlying population projection for the dependency ratios are from Census Series E, which is the lowest population growth projection. The labor force participation projections and dependency ratios are from Dennis Johnston, "Illustrative Projections of the Labor Force in the U.S. to 2040" in *Economic Aspects of Population Change*, Commission on Population Growth and the American Future, research reports vol. II, p. 172, table 5.

°Aged dependency: persons 65 and over not in the labor force/total labor force; total dependency: all persons not in the labor force/total labor force.

rough indication of the likely burden of the costs of the social security system on the working population in those years. The projections[15] do indicate a slowly increasing ratio up to the year 2000 and, subsequently, sharper rates of increase.

When assessing the potential burden of future workers, however, one should also take into account the magnitude of other claims. The shifting age structure does mean a higher portion of aged, but it also means a lower portion of the population in the youngest—0 to 18—age groups, which also make dependency claims on the working population. The total dependency ratio gives a crude indication of the overall dependency burden on future workers. The projections show that this ratio will decline sharply to the year 2000, and that even in 2020 it will still be considerably below the dependency ratios of the present and the recent past. While the relative burden of social security costs will rise, it is likely that the social costs of programs associated with the younger dependency groups will fall relatively. I know of no study which attempts to assess future cost of social security in the context of likely costs of other social programs, but the above crude indicators suggest that alarm about explosive social security costs needs to be balanced by more realistic assessments of overall social costs.

The Relative Income Position of the Aged

While concern about the future costs of social security appears to have been growing as a result of recent developments, relatively little attention has been focused on the fact that the recent increases in benefits reflect a fundamental shift in the implicit social judgment about what the relative income position of the aged portion of the population should be. Since 1968 the relationship between average covered earnings before sixty-five and benefits has been increased by over 50 percent.

In 1968 it was estimated that a single retiree who had worked in manufacturing would qualify for social security benefits equal to about 0.29 of his earnings in manufacturing the year before retirement—this sort of figure is referred to as the replacement ratio. By January of 1972 it was estimated that a single retiree who had been working in manufacturing would have a replacement ratio of 0.34.[16] My rough calculation is that by July 1974 a single manufacturing retiree would have a social security benefit equal to 0.38 of his wage in the year prior to retirement. This, then, amounts to a rise of 30 percent in the replacement ratio for such workers. While some feel that a replacement ratio of 0.38 is still too low, the 30 percent rise in this ratio over six years represents a substantial improvement in the relative income position of such over-sixty-five workers.

SSI Absorbs One of the Basic Social Security Functions

In reviewing the shortcomings of the system as constructed before 1972, it was noted that one of the two basic functions of the system was to redistribute income within cohorts of the aged so that some sort of income floor would be provided for the poorest. This, however, is exactly the function of the SSI program. With the creation of SSI—a uniform national low-income support program for the aged—we now have two separate policy instruments with which to perform the two functions that the single social security program had previously sought to perform. SSI makes a good part of the income redistribution functions of the social security system redundant. Rather than having to live with a system compromised in its ability to perform either of its functions fully because of the constraints imposed by the other function, it is now conceptually possible not only to fashion each program to perform a single function effectively, but also to integrate the programs rationally.

The Cost of Social Security Myths Has Risen

The price which society pays for maintaining the myth of social security as an insurance program has risen substantially as a result of the changes initiated around 1972. In order to finance the rise in benefits and extension in coverage, it has been necessary to raise sharply the level of the payroll tax. The burden of the payroll tax on the lower-income groups has, as noted above, been substantially increased. The Congress could have financed all or some of these changes through general revenues, thus placing less of the burden on lower-income workers. In choosing to stick with a social security tax as the basic financing instrument, Congress has forced the low-income worker to shoulder a heavy burden in order to maintain the appearance of a social insurance program.

While the level of earnings at which the retirement test begins to reduce earnings has been increased considerably and the 100 percent marginal tax on earnings caused by the retirement test over a segment of the earnings range has been removed, the fact that benefits have increased means that the range of earnings over which the retirement test will be reducing earnings—and thereby operating as a marginal tax rate—has also been increased.[17] Therefore, the cost—in terms of adverse work incentives—of "proving" by means of the retirement test that the system is an earnings replacement system has increased.

Priests and Reformers

The 1972 amendments and related developments are viewed rather differently by the priests of social security and the Johnny-come-lately reformers.

The Priests' View

The originators of the social security system and the supporters of the concepts as originally conceived—many of whom have done yeoman labor in the administration of the program, in congressional lobbying for it, and in academic analysis of it—are those I will characterize as the priests of social security, in part because their rhetoric takes on priestly tones and often involves many appeals to the original scriptures of the founding fathers of the system. In general, the priests see aspects of the 1972 amendments as realizations of their fondest hopes; in their eyes the system has matured and reached its finest flowering. They feel this is so primarily because: (1) the 1972 developments have broadened the coverage of the system to include nearly all workers and classes of dependents; (2) benefit levels have been substantially increased and brought near to a level which might be deemed adequate relative to general living standards; and (3) indexing of the benefit levels—that is, increases coming automatically with price level rises—provides systematic protection against inflation.

The priests appear somewhat uneasy about the creation of the Supplementary Security Income program. They recognized the need to do something about the patchwork of federal and state programs of old-age assistance and aid to the blind and disabled. However, they fear that SSI may perhaps be a mistake, particularly because it is to be administered by the Social Security Administration. Since it is a means-tested program— that is, in order to determine eligibility and benefits, income and assets, or means, must be determined—it may contaminate the image of the Social Security Administration. As long as those programs were largely run by the states, social security was not touched by the stigma of welfare; now, with SSI, the carefully preserved distinction between social security as social insurance and the other programs as welfare is perhaps blurred in the public mind. The priests could not very well fight hard against the passage of SSI, since it clearly meant a rise in cash income for many aged persons, so they have accepted it with what I perceive to be less than great enthusiasm.

The Reformers' View

The Johnny-come-lately reformers are social analysts, primarily economists, whose interest in the problems of social security has increased considerably in recent years—thus the priests call them Johnny-come-latelys. They tend to look at the program as one form of income redistribution, both within generations and across generations, and to put considerable weight on technical concepts of efficiency and equity. In their view the changes in the system related to the 1972 amendments have heightened the contradictions already inherent in the pre-1972 structure and have brought into sharper relief the high costs of the social myths upon which the system is said to be constructed, as well as the fact that those costs are borne in particular by lower income persons. The raising of the payroll tax in order to finance higher benefits has, in their view, broadened the scope of regressive federal taxation and, combined with the reductions in the federal income tax—which is more progressive in its impact—has made the overall structure of federal taxation more regressive.

The rise in benefits has, as noted above, spread the negative work disincentives caused by the implicit tax over a broader range of older persons. The retirement test is repugnant to reformers not only because of its negative work disincentives, but also because of its inequitable impact. For example, those over sixty-five who must rely on earnings as a major additional source of income receive reduced social security benefits; yet, other income—of the same, or greater, amounts—from nonearnings sources leaves social security benefits unaffected.[18]

Finally, the introduction of SSI, in the view of the reformers, makes the redistributive features of the social security benefit structure redundant. Now, they argue, the myth that the single, unitary system can adequately serve both the income maintenance and intergenerational transfer functions is dispensable, and each element—SSI and social security—can be reformed to serve its single function more effectively.

Point and Counterpoint on Reform

The Johnny-come-lately reformers argue that, first and foremost, it should be explicitly recognized that social security is not insurance. Once this fact is recognized, the system can be financed through a more progressive system of taxation. There are a number of proposals for achieving a more progressive form of financing,[19] but I will not attempt to spell them out here, especially since the main argument can be simply stated:

> It is misleading to think of payroll taxes as individual contributions destined to be returned to the contributor at a later date; it is far more accurate to think of the social security system as a national pension scheme, whose benefit levels are determined by the national priority accorded to the needs of the retired, the disabled, and survivors and whose costs are paid for by a tax on current earners. Once this point of view is accepted, there is no logical reason why the tax used to support the pension system should impose hardship on the poor. The arguments for financing pensions out of a progressive tax that exempts the poor are just as strong as those for financing other government expenditures in this way.[20]

The reply of the priests of social security to this argument deserves quotation at length, both because it is not easily summarized and because it is important to have a sense of the quality of the rhetoric. Professor J. Douglas Brown of Princeton University, one of the founding fathers of social security, comments:

> To understand the effectiveness of contributory social insurance in meeting human risks, it is necessary to treat it as an integrated mechanism. Wage earners are willing to contribute because they will receive benefits as a matter of right when they or their families need them most. For centuries, working people have learned that one cannot get something for nothing; at least, you cannot count on it. . . .
>
> Contributions and benefits in social insurance are not separable entities,

artificially stuck together, but are, rather, inseparable, interlocking elements in a single concept. Without this interlock, you end up with a program of doles financed by general taxation. It was such a scheme, under the name of the Townsend Plan, which we were desperately seeking to avoid in 1934–35. . . . This close integration of contributions and benefits in the concept of contributory social insurance, paying benefits as a matter of right, is the reason why those of us who have worked longest in the development of the OASDI [social security] program oppose altering the rate of contribution for lower-income participants according to some ancillary test of need.

That is, Brown is saying, to finance more progressively would be to introduce a means test, undercutting the contributory insurance feeling workers have:

You see where our differences lie. I am also convinced that the feeling of self-respect is vital to social insurance to make it work. People are willing to pay these payroll taxes because it gives them a feeling of self-reliance. . . . The association of the benefit with the payment or a contribution which makes it a matter of right, is a powerful mystique. It is an integral part of the concept of social security.[21]

The Johnny-come-lately reformers, in turn, put forward another proposal. All right, they say, if the contributory principle is central to the viability of the social security system, let us explicitly recognize it and, then, follow it correctly by splitting the two functions of the system. SSI can be improved and take the place of the income maintenance function of social security. The social security benefits can be closely related to payroll taxes actually paid over the working lifetime prior to sixty-five. There would be no skewing of the benefits toward the low-income workers: their special needs would be met through SSI. After the age of sixty-five all workers would receive benefits which would be the same proportion of their paid payroll tax. The system would operate as a federalized pension insurance program. There would be no retirement test, since the federal pension would simply reflect past payroll tax payments. This dual system of social security for pensions and SSI for low-income needs determined by the worker's current income from all sources would perform the two functions of the current system with greater efficiency and equity; moreover, neither function would be compromised by the constraints of the other. The issue of the regressivity of the payroll tax would evaporate, since benefits would be strictly tied to the tax.[22]

The priests of social security respond in horror to such a proposal. With respect to the aspect of an improved, separate SSI, Wilbur Cohen—former secretary of Health, Education, and Welfare—stated:

I . . . oppose any wholesale substitute for the social security system, whatever its name (such as a negative income tax, a guaranteed income or what have you) that makes payments only to the poor. A program for the poor will most likely be a poor program.[23]

J. Douglas Brown conjures more vivid imagery to counter the reformers' proposals to tinker with the time-tested system:

> It is said that a panel of aerodynamicists, after careful research, found that the wings of the bumblebee provided insufficient lift to support the bumblebee in flight. It is fortunate that the bumblebee, in its million years of evolution, did not know about this scientifically determined shortcoming.
>
> The aerodynamicists made two mistakes.
>
> One, they intensively examined the bumblebee's wings without taking the time to understand the way a whole, live bumblebee functions.
>
> Two, they failed to realize that living things, through long response and adjustment to conditions, develop the capacity to do what is necessary for effective survival. . . .
>
> As with bumblebees, so with many social institutions, if they are dissected into their separate parts, those parts appear to a specialist to be ill-designed and unworkable. But through long evolution as integrated entities, the institutions have gained a mysterious capacity to survive and function effectively.
>
> Among such social institutions are the Government of the United States, the U.S. Constitution, the U.S. Senate, the Roman Catholic Church, Harvard University, and contributory social insurance. Of these, only the Catholic Church is older than the early beginnings of the contributory mutual benefit associations for the protection of workers out of which social insurance systems developed.[24]

This brings us to the central tenet of the priests of social security. A system which explicitly recognizes the separate functions of the current system—shifting funds from earnings to later life on the one hand and income maintenance on the other—will be socially divisive. The system must be shrouded in the social myth of contributory social insurance in order to operate. If one makes explicit the system's functions, the system will become a political football. The social myth exacts a price—that is, it is a regressive system in which the poor bear a disproportionate burden to support that myth; however, they argue, if one removes the myth, the social contract will dissolve.

George Rohrlich comments: "In a nutshell, what one finds lagging, if not altogether missing, in our current notion of distributive justice is a sense of social solidarity."[25] The priests seem to be saying: the whole ingenious structure of social security is fragile; thus do not tamper with, do not be excessively tidy about the details of, the system. If it were made clear to the general public either that the system is an intergenerational transfer mechanism—the young supporting the old in each period, which is the essence of the reformers' first proposal—or that the system redistributes income within the aged cohort from high earners to low earners—which is essential to the reformers' second, dual system proposal—social conflict will emerge, and the system will disintegrate. It is working, they argue, so leave it alone.

Is the social myth a necessity? This is the deep issue in the debate over social security, the possible kernel of truth to be found in the warnings of the priests of social security not to ignore the original scriptures. What is the cement which holds together a social system? What is necessary to avoid conflict between the young and the old or the rich and the poor? Must we have the confidence man in order to build social institutions? While I would like to think not, I cannot argue the point with much persuasion.

Confidence Men and Social Institutions

Is the social myth a necessity? This is the deep issue in the debate over Social Security, the possible kernel of truth to be found in the warnings of the priests of Social Security not to ignore the original scriptures. What is the cement which holds together a social system? What is necessary to avoid conflict between the young and the old or the rich and the poor? Must we have the confidence man in order to build social institutions? While I would like to think not, I cannot argue the point with much persuasion.

Melville, whose whole book plays with the ambiguities of confidence—both private and public—concludes his work:

> The cosmopolitan [talking to an old man] said sadly: "Though this is a theme on which travellers seldom talk to each other, yet, to you, sir, I will say, that I share something of your sense of security. I have moved much about the world, and still keep at it; nevertheless, though in this land, and especially in these parts of it, some stories are told . . . to make one a little apprehensive, yet I may say that, neither by land nor by water am I ever seriously disquieted, however, at times, transiently uneasy, since, with you, sir, I believe in a Committee of Safety, holding silent sessions over all, in an invisible patrol, most alert when we soundest sleep. . . . In short, I never forget that passage of Scripture which says "Jehovah shall be thy confidence." The traveller who has not this trust, what miserable misgivings must be his; or, what vain, short-sighted care must he take of himself."

. . . .

NOTES

1. Herman Melville, *The Confidence Man* (Indianapolis, Ind.: Bobbs Merrill, 1971).
2. U.S., Department of Health, Educatin and Welfare, *Social Security Programs in the United States*, DHEW no. (SSA)73-11915 (1973), p. 30.
3. See Paul Samuelson, "An Exact Consumption-Loan Model of Interest," *Journal of Political Economy* 66 (December 1958), pp. 467–482: or "Social Security," *Newsweek*, 13 February 1967, for the theoretical justification for such a social mechanism.
4. For example, if an individual works for three quarters of each year in the

public sector which is not covered and for one quarter in a covered job, he still qualifies for social security benefits. Moreover, he will get the same retirement benefits as someone his age who worked at an equal wage for all four quarters in the covered sector. The first individual will have paid one-fourth the amount of social security taxes as the second.

5. This should not obscure the fact that under the law—both as currently conceived and as it stood in 1971—all workers will receive more in benefits than they pay in social security tax. John Brittain estimates that an average worker will get about 4 percent real rate of return on the payroll taxes he has paid. Any such estimates require a number of assumptions, but Brittain's seem broadly reasonable. See John Brittain, "Statement," in *Future Directions in Social Security*. U.S. Congress, Senate, Special Committee on Aging (Washington, D.C.: Government Printing Office, 1973), part 3, p. 176.

6. The law was subsequently changed in several steps. The current law allows $2,400 of earnings before benefits are reduced; after that, benefits are reduced fifty cents for each additional dollar earned. This means that while the 100 percent tax range no longer exists, the 50 percent tax range still does.

7. See, Julian Abbott, "Covered Employment and the Age Men Claim Retirement Benefits," *Social Security Bulletin* 37, no. 4 (April 1974), pp. 3–16; and the works cited therein.

8. For a fuller discussion of this issue, see U.S. Congress, Senate Special Committee on Aging, *Future Directions in Social Security* (Washington, D.C.: Government Printing Office, 1973), part 5, pp. 375–393.

9. See John Brittain, *The Payroll Tax for Social Security* (Washington, D.C.: Brookings Institution, 1972), chaps. 2 and 3.

10. Ibid., pp. 10–11.

11. A convenient summary and overview of this period can be found in Robert Ball, "Social Security Amendments of 1972: A Summary and Legislative History," *Social Security Bulletin* 32, no. 3 (March 1973), pp. 3–25.

12. The annual exempt amount of earnings—the retirement test threshold—was legislatively increased from $1,680 to $2,100 in the 1972 amendments and then to $2,400 in 1973.

13. For details, see Charles Schultze et al., *Setting National Priorities: The 1974 Budget* (Washington, D.C.: Brookings Institution, 1973), pp. 45–63.

14. Mary J. Wilson, "Social Security: An Inflation Hedge?" *New York Times*, 13 January 1974.

15. It must be remembered that such projections are quite sensitive to assumptions made about how the labor force participation of the aged will change in the future. Since, as noted above, the decline in the aged male labor force participation rate has been particularly precipitous over the last two decades, assumptions about future aged labor force participation rates are particularly difficult to make with any confidence.

16. The 1968 and 1972 replacement ratios are cited as they were reported by the National Retired Teachers Association and the American Association of Retired Persons in *Future Directions*, part 5, pp. 334–342. The replacement ratio is lower than the ratio of benefits to average covered earnings because, in general, the earnings of a worker in the year prior to retirement will be greater than the average over the period of his covered earnings. Thus the denominator for the replacement ratio is larger than for the ratio of benefits to average covered earnings.

17. With the earnings test in effect in 1970 and the single worker minimum benefit at that time, the retirement test would have operated to reduce benefits for anyone with earnings between $140 and $250 per month. For someone with the maximum equivalent of the current maximum—that is, the current

maximum discounted by the percentage legislative increase since 1970—the retirement test operated for monthly earnings between $140 and $350. With the current retirement test, at the minimum single worker benefit the retirement test on earnings operates between $200 and $388 per month in earnings and at the maximum benefit it operates between $200 and $591 per month in earnings. Thus the range over which the implicit marginal tax rate in the retirement test operates has been expanded.

18. The estimated cost of removing the retirement test is about $4 billion annually which, if financed by the payroll tax, would require adding about one-fourth of a percentage point to both the employee and employer contributions. To the extent that removal of the retirement test did result in increased earnings among the aged, some of these tax costs would be recovered through the federal payroll and income taxes. Proposals have also been put forward to make all income, regardless of source, subject to the retirement test. This has been rejected by the priests because, among other reasons, "the idea that Social Security benefits are intended as a partial replacement of earnings from work would be diluted or lost." See, National Retired Teachers report in *Future Directions*, part 5, p. 379.

19. See Michael Taussig, "The Social Security Retirement Program and Welfare Reform," in *Studies in Public Welfare*, U.S. Congress, Joint Economic Committee (Washington, D.C.: Government Printing Office, 1973), paper no. 7, pp. 37–38; Schultze et al., *Setting National Priorities*, pp. 57–64; Brittain, *Payroll Tax*, chap. 5.

20. Schultze et al., *Setting National Priorities*, p. 60.

21. J. Douglas Brown, "Statement," in *Future Directions*, part 3, pp. 188–202.

22. Taussig, "Social Security Reform," pp. 29–35, spells out the details of this dual system quite clearly, drawing on earlier work by James Buchanan, "Social Insurance in a Growing Economy: A Proposal for Radical Reform," *National Tax Journal* 21, no. 4 (December 1968), pp. 386–395.

23. Wilbur Cohen, as cited in Wilbur Cohen and Milton Friedman, *Social Security: Universal or Selective?* (Washington, D.C.: National Debate Seminars, American Enterprise Institute for Public Policy Research, 1972), p. 12.

24. Brown, "Statement," p. 189.

25. George Rohrlich, "The Place of Social Insurance in the Pursuit of the General Welfare," *Journal of Risk and Insurance* 36, no. 4 (September 1969), p. 348.

Intergenerational Transfers and the Bureaucracy

JUANITA M. KREPS

While people believe that retirement benefits received by the aged from the government are financed by funds paid in by those older people during their working years, in reality the payroll taxes of middle-aged workers are used to benefit current retirees. A question which has been raised is whether an increased reliance on government and private pensions has affected relationships between the aged and their children. Before social security was established, the middle generation supported their aged parents directly. The middle generation is still the source of support for the aged, but the financing is now indirect and impersonal. In this article Kreps discusses the present sources of income of the aged and the potential effects on family relationships.

A decade ago a small group of scholars met at Duke University to consider some aspects of the changing reciprocal relations among members of families living in industrialized countries. Within that context one analysis underscored the major economic characteristic of such current reciprocity: the reliance of both retirees and youth on the middle generation of workers for current output, the allocation of this output being made via a transfer of money claims between whole generations rather than between members of the same family. Governmental arrangements for retirement benefits, financed by payroll taxes on those at work, now largely replace intrafamily support; each generation of workers is taxed, presumably in order to provide for its own future retirement. But in reality annual tax receipts are used to pay benefits to current retirees.[1] Hence, as Kenneth Boulding notes, "The support which the middle-aged give to the young can be regarded as the first part of a deferred exchange, which will be consummated when those who are now young become middle-aged and support those who are now middle-aged who will then be old. Similarly, the support which the middle-aged give to the old can be regarded as the consummation of a bargain entered into a generation ago."[2]

In turning now to a consideration of the linkages of old people with their children and with the bureaucratic organizations—an inquiry designed to help describe the quality of life of the aged—we come up against the question of how old people cope with the bureaucracy in all its complexities. Do the elderly's own children and grandchildren provide the means of entry into the social order and a buffer against the pressures of bureaucracy? Or have these functions, too, become a part of the formal organization, so that information and advice are now provided primarily by professionals in the health and welfare fields?

Further questions, partly economic in content, are raised. As the bulk of the aged person's money income comes to be guaranteed through governmental transfers and private pension arrangements, does he not shift his financial reliance away from his children, depending instead on his past earnings record and the actions of Congress? Moreover, if independent retirement incomes enable the elderly to maintain their own homes, often quite distant from the location of their children, will these living arrangements not reduce further the family linkages, while making dependence on the bureaucracy ever more pronounced?[3]

One possible effect of the aged's decreased financial reliance on their own children would be a change in the quality of the intergenerational relationship, from one of dependency to one based on mutual interests, affection, and psychological support. To the extent that aged parents cease to be an economic burden to their children, vying for the family's limited resources, frictions within the family should be greatly reduced. In the same manner financial provision for young adults not yet in the work force (through scholarships, stipends, training allowances, etc.) which enables youth to live on their own funds, apart from their parents, minimizes intrafamily conflict.

The freedom from the burden of providing economic support directly to one's aged parents is of course counterbalanced by the necessity of paying taxes out of which the economic support is funded. Thus the middle generation's escape from financial responsibility for the aged (and the aged's escape from dependence on their children) is illusory. But the illusion is important nonetheless—perhaps more important than the reality. For the payment of taxes is compulsory and the receipt of benefits is virtually universal. As a result the aged's income is guaranteed, being dissociated from any caprice of their own children. The independent source of income allows the aged to live separately and make their own decisions for longer than would be the case if economic resources were shared within a family unit. It allows the middle generation greater independence of action as well. By insuring that elderly parents have incomes regardless of any uncertainties that befall their children, social security transfers permit the middle generation greater freedom and control over their own financial decisions. Again the parallel between the middle-aged and youth may be appropriate: each generation would increase its range of independent decisions if transfers of income to youth were intergenerational rather than intrafamily.

There can be little doubt that the growing economic independence of the three generations, each from the other, affects the nature of the interrelationship between the children, parents, and grandparents of a particular family. One of the major bases of both cooperation and conflict is being removed. But when it is no longer necessary for grandparents, parents, and children to join forces and work through the process of allocating family resources, will a joining of forces actually occur? Except for periods of psychological stress, illness, and the like, will there be a sufficient mutuality of interest to hold the three groups together on a continuous basis?[4] Even if the elderly's children provide a buffer against the pressures of the bureaucracy, these linkages may well be intermittent, occurring primarily in times of crises.

Any trade-off between increased financial independence and a geographical (and perhaps psychological) estrangement of the elderly from their children can be appraised only if the terms of the trade-off can be defined. Research would reveal the extent of the aged's reliance on their children for entry into the social order; similarly a review of the data will indicate the components of the aged's income and the extent to which they are financially independent of their children. . . . The discussion immediately following focuses on the second issue, i.e., that of the elderly's income sources. After the financial picture is drawn, attention is given first to the manner in which the allocative mechanism, in concert with the process of economic growth, produces significant intergenerational income differentials; and second, to the possible conflict between generations (as distinct from differences of view between the aged and their own children) arising from the allocation process.

The Changing Composition of the Elderly's Income

The shift from intrafamily to intergenerational support can be demonstrated by the growth in the proportion of the aged's income provided by social security and other income-maintenance benefits. This increasing component of income in the form of benefits reflects both the maturing of the nation's social security system and the secular decline in the labor force activity of older men. To illustrate the latter: from a labor force rate of about two in three older men at the turn of the century, the proportion had dropped to one in three by 1960, and has since fallen to one in four.

In aggregate terms the elderly's earnings of $7–8 billion at midcentury was several times the size of their total benefits. By 1958 total income going to the population aged sixty-five and over had risen substantially and about two-fifths of the total came from social security benefits. Even with the addition of other public transfers of income, earnings were higher than benefits during most of the decade. By 1960, however, when the aged's aggregate income had reached $33 billion, the ratio of earnings to benefits had reached one to one.

During the past decade the composition of income has mirrored even stronger trends toward transfers, with less than one-third of the total coming from earnings by the end of the 1960s. Social security payments constituted over 30 percent, with railroad retirement and government pensions adding 6 percent, public assistance 5 percent, and veterans' benefits 4 percent. Thus more than 45 percent of the aggregate income of the elderly came from public transfers in a year when only about one-fifth of all old people were working. The addition of private pensions swells the income from transfers to about half the total amount received.

Social security coverage, along with public benefits provided for civil servants and railroad employees, is now virtually complete, and recent increases in the size of benefits will have the effect of making this source of income an even more significant portion of the elderly's aggregate income. The decline in labor force activity of men over sixty is expected to continue with further erosion of earnings. Even now, the elderly's wages are those received by persons in their late sixties; most older people have no earnings, but must rely almost exclusively on social security benefits and on Supplemental Security Income administered by the Social Security Administration.

Total money incomes going to the aged are relatively low, despite social security's coverage. Of the more than 21 million aged Americans representing approximately 10 percent of the 1972 population, 4.3 million were classified as poor by current standards. This means that almost 20 percent of the poor were aged. There is also a substantial amount of hidden poverty among the elderly. More than 2 million old people live with their families—families whose incomes are above the poverty level. Adding these to those officially classified as poor, the number of aged poor rose to 6.3 million, which represented almost one-third of all people age sixty-five or older in 1972.[5] The median family income of the aged is much lower than that of younger families; indeed, the aged's family income was less than two-thirds that of the national average. For whites of all ages in 1974 median family income was $13,356; for those over sixty-five the median was only $7,519. For blacks of all ages the median was $7,808, while that of the black elderly was $4,909.[6]

Monthly social security benefits and the number of people covered under Old Age, Survivors and Disability Insurance have risen substantially during the past two decades. Currently about 17 million men and women aged sixty-two and over receive monthly OASDI payments. Average monthly benefits paid to retired workers in September 1975 were $226 to male and $131 to female beneficiaries, many of whom had taken retirement prior to age sixty-five.[7] Wives and husbands of retired workers, most aged sixty-two and over, received $105 a month on the average,[8] and widows and widowers, $192.[9]

Improvements in the level of benefits have been accompanied by increases in payroll taxes on workers, the benefits being financed from these receipts. The most recent rise in social security taxes again drew attention to the volume of transfers to retirees from workers, particularly low-income workers, who are taxed a higher proportion of their earnings than are those workers who earn higher salaries. The regressive nature of payroll taxes, a source of constant criticism from students of public finance, led to a recent tax revision that mitigated the initial impact on low-income workers.

Allocative Mechanism and Intergenerational Differences in Income

Recent legislation has provided for substantial increases in average social security benefits, has federalized old-age assistance, and has tied social security payments to the cost of living—all of which will tend to reduce intergenerational differences in income levels. But the basic distributive scheme will nevertheless continue to favor those currently at work over those currently retired, at least as long as economic growth continues.

Economic growth is made possible from an increase in the quantity or an improvement in the quality of resources, and from the development of better combinations of resources in the production process. Thus higher real income may result from improved technology, a better educated or more skilled labor force, or heavier investments in capital equipment. When such forces raise the level of output, year after year, consumption levels can be raised for the society as a whole. But the fruits of growth are not conferred evenly over the population; the impact of growth on income and consumption levels may, in fact, accentuate intergenerational differences in economic levels.

A systematic tendency for incomes of the retired to lag behind those of employed persons was demonstrated earlier in a model developed by Blackburn,[10] in which he shows that the relation between the level of consumption of retirees and that of workers depends, *ceteris paribus*, on the rate of growth. Specifically Blackburn assumed an average age of labor force entry of twenty, retirement at sixty, and death at age eighty. On the average, then, people work forty years and spend twenty in retirement. Assuming further a 5 percent rate of interest, and supposing that the worker throughout his labor force years saved that fraction of earnings necessary to provide a retirement consumption level equal to the level *of that year*, he notes that:

1. Consumption at the beginning of the retirement period, as a

proportion of average consumption of workers, would be 100 percent only if the growth rate were zero.

2. If the income growth rate were 1 percent, the worker would enter retirement on 77 percent of the average workers' consumption level; if the growth rate were 2 percent, on 60 percent of workers' consumption; if 3 percent, 48, and if 4 percent, 35 percent of workers' consumption.

3. Since workers' incomes would continue to rise in accordance with economic growth, the divergence of incomes would continue during the twenty-year retirement span. Half way through the retirement period, for example, the retiree would have a consumption level equal to 45 percent of an average worker's level if the growth rate is 2 percent, and 36 percent if growth is 3 percent (pp. 59–60).

The significance of this tendency of earnings to reflect current growth, while retirement benefits (public and in most cases private) are based on some portion of the earnings of an earlier, less productive era, has been obscured by the debate over tying benefits to the cost of living. Throughout recent discussions of the inflationary spiral and its impact on the purchasing power of the fixed-income aged, the growth question was ignored. From congressional hearings one might easily conclude that once benefits were adjusted automatically to price increases, erosion of the financial position of the elderly would cease. Yet the relative deterioration in retirement income occurs even when cost-of-living adjustments are made. In brief, the faster the pace of technology and the higher the rate of economic growth, the greater the disparity between earnings and retirement benefits, under present allocation arrangements.

The manner in which savings are accumulated (privately, or through tax deductions) does not affect the process of widening generational differences in income, although the form of investing the savings will of course affect the return received. To the extent that savings are invested in equities which keep pace with economic growth, some of the difference in current and past earnings could be offset. But since the gap results from the fact that succeeding generations enjoy progressively higher earnings, whereas the retiree's savings have been derived from lower incomes, the consumption levels of retirees are bound to be lower than wages unless a bureaucratic reallocation of aggregate income occurs.

The relative deterioration in the incomes of retirees, occasioned by growth in earnings and perpetuated by the distributive arrangements, could be at least partially offset under a different allocation scheme. If a share in growth were imputed to retirees through some strategy such as the social credit plan introduced by Spengler,[11] the erosion of standards during the retirement period could be prevented. However, such action appears unlikely and in any event would not take account of the gradual rise in earnings during work life. Because of the rise in consumption levels through the middle years, peak incomes are generally received near the end of work life; the drop that accompanies retirement is a sharp one, although the level to which income falls may be comparable to an earlier one in the life cycle.

Since our system of economic incentives is couched in terms of wage increases based on the rise in productivity, it is difficult to imagine any leveling of earnings during the work life. On the contrary, wage differentials may be increasing. Recent study indicates a slow but persistent increase in the concentration of earnings during the 1958–70 period,[12] which may be in part a reflection of a greater range between wages earned early and those earned late in work life. As a long-run problem, intergenerational differences in income may become more acute, giving rise to age-related distributional questions to which the society has not given serious attention. Resolution of differences in these views will be found in the political arena, however, rather than within families.

Sources of Intergenerational Conflict

The reduction of labor force participation of elderly men and, in particular, the downward drift in the retirement age of males lengthens the retirement period during which support is drawn from past earnings. As the numbers of retirees grow relative to the size of the working population, and as school age is extended to a later age, the dependency relationships are affected even though, as Philip Hauser points ost, the dependency ratio itself is expected to drop by 1980, rise by 1990, and drop again by 2000.[13] Although the heavy influx of women into the labor force during the twentieth century has offset the decline in work activity of younger and older men, the concentration of work in the middle years has nevertheless sharpened the economic distinctions between generations. Youth now has an extended period of schooling, the cost of which is increasingly the responsibility of the whole society, and retirees' incomes, as we have seen, are largely independent of family connection. During this century about five years of nonworking time have been added at the beginning and another five years at the end of work.

When the support patterns for these longer periods are clearly identified as flows of income between generations, some basis for conflict between generations emerges, replacing perhaps an earlier intrafamily conflict over the allocation of the family's resources. The probability of intergenerational debate concerning how the nation's output will be distributed is heightened when the allocative mechanism tends to award current income to current participants in the economic process, and when this process is well understood by members of the three generations.

It is not surprising, therefore, to see references in the popular press to the burdensome load of social security taxes on the workers. Setting the economic well-being of the younger family against that of the old person, it is easy to show that the drain of tax dollars in the latter's direction is a source of a genuine hardship, particularly on the low-income worker. One article, devoted to the cut in take-home pay resulting from 1973's increase in the payroll tax rates and base, publicized some interesting projections. Assuming that wages continue to rise and social security benefits rise sufficiently to cover an estimated 2.75 percent a year cost-of-living increase, the maximum monthly benefit for a worker retiring at sixty-five in 2011 would be $1,819. Adding 50 percent for a dependent wife, the couple's monthly benefit would be $2,729, or an annual social security income of nearly $33,000.[14] From the viewpoint of the worker paying taxes, the need for supporting old people in such supposed affluence would surely be questioned.

A review of the tax rates and wage bases indicates that the amount paid by low-wage workers has become quite a significant proportion of earnings. From the time of the passage of the legislation in 1935, when the tax was 1 percent on employer and employee for earnings up to $3,000, the tax has risen to its present level of 5.85 percent on each, on all wages up to $15,300. Total taxes collected from an individual worker earning as much as the taxable base have thus grown from $346 in 1965 to $1,790 in 1976.

The worker whose income falls at $15,300 or below has been taxed on all his earnings, whereas the wage earner who is paid $30,600 is taxed on only half of his. The percentage of income paid in social security tax has been higher, the lower the income. Taking into further account the proposition generally held by economists that the worker actually bears the cost of the tax on the employer as well as the one levied directly on him, his total liability is now 11.7 percent of all wages up to the taxable base.

As mentioned earlier, the regressivity of the payroll tax has brought sharp criticisms, even from proponents of higher social security benefits.[15] Proposals have been made for shifting the cost altogether to general revenues; for shifting a portion of the costs, perhaps one-third, to general revenue funding; and for exempting low-income families (those on income at or below the poverty threshold, at least) from the payroll tax, just as they are exempt from the federal income tax. Counter-arguments have held that the regressive impact of the tax is largely mitigated by a progressive benefit return;[16] hence, on balance, the system is acceptable. Under the tax reduction act of 1975 families with children were given an income credit that had the effect of eliminating their OASDI tax when wages were under $4,000 per year. Between $4,000 and $8,000 the tax is progressive, between $8,000 and $15,000, proportional, and over $15,300, regressive.

The fact that the size of the benefit is subject to change by congressional action is nevertheless recognized. Older people correctly perceive that insofar as their economic status is dependent on their social security benefits, that status is in the hands of the bureaucracy. Political pressure thus becomes the medium through which one improves his retirement benefit, *once he is in retirement*, just as political pressure is the means by which he holds payroll taxes in check *while he is in the work force*. The interesting question arises: How much conflict of interest over income allocations do the two generations perceive? If the conflict appears to be significant, what impact does it have on each generation's view of the other, and more importantly, on each one's view of those family members who are in the other generations?

How Much Conflict?

On this century's changing pattern of intergenerational support, a simplistic appraisal might conclude that the bureaucracy has assumed the family's earlier function of allocating scarce resources among the generations and with this preempting of the distributive role the voting booth has replaced the family budget conference. Given the depersonalization of this allocative process, moreover, each generation can now be expected to vote for its own interests, despite the recognition that its higher incomes would be gained, temporarily, at least, at the expense of the economic welfare of the other generations, which contain members of the same family.

Institutionalization of income allocation between generations has indeed occurred, with the incomes of retirees (and even those of young adults) being more and more often determined politically. And there is some evidence of generational solidarity on issues such as tying social security benefits to the cost of living and, more recently, complaints against the rise in payroll taxes. At the local level some of the rising sentiment against bond issues and property-tax revaluation has been attributed to the fact that older property owners have articulated their own interest. But these examples hardly make a generational war.

Stronger action by the elderly might be voiced, perhaps, if they thought their political action would be effective. For it seems unlikely that today's aged would interpret their position of, say, being against property taxes as being against the young or their middle-aged parents. Certainly there is no evidence that in their plea for stabilizing the value of retirement benefits the elderly have felt any conflict of interest with the middle-aged taxpayer. The Congress was under attack for letting living costs rise and erode benefits; but the trade-off of income for the aged versus income of the worker went unacknowledged.

The mystique of retirement benefits—the notion that the retiree has paid for them while working, and the money has been held in trust, drawing interest—bolsters the belief that the amount paid out is no drain on current workers, who are merely building up their own dollar accounts. Even the coupling of a rise in benefits with a rise in payroll taxes can be explained by the need for today's worker to put in more dollars for his own future retirement, rather than a need to increase revenues for the current generation of retirees when benefits are raised. Until the retiree has a clearer understanding of social security financing, intergenerational conflict will be happily minimized. It may well be that the explanations economists think necessary are in fact unwise.

Among people now at work the view that retirement benefits will accrue because one pays social security taxes during his working years (rather than because the money paid is in any way earmarked for his individual account) is widely shared. Thus a clear understanding of benefits as a transfer of money claims does not negate one's feeling of entitlement. In the future the issue in any intergenerational difference of view on transfers will not be the right to a benefit in old age but the amount of that benefit. In the resolution of that question the generations must confront the allocative issue. Since total money income cannot exceed the aggregate volume of goods and services produced (without inflationary pressure), an increase in the claims of one generation means a decrease in the claims of another. Debate over one recent 20 percent increase in social security benefits, accompanied by an increase in payroll taxes, is illustrative.

Yet even when the financing of public transfers to the elderly is clearly understood, some of the ambivalence remains. Those paying higher taxes are in a sense insuring that their own benefits will be higher; benefits have never been reduced, and tomorrow's retirees assume that gradual improvement will continue. Moreover, workers with aged parents are unlikely to protest an increase in payroll taxes when, at the same time, they see their parents' incomes increase.

Rather than a hardening of generational lines on the income issue, debate is more likely to continue on the issue of the extremely low incomes of persons of all ages. Within this group the elderly have a disproportionately heavy representation, as earlier discussion indicated. Insofar as the public attends to the income dilemma of the poor in general, the solutions will not be divisive of the generations. On the contrary, children and aged widows below the poverty line would receive the same attention. Moreover, particular legislative actions (notably HR 1 as it finally passed) often separate out certain age groups for income supplements, leaving other equally poor persons without relief. The failure of the Ninety-third Congress to legislate federal standards for all welfare recipients was perhaps not surprising, given our history of state control and state financing. What was surprising was the enactment of federal standards for the elderly. We have yet to see whether this action on behalf of the aged, but not for children, will produce complaints that one generation is gaining over another.[17]

Alternatives to Conflict

As Professor Sussman has indicated,[18] the functions of the family and bureaucracies often overlap, resulting in competition over roles. He further points out that "the family can optimize its possibilities of survival and sustain intact its interactional system and territory if members develop managing, manipulating, and mediating skills in linkage activity."[19]

Along with the expansion in bureaucratic roles that has preempted many of the functions formerly performed within families, is there evidence that the somewhat disenfranchised family is indeed helping the individual to adapt to the bureaucracy or influencing the larger society on behalf of the individual? As it has yielded to the bureaucracy the role of allocating family income between generations, has the family assumed the role of mediating between bureaucratic structures and individual need?

Such a mediating role is clearly needed, particularly in the case of the elderly person. His reduced physical mobility means increased dependency on others for transportation to the location of the services, even when the services are provided at public expense. The even more complicated process of proving his eligibility for services (or cash payments for Supplemental Security Income, for example) taxes the patience of the most persistent and knowledgeable citizen. Misinformation, fear of governmental reprisal, pride in the ability to handle one's own affairs all militate against the older person's taking full advantage of mandated services.

Children or other relatives of the elderly could play a major role in bringing the parent and the bureaucracy together and in interpreting for the aged person the range of options available to him. Since it is clearly to the advantage of the middle-aged as well as their parents to utilize all the services that are provided at public (that is, largely the middle-aged's) expense, the children's investment of time and effort in making the necessary arrangements for their parents is well spent. To the extent that the family's role of direct support is replaced by the responsibility for seeing that the support is in fact forthcoming and that it is adequate, the family role continues to be important, though markedly different from the one assumed earlier.

The role of watch-dog of the bureaucracy has a certain popular appeal at present. Concern with major problem areas—racism, poverty, inflation—is fed to an ever-increasing pitch by the media. But equal attention to the fine details of legislation which govern the income and services of particular groups of people is not readily apparent. For while it is easy to be righteously indignant about issues such as Watergate, it is difficult to interpret the terms of welfare legislation, and far more difficult to see that unsatisfactory legislation is rewritten.

There are some optimistic signs, however. It is increasingly clear that blacks are now demanding a more careful consideration of their income needs in old age; that working women are far more sensitive to social security coverage than nonworking wives; that recent retirees are better educated and more attuned to bureaucratic systems than the very old. Specific incidents reveal the attention paid to policing the law. One research firm, concerned with the extent to which mandated services failed to reach eligible clients, proposed that the government be held responsible for delivering the services it owed to the citizens in the same way that citizens are held responsible for paying taxes owed the government. Needless to say, spokesmen for governmental agencies were appalled at such a prospect.

Yet such a calling of the bureaucracy to account is quite likely when strong advocates are involved, and the resulting impact can be quite marked. The consumer movement in this country now has power to influence not only the government but private industry as well. The civil rights movement had unprecedented influence. The women's movement has brought a raft of new governmental and industrial policies.

In examining the family's role in reshaping the bureaucracy (as opposed to redefining its own role to accommodate to the increased power of the bureaucracy), the questions need to be sharply focused. To what extent is the family attempting to bend other institutions to serve its needs? What would be the evidence? Since the family's action is by definition a single attempt at a local level, the impact of such action does not attract attention in the manner of a group movement. The voting behavior of family members of certain ages would reveal their views toward institutions and policies: older people's vote against bond issues for school construction are a case in point. But there the vote is along generational rather than family lines.

Survey might reveal the degree to which the family is a force which countervails the power of the larger institutions in the economic sphere. If the adults in the family usually agree on important issues, such as the relative levels of living appropriate for the older and the middle generations, one might conclude that family pressure on the bureaucracy would reflect this preference. In such a case, intergenerational conflict on economic issues would be minimal and the bureaucracy would simply provide the mechanism through which aggregate allocations were made.

Some Questions

In the United States, where social security is newer than in many Western European countries, the maturing of the system is only now occurring. With that maturation economic support during old age has come to be financed largely through transfers of money claims from those currently at work and paying payroll taxes to those now retired. These public transfers are supplemented by savings and private pension claims which, although substantial for higher-income workers, constitute a minimal portion of the retirement income of the low- and middle-income wage earner; and by the needs-based Supplemental Security Income, available when incomes are extremely low. These forms of income maintenance in old age have largely replaced intrafamily support in which the wage earners provided income for their own aged parents and have enabled most older people, having their own financial resources, to live apart from their children and grandchildren.

The question posed here—whether, given this bureaucratization of economic support, the elderly nevertheless rely on their children and other relatives to provide entry to the social system and to act as a buffer against the bureaucracy—is of course not an economic question. However, the extent of the aged's reliance on their own children (as opposed to the bureaucratic arrangement) can be researched once again, taking into account the most recent changes in institutional setting.

An important question is posed by changes in the economic framework. Have the shifts to intergenerational (as opposed to intrafamily) support resulted in conflicts of interest that set one generation against another? The tentative answer is no, in part because the allocation process has been poorly understood; the payment of taxes is thought to give one his own future claims to benefits. To the Congress it is clearly necessary to balance the needs of the generations in the overall allocation of money claims. Although there has been little evidence that this balancing has led to conflict between the generations, there is a growing tendency to make the choices explicit: emphasis on priority setting may well generate strong differences in viewpoints.

The fact that the elderly do not perceive their interests as being inimical to those of the middle-aged and the young could change in time, particularly if the gap between earnings late in work life and retirement income grows. A sharp decline in income with the cessation of work could well evoke protest; hence the persistent tendency for earnings to grow and for retirement incomes to lag behind—tendencies inherent in the process of growth and the way its fruits are allocated—may bring into focus an intergenerational point of conflict which has not yet been emphasized, except by economists.

A second question has to do with the impact of this shift in income sources on intergenerational family ties. Does the removal of the income-allocation issue from the family lessen conflict and thus improve family relations? Or by eliminating one of the needs for persons of different ages to rely directly on one another, does the bureaucratization of financial support remove an important link between the aged and their children and grandchildren?

The new role that needs to be assumed, given the bureaucratization of income support, is that of supervising and holding accountable the larger institutions. If the family is able to intervene on behalf of its older members, interpreting governmental rules and even protesting the rules when necessary, the rights of the aged and the viability of the family are assured. The allocation of retirement income along generational lines has the advantage of allowing older people and the middle-aged greater independence of decision making and more freedom of action than could ensue in an intrafamily setting. Family linkages with the bureaucracy would seem essential, however, if the aged are to have full access to the range of services and income supports that are now promised them.

NOTES

1. J. M. Kreps, "The Economics of Intergenerational Relationships" in *Social Structure and the Family: Generational Relations*, ed. E. Shanas and G. F. Streib (Englewood Cliffs, N.J., 1965), pp. 276–88.
2. K. E. Boulding, "Reflections on Poverty," in *The Social Welfare Forum* (New York, 1961), pp. 45–58.
3. See M. B. Sussman, "Relationships of Adult Children with Their Parents in the United States," in *Social Structure and the Family: Generational Relations*, ed. E. Shanas and G. F. Streib (Englewood Cliffs, N.J., 1965), pp. 62–92. More recently Dr. R. A. Ravich of the Cornell Medical School was quoted in the press as saying that "Institutions exist to destroy the family. . . . The more the family goes downhill, the more the power of the institutions increase."
4. For a discussion of the interrelationships of the generations, particularly the degree of communication and frequency of contact of the elderly with their children, see the works by E. Shanas, notably *Family Relationships of Older People*, Health Information Foundation Research Series 20 (New York, 1971); and the research reports from a cross-national study of elderly people conducted in Britain, the United States, and Denmark by E. Shanas, P. Townsend, D. Wedderburn, H. Friis. P. Milhøj, and J. Stehouwer, *Old People in Three Industrial Societies* (New York, 1968).
5. U.S. Senate Special Committee on Aging, Information for Initial Hearings, "Future Directions in Social Security," mimeographed (January 15, 22, 23, 1973).
6. U.S. Bureau of the Census, *Current Population Reports*, Series P-23, No. 59, May 1976.
7. *Social Security Bulletin, Annual Statistical Supplement*, 1975.
8. Ibid.
9. Ibid.
10. J. M. Kreps and J. O. Blackburn, "The Impact of Economic Growth on Retirement Incomes," Hearings Before the Special Committee on Aging (Washington, D.C., 1967), pp. 58–64.
11. J. J. Spengler and J. M. Kreps, "Equity and Social Credit for the Retired," in *Employment, Income and Retirement Problems of the Aged*, ed. J. M. Kreps (Durham, N.C., 1962), 198–231.
12. See P. Henle, "Exploring the Distribution of Earned Income," *Monthly Labor Review* 95 (1972):16–27.
13. Philip Hauser, "Extension of Life—Demographic Considerations," mimeographed (paper delivered at the 25th Annual Conference on Aging, Ann Arbor, Mich., 1972).

14. *U.S. News and World Report*, December 18, 1972, pp. 39–43.
15. See J. A. Brittain, *The Payroll Tax for Social Security* (Washington, D.C., 1972); J. A. Pechman, H. J. Aaron, and M. K. Taussig, *Social Security: Perspectives for Reform* (Washington, D.C., 1968).
16. R. J. Myers, "Employee Social Insurance Contributions and Regressive Taxation," *Journal of Risk and Insurance* 34 (1967):611–15.
17. Earlier, a secretary of Health, Education and Welfare commented on the fact that larger governmental expenditures were being made for the elderly than for children. He included social security benefits in the total amount going to old people and was immediately under attack for doing so. But the significant point raised by his comment lay in the allusion to intergenerational differences in public benefits and in his obvious concern to balance the needs of the young against those of the old.
18. M. B. Sussman, "Family, Bureaucracy, and the Elderly Individual: An Organizational/Linkage Perspective," in *Family, Bureaucracy, and the Elderly*, ed. E. Shanas and M. B. Sussman (Durham, N.C., 1977), ch. 1.
19. Ibid.

Economic Crises for Women: Aging and Retirement Years

JAYNE BURESS BURKS

The financial resources for women of retirement years are scarcer than those available to men. One reason is that women have been encouraged to maintain only a peripheral participation in the labor force. In addition, societal values have kept women from earning equal pay during the "productive" years. Inheritance laws, social security regulations, and payments of pensions and annuities to women all discriminate against the older woman. New societal arrangements are called for to allow the jobs of economic support, parenting, and home maintenance to be shared, so that women will not be penalized by an unfair distribution of retirement income.

For more than a decade the women's movement has been forcing upon the attention of the entire society the fact that we are, and have been from our beginnings, a male-dominated society. What it means to be a woman in a society which is run by and for men has been the subject of a growing body of literature. Too familiar to bear repetition here are some of the financial consequences for women in other periods of life, and we would like to focus in this paper particularly on the financial status of women in the older age group.

Financial problems for the older woman are now the number-one problem. We could possibly change that statement to say that financial problems for the older *person* are the number-one problem and be equally correct. The structure of society and the values and priorities which operate to determine the life chances of members of this society leave the older person very much disadvantaged. But in addition to this more general condition of being old in a youth-oriented society is the more particular problem of being a woman in a male-dominated society and even especially being single in a society which generally subscribes to the idea that a woman will be provided for by her husband. All these conditions operate to make the financial plight of the older woman an often desperate situation, and one cannot think of this even as a financial "crisis," which seems to have the connotation of turning point. For today's older woman there seems to be no present plan to improve her plight. For younger women, who will occupy this status in future decades, the more

SOURCE: This article was originally presented as a paper at the 1977 meeting of the Midwest Sociological Society and is reprinted here by permission of the author.

equitable distribution of job opportunities and the improvement of women's earning power, if this does in fact come about, may make being an older woman less of a financial disaster than it now is.

Part of the problem of course is simply the institutional arrangements for aged people that have emerged from the industrial society in which we live. Our own attitude toward the value of work seems to underlie our tendency to pass on any increments in productivity to those who are, in fact, the producers or the job-holders in society. The affluence of society itself seems to create a situation from which older people cannot anticipate benefits, according to Juanita Kreps, who has worked with the problem of the economics of the older person.

> Paradoxically, the higher per capita income rises, the more acute become the income problems of certain groups of people, i.e. those groups who are not current participants in the economic process. For the higher income reflects higher productivity per man-hour, and such increases in our economy are expected to accrue to the workers who are actually at work rather than to those of the preceding or succeeding generations of workers.[1]

This means that those who are not employed are dependent upon the transfer of income from the productive workers for their subsistence and makes the position of "unemployed" a very much devalued status. Unemployment during a person's productive years is seen as a personal calamity even when it is the result of economic exigencies over which the individual has almost no control, and it is fairly common in our society to hear expressed the attitude that those who are unemployed are shiftless and lazy and thus are not deserving of the fruits of hard work. Unemployment compensation is given penuriously and demeaningly to underscore the attitude that only those who work are fully entitled to the benefits of an affluent society. The personal calamity of the unemployed worker though becomes an institutionalized state for the person who has reached the age when he is no longer able and/or permitted to be a part of the work world. As longevity has increased and as retirement ages have decreased, more and more people are spending a considerable number of years in this nonworking state.

> Taking into consideration the trends toward increasing longevity and decreasing age at retirement, the proportion of the individual's life spent in the labor force will soon be less than half.[2]

As Golda Meir said on the occasion of her seventieth birthday, "Seventy is not a sin." To be an older person in our society should not be punishable by extreme deprivation, yet our societal arrangements seem to make this the incredible reality for too many of our citizens. There are over 22 million people over sixty-five in our society presently and approximately one-third of them (7.3 million) have incomes at poverty levels. More than twice as many aged women as aged men live at poverty levels of income.[3] Our national policies toward old age turn out to be sexist as well as age discriminatory.

In 1967 the average income of people over sixty-five was less than half of that of the average of the total population,[4] and in the ensuing decade of galloping inflation and increasing wages of the workers, the gap between the two groups in income has widened, in spite of some increase of social security benefits during this time. In generations past the transfers of income from one generation to another occurred mostly in the family setting and depended upon attitudes of familial love and duty to ensure the elderly person a retirement period of participation in the fortunes of the younger generation. Increasingly the transfers of income are not tied to kinship but are occurring between workers and nonworkers. Our own reluctance to allocate a greater share of national income to the support of those outside the earning ages is again reflective of the fact that our priorities are not directed this way. The needs of youth for support and education and for maintenance, provided while they also are outside the earning ages, are much more heavily subscribed to. Even the elderly, as much in tune with the shared values of this society as any group, would feel that the needs of the younger members come first. But when we compare our sense of responsibility to that of other industrial societies, it is an embarrassment to discover that in the United States, where per-hour income is more than twice as high as that of West Germany and at least a third higher than Sweden, the average old-age benefits, as a percentage of workers' wages, is considerably less than in these countries. In West Germany 31.4 percent, in Sweden 22.4 percent of average wages for all workers are devoted to old-age benefits. In the United States the figure is 18.2 percent.[5]

The problem becomes compounded for women when we look at the way in which old-age benefits (including pensions, annuities, and social security payments) are computed and distributed. Old-age benefits in this work-oriented society are distributed on the basis of work done, that is, wage-compensated work, during the productive years of one's life. Thus old-age or retirement pensions and transfers of income are really *workers'* pensions and are determined by that status, not because of age. If you have not "worked" you do not qualify for these benefits. If you have had to work for low wages, you will receive a proportionately lower old-age income. If you have not worked "long enough," you may not qualify for these benefits. "Long enough" in terms of receiving national social security payments is forty quarters, or ten years. "Long enough" varies from company to company in qualifying for private retirement pensions. If you have not worked outside the home, if you are a woman, you are dependent upon the benefits accrued to your spouse during his working years, this benefit being further qualified by your relationship to said spouse and whether said spouse is still living. If you are not supported by a male, the policies of the society in terms of your old-age income may have disadvantaged you even more.

It has been documented too frequently to be any kind of a surprise that women's incomes are lower than men's incomes in this society. First, of course, because the types of jobs that are ordinarily held by women are paid less well than jobs ordinarily held by men. But even when women work at the same profession and qualify with the same amount of educational preparation, average incomes for women are less than those for men. When retirement income is based upon proportionate amounts of earlier earned income, the lifelong difference in earning power becomes even more evident. To see women as basically not equal participants in the work world is to set up a financial plight for women in their later years that is inexcusable.

To get at some notion of the present financial status of the older woman it is instructive to look at some of the facts about women now in the productive years. We have available some information about the work and income levels of women who are presently working and earning, and can get some idea of the income that could become available to them in their retirement years by simple extrapolation of today's conditions. However, it is well to remember that women who are today in the older age groups, and in fact those who will be moving into these age levels in the next few decades, will have worked even less and earned smaller proportionate incomes in comparison with men than today's young woman. Women who are currently in the over-sixty-five age group were born before 1910. For these women the women's movement is too little and too late, and the opportunities for earning equal pay and achieving equal treatment in the occupational world for which women are now struggling will not improve their situation. These women have had a life experience that did not include working outside the home, but followed the traditional pattern of childbearing and homemaking. In an earlier agricultural or preindustrial setting, where much of production took place in the home, there was no question that women made a sizable contribution in the economic sphere. With urbanization and industrialization, production has been seen as taking place outside the home. The necessity to keep women in the home to raise children and to perform the supportive and maintenance tasks for the workers has not been seen as part of the cost of production. In military settings or other all-male work forces, the jobs of housekeeping (providing for meals, living quarters, purchasing and maintaining clothing and equipment, etc.) are seen as one of the costs of the operation. No one would think that those who are designated to perform these tasks are "not working." But in the institutionalized arrangements that have emerged in our society, this part of the cost of production becomes invisible, and the workers (wives) who perform these tasks are not considered part of the work force. The industrial economy has utilized the services of these women without ever becoming aware of the contribution they have made.

To look at the record of earnings and work status of the most recent available data for women will at least give us some idea of how present participation in the economic institution will affect the retirement status of these women. There are 868,224 women over sixteen in the St. Louis metropolitan area[6] as of 1970, and fully 58 percent of these women are not in the labor force. Close to 15 percent have never worked, most of these in the upper age groups. Of those who in 1970 made up the 42 percent of women who were considered to be in the civilian work force, 5.6 percent were unemployed and another 31 percent were part-time workers, that is, were working less than thirty-five hours a week. Part-time work does not qualify the worker to receive the "fringe benefits" in company retirement pensions (or indeed in any other health insurance and unemployment compensation benefits of full-time workers). This compares with the over-sixteen male population with participation in the labor force as of 1970 of 77 percent, with only 4.5 percent unemployed. The question now is what provision do we make for retirement income for the 58 percent of women in the St. Louis metropolitan area who are not in the work force? What particularly for the 15 percent we can assume to be mostly in the upper age groups who have never worked? Has society's expectation that woman's place should be seen as in the home, rather than in the work world, disadvantaged her financially? Of course it has. It has, in fact, completely deprived her of a right as an individual to receive any transfer of funds for support in her older years, except as she is related to a male worker as his dependent. Has the societal value for women who do work, to see working as a secondary priority to be engaged in as a low-pay or part-time activity, disadvantaged her financially in her retirement years? Of course it has. Part-time work is notoriously poorly paid in terms of actual per-hour income and poorly compensated in addition by the exclusion of part-time workers from workers' benefits, including retirement income. Her preference, and society's pressure, to put responsibility for child raising and homemaking ahead of her ability to earn a wage outside the home enables society to say to her in her old age, "But you didn't work, so you cannot expect compensation for retiring from earning."

The status of women as workers, that is, in terms of their actual participation in the labor force, is one way to focus on the problem. Perhaps even more revealing is to look at the data on the actual amounts of money women are receiving for their work. Since retirement income is based upon levels of income during productive years, this information will also help clarify the status of the older woman. In the St. Louis metropolitan area by the most recently available data (1969), already outdated by inflationary tendencies, the median income for men employed full time was $9,152. For employed women the comparable figure was $4,822.[7] In every occupation studied, from professional to the private household worker, the median income for men was greater than for women. To give us some idea of what this means for retirement income, an example maximum monthly social security payments available as of 1975 would be $386 if you had earned $5,000 per year for the required number of years, $445 if you had earned $10,000 per year.

It is common to think, however, that this disparity in earning power of men and women does not result in unfair distribution of life-support income since women are seen as benefiting as wives from the higher income made available to heads of households. However, there are nearly 70,000 families in the St. Louis area with female heads, and 31 percent of these have incomes of less than poverty level. It means that male heads of households are seen as deserving and needing higher income because of this responsible position. With the same responsibilities, females make do with female wages, which are supposedly low because women are supported by male heads of households!

The financial status of women as dependents of workers is somewhat rosier than that of the unmarried woman, reflecting again a societal preference that women are to be regarded as dependent upon males rather than as individuals with equal rights and status. To puncture the myth that all women are being well taken care of by the male population, however, it is instructive to see that of all females over fourteen living in the St. Louis area, only 60 percent are married, and this number includes those who are married but separated from their spouse, a situation which often means frank desertion with no support being provided by the absent husband. In the St. Louis area, 23 percent of the women over fourteen are single and thus not beneficiaries of a male's higher retirement benefits. Widows are entitled to the social security benefits earned by their spouses during their productive years. Wives who are past sixty-five and whose husbands are still living may collect up to 50 percent of the amount of retirement benefit their husband is entitled to, a lesser amount if they begin to collect this amount at sixty. However, a divorcee may only collect such benefits if she "earned" it by being married to her spouse for [ten] years. If the divorce took place before their [tenth] wedding anniversary, she will not collect any benefits at all. And of course both widows and divorcees, an ever growing company in today's society, may forfeit their former spouse's social security benefits if they remarry. If the widow past sixty remarries, she will forfeit 50 percent of her deceased husband's retirement benefits, or she may decide to forfeit all her deceased husband's benefits and collect on her present husband's benefits as his wife, if this is higher. (Some segments of society have felt some righteous indignation over the fact that some older people are electing to cohabit rather than marry. They might take a look at the income issues and see that older couples' combined social security retirement income will take a 25 percent decrease if they marry, since the wife must forfeit 50 percent of her deceased husband's retirement benefit.) The financial plight of the woman who divorces before she has been married [ten] years, remarries, and later divorces the second husband before [ten] years of marriage have elapsed is not pleasant to contemplate. It is possible that a woman could spend nearly [twenty] years as dependent and yet never be entitled to any dependent benefits.

In recent years some legislation has been passed to help alleviate the no-income position of many older persons, mostly women. The social security system was not, in fact, designed to provide an adequate income for older persons, but was seen as a way to provide supplemental income. However, the present generation of over-sixty-five persons has been essentially unable to overcome the economic collapse of the Depression years, and the years of inflation following World War II. They have been unable to build up savings and for this reason, for about one-third of them, social security is their sole source of income. For the elderly women (and men) who do not qualify for social security payments and have no other income resources, there is now a program of Supplementary Security Income which will provide a modest amount ($157.50 per month), reduced by certain situations, such as if the destitute person is living in someone else's home or if such a person earns as much as $65.00 per month. Medicare and Medicaid programs have been of great help in enabling older persons to have health care for acute diseases. Of course the more usual diseases of old age, which are chronic in nature, are not well covered, since 190 days of hospitalization in one lifetime is the maximum coverage. These programs (Supplementary Security Income, Medicare, and Medicaid) are not social security programs, although this agency handles the administration of these programs. Monies for these programs come from general revenue sources.

In certain other situations even the woman who works may not be able to earn social security benefits on her own account. If a husband and wife operate a business together, even if it is a partnership arrangement, only the husband may report earnings for social security credits. A husband may not hire a wife to work in his business and report her earnings for social security credit. Our governmental policies which discount the financial needs of older women seem to go on and on. If a husband is hiring his wife or working in a partnership with her, *he*, but not *she*, is entitled to put 15 percent of their income, or $1,500.00 maximum, into a tax-free Individual Retirement Account. Legislation is now being proposed which would allow the partnership to set aside a maximum of $500.00 for the wife who is in this situation. I suppose this can be seen as a step in the right direction, but it does bemuse one to see that there is an admission that the present arrangements are unfair, but the unfairness is continued in the new proposed legislation by this unequal allowance for husband and wife.

Income for retirement years coming from non-social security sources continues the story of the disadvantaged position of the older woman. Income from private pension plans for workers often stops at the death of the worker, and because wives regularly seem to outlive their husbands by several years, she has again been victimized by her dependence on *his* work for *her* life support during her older years.

In addition to the fact that women have earned less during their productive years, the benefits in monthly income from pension or retirement plans to which workers have contributed are disproportionately distributed on the basis of sex. Retirement benefits from the *same amount* of earnings will be paid out at higher monthly stipends for men than for women. As anyone can explain very glibly, actuarial tables demonstrate that women live longer than men, so "on the average" the benefits are equal in actual dollars paid out as the woman collects her smaller amount over a longer period of time. To the insurance industry, the explanation is simple and reasonable. To the older woman, who is unable to persuade the landlord or the grocer that she should pay less per month than a man the same age, this policy means again that women are expected to get along on less and to live at a lower standard than men.

Another example of financial discrimination towards the older woman, though hardly a case of financial crisis, involves inherited income accruing to widows of men in the upper socioeconomic classes. We find that once more the advantage lies on the side of the party with the higher earned income, in effect the male, who has in many cases been the only earner of wages and almost invariably has been in the past the primary source of income in a marriage. This means that if a woman precedes her husband in death, the entire combined holdings of the couple from their life together is considered to be the property of the husband, even if there is joint ownership of property or other assets, and thus there is no tax occurring at her death and the entire amount is totally in his control. If a man dies first, which is of course more usual, again their entire accumulated holdings are considered his estate upon which taxes must be computed. As an attempt to redress this patently unfair situation, a widow is granted a sizable exclusion upon which the estate is not taxed, and of course other parts of the estate which she can document were due to her own working wages outside the home or were inherited by her exclusively. It is common for men with considerable estates not to leave the entire amount to the widow, but to arrange for her to perhaps receive life income from the portion over the exclusion amount. Ownership of this excess portion will perhaps be put in trust for their common children, *or* for any other cause which he, the husband, designates. Thus while men retain control of the couple's entire estate if they are widowed, women in the same circumstances usually do not control the full amount of their jointly amassed holdings. If the estate is willed entirely to the wife, estate taxes will be assessed and then when the estate passes to their heirs the estate will again be taxed. Again this reflects the higher value the society places on who earned the money by work outside the home, at the same time that it has managed to obstruct or disapprove of women participating in earning money in anything like an equal fashion.

Since the housewife who has not worked outside the home will not have an estate (unless of course she has inherited money or property), if she dies intestate, her husband will retain full control over all their holdings. In Missouri, if the husband dies first and has not made out a will, his wife will inherit one-half of the estate and one-half will be disbursed to children and/or relatives, including her husband's parents, siblings, or any of their descendants. Only if there are no other qualifying surviving relatives will his wife inherit all the estate. In Illinois the widow in these circumstances will receive one-third and his descendants will receive two-thirds of his estate; or if there are *no* descendants the widow will inherit all. The law extends some protection to the widow whose husband may choose to exclude her from his will by allowing her to set aside his will in favor of receiving one-third of his estate if there are descendants, or up to one-half if there are no descendants. The law of course, in fairness, does not specifically discriminate in terms of wife or husband. The law states that these apportionments are made to the "surviving spouse." It is rather the life experience and the roles that men and women occupy throughout their lives that have determined that the wife generally has had no estate large enough to be probated. Whatever contribution a woman may have made to the financial success of a marriage is not recognized, and her resources then as the surviving spouse are very much different than his resources, should he be the surviving spouse.

In all these instances the financial plight of the older woman appears to come as a sort of unintended consequence or latent effect of society's values and priorities. There is no concerted conspiracy to do the older woman in; it simply occurs because of the policies and practices which have emerged in the industrial society. Women are told again and again that they are valued as mothers and wives and that they make real contributions to the society by fulfilling these functions. Yet the society does not arrange to recognize this function as "work," and since work is the basis for retirement and retirement benefits, the society seems to discount the needs of women as individuals. Seeing this nonwork function of homemaking and child rearing as the primary and important function of women enables the society to hold on to the myth that women then do not need to earn as much as men if they *do* work since they are primarily dependent upon a spouse. This myth then makes it easy to say that the "heads of households" naturally need to earn a higher income than those who are in the labor force in a secondary and peripheral way. However, it turns out that this allocation of income potential on the basis of *functions* is not the basis of the discrepancy in income, but rather this discrepancy is exactly a matter of sexual discrimination. If a woman fulfills the function of "head of household," she is not given a higher income because of these responsibilities. Her household is expected to live on the lower income that she earns because she is a woman. If a man is single and *not* head of household, he will not earn less because of this. He is compensated at higher earnings than women because he is a man.

It is hardly any surprise that the financial situation of elderly men and elderly women shows wide divergence and that "the system" which has affected the financial status of women throughout life stages has placed the older woman in a state of real financial jeopardy. Irving Rosow, writing in 1962,[8] discovered that 25 percent of the women over sixty-five had no income at all. Another 50 percent had incomes of less than $1,000 per year. In fact, only one out of twelve women over sixty-five had as much as $2,000 income annually. In the 1970 census we find the situation appears not to have significantly improved. In the age cohorts over sixty-five we find that both males and females become increasingly destitute the longer they live and that women, because they have so few resources and because they tend to live longer, are living lives of pinching poverty. Among those whose incomes in 1970 were less than $1,000 per year, we find 5.4 percent males and 26.5 percent females. As the years go on, we find that 15.5 percent of the males over seventy-five are forced to survive in this extreme penury. Among the women, an unbelievable 39 percent are surviving on less than $1,000 per year.[9]

There is no question that part of the problem with which we are dealing here is simply the problem of aging. And in this sense it is a problem of all of us since, given the normal circumstances of living, we may all anticipate living into retirement years. We are a society which has achieved an affluence sufficient to enable us all to enjoy an old age with adequate provision for our material needs. If we cannot use the services of all our people, then we must prepare to pay the bills and supply the money to those who are not able or not permitted to earn income for their needs. It has been estimated that about half of our over-sixty-five citizens are physically able to work. Yet only if they are self-employed or are willing to work on the periphery of the labor market at low-skill, low-pay jobs will they be allowed to continue to earn income. The remarkable exception to the mandatory retirement regulations which most of us have to subscribe to are those in the political sector, who pass the laws which set these mandatory limits. It is a bit ironic that they are able to see themselves as capable and fit to continue their careers, while others in society are considered obsolete.

Our problem with dealing with old age is a moral problem as much as it is a fiscal one. We allocate our national resources according to a view of public and private needs, and in the priorities we have set up and the values we subscribe to, we have apparently allowed the needs of older individuals to become almost invisible. To the deficits in terms of physical and emotional resources that old age normally brings, we add the burden of living in a financially disadvantaged state as well.

But to the economic problems that all older people suffer we have somehow managed to create some special economic problems for the older woman. The women's movement has been working very hard for goals of equal pay, equal work opportunities, and equal advancement for women in the world of work. As more and more women move into careers formerly reserved for men and as we begin to see a real equalization of incomes for men and women who are doing the same jobs, we may expect to see an improvement in the financial picture for the older woman. However, we have not yet reordered our priorities to allow women to choose the alternate course of remaining outside the work world and engaged primarily in the more traditional role of child rearing and homemaking, without being disadvantaged by her choice. For this woman who remains dependent upon a man for support, our old-age arrangements have too often meant a state of abject poverty, and it is ironic that it is this role that society generally sees as the proper sphere for women. Even though, with smaller families and more simplified house-keeping, the usual woman finds herself less occupied over her lifetime with the mechanics of this role, still her primary commitment to the traditional feminine adult life pattern dictates that she will be disadvantaged economically in her later years. Her willingness, indeed preference, for putting motherhood and caring for others in her family ahead of her own ability to achieve in her own individual career has been repaid by society seeing her contribution as having no monetary value. And to her devaluation of self-interest in support of the interest of spouse and children, she has found her needs devalued by society.

Retirement then for women, as for men, must be seen as an age in which the society provides the transfer of monies from the earning sector to the nonearning sectors of society. The women's movement, and the interests of all women, demand that the allocation of these funds be done without unfair discrimination based on sex. If we continue to insist that retirement income is to be allocated on the basis of earnings during productive years, then it is time to equalize the earning potential of men and women. It is time to grant social security credits towards retirement benefits for time spent outside the labor market on the supportive service of child rearing and homemaking. It is time to allow flexible work schedules that will allow men and women to share the jobs of parenting and home maintenance without penalizing women so that retirement income is unfairly distributed.

NOTES

1. Juanita M. Kreps, "Economics of Retirement." In E. W. Busse and E. Pfeiffer, eds., *Behavior and Adaptation in Later Life*. Little, Brown, Boston, 1969, p. 86.
2. Kurt W. Back, "The Ambiguity of Retirement." In Busse and Pfeiffer, op. cit., p. 111.
3. Erdman Palmore, "Sociological Aspects of Aging." In Busse and Pfeiffer, op. cit., p. 42.
4. Ibid., p. 39.
5. Juanita M. Kreps, op. cit., p. 77.

6. Jane Altes, "The Demography of St. Louis Area Women." Table 16, p. 17. Unpublished paper.
7. Ibid., Table 24, p. 22.
8. Irving Rosow, "Old Age: One Moral Dilemma of an Affluent Society." *Gerontologist*, 2 December 1962, pp. 182–191.
9. U.S. Bureau of the Census. Vol. I, Characteristics of the Population. Part I, U.S. Summary, Section 2, Table 245.

REFERENCES

Altes, Jane. "The Demography of St. Louis Area Women." Manuscript. 1976.

Back, Kurt W. "The Ambiguity of Retirement." In *Behavior and Adaptation in Later Life*, E. W. Busse and Eric Pfeiffer, eds. Little, Brown, Boston, 1969, pp. 93-114.

Butler, Robert W. *"Why Survive: Being Old in America."* Harper & Row, New York, 1975.

Chesler, Phyllis, and Goodman, Emily Jane. *Women, Money, and Power*. William Morrow, New York, 1976.

Cumming, E., and Henry, W. *Growing Old: the Process of Disengagement*. Basic Books, New York, 1961.

Institute of Gerontology, The University of Michigan, and Wayne State University. "No Longer Young: The Older Woman in America." Occasional Papers in Gerontology, no. 11.

Kline, Chrysee, "The Socialization Process of Women." *Gerontologist*, vol. 15, no. 6, December 1975, pp. 486–492.

Kreps, Juanita M. "Economics of Retirement." In Busse and Pfeiffer, op. cit., pp. 71–91.

Kreps, Juanita M. and Spengler, Joseph J. "Equity and Social Credit for the Retired." In *Employment, Income, and Retirement Problems of the Aged*, J. M. Kreps, ed. Duke University Press, Durham, N.C., 1963, pp. 198–229.

Palmer, E. *Normal Aging*. Duke University Press, Durham, N.C., in press.

Spengler, Joseph J. "The Aged and Public Policy." In Busse and Pfeiffer, op. cit., pp. 367–383.

Rosow, Irving. *Socialization to Old Age*. University of California Press, Berkeley, 1974.

Rosow, Irving. "Old Age: One Moral Dilemma of an Affluent Society." In *Gerontologist*, vol. 2, no. 4, December 1962, pp. 182–191.

St. Louis Post Dispatch, June 3, 1975. "U.S. Population Aging Rapidly."

St. Louis Post Dispatch, July 25, 1976. "Age Old Question: How to Survive Old Age."

U.S. Bureau of the Census, 1970. Characteristics of the Population. Part I, U.S. Summary Section.

11

Health Care and Institutionalization

As a person grows older, there is a gradually increasing risk of disease and impairment in functioning (Shanas and Maddox, 1976, p. 593). However, the illnesses of old age are different from those of youth. While younger people are more likely to suffer from acute illnesses that last a short time, the aged are more likely to suffer from chronic, often degenerative conditions. The most prevalent are heart disorders, arthritis, and rheumatism. Both the type and amount of illness affecting the aged have implications for the kind of health care they receive.

The Aged and the Medical Profession

Since older people do have higher rates of illness than younger people, they generate a high demand for health services. The problem is that the organization of health care services is not geared toward the care of chronic illness. Rather the medical profession as a whole is oriented toward the treatment of acute illnesses for which there are recognizable cures. This is partly a structural condition of the way in which health care services have developed in this country, since health care is concentrated in hospital settings rather than being oriented toward community-based preventive and re-habilitative care.

A more subtle issue concerns the attitudes of health care profession-als toward their work. There is a widespread feeling among the aged that most doctors are not interested in them, and this percep-tion may be accurate given the ways physicians are trained to define their work and their primary duties. One study of medical students found that a young physician's most important self-definition was as an active person who could respond quickly and that the greatest sense of satisfaction came from seeing a patient recover (Becker et al., 1961). Quick solutions cannot be posed for chronic diseases, and it is difficult or impossible to define a patient with a chronic illness as cured. In addition, doctors are trained to recognize the symptoms of poor health rather than the eroding consequences of normal aging. The article by Coe describes the attitudes of health care professionals toward the aged.

The recognition of these problems of the organization and attitudes of health care professionals has led some people to suggest that a specialty in geriatric medicine should be encouraged. This is a controversial issue, and there are pros and cons on both sides. The argument supporting specialization in geriatrics concerns the problem of wide variations in the diagnosis and treatment of the illnesses of the elderly. One aspect is that the occurrence of multiple chronic disorders can cause symptoms to be hidden from the untrained physician. As shown in Table 1, a relatively high percent of older people have more than one chronic disorder, and this tendency increases with advancing age. The greater the number of existing chronic diseases, the more complex the issue of diagnosis.

In addition to problems of misdiagnosis resulting from multiple chronic conditions, symptoms of many illnesses take a different form in the aged than they do in younger people. For instance:

> An older person with hyperthyroidism may appear apathetic, not hyperactive; tuberculosis may proceed in silence; appendicitis may occur without the characteristic abdominal tenderness . . . , without fever, and without an elevated white count; an older person may even have a heart attack without chest pain and may instead appear confused, disoriented, and seem like the victim of a stroke (Butler, 1976).

TABLE 1   Number of Chronic Disorders by Age

No. of specified* chronic diseases	% of persons 65–74 years	% of persons 75–79 years
0	29.7	22.4
1	29.9	25.9
2	27.3	32.9
3	11.7	17.0
4	1.2	1.8

*Included as chronic disorders are heart disease, hypertension, osteoarthritis, rheumatoid arthritis, stroke with paralytic residuals, and diabetes.

Source: E. L. White and T. Gordon, Related aspects of health and aging in the United States, in *Colloquium on health and aging of the population, Interdisciplinary topics in gerontology*, vol. 3 (Basel: S Karger AG, 1969).

In addition, cancer in the elderly causes only weight loss and anemia, not the usual vomiting, jaundice, and coughing.

A second problem is that two physiological factors require that the older person be administered drug treatment at lower dosage levels. First, the ratio of muscle tissue to fat decreases as a person ages. Second, the kidneys are less efficient in old age. Thus, if you administer a sedative to the average older person at ten or eleven o'clock at night, it could cause him or her to sleep or be confused for the entire next day (Johnson, 1970, p. 34).

The main argument against establishing a geriatric specialty is that medicine is already overspecialized. Opponents state that a preferable solution is to have more primary-care physicians who have known an individual over a long period of time and are aware of a person's lifetime health history. The medical profession is moving slowly in both directions. More emphasis has been placed on encouraging young physicians to choose family practice as an area of specialization, so an increasing number of primary-care physicians should be available in the future. Further, an increasing number of medical schools are including courses in geriatric medicine in their curriculum. In 1974 not one of 119 medical schools connected with the Association of American Medical Colleges had electives which focused on problems of the elderly. Two years later 45 schools reported they had added courses dealing with geriatrics. However, in the field of geriatric medicine there are still relatively few courses being offered, few knowledgeable professors, and little information in textbooks.

Institutionalization of the Aged

It is quite possible that improvements in medical care for the aged, specifically including increased emphasis on rehabilitative care in the community, could decrease the number of people who need to be institutionalized. However, the long-range trend over the past century, a trend which has accelerated in the past ten years, has been in the opposite direction: in a ten-year period the number of nursing homes doubled and the number of beds tripled. The reasons for this trend are twofold: an increasing demand for beds as the aging population increased, and guaranteed payments to nursing homes financed by Medicare and Medicaid (Butler and Lewis, 1977, p. 244). The fact that we, as a nation, are placing more older people in nursing homes means that we need to become vigilant about both the effects of institutionalization on the individual and the existing conditions in nursing homes.

The decision to institutionalize an older person should be made with great care, given the statistics on survival in a nursing home. Most older people dread entering a nursing home, viewing it as a prelude to death. Their concerns are justified, for one-third of all nursing-home patients die within their first year (Butler and Lewis, 1977, p. 245). The average length of stay in a nursing home is 1.1 years. Of course, most of the people who enter nursing homes are very ill to begin with. However, illnesses are often exacerbated by the treatment patients receive. The following excerpt illustrates how the emotional shock of institutionalization can increase the vulnerability of the patient to physical illness:

> One eighty-three-year-old depressed lady was placed in a nursing home due to increasing inability to care for herself in her little apartment. The home was described as a hotel and the stay as temporary. She became confused the first night when she was unable to find the bathroom, fell, and suffered contusions on her head and arms. She remained awake all night, which disturbed her roommate. In the morning she was seen by a physician, who prescribed Librium 10 mg.t.i.d. Her gait became unsteady and she became confused and mildly disoriented. She thought that she was home and that strangers had invaded the house and were stealing her possessions. In the afternoon she became agitated and began to abuse her roommate verbally at first and later physically. The physician was called, and over the telephone he prescribed Thorazine 25 mg. P.R.N. The patient's agitation finally subsided and gave way to psychomotor retardation, withdrawal from others, suspiciousness, sullenness, increased time in bed, and refusal to eat. Five days after admission she was unable to be moved out of bed. Her temperature was 103.8 F. The patient was noted to be semicomatose and dehydrated, and her skin was flushed. She was sent to a general hospital where she was found to have bronchopneumonia. She died within thirty-six hours after admission (Stotsky and Dominick, 1970, p. 38).

While some abuses in nursing homes are unintentional, there is evidence that a good deal of intentional abuse of patients also takes place. Even when a patient is not physically abused, life in a nursing home is often unpleasant, and many patients simply retreat into their own private worlds rather than continue to attempt to humanize a dehumanizing situation. The article by Fontana describes the setting, people, and daily interaction in what is probably a typical nursing home. In the final article, Stannard identifies the conditions which subtly encourage abuse in a nursing home.

The health care of the aged can be provided either in the individual's own community or within the confines of an institution. Regardless of where this care is provided, it will be increasingly necessary for the medical profession to take note of the special needs of the aged and reorganize the delivery of health care services. In addition, health care professionals need to be sensitized to a variety of physiological and emotional factors concerning the health care of the aged.

REFERENCES

Becker, Howard S., Blanche Geer, Everett Hughes, and Anselm Strauss. 1961. *Boys in white: Student culture in medical school*. Chicago: Univ. of Chicago Press.

Butler, Robert N. 1976. *Medicine and aging*. Testimony before the U.S. Senate Special Committee on Aging. Washington, D.C.: U.S. Government Printing Office.

Butler, Robert N., and Myrna I. Lewis. 1977. *Aging and mental health*. St. Louis: C.V. Mosby.

Johnson, Amos N. 1970. The physician's role in the care of the aging. *Gerontologist* 10 (Spring):33–37.

Shanas, Ethel, and George L. Maddox. 1976. Aging, health, and the organization of health resources. *Handbook of aging and the social sciences*. New York: Van Nostrand Reinhold.

Stotsky, Bernard A., and Joan Dominick. 1970. The physician's role in the nursing and retirement home. *Gerontologist* 10 (Spring):38–44.

Professional Perspectives on the Aged

RODNEY M. COE

This article examines the nature of the social encounter of health care practitioners and aged patients. In analyzing physicians' attitudes toward the aged, the author finds that they view aging as an inevitable deterioration of physical and mental processes. They also see older people as rigid and unable to adjust to change. In part these attitudes among physicians as well as other health care professionals are colored by the fact that they deal with the deteriorated aged rather than the aged who are well. The consequences of these attitudes are potentially harmful to the aged patient, since they lead to therapy which is largely custodial or palliative. Further, both professional health care workers and aged patients are likely to approach their encounters with each other negatively. The problem is further exacerbated by the lack of communication and coordination among the several specialists often involved in the treatment of the chronically ill person.

Health and medical services for the aged citizen in the United States are in the midst of a major social change. The recently passed amendments to the Social Security Act are broad in scope and introduce radically different philosophy and procedures. To be sure, no one is quite certain as to the consequences of the Medicare amendments—their effect on the level of health of persons over age sixty-five, on rates of the utilization of community health resources, or on the attitude of the public toward the change. These consequences, however, are easily documented and probably will be the focus of considerable research effort in the future. Nevertheless, concern for rates of utilization, provision of facilities and services, and costs of programs, however important they may be, tend to ignore a fundamental issue in the delivery and acceptance of medical care services—*the nature of the social encounter of the physician and his patient.*

There have, of course, been many surveys of the attitude of patients with respect to the medical profession in general, to physicians specifically, as well as studies of patient satisfaction or dissatisfaction with the care they have received. Most of these studies have concluded that the public tends to be critical of the medical profession in general, but people tend to accept uncritically their own physician as "being different"

SOURCE: Copyright 1967 by the Gerontological Society. Reprinted by permission from *Gerontologist*, Vol. 7, No. 2 (1967).

(Freidson, 1961). Then, too, individuals usually are fairly well satisfied with the care they receive from their personal physicians (Anderson and Sheatsley, 1959). On the other hand, there have been few studies which examine the attitude of physicians toward their patients. Since physicians and other health personnel such as dentists, nurses, and physical therapists can expect to encounter an increasing number of older people in their practices, it would seem important to study the kinds of attitudes health professionals hold toward the aged and aging patients.

The Nature of the Therapeutic Encounter

Before examining some results of this pilot investigation, it may be well to review some basic features of the therapeutic encounter.[1] Generally speaking, the encounter may be viewed as a system of complementary roles in which each person brings to the encounter a set of attitudes, beliefs, and expectations in regard to how he and the other person should behave (Parsons, 1951). For his part, the patient experiences certain symptoms by which he defines himself as sick. He recognizes that being sick is an unnatural and undesirable condition and seeks out competent professional help because he is technically unqualified to help himself. In placing himself in the care of the therapist, the patient expects that on the basis of expertise, the practitioner will employ some specific therapeutic intervention to eliminate the source of sickness and do so without harming or otherwise taking advantage of the patient. The therapist, on the other hand, also brings to the ecounter certain attitudes and beliefs derived from past associations and experiences. Essentially his expectations are that, since the patient has initiated the encounter, he must be aware of his state of ill health, and, therefore, should be willing to cooperate, i.e., follow orders, because he "wants to get well" and resume his normal roles. In addition, the therapist believes the patient must trust him in order that the appropriate therapeutic procedures may be willingly carried out.

But the therapeutic encounter often may be conducted in highly emotionally charged states, both for the patient and for the therapist. The patient may be fearful or anxious over the meaning of his present illness in terms of his chances for rapid recovery and its effects on his future. His focus of concern on himself as a person is expressed in a number of ways depending on a variety of socio-cultural and social-psychological factors. The therapist, on the other hand, despite his training to control expressions of emotion, also is subject to some anxiety derived from his assumption of responsibility for care of the patient and from uncertainty over his judgment in regard to accurate diagnosis and treatment. According to this model of therapist-patient interaction, the expectations of both the therapist and patient are met and their respective anxieties are quieted when, upon application of the appropriate therapy, the patient rapidly recovers and resumes his normal activities.

This classical model of the therapist-patient relationship is, of course, based on the characteristics of acute, infectious diseases over which the medical profession has largely gained control. However, in view of the dramatic shifts in morbidity and causes of mortality, this acute-care model is no longer always appropriate. One must also view the encounter in terms of the characteristics of chronic diseases. This type of medical problem presented to the practitioner is one about which he may have only incomplete knowledge of etiology and appropriate, effective treatment. Thus initially there may be a heightened uncertainty about the course of therapy to be taken and a resultant increased use of palliatives. Moreover, the disease is such that it usually cannot be overcome in one or two treatments, and it may require a long period of medical supervision. But the kind of supervision needed does not always require a physician, and certainly the procedures do not always require his attention. These can be delegated to others whose expertise is called for, such as physical therapists, nurses, and social workers; i.e., management of chronic diseases is a "team" function (Wessen, 1964). Thus the therapist does not and cannot meet the patient's expectations for rapid recovery. Furthermore, the therapist's uncertainty (or perhaps his disinterest in an unexciting case) is often communicated to the patient (Coe and Wessen, 1965).

The patient's perception of therapeutic inefficacy acts to reduce his faith in the therapist and increase his anxiety over the illness, the mounting costs of prolonged treatment, perhaps also over the spectre of permanent disability or even death. Thus he may not follow the therapist's instructions since they aren't effective anyway, or the patient may "shop around" for a better therapist. In either case, the patient does not meet the expectations of the therapist either. The result is a mutual dissatisfaction and, perhaps, an eventual breaking off of the encounter.

Professional Perspectives on Aging

The data for this pilot study are taken from transcripts of tape-recorded discussions held separately with a small group of physicians, dentists, physical therapists, nurses, and social workers. In these discussions a group leader (a staff member of the Gerontological Society) asked essentially the same questions of each group. The subsequent discussion by members of the group was recorded and transcribed. The statements made were then classified according to several categories including (1) perceived characteristics of aging as a process, (2) attitudes toward the aged, (3) opinions concerning the appropriate medical management of illness in the aged, (4) perceived gaps in the treatment of the ill and aged, and (5) opinions about what is needed in the future training of practitioners. The statements in these categories were then compared according to the profession of the respondent. For purposes of this report, the first three categories are the most important and are discussed below. The

health professions were arrayed according to their degree of "professionalization" (Hughes, 1965). In this case, the most professionalized group
were the physicians, followed by dentists, physical therapists, nurses, and
social workers.

One of the generalizations from the data of this pilot study which
stands out most clearly is that attitudes of health professionals toward
aging are closely bound to professional ideology. Physicians tended to
view older patients (and probably younger ones, too) in terms of the
disease process. This, of course, is the typical approach taken with respect
to the classical-care model. Also "functionally specific" in their viewpoint
were dentists. With physical therapists and nurses, particularly the latter,
one observes the introduction of social-psychological variables as important, whereas social workers tended to ignore physical disease characteristics and focused on socio-emotional and socio-cultural components of
aging.

Perspectives on the Aging Process

The most characteristic view taken by physicians was that aging is "an
inevitable deterioration of physical and mental processes . . . a terminal
process." Thus failing eyesight or hearing, incontinence, and lapses in
memory characterize aging. In speaking about lapses in memory, one
physician stated that they

> are a normal part of aging; this aging process is a terminal process. There is
> going to be downhill progression . . . families can just accept the inevitable.

There also was considerable agreement among physicians that although
aging is a process of deterioration, it is accelerated by changes in the
environment, particularly admission to the hospital or nursing home,
because older people are "rigid and inadaptable and find it difficult to
adjust to change." Dentists also equated aging with deterioration but
almost entirely in terms of loss of teeth. Thus the replacement of lost teeth
is "useless and a waste of money" since the patient won't adjust to new
dentures anyway.

To a certain extent, physical therapists also viewed aging this way as
this statement indicates:

> [Even the well aged] . . . while they are well today, we know that in a month or
> six months—at some time—they are not going to be well.

On the other hand, physical therapists and nurses, too, included consideration of "psychiatric overlay" as part of the health problem in aging. Thus
motivation becomes important in sustaining the desire of the aged patient
to "maintain a plateau of activity," especially since the increments of
recovery are so small. In addition, nurses were concerned with how
slowly the aged patient adjusted to institutional routine.

> The older person should not be expected to adjust to drastic changes in routine. With the older persons who come in and are going to be here for months and months and months, really what we try to do is to change their entire way of living . . . and that's wrong. . . . Hospital procedures should be explained to the patient. The older they are, the more carefully you have to explain them and the more time they need.

Social workers also implied that deterioration was an aspect of the aging process, but it was more a "social deterioration." For example, problems such as "increased dependency," progressive "loneliness," lack of attention, or of motivation were cited as characteristics of aging.

> It always seems they are old, they are sick, they are poor and they are alone and this is a tragic situation. . . . The problem is dependency, their total dependency, financial, social, emotional. . . . There is a greater problem in aging because of the advancing dependency.

These comments clearly point out the negative perspective on aging, an irreversible process of decline, yet the substance of the attitudes varied greatly. One might also point out that these statements, particularly the last one, should be evaluated in the context that these practitioners deal only with the sick deteriorating patients—since presumably the well aged do not require their services—thus this may have an important effect on their perspectives.

Perspectives on the Aged Patient

Except for the specific content of their expressions of attitudes toward the aged patient, all the respondents were agreed that the older person tended to be rigid in behavior and inadaptable to change, either in environment or in habits. Physicians and dentists usually expressed this attitude in reference to dealing with the patients' specific medical or dental problem. For example, a physician reported that in treating an elderly patient, "their appointments take about twice as long as the average patient. . . . One of their main problems is the impaired senses. They don't remember, they can't see, and they can't hear . . ." Dentists expressed essentially the same view:

> Most of your difficulties with older people are dentures. Older people are not able to tolerate new things like the younger people will. . . . A younger person, for example a twenty-year-old, can take a denture and go right out and wear it with very little trouble. Tolerance is real high. But an older person is not going to tolerate them like a twenty-year-old.

Moreover, both professions saw patients as basically wanting to talk and not particularly in need of health care services. For physicians the problem was *how* to treat a recalcitrant patient who was "essentially healthy." For dentists the question was *whether* to treat in view of the inadvisability of replacing teeth.

Two points related to their belief about aging as a progressive decline seem to be held by physical therapists. First, they tended to emphasize the relative slowness in recovery; and second, they emphasized the need to motivate the patient.

> The well aging are all sick. . . . The person is not as well as he was ten years ago so that relatively we all have a plateau of activity and we just drop off as the years go on. . . . [In treating a patient] . . . the most important thing is to establish a reasonable goal . . . to set minimum goals and keep going until the patient really reaches a plateau. This goal has to be set realistically with his physical limitations and with the social circumstances and also economic. In working with older people, you have to consider that they are set in their ways.

If one sets minimum goals, then, and progress toward these goals is only slowly made, there clearly is a need for motivating the patient to continue to progress, but also to keep up the therapist's interest in the case. On the one hand, many therapists see this as part of their therapy by never disclosing to the patient their disappointment, by exhibiting enthusiasm, but most of all by being patient in the therapeutic process. Other therapists see their jobs strictly as a manipulation of bones and muscles. One therapist reported that

> In the case of the patient who won't stand, won't talk, won't write, I take him to the psychiatrist and let him get the patient to the point where he will stand, he will talk, and he will write. I don't think it is worth my time because you have to have the patient's cooperation.

In several respects, nurses expressed views similar to the physical therapists. Nurses indicated a belief that aged patients were slow, and that it was sometimes hard to deal and to communicate with them. They also indicated that there were annoyances associated with treating the aged because of their complaining, demanding, incontinence, inability to feed themselves, etc. The interesting difference between the nurses and physical therapists was that in the case of the nurses, these attitudes are transferred to others, especially students.

> Student nurses do not like the factor of not seeing rapid improvement in chronic patients. They prefer acute patients who recover more rapidly. . . . You always hear bad things [about chronically ill patients] but you never hear the good things, and most students believe before they even get there that they won't enjoy working on the chronic disease unit.

Thus for nurses there was apparently a generally negative attitude toward providing care for the aged patient as well as a perception of small reward. This view apparently is also transmitted to other students both by fellow students and by instructors.

In the view of social workers, there appeared to be two types of attitudes. One is that the aged person is not different from any other patient in any other age group. It was a matter of looking into presented problems in the context of the characteristics, i.e., personality, of the patient. The other view sets the aged off from others by virtue of the uniqueness of the problems presented, especially as related to dependency.

> The problem arises when the aged person living alone starts getting senile and cannot take care of his housekeeping chores or has delusions or gets lost. . . . It is questionable whether we can consider them self-sufficient and capable of living alone. . . . Yet public institutions say they belong in mental institutions and mental institutions say they belong in public institutions and we are sort of left in the middle holding the bag. . . . With this kind of person who is not able to swing it in independent housing, there is no place for them to go.

The consequences of this perspective leave the social worker "overwhelmed" with the problem which is "pretty discouraging and depressing to the worker." The inability to marshal sufficient resources to aid the aged patient in independent living—a major social-work goal— apparently leaves the impression of futility so that "many look on working with the aged as something that is almost useless and a waste of energy."

Perspectives on Therapy

In view of the general tendency for the health professions to consider aging as an irreversible decline and the aged patient as difficult and/or depressing, one might expect also that palliative measures or custodial treatment would be considered the most appropriate form of treatment. In a sense, this is the case; yet remnants of the ideology of specific disease-oriented therapy and subsequent rapid recovery are still present, most strongly for physicians and least for social workers. Physicians, for example, felt that repair of physical defects would eliminate all problems.

> One thing that seems terribly important is to try to maintain these people. So many varicose veins, hemorrhoids, prostate trouble, cystociles or rectociles. I think these people become discouraged . . . and that contributes quite a lot to aging. If you repair these things, take care of hemorrhoids, repair the cystociles, a lot of people go right along because everything is all right.

On the other hand, physicians were reluctant to prescribe new glasses for "eyes that wouldn't see," or hearing aids for "ears that wouldn't hear." Rather, the approach seemed to be "just treat them with the needle twice a day—the placebo effect." Dentists took a similar stance in regard to the use of palliative measures. One stated he thought it was "a big mistake to try and do anything for these people other than alleviate the immediate problem."

Physical therapists again returned to the theme of establishing modest plateaus of functioning. There was agreement that being able to walk, independently or with assistance, was of major importance. In part, this was for functional reasons, i.e., it leads to a condition of self-care, but it also had a psychological function. One therapist indicated that "walking is the supreme goal in all geriatric patients, no matter what's wrong with them. If I can walk, I am not dead." In treatment procedures, physical therapists for the first time showed a sensitivity to the necessity for establishing rapport with the patient. A key to motivating the patient to succeed was "to get the patient to like you so they will do things for you."

> The big thing in geriatric care is the "hands on" technique, to touch them, to see about range of motion, get them up, assist them, not by putting on the lamps and running them for twenty minutes and then going on to the next one.

In the responses of nurses, there is a curious ambivalence in regard to treatment of the aged. On the one hand, there is an explicit recognition of the social and psychological factors of aging as indicated in the previous quotations. Yet treatment is viewed in terms of physical care. Thus nurses stressed viewing patients by type of disease, i.e., you don't "handle" a heart patient the same as a stroke patient. They also tend to emphasize making the patient comfortable and employing good bedside care techniques. Moreover, a key to successful therapy is appropriate nutrition.

> There is much that can be done to insure better nutrition for older people and this is an area that really needs a lot of work because it's basic to everything that they are going to have done for them. Nutrition is not only important for maintaining health, but they are going to feel better and respond better to whatever treatment is being tried on them.

Thus the nurses' views are in conflict, some stressing the "custodial approach," others focusing on rebuilding health through proper nutrition.

Finally, for social workers the solutions to the problems of the aged person apparently depended upon implementing coordinated services for the aged. These services, not unexpectedly, revolve around keeping the patient out of the institution. For example, homemaker services, home care, house cleaning, shopper services, transportation, social and recreational needs were seen as items of great importance. This may be analogous to the therapeutic intervention in the classical medical model. That is, if these services could be made available, institutionalization could be averted and other problems of aging would disappear.

Conclusion and Implications

From the data analyzed in this pilot study, of which only a few examples were presented here, some tentative conclusions may be drawn.

1. Perception of the aged patient by the professional tends to be circumscribed by particular interests and competencies of the professional, but it varies among them in content—from emphasis on physical problems to emphasis on disturbed social relationships.

2. Aging as a process is viewed by all professional groups as a deteriorative change, but again with varying substantive emphasis from physical and mental deterioration to social isolation and dependency.
3. Professionals tend to view the aged as rigid, inadaptable, and slow to respond to treatment.
4. Therefore, therapy is largely custodially oriented or, at best, palliative in nature, especially when therapeutic intervention does not produce rapid results.

There are perhaps two major implications of these generalizations. The first concerns the nature of the therapist-patient relationship. It does not appear that a therapist could meet any expectations of the aged patient if the above-described stereotypes were very strongly held. The practitioner would, so to speak, have developed a negative "set" about older patients even before actually seeing a particular aged patient. If the therapist believes that his ministrations are likely to fail (in the classical sense of promoting rapid recovery) because older patients "have only one way to go," and if the therapist does not believe the patient will follow instructions because he is so intractable, it is unlikely that the therapist could approach the encounter with any appreciable enthusiasm. Moreover, the therapist is often beset by doubts of his ability to deal with chronic diseases, which further reduce his willingness to accept the case. Consequently, either half of the dyadic relationship may tend to approach the encounter negatively with few realistic expectations about the prognosis of therapy for the disease.

The second implication concerns the effects of the stereotypes on the professionals themselves. It was noted above that the management of chronic diseases requires coordination of effort on the part of several therapeutic specialists. It is difficult to see how this coordination can occur, however, when it is hampered by isolated approaches to the problems of aged patients and by lack of communication among the professionals. Some of the data presented earlier suggested that each profession defined the substantive problems of aging in a somewhat different fashion and consequently placed a different emphasis on the presumptions about effective treatment programs. These differential perspectives contribute to problems of communication. In addition to the relative differences in status among the professions which tend to channelize communications along disciplinary lines, the narrow perspective on the problems of the treatment of the aged patients tends to discourage any but formal communication among the therapists (Wessen, 1958). As a result, the particular professional stereotypes are seldom brought under close scrutiny by other participating professionals, but rather tend to be reinforced by communicating only with one's colleagues. Thus stereotypes continue to influence professionals' perspectives on the problems of aging and of treating the aged patient and also hamper effective coordination of the variegated services required by the aged patient.

What is clearly called for by this oversimplified description of the therapist-patient encounter is better understanding not only of chronic disease *per se* but also of its impact on the social relationship between the therapist and the patient. To this end, this study has examined some attitudes by members of several health professions toward aging as a process, the aged as patients, and perceptions of appropriate therapy. The conclusion would be that stereotypes of these phenomena must be modified before therapists will be able to deal effectively with the health problems of the aged and before aged patients will be able to regain their confidence in medical treatment.

NOTES

This article is a revised and expanded version of a paper read at the meetings of the 7th International Congress of Gerontology, Vienna, Austria, June 1966. This pilot study has been sponsored by the Gerontological Society under funds granted by the U.S. Public Health Service, Contract Number 86–63–184; the Medical Care Research Center, a joint agency of the Social Science Institute of Washington University, The Jewish Hospital of Saint Louis, The Saint Louis University School of Medicine, and the Saint Louis County Health Department, under funds granted by the U.S. Public Health Service, CH 00024; and by the Midwest Council for Social Research in Aging.

1. What is called here the "therapeutic encounter" is mostly a reflection of the characteristics of the doctor-patient relationship. The more general label of the therapeutic encounter has been adopted for two reasons; first, on pragmatic grounds because this report concerns the attitudes of other health professions as well as physicians, some of which exhibit slight variations on the doctor-patient theme; second, and more importantly, the nature of the medical management of chronic diseases requires the use of several kinds of practitioners, especially those discussed in this report.

REFERENCES

Anderson, O. W., and P. B. Sheatsley: *Comprehensive medical insurance—a study of costs, use, and attitudes under two plans.* Health Information Foundation, New York, 1959.

Coe, R. M., and A. F. Wessen: Some social-psychological factors influencing the use of community health resources. *Amer. J. Pub. Hlth.*, *55*: 1024–1036, 1965.

Freidson, E.: *Patients' views of medical practice.* Russell Sage, New York, 1961.

Hughes, E. C.: Professions. In K. S. Lynn (editor), *Professions in America.* Houghton Mifflin, Boston, 1965.

Parsons, T.: *Social system.* Free Press, Glencoe, 1951.

Wessen, A. F.: Hospital ideology and communication among ward personnel. In E. G. Jaco (editor), *Patients, physicians, and illness.* Free Press, Glencoe, 1958.

Wessen, A. F.: Some sociological characteristics of long-term care. *Gerontologist, Part II 4:* 7–14, 1964.

Growing Old Between Walls

ANDREA FONTANA

The author of this article worked as a janitor in a nursing home to understand life within an institution from the perspective of those confined and those in charge. As a staff member, he took part in employee gripe sessions and learned how patients became defined as "work objects." Through his work in the wards he came to know and gain insights into the patients. This article describes the routinely insensitive treatment of the institutionalized aged and how they react to it. Few patients manage to survive the heavy odds against them and keep a lucid mind.

The patients lined up to get some cake and the band played "Happy Birthday to You" to no one in particular.

—field notes

I had a dream the other day. I dreamed that I was an old man lying on my bed by the window overlooking the front lawn of the building I was in, the Sunny Hill Convalescent Center. Beyond the blue window I could see people in the distance; I could see children running; I could imagine the sound of laughter. I lay there semiawake, listening. I could not quite understand what was going on because, you see, like all convalescent-center patients, I was confused. Besides, my roommate was stretched out on his bed hollering with a voice one would never guess could come out of such a thin, emaciated, wrinkled man. He had urinated all over himself again and in the heat of the summer day it was grossly uncomfortable, since any initial cooling sensation which he might have derived from such an action had quickly given way to an intolerable acid stench. He was yelling like a man alone in the middle of an ocean, about to drown, and he well might have as there was no sign of land anywhere to be seen, or in this case, there were no nurses within the horizon.

When I suddenly woke up, I really was at the Sunny Hill Convalescent Center, but fortunately not as a patient. I had taken a summer job at the convalescent center as a janitor (actually, housekeeper was the definition given to my job) with the intention of studying the setting, and coming back later as a researcher, which I did the following summer. This chapter is based on the data gathered in these periods.

SOURCE: These excerpts are reprinted from *The Last Frontier* by Andrea Fontana, Sage Library of Social Research, Volume 4, © 1977, pp. 143-145, and pp. 147-167, by permission of the Publisher, Sage Publications, Inc. (Beverly Hills/London).

Having worked at the center proved very helpful to my research in three ways. First, I was part of the staff, thus being able to partake in "backstage" interaction.[1] By this I mean that I took part in "gripe sessions"; I listened to the aides' accounts, not in an official form or through formal work relations, but relaxedly over a cup of coffee, from one "low-rank" employee to another. In this fashion I learned how Joe did not have a bowel movement in two days, why Bill was so confused after the new medication, or why that "old bitch" down the hall wouldn't eat unless you pinched her nose closed; things one would not find in records or would not be told to an "outsider." This gave me an understanding of how the aides felt and allowed me to sit right in with them during breaks or to walk around with them while they worked in the center.

Second, I was able to spend time with the patients while cleaning their rooms, and I came to know some of them well. While this does not matter with some patients, who would talk to anybody willing to listen, it is important with others, who become suspicious and taciturn.

Third, I viewed the patients as a staff member, thus coming to see the patients in terms of my job. That summer I had a lot of patients classified:

> This one spits on the floor all the time; I'll have to give him a butt can. That one throws his food all over the floor; it'll be hard to mop. Old Anne always had a puddle of urine under her wheelchair. Sarah will walk away with the mop and the bucket if I don't watch her; Dan will talk my leg off so I'll skip his room today.[2]

I came to see the patients as "work objects" rather than as human beings. But I also slowly became aware of other important concerns which made me realize the meaning of growing old between the walls of the convalescent center for the patients. This chapter is not an ethnography of the operations of a convalescent center;[3] it is not a collection of survey data on convalescent centers;[4] it is not a critical indictment of convalescent centers;[5] this chapter intends to explore what happens to the meaning of the "golden years," to the "consummatory period of life" for that handful of elderly[6] who come to "convalesce" in the waning years of their lives.

. . . .

The Stage

The proscenium upon which this drama of life is played serves an important function as the setting for the interaction between the staff and the patients. Thus, before being introduced to the actors, as the curtain pulls back, the reader will be presented with a vision of the center itself. The brochure advertising the center reads:

> At the Sunny Hill Convalescent Center the guest wants for nothing . . . screened sunbathing and patio areas, television, telephone facilities,

planned recreational activities and beautiful six-acre site are at the disposal of the guests . . . especially noted for the delicious food prepared in the spotless, modern kitchen.

However, as one looks closely around the center, the picture which emerges is quite different. The convalescent center is located in the middle of the small town of Verde, which is about twenty miles away from the nearest city. Although centrally located, the center is isolated from the town because it is situated atop a steep hill, which is accessible only by a road leading to the center; no other building is located on the hill.

The center comprises two wards, situated one below the other on the slope of the hill. The lower ward is a long one-story construction, while the upper one is a two-story building; both appear fairly new from the outside. The "six-acre" site is indeed there, but the "sunbathing and patio areas" are small and enclosed by a high chain-linked fence.

The inside is almost identical in both wards. It consists of a long corridor running the length of the slightly V-shaped buildings. Rooms with two beds in each are located at both sides of the corridor, with adjoining toilets between two rooms; the same toilet is at times shared by two men in one room and by two women in the next. Both wards have a large recreational lounge, with a view overlooking the town through a large, dark blue-tinted picture window. The recreation lounge is furnished with sofas, armchairs, chairs, and a television set.

Both wards have a kitchen right across from the recreation room. The upstairs kitchen is used only for warming up food, since all the cooking is done in the downstairs kitchen. Small dining rooms are adjacent to the kitchens. The kitchens contain some old, greasy-looking gas stoves, a large sink, a hot-water sterilizing unit (for dishes), refrigerators, and other assorted equipment. Both wards have a nursing station, which is a smallish place located behind a long counter. At the end of each corridor is a large bathroom containing a tub and a shower in which the aides wash the patients (four bathrooms in all). The lower ward has a small waiting hall for incoming visitors. This room can be separated from the rest of the ward by a heavily blue-tinted glass sliding door.

The only telephones available are in the offices and nursing station and are to be used only by the staff on official business. I only witnessed a couple of "emergency" personal calls by employees and none whatsoever by patients. All doors are locked at all times, and the staff are forever unlocking and locking doors and closets in their daily rounds. A couple of times the outside door was accidentally left unlocked, and a patient managed to "escape" but was soon found wandering in downtown Verde. One time I saw Wilma, a sixty-year-old ex-ballerina (she had a tracheotomy operation so she cannot speak and has a small hole at the base of her neck), gingerly vault over the high chain fence, and I had to unlock the gate and guide her back inside. One final point: One of my duties was to wash breakfast dishes in the "spotless kitchen," and the only spotless thing about the kitchen were my hands after I had summarily rinsed off a pile of muck-covered plates.

The Actors

Having described the setting, it is time to introduce the cast. The staff consists of an administrator, who manages the facility, a bookkeeper, two janitors, a laundry person, the kitchen staff (a cook, two second-cooks, and part-time helpers), and the nursing staff.

The director of nurses is a registered nurse who is in charge of another nurse and the aides. The other nurse is a licensed vocational nurse managing the lower ward when the registered nurse is in the upper one, which is most of the time. The remainder of the staff is composed of nurse's aides.

The aides are either white women from nearby towns or Indian women from the reservation three miles away. The turnover is great due to the harshness of the job, the extremely low pay, and the nature of the place. I witnessed quite a few cases of aides who left aghast after their first day and never came back. Actually, that almost happened to me, as I was not yet trained in the arts of doing field research while cleaning toilets. There are two kinds of aides: the old "battle axes" who have seen it all, have been there forever, and are not shaken by anything that happens; the others are much younger women, usually fresh out of high school, often on their first job, who live in the town of Verde, where no other jobs are available, or are just filling a gap while waiting for a better job to materialize.

The other people on the payroll as staff members do not work in the center but make periodic visits. There are three doctors, each caring for a certain number of patients, who come by to visit the patients every other week (at the time of the research, the doctors were allowed to bill MediCal twice a month per patient). There are others: a hairdresser, who comes over from the reservation once a week; a social worker, who comes every other week; a handyman, who is on call; and a dietician, who is consulted by telephone.

The rest of the cast is made up of the patients. The patients are not identified in any visible way and are not divided in the wards in any fashion. The only rule is to have two individuals of the same sex in a room, but if one is senile and incontinent and the other is not, it is of no concern to the staff; contingencies such as availability of rooms are much more pressing. Usually the center is filled to capacity; even the room supposed to be used as an emergency room has a patient in it, an old blind wrestler, who must at one time have been a giant, but now has stumps where legs used to be and has lost most of his cognitive ability on various rings across the country years ago.

Not being able to identify the patients at sight[7] was a problem for me, but it was not a problem for the staff, who classified the patients in terms of physical attributes related to their daily work routine. There are the "up and about," those patients who can walk and get in and out of bed by themselves, walk to the dining room for meals, go to the toilet, etc. The others are called "in chair," meaning that they are confined to a wheel-chair and that they must be helped in and out of bed; they need containers to urinate in while sitting in their chair, etc. Another classification is that of "feeders" and "nonfeeders." "Nonfeeders" are those patients (whether "in chair" or "up and about") who are capable of eating in the dining room by themselves, whereas "feeders" need to be hand-fed by an aide. With this system of classification, the nurses and aides can categorize patients in terms of "work time." An "up-and-about nonfeeder" will require little of their time, while an "in-chair feeder" will take a lot more time: he will have to be fed, have his diapers changed, and his bed sores medicated. Most "in-chair" patients spend a lot of time in bed, hence developing bed sores. At one time I wondered out loud why they bothered getting them out of bed at all, and the licensed vocational nurse said that it was required by MediCal that all patients be up and out of bed for at least two hours daily. The classification system is an effective tool in planning one's daily work schedule. This is no different from my classification of patients while I was a janitor (spitter, wet-the-floor type, mess-up-the-toilet type, and so on).

As a researcher, such classification would have proved of little value, since even among "feeders" the difference in people and their behavior was remarkable. It varied from the old woman who was in an advanced state of senility, passively allowed the aide to feed her, and sat staring at some spot in front of her all day long, to the rebellious old woman who would "make faces," close her mouth, throw food on the floor, and curse the aide.

The behavior of the patients was markedly different outside of the categories of "work time" invoked by the staff. By this it is meant that categorizing patients in classes based upon the care they require does not account for those periods which place no (or minimal) demands upon the staff. These periods comprise a large part of the day of the patients, and are spent in different ways by them.

Many elderly patients no longer have to worry about the problem of how to occupy their time in meaningful ways because their selves have escaped long ago, leaving behind babbling biological husks which are carted about by unkind hands and spend their time strapped to beds or wheelchairs. But there are others. And it is to these and to their attempts to keep their selves from escaping their weakened frames that attention shall now be paid.

The Interaction

"But I don't want to go among mad people." Alice remarked. "Oh, you can't help that," said the Cat: "We're all mad here. I'm mad, you're mad." "How do you know I'm mad?" said Alice. "You must be," said the Cat, "or you wouldn't have come here."[8]

The Cheshire Cat must have been a convalescent patient at some time or another since its statement to Alice captures the approach to the patients at Sunny Hill. It must be mentioned that Sunny Hill has a mental health license, hence mental patients can be found mixing freely with those whose only fault is to be old.[9] There are three kinds of interaction which are relevant to the understanding that shapes the everyday lives of the patients: staff-to-patient interaction, patient-to-staff interaction, and patient-to-patient interaction.

Staff to Patient

Staff-to-patient interaction is characterized by what Strauss and Glaser call "work-time."[10] The same problem noticed by the two sociologists in their study of a hospital ward is found at the Sunny Hill center: The patients and the staff's conceptions of time are very often at variance. There are not enough nurse's aides, and they consequently have a very busy work schedule and minimal time to give the patients any attention as human beings; the patients are work objects, as is exemplified by their categorization in terms of work (feeders, etc.).

Given that the staff-to-patient interaction takes place in terms of work, a typical daily work routine will be described. The aides begin getting the patients out of bed and into their wheelchairs at about 6:30 a.m. At 7:00 the day-shift aides come in and finish preparing the patients for breakfast. The aides distribute trays to the patients who sit in their rooms in their wheelchairs, while the ambulatory cases walk to the dining room. Next, the aides feed the "feeders":

> I was going around with Mary and Glenda feeding the patients. Mary was literally stuffing food in a woman's mouth, and the semi-liquid yellowish substance was dribbling down the woman's chin onto her nightgown, which had been washed so many times that it was now an amorphous gray sack.
>
> Louise was feeding lunch to an old patient, and she explained to me that he always refused his water and that was bad for his kidneys. After having finished feeding him, she held a glass of water to his mouth, which he shut tightly. So Louise turned to me and said, "See, I told you so" and left, making no further effort to give the man a drink.[11]

During breakfast the licensed vocational nurse goes around with a medicine cart slipping pills in bowls of cornflakes or oatmeal, while the janitor mops up the floor between the chairs, cleaning spilled oatmeal, wheelchair scuffs, and small puddles of urine underneath some of the chairs because the patients' requests to go to the toilet are being ignored by the aides. The aides are still feeding "feeders" down the wing somewhere (some patients do not ask for help to go to the toilet anymore, they just urinate in their wheelchairs).

After the chaos of breakfast, with things and people running around, everything calms down. The patients are dressed (or they dress themselves, or are put back in bed) and either sit in their rooms or are wheeled into the lounge room where the television is broadcasting its usual variety of morning quiz shows. The patients look at the television, but most of them are just staring at a box with light and colors:

> I often asked some of the wheelchair patients (the "better" patients do not come and watch TV) if they liked the program or what program they were watching and either received no reply or something like this—"Bob, is this a good show?" "...g...o...od," "What show is this, Bob?" "...go...o...od...sh...sh...ow."

The 9:00 aide is here now[12] and she begins to make beds on her assigned wing. Some days I go around with her:

> Today the 9:00 aide is Louise and I join her. She is making beds in and around patients. As I talk to her, she is going right on making beds and talking to me. Some of the patients are up and in the wheelchairs, but others are in bed. Louise picks them up and sits them in a chair, then proceeds to make the beds. After having changed the linen and the plastic sheet, Louise puts the patients back to bed, either saying nothing to them or things like—here you go—that's good—, while carrying on a conversation with me or with another aide if there is one nearby.

After the morning activities, the mealtime bedlam of rushing food trays, cleaning up floors, and pushing around patients begins all over. After lunch it is quiet again as some patients are wheeled into the lounge room to watch some soap operas while others are put to bed to take a nap.

At 3:00 p.m. the evening shift comes in while the day shift retires to the dining room to fill in their daily reports on the patients. These reports summarize the activities of the patients in terms of physical and mental functions. Emphasis is given by the aides to things such as b.m.'s (bowel movements) and unusual behavior; since each aide fills only some charts, there is a continuous negotiation on whether Billy had a bowel movement today or whether Elma had a quiet day or was restless. The reports are jotted down in about twenty minutes and the charts returned to the nursing station.

These reports are very important for the patients since the nurse in charge compiles her monthly reports by summarizing the aides' reports. The social worker also uses the aides' reports to give her account of the patients, and the various reports are used by the doctors to determine the status of the patients. A doctor comes in, sits behind the nurses' station, and inquires about his breakfast, which is promptly served. Having thumbed through the charts for a while, he walks quickly up and down the corridors, asking from time to time, "How are you today, Mr. Smith, and you, Mrs. Jones?" Without waiting for an answer, he keeps on walking. At times he visits one or two patients who may be experiencing serious problems, and then he is gone, not to be seen for another two weeks.

The following is an example of how the information in the reports is acquired in many cases. Mr. Anderson's medical records stated that he had been committed to the convalescent center as a manic-depressive case. The records made mention of the fact that he had been a former patient and had left to go to a boarding house. However, Dr. Bell (his doctor throughout this whole period) brought him back to the center, since Mr. Anderson was in a severe state of depression (listed as spitting and cursing at doctors and nurses).

I thumbed through the reports of the aides and found that Mr. Anderson was often reported as "depressed" (aides have five choices in their chart: satisfactory, confused, depressed, irritable, noisy). On the back of the report, under "nurses' progress notes," it was often generally stated that Mr. Anderson had shown signs of depression, and occasionally he was reported as having said things such as, "If I had a gun I would shoot myself."

I happened to be present during one of Mr. Anderson's "depressive" conditions.

> Mr. Anderson said that he could not understand why they locked the windows, that all it would take to get out would be a kitchen knife used as a screwdriver. The aide wrote down in her report that he was very agitated and talked about escaping from the center.

My impression of the "incident" was entirely different. I had heard Mr. Anderson make the comment about the windows to an aide.[13] The incident assumed new meaning in the aide's account of it. Dramatic overtones kept piling on until what had seemed to me a frustrated remark about the futility of certain security measures became a dramatic plan to escape from the center. The incident shows that the interpretation of Mr. Anderson's behavior as deviant was taken by an aide who had a preconceived notion of his depression and was in a hurry to finish her report. Her account became of extreme importance since the other members of the staff rely solely upon such reports to pass judgment on the patients.

After this example of "form filling," it is time to return to the daily scheduled events. The daily work routine is now in the hands of the evening shift. The circle starts all over again—getting patients up from their naps, making beds, getting patients ready for dinner. It is 5:00 p.m., the last meal of the day, the last moment of a kaleidoscope of colors, odors, noises. Food is served, forced into mouths, spat out, cleaned up, dropped on the floor, aides yell at patients, and patients scream in the hall, in their rooms, in their chairs, and then, silence again. Some patients, a few, walk back to the lounge room, the others are put to bed, the day at the center is over.

The rush imposed by a heavy work load leads the aides to treat the patients in the same fashion. It becomes legitimate to stuff food down their throats because the goal has become serving the meal, not nourishing the patient; or to lift them in and out of bed as if they were inanimate dummies because the goal is bed making not making the patient comfortable. The patients thus end up suffering from "organization contingencies" similar to those found by many sociologists in other settings.[14] But what is suffering here from problems stemming from work-flow contingencies is not a car malfunctioning from shoddy workmanship, but human beings who by being treated as inanimate objects end up becoming inanimate objects.

Patient to Staff

Patients find themselves competing for the staff's attention. The patients are not rushed by a busy work schedule, on the contrary they have nothing but time on their hands. Apart from the scheduled rounds of activities such as meals, baths, haircuts, etc. there are scarcely any other goings-on available to the patients. The patients who still have the physical and mental capabilities to do so return to their rooms after the scheduled activities are over; others never leave their room; the rest, who fall somewhere in between, are carted to the recreation room to watch television.

Confined to a restricted setting beyond their control, the patients attempt to break the monotony of the empty periods of waiting for the next scheduled activity. The patients employ various strategies to attract the attention of the aides. They wave their hands or call the aides by their first names; one of the patients kept calling to me "Curly," but after a while I realized he was saying "Girly" since he was almost blind and assumed that the person walking by was an aide. "Bob waves his hand at the aide who is passing by and mumbles—toilet—she looks at him and says—oh you don't have to go—and goes on." When they attract someone's attention, usually a new aide or me, they smile and ask for a glass of water (or milk) or for a dime to buy a Coke. Five minutes later, up goes the same hand, and the same person asks for another glass of water. Doing beds or cleaning rooms is also a good time to attempt to engage the aide in conversation because she cannot just turn around and leave. These attempts to create diversions in the period between meals, or between a meal and a bath, are treated by the staff unanimously in the same fashion—they are ignored unless they become a problem which will disrupt the daily schedule: things such as a patient defecating in the hallway or pulling another patient's hair can no longer be ignored as they would soon attract the attention of the licensed vocational nurse or the administrator.

Patient to Patient

In examining the two previous kinds of interaction it was found that interaction between staff and patients was characterized by a work schedule and that between patients and staff by attention on one side and disinterest on the other side. The interaction among patients is mainly characterized by its absence. Patients do not have anything to do with each other. To fraternize with other patients would mean to place oneself at their level, to admit that one indeed belongs here.

Thus the others are ignored. Once I asked Al, who was a great sports fan, why he did not watch the ball games on television. He replied that he would not go into the recreation room during the day because he did not like to see and smell the result of other incontinent patients, and the aides would not let him watch the night games.

I was talking to Mr. Anderson, who was so talkative that I wondered why he did not speak to his fellow patients. He said that there was nobody to talk to because they were all senile or crazy. This was said right in front of Mr. Stern, his roommate, who had turned his wheelchair away from us and seemed very absorbed in a magazine, but who was really listening to our conversation since he was not turning the pages of his magazine.

At Christmas I had sent Mr. Adams a set of checkers, and when I returned to the center the next summer, he invited me to play with him. The checker set had not been opened yet, and Mr. Adams said that there was nobody to play with at the center. Later I discovered that this was not true since I played with other patients. When I mentioned this to Mr. Adams, he claimed that they were not good enough players to play with him. But neither was I, because after an initial doubt as to whether I should let "poor old Mr. Adams" beat me at checkers, I realized that I had as much of a chance of beating him at checkers as I would have had of spotting Bobby Fischer a rook and then beating him at chess.

When interaction between patients does take place, it is not of a desirable kind. The following examples illustrate this point. The administrator decided to put Mr. Adams and Mr. Ritter, two of the "better" patients, in the same room. This arrangement did not last long. Both fellows liked their privacy and the freedom of doing what they liked in their rooms. They were known to become easily irritated by other patients and to keep to themselves most of the time. They tolerated each other for a while but began complaining about each other's quirks privately (often to me). The complaints were mostly about things such as, "It's hard to understand him, he stutters," or "He's always listening to that damn radio and it bothers me." This eventually led to open confrontation, which occurred when they were both listening to their favorite program on their transistor radios and tried to outdo each other by a battle of volumes. The nurse rushed in to see what was going on, and as a result Mr. Adams went back upstairs to a new room.

This was where I left him. He was rooming with a wheelchair/incontinent patient (almost paralyzed by a stroke and unable to speak). Mr. Adams preferred it that way since he was practically by himself in the room. He had more personal possessions than most patients; he had a radio, an alarm clock/barometer, which he had put together himself (as he often told me), and the most prized of all—an armchair which reclined in three positions.

At times, the interaction between patients became violent as when somebody grabbed hold of a hank of hair and pulled as hard as he or she could. A couple of times punches were thrown by some patients, but these flare-ups were rare. What caused most of the problems was the mixing of mental cases with normal patients as shown by the following example.

Mr. Reid, an obtrusive, large fellow in his late fifties, had been declared insane by the courts following a bout with the law over a charge of attempted rape. He had been on his best behavior, and his improvement had gained him a transfer from the county mental institution to the Sunny Hill Convalescent Center.

Mr. Reid did not show signs of improving when he reached the center; on the contrary, he managed to alienate the young aides by continually exposing his genitalia and propositioning them. The old "battle axes" just laughed at his antics, and they laughed even harder when we found him in a bathroom while Wilma, the ex-ballerina patient, was performing fellatio on him. It was assumed that she had been a willing partner, and jokes about it stirred laughter and crassness.

Two months later, the laughter turned hollow with tragedy when the night aide discovered Mr. Rooney, the quiet, thin elder who roomed with Mr. Reid, dying in agony while "every orifice in his body was bleeding," as the nurse puts it. Then and only then, was Mr. Reid sent back to the county medical institution.

The Prisoners

"There is a good deal to be said for internment. It keeps you out of the saloon and helps you to keep up with your reading."[15] P. G. Wodehouse took his confinement to a lunatic asylum by the Nazis with a humor worthy of his novels. Some of the patients at the center would certainly agree that internment keeps you out of the saloons; as a matter of fact, that was exactly why some of them were there. They would also agree that there is plenty of time to keep up with one's reading, but they would not sound as pleased about it as Wodehouse did.

The patients respond in different ways to their confinement in the center. Those who manage to survive the heavy odds against them and retain a lucid mind are few indeed. They may or may not have reconciled themselves with spending the remainder of their days at the center, but they all agree that their stay is against their will, that they are for all practical purposes being kept prisoners in the center.

Mr. Anderson is a tall, thin man in his early eighties; his vivid, alert eyes peer at you from his hollow cheeks, and his long, bony hands are tightly held in his lap. He walks slowly, slightly hunched, but he walks.

Mr. Anderson used to live in a boarding house. One day the people who managed the house told him that he had to go to the doctor for a check-up. He was taken to the center and has been there ever since. He feels that this is illegal, and that the doctor signed his release to the center because he is a good patient, ambulatory and quiet, and they wanted his money. He has written to his daughter about it but has received no reply.

Mr. Anderson told me his story in a calm, resigned manner. He feels as if he were in a prison. He spends his days voraciously reading old novels and magazines. Mr. Anderson said that when he reads he loses track of time, and before he knows it, it is time for lunch or dinner. At times, however, he feels very depressed about being in the convalescent center; then he closes the door and stares out of the window since he doesn't feel like reading.

Mr. Ritter, a tall, heavy-set fellow in his late fifties, is another case. He used to be a minor-league pitcher, and he went on to become a professional heavy-weight fighter. He has pictures of himself and his brother (a fighter also) in their boxing attire. Mr. Ritter told me about his fights, the most famous one being against Jim Braddock. His left ear, with its "cauliflower" look, testifies to his fighting years. He likes to talk about his boxing days—the ring, the victories, the ones that got away, and the traveling from city to city between fights.

Mr. Ritter's chart tells its readers that he has a psychotic mental disorder caused by chronic alcoholism. He was placed in custody in 1971 as decreed by court order after psychiatric examination. The examiner reported, as can be read in the chart, that Mr. Ritter was confused. He had trouble subtracting numbers from 100 in descending order, seven at a time (he became confused at 93). He also forgot to mention Kennedy when listing our presidents backward. The examiner's report in 1972 showed no signs of progress; instead Mr. Ritter had become more confused, at least according to the test. He has to be reexamined every year to determine whether his mental state warrants commitment. While no cure or therapy is prescribed for Mr. Ritter, he is being administered quite a few phenobarbital drugs as sedatives on an "as-needed" basis.

Mr. Ritter blames his sister-in-law for his having been committed, unjustly in his opinion. He says that he was in his trailer when a couple of sheriff deputies came over and asked him to go for a ride with them. The next thing he knew, he was in the courthouse, and these fellows in white coats kept asking him funny questions and writing down something on a pad before he had a chance to answer. From there, he was taken to a boarding house where he stayed for a year, without liking it very much, and finally he was transferred to the convalescent center without being given any explanation for the move. Mr. Ritter feels that he is being kept at the center as a captive, but he is resigned and he will not attempt to escape. He spends his days mending old trousers or sewing buttons on shirts and listens to the radio from time to time.

The last case examined is Mr. Adams, who is not resigned to spending the rest of his life at the center. He kept telling me over and over that he had a little money saved up and would move if he could find a nicer convalescent center. He emphasized that there is nothing wrong with his mind, and he does not like being "cooped up" with a lot of crazy people. He asked me to buy him some stamps so that he could write to a lawyer in the city and see if he could get out of there. I asked the registered nurse and the administrator if I could buy the stamps, and they showed concern that he might give me letters to mail without their knowing about it.

I asked the registered nurse why Mr. Adams could not be transferred to a "normal" convalescent center (one not having a license for dealing with mentally disturbed patients). She replied that Mr. Adams is overbearingly crabby and complains continually and that she did not think that he would work out in a "normal" convalescent center.

Mr. Adams is confined to a wheelchair due to polio, but he can walk a little if he holds on to his wheelchair. He used to work in the valley, dealing with fruits and vegetables. He liked to drink, and one day was found in his cabin more dead than alive from overdrinking. He was taken to the hospital and from there he was moved to the convalescent center.

Mr. Adams is a great baseball fan and spends most of his time reading the sports page and listening to games on his radio. He also likes to talk very much to the staff (not to other patients). He stops whomever he can and begins to talk about baseball. I was his favorite "target," being a man and hence supposedly knowing more about baseball than the aides (all women). One day I decided to take Mr. Adams to a ball game; however, the administrator was very cold about it. She said that Mr. Adams was too excitable, and that after all, I was not a relative, and it would have been hard to obtain permission, and the responsibility was too great, and so on until I gave up the idea.

Mr. Adams is very bitter about the center. He feels that the owners take advantage of the patients (such as keeping money allocated for buying new clothing for the patients, and using instead clothing of recently dead patients). He does not like to share a room, and the fact that the place is centrally heated and he has no control over regulating the temperature bothers him. He resents the high degree of control that the administrator has over the place, and on various occasions he has had arguments with her.

The regularity with which the "better" patients view themselves as prisoners seems to indicate that believing that they are being held by some conspiracy in a place in which they do not belong allows these individuals to reconcile themselves with their being at the center. Even Mr. Adams' claims to be trying to move are largely rhetorical. I have been in and out of the center for three years now, and he still makes the same claims about leaving, and calling a lawyer, and so on. But as long as the "better" patients view themselves as prisoners, they can survive in the center: The other people here are not their equals, and the staff's treatment is a part of the conspiracy to keep them here.

These are the only individuals who can still view their lives in cognitively meaningful terms. Their lives become seen as a sequence of scheduled events with large gaps of time to be filled in between. One cannot speak of leisure in a setting such as this, a setting which cannot be left freely. The "waiting periods" between scheduled events are filled with activities such as reading, sewing, listening to the radio, etc. These tasks become paramount because they are the only tasks that the patients can themselves choose and regulate to a certain extent. Due to this, a curious thing happens: leisure becomes equated with sustenance activities, reversing definitions which separate the two. The patients look forward to lunch, to dinner, to their monthly haircut, etc. as the most entertaining events in their lives. The remainder of the time, the "free" time, which should be their leisure time, becomes mere filler, and activities are only useful to "kill time" until the next scheduled events will break the monotony of waiting.

The Others

There are other patients at the center who hang on to a remainder of self. It is often impossible to know how much lucidity they retain because it is hard to crack the solid wall that these patients have erected between themselves and the institution. At times, only at times, a crack appears, and one can catch a glimpse of life beneath the dull outside.

I was able to follow the case of a patient before she had set in place the last brick that would forever entomb her alive inside the wall. Mrs. Leister had come to the center willingly because she had a heart condition and felt that she would want medical care nearby all the time. When she came in, she was an active and talkative lady. She walked up and down the corridors, talked to people, smiled a lot, and chirpily moved about. One day she was very excited because her daughter was coming to visit her from back East. She showed me a picture of her daughter and told me all about her daughter's husband and children. That very day I witnessed the kind of interaction that was to force Mrs. Leister behind her wall.

The aide came into the room without knocking and left the door opened behind her. Mrs. Leister was fully dressed, but she was lying on the bed awaiting her doctor's visit. The aide, taking no notice of either of us, began making the bed around Mrs. Leister. The doctor walked in and nodded good morning to the aide. He had no way of knowing who I was since he had never met me before, thus I was a stranger of the opposite sex of the patient he was examining; nevertheless, he casually unbuttoned Mrs. Leister's blouse while asking her about her health and began listening with a stethoscope to her heart. He left after a few minutes, and the nurse resumed making the bed while telling me what a terrible doctor that was.

That day Mrs. Leister had her first taste of what it is like to be treated as an object. When she attempted to be a human being, she was met by the unyielding iron hand of regulations. No, she could not go outside the center and take walks, that was against regulations; no, she could not watch television in the evenings, that would disturb the other patients, and it was not allowed; no, there was no portion of the six acres around the center that was set aside for gardening by the patients. Other patients spoke curtly to Mrs. Leister or returned her conversation with an idiotic grin. Old Maria, in her ramblings, once more reverted to the language of her youth when she was a prostitute in the streets of New York, and invested Mrs. Leister with a barrage of profanities, which brought laughter and a thorazine shot from the "battle axe" on duty.

Four months later, Mrs. Leister was spending all of her time on her bed. She no longer walked up and down the corridors. "I can look at the sky from here," she told me, perhaps in her last attempt to have something of her own.

Others who have been at the center longer have finished their wall and devised small ways to show that the center is an abhorrent entity outside of themselves. This enables them to keep a distance between themselves and the center. Goffman observed these behaviors on the part of patients in his work *Asylums* and called them secondary adjustments:

> Secondary adjustments provide the inmate with important evidence that he is still his own man, with some control of his environment; sometimes a secondary adjustment becomes almost a kind of lodgment for the self, a *churinga* in which the soul is felt to reside.[16]

The following show some of the small ways in which secondary adjustments emerge at the center.

Old Mr. Walters used to roll his wheelchair back and forth, while banging continuously on the wall with his fist. He did not speak apart from yelling his head off when his pants were wet with his own urine. At Christmas one of the aides brought in a tom-tom to redress Mr. Walters' banging. Mr. Walters, upon receiving his "gift," suddenly looked very somber, then he threw it aside in disgust and began weeping. A senile old man? Maybe.

Mr. Jackson wheeled around his chair mumbling discontent to any and all and expectorated on the floor whenever and wherever he felt like it. Moved by my research instinct, and by the fact that I had to clean the floors, I tried to befriend Mr. Jackson. I began helping him around with his wheelchair whenever he needed help; I tried to carry on small talk while cleaning his room; I turned old tomato cans into spittoons and moved them near him wherever he was. It took me many weeks, but Mr. Jackson began replying to my small talk and he began using the spittoon. But I had to leave, and when I came back the next summer, Mr. Jackson was still there, back to silently spitting on the floor.

Benny Barons had been a good musician. He used to play the saw with a famous band in the 1930s and 1940s. He now sat gloomily and scowled at the world. One of the assistant cooks brought out a checker set and placed it on the table in front of Benny and with no words being exchanged, a checker game began. The cook was slightly ahead in the game when culinary duties called. I took over the game and tried to talk to Benny, with no response. No one else was in the dining hall at the time so we played in silence for a while. Benny would not answer when asked, "Is it my move?" but would not move if it was not his turn. After a while, I purposely made an obvious mistake, and Benny won the game while I was complaining about my stupidity. Again no response. I left him and mentioned the strangeness of the game to the registered nurse, who feigned surprise that he would be capable of playing at all. She told me that he never speaks; he just sits and frowns.

And the rest of the patients? They are shadows who no longer possess a cognitive self. They wander aimlessly through the corridors or sit whimpering in a wheelchair, or groan as their bed sores grow redder. When one displays a spark and begins to rage against a ghost from the past which torments him, another pill is popped in his mouth. Slowly, the eyes turn glassy again and, as order and discipline are restored, the patient, a babbling idiot once more, slowly shuffles away.

. . . .

In attempts to interact at the center, a new patient is confronted with other patients and staff. Some patients withdraw within themselves and present a cold, often hostile front toward other patients, as in the cases of Mr. Adams and Mr. Anderson. The remainder are not able to interact competently. A new patient then turns to the staff for interactional purposes. But it has been shown that the staff is too busy accomplishing their daily tasks to stop and consider the patients as human beings. Being treated either as a work object by the staff or as nonexistent by other patients does little to sustain one's conception of wholesomeness. Previous values are shattered and meanings vanish in this environment where the world can only be seen through locked doors and the distorting bluish tint of a picture window.

In attempting to understand why patients present such a hostile front to others rather than unite and share the burden of their destiny, an analogy must be drawn. Seymour Martin Lipset and his associates,[17] in studying the typesetters union, discovered that typesetters fraternized with other typesetters in their off-duty activities. Lipset and the others attributed this to a problem of perceived status versus accorded status.

A group feels that it belongs to a certain status category and, therefore, believes that it should be its right to interact with groups in the same status bracket. However, the rest of society accords the group a status inferior to that which it itself perceives. The group is, in other words, rejected by others who feel superior to it and, in turn, rejects groups which it perceives as inferior.

In the center, a single patient can be considered the equivalent of the whole group of typesetters. The patient feels that he belongs to a certain status—being sane—and attempts to interact with individuals whom he considers sane: doctors, nurses, aides, janitors, etc. But they perceive the patient as belonging to an inferior status—work-object, insane, senile, etc.—and refuse to interact with him. On the other hand, the patient perceives the other patients as inferior because he assumes them to be bona fide patients deserving of being in the center and thus refuses to interact with them. The patient has only one group left with which to interact: himself.

. . . .

NOTES

1. Erving Goffman, *The Presentation of the Self in Everyday Life* (Garden City, N.Y.: Anchor, 1959).
2. For a detailed account of patients in hospitals in terms of time and work, see Barney Glaser and Anselm Strauss, *Awareness of Dying*. Chicago: Aldine, 1965; *Time for Dying*. Chicago: Aldine, 1968; and *Anguish*. Mill Valley, Ca.: Sociology Press, 1970.
3. For a detailed ethnography of a convalescent center, see Jaber F. Gubrium, *Living and Dying at Murray Manor*. New York: St. Martin's Press, 1975.
4. Matilda W. Riley and Anne Foner, *Aging and Society* (New York: Russell Sage, 1968) Vol. 1, Chapter 25.
5. Claire Townsend, *Old Age: The Last Segregation* (New York: Grossman, 1971); Mary Adelaide Mendelson, *Tender Loving Greed*. New York: Alfred A. Knopf, 1974.
6. Less than 5 percent of the people over sixty-five years of age in the United States are institutionalized. See *Social and Economic Characteristics of the Older Populations 1974*, U.S. Department of Commerce, Bureau of the Census. Washington, D.C.: U.S. Government Printing Office, 1975.
7. However, I had access to all the medical records of the patients.
8. Lewis Carroll, *Alice in Wonderland* (New York: Random House, n.d.), p. 87.
9. In the latter part of my research an increasing number of young mental patients began replacing the old ones in the upper ward. At times I was mistaken by a new aide or a delivery man for a patient because I did not wear a white coat and wandered around the facilities.
10. Barney Glaser and Anselm Strauss, *Anguish*, op. cit.
11. This quote and the remainder in the chapter, unless otherwise noted, are from my field notes taken in the summer of 1974.
12. There are four aides on day shift (7:00 to 3:30), two per wing on each ward, plus two 9:00 aides (9:00 to 5:00).
13. The aide is an older lady in her sixties; she has been at the center for many years and somehow feels responsible for all that goes on in there. This leads her to become easily excitable, as I had the opportunity to witness many times.

14. See, for instance, Abraham Blumberg, *Criminal Justice*. Chicago: Quadrangle, 1967.
15. P. G. Wodehouse, quoted in George Orwell, "In Defense of P. G. Wodehouse," in *The Orwell Reader*, New York: Harcourt Brace & World, 1949:316.
16. Erving Goffman, *Asylums* (Garden City, N.Y.: Anchor, 1961), p. 55.
17. S. M. Lipset, Martin Trow, and James Coleman, *Union Democracy* (Garden City, N.Y.: Anchor, 1956).

Old Folks and Dirty Work: The Social Conditions for Patient Abuse in a Nursing Home

CHARLES I. STANNARD

Using the method of participant observation, the author of this article examines the conditions which lead to patient abuse in a nursing home. The everyday conditions of work serve to keep the nurses from seeing or hearing about the abusive treatment of patients by the aides. These conditions also provide the nurses with routine ways to deny its occurrence when claims of abuse are made. The conditions are the invisibility of aide-patient interaction, the gap of hostility and suspicion that separates the nurses from the other employees, and the character and behavior of the aides and patients which provide the nurses with a rationale to deny allegations of abuse. The author concludes that, on the basis of the sociological literature on nursing homes, state mental hospitals, and hospital wards for the aged, similar processes leading to abuse may exist in a variety of institutions dealing with powerless clients.

This report will try to show how patient abuse can occur in a small, proprietary nursing home without the nurses who work there being aware that it is a recurring problem. I will try to show how the everyday conditions of work in the nursing home and people's reactions to them not only prevent the nurses from seeing much of the abuse that goes on, but also, by impeding the development of trust and communication among the groups who work and reside there and coloring the relations that obtain among these people with distrust, hostility, and cynicism, these conditions keep the nurses from hearing about abuse. These same conditions, finally, also provide the nurses with a variety of reasonable denials of the occurrence of abuse when infrequent allegations of its use by orderlies and aides are made. These denials and differentials in the awareness of abuse reduce its visibility to the nurses, making it appear random and infrequent, thereby masking the fact that it appears to be a patterned response of the aides and orderlies to their recurring problems of controlling the patients. In so doing, they serve to perpetuate the abuse (Coser, 1969; Moore and Tumin, 1949).

SOURCE: Reprinted by permission from *Social Problems* 20:3 (Winter 1973), pp. 329–342. Copyright 1973 by The Society for the Study of Social Problems.

The data on which this analysis is based were gathered by participant observation in a sixty-five-bed proprietary nursing home located in a suburb of a large midwestern city. Participant observation involves the researcher entering a group or organization, observing interaction patterns, and discussing the meaning and import of the interactions with group members (Zelditch, 1962). The aim of such research is to develop a systemic or holistic model of the group under investigation (Becker, 1958; Weiss, 1968). This leads to an emphasis on the similarities and commonalities in the patterns of interaction, rather than an emphasis on the differences or variations, as is the case in other modes of research, especially survey research (Becker *et al.*, 1961:22).

Initial contact with the nursing home began in the fall of 1967. From September to December, I made a dozen visits to the home; more intensive contact began in June 1968, and lasted until February 1969. During this period, my identity was that of a sociologist writing a book on nursing homes. Later, in the summer of 1969, I worked as a janitor in the home for six weeks.

Personnel Problems: Marginality, Turnover, and Absenteeism

The greatest problem the nursing home faced was securing and maintaining an adequate staff. The people who worked there reflected the unattractiveness of this type of work and the low wages the home paid, problems that appear common to nursing homes (U.S. Department of Labor, 1969; Kansas State Department of Health, 1964:82). Most of the people who worked in the nursing home occupied marginal positions in the labor market. Most nonsupervisory employees were from the urban lower class. Of these, the bulk were black women who were divorced or widowed. Whites working in the home were often migrants from the rural South. With the exception of a few middle-class high-school girls who worked as aides during the summer, the employees had little in the way of education, training, or skills.

Even the supervisory personnel often lacked training or accreditation. Of the five registered nurses (RN) employed at the home, two were no longer licensed, though this did not prevent them from performing the same duties as the licensed nurses. Only one licensed practical nurse (LPN) had received formal training for that position; the others became LPNs by passing a special waiver examination created to increase the number of LPNs in the state.

Some of the people who worked in the home had "spoiled identities" (Goffman, 1963). These included former mental patients, several men who had criminal records (one was on probation while working at the home), a former alcoholic, several men who appeared to be homosexuals, several people whose bizarre behavior seemed to indicate mental illness, and several men who appeared to be drifters in need of temporary employment.

Nonsupervisory personnel did not develop strong commitments to their jobs or to the home. This is suggested by the turnover and absenteeism among employees. The nursing home had a very difficult time maintaining a numerically adequate staff. During 1968, 225 people worked at the home. Since 45 people constituted a full complement of employees, the turnover was extremely high, 500 percent.

A record was also kept of the total number of bimonthly pay periods a person worked at the home during 1968. These were tallied for those people who were working there in December 1968, which gives some measure of the degree to which people were likely to stay on at the home and provides an indication of the amount of continuity and experience among the staff. The distribution was found to be distinctly bimodal: an employee either worked at the home a relatively short time—two months or less—or he worked the entire year. Thus, of the 45 people employed in the final pay period of 1968, 56 percent worked two months or less and the bulk of these people (15 out of 24) worked a month or less at the home. At the other extreme, a third of the employees worked the entire year.

The tendency to remain employed at the home was not evenly distributed among the employees. Those in supervisory positions were much more likely to stay on than those in nonsupervisory positions. Eight of the 15 who worked the entire year were RNs or LPNs. The nine supervisory people working at the end of 1968 averaged 21.6 pay periods of employment, while the other employees (aides, orderlies, janitors, kitchen help) averaged only 7.8 pay periods.

Absenteeism was also a chronic problem. In order to estimate the amount of absenteeism in the home, a sample of three months—April, May, and October—was chosen randomly. For each day of these months, a count was taken of the number of absences as noted on the official payroll sheets. A record was also kept of the particular shift on which an absence occurred (day, evening, and night), and whether the person was directly engaged in patient care (RN, LPN, aide, orderly) or supporting patient care (janitor, cook, dishwasher, laundryman). This distinction is important because absences among those in the support group created different problems for those in charge of the home. The data on absenteeism are presented in Table 1.

Like turnover, absenteeism was extremely common among the employees. On the day shift someone was absent 86 percent of the time; on the evening shift an absence occurred 80 percent of the time; 14 percent of the time someone was absent on the night shift; and 70 percent of the time someone working in the support group was absent.

Furthermore, on many days there were multiple absences. On the day shift two people were absent 20 percent of the time; three or more people were absent 42 percent of the time. At one time during the period sampled, more than one-third of the people scheduled to work did not show up.

The other shifts, with the exception of the night shift, fared only slightly better. On the evening shift two or more people were absent 46 percent of the time; three or more people were absent 26 percent of the time. One evening during the period sampled, two-thirds of those scheduled to work on this shift did not show up. Among those working in support activities, two or more people were absent 36 percent of the time. Absences among these employees were more of a problem because many of the tasks of this group could not be neglected or shared if the patients were to be cared for. The meals had to be cooked, the dishes cleaned and stacked, meals set up, and the linen and laundry cleaned. This made an absence on this shift doubly troublesome because it meant that someone, usually an aide, had to be taken from her job and assigned to one of these tasks, thereby creating a shortage among those caring for patients.

Personnel Problems and the Role of the Nurse

The problems of maintaining a sufficient staff to run the home, while affecting everyone in the home, had their greatest impact on the RNs who ran the home on a daily basis. The vulnerability of the nurses to the effects of the personnel problems lay in the centrality and visibility of the nurse's role.

The prime responsibility for the day-to-day provision of patient care and the operation of the home rested with the nurses. They held themselves responsible for the type of care administered and were held responsible for this by all the people who interacted within the home. The owner, the patients' doctors and relatives, the other employees, and the patients, all looked to the nurses for information, direction, decisions, help, and guidance in the daily affairs of the home.

The central problem for the nurses was that though they were charged with the responsibility for the type of care the patients received, in actuality they provided little of this care themselves. Rather they were, like their counterparts in general hospitals, administrators (Mauksch,

TABLE 1 The Number of Absences by Shift Worked for April, May and October

Shift	7–3		3–11		11–7		Support°	
NUMBER OF ABSENCES	DAYS	PER-CENT	DAYS	PER-CENT	DAYS	PER-CENT	DAYS	PER-CENT
None	13	14	19	20	79	86	28	30
One	22	24	31	34	13	14	31	34
Two	18	20	18	20	—	—	21	23
Three or more	39	42	24	26	—	—	12	13
Total	92	100	92	100	92	100	92	100

°Includes all employees not engaged in patient care: cooks, janitors, dishwashers, laundrymen.

1966; Corwin and Taves, 1963) who organized, coordinated, and directed the activities of the aides. With the exception of giving injections or other specialized medical procedures such as subcutaneous feedings and examining sick patients, the aides took care of the patient's needs. The bulk of the nurses' time was taken up with administrative duties, which included, when the owner was not present in the home,[1] ordering supplies, hiring employees, and dealing with people seeking admission to the home for themselves or a relative.

This meant that in order for the nurses to fulfill the mandate of their position (Hughes, 1958), they had to rely heavily on the performances of the other employees in the home. If these people did not perform well, the nurses were held accountable by the other status groups, especially the relatives. The problem for the nurses was that the unreliability of the other employees and the patients themselves[2] continually called into question their ability to fulfill this mandate to provide good care for the patients.

The plight of the nurses was manifested in bitter cynicism and adamant custodialism. They were extremely cynical, doubting the intentions, sincerity, and capabilities of all the other people who interacted with them in the home and continually imputing illegitimate motives to these people's actions. The nurses were most suspicious of the other employees, regarding them as unreliable, untrustworthy, dishonest, and immoral. Thus they were skeptical when an employee called in sick or offered mitigating circumstances as an excuse for an absence. One time an aide called in and told the nurses that she would not be coming to work because a relative had died. She was especially suspect because it was Monday morning. A nurse commented that the aide was probably hung over from the weekend, and also said that this particular relative had "died" before. Because theft was a recurrent problem, the nurses warned new employees to keep their money and wallets on their persons at all times when in the home. Patients' relatives were also told to remove any of the patients' valuables from the home or to put them in the owner's office in the basement so they would not be stolen. The nurses were also doubtful of the ability and willingness of the employees to work and felt that many of the people who worked there were lazy, stupid, or just did not want to learn how to do their jobs well. Finally, they doubted the moral probity of the employees and saw them living immoral lives, replete with illicit sex and excessive drinking. As one nurse said of the aides: "They have the morals of an alley cat."

The employee problems affected the nurses' relations with other status groups in the home by creating conflicts with them. Because of these conflicts, the nurses saw these people as ignorant of their difficulties in running the home and unsympathetic to their plight. What is important to note about the complaints the nurses had with these people is that these complaints were directly related to their difficulties in running the home, which, in turn, stemmed in large measure from the problems with the employees.

The nurses were irritated by doctors who were reluctant or unwilling to prescribe tranquilizing drugs for fear of "snowing the patients under," which made it harder for the nurses to control the patients and prevent them from disrupting the daily routines of the home or from escaping or injuring themselves. In dealing with these doctors, the nurses would try, often unsuccessfully, to persuade them of the importance or necessity of tranquilizers for problem patients. The relatives created similar problems for the nurses by refusing to let them restrain the patients, thereby increasing the potential for an accident or escape, both of which reflected badly on the nurses. Complaints about the care given by the home were taken to indicate ill will on the part of the relatives. The Health Department was always finding what the nurses regarded as trivial faults in the home—burned-out light bulbs, dirt in closets, inadequate charts—but overlooked the real problems the help created. The nurses viewed the owner as unsympathetic and unconcerned with the home. He demonstrated this to them by his low involvement in the affairs of the home, his hiring and wage policies, his occasional attempts to fire employees the nurses regarded as reliable and competent, and by his allowing his mother-in-law to meddle in the affairs of the home, always an upsetting experience. Finally, the patients, by their constant rule-breaking and their complaints to their relatives, also frustrated and irritated the nurses.

A custodial ideology dominated the home. The nurses emphasized the hopeless conditions of the patients, their enfeebled mental states, and the necessity of controlling them with drugs and cloth restraints. Care thus was defined minimally in terms of tending to the bodily needs of the patients and keeping them and the home clean and orderly—"pediatrics senior-grade" in the words of one nurse. The personnel problems even made achieving these minimal goals uncertain (cf. Stannard, 1971; chap. 3).

The Social Conditions for Patient Abuse

Most people who worked in the nursing home regarded patient abuse as wrong and evil. The nurses felt especially strongly about this. They claimed that such activities happened infrequently in the home and that when they discovered an instance of abuse, they fired the person responsible for it right on the spot. The head nurse claimed that she had come across such behavior only a few times during her three-year tenure at the home, and each time she did, the person perpetrating it was fired immediately. During the research, this happened only once, when a LPN observed an aide kicking a patient and fired her. Because of its purported infrequency, the nurses did not regard patient abuse as a problem.

The aides felt the same way as the nurses, that in view of their deteriorated physical and mental conditions, the patients should be humored and helped, not hurt. Yet patient abuse did occur in the home.[3] This happened when a patient assaulted an aide or was perceived as deliberately making her job more difficult than it had to be. Kicking, biting, punching, or spitting at an aide were, in the aides' minds, inexcusable and punishable behavior. Likewise, a patient who defecated on the floor or in a wastebasket when, according to the aide, she was perfectly able to use the toilet, was liable to receive abusive treatment. The fact that the patient violated institutionalized expectations of proper patient behavior temporarily neutralized or suspended (Sykes and Matza, 1957; Matza, 1966) the norm prohibiting abuse of patients. In so doing, it momentarily freed the aide from the restraining power of the norm and allowed her to use illicit force in dealing with the patient.

Why were the nurses unaware that aides and orderlies occasionally abused patients? There are several reasons for this. First, the way work was organized left the aides physically isolated with patients. Second, the nurses' hostility toward and suspicion of the other employees reduced the amount of interaction and communication between these two groups. Three, the character of the patients and personnel of the home provided the nurses with ready "accounts"[4] for allegations of abuse. These accounts worked by denying the claim of abuse and imputing malice or ignorance to the person making the claim.

Work in the home was organized so that aides, for the most part, had a set group of patients for whom they alone provided care. The aides received very little direct supervision from the nurses, who were occupied with administrative duties at the nurses' station. As a result, much of what went on between the aide and the patient was not observable to the other aides or to the nurses. The patient's room, the toilets, the tub rooms, were areas where important interaction occurred between aides and patients that were also "private" or could be made so by closing the door (Schwartz, 1968) to suit the aide's or patient's needs. This isolation reduced the chances that the aide would be detected acting improperly with a patient.

Of course, this isolation of aide-patient interaction could be effective only to the extent that the patients did not verbalize their mistreatment to other aides, nurses, relatives, or doctors. Thus this factor was important especially with those patients who were unable or unwilling to communicate with people about their experiences in the home.

However, this isolation did not prevent abuse from being observed occasionally. Once in a while an aide observed another aide abusing a patient. In some instances the aide was sympathetic to the other aide, feeling that her actions were justified by the patient's actions. In those instances where the aide felt that the other aide acted improperly with a patient, she either did nothing at all or told the other aides about it. When the latter happened, the aides spoke about the personal attributes ("meanness") or objective conditions (widowed and living alone, too old for this type of work) of the aide which they regarded as responsible for the aide's actions.

The aides rarely reported such actions to the nurses. One reason was the solidarity and cohesiveness that obtained among the small group of regular and steady employees, who did not want to harm another aide and be responsible for someone losing a job. Among the less well integrated employees, it can be that their lack of integration into the core group of aides left them uncertain about how they were to act and vulnerable to sanctions from the more experienced aides, primarily in the form of lack of cooperation and information about their jobs, and thus unlikely to report abuse to the nurses.

Equally important in restricting information about abuse were the hostility and suspicion that separated the nurses from the other employees, especially the aides. The nurses publicly communicated their dislike, distrust, and low opinion of the lower-level employees, particularly the aides, to these people as they griped about their unreliability, inferiority, immorality, and low intelligence at the nurses' station and other places where the nurses gathered. They literally treated these employees as "nonpersons," derogating their characters openly and in their presence, thus minimizing communication and interaction between them and other employees.

Finally, sometimes patients, their relatives, or an employee complained to the nurses about mistreatment. The usual response of the nurses to such claims was to deny the occurrence of abuse. They did this by making a counter-claim about the person making the complaint, denied the legitimacy and validity of the contentions, and accounted for them by referring to discrediting attributes of the person making the allegation. Thus the nurses argued that the patients who made such complaints were trouble-makers or crazy and did not have to be taken seriously. Similarly, they felt that relatives who took up a patient's case were ignorant of the situation in the home, dupes of a crazy patient, or crazy themselves, and did not have to be taken seriously. When an employee made such an allegation, the nurses and owner imputed ulterior motives to him and in so doing debunked his claim; or they received it skeptically and did nothing.

The various accounts that the nurses offered to deny such claims of maltreatment were based on their definitions of reality in the home. They formed a common "vocabulary of motives" (Mills, 1941) that stemmed from the basic characteristics of the work force and patients in the home. From the nurses' perspective, both the employees and patients had in common the fact that they were likely to have discrediting attributes or characteristics which made them untrustworthy and unreliable, characteristics which were responsible for their being in the nursing home in the first place. Furthermore, both groups manifested these attributes daily and in so doing made life miserable for the nurses. The employees did not come to work; when they did, they did not perform well; many had elements in their pasts such as criminal arrests, a history of drunkenness, illegitimate children, etc. that were shocking and stigmatizing in terms of the nurses' conventional standards. The patients were unreliable by definition, since one of the reasons for their incarceration was the fact that they could not care for themselves in the outside world (Goffman, 1961:76) and exhibited their incapacities and incompetence daily by their helplessness and frequently bizarre behavior.

Accounting for Abuse: An Example

The interplay of these factors can be seen in the two radically different interpretations of an event that arose during the research. The nurses and owner interpreted the event one way; the aides and other employees another way. The event that precipitated these rival interpretations was the scalding of a patient one evening. Two weeks after the scalding, the patient died in the intensive care unit of a local general hospital. His demise was directly attributable to the scalding in the nursing home.

According to the nurse who was working the evening of the scalding, it was the result of a complicated series of events that began on the day shift. On that day, the man who worked in the laundry did not come to work. Because of this, the nurses on the day shift had to assign an aide to work in the laundry, which was located in the basement of the home. One of the duties of the person doing the laundry was to bring the clean linen and laundry to the floors where the aides and orderlies worked. For one reason or another the person who did the laundry that day neglected to do this for the evening shift, so that shift was short of linen, towels, clothes, and diapers for the incontinent patients.

That night the evening shift was also short of help; there were four people to do the work of nine. The shortage was so great that even the RN on that shift was putting patients to bed. Early in the evening an orderly went to put a patient, Mr. Jones, to bed. The patient had soiled himself and his bed. According to the nurse, the orderly had the "good sense" to clean him and change his linen, something not every employee could be relied on to do. He undressed the patient and put him in a bath tub. After washing him, the orderly went to get a towel and clean linen, but there were none in the linen closet. The janitor who worked on the day shift happened to be on the floor at the time, so the orderly asked him to watch the patient while he went to the basement for some clean towels and linen. Instead of watching the patient, the janitor took some trash cans out to the garbage bin behind the home. He and the orderly returned to the floor at about the same time and found Mr. Jones sitting in a tub of hot water with the faucet on. Both of them panicked when they saw this.

They picked the patient up, wrapped him in a clean sheet, and put him to bed. They did not tell the nurse what had happened.

About an hour after the patient was scalded, the evening nurse came to the second floor and "just happened" to look in on Mr. Jones. There, lying in bed, was Mr. Jones with the skin and tissue on his legs and lower trunk "coming off in hunks." After recovering from the horror of her gruesome discovery, the nurse called an ambulance, and he was taken to a local hospital.

No one knew for sure what had happened while the patient was alone in the tub. The nurses and the owner theorized that Mr. Jones, in his mental confusion, was attracted by the shininess of the faucet and reached out for it, accidentally turning on the hot water. Because of the pain and his confusion, he was unable to turn off the water. Thus he sat there while the tub filled with hot water until the orderly and janitor found him.

Some time after the patient died and an inquest was held which cleared the staff of any criminal charges, another version of the events of that evening surfaced. According to this version, the orderly put the patient into the tub of hot water in order to punish the patient for cursing him.[5] The shortage of help that night gave the orderly the chance to use this form of punishment on Mr. Jones, a form he had learned while he was working in a mental hospital. This version was relayed to me by the janitor who was on the floor at the time. He said that he, another janitor who came to the floor, and the orderly got together and fabricated the other story to protect the people who owned the home and those that worked there. In the interim between the scalding and his telling me this, the orderly and other janitor had quit working at the home.

Shortly after hearing this, I left town for several days. On returning I told the charge nurse what I had heard. During this interval, the janitor who told me this was fired, along with two aides. He and the aides were drinking in the home one evening and created a disturbance for which they were fired. According to the nurse who was on duty at the time, they were all a "bunch of wiseass kids." The janitor and one of the aides then purportedly went to Philadelphia together.

My version of the causes of the scalding upset the charge nurse, who said that she had heard something similar from the aides but did not pay any attention to it. She was puzzled when the scalding occurred because, as she said: "There have been thousands of baths in that tub and nothing ever happened before." It was this uneasiness that prompted her and the evening nurse to question the people who were on the floor that evening several times. To her, my tale only provided more confirmation of the poorly developed moral sense of the "colored." She said: "They only tell you what they think you want to hear."[6] She decided to tell the owner what I told her and let him decide what to do.

The next day I saw the owner of the nursing home. The nurse had told him the new version of the events of that evening. He told me that the janitor had already told him his story just before he left for Philadelphia. The owner said that he told the janitor that he should tell his story to the police and not to him.

In the owner's mind, the scalding was the result of a chance and tragic conjunction of events in the home: the absence of the laundryman on the day shift, which eventuated in a shortage of linen, towels, and clothes on the second floor that evening; the patient soiling himself; the shortage of employees to watch over the patient while the orderly went to the basement; the *"non compos mentis"* status of the patient, which led to his reaching for the faucet and turning on the hot water, his inability to turn off the water, and the debilitated condition of his skin. These were the causes of the patient's death, not the deliberate actions of an employee.

He responded to the janitor's claim that the death was not an accident by arguing that the janitor made up the story to blackmail him, and said that the janitor's girlfriend, the aide he went to Philadelphia with, put him up to this. She was angered at the owner because he was making her move out of the room she rented in his home and was working through the janitor to get back at him. Such behavior was not unusual from the people who worked at the home and, in fact, one might expect the type of people who worked there to try to make private capital out of such a tragedy. He said that just that week a former employee had made a threat on his life. Not believing the janitor's story and not feeling personally responsible for reopening the investigation (this was the janitor's duty), he was content to "let sleeping dogs lie." Though challenged, the official version managed to maintain its integrity because it did not contradict the nurses' and owner's version of normal events in the home.

The janitor's version made sense to the aides and other employees because it was consonant with their perceptions of reality in the home. Patients did assault aides and orderlies verbally and physically. Sometimes when this happened an aide or orderly retaliated with force. To them, the scalding was an example of this type of interplay between aide and patient, more extreme than most, but still one of a class of events with which they were familiar. What made this event unusual was the extremity of the orderly's response against a patient who, in the words of one aide, "didn't know any better" and therefore was not responsible for his actions. The aide said that the orderly should have known that this patient was crazy. If he did, he would have known that crazy patients are not punished for cursing aides.

The events surrounding the scalding of Mr. Jones highlight the effects that the hostility, cynicism, and distrust of the nurses and owner had on relations and activities in the home. The nurses and owner were reluctant to take seriously allegations of abuse in the home. They rebutted such assertions by referring to discrediting elements in the character of the person making the complaints. In essence, they adopted the principle that "seeing is believing" with regard to abuse, while their low frequency of interaction with aides or patients made such observation unlikely.

On the side of the lower-level employees, there was the tendency to look the other way when another employee abused a patient. Their involvement in their roles was so minimal that they not only seldom reported abuse to the nurses, they seldom even sanctioned the person doing it, even if they thought it was unjustified.

The end result of these corresponding attitudes of suspicion and resentment was that some of the abuse that could have been detected and punished in the home went undetected and unpunished at the supervisory level. These attitudes acted as an information screen (Caplow, 1964) that prevented the nurses from seeing that abuse was a recurrent response of the aides to their problems with patients.

Discussion

Here I would like to extrapolate from the single case study and suggest that similar processes with regard to abusive behavior may be present in a variety of similar institutions. The literature on nursing homes (Henry, 1963: chap. 10; Coe, 1965; Bennett and Nehemow, 1965; Glaser and Strauss, 1968: chap. 4), on the social structure of hospital wards dealing with the elderly (Coser, 1963), and on state mental hospitals (Rowland, 1938; Belknap, 1956; Dunham and Weinberg, 1960; Salisbury, 1962; Strauss *et al.*, 1964: chap 5) suggests that the social organization of these different institutions is not very different from that found in our nursing home. All these institutions deal with clients of low social worth who are relatively powerless, whose prognosis for recovery is pessimistic, and whose credibility is tarnished. The disruptive effects of employee turn-over, absenteeism, and poor role performance are common in these institutions (Belknap, 1956; Kahne, 1968; Coser, 1963), treatment is defined in custodial (cf. Smith, 1965) rather than therapeutic terms, and hostility and mutual antipathy characterize the relationships between the professional and supervisory staff and those individuals who deal directly with the inmates of these institutions.

The people who work in these institutions, including the professionals, tend to occupy marginal positions in the labor market. The occupants of the lowest positions, the aides and orderlies, who have the greatest contact with inmates share a latent culture (Becker and Geer, 1960) due to their lower social-class origins, which regards the use of force and aggression as a legitimate means of resolving conflicts (Blumenthal *et al.*, 1971). Because of their social class and low levels of education, these people do not entertain sophisticated and complex notions about human motivation and mental illness. Their interpretations of patients' actions are likely to be based on lay rather than medical ideologies (Strauss *et al.*,

1964:95–6). This increases their likelihood of using already established and familiar means of handling difficulties with patients, namely force.

Conflicts between staff and patients are likely because these organizations cannot rely on rewards or the internalization by the patients of their goals or norms to generate a commitment to their rules (Etzioni, 1961). As a result, those people who work most closely with patients find control of the patients to be their greatest problem and abuse to be one way of coping with it.

The professionals and semiprofessionals who work in these institutions are the less successful members of their professions. Work in custodial mental hospitals and nursing homes does not bring professional recognition and is regarded as a step down by their professions in general. Once in these institutions, they find themselves with patients they cannot help, confronted by staff problems which make it difficult or impossible to achieve the goals expounded by their professions. The lofty goals of help and service learned during their professional training give way to more realistic goals of custody and order maintenance.[7] Rather than taking active leadership in caring for patients, they withdraw from this aspect of their role, become cynical, and concentrate their attention and energy on activities which reduce their contact with patients and lower-level employees. Patient care becomes the almost exclusive province of the lower-level employees to whom the professionals delegate a great deal of discretionary power. This insulates the lay perspectives of the lower-level employees from the more sophisticated and potentially ameliorative ideas of the professionals.

In such a context, the supervisory and professional staff will seldom see abusive behavior on the part of the other employees. Furthermore, they will probably develop a culture of accounts to deal with reputed cases of abuse which will enable them to deny the routine nature of abuse. In fact, these organizations may necessitate such a culture of accounts.[8] The professionals who stay on in such organizations will be those who have been successfully socialized to this culture. Those who do not accept the definitions and premises of such a culture are forced to leave the organization because of the dissonance created by the discrepancy between their self-images as professionals and the acknowledgment of what is really going on in the organization. The end result of these processes is the continuance of abuse.

NOTES

1. The owner of the nursing home was seldom at the home for more than a few hours each day. Some days he would not even come to the home. One time he did not come to the home for several weeks. During this period the nurses

could not reach him directly because he moved to a neighboring town, had an unlisted phone installed, and did not give the nurses the phone number. The only way they could reach him was to call his mother, who would relay the message to him.

2. The patients in the home generally were quite infirm. Many were bedridden, incontinent, and suffering mental impairments.

3. Abuse refers to behavior which would lead to negative sanctions if it were observed by a nurse. This definition is similar to the definition of deviance of Black and Reiss, Jr. (1970:63). Pulling a patient's hair, slapping, hitting, kicking, pinching, or violently shaking a patient, throwing water or food on a patient, tightening restraining belts so that they cause a patient pain, and terrorizing a patient by gesture or word are examples of abusive behavior. During the research, I occasionally witnessed aides abusing patients in one or another of these manners. Most of the data on abuse comes from discussions with aides about the way they and their fellow workers dealt with the patients.

4. "An account is a linguistic device employed whenever an action is subject to valuative enquiry. Such devices are a crucial element in the social order since they prevent conflicts from arising by verbally bridging the gap between action and expectation. Moreover, accounts are 'situated' according to the statuses of the interactants, and are standardized within cultures so that certain accounts are terminologically stabilized and routinely expected when an activity falls outside the domain of expectations" (Scott and Lyman, 1968:46).

5. This patient never spoke to people except in anger or fear, when he would utter a barely intelligible curse, usually "son of a bitch." The only person to visit him was his wife, who rarely came to the home.

6. The nurses were all white and strongly prejudiced against blacks. Their racism was part of the culture of accounts they developed; but it should be noted that they were hostile to and cynical about white employees as well.

7. Powelson and Bendix (1951) find this is the case for psychiatrists who work in prisons. The situation also seems analogous to that of lawyers. Carlin (1966) found that the less successful lawyers often found themselves in situations where the corruption of their professional ethics and goals was possible and reasonable.

8. Suggested by Merton Kahne in a personal communication.

REFERENCES

Becker, Howard S. 1958. "Problems of inference and proof in participant observation." American Sociological Review 23 (December):652–660.

Becker, Howard S. and Blanche Geer. 1960. "Latent culture: A note on the theory of latent social roles." Administrative Science Quarterly 5 (September):304–313.

Becker, Howard S., Blanche Geer, Everett C. Hughes, and Anselm L. Strauss. 1961. Boys in White. Chicago: University of Chicago Press.

Belknap, Ivan. 1956. Human Problems of a State Mental Hospital. New York: McGraw-Hill.

Bennett, Ruth and Lucille Nehemow. 1965. "Institutional totality and criteria of adjustment in residences for the aged." Journal of Social Issues 21 (October):44–78.

Black, Donald J. and Albert J. Reiss, Jr. 1970. "Police control of juveniles." American Sociological Review 35 (February):63–77.

Blumenthal, Monica D., Robert L. Kahn, Frank M. Andrews, and Kendra B. Head. 1971. Justifying Violence. Ann Arbor, Michigan: Institute for Social Research, University of Michigan.

Caplow, Theodore. 1964. Principles of Organization. New York: Harcourt, Brace and World.

Carlin, Jerome E. 1966. Lawyer's Ethics. New York: The Russell Sage Foundation.

Coe, Rodney M. 1965. "Self-conception and institutionalization," pp. 225–243 in Arnold M. Rose and Warren A. Peterson (eds.), Older People and Their Social World. Philadelphia: F. A. Davis.

Corwin, Ronald G. and Marvin J. Taves. 1963. "Nursing and other health professionals," pp. 187–212 in Howard E. Freeman, Sol Levine, Leo G. Reeder (eds.), Handbook of Medical Sociology. Englewood Cliffs, N.J.: Prentice-Hall.

Coser, Lewis L. 1969. "Visibility of evil." Journal of Social Issues 25:101–109.

Coser, Rose Laub. 1963. "Alienation and social structure," pp. 213–265 in Eliot Freidson (ed.), The Hospital in Modern Society. New York: The Free Press.

Dunham, H. Warren and S. Kierson Weinberg. 1960. The Culture of the State Mental Hospital. Detroit: Wayne State University Press.

Etzioni, Amitai. 1961. Complex Organizations. New York: The Free Press.

Glaser, Barney G. and Anselm L. Strauss. 1968. Time for Dying. Chicago: Aldine.

Goffman, Erving. 1961. "On the characteristics of total institutions: Staff-inmate relations," pp. 68–106 in Donald R. Cressey (ed.), The Prison. Holt, Rinehart and Winston; 1963. Stigma. Englewood Cliffs, N.J.: Prentice-Hall.

Henry, Jules. 1963. Culture against Man. New York: Random House.

Hughes, Everett Cherrington. 1958. Men and Their Work. New York: The Free Press.

Kahne, Merton J. 1968. "Suicide in mental hospitals: A study of the effects of personnel and patient turnover." Journal of Health and Social Behavior 9 (September):255–266.

Kansas State Department of Health. 1964. Kansas Long-Term Care Study. Topeka, Kansas.

Matza, David. 1966. Delinquency and Drift. New York: Wiley.

Mauksch, Hans O. 1966. "The organizational context of nursing practices," pp. 109–137 in Fred Davis (ed.), The Nursing Profession. New York: Wiley.

Merton, Robert K. 1957. Social Theory and Social Structure. New York: The Free Press.

Mills, C. Wright. 1941. "Situated actions and vocabularies of motives." American Sociological Review 5 (December): 904–913.

Moore, Wilbert E. and Melvin M. Tumin. 1966. "Some social functions of ignorance." American Sociological Review 14 (December):787–795.

Powelson, Harvey and Reinhard Bendix. 1951. "Psychiatry in prison." Psychiatry 14 (February):73–86.

Rowland, Howard. 1938. "Interaction processes in the state mental hospital." Psychiatry 1 (August):323–337.

Salisbury, Richard F. 1962. Structure of Custodial Care. University of California Publications in Culture and Society, vol. 8. Berkeley: University of California Press.

Schwartz, Barry. 1968. "The social psychology of privacy." American Journal of Sociology 73 (May):741–752.

Schwartz, Morris and Charlotte Green Schwartz. 1955. "Problems of participant observation." American Journal of Sociology 60 (January):343–353.

Scott, Marvin B. and Stanford M. Lyman. 1968. "Accounts." American Sociological Review 33 (February):46–52.

Smith, Dorothy E. 1965. "The logic of custodial organization." Psychiatry 28 (November):311–323.

Stannard, Charles I. 1971. Old Folks and Dirty Work: The Social Organization of a Nursing Home. Unpublished Doctoral Dissertation, Northwestern University.

Strauss, Anselm L., Leonard Schatzman, Rue Bucher, Danuta Ehrlich and Melvin Sabshin. 1964. Psychiatric Ideologies and Institutions. New York: The Free Press.

Sykes, Gresham M. and David Matza. 1957. "Techniques of neutralization: A theory of delinquency." American Sociological Review 22 (December): 664–670.

U.S. Department of Labor, Bureau of Statistics. 1969. Industry Wage Survey: Nursing Homes and Related Facilities, October 1967 and April 1968. Washington, D.C.: Government Printing Office.

Weiss, Robert J. 1968. "Issues in holistic research," pp. 342–350 in Howard S. Becker, Blanche Geer, David Riesman and Robert J. Weiss (eds.), Institutions and the Person. Chicago: Aldine.

Zelditch, Morris, Jr. 1962. "Some methodological problems of field studies." American Journal of Sociology 67 (March):566–576.

12

Death and Dying

According to Elizabeth Kubler-Ross (1970), the fear of death is universal. The ancient Hebrews regarded the body of a dead person as something unclean, not to be touched. The early American Indians shot arrows into the air to drive away evil spirits from the body of a dead person. It has even been suggested that the tradition of the tombstone may have originated from a wish to keep bad spirits down in the ground. Each society develops its own cultural forms to contain the disrupting impact of the death of its members.

Cultural Variations in the Meaning of Death

While death has obviously always been present in all societies, the characteristics of those most likely to die has changed greatly. In preindustrial societies with high birth rates and low life expectancy, the primary concentration of death is at the beginning of the life span. High infant mortality makes the occurrence of death commonly visible to all members of the society. For example, among the Sakai of the Malay Peninsula, approximately 50 percent of the babies born die before the age of three. Among Indian males born in the 1940s, 35 percent die before the age of ten. Among the Kurnia tribe of Australia, 40 to 50 percent of all children die before the age of ten. These societies must organize their customs around death's commonly recurring presence (Blauner, 1966).

One means of containing the impact of mortality is to reduce the real or ideal importance of those who die. This is done in many preindustrial societies by not recognizing infants and children as people. Up to a certain age, they are believed to belong to the spirit world from which they came. Thus upon their death no funeral is held. The historian Aries (1962) has noted that during the period of high infant mortality French children were neither valued nor recognized as separate individuals and that the concept of child-hood as a separate phase of the life cycle did not evolve until infant mortality rates dropped.

In modern industrialized societies, death has become largely the province of the aged. Modern cultures have coped with the death of the aged, minimizing its disruptiveness, by disengaging the elderly from the vital functions of society. In this way the societal institutions can continue to function, with new, younger members taking the place of older people in the family, the economy, and the community. The trend of bureaucratization which accompanies industrialization has further diminished the visibility of death. The custom of dying in one's home surrounded by family has largely been abandoned. Instead the dying are removed to hospitals which are organized to hide the facts of dying and death from both patients and visitors. Studying the handling of death in a county hospital, Sudnow (1967) quotes a text in hospital administration:

> The hospital morgue is best located on the ground floor and placed in an area inaccessible to the general public. It is important that the unit have a suitable exit leading onto a private loading platform which is concealed from hospital patients and the public.

The first two articles present two perspectives on our attitudes toward death. Pattison believes that our society can be classified as death denying and that this denial of death is symbolic of an inability to accept our own inevitable mortality. In contrast, Marshall shows that in a conducive environment, such as a retirement community, people accept and even desire death if they believe they will be allowed to die with dignity.

Changing Attitudes toward Death

The pioneering work of Kubler-Ross stimulated our awareness that societal attitudes toward death may be harmful not only to the dying but to the living. In contrast to the Sudnow study, in her book *On Death and Dying* Kubler-Ross describes a remembered death scene from her childhood:

> I remember as a child the death of a farmer. He fell from a tree and was not expected to live. He asked simply to die at home, a wish that was granted without questioning. He called his daughters into the bedroom and spoke with each one of them alone for a few minutes. He arranged his affairs quietly, though he was in great pain, and distributed his belongings and his land, none of which was to be split until his wife should follow him in death. He also asked each of his children to share in the work, duties, and tasks that he had carried on until the time of the accident. He asked his friends to visit him once more, to bid good-bye to

them. Although I was a small child at the time, he did not exclude me or my siblings. We were allowed to share in the preparations of the family just as we were permitted to grieve with them until he died. When he did die, he was left at home, in his own beloved home which he had built, and among his friends and neighbors who went to take a last look at him where he lay in the midst of flowers in the place he had lived in and loved so much.

In this scene death is clearly a part of life. Kubler-Ross concluded from her earliest experiences that when people are allowed to mourn naturally, the loss of a loved one is easier to accept.

Pursuing a subject she felt had been greatly neglected, Kubler-Ross interviewed over two hundred dying patients. She found remarkably similar responses in their reactions to their impending death. For most individuals the initial response is denial. "Oh no, not me. It can't be true." According to Kubler-Ross, denial functions as a buffer after unexpected shocking news, allowing the patient to collect himself and mobilize other, less radical defenses. When the first stage of denial cannot be maintained any longer, it is replaced by feelings of anger, rage, and resentment. This stage is difficult for family and medical staff to deal with, since anger is displaced in all directions and projected on the environment almost at random. In the third stage, the patient bargains in an attempt to enter into some sort of an agreement that may postpone the inevitable happening. Eventually rage and anger are replaced with a great sense of loss, and the dying person sinks into a depression. If the patient has had enough time and has been given help in the previous stages, he or she will eventually reach a stage of acceptance. This is not a happy stage, but rather one devoid of feelings. It is as if the pain is gone, and the struggle is over. This is the time when the family may need more help and understanding than the patient.

Not all dying persons reach all the stages, nor do they necessarily proceed in that order. Some researchers have become concerned about some rather unexpected reactions to Kubler-Ross's research. As her ideas have become popular among health professionals, as well as the dying and their family members, the stages are in danger of becoming a self-fulfilling prophecy (Kalish, 1976). Some hospital staff have been observed trying to manipulate their dying patients through the five stages, and patients occasionally become concerned that they are not progressing adequately. Further, there is the moral issue of whether acceptance is, in fact, the proper way to die. Some say the message summed up in the lines by Dylan Thomas "Do not go gently into that good night . . . Rage, rage against the dying of the light" is a preferable attitude to hold toward impending death.

As we have become more aware of the negative aspects of denying death, new options for the dying have begun to be explored. Already successful in London and recently operative in the United States and Canada is the hospice. The hospice movement began in England in 1967 with the opening of St. Christopher's Hospice. The basic hospice philosophy is to reduce the pain and discomfort of the dying person and allow the patient to die easily and at peace, surrounded by people who care. The article by Saunders describes the philosophy and format of St. Christopher's Hospice.

Kubler-Ross believes that if people do not accept their own mortality, they will lead empty, purposeless lives. By behaving as if we will live forever, we inevitably fail to reach out to other human beings, and the potential for growth within ourselves is lost.

REFERENCES

Aries, Philippe. 1962. *Centuries of childhood: A social history of family life.* New York: Alfred A. Knopf.

Blauner, Robert. 1966. Death and social structure. *Psychiatry* 29:378–394.

Kalish, Richard A. 1976. Death and dying in a social context. Pp. 483–507 in Robert H. Binstock and Ethel Shanas (eds.), *Handbook of aging and the social sciences.* New York: Van Nostrand Reinhold.

Kubler-Ross, Elizabeth. 1970. *On death and dying.* New York: Macmillan. 1975. *Death: The final stage of growth.* Englewood Cliffs, N.J.: Prentice-Hall.

Sudnow, David. 1967. *Passing on: The social organization of dying.* Englewood Cliffs, N.J.: Prentice-Hall.

Attitudes toward Death

E. MANSELL PATTISON

As early death has been largely conquered by medical science and as life expectancy has increased, death has become less visible but more taboo. Just as sex was the forbidden subject of the Victorian era, death is the unmentionable topic of the twentieth century. There are four distinct cultural attitudes toward death: death denying, death defying, death desiring, and death accepting. The first is the most common in our time. We must recognize and accept our natural ambivalence, our feelings of love and hate, toward the dying and become death accepting before we can come to terms with our own human nature.

When I was ten years old I lived on a farm. One day I found a bird with a broken wing. I took the bird home, nursed it, fed it, gave it care and attention for three days. Then it died. I cried. I put the bird in a shoe box and buried it in the garden. The grave was marked with a stick, covered with flowers. For a day or so I mourned and then the bird was forgotten. Except that *I* remember.

When I was twenty years old, I went to work as an orderly in a hospital. My first night at work I was summoned to assist another orderly on a "man's job." The two of us walked briskly onto the ward. All the doors were shut, visitors gone, the nurses standing hushed at their station. They nodded silently toward a closed door. My colleague and I stepped inside the room. There lay the emaciated corpse of an old man. We pulled the tubes and needles. Taped the eyes and mouth. Stuffed the orifices. Tied the limbs to body. Placed the corpse on a stretcher. We peered out the door. The nurse nodded—no one in sight. We whisked down the hall to a waiting elevator, held for us to arrive. Down to the basement, into the morgue. Then back to the ward. Everyone was moving about—lively, animated, busy at the job of healing people. The vile threat had been removed.

Two years later I was working in a mortuary. It was time to move a casket from the "preparation" room. We adjusted the clothes. Coiffured the hair. Added some touches of cosmetic. Folded the hands. "Ah, so lifelike," we said. Up to the "slumber" room. We adjusted the lights, the piped-in music, and the temperature. Sprayed the room with subtle perfume. And drew a "slumber veil" across the casket so the "loved one" was not seen too clearly, nor touched. Perfect.

A decade later Grandfather died. He lay in the mortuary. We arrived

SOURCE: From E. Mansell Pattison, *The Experience of Dying*, © 1977, pp. 5–17. Reprinted by permission of Prentice-Hall, Inc., Englewood Cliffs, New Jersey.

with the children, all small and not acculturated to civilized ways. As we walked in the entrance, they loudly pointed to the pretty flowers, stained glass windows, and marble statuary. What a nice place! The receptionist frowned at our entrance. We found the right room with relatives already there. "Where's Grandpa?" the kids asked. There were silent nods toward the casket. "Oh, here he is!" Curious childish fingers pulled away the "slumber" veil. They patted his chest. Pulled his nose. Felt his whiskers. "It's Grandpa, alright. But it's just his body—he isn't here." And with that, the little cousins fell to childish chatter and games.

In these personal vignettes I have tried to capture the contradictory attitudes that we face in our culture: the inevitable experience of death, loss, and grief; the avoidance and seclusion of death; the denial of the reality of death through almost macabre rituals; and finally the profound simplicity that death is.

Why are we concerned about issues of death and dying? There are two reasons.

First, death is a major life event that stresses our human existence. The failure to cope appropriately with death and to resolve the subsequent loss and grief process is likely to lead to emotional maladaptation (Bowlby, 1960). The loss of a parent when one is a child is a severe stress that may profoundly compromise healthy development (Furman, 1974; Moriarty, 1967). The loss of important people in adulthood may precipitate not only depression but other neurotic and psychotic reactions (Carr et al., 1970). The loss of a spouse in old age is likely to precipitate illness and death in the surviving spouse (Parkes, 1972). In his book *Death and Neurosis* Meyer (1975) summarizes the cumulative evidence that failure to cope with death is the seedbed of neurosis. It is not that death per se is neurotogenic. In his classic article on the importance of grief, Lindemann (1944) reported that it was the *failure* to mourn appropriately that precipitated neurotic reactions. But we cannot appropriately cope with death unless we can face death.

Second, just as death has been ignored, so have the dying. "There's nothing more I can do for you. You're going to die." So said the doctor, leaving the patient, family, nurses, and friends in a dilemma of confusion. Our culture has made the process of dying a medical problem, yet no one takes responsibility. A general practitioner, Dr. Merrill Shaw (1956), who was himself dying of rectal cancer, pinpoints the problem:

> The period of inactivity after a patient learns that there is no hope for his condition can be a period of great productivity. I regard myself as fortunate to have had this opportunity for a "planned exit." Patients who have been told there is no hope need help with their apprehension. Any doctor forfeits his priesthood of medicine if, when he knows his patient is beyond help, he discharges his patient to his own services. Then the patient needs his physician

more than anyone else does. The doctor who says merely, "I'll drop in to see you once in a while, there's nothing more I can do," is of no use to the patient. For the patient goes through a period of unnecessary apprehension and anxiety.

The problem is this: death has been taboo in our culture.

Cultural Antecedents

Death has not always been taboo in Western culture. Even a casual visit to Europe reveals death in paintings, statues, carvings, graves, and monuments—a historical litany of Western civilization's preoccupation with death throughout our cultural history. Aries (1974) has recounted this history, rooted in the Judeo-Christian heritage, in which the mortality of the human being stood center stage in the life of the culture. But as Feifel (1963) has documented, since about 1900 there was increasing denial of mortality and the reality of death. So by midcentury, death was no longer admitted into the thought of civilized people. Death had become taboo.

What factors may account for this process? Parsons and Lidz (1967) point out that after 1900, in America at least, there were no more wars fought on our soil. We did not immediately observe and experience violent death. Public executions were banned. Medical science conquered the infectious diseases of childhood, so the threat of infant mortality was largely removed. We expect that all of our children will live to be adults, and we do not need to sire ten children that two might survive. Trauma of childhood and the fatal dangers of frontier life have vanished. Whereas in 1900 people died at age forty and many children were orphaned, parents now live to age seventy or more and usually see their grandchildren. Yet our aged and feeble no longer live in the family home or neighborhood but are sequestered in retirement colonies, decaying neighborhoods, or nursing homes. We are a culture of youth; the aged and dying do not exist. Thus there is much in our culture that removes death and dying from the midst of our everyday life.

But that which is taboo and repressed reemerges in perverse forms to create neurosis. In Victorian times, cultural denials and taboos centered on sexuality. As Freud so aptly observed, sexuality then emerged in perverse form and became the nidus for the generation of psychopathology. Sexuality has been readmitted into human discourse, but death has become the taboo. As a result, we see preoccupation with death in its perverse forms. The lurid desecration of death in pornographic form that dehumanizes dying is seen in movies such as *The Loved One*, *Straw Dogs*, and *Clockwork Orange*. The intimate close-up gore of brutal killing is the nightly fare on television prime time. Thus we do not escape death, but it returns as a preoccupation of our culture, which both denies death and is obsessed by its observation. It is not surprising then to find much scientific data to support the notion that death is neurotogenic in our time. The problem is succinctly put by anthropologist Sir Geoffrey Gorer (1965):

> Pornography would appear to be a concomitant of prudery . . . pornography has been concerned with sexuality . . . copulation and birth were the unmentionables . . . in the twentieth century, however, death has become more and more unmentionable *as a natural process* . . . preoccupation with such processes is morbid and unhealthy, to be discouraged by all and punished in the young. . . . If we dislike the modern pornography of death, then we must give back to death—natural death—its parade and publicity, readmit grief and mourning.

Beside the return of the repressed, other factors bring death back into our attention. First, medical technology has prolonged the process of dying. For the first time in history we have made it possible for people to live on borrowed time. Cancer can be suppressed with drugs, hearts transplanted, kidneys supplanted by dialysis machines. The dying process can be weeks, months, or even many years (Crane, 1975; Ford, 1970).

Second, man is faced with the threat of massive nuclear annihilation. As Robert Lifton (1964) notes:

> In every age man faces a pervasive theme which defies his engagement and yet must be engaged. In Freud's day it was sexuality and moralism. Now it is technological violence and absurd death. We do well to name the threat and analyze its components.

Third is the crisis of meaning. The challenge of traditional values and their religious supports has left many facing an existential dilemma of providing purpose to keep on living. The towering existential philosophers of our time, Camus and Sartre, have labeled life absurd. The challenge they throw down to modern man is stark: the only important question is whether there is reason to live.

Without an ultimate justification for life, the only value becomes living itself. Thus we see an almost panicky tenacity to hold onto one's life. It is no longer fashionable to give one's life for family, friend, neighbor, or country. Life is all I have, so I had better hang on to it.

As a result, modern medicine has become servant of the culture, devoted to the preservation of life at all cost, and death is viewed as an intrusion onto the medical scientific quest for eternal existence. The maintenance of life per se as our ultimate value is reflected in science fiction, in movies such as *2001*, and the cryogenic societies that would hope to preserve life through freezing and then the wait to thaw! The denial of death is inadvertently well stated by an eminent medical scientist (Goldfarb, 1965) as follows:

> I, myself, tend to adhere to the concept of death as an accident, and therefore find it difficult to reconcile myself to it for myself or for others . . . people do not forgive themselves easily for having failed to save their own or other's lives.

Cultural Attitudes

Our behavior throughout life is determined by our culture, and the same is no less true of our behavior toward death. Primitive cultures do not perceive death as a final biological state. The worlds of the gods, both in heaven and hell, exist in a continuum with the middle world of mortals. Life and death are part of an eternal process. Mortal man is part of the larger ongoing continuity of existence. Consider this African poem:

> Listen more often
> To things than to beings;
> The fire's voice is heard
> Hear the voice of water.
> Hear in the wind
> The bush sob
> It is the ancestor's breath.
> Those who have died have never left,
> They are in the woman's breast
> They are in the wailing child
> And in the kindling firebrand
> The dead are not under the earth.
> They are in the forest, they are in the home
> The dead are not dead.

In contrast, Western culture holds death to be an inevitable termination and destruction of existence.

At present we may observe four distinct different cultural attitudes toward death: death denying, death defying, death desiring, and death accepting.

The *death-denying* attitude has been most common and pervasive in our time. I have already noted many manifestations of death denial in our culture. It is curious to note that the care of the dying has been handed over to the medical profession and to hospitals. Yet Feifel (1965) reports that physicians deny death more vigorously than the general populace. Even psychiatrists, who are trained for sensitivity to human emotion, avoid death; they just use more abstruse mechanisms. Thus Wahl (1958) notes:

> It is interesting also to note that anxiety about death, when it is noted in the psychiatric literature, is usually described solely as a derivative and secondary phenomenon, often as a more easily endurable form of the "castration fear" . . . it is important to consider if these formulations also subserve a defensive need on the part of psychiatrists themselves.

We can observe the threat of death in many psychotherapy settings: how a patient's threat of suicide cows the therapist; how the psychiatrist puts him- or herself in physical danger with a violent patient; the therapist's reluctance to allow a patient to expose the deepest threatening fantasies and psychotic thoughts that intimate the annihilation of the self. How often as a young psychiatrist I despaired in my work in prison, facing men with life sentences or, worse, sentenced to death. How did one, did I, relate to dead lives?

The denial of death is seen in hospitals—in the apprehension and avoidance of the dying patient. Often hospital staff suggest that it is unwise to talk to dying patients about their dying because the patients will become nervous, upset, hurt, anxious, or injured. Kübler-Ross (1970) reports that only 2 percent of dying patients rejected the opportunity to discuss their dying, but that many staff became emotionally upset. Similarly, I have found that most dying patients are not only willing but want to share their dying experience with others. It is rare that such discussions upset the dying person. But I have seen many nurses, physicians, and mental-health personnel become nervous, anxious, upset, and distraught. At times they angrily denounce my inhumaneness for frank discussions with the dying. May it be that the fear and anger is not concern for the patient, but a projection of the anxieties that professional persons experience about their own feelings of death?

The *death-defying* attitude is rooted in our traditional Judeo-Christian heritage. St. Paul sounds the keynote: "Death is swallowed up in victory. O death, where is thy sting? O grave, where is thy victory?" (I Corinthians 15:54). The poet Dylan Thomas is more poignant in his themes like "Death, Be Not Proud" or "Rage, rage against the dying of the light." We can all recall many instances of people who have fought for causes, ideologies, families, or countries in defiance of the fact that they die in the doing.

The *death-desiring* attitude is much more common in our culture than we admit, for it is not considered acceptable to desire death either for oneself or for others.

A desire for death may be a means to resolve life conflicts, or to kill oneself for revenge or retaliation. We are now aware that there are multiple overlapping motivations for suicide and degrees of death desiring (Wolman, 1976). Along a related line there are neurotic and psychotic fantasies of a different life in death. For example, one may seek reunion with loved ones in the magical union of death. In Othello and in Aida, the lovers will be reunited eternally in death.

Still a different death-desiring attitude is found in those who are severely debilitated, disabled, and the unhappy elderly, who seek release and escape from the misery of their lives. And there are those happy people who have reached fulfillment and look toward death as the satisfying and acceptable end of their lives.

We also must be aware that there are many circumstances where we may desire the death of others. We may have a humane desire to see the end of suffering and misery. We may desire relief from personal, emotional, and financial responsibilities and burdens. There may be people who are a source of anger, frustration, or resentment, whose death may be a welcome termination of relation. Death-desiring attitudes and emotions may be neither neurotic nor abnormal. Yet this may still remain the most taboo attitude toward death.

Death-accepting attitudes place death in perspective as a part of life and integral to existence. Death as the concluding episode of one's life plan is eloquently described by Bertrand Russell (1956):

> An individual's human existence should be like a river—small at first, narrowly contained within its banks, and rushing passionately past boulders and over waterfalls. Gradually, the river grows wider, the banks recede, the waters flow more quietly, and in the end, without any visible break, they become merged in the sea, and painlessly lose their individual being.

This might be termed "death as conclusion." But this is a romantic view, for as Schneidman (1971) points out, this view makes accidental death or early death a tragic and nonnatural event—the romantic progress of life has been interrupted!

A very different death-accepting attitude might be called *death integrating*. Existential thought has placed death at the center stage of life. Death is not physiological termination. It is our frail mortality. It is not the threat of body stoppage. It is threat of one's own nonbeing. Heidegger puts it that we are faced with a basic anxiety about our authentic potentiality for being-in-the-world. If we do not face and come to terms with the existential frailty of our existence—the fact that we plan life trajectories that will lead us to old age . . . when our life may be snuffed out at any moment—if we deny this fragile life, we become vulnerable to all the neurotic processes of denial. In *Life against Death* Norman O. Brown (1959) argues that neurosis arises from our incapacity to die. Once freed from avoiding our own nonbeing in death, we can joyously embrace life. In his book *Denial of Death*, Ernest Becker (1973) states that it is the resignation to and acceptance of our limited existence that is the central task for achieving maturity. Jacques Choron (1964) notes: "Postponement of death is not a solution to the problem of the fear of death . . . there still will remain the fear of dying prematurely." So it is not the integration of death of which we speak, but the integration of a sense of being-meaning that is at issue. As Becker (1973) says:

> Fear of death is not the only motive of life; heroic transcendence, victory over evil for mankind as a whole, for unborn generations, consecration of one's existence to higher meanings—these motives are just as vital and they are what give the human animal his nobility even in the face of his animal fears.

Becker suggests what has been a traditional religious solution, and one that finds its expression in the Judeo-Christian heritage: "For whosoever will save his life shall lose it; and whosoever will lose his life for my sake shall find it" (Matthew 16:25). Death integration is perhaps then not an individual psychological solution, but can be integrated only within a transcendent belief.

In summary, cultural attitudes toward death rarely exist in pure form, any more than personal attitudes exist in pure form. Indeed, since the mid-1960s we have moved from a rather death-denying culture toward a more open death-integrating one. Perhaps it is the complexity and constant shift of many attitudes toward death of which we must be aware.

Death Denial and Death Acceptance—a Dialectic

Who is afraid to die? What is it we fear? We are asked to understand and respond to the dying person. Yet to understand another person in his or her life requires that we understand that same conflict, same feeling, same situation, located within ourselves—for all humans partake of universal feelings and reactions. To understand dying in others demands that we deal with dying within ourselves.

Freud (1915) suggested that the unconscious does not recognize its own death, but regards itself as immortal: "It is indeed impossible to imagine our own death; and whenever we attempt to do so, we can perceive that we are, in fact, still present as spectators." In this Freudian view, we fear the unknownness of death. On the other hand, more recent observations suggest that death anxiety does not pertain to physical death but is the primordial feeling of helplessness and abandonment. The fear of the unknown of death is the unknown of annihilation of self, of being, of identity. Leveton (1965) describes this sense of "ego chill" as "a shudder which comes from the sudden awareness that our nonexistence is entirely possible."

This unknown threat cannot be processed within the self. Robert Jay Lifton (1964) has graphically described his personal reactions while interviewing the survivors of the Hiroshima atomic bomb. At first he was profoundly shocked and emotionally spent as he sensed his own human frail mortality, but as the interviews went on he found himself becoming detached as a scientific observer. He did not become insensitive but found himself inexorably developing a sense of "psychic closing off"—the development of a distance between the experiencers of death and his own personal relationship to death—for him to function effectively as a physician and as a scientist.

This personal account from Lifton is a critical observation: *we cannot for long look at our own nonbeing.* In fact, the central theme of Becker in *Denial of Death* is that life is an unordered chaos in which there is no predictability or sense. To survive, says Becker, the human organism *must repress* his or her sense of frailty, must submerge his or her awareness of mortality, and must construct a mythology of existence—which we call our mature sense of reality. Reality is *not* out there to be rationally comprehended. Reality is the construction we make to exist. To sense our own nonbeing is perhaps vital, but we cannot for long look directly at it. It is like the sun. We can only look directly at the sun for a few fleeting blinding moments at one time. For the most part, we look at the sun indirectly. In the same fashion, we look at our own nonbeing indirectly.

What is the practical import here? To talk to, work with, and understand the dying person evokes intense personal feelings. As Weisman (1970) notes, the care of the dying arouses some of the most pervasive fears of all people—extinction, helplessness, abandonment, disfigurement, and loss of self-esteem. We could not long survive, much less serve our fellow beings if we had to struggle continuously at the raw edge of our own existence.

Too often we have encouraged the denial of death—but the remedy is not a defenseless wallowing in the blinding acuteness of our own mortality. Rather, there is that psychic distance to be achieved— *compassionate detachment. Appropriate repression* of our death anxieties is a necessary prelude to effective professional care. Here I mean the capacity to bring into consciousness the fundamental awareness of death anxiety, feeling acceptably comfortable about one's own finite mortality, and thus able to allow the fundamental concerns to lie out of conscious sight most of the time. When necessary, or when evoked by life circumstance, one can then respond without conflict to the stirrings of one's own concerns about death.

Professional Distortions

A posture of compassionate detachment is difficult to attain and maintain. Over the past decade of professional interest in the problems of the dying, two major distortions of compassionate detachment have emerged.

The first is *exaggerated detachment.* Instead of denial of death in a gross and crass manner, emotional distance is achieved through professionalization. Dying is made an object of scientific inquiry. Death is made a disease—a thing. Death is no longer a threat because it can be therapized. So we can now turn to the "right treatment of dying." Dying is no longer a subjective experience of persons but an impersonal objective external problem. Such people often demand that specific regimens be set up for dying persons. People are now supposed to die in the "right way." They look for logical and rigid patterns of progression of dying so that they can rigorously follow the scientific course of action. I have had such professional people seek my consultation because dying persons were not in the right stage, not reacting the right way, or otherwise failing to respond to the professional and scientific treatment of the dying. In a word, dying is made acceptable through professional *objectification.*

The second distortion is *exaggerated compassion.* Here, instead of separation from the dying there is fusion with the dying. Such professionals not only identify with the dying person but may seek in their work to undo past guilts, relieve past shame, restore personal self-esteem, rework their own prior death experiences, anticipate their own death anxieties. They live, die, and are reborn with each dying person. Such vicarious identification is also a defense. The dying person is me . . . but then the miraculous occurs, for when the dying is dead, I am still alive. I have beaten death after all. Such professionals often become personally and professionally overinvolved in the life of the dying person. I have seen these persons angrily denounce any distance or detachment they see in others who work with the dying. How can you have compassion if you are not totally involved? Here, dying is made acceptable through professional *subjectification*.

Love and Hate: The Ambivalence Toward Dying

In the recent past we have hated and despised death—and now at least some would have us welcome, embrace, even love death! I am reminded of those who hate or love the fact that they were born. But birth *is*, we had no say. Even so, death *is*, we have no say. Feelings of love or hate are irrelevant. Life *is*.

However, feelings of love and hate are most relevant to people. All important relationships are a mixture of love and hate. No important person fails to disappoint and frustrate us. The very depth of loving importance increases the probability of disappointment. For the most part we accept and tolerate the negative hateful emotions and tend to experience in our consciousness only the positive ones. But it is clear that all of us harbor love and hate together. Our capacity to accept, tolerate, and even utilize the ambivalence of our feelings is one major hallmark of emotional maturity.

The importance of universal ambivalence is central to our attitude toward the dying. The dying person who is important to us evokes not only feelings of tender loving compassion but also feelings of anger, despair, frustration, disappointment, even hatred. If we expect that loving feelings are the only dimension of caring for the dying, we shall delude ourselves and fail to cope appropriately with the arousal of hateful feelings.

The process of appropriate grief and mourning revolves around the successful recognition and integration of our love and hatred toward the dead person we mourn. Thus our attitudes toward dying are rooted in our attitudes toward ourselves and toward others; an integration of the likeable and the despicable. So it turns out that the process of dying is a part of our life that can be best understood as we understand the nature of human nature.

REFERENCES

Aries, P., *Western Attitudes toward Death: From the Middle Ages to the Present*. Baltimore: Johns Hopkins Press, 1974.

Becker, E., *The Denial of Death*. New York: Macmillan, 1973.

Bowlby, J., Separation anxiety: A critical review of the literature. *Journal of Child Psychology and Psychiatry* 1:251–275, 1960.

Brown, N. O., *Life against Death*. Middletown, Conn.: Wesleyan University Press, 1959.

Carr, A., D. Peretz, B. Schoenberg, and A. Kutscher, eds., *Loss and Grief: Psychological Management in Medical Practice*. New York: Columbia University Press, 1970.

Choron, J., *Modern Man and Mortality*. New York: Macmillan, 1964.

Crane, D., Decisions to treat critically ill patients. A comparison of social versus medical considerations. *Health and Society* 53:1–34, 1975.

Feifel, H., The function of attitudes towards death, in *Death and Dying: Attitudes of Patient and Doctor*. New York: Group for the Advancement of Psychiatry, 1965.

———, The taboo on death. *American Behavioral Scientist* 6:66–67, 1963.

Ford, A. M., Casualties of our time. *Science* 167:256–263, 1970.

Freud, S., Thoughts for the times on war and death. Collected papers, vol. 4. London: Hogarth, 1915.

Furman, E., A *Child's Parent Dies*. New Haven: Yale University Press, 1974.

Gatch, M., *Death: Meaning and Mortality in Christian Thought and Contemporary Culture*. New York: Seabury Press, 1969.

Goldfarb, I. A., Discussion, in *Death and Dying: Attitudes of Patient and Doctor*. New York: Group for the Advancement of Psychiatry, 1965.

Gorer, G., The pornography of death, in *Encounters*, eds. S. Spender, I. Kristol, M. Lasky. New York: Simon & Schuster, 1965.

Grotjahn, M., Ego identity and the fear of death and dying. *Journal of the Hillside Hospital* 9:147–155, 1960.

Heilbruun, G., The basic fear. *Journal of the American Psychoanalytic Association* 3:447–466, 1955.

Kubler-Ross, E., *On Death and Dying*. New York: Macmillan, 1970.

Leveton, A., Time, death, and the ego-chill. *Journal of Existentialism* 6:69–80, 1965.

Lifton, R. J., On death and death symbolism: The Hiroshima disaster. *Psychiatry* 27:191–210, 1964.

Lindemann, E., Symptomatology and the management of acute grief. *American Journal of Psychiatry* 101:141–148, 1944.

Meyer, J. E., *Death and Neurosis*. New York: International Universities Press, 1975.

Moriarty, D. M., *The Loss of Loved Ones*. Springfield, Ill.: C C Thomas, 1967.

Parkes, C. M., *Bereavement: Studies of Grief in Adult Life*. New York: International Universities Press, 1972.

Parsons, T., and V. Lidz, Death in American society, in *Essays in Self-Destruction*, ed. E. S. Scheidman. New York: Science House, 1967.

Russell, B., *Portraits from Memory*. New York: Simon & Schuster, 1956.

Schneidman, E. S., On the deromanticization of death. *American Journal of Psychotherapy* 25:4–17, 1971.

Shaw, M., Dying of cancer. Horror attitudes most harmful. *Seattle Times*, March 24, 1956.

Wahl, C. W., The fear of death. *Bulletin of the Menninger Clinic* 22:214–223, 1958.

Weisman, A.D., Misgivings and misconceptions in the psychiatric care of the terminal patient. *Psychiatry* 33:67–81, 1970.

Wolman, B. B., *Between Survival and Suicide*. New York: Gardner Press, 1976.

Socialization for Impending Death in a Retirement Village

VICTOR W. MARSHALL

This article examines how people legitimate death, so that they can continue the routines of everyday life. The author combined participant observation with intensive interviewing of the residents of a retirement community to analyze their attitudes toward death. He found that people were prepared for and even desired death if they felt they had fulfilled their obligations in life. Deaths occurred frequently in the community, and they were observed quietly and discreetly, allowing people to go on with the business of living. Day-to-day life provided residents with role models with which to anticipate their own dying. When fear was expressed, it was not of death per se but rather of dying ignobly. The author concludes that impending death can, under the proper conditions, be a matter-of-fact aspect of human life.

Sociologists and gerontologists have frequently noted that the necessity for learning new social roles continues throughout the life cycle. Thus Riley et al. (1969) argue that, in addition to myriad small adjustments, "major adjustments are also required as the occupational role gives way to one of leisure-in-retirement; as the combined roles of spouse-and-parent shift, after the children leave home, to the role of spouse without parental responsibilities, and later to widowhood; as relationships to descendant kin proliferate to grandchildren, great-grandchildren, and numerous in-laws; and as preparation is made for ultimate death." This paper focuses on the last of these "major adjustments"—"preparation . . . for ultimate death"—and argues that congregate living facilities can provide optimal settings for this form of socialization. It views a retirement village as a relatively "non-total" (Goffman, 1961) "people-processing institution" in which residents themselves devise means for their collective socialization for impending death. I suggest that we can learn from this setting about the conditions favorable to successful socialization.

Legitimation of Death

In their most general terms, the arguments which follow stem from the perspective of Berger and Luckmann (Berger, 1969; Berger and Luck-

SOURCE: Victor W. Marshall, "Socialization for Impending Death in a Retirement Village," *American Journal of Sociology* 80 [1975]: 1 1124–44. Reprinted by permission of the University of Chicago Press. © The University of Chicago.

mann, 1967) concerning the symbolic ordering of biography. As these authors put it (1967, p. 100): "The symbolic universe provides order for the subjective apprehension of biographical experience. . . . the individual passing from one biographical phase to another can view himself as repeating a sequence that is given in the 'nature of things,' or in his own 'nature.' That is, he can assure himself that he is living 'correctly.' . . . As the individual looks back upon his past life, his biography is intelligible to him in these terms." In short, the individual is able to view his own identity as nonproblematical if it can be incorporated within shared, taken-for-granted reality and viewed as a typical life in a typical situation. Moreover, the individual is fundamentally motivated to seek an incorporation of his biography into taken-for-granted social reality: to do otherwise would subject him to the anomy or meaninglessness of a nonvalidated (by others) reality (Berger and Luckmann, 1967, pp. 64, 102; Berger 1969, pp. 23–24; McHugh, 1968, pp. 50–53).[1] The individual, then, seeks to *legitimate* his biography in terms of socially shared reality or, in Berger and Luckmann's words, the "symbolic universe," which constitutes the taken-for-granted reality of the individual and his fellowmen. Death postulates a key problem for the legitimation of biography (Berger and Luckmann, 1967, p. 101):

> A strategic legitimating function of symbolic universes for individual biography is the "location" of death. The experience of the death of others and, subsequently, the anticipation of one's own death posit the marginal situation par excellence for the individual. Needless to elaborate, death also posits the most terrifying threat to the taken-for-granted realities of everyday life. The integration of death within the paramount reality of social existence is, therefore, of the greatest importance for any institutional order. This legitimation of death is, consequently, one of the most important fruits of symbolic universes.

Any symbolic universe may be employed in legitimating death, a process which may be seen as two-faceted, for both the death of others and the impending death of the individual must be made understandable (Berger and Luckmann, 1967, p. 101): "All legitimations of death must carry out the same essential task—they must enable the individual to go on living in society after the death of significant others and to anticipate his own death with, at the very least, terror sufficiently mitigated so as not to paralyze the continued performance of the routines of everyday life."

In 1969–70 I studied a retirement village, Glen Brae, through participant observation and intensive interviewing techniques. This setting can be viewed, at a micro level, as a small society in reference to Berger and Luckmann's discussion of the need for legitimation of death if life in society is to carry on. Moreover, this is a society in which death is prevalent and where the members, because they are in their later years, experience most poignantly the need for legitimating death. Glen Brae will be described shortly. I turn first to evidence that in such a society death does appear to be successfully legitimated for most participants.

Successful Legitimation of Death

The legitimation of death is a fairly successful accomplishment at Glen Brae. For whatever reasons, most residents of the retirement community are able to accept that death—whether that of others, their own, or both—is legitimate. I do not mean that death is viewed in isolation as a positive event (although this might be the case for some) but, rather, that it is viewed as appropriate, given contextual factors and the logical alternative—continued life. Perhaps the greatest evidence of such legitimation lies in the ease with which residents could formulate thoughts about death and dying—including their own—to me as an investigator. Certain specific indicators provide additional evidence.

The residents in the study were asked if they would like to live to be 100 years old. Of seventy-nine respondents, none answered with an unconditional yes. Conditional yes answers were given by nineteen residents,[2] while sixty gave unconditional no answers. Conditional replies indicate that the individual entertains certain formulable reasons why continued life to that age *could* be appropriate but no certainty that these reasons will obtain. Negative replies indicate that the subject can formulate no adequate or legitimate reasons why life extending to age 100 would be appropriate or more appropriate than death; they do not indicate whether continued life within that parameter is viewed as legitimate. This indicator, then, gives a very conservative measure of the legitimation of death.

Additional evidence that death is legitimated in the Glen Brae community by most residents comes from responses to three attitudinal questions.[3] The fact that these have been asked of a representative national sample by John Riley (1970; see M. Riley and Foner [1968, pp. 332–37] for additional discussion of findings) allows for comparison. Just over half of Riley's respondents were under age forty-one, but the insignificant effects of age on the responses given can be seen by comparing the overall results with those for persons age sixty-one plus (Table 1). It is clear from this table that the great majority of Glen Brae residents have legitimated death, at least in a general way, and, further, that the extent to which they have done so exceeds that found in the overall population. This is not, as far as can be ascertained, attributable to the higher educational level of the Glen Brae population. Riley found college-educated people over sixty-one less likely to agree that death always comes too soon (29 percent vs. 59 percent for those with less education), but the proportion of the college-educated group agreeing with the statement is still more than twice that for the Glen Brae residents. At Glen Brae a higher level of education is associated with a decreasing proportion of residents agreeing

TABLE 1   Comparison of Riley's Sample for Selected Indicators

	Percentage agreeing with statement		
	GLEN BRAE	RILEY, AGE 61+	TOTAL RILEY
Would you agree or disagree with the following statements?			
Death is sometimes a blessing.	98	91	89
Death is not tragic for the person who dies, only for the survivors.	91°	85	82
Death always comes too soon.	12†	51	53
Total N	79	249	1,428

°Excludes 11 "don't know" and six uncodable responses; includes 16 responses indicating that death is tragic for neither the person who dies nor the survivors (based on probing apparently not done in the Riley study).

†Excludes one "don't know" response.

that death always comes too soon, but the trend does not reach significance. Level of education makes no discernible difference in the responses to the question concerning the tragic aspect of death. We are left, then, with some indication that death is highly legitimated in this community—and with the task of seeking an explanation for this fact.

It is important to recognize that legitimation of death is not a defeat—or not necessarily so—for many residents. It can signify a genuine feeling of appropriateness, as indicated by the remarks of an eighty-one-year-old widow when asked how old she would like to live to be: "Heavens! I've lived my life. I'd be delighted to have it end. The sooner the better. I nearly went with a heart attack. It would have been more convenient to go when my daughter was in ——— rather than in ———. I feel I've lived my life, and I don't want to be a care to anybody. That's why I'm glad to be here [in Glen Brae]. No, I don't want to mourn when I go. I've had a good life. It's time."

Others see little point in living longer, and death does not seem to enter into their considerations. As another resident put her response to the question "Would you like to live to be 100?": "No point. I have no one dependent on me. And I've looked after my few descendants I have. And

I haven't any great problem to resolve." This woman is eighty-eight and feels "it's time people shuffled off by 90."

Another says of her husband that he died well: "I mean he had never done anything to regret. Nothing to complete. Nothing to make right."

A woman who would like to live until "the day after tomorrow" says that, although she is "disgustingly healthy," "you get tired of the routine." These examples suggest people for whom the legitimation of biography is highly important for the legitimation of death. Death itself is not a big problem for them, except perhaps in not coming soon enough. This can be seen more clearly in the following analysis.

For a subset of the Glen Brae residents surveyed, good evidence that they have legitimated their own deaths comes from cross-tabulating their responses to two questions. These are a fixed-choice question asking the individual to estimate how old he thinks he will live to be and a direct question, "How old would you like to live to be?" The first question, involving the selection of a statement representing the respondent's estimate of how old he will live to be, produced codable data for fifty respondents. The question on how old people would like to live to be produced many "don't know" responses but codable responses for thirty-two residents. Answers were transformed into years the respondent desired to add to his present age, and then the categories were collapsed. The categories are somewhat different from those for the life-estimate question, because of the language employed by the residents. The difference in coding in fact enhances the utility of the data for purposes of comparison. Regrettably, the low usable response on both questions leaves us with a cross-tabulation containing only twenty-four cases (Table 2).

Of those twenty-four, only four expressed a desire to live longer than was anticipated. Kendall's rank-order correlation test shows a significant correlation of the ranking, indicating that the number of years individuals desire to live adjusts to the number they anticipate living.[4] But the more important finding lies in the display itself. At least ten respondents

TABLE 2   Desired Life Expectancy in Relation to Anticipated Life Expectancy

	Anticipated remaining years of life		
	10+	5–10	LESS THAN 5
Respondent would like to live an additional			
10+ years	3	1	0
5–9 years	3	1	3
0–4 years	1	6	6

Note.—Kendall's tau $B = .404$, significant beyond .003. The selectivity on the question asking the individual to specify the number of years he would like to live suggests caution in the interpretation of this table.

indicated a desire to live less long than they anticipated living. The remaining ten individuals wished either to die at a time when they expected to or to live beyond that time.

These data provide striking evidence that, for a sizable proportion of the residents, death is legitimated as more reasonable than continued living.[5] For many, the evidence goes beyond mere acquiescence to or acceptance of impending death and indicates a positive desire for death rather than continued living beyond a specific age. This and the attitudinal indicators concerning the lack of tragedy and the blessings of death, together with the fact that no respondents expressed an unqualified desire to live to be 100, provide strong evidence that death is legitimated for many residents of Glen Brae.

The remaining sections of this paper seek to establish the importance, in providing acceptance of death, of the social organization for death and dying which is fostered at Glen Brae. This analysis is focused at the level of the community. A complementary analysis at the level of the individual in interaction with others appears elsewhere (Marshall, 1972b). My point in this paper is that the particular features of an age-segregated environment, rather than age segregation itself, significantly affect the degree of successful legitimation.

The Research Site

The data used in this analysis stem primarily from extensive field research supplemented by interviewing in the retirement village of Glen Brae (for other reports, see Marshall [1972a, 1972b, 1973a, 1973b]). This retirement community is a rambling, modern, 300-apartment structure housing about 400 residents in a campus-like setting in a suburban environment near the eastern seaboard of the United States. Residents purchase their apartments on a "life-care" principle which includes their right to receive care in an attached nursing-care facility should this become necessary. More than two-thirds of the residents were born in the state where they now live or in a neighboring one. Their age ranges from sixty-four to ninety-six, the average age being eighty. As in most similar communities, they are educationally privileged, with less than one-fifth having no more than a high school education. By major breadwinner, 58 percent of the sample (which is representative) are from business and 38 percent from professional families. Their religious adherence is mixed but almost exclusively Protestant. Fully 78 percent are female; 28 percent are married, 46 percent widowed, and 27 percent single (77 percent of the males but only 15 percent of the females are married; all other males are widowed, while about one-third of the females were never married).

As it has been noted that retirement communities tend to have a natural history and a life cycle of their own (Rosow, 1966; Carp, 1972), it is important to note that at the time these data were gathered the community was moving from its fifth to its sixth year. The "sea of mud" phase (Rosow, 1966) which began the life of the community was over. My description of the development and functioning of institutions within the community for socialization for impending death is thus based not only on extensive interviewing (an average of three hours per respondent) and observational data gathering but also on a reconstruction from interview material and documents available to me.

Much of orderly social behavior depends on common definitions and assumptions about the location of events in time (Moore, 1963, p. 8; Lyman and Scott, 1970, pp. 194–99). I am speaking of time not as a boundary condition but as a sequence of activities. Moore (1963) speaks of the "timing" of organizational life, referring to the synchronization, sequencing, and frequency of activities. Lyman and Scott (1970, p. 195; see also Calkins, 1970; Gustafson, 1972) speak of the pace and sequence of temporal orderings. At Glen Brae time is structured so as to be both full and involving the residents. In large measure, Glen Brae residents structure their own time. The lives they lead are worked out by themselves instead of being structured for them by the administration.

The daily routine of living at Glen Brae is broken up by mealtime, but meals are not highly structured. Individuals dine at tables of their choice and at times of their choosing during extensive dining hours. They may also dine in their own kitchen-equipped apartments or in a snack bar. In the dining room, meals are served by waitresses; this, coupled with the freedom to choose one's table partners, leads to broad-ranging and extensive informal interaction. A hostess will introduce newcomers or isolates who might wish to share a table with another resident. Varying table sizes and freedom to choose one's companions encourage the residents to treat dining as a social occasion.[6] As meals are paid for in the rental package, it is also a simple and inexpensive matter to arrange a small gathering in an apartment for a drink or two before dinner. In proximity to the dining room are the residents' library and a lounge, which provide additional social opportunities.

Dining arrangements are paradigmatic of the informal social organization of Glen Brae. Recreational pursuits are similarly flexible. Throughout the day one will see residents busy at lawn bowls or shuffleboard, swimming, engaged in bridge games in the many lounges, or tending their small flower gardens outside their apartments. The sameness of daily life is broken on a regular basis by activities which, though routinized, are scheduled at a different pace. These include concerts, movies, and lectures. These activities, which provide a range of social opportunities, are planned by the residents themselves, through their own "house government," the Forum.

The Forum itself provides another opportunity for residents to initiate their own form of social organization in the community. It meets annually and at other times according to need, and its many committees are active throughout the year.

Not the least important of the Forum-initiated activities is a "corridor-chairman" system. For each corridor in the village the Forum appoints one individual to act as "den mother." This person checks the health status of each resident on his or her corridor each day and can mobilize formal and informal community support when needed. Attempts are made to incorporate isolates. Particular watchfulness is exercised in situations of potential crisis, such as the death of a spouse or friend; thus the corridor-chairman system is able to act as a kind of informal "widow-to-widow" crisis intervention system (Silverman and Englander, 1973). In a general way the system serves to define the atmosphere of the community as one of mutual support.

A resident newspaper, the *Glen Call*, is published quarterly, providing a calendar of upcoming events, a commentary on past events, and an opportunity for the community's poets, gossips, and social critics to develop a sense of community. An article in the *Glen Call* illustrates the informal character of social activities at Glen Brae: "July and August are somnolent months at Glen Brae, a marking-time period for those who spend summer here, a time for friendly games of cards, swimming and bowling for those who are athletically inclined, a time to get better acquainted with one another."

In back issues of the *Glen Call*, the origins of many regular and irregularly scheduled activities can be seen. These were not initiated by the administration to carry out an activities policy; rather, they arose over the five years during which the community of Glen Brae residents developed a reasonably full routine of activities. The Forum was itself initiated by interested residents, and many of the activities listed above are under its sponsorship. There is generally "something doing" for Glen Brae residents. Time, as a sequence of activities, is full, the pace is swift, the time between activities and events of note short. However, it is important to note that the individual resident can adapt himself freely to the temporal routines. The resident who wishes to fill his time can do so; the resident who does not wish to be active need not take part in the social activities.

Glen Brae as a Place to Die

A move to Glen Brae is the last move for most of its residents, making it a place where people go to die, although this fact might be obscured by the emphasis on living. An early issue of the *Glen Call* quotes the medical director: "Our philosophy at Glen Brae is that this is a place to come to and live; not to die. It is one of keeping residents healthy, active, virile and mentally alert."

But people do die at Glen Brae, and they go there knowing they will die there. Moreover, the move to the retirement village serves to heighten the resident's awareness of his finitude. The move is fundamentally a calculation involving the life estimate, both on the part of the resident and on the part of the management, and both parties realize this. Also, for both parties, this realization is heightened by financial factors.

Glen Brae is financed by the death of its residents, a fact which sets up an ironic conflict of interest, at least on a theoretical level.[7] An insurance company holds a mortgage on the multimillion-dollar physical plant. This is being amortized through the initial fees, or "founders' gifts," which residents pay to guarantee a lifetime lease. Monthly rates are calculated for the sole purpose of meeting operating expenses. An initial twenty-five-year mortgage was negotiated on the basis of estimated turnover of apartments; however, this estimate was overly "optimistic," as the residents did not die as quickly or frequently as anticipated. The mortgage has been rewritten on a thirty-year basis. Thus the administrators of Glen Brae can and do speak with pride of their ability to keep people alive longer than might be expected in less advantageous surroundings; but their pride must be somewhat tempered by the consequent financial difficulties.

I have no data on the basis for the initial actuarial estimates, but I suspect that the planners' "optimism" was due to a failure to take account of social class (see Mayer and Hauser, 1953) and health selection factors (Gove, 1973). The estimates for the revised thirty-year mortgage take account of the fact that "the occupants would probably exercise selection similar to that of purchasers of annuities. That is to say, an individual or couple in ill health would probably not pay the relatively large sum required as a Founders' Gift since there would be no refund in the event of their early death" (from administration records).

The chief administrator of Glen Brae attributes the unexpected longevity of its residents to two factors: freedom from worries and the availability and utilization of excellent medical care facilities, reasons that are seconded by many residents. One of them articulates well the residents' understanding of this problem: "I've heard you get such beautiful care here you haven't a chance of dying. Here's the administration wanting you to die because they want to sell apartments, and the medical staff wanting you to live."

In any case, heightened longevity can cause problems for the residents as well as for the administration, especially with the steep rise in monthly rates which has characterized the history of the community.[8] Payment of the founder's gift commits the resident to further investment of his resources in the form of the monthly rental fee. But the amount of further investment is uncertain, as it depends on relative stability or predictability of the fee and on actual life expectancy, the latter of which can be only subjectively estimated. If the Glen Brae resident greatly underestimates his life expectancy,[9] he may literally exhaust his financial resources. One resident vividly captured the dilemma as she spoke of trying to manage her limited resources: "I just got my bank statement, and it isn't too high.

I'll have to be careful from now on. If you knew how long you had [to live] you could figure it out to the cent. But you can't."

It is clear from many interviews with residents that even those with extensive personal financial resources are keenly aware of this dilemma, because they see it affecting other, less fortunate members of their community. Another resident claimed: "I think with the rapid increase in rates here that there are people in great anguish that they will not die until they've spent everything they've got—you see, if you could just make it come out even it would be very nice."

The large financial investment involved in a move to Glen Brae emphasizes subjective life expectancy and is closely related to awareness of finitude. As one resident declared, "They come here to die, you know, to spend their last days." He claims, "It's a form of insurance to come here—based on life expectancy."

Community Organization for Death and Dying

The administration has not made plans for the management of dying and death as a community event. But by the time Glen Brae had been in existence for a year, the residents had begun to organize as a community of the dying. This was expressed in a 1966 editorial in the *Glen Call* by the president of the Forum, which I cite in full:

> Most of us have been residents in Glen Brae for more than a year. We realize its present and ever increasing beauty. Friendships are being formed. Life is taking on new and important meaning. It is a rewarding way of life.
>
> And new responsibilities are ours too. Fifteen deaths have occurred to date, which was the predicted actuarial estimate.[10] The rate will increase as we grow older. With 100 new residents arriving next year[11] it is forecast that we can expect a death amongst us as frequently as one every two weeks. This is a sober thought.
>
> Our responsibility, therefore, involves a point of view, a determination. Either Glen Brae will turn into a place shrouded in a funeral parlor atmosphere of tears and perpetual sadness, or it will play its intended role—the best place to be when crises occur. It is suggested that each of us look toward the future and be prepared, that we respect the faith of others, the wishes of the survivor, and above all else that we reduce to a minimum the prolongation of sorrow, the discussion of pain, loss, tragedy. It is up to us, not management, to make Glen Brae the haven we desire.

This early statement characterizes the present treatment of death at Glen Brae, that treatment being informal and resident-initiated social organization for death and dying. Deaths at Glen Brae are marked only by a discreet notice placed on the bulletin board and a name-only obituary listing in the *Glen Call*.

Funerals are held elsewhere, and survivors make every effort to prevent their grief from casting shadows on their fellow residents. A resident whose husband is still alive says, "This angers me here—that there is so little external appearance of grieving. This angered me ever since I came; that people would lose a spouse, and in most cases go along doing interesting things."

But I would judge that the majority of residents approve of the low-key management of death and grief. In the words of one, "Here we are in the midst of death, so to speak, because you see notices often. I think death is very philosophically treated here." Another resident maintains that when a spouse dies, the widow takes it "very well. [Other] people rally round—make dates for lunch with them. It's wonderful how widows don't have to move."

May (1967, p. 58) has written of the effects of death on the human community:

> The awareness of death also has another value, and this is that it is the ultimate source of human humility. The fact that you and I at some time will die puts us, in the last analysis, in the same boat with every other man, free or enslaved, male or female, child or adult. The facing of death is the strongest motive, and indeed requirement, for learning to be fellow men. . . . in the long run, we are all in the same boat. This is what Theseus meant in Sophocles' play *Oedipus at Colonus* when he said: "I know that I am only a man, and I have no more to hope for in the end than you have."

The fact that all at Glen Brae are approaching death seems indeed to be a humanizing factor. Most residents would agree with May as he continues: "[Death] places us all in need of mercy and forgiveness by the others, and makes us all participate in the human drama in which no man can stand above another."

The "common-fate" approach of Glen Brae residents to their impending death was perhaps helpful in their reaction to a less-than-subtle reminder of their finitude from the administration: a questionnaire given to all residents rather blatantly soliciting information as to funeral arrangements. It represents an effort to effect efficient disposition of a body upon the death of a resident in keeping with his own wishes. Detailed questions are asked concerning preference for cremation, open or closed casket, obituaries, and other pertinent matters. As far as I could tell, the questionnaire is received with humor by most residents (although some have still not completed it). For example, the following poem appeared shortly thereafter in the *Glen Call*:

Ode to Immortality

(In answer to a questionnaire about our demise. To be sung to first verse of "Yankee Doodle.")

> They asked you all to make your will.
> We hope you're well provided,
> So, favorite son, and daughter, too,
> Will not think you're one-sided.

Have you kept out your favorite dress?
Please don't let it get spattered,
And if you think you'll live too long,
Be sure it won't be tattered.

Will men be wearing double breast,
Or will they be that formal?
Or, do you think a business suit
Will make them look more normal?

Lead righteous lives, dear girls and boys
And don't commit outrageous sin,
So when you reach the pearly gates,
St. Pete will say, "Come in, come in."

At Glen Brae, as anywhere else, dying is a social event in that people die in the context of others who define their dying in ways amenable to a sociological role analysis (Glaser and Strauss, 1965, 1968, 1971). Glaser and Strauss (1968, p. 6) use the term "dying trajectory" to refer to an individual's socially defined course of dying. As socially perceived, the dimensions of dying "depend on whether the perceiver initially *defines* someone as dying and on his expectations of how that dying will proceed. Dying trajectories themselves, then, are perceived courses of dying rather than their actual courses."

In this respect we may note with Sudnow (1967, p. 62) that "the characterizations 'he is dead' and 'he is dying' . . . are the products of assessment procedures, i.e., constitute the outcomes of investigative inquiries of more or less detail, undertaken by persons more or less practically involved in the consequences that discovery of those outcomes foreseeably have."

The definition of a resident as dying has interactional consequences. At some point, the dying of a resident at Glen Brae will lead to his removal to the extended-care facility, which is somewhat separated from the residential section. However, because the extended-care facility handles many short-term emergencies, a move there is not necessarily clearly indicative to other residents of impending death. The administration has the authority to move a seriously ill resident to the extended-care facility and lease his apartment to someone else. This action usually signals impending death; sometimes it simply represents a prognosis of continued severe disability requiring extensive nursing care. The administration claims that sometimes this procedure leads the person himself to get upset and "see himself as dying."

Because I did not conduct research in the extended-care facility itself, I have not gathered data as to the definitional properties of the very last phase of dying. I feel, however, that the provision for removing the seriously ill from the residential section of Glen Brae serves the function, for other residents, of effectively removing the vivid presence of death (Friedman, 1966). This is not to say that the residents are not aware that they live in the midst of death. It would be impossible for them not to be aware of that, given the fact that many among them die. But their awareness of the hard, cold fact of death, as opposed to their strong awareness of finitude, is probably somewhat buffered by this geographical segregation of the terminally ill.

In summary, Glen Brae is a place where people go to live out the last days of their lives in a relatively problem-free environment. The cost of freedom from housekeeping and medical service worries is heightened awareness both of the dying of other members of the community and of one's own finitude. Yet the residents of Glen Brae have developed a system of mutual support and a normative pattern of behavior with regard to death. In the next section, I explore the effects of this social organization of death and dying on the anticipation of death and dying.

Plans for Death and Dying

Living in the community of the dying provides Glen Brae residents with role models with which to anticipate their own dying. Experience with the death of kin performs a similar function. There thus exists, for many residents, a conception of the appropriate course of dying. As one subject put it: "I think the thing that is feared is dying, not death. You see you want to die nobly, and you're afraid you won't be able to." Another, describing what she would like to accomplish in her future, said: "I haven't any idea. I hope to live comfortably and not be too much of a care to my children. And to die 'gracefully.' I aim to die without yelling, 'Hey, I'm going.'"

Persons highly aware of finitude live in anticipation of the most important status passage they have ever anticipated—that from life to death.[12] Living in a congregate residential facility for the aging and dying quite naturally encourages an appreciation of this fact:

> The older you get and the more you are in a place like this, and the more you see, you begin to wonder what's going to happen to you, what's in store. . . . You are aware that people are dying all the time—or that they won't last much longer. Since I've been here there have been seven people whom I knew more or less well who have gone.

> ———

> Until I was 87 [the previous year] I never thought about how old I was. Now that I am here and am with a lot of older people I know how old I am. I was busy—I just didn't think about it. I was well until I got here. Then I had accidents, was in the infirmary. Then I began to think.

When people begin to think about their impending deaths, they frequently talk with others about it; this proves beneficial in assisting them to come to terms with it. Glen Brae is, in a sense, organized to provide such assistance by encouraging a high level of social interaction which allows death to be dealt with informally. The community also, however, provides models which enable the individual to anticipate with greater clarity what his own death might be like, and thus to structure his own planning for death.

Glen Brae residents see slow and painful deaths but also quick and painless ones. One resident told me that, on learning she had a heart condition, she felt great relief, for now she could anticipate not only that she would not live too much longer (and suffer decline of mental or physical health) but also that her death would probably be the relatively painless, and frequently unexpected, death from a heart attack. Other respondents echoed the same preference for a quick and easy death:

> I hope . . . when the end comes it'll be snappy. You know, I know one person here who carries a cyanide pill with him. . . . I think he dreads a terrible siege.

> I hope that when that time comes it will come fast. I've given the doctors instructions that way.

> I don't know what I hope to accomplish. I hope for a quick death when it comes.

> I'd just like to go to sleep and never wake up. Kind of cowardly, but I haven't anyone to say goodbye to.

> Everybody wishes they'd have a sudden heart attack. No one wants a lingering incapacity.

These quotations reflect a concern not with the legitimation of death— we have seen that most residents have legitimated their impending deaths—but with the appropriate style of dying. Living in a community of the dying, these people "know" what is a good and what is a bad style of dying. Being ready to die, they want their dying to be of no trouble to themselves or to anyone else. As one widow said, "I hope I don't struggle or make a scene."

This concern has been translated by many into direct requests that heroic measures not be taken to sustain their lives. A series of meetings have been held with the medical staff to discuss a variety of issues concerning health care. A recent issue of the *Glen Call* reported:

> The problem of care in a terminal illness came up in every one of the 13 meetings. . . . No heroic measures, urged several residents, and the doctors assured us they would honor our wishes. "With or without your signature on the blanks obtainable in the clinic [for stating such wishes], we will treat each resident as we ourselves want to be treated. Only oxygen, nutrition and pain relief; no heroic measures." In this way the doctors set at rest many of our worries and fears.

Death thus becomes something that is to a certain extent planned for

(Miller, Galanter, and Pribram, 1960, pp. 141–42), and in more aspects than noted above. Approximately 90 percent of the Glen Brae residents feel that it is better to plan for death than to ignore it; a similar proportion have already made plans for their own deaths. (Riley and Foner [1968, pp. 336–37] report a similar proportion of old people feeling it is best to plan, but fewer who do.) The administration of Glen Brae requires them to do so, as we saw in the discussion of the questionnaire requesting a report of such plans. Actual plans range from spiritual ones, which, however, are infrequently mentioned at Glen Brae, to concrete details for funerals and interment:

I'm getting a stone up in the cemetery with my name on it. All but the date.

———

[My wife] and I bought a plot and a stone five or six years ago. The stone's up now.

———

I had the man from the funeral home yesterday—after Mrs. ——— [another resident] died. It gets us all scared. She's probably been dead 24 hours. They found her in her bed.

———

I joined that organization that is trying to have simple cheap observances. I've arranged to give my eyes to the cause of science. I think all of us have done something like that. I'm just changing my will.

Of the few who have not made specific plans for their impending deaths, some know that this is being attended to by their children. One widow thus turned to spiritual preparation: "[Making plans for death] is up to my family. You know, you teach your children, 'Now I lay me down to sleep. I pray the Lord my soul to keep. And if I die before I wake, I pray the Lord my soul to take.' Now that is becoming to be my prayer."

Planning at Glen Brae for death and dying takes place in an expectational milieu where impending death has been legitimated and where it is accepted that the act of dying is not supposed to be prolonged or to cause great disruption in the lives of others. The details of the ritual markings of residents' deaths have, for the most part, already been planned by themselves. While the great majority of Glen Brae residents feel that others close to them will be affected by their deaths, only about 15 percent feel that the lives of others will be seriously disrupted. In general, there seems to be an effort to minimize any hardship for others that would be caused by their deaths (just as others are relieved of the care of their parents when the parents move to a retirement community). Like the majority of Glen Brae residents, one respondent, for example, would prefer to have family members present at her death—"someone to hang on to." However, she continued, "on the other hand, there again, if I thought that my going would be terribly hard on my husband and son, then I'd want to spare them that. I'd rather die alone."

Routinization of Death

We have seen that Glen Brae is a community setting in which the residents are remarkably successful in legitimating their impending deaths. The success of Glen Brae in this regard is partially due, I have tried to show, to the low-keyed but resourceful approach taken by the residents themselves as they organize aspects of their lives so as to deal with death and dying.

The low-keyed approach, as I have demonstrated, was working out well in the early years of the community, and it continues as a deliberate practice. Thus, when a resident dies, the surviving spouse carried on: "Most of the time, outside of going to the funerals, they pick up and go on in very remarkable fashion. And they do it purposefully—for the other residents. It's very obvious."

This is not to say that conversational resources are not available when needed: "There are several people who have come here rather soon after they have lost a mate. They will speak about that, and interestingly enough when that happens you are almost under a compulsion to explain that you have lost one also." The loss of spouses is discussed, but "in a little way, not in a great way. I think most of the people here are quite reserved. Generally speaking, it's a happy attitude here." As a result, death can continue to be taken for granted by the residents: "I think it's an accepted thing. They talk about it the same as a game of bridge. I've been surprised with this group. They don't resent [death], do they? . . . It's an accepted fact. You see that when people read a notice of a death on the bulletin board. It might just as well have been about anything else."

This comment testifies to the degree of success of socialization for death within the Glen Brae community. Death is not built up into a great philosophical problem for the residents. That they will die is taken for granted by them; why they die is legitimated conversationally. Glen Brae residents learn not to make a great fuss about their dying. Thrown together with a large number of others facing the same fate, they have developed a community of tacit understanding which legitimates their impending deaths. In this sense they are like the residents of Moosehaven described by Kleemeier (1954): "As there is sickness in Moosehaven, so there is death. It comes often as an old friend. There is a comfortable matter-of-factness about the way Moosehaven people face death. There is no false sense of values which denies the inevitability of death. Nor is there morbid preoccupation with it."

At Glen Brae, I, too, could learn a great deal about dying that could be applicable to myself, despite my own long life expectancy. I learned that under favorable conditions I would be able to anticipate my own death with equanimity.

Conclusion

Speaking of death as a community event, a resident of Glen Brae said, "It's a very 'understanding' community. Everybody is in the same conditions of their lives." But that is not enough to provide socialization for impending death. To comprehend the way "understanding" becomes operative in dealing with impending death, we have to look at the way the community organizes itself to deal with death. Given the absence, in this analysis, of a wider spectrum of community settings for the aged, I can offer no definitive list of community organization variables which enhance socialization for death. However, some suggestions can be made.

A major adjustment that faces the aging individual is, I have argued, adjustment to his impending death. This is thought of as a process of legitimation, by which the aging individual comes to accept death, including his own impending death, as appropriate and nonproblematical within a shared system of meanings. To legitimate impending death in this manner allows the individual to go on living with others while facing his death with equanimity. The legitimation of death, like any process of legitimation, is best accomplished in a conversational process, for any reality is maintained primarily through conversation (Berger and Kellner, 1964).

One is also better able to face his impending death if he can observe, in a kind of role-modeling process (Hochschild, 1973, p. 80), that the deaths of his fellows occur within a taken-for-granted framework where they are considered appropriate. The rendering of death as appropriate must be a community event in which the individual can himself participate. If community involvement in the social organization for death and dying is to be developed, there must be an underlying substratum of community involvement and social interaction. Simply put, if individuals are to deal with their own deaths in their communities, they must have opportunities to interact, to talk about death and dying, and to deal with it in a process of reality construction. Hochschild (1973, p. 79) characterized another community of the aged and dying in this manner. Describing Merril Court, a low-income apartment project for the aged, she says: "[Death] was a fact of life . . . and there was no taboo against talk about it. . . . Although each individual faced death essentially alone, there was a collective concern with, as they put it, 'being ready' and facing up, a concern the young could not share with them in quite the same way. The deaths of fellow residents meant a great deal to the community and they reveal a great deal about it."

Hochschild's valuable analysis demonstrates that persons of lower-class backgrounds and low educational level can, given the appropriate community setting, successfully socialize each other for impending death. Her study thus lends indirect support to my stress on organizational factors rather than factors of selection as the important determinants of successful legitimation.[13]

Merril Court, like Glen Brae, is a community where residents maintain an active formal and informal social life with one another. Residents maintain watchfulness over their fellow community members for sickness and death (Hochschild, 1973, p. 53). Such mutual concern probably cannot be legislated by the administration of any congregate facility for the aging, but it can arise when a degree of independence and social interaction is fostered as a foundation. We have seen, for instance, that such prosaic administration policies as those concerning dining arrangements can contribute to building such a foundation.

Two additional features of Glen Brae have reinforced both the awareness of residents that they are in fact a community of the dying and their community response to this awareness. These are the financial dilemma caused by the founder's gift-rental system and the fact that residents do have options when planning the material concomitants of their deaths, such as funeral and burial. Both features involve residents in concerns about finitude and death. Both ask residents to assume some control over their final years. I noted earlier, in quoting Rollo May, that facing death is the strongest motive for learning to be a fellow man. Paradoxically, then, the financial dilemma in a way enhances the process of socialization for death, just as ensuring that one's departure from this world will cause no bother for others leads to a personal feeling that one's house is in order.

The vivid presence of death probably does not in itself make for an understanding community wherein death can be legitimated. Legitimation of death will probably occur only when community characteristics are favorable. I believe that an administration, although it cannot legitimate death, can provide conditions conducive to community involvement which in turn can provide the interactional substrata for community socialization for death. This paper cannot substantiate that argument, for to do so would require comparative data from a variety of congregate residential facilities, data which I do not have. My paper thus represents a case study in an area rich in research opportunities.

Beyond giving some suggestions as to the organizational factors which enhance socialization for death, I have, however, attempted to document the important fact which seems not often to be accepted by those who work with or study the aged and dying: that impending death can be and often is accepted as a matter-of-fact aspect of individual human lives. Legitimation of death does not mean resignation. It means acceptance of one's impending death as appropriate. Impending death can be seen as an appropriate end to one's biography and, like any portion of biography, the end will most likely be seen as appropriate when consensus is developed between an individual and his community.

NOTES

This research was supported by the Canada Council and Princeton University. I am grateful for the perceptive criticism of an anonymous referee for the *AJS*, which led to extensive revision of this paper.

1. Anomy as employed here should not be confused with alienation. The distinction is underscored by Berger (1969, pp. 86–87) and by Berger and Pullberg (1965): "alienation is the process by which man forgets that the world he lives in has been produced by himself." Anomy occurs when events cannot be subsumed under the socially shared reality (Berger and Luckmann, 1967, p. 102). This usage reflects but one (the meaninglessness) dimension of anom*ie* as discussed by McHugh (1968, p. 53).
2. Includes one "don't know." None of the twenty-seven Glen Brae residents in a pilot study gave an unconditional yes.
3. The third of these questions, which asked for agreement or disagreement with the statement "Death always comes too soon," was followed by a probe for reasons why death might not come too soon. Similarly, the question asking if the individual would like to live to be 100 was followed by the question "Why not?" Elsewhere (Marshall, 1972*a*, 1972*b*) I present a typology of such legitimations and show that the type is related to the individual's age, personal estimate of life expectancy, sex, marital status, friendship ties, perceived health, and length of time in the community. The principal legitimation types hold that death is preferable to continued life because of declines in physical and mental health, fear of becoming a burden, and loss of the ability to remain active. Religious legitimations are notably absent at Glen Brae, whereas limited data from a Catholic home for the aged suggest that they are the most prevalent type there. The association of duration of residence with changes in the prevalence of particular legitimations, together with the existence of the different types in two different settings, provides evidence that not only the existence but also the type of legitimation is influenced by community life. This inference is explored in Marshall (1972*b*).
4. This direction of causation is inferred.
5. If ability to produce a codable response to the two indicators is viewed as indicative of an active concern with impending death, the cautious interpretation here would be that most of those for whom impending death is of great concern have legitimated their impending deaths.
6. Compare the table excitement in Thomas Mann's *The Magic Mountain*. In contrast, Gustafson (1972) found in a nursing home that "although no staff member or relative will directly discourage the patient from making new friends . . . , he is often not expected or encouraged to do so. . . . Admission to the home is usually treated as the end of one's social career."
7. I investigate this further in Marshall (1973*b*).
8. This is complicated by the additional gamble on the part of the administration that the resident has enough money to continue paying his monthly rental fee. Applicants are screened for financial status. Unfortunately, the administration did not accurately estimate the steep rise in operating expenses (see Marshall 1973*b*).

9. Because most in fact do, I investigate in Marshall (1973a) the manner in which estimates of life expectancy are formed.
10. It was in fact less than the estimate.
11. Refers to an expansion of Glen Brae.
12. I am not attempting here to put forth a formal theory of dying as a status passage. A characterization of the formal properties of dying itself as a status passage has been given by Glaser and Strauss (1971, pp. 8–9), who describe these properties thus: "Dying is almost always unscheduled; the sequence of steps is not institutionally prescribed; and the actions of the various participants are only partly regulated. . . . Dying (though not necessarily death itself when it comes) is usually defined as undesirable and is usually involuntary. Among the other relevant but highly variable properties are: the degree to which the signs are disguised; the clarity of the signs; . . . the amount of control which the participants . . . have" (see also Gustafson, 1972).
13. An anonymous *AJS* reader of an earlier draft of this paper rightly pointed out that I present no direct evidence that the residents of Glen Brae do not arrive there already having legitimated their impending deaths. Elsewhere (Marshall, 1972b) I address this issue theoretically and give evidence that legitimation of death becomes a concern for most residents after they have arrived at Glen Brae, for it is only when the realization develops that their time is running short that legitimating death becomes a relevant concern (see also Marshall, 1973a).

REFERENCES

Berger, Peter. 1969. *The Sacred Canopy*. Garden City, N.Y.: Doubleday Anchor.

Berger, Peter, and H. Kellner. 1964. "Marriage and the Construction of Reality." *Diogene* 46 (2):3–32.

Berger, Peter, and Thomas Luckmann. 1967. *The Social Construction of Reality*. Garden City, N.Y.: Doubleday Anchor.

Berger, Peter, and Stanley Pullberg. 1965. "Reification and the Sociological Critique of Consciousness." *History and Theory* 4 (2):196–211.

Calkins, Kathy. 1970. "Time: Perspectives, Markings, and Styles of Usage." *Social Problems* 17 (Spring):487–501.

Carp, Frances. 1972. "Mobility among Members of an Established Retirement Community." *Gerontologist* 12 (Spring):48–56.

Friedman, E. 1966. "Friendship Choice and Clique Formation in a Home for the Aged." Ph.D. dissertation, Yale University.

Glaser, Barney, and Anselm Strauss. 1965. *Awareness of Dying*. Chicago: Aldine.
———. 1968. *Time for Dying*. Chicago: Aldine.
———. 1971. *Status Passage*. Chicago: Aldine-Atherton.

Goffman, Erving. 1961. "On the Characteristics of Total Institutions." Pp. 1–124 in *Asylums*, edited by Erving Goffman. Garden City, N.Y.: Doubleday Anchor.

Gove, Walter R. 1973. "Sex, Marital Status, and Mortality." *American Journal of Sociology* 79 (1):45–67.

Gustafson, Elizabeth. 1972. "Dying: The Career of the Nursing Home Patient." *Journal of Health and Social Behavior* 13 (September):226–35.

Hochschild, Arlie. 1973. *The Unexpected Community*. Englewood Cliffs, N.J.: Prentice-Hall.

Kleemeier, Robert. 1954. "Moosehaven: Congregate Living in a Community of the Retired." *American Journal of Sociology* 59 (4):347–51.

Lyman, Stanford, and Marvin Scott. 1970. "On the Time Track." Pp. 189–212 in *A Sociology of the Absurd*, edited by S. Lyman and M. Scott. New York: Appleton-Century-Crofts.

McHugh, Peter. 1968. *Defining the Situation*. Indianapolis: Bobbs-Merrill.

Marshall, Victor. 1972a. "Continued Living and Dying as Problematical Aspects of Old Age: An Empirical Study." Paper presented at the Ninth International Congress of Gerontology, Kiev, USSR.

———. 1972b. *Continued Living and Dying as Problematical Aspects of Old Age*. Ph.D. dissertation, Princeton University.

———. 1973a. "Awareness of Finitude and Developmental Theory in Gerontology: Some Speculations." Paper prepared for the Berkeley Conference on Death and Dying, July 1973.

———. 1973b. "Game-analyzable Dilemmas in a Retirement Village: A Case Study." *International Journal of Aging and Human Development* 4 (4):285–91.

May, Rollo. 1967. *Existential Psychotherapy*. Toronto: CBC Publications.

Mayer, Albert, and Philip Hauser. 1953. "Class Differentials in Expectation of Life at Birth." Pages 281–84 in *Class, Status, and Power*, edited by R. Bendix and S. M. Lipset. Glencoe, Ill.: Free Press.

Miller, George, Eugene Galanter, and Karl Pribram. 1960. *Plans and the Structure of Behavior*. New York: Holt, Rinehart & Winston.

Moore, Wilbert E. 1963. *Man, Time, and Society*. New York: Wiley.

Riley, John. 1970. "What People Think about Death." Pages 30–41 in *The Dying Patient*, edited by O. Brim, Jr., H. Freeman, S. Levine, and N. Scotch. New York: Sage.

Riley, Matilda, and Anne Foner. 1968. *Aging and Society*. Vol. 1: *An Inventory of Research Findings*. New York: Sage.

Riley, Matilda, Anne Foner, Beth Hess, and Marcia Toby. 1969. "Socialization for the Middle and Later Years." Pages 951–82 in *Handbook of Socialization Theory and Research*, edited by David Goslin. Chicago: Rand McNally.

Rosow, Irving. 1966. Discussion following Maurice B. Hamovitch's paper. Pp. 127–35 in *The Retirement Process*, edited by F. Carp. Public Health Service Publication no. 1778. Washington, D.C.: Government Printing Office.

Silverman, Phyllis, and Sue Englander. 1973. "The Widow's View of Her Dependent Children." Paper prepared for the Berkeley Conference on Death and Dying, March 1973.

Sudnow, David. 1967. *Passing On: The Social Organization of Dying*. Englewood Cliffs, N.J.: Prentice-Hall.

Dying They Live:
St. Christopher's Hospice
CICELY SAUNDERS

Dying patients are not easily given appropriate care in a busy general ward of a hospital. Doctors and nurses are trained to respond to acute conditions and to prolong life by all available means, not to respond to the needs of the dying. This article describes St. Christopher's Hospice in England and the hospice movement, whose goal is to help people die easily and at peace. A home-care program is provided for those who are able to remain with their families. For those who enter the hospice, every effort is made to make them feel welcome and valued, however ill they may be, and to involve their spouses and relatives in the life of the hospice. Through efficient medical treatment and careful coordination of services, the hospice seeks to rescue patients from the common alternatives of frightening pain or too heavy sedation. While patients and families are not protected from sadness, the hospice philosophy teaches that the living and dying are linked together.

Life Has a Pattern

Mr. B. was sitting by his bed in one of the small number of single rooms at St. Christopher's Hospice. Now sixty-three, he had, for many years, been a firefighter in London. He had been admitted two weeks before with a fungating and offensive recurrence of a carcinoma of the floor of his mouth. He had had surgery four and a half years earlier, followed by radiotherapy and chemotherapy. His previous hospital had now decided that further treatment of this nature was inappropriate and had asked the Hospice for admission to alleviate his terminal distress. His pain was by now well controlled, and the odor, previously his greatest distress and humiliation, no longer noticeable. We greeted each other, and after he had reported that his previous symptoms were under control, we went on talking.

> "What do you do with yourself all day?"
> "I read a bit and watch television; my wife and daughter spend a lot of time visiting me."
> "Do you get bored?"
> "No. I am contented—all my life I've been as you might call it, succoring people, helping others; now I am on the receiving end."

Source: From *New Meanings of Death*, edited by Herman Feifel. Copyright © 1977 by McGraw-Hill, Inc. Used by permission of McGraw-Hill Book Company.

"Do you find that hard?"
"No—I don't now—life has a pattern."

A few days later I joined him in a three-cornered conversation with his wife. She told me about the rest of the family and that her elderly mother was in a nursing home. Mrs. B. saw her often, and she told me that her mother and her roommate, both now in their eighties, were good and cheerful companions and that they were happy there. She went on to tell me how the second old lady had arrived about a year ago, severely incapacitated from a recent stroke, and so unhappy that she had asked first her own daughter and then Mrs. B. if they would bring her in some pills so that she could kill herself. "Now," said Mrs. B., "she has changed her mind; she can walk with a frame and can do crochet. She does not want to die now, her whole outlook has changed."

His wife reported to me later that, although it had been hard to bear, Mr. B. had not been overcome by his previous distress. Indeed she felt that all along he had been supporting her. Now the whole family joined in his relief and were able to relax. His freedom from pain had enlarged his capacity to use this part of his life's pattern to the full.

Mrs. B. is fortunate in that her mother is in a capable and compassionate nursing home where an old lady has been helped from a desperate wish to die to a cheerful readiness to live. A similar change of attitude in an elderly patient is shown in the conversation notes of Mrs. D., aged eighty-two years, and a patient in St. Christopher's. Her physical condition was deteriorating throughout the time covered by this record yet her outlook was developing all the time. Once she reached acceptance she did not lose it again. A few days before her death (three weeks after the last entry) she was overheard discussing the world to come with her friend, the long-stay patient in the next bed. "Wouldn't it be good if we both went together," she was heard to say, and the subsequent conversation made it plain that their expectation was to go to a place of excitement and interest. In fact, Mrs. D. died thirty-six hours after her friend, staying long enough to comfort the nurses and the many friends of that much-loved patient.

"Life has a pattern," said Mr. B., and no one meeting him could doubt that this pattern had been accepted or that the acceptance had enabled good to emerge from what was indeed a desperately hard situation. Those who meet and listen to such people as Mr. B. and Mrs. D. have seen repeatedly how much strength there is in accepted weakness and how often it is the person who is "on the receiving end" who is giving courage to those around him or her.

Patients who have intractable pain or other terminal distress from malignant disease and the elderly with deteriorating illnesses or diminishing powers are the two groups who are most often referred to in the literature demanding the legalization of some form of voluntary euthanasia. It is claimed that the only way in which they can die with peace and dignity is for them to be given, when they ask and with due formalities and safeguards, a lethal injection. It is taken for granted that many *will* ask, and the complex issues behind this suggestion are rarely explored. Little account is taken of the inconsistencies of the ill or of their vulnerability to the suggestions of others. Family discussions and divisions, doubts, and guilts are ignored, and no account is taken of the great difference between experiencing a situation and watching it from without. The suggestion that a declaration should be made earlier in life ignores this fact. It also takes little account of the shock reaction of the well on seeing the very ill and the frequency with which they project their own feelings upon the sick person.

It is also taken for granted that dying people will suffer inevitably increasing pain or other physical symptoms which cannot be relieved or which can be alleviated only at the cost of the impairment of their mental faculties. It is implied that the elderly will inevitably deteriorate to a stage of senile dementia, confused, incontinent, and a travesty of the persons they were. Sadly, these assumptions are all too often reinforced by stories of truly horrendous cases, where pain was not controlled and all drugs appeared to have lost their effect: where people were subjected, apparently with no choice, to more and more surgery or life-supporting measures which were at best inappropriate and at worst correctly described as forms of torture no one would have permitted an animal to undergo. Far too many elderly people end their days in pitiful and degrading isolation, with the reality around them so distressing that they retreat into confusion and do not even recognize those they love. It is no help to this discussion if we deny the distress which many people are suffering at this moment.

Such patients are not easily given appropriate care in a busy general ward. Often it is not the right place for them nor do their needs arouse the interest of many of the doctors who look after them. One reason for this is no doubt the fact that such patients are not seen often where most medical education takes place. Ann Cartwright's study, *Life before Death* (Cartwright et al., 1973), gives the details of the last year in the lives of 785 people, a random selection from different areas in the United Kingdom. Only 2 percent of her sample died in teaching-hospital beds. Such wards are geared to active diagnosis and the treatment of acute conditions, and their implicit standards do not help students to learn how to help people who are dying. Many of the staff feel that treatment must mean active therapy designed for cure or rehabilitation and that ethically this can never be discontinued. We may add that it is implied that "satisfactory" patients should get better or at least die without fuss before those treating them have come to the end of their (largely irrelevant) resources. It is often thought that the strong analgesics which some patients need desperately for adequate relief are virtually unusable because of ill-understood risks of tolerance and dependence. Even when they are given, it is implied that they are somehow a disgrace. As one medical student told us, "In our hospital, the patients have to earn their morphine." If we add to this the implicit demands that patients should not ask awkward questions and that families should be unobtrusive and not disturb others with grief or anger, we see some of the reasons for the sad state of many dying people, well documented in the press and rightly causing public disquiet. It is being said that the only compassionate and realistic answer is for these people to have the right to die when they ask to end their intolerable existence.

Doctors are committed to the service of health and to the relief of suffering (World Health Organization, 1948). To prolong life by all means available to intensive care, regardless of its quality, is not to serve health but rather to fail to balance technical possibilities with informed clinical judgment. It has been said that to refrain from all possible active treatment is "passive euthanasia." This is a misleading definition, and one which the British Medical Association and the Church of England's Board of Social Responsibility Working Party have both refuted (British Medical Association, 1971; Church Information Office, 1975). As the Working Party says:

> In its narrow current sense, euthanasia implies killing and it is misleading to extend it to cover decisions not to preserve life by artificial means when it would be better for the patient to be allowed to die. Such decisions, coupled with a determination to give the patient as good a death as possible, may be quite legitimate. Nor should it be used to cover the giving of drugs for the relief of pain and other distress in cases where there is a risk that they may marginally shorten the patient's life. This too we think is legitimate.

Such decisions have always been part of clinical judgment; no doctor is committed to preserving life whatever its quality, and to ease the distress of dying is undoubtedly part of medical treatment (Devlin, 1960).

The doctor has to serve health, and surely there comes a time for the very old and for people with such illnesses as we are discussing when it can be said truly that to die has become the "healthy" thing to do. The two extremes of dying in pain and being killed do not exhaust the possibilities for the stricken patient (Horder, 1936). There is another way, the way of giving appropriate and understanding medical care and compassionate and personal nursing care arising from true social concern.

The Working Party considered that:

> If all the care were up to the standards of the best, there would be few cases in which there was even a prima facie argument for euthanasia; better alternative means of alleviating distress would almost always be available if modern techniques and human understanding and care of the patient were universally practiced. It should be the aim to improve the care of the dying in hospitals and hospices and in their homes to as near this standard as the money and the staff available will allow.

It believes that, at present, ignorance and mistaken ideas are a greater obstacle than shortage of money and staff, and that to justify a change in the law to permit euthanasia it would be necessary to show that such a change would remove greater evils than it would cause. It listed among these evils: the pressure it would place on patients to allow themselves to be put away, recourse to euthanasia in many cases in which it was far from morally justified and performed for the wrong reasons, and grave weakening of confidence in doctors by a majority of patients.

Finally, the Working Party wrote, "that in the rare cases (if such there be) in which it would be justified morally it would be better for medical men to do all that is necessary to ensure peaceful dying and to rely on the flexibilities in the administration of the law which even now exist than to legalize euthanasia for general use."

What has come to be called "the Hospice movement" has set out to give such people all the care that will help them to die easily and at peace, to spread knowledge and concern of its potentials in special units or hospices, in general hospitals, and in the patient's own home.

. . . .

Given to Hospitality

Men and women can fulfill their lives in passivity and weakness as well as in strength and activity. Those who welcome each patient to St. Christopher's do so with the conviction that he or she is an important person and that hospitality to a stranger is a prime necessity.[1] Those concerned take care to know the name of newcomers before they arrive, and a senior nurse joins the stewards at the ambulance to welcome them personally. The patient is lifted directly into a warm bed, and his family travels in the lift with him to the ward. It is impossible to overemphasize what such a welcome means to a mortally sick person who has so often felt alien and rejected. He has been the "failure" who cannot get better in the acute ward, feeling obscurely that it is his own fault, or he has suffered long pain at home which has led to despair of ever finding peace. A great deal has happened to bring relief to patients by the time the doctor comes to speak to the family—the nurses have already introduced them to their neighbors and begun to settle them in their own place. Patients will not be moved so long as they stay in that ward; their bed has their name on it instead of a number, and they are encouraged to put out small personal things on their locker. Everything is done to establish their identity, however ill they may be. Even those patients who are already confused or unconscious seem to show that they know they have been greeted as persons and not merely admitted as cases. "Our own name helps us to know that we belong." The first greeting by name and its repetition on each ward round and at every contact between a staff person and a patient emphasizes his relationship to the community. In one of the first annual reports after the Hospice opened it was written, "Every time we greet a new patient we see the colorfulness of the Hospice afresh and find that it is all very good." Each time it has been new also for the patient at the moment when we say, "Come just as you are—you are welcome."

Not all patients are easy members of the ward community they enter, and there are some who need to work out their way of living and dying in the privacy of a single room. But a hospice must welcome people simply on the grounds of their need and of their common humanity and has to find a way to enable each one to have his or her own appropriate way of dying.

Two people make a meeting. It cannot take place where one of them is obscured by a professional role. We are all acquainted with the superficial greeting of a patient which expects the gratified answer and is much taken aback by anyone bold enough to express his real feelings. Many medical students who meet hospice patients on teaching rounds ask how they can begin to transfer this experience back to their teaching hospitals. It is suggested that a simple beginning could be a resolution always to say "Good morning" to patients by name, especially to those who are dying. The student, like everyone else who feels that he is facing a situation where he has little to give, will feel tempted to pass by, feeling that they can be no better than a useless disturbance. If they can convey the attitude, "I am not only concerned with what is yours (your diagnosis, your response to treatment, and so on) but with you as a person (however despairing you are, however unattractive)," much can develop from this one moment of mutual recognition.

Neither students nor relatives can meet those patients who remain swamped by distress or become smothered by treatment. The result of the proper control of terminal physical distress, seen repeatedly in every place where this skill is practiced, is for the patient to go on living in relationship with those around him. So many of us have known bitter regrets that we have not learned love until too late; so many families find words to express their care only when the patient can no longer hear them. The extra time for such communication is frequently used for reconciliations or even new beginnings. As one daughter wrote, "I came to know my father better during these visits—as a man and not just my father . . . you at St. Christopher's helped us to look more honestly at ourselves and offered constructive help when we asked for it . . . to be aware of death without being afraid of it seems to make one that much more aware of life." None of this, nor the many encounters between families which it represents, would have happened if the patients had remained imprisoned in the distress with which they were admitted.

Much of the communication at St. Christopher's may at first sight look superficial. Visiting students find themselves busy serving meals and giving so much practical care that they do not feel they can sit down and have the long talks they somehow thought would make up their experience. But the part of life before death is like the rest, it is full of ordinary and exasperating things. Feeding a person who cannot even manage to get a spoon to his mouth can be a chore to the worker and a humiliation to the patient; it can also be a social occasion when the worker can just come as a neighbor. We all feel clumsy at times and must often say the wrong or hurtful thing, but as we keep coming for such simple errands we have the opportunity for a new beginning. The place to find meaning is so often in the ordinary, in the endlessly repetitive and insignificant. A true meeting between two people is a gift coming unbidden into the midst of such action.

Humiliation and exposure are the lot of many of the very ill. We can help them to feel valued in the way we give the things of everyday life. Few infusions are to be seen in a hospice—many people, families included, are to be seen giving food and drink, slowly and kindly. Patients do not feel thirsty, and do not look dehydrated, and the drink they need is given in a manner which draws them near to others. Drips and tubes may seem a quicker and more efficient way to keep up a fluid intake, but at this stage personal contact matters more than electrolytes and can give refreshment where, before, everything was drought and isolation.

When we visit a dying person we may meet the unexpected. Most people are honest as they face death, and they are likely to have dropped much of the mask we all tend to wear in our daily encounters with others. They will not let us be sentimental, and they are usually realistic and challenging, whether or not they *know* what is happening. If we can use our skills as vehicles to bring us close to the person we are trying to help, we may find we are uncomfortable, but we will surely gain from the exchange.

We have considered a patient's relationship with St. Christopher's as a person, for that is what first arrests the attention of both the patient and his or her family. But the staff would not be able to greet them with such confidence nor offer such immediate security if the personal meeting were not accompanied by careful coordination of all the Hospice can offer and by the efficiency of its treatment.

Admission and Continuity of Care

About 40 percent of St. Christopher's patients are transferred directly from a hospital; the rest are admitted from their own homes. They are sent with uncontrolled pain and other symptoms, with emotional distress, and with social and interpersonal difficulties which those previously caring for them were unable to help. They are not a random selection of people dying in this part of London; they are a group who present themselves with unrelieved distress.

Every effort is made to enable them to stay at home as long as they wish, to come at the optimum moment for them, and to return home if possible. An admission meeting considers all applications daily, and patients come in according to their need. Those in distress at home have priority over those already in a hospital, and discharged patients are always readmitted immediately. St. Christopher's social worker may begin his or her contact with the family and with other workers involved before the patient comes in, and many families visit to see the place to which their relative is to be admitted. The Domiciliary Service staff go to assess the home situation whenever it is indicated, and report daily to this meeting.

Continuity of care has priority and may not be easy to establish with those previously treating the patient. Notes may be confusing. Liaison between the various departments of a hospital are not always good, and there may also have been much delay in writing to the family doctor on a patient's discharge. Letters and reports are held up and, when they come, little is said in them of what the patient or family has been told to expect. The Hospice doctors sometimes have to be most importunate in obtaining vital medical information. This is often more easily dealt with when the patient is seen first at home, but some admissions are urgent, as when the family doctor has only contacted the Hospice when the situation has broken down irreparably. St. Christopher's is usually able to offer help at once, for it can take over 550 admissions a year with a median length of stay of only ten days.

The Home-Care Program

The patient and his family may be referred by the hospital who has treated him or directly by the family doctor. In any case the latter will be contacted before a home visit is made, and he will continue to be involved with the patient's care, consulting and cooperating with the Hospice nurses and doctors. Four specially trained nurses and a part-time doctor with experience in general practice carry a case load of over seventy patients each month, covering an area of six miles or so from the Hospice, which is in a heavily populated area. Family doctors are now asking more often for assessment visits to be made early in the illness, enabling the home-care staff to get to know the family before matters become desperate. Some patients are seen only once or twice at home before they need admission, but in that time come to terms with what many of them know is the final farewell to their home. Others may remain at home for many weeks or months, and a considerable number are able to remain there until they die.

The clinic staff reports in full to the wards as they hand over care of the patient when he or she is admitted. As far as possible, the problems that arise as one group of staff replaces another are faced and dealt with by direct consultation. Thereafter, clinic staff will continue to attend open ward meetings, and may continue to pay social calls on their patients in the ward.

Peggy and her husband lived in a first floor flat in a housing estate in Bermondsey. She was well known to all her neighbors and much loved for her warm and friendly nature. Two months before her death her doctor asked St. Christopher's for help in the control of her pain and St. Christopher's nurses became almost daily visitors to the flat. Peggy was a tiny slip of a thing with the spirit of a giant. She was determined to remain at home because her husband suffered from arthritis and found it hard to get about. The door of the flat was always open and neighbors came and went through the day. Nursing care was given by the District Nurses three or four times a day; a night nurse took over at dusk.

The role of St. Christopher's was to assess Peggy's constantly changing needs and to adjust her drugs accordingly. All the expertise gained in our wards was used to keep this young woman at home. It was a triumph of cooperation between the General Practitioner, the District Nurses and ourselves. Peggy died early one morning after a peaceful night's rest. She slipped quietly into eternity conscious to the last. The morning of her funeral was crisp and cold. Her body lay in her own home surrounded by masses of flowers, the narrow hall was lined with them and sprays and posies extended along the open balcony and down the stairs, spilling out in a cascade on to a forecourt below. Neighbors leaned over the balconies on every floor as the coffin was carried out: the traffic in Jamaica Road piled up in both directions as the cortege crossed the road to the church opposite: local shops closed their doors briefly during the funeral service and those who could not get into the church stood about on the pavement as the bell tolled. We are glad that we made it possible for Peggy to remain at home and to die surrounded by family and friends (from the Domiciliary Service).

"You Welcomed Us As Well"

When patients enter the hospital, they leave their own community and much of their identity. We are all bound up in our homes and our possessions, our work and our hobbies, and we feel stripped and humiliated if our clothes and personal belongings are removed. The emphasis on possessions, clothes, and idiosyncrasies in a hospice is a way of maintaining identity. Many hospital wards do little to integrate their patients into a new community in which they have an active part. The way a patient is welcomed into the new life of a hospice can be a reaffirmation of his own home and community, even though he may never return to them.

People matter more than things, and a patient is, above all, part of a family and circle of friends. St. Christopher's tries to welcome the family as wholeheartedly as it greets the patient who is part of it. The staff in the wards as well as those in the Domiciliary Service frequently spend as long or longer with the family members as with the patients. Much of this is on a simple and friendly level, but many ward groups and discussions are guided by the social psychiatrist who has been part of the Hospice team from the beginning.

Patients are referred to the psychiatrist by the nurses as well as by the doctors, and his advice may be sought by anyone. Over the years he has found that he sees approximately 15 percent of all patients, and there are others whom he discusses with the ward staff but does not meet directly. He is involved in ward and general staff meetings and with a small senior staff group as well as in a regular seminar with visiting students and graduates. He also acts as consultant to the group working with the social worker to identify and visit those families in special need of support in their bereavement.

Two years ago he established a patients' group. It meets weekly for an hour's discussion, and friendships formed there may extend to other contacts during the week. The number attending varies from as few as four to as many as fifteen. The core is composed of long-stay patients who may come regularly for many months and who welcome and absorb into the group a number who only come once or twice before they are too ill to attend. Family members sometimes join, and a discharged patient returns faithfully. Various subjects are brought up; sometimes discussion is general, at other times it is focused on life and death in the Hospice. The loss of a member of long standing is faced and talked about because the members as a whole feel secure enough to grieve together and to look at the implications for themselves. On other days they concentrate on learning from or instructing those who visit them. It is a coveted honor for staff or visitors to be invited to join in one of the meetings, and although small in number, this group has an impact on the life of the Hospice as well as on that of its members.

Since St. Christopher's opening eight years ago, Dr. Parkes, the psychiatrist, has carried out a number of psychosocial studies. He recently (1975) completed a comparative study of thirty-four families of cancer patients who died at the Hospice, matched with thirty-four families of patients who died elsewhere. Statistically significant differences favoring the group from the Hospice were:

1. Greater mobility of the patient.
2. Less pain rated as severe (but not bought at the cost of greater drug-induced confusion).
3. Less anxiety among spouses during the period of terminal care with fewer somatic symptoms.
4. Spouses spent much more time at the patient's bedside and much more time talking to staff, other patients, and visitors. They were more likely to have helped to care for the patient and more likely to know a doctor's name.
5. Doctors and nurses at St. Christopher's were less likely to be seen as "busy" or "very busy" than staff elsewhere.
6. Despite the fact that two to three patients died each week on each

floor at the Hospice, only 6 percent were said to have been upset by the death of another patient. The same figure was given for those in other wards, none of which were for "terminal care."

7. Twenty-seven from each setting completed a checklist which allowed them to agree or disagree with general statements regarding the hospital in which their spouse died. The statement which best characterized St. Christopher's was "The hospital is like a family," which was checked by 78 percent of the St. Christopher's families and 11 percent of the rest.

This family feeling explains why some relatives have returned to work as volunteers, often for several years service. For others, the connection continues informally; letters are exchanged, visitors come back to talk to the ward or reception staff they know, or they appear at Open Days, sometimes years later, to bring their friends to see the Hospice. Many respond to the card sent to all next of kin on the first anniversary of a patient's death. It is of one of the Resurrection pictures in the Hospice with the words "We are remembering you at St. Christopher's." The list of names put on the notice board outside the chapel each week makes this a fact and not merely a pious fiction.

A few relatives come regularly to the Sunday chapel service, others come for festivals or anniversaries. An increasing number come to a monthly social club, which is also attended by members of staff and their families. This club has gradually built up until space is becoming a problem, and it expands into a large general party each Christmas and midsummer. In many ways the life of the Hospice resembles that of a village, a place which shares the good and the sad and which does not lose its interest or attraction for those who once belonged. Nurses return to show off their new babies, students call back for a meal, and the friends who support the work by their prayer and gifts return each year at Open Days to see the new developments and to meet old acquaintances. The follow-up of the bereaved and the sad fits naturally into such a context, and surprisingly few of them have made dependent and clinging relationships with the Hospice.

Another of Dr. Parkes's studies (1975) set out to assess the reliability of the method developed to identify the wives and husbands who were likely to get into difficulties after bereavement. Of seventeen spouses who had a "poor outcome," thirteen had been correctly predicted. Those who were expected to need help urgently were all followed up, the next group were assigned at random to two groups. One was supported by visits from St. Christopher's staff or volunteers who were known to them, and the other was not. Both were visited twenty months after bereavement when the "unsupported" group were found to have almost twice as much depression as the "supported" group. They also had significantly more physical symptoms of anxiety.

A Center for the Control of Chronic Pain

Mr. B. needed constant adjustments of his medication, especially during the last few days of his life. Specialized care was essential to ensure that his potentially great distress was anticipated and alleviated.

The Hospice has been concerned with the nature and management of chronic and terminal pain ever since the years spent by the medical director in St. Joseph's Hospice (Saunders, 1965). Ever since its first planning and through the development of the teaching program, the work has been based on growing experience and on a series of studies and clinical trials (Saunders, 1963, 1975; Twycross, 1974). Every year the medical and nursing notes of all the Hospice patients are summarized by a doctor and analyzed by a nurse, neither of whom is involved with ward care. Only a small number (1.5 to 2 percent) are reported as continuing to complain of unrelieved pain during their time in the wards. A further study has been carried out by Parkes. His research worker has never worked in the Hospice, visits from the Tavistock Centre for Human Relations, and is not identified with St. Christopher's. She interviewed the families of forty-five patients who had died in the Hospice and 100 who had died elsewhere in the area. Thirty-six percent of St. Christopher's patients were recalled by their families as having severe, unrelieved pain before their admission; the other families rated 20 percent. After admission the St. Christopher's families recalled pain in 8 percent while at the other hospitals the figure remained at 20 percent. It is scarcely surprising to find that the figure given is higher than that rated by the staff. We must all have spoken to families whose relative is lying quietly unconscious and heard them say, "We long to see him out of his suffering," and had to try to explain that so far as we can tell he is now no more aware of any movement or noise than when he was snoring in healthy slumber. The Hospice recognizes that there is still further work to be done in the control of pain and other physical distress, but there is reason to say that at present greater success is achieved than is usual elsewhere.

Hospice doctors and nurses recognize and consider the differences between acute pain which forms the basis of much teaching in therapeutics and that of chronic or terminal pain (LeShan, 1964). Orientation is that use of analgesics should be only a part of a multifaceted approach. Terminal pain needs to be considered as an illness in itself, to be diagnosed and treated with attention to detail, according to a rational plan of treatment and with an individual approach to the whole spectrum of a patient's distress, social and emotional as well as physical.

Eighty percent of the patients referred to the Hospice have pain sufficiently severe to need narcotics for its adequate relief. Many have had unrelieved pain for long periods, and it may take time before they learn to expect relief rather than distress. Both are self-perpetuating, and the doctor should so anticipate the onset of pain that the patient does so no longer. Drugs balanced to need and given regularly so that pain does not occur prevent the vicious spiral of pain, tension, increased pain, and a higher dose of analgesic. The best treatment of terminal pain is its prevention. Of 108 patients admitted to a controlled clinical trial of two different narcotics in the Hospice, 61 percent reported to the nurse observer that they had no pain at any time when she visited them ten days later. None of the remaining 39 percent reported unrelieved, severe pain, although all had been admitted to the trial because of pain. A series of studies being completed has included a controlled clinical trial of morphine and diamorphine given orally in a cocaine elixir with a phenothiazine in which it was found that there was no clinically observable difference between the two opiates when given regularly. This study and further work on the absorption of these drugs when given orally and retrospective studies of a group of patients who received opiate drugs over long periods in the Hospice and in their own homes will soon be published. This work is at last bringing objective science into a field too long confused by myth and misconception (Twycross, 1974). Too many patients have suffered unrelieved pain because their doctors considered that the drugs which could have given them comfort were virtually unusable.

Parkes's work quoted above has shown not only that the patients are given better pain relief in the Hospice but also that this is not bought at the expense of alertness or the possibility of living in as full a manner as their physical condition allows. The proper balance of the analgesics and the adjuvants to the patient's need will rescue him from the two alternatives that are usually offered, frightening pain or too heavy sedation.

. . . .

"Everything That Went Before and Anything That May Come After Will Be Worth It for That Day"

Mr. B. died five days after . . . his birthday party. His wife had prepared a small celebration and came in to find that, according to Hospice custom, a birthday cake and party had been organized by the ward. The party continued for much of the day. The writer was away but was told about it afterwards by Mrs. B. She said, "Everything that went before and everything that may come after will be worth it for that day". . . .

This shows much of what St. Christopher's means for the staff and is an illustration of what enables them to continue with such work at the level of caring demanded and given. "Efficiency is very comforting," said one relative. It is comforting to the family and also comforting to the staff to see pain relieved and relationships reaffirmed. Much weariness and mental suffering may still remain, but it is deeply rewarding to meet people who are making such achievements of life's pattern and to join in such occasions. We cannot take away the whole hard thing that is happening, but celebration is still an important part of life, and each

Hospice occasion is a salute to this kind of courage. There is no need for the staff to idealize their patients, the daily reality of troubles accepted and overcome is enough. Neither patients, families, nor staff are protected from sadness, but in sharing it as they do they find that living and dying well are linked together and are constantly opening up new and creative possibilities.

IN THE MIDST OF LIFE[2]

Death and I are only nodding acquaintances
We have not been formally introduced
But many times I have noticed
The final encounter
Here in this Hospice,
I can truly say
That death has been met with dignity
Who can divine the thoughts
Of a man in close confrontation?
I can only remember
One particular passing
When a man,
With sustained smile
Pointed out what was for him
Evidently a great light
Who knows what final revelations
Are received in the last hours?
Lord, grant me a star in the East
As well as a smouldering sunset.

NOTES

1. "I won't be forgotten *here*"—a patient on admission.
2. By Sidney G. Reeman (a patient in the Hospice who died on March 3, 1975, and who wrote over 50 poems during his 4-months stay).

REFERENCES

British Medical Association. *The problem of euthanasia*. London: British Medical Association, 1971.

Cartwright, A., Hockey, L., and Anderson, J. L. *Life before death*. London and Boston: Routledge & Kegan Paul, 1973.

Church Information Office. *On dying well*. An Anglican contribution to the debate on euthanasia. London: Church Information Office, 1975.

Devlin, Lord Justice. Lecture to the Medical Society of London, 1960.

Horder, J. Parliamentary debates, House of Lords, 1936, 103, 466–506.

LeShan, L. L. The world of the patient in severe pain of long duration. *Journal of Chronic Diseases*, 1964, 17, 119–126.

Parkes, C. M. P. *Evaluation of family care in terminal illness.* Alexander Ming Fisher lecture, Columbia University, New York, 1975. In *Man and medicine.* New York: Columbia University Press, 1977.

Saunders, C. M. The treatment of intractable pain in terminal cancer. *Proceedings of the Royal Society of Medicine*, 1963, 56, 195–197.

Saunders, C. M. The last stages of life. *American Journal of Nursing*, 1965, 65, 70–75.

Saunders, C. M. Alexander Ming Fisher lecture, Columbia University, New York, 1975.

Twycross, R. G. Clinical experience with diamorphine in advanced malignant disease. *International Journal of Clinical Pharmacology, Therapy and Toxicology*, 1974, 9, 184–198.

World Health Organization. *The declaration of Geneva.* Geneva, Switzerland, 1948.